HOKUSAI
Life and Work

HOKUSAI

LIFE AND WORK

RICHARD LANE

BARRIE & JENKINS

LONDON

This book is dedicated to Hokusai's shade
(which I suspect of viewing our activity with great glee, if feigned disinterest)

First published in Great Britain in 1989 by
Barrie & Jenkins Ltd
289 Westbourne Grove, London W11 2QA

British Library Cataloguing in Publication Data

Lane, Richard, *1926*–
   Hokusai.
   1. Japanese graphic arts. Hokusai—Critical
   studies
   I. Title
   760'.092'4
   ISBN 0 7126 2506 2

This book was designed and produced by
JOHN CALMANN AND KING LTD, LONDON

Designed by Harold Bartram
Typeset by Fakenham Photosetting Ltd, Norfolk
Printed in Hong Kong by Imago Publishing Ltd

Contents

I
Edo:
Year of the Dragon

CONFIDENT, self-centred, ebullient, and resolutely cut off from the rest of the world: this was Japan of the Edo Period (1603–1868). Yet it was this very isolation that served to produce one of the most remarkable civilizations known to man, with not the least of its wonders *ukiyo-é*, literally 'pictures of the floating world', which sought to portray in prints, paintings and illustrated books the transient pursuits and pleasures of Edo society. Ukiyo-e (pronounced 'ookeeyóh-eh') was, in a sense, the prototype and epitome of pop-art, rooted in the reality of commonly held daily experience, in the vibrant plebeian culture of the times. For the most part it was a vivid and evocative reflection of the life of the people, rather than of the psyche of the artists.

The year 1760 was hardly an auspicious one for Edo—that booming metropolis now called Tōkyō and, with well over a million in population, probably the largest city in the world. In early spring great fires swept through the centre of town from Asakusa to Shinagawa; and two days later spread further to the north and east—from Kanda and Asakusa to Fukagawa—later even consuming Shiba in the south. The ensuing summer was inordinately hot and arid, with widespread crop failure. And in the autumn of this inauspicious year—the Year of the Dragon, Horeki X in the Japanese calendar—Hokusai was born.[1]

In feudal Japan formal biography was reserved for eminent personages, not plebeian artists, and little is recorded of Hokusai's early background. We do know that he was born on the eastern outskirts of Edo, across the Sumida River, on the twenty-third day of the Ninth Month: 31 October in the modern calendar. This part of town, known as the Honjo District, lay just north-east of Fukagawa; both were sea-level areas often visited by floods. The region had in former times been part of Katsushika County, and from this the Master was to take his later *nom d'artiste*, Katsushika Hokusai (the 'u' of Hokusai is silent and the name pronounced roughly 'Hoak-sigh' or Hoax-eye').

Although not in the commercial centre of Edo—the effective capital of Japan from 1603, renamed Tōkyō, 'Eastern Capital', only with the Restoration of the Emperor in 1868—Honjo was by Hokusai's time firmly a part of the *shitamachi*, 'downtown' quarter. It had, indeed, been settled as early as 1659 when the Ryōgoku ('Double-Provinces') Bridge was built to connect it to downtown Edo, and the quarter was developed as a residential area for the lesser samurai—and for the tradesmen and artisans who catered to them.

The seat of plebeian culture lay in these very flatlands flanking the Sumida River—the lower 'old town' as distinct from the safer, more elevated and salutary areas away from the Bay, occupied by the more affluent samurai classes. More specifically, Hokusai's birthplace was beside the Wari-gesui Canal, one of several such narrow waterways—some nine feet in width—which characterized this low-lying quarter.[2]

Hokusai's parentage is unknown, though his original surname may have been Kawamura (the name which appears at the foot of his tombstone). He seems to have been adopted in childhood by the prestigious Honjo artisan-family Nakajima. But he was never acknowledged as heir, nor even apprenticed to the family trade of mirror-making for the Shōgun Family.[3] This may support the hypothesis that, though the true son of Nakajima, he had been born of a mistress. Another theory (based on an elliptical diary entry by the novelist Bakin) is that Hokusai was adopted by Nakajima, who may have been his uncle, at a later date, in his late teens.

The artist's childhood experiences were possibly unhappy: he never spoke of them. But he was fond of remarking the fact that his mother was of samurai stock, granddaughter of an ill-fated retainer to Lord Kira, villain of the famous *Chūshingura* vendetta: a connection which may well have

1 Map of Edo/Tōkyō in the Age of Hokusai. (Triangles indicate the artist's known places of residence.)

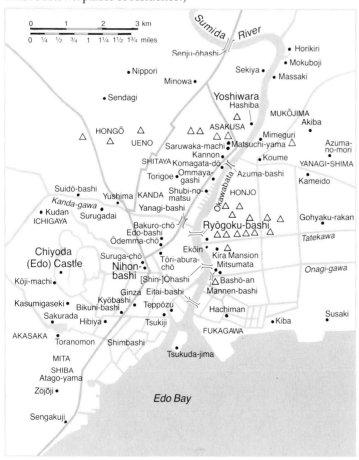

influenced Hokusai's addiction to this theme in his early career, in several series of prints and book-illustrations. (The topic was also of perennial interest to his audience and to that of the Kabuki dramatist—see Plates 84–87, 95.)

Hokusai's childhood name was Tokitarō, which, a decade later, he retained in some of his early publications. In the famed colophon to his *Hundred Views of Fuji* of 1834 he writes, 'From my sixth year I have had a passion for sketching the form of things . . .' This passion was to last throughout his life. In his handbook for artists, *On the Use of Colouring*, published the year before his death, he says: 'From my sixth year until my eighty-eighth, revelling in independence. . . . How can I recreate on simple sheets of paper all these things that crowd my mind. . . .' His sixth year would have been the Second Year of Meiwa, 1765, when, quite by coincidence, the Japanese colour-print was just in the process of being re–created under the aegis of the great Harunobu.

Little is known about this early period, we have only the stray bit of information—gleaned from old temple-records—that the artist lost a younger sister in the following year, at the age of six.[4]

We know nothing further of the artist until his early teens, when his name was changed to Tetsuzō and he took up his first job as delivery-boy to a lending bookshop, one of over six hundred such shops that served the needs of the literate middle and upper classes in Edo. The book-pedlars and their shops played a crucial role in disseminating literature, the youthful salesboys carrying their wares to all manner of readers—an experience that was to find graphic replay in Hokusai's later work. Only a few of the larger bookshops (who often did publishing of their own) actually received customers, and the artist's principal task must have been to carry, on his back, a goodly stock of books for lending. Even the lowly delivery-boy had soon to become something of an expert on popular literature—and its illustration—if only to advise clients on the current best-sellers.

It was some time after this—around the age of 14—that Hokusai took up his first 'professional' work, as apprentice to a woodblock-carver. This trade (which tended to be a small, family operation, on sub-contract to the publishers) comprised the basis of all published forms, whether print or book, of ukiyo-e, the images which were to constitute the artist's lifework.

It is worth examining here the process of Japanese woodblock-printing. Both the author's and the artist's final, thin-papered manuscript was pasted, face-down, on a fine-planed block of hard cherrywood, and the blank spaces carved and gouged away leaving the text or picture in relief. This was then printed by inking the block, lowering a sheet of tough, handmade paper on to it, and then rubbing the back of the paper forcefully with a lightly oiled, stiff *baren*-pad. The woodblock-artisan's task was thus a most exacting one, requiring not only sharp eyesight but also great patience and unfailing dexterity. And though we may sometimes oversimplify by referring to this as 'engraving' it was actually woodblock-carving—a much more difficult and time-consuming process.[5]

It is clear proof of the young artist's assiduous application and technical aptitude that he was permitted to carve his first text already in 1775, after less than a year of apprenticeship. The subject was a *sharé-hon*, one of the light novelettes devoted to life in the Yoshiwara, Edo's elegant pleasure-quarter. It is notable that the young Hokusai was able to reach a near-professional standard in this very specialized skill at such an early age. No wonder, in view of this background, that Hokusai was to prove the most precise, the most exacting of all Japanese print-designers: he knew his *métier* from the ground up. By the same token the artist proved a great perfectionist, in later years expending much effort in trying to persuade his own block-cutters and publishers to meet certain high standards that were, by then, already beginning to die out. Thanks to this experience Hokusai gleaned a fine appreciation of the complex process of ukiyo-e production: from preliminary sketch to final drawing, followed by meticulous carving of the wood-blocks, on through final proofing, printing, publicity and sales; but most important of all, he acquired a clear perception of the specialized requirements of book and print design: so different from the freedom of action enjoyed by the *painter*.[6]

From such early apprenticeship—first book-sales boy, later engraver—Hokusai came to know intimately both the tastes of his future public and the technical background of his art. Given his native genius, had he only been a less stubborn man, a less exacting personality, fame and riches should have come his way apace. The fame was to come—though only years later; but the riches only rarely, if at all.

NOTES

1 It is from this connection that the artist was to receive not only his childhood name Tokitarō ('Time/Dragon-First-born-son') but also to take several of his later *noms d'artiste*.

2 For those familiar with Tōkyō/Edo, reference to the map (Plate 1) may be edifying; for most, it may be more meaningful to cite Hokusai's birthplace as about one kilometre east of the Ryōgoku Bridge of our Plates 8, 94, 251, and a little north of the Tatekawa lumber yards of our Appendix Fig. 83. 'Katsushi-ka', incidentally—written with phonetically employed characters of no particular significance—is an ancient word for 'cliff-beach', probably deriving from the language of the pre-Japanese Ainu race.

3 Note that the traditional Far-Eastern *mirror* was made not of glass but cast in bronze with a silvered surface—which had to be frequently polished. Mirrors tended to be rather expensive—the back was decorated with intricate, delicate designs—and were made for toilette use, not wall decoration. For samples depicted by Hokusai, see Plates 2, 72, 134, 319; and there are also designs for mirror-use in the artist's *Models of Modern Combs and Pipes* of 1822–3. (With the eighteenth century, small hand-mirrors were sometimes made of glass, imported, for example, from Venice. See Plate 6.)

4 By Japanese reckoning, a child was 'in his first year' at birth and hence 'age one'. Specific ages have been adjusted here to modern usage, where feasible.

5 The problem with the term 'woodblock-carver'—and even 'block-cutter'—is not only that it is cumbersome and ambiguous compared to 'engraver', but that, to the casual reader, it may give the erroneous connotation of 'sculptor'. Indeed, some generalist writers have mistaken this very point: thus E. Grilli (*Hokusai*, 1955, p. 4—adapted from I. Kondō) writes that Hokusai 'is said to have been apprenticed to a sculptor. . . .' Further, in M. Narazaki's *Studies in Nature: Hokusai-Hiroshige*, 1970, we find the statement, ' . . . in his mid-teens he was apprenticed to a woodblock artist'—this, presumably a mistranslation for 'woodblock-artisan'. Students may also have been misled by the note in K. Toda's *Ryerson Catalogue* (1931, p. 227), speaking of Hokusai as 'an engraver of printing clocks. . . .' This is simply a misprint for 'blocks'. (For a sample page of Hokusai's actual woodblock-carving, see Appendix, Fig. 171.)

6 For the reader familiar with the techniques of modern, *sōsaku-hanga* print-artists, it may be pertinent to cite that there is no evidence that Hokusai ever subsequently engaged in the engraving (or printing) of his own designs. This would not, indeed, have been usual in feudal Japan, where the various trades (including that of print-designer) were rather strictly delimited.

II
The Making of an
Ukiyo-e Master (1)

WHETHER as book-pedlar or as woodblock-carver it may be assumed that the young Hokusai spent his spare time in assiduously studying and copying the illustrations of the varied 'floating world' publications that passed through his hands. This period of the mid-1770s was indeed the beginning of the Golden Age of ukiyo-e. In the field of book-illustration and prints, the older masters Kiyonaga and Shigemasa were manifestly Hokusai's earliest models; it was also a time when the Kabuki actor-print was flourishing under the aegis of Shunshō and his Katsukawa School.

The Era of An-ei/Temmei (1772–88) was a particularly active one in the Japanese intellectual world. Since the 1620s Japan had been deliberately closed off from the West. Contact with foreigners was barred, the Shōgun permitting only limited trade delegations from China, Korea, Okinawa and Holland. But in the late eighteenth and early nineteenth centuries there was a revival of interest in Western civilization, especially in things that could be studied visually. Dutch scientific books, notably those on anatomy, were circulated and under the leadership of the *rangakusha*—students of Western learning—Japanese scholars and physicians for the first time came into intimate contact with European knowledge. Traditional science and medicine began to be revolutionized, and the art world soon followed: students and imitators of European painting and etching were already consolidated under their own schools by the 1780s. Most important for ukiyo-e, the Occidental device of *perspective* came gradually to be assimilated into the artist's subconscious; and the detailed, realistic technique of copperplate engraving also strongly influenced the new trend towards realism in Japanese art.

It was this powerful European influence—stemming from the Scientific Revolution—that succeeded in overwhelming the strongly decorative tendencies of Japanese art and produced, in the end, the print masterpieces of Sharaku and Hokusai. It is doubtless because of this influence that the later Japanese landscape print is immediately appreciable to the Western viewer, whereas the work of the earlier masters may seem only quaintly stylized pictorialism. Indeed, it was this stimulus to break out of the conventional Japanese mould of art that permitted Hokusai to extend his creative powers, to reach beyond the bounds of his tradition and achieve an amalgamation at once dramatically creative, yet withal eminently Japanese.

Not unexpectedly, Hokusai was hardly likely to be content for long with the demanding—if fascinating—craft of reproducing the work of others. Thus some four years later, in 1778, at the age of 18, we find him apprenticed to the master of the ukiyo-e actor-print, Shunshō, whose studio-workshop was at Ningyō-chō, near the centre of Edo. We

have no record of how this important development transpired: probably there were introductions of some kind; but it was surely the artistic potential of the young Hokusai that effected his entrance into such a major atelier. In fact, it may be that Hokusai's adoption by the Nakajima family occurred at this date. In that case, it would have been this prestigious connection that enabled him to enter the Katsukawa School, which normally entailed a substantial initiation fee. Subsequently, when Nakajima's own eldest son died early, it should have been Hokusai's duty to return and take over the family craft. However, he must have declined this honour, preferring to remain a lowly ukiyo-e artist, even though this meant breaking his financially rewarding connection with his adopted family.

Most artistic groups in Old Japan were organized as schools under a famed master, with his sons (rarely daughters) and pupils serving long periods of apprenticeship, including, for the pupils, much menial work, before achieving individual recognition and, sometimes, independence or a sub-school of their own. As with the feudal society itself (*samurai* means, after all, 'he who serves'), allegiance to the master and to the style was *de rigueur*—and it was to be here that Hokusai was later to meet his first obstacle in the pursuit of his own path. A brief digression will thus be necessary to understand just what the situation of the fledgling artist was like.

Shunshō was 52 at the time Hokusai entered his studio in 1778 and in his prime, both in the production of vividly realistic actor-prints—breaking with the conventionalized patterns of the traditional Torii School—and in his more personalized art of the *bijin-ga* hand-paintings of beautiful women. Indeed it is noteworthy that Shunshō, following his own teacher Shunsui and his predecessor Chōshun, was that *rara avis* among ukiyo-e print-artists, a master of hand-painting as well. In that sense, also (though Hokusai was not later to continue his work in the actor-print), this Shunshō connection was a crucial one in the artist's development.

The great innovation in the Kabuki print under the aegis of Shunshō had been the new conception of the actor as an individual—not just a stage-type—visualized in a stylized yet nonetheless realistic manner, skilfully expressing a particular actor's quirks and mannerisms. Such a trend was developed further not only by Shunshō himself but also by his leading pupils, with competition later from the rival Utagawa School under the leadership of Toyokuni and Kunimasa, as well as by such independent masters as Sharaku and Enkyō. This emphasis on the realistic portrayal of the individual necessarily required daily contact with the actors themselves (in addition to the customary detailed knowledge of the plays and the theatre). A Kabuki artist thus became a kind of journalist, married to his subject and free to work on other themes only when such rare commissions came in. Hokusai, during his apprentice period, had to take on whatever task was given to him, not only the production of occasional print-designs of his own, but also the menial work of the studio which was the lot of any beginner.

Although the name Hokusai is known throughout the world today, it is well to remember that he entered a school (or workshop) already staffed with strong competition: Shunkō, Shunjō and Shun-ei, for example, produced some of the finest actor-prints known during the 1770s and 1780s—a genre in which, for that matter, Hokusai never succeeded in surpassing them. Indeed, their mentor Shunshō himself was so prolific, definitive and long-lived an artist that he could very easily have carried the banner of his school single-handed.

However, in the communal society of Japan at least, the establishment of a school, and the development of a strong group of disciples, was deemed an important element of a successful artist's prestige. In such a society, the lone genius, though he might have patrons and aficionados, was always considered an outsider. So when, within a year of beginning his apprenticeship, we find the young Hokusai already publishing actor-prints, we must assume this was because Shunshō took a special interest in the budding artist; it was the first major step in Hokusai's creative development.

Indeed, although Hokusai aficionados may enthuse over newly discovered early prints bearing the artist's first *nom d'artiste* Katsukawa Shunrō, such works are, usually, only barely competent: interesting as 'early Hokusai' rather than as specimens of this particular genre (Plate 13, Figs. 1–3). Significantly, however, the pen-name given to the young artist was *Shunrō* ('Spring-brilliance'), the first part clearly derived from the name of the master Shunshō ('Spring-brightness'), the second part from the teacher's alternative name Kyokurōsai, which was something of an honour.

The young Hokusai did not suddenly revolutionize this established atelier, but his early works are certainly of interest. At least three actor-prints are known of his debut-period, the Eighth Month of 1778. That of Plate 13 is probably the right panel of a triptych. Like many of these early works, it is known only in incomplete specimens: an indication that sales did not warrant more extensive editions. The print is a good, professional example of Katsukawa work, the background well realized, and the actor's pose well expressed.

One may, indeed, remark the beginnings of a distinctive style, even within the confines of the conventions decreed for the Kabuki print. Yet while we here glimpse something of the artistic beauty inherent in the female impersonator of the Kabuki drama, we miss the dramatic power of the mentor Shunshō—or even of Hokusai's elder confrères

2 'Yaozō III in Seven Roles'. *Hosoban* actor-print for children, designed for making cut-out doll; *c.* 1792. Signed Shunrō. (The 'ivy-leaf under Fuji' seal of Hokusai's publisher Tsutaya—whose shop appears in Plate 44—will be seen at right.) (For another Hokusai cut-out print, see Fig. 16.) (Note: for print sizes, see Appendix, p. 279. Data on signatures are given in text or caption only where of special interest. Full details will be found in Appendix. For provenance of

the originals, see Acknowledgements, p. 317.)

3 Ebizō I [= Danjūrō V] as Bandit, and Hangorō III as Itinerant-priest. *Hosoban* diptych; Eleventh Month, 1791. Both prints are signed Shunrō. (For other Hokusai actor-prints of this period, see Figs. 1–4; all Figs. appear in Appendix.)

within the same school. But Hokusai's development as an artist of Kabuki was leisurely. It is only in the late works of his Shunrō Period that he really begins to assert his individuality; just possibly, self-expression may even have been purposely restrained by the regimen of the school.

One curiosity of Hokusai's later actor-*oeuvre* is the *omocha-e* or 'cut-out print' of Plate 2, quite literally intended to be clipped up as a child's plaything. Here we view a famous Kabuki actor's 'Seven Instant Changes' of role, each effected by a simple change of costume, yet achieving (for us, necessarily, in the mind's eye) a surprising variation of mood and atmosphere, despite utilization of the same actor's face and pose. The artist, while working within the nominal confines of the traditional actor-print, has managed to extend the form beyond its customary boundaries to—in the end—a three-dimensional conclusion.

From this later period, too, dates the rare diptych of Plate 3, which gives interesting hints of the direction Hokusai's work might have taken had he remained in the Katsukawa School.[1] While superficially resembling the style of Hokusai's elder confrère Shun-ei, such prints also begin to reveal something of the artist's own specific character: the forceful and somewhat rough manner of forming outlines, the emphasis on frozen movement, the sense of latent, restrained power concealed within the minature framework. One can well envisage the artist as growing in stature as a master of the theatre, competing on a level with Sharaku

and Toyokuni, perhaps achieving his own school; and with it being dragged down with the decadent conventions of the later Kabuki print. (Indeed, Hokusai's few later actor-prints well support this thesis, see for example Plate 194.) Fortunately, he was subsequently to break out of this mould, turning from the theatre to that other world of ukiyo-e beauty, the *bijin-ga* or genre figure-print, to produce some of the masterpieces of the second Golden Age of 'floating-world art', the 1790s.

This is not, however, our last word on the Shunrō Period for, one way or another, the artist did manage to escape, now and then, from the confines of the theatre and search out subjects and styles more suited to his own taste and natural talent.

NOTE

1 Dates for Kabuki works are those of the actual theatrical performance, for which the print was—usually but not always—published simultaneously. Such dates are cited here in a compromise between Eastern and Western reckoning. Thus, for Plate 3, in the lunar calendar of Kansei III the Eleventh Month corresponded to 26 November–24 December; but often the Eleventh—and always the Twelfth Month—extended into the next year in the Gregorian calendar (assuming that the play ran on to the end of the month, not necessarily the case). Sometimes, accuracy is more critical: thus the death of Hokusai's mentor Shunshō is often cited loosely as 1792, whereas it actually fell on the eighth day of the Twelfth Month—running well into 1793 (19 January, to be exact). (Correct, for example, R. Keyes, 'Hokusai', in *Encyclopedia of Japan*, 1983, and L. Bickford, 'The Katsukawa', in *Impressions* No. 14, 1988, p. 1.)

III
The Making of an
Ukiyo-e Master (2)

1

MORE suited to Hokusai's natural talent—and certainly of more general interest than the early Kabuki designs—are his occasional prints that feature less formalized aspects of legend and of the floating world. Such works point, indeed, towards the varied subjects and approaches that were to characterize the artist's long future career. Most of these prints are again rare: another indication that popular demand seldom warranted publication beyond the initial run, customarily only some two hundred copies.

Possibly Hokusai's most perfect print of this early period is—rather surprisingly—his masterful depiction of the two massive professional wrestlers Dewanoumi and Kimenzan (Plate 16). The art of *sumō*, Japanese-style wrestling, which flourished along with the other performing arts in the 1780s, was more like a ritualistic morality play than a sport, and Hokusai's tableau captures the essence of the stylized melodrama of the contest. There are also possibly subconscious overtones of the erotic Hindu elephant-god Ganesa in the way the two wrestlers stoically embrace—each trying to assess his opponent's weak points before attempting a throw.

Likewise from this period date several series of humorous prints that reveal Hokusai's fascination with the comic—even slapstick—side of life (Plate 4). This type of scene was to form a significant part of his *oeuvre* in the miniature and illustration formats; and its rising popularity is typical of the mounting trend towards hedonism, even decadence, that was to characterize the succeeding century in Japan.

4 Man and Wife in Tipsy Dance. From the early print-series 'The Mibu Farces'. Small-*chūban* size (slightly trimmed); *c.* mid-1780s. Signed Shunrō. (For another of this series, see Fig. 6.)

5 Young Kintoki with Eagle and Bear-cub. *Ōban*-size print (slightly trimmed); *c.* late 1780s. Signed Shunrō. (Note: the '*tomoe*-under-mountain' seal of the publisher Eijudō—whose shop appears in Plate 232—is seen at bottom.)

Legend, children and animals were to be other frequent themes of Hokusai's maturity and we find outstanding work already at this early period. The depiction of the Herculean young Kintoki, for example (Plate 5), both subduing and playing with the wild eagle and bear-cub, goes back for inspiration to the great Kiyonaga, but none the less reveals a solid sense of triangular composition that is typical of Hokusai's dynamic method.

Other interesting Hokusai works of these years are the several series of figure-prints in smallish *chūban* size, featuring the fair beauties of the Floating World of Edo life and leisure. Some thirty prints are known, parts of series that presumably never saw completion. This is a feature that will characterize much of this master's print-production, reflecting an urge to publish that was always far greater than the market could support.

Among the more notable of these series is the *Fūryū otokodate hakkei* (Eight Views of Stylish Gallants), of the late 1780s, of which some five designs are known. These prints feature modern young heroes of the age, usually with their lady-loves. The style is again taken directly from a master of the figure-print, Kiyonaga—with some influences from Shunshō and Shunchō—but the design represents a striking stage in the artist's attempt to escape from the restric-

tions of the actor-print. The scene shown here (Plate 6)—a courtesan and her lover in a house of assignation—is typical of the series and a familiar one in ukiyo-e; it was to be raised to even greater heights in Hokusai's work of the next decade. The young hero Bunshichi (leader of a gang of Ōsaka gallants) has borrowed the pocket-mirror of his love, the courtesan Shimizu, who adjusts his coiffure. Through the window is viewed a flight of wild geese—a reference both to his nickname Karigane ('Wild Goose') and to one of the traditional 'Eight Views' of the series-title.

Also in the Kiyonaga/Shunchō manner, but impressive designs in their own right, are the prints of the *Haikai shūitsu* (Haiku Masterpieces) series. At least three designs from this rare series are known; our example (Plate 7) features a most effective foreground scene; the background landscape is hardly integrated, yet the total effect is masterful and well matched to the accompanying verse (the nominal purpose of the series):

'One speaks out and / the lips turn cool / before the autumn breeze'.[1]

Mention should also be made of Hokusai's rare figure-work in the long narrow 'pillar-print' format such as Plate 14. Here again he is glimpsed working in the shadow of the masters Shunshō and Kiyonaga, but with most elegant

6 Courtesan and Lover. From the series *Eight Views of Stylish Gallants*. *Chūban*-size print; *c.* late 1780s. Signed Shunrō. (For others of this series, see Figs. 10–11.)

7 Maidservant and Geisha by the Sumida River. From the series *Haiku Masterpieces*. (For details see Appendix, Prints, No. 14.) Small-*chūban*-size print; *c.* late 1780s. Signed Shunrō. (The circular seal at lower left is that of the early print-dealer Hayashi.)

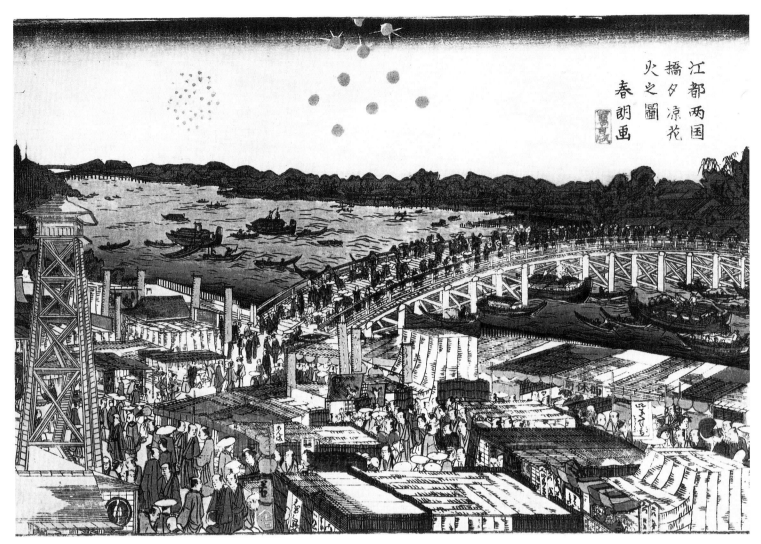

江
都
両
国
橋
夕
涼
花
火
之
圖
春
朗
画

8 'Fireworks at Ryōgoku Bridge'. *Ōban*-size print; *c.* 1790. Signed Shunrō. Note: although the version shown here is the most effective and well printed, the alternative, Eijudō edition probably represents the earlier issue. There is also a later edition of this print, with altered title and colouring. (For other early Hokusai *uki-e* see Plate 17 and Fig. 12 ff.) Where, as here, title is on original print, translation is given in quotes. Translations are not necessarily literal or complete.

results. It is also during this period that we see a beginning of production in that staple genre of the miniaturistic print, *surimono*, private editions of luxurious paper and printing, intended for use as personal gifts and New Year's greetings by the poetasters and verse-masters who commissioned them (Plate 18, Fig. 7).

<h2 style="text-align:center">2</h2>

It was, significantly enough, in the later half of this Shunrō Period that the artist commenced his first positive efforts in the landscape genre. As with all this artist's early work these prints represent serious, draughtsmanlike designing, executed with skill, but with only limited creative imagination. Unsigned, they might pass for the standard work of Shigemasa or Masayoshi (if not for the more distinctive *oeuvre* of the senior master in this genre, Toyoharu). But there is as yet little foreshadowing of the magnificent Hokusai views of four decades later.

Perhaps Hokusai's most interesting design in this, the *uki-e* or 'perspective-print' genre, is that of Plate 8. For

such a traditional 'Fireworks' theme the print shows unusual emphasis on the foreground details of the stalls and sideshows set up to attract the crowds that attended this midsummer event. In the receding lines of shops, bridge and river will be perceived the essence of the *uki-e*; but in the fire-tower and environs at left, one can see how imperfectly the principles of Occidental perspective were comprehended. (Beyond the willows at far right lies Honjo, site of the artist's birthplace and of several of his numerous, always temporary abodes.)

Such prints belong to that curious category called not only *uki-e* but also *kubomi-e*—'trompe l'oeil pictures'—an adaptation of Occidental perspective as only partially understood by Japanese artists, on the basis of limited contact with European etchings and engravings. These may appear only quaint to us today, but in Japan of that time they were considered most avant-garde—just as Hokusai's own later *Fuji* prints were to seem in the Paris of the 1880s.

Uki-e (literally, 'floating pictures') were originally designed primarily to be viewed through lens and mirror, in a type of panoramic peep-show imported from Europe with the early eighteenth century.[2] Though doubtless not a major genre in themselves, these perspective-pictures nevertheless represented a widening in the horizons of the ukiyo-e artist, when compared with the limited and essentially indoor tradition of his usual subject-matter: the

Yoshiwara courtesans and the Kabuki actors. This new *plein-air* theme was, indeed, to prove the salvation of ukiyo-e in the coming generation, by which time the traditional range of the school had almost reached a dead end.

Hokusai's prints in this category were modelled on the pioneer work of Toyoharu in developing this ukiyo-e genre during the 1770s and 1780s, but with a greater emphasis on architectural structure and detailed attention to intricate composition. The designs are at once powerful and imposing, if lacking the delicacy of the earlier master. The example here (Plate 8) seems likely to have been the most popular of Hokusai's works in this form, being known also in alternative editions with different title and sky effects. And another of the artist's *uki-e*—depicting the Asakusa Temple—was even copied by the minor master Shūchō a few years subsequently: a rare example of Hokusai's early work already influencing a fellow-artist.

Such designs served to form Hokusai's introduction to the nascent landscape genre which, a generation later, was to make his name renowned worldwide. For the moment, however, the landscape was not an independent category of the Japanese print, but hovered somewhere between the genre scene and the historical tableau, with little appreciation of the natural grandeur of landscape itself. The popular landscape-print was only to come into its own with the boom in plebeian travel from the late 1820s. The more immediate successor to the *uki-e* in Hokusai's work was to make its appearance in his varied illustrations to the historical novels of the following decade—the artist taking ample advantage of experience gained both in the *uki-e* and the actor-print genres, as well as in the earlier picture-novelettes (to be discussed below).

In fact, if one were to search for a more distinctive precursor to the later Hokusai, it would be found in his rare adaptations of the supernatural to the 'perspective-picture', as in Plate 17. Here the subject has precedents in prints of Toyoharu, and in books by Sekien, Shunshō and Shun-ei; but Hokusai forcefully transforms the architectural emphasis of the usual *uki-e* to the ghostly apparitions, and to the cowering humanity depicted (composed, significantly, not of timid maidens but of grown men). The viewer is drawn into the scene not simply by a device of *trompe l'oeil*, but by a feat of verisimilitude that acts very much in the way a first visit to a circus Haunted House acts on a child. Naturally, when compared with the works of the artist's maturity, even from a decade later, the design is again lacking in unity: the carefully delineated landscape background, with its impressively perspected rows of trees at left, is largely irrelevant so far as the main theme is concerned; the pairing of ghosts at left and top is confusing; and there is no real centre of focus. Yet withal, the print is an early masterpiece; and (this being an age when ghosts were very much alive for the average citizen) it is a theme that Hokusai was to return to often in later years, with increasing mastery.[3]

After this examination of some typical examples of Hokusai's *oeuvre* in this formative decade and a half, it may be useful to pause a moment for an overview. To summarize, we can say that the artist's style during his Shunrō Period

tends to fall into three distinct categories. The first lies in direct imitation of his own prime teacher Shunshō—and less directly of Kiyonaga and Shigemasa—and lasted from 1778 to about 1782. The second period—up to 1787—is one featuring greater skill within the Katsukawa tradition (but with unexplained hints of possible problems in certain of the roughly executed 'Gumbatei' prints of 1785–94, when the artist at times used this additional *nom de plume*). And thirdly we may conclude with the period running to 1794, when the artist has developed his own style and begins to express his individuality with greater force, gradually freeing himself—particularly after the death of Shunshō early in 1793—from the bonds of feudal obligation.

The specific formats and subject-matter of Hokusai's work in this period are detailed in the Appendix, Prints, Nos. 1–28, but the total of well over two hundred extant prints is only a tentative one, for no comprehensive survey has yet been made of Hokusai's *oeuvre*—scattered in museums and collections throughout the world. Indeed, since many of his early works are known today only in a single specimen, it is quite possible that up to half of his earlier productions, never reprinted after an initial run of some two hundred examples, just did not survive.

Of these two hundred or more extant works, over 120 are in the narrow *hosoban* format (for print-sizes, see p. 279)—predominantly actor-prints, plus some wrestlers, warriors and children (see Plates 2, 3, 13 and Figs. 1–4); at least 45 are vertical *chūban* (a somewhat larger, squarish size), representing figure-prints, children and warriors; some four comprise the slightly larger, vertical *aiban* size— *sumō* wrestlers (Plate 16 and Fig. 9). At least 13 are in the larger, horizontal *ōban* format—figures and *uki-e* landscapes (Figs. 12–14); some 16 are comprised of vertical *ōban* prints—of figures, children, warriors and Gods of Luck (Plate 5); at least eight appear in the long, narrow 'pillar-print' format—a kind of 'poor-man's *kakemono*', featuring scenes suitable for hanging in the parlour—figures, animals, Gods of Luck (Plate 14, Fig. 5); and perhaps a dozen are comprised of *surimono*, especially calendar-prints (Plate 18, Fig. 7). Such rough figures represent but an interim report, since new treasures are discovered every season— sometimes, every month; with this prodigious artist, there is no way of knowing what will turn up next.

3

Hokusai's work in the Katsukawa School included not only prints (and possibly paintings) but also book-illustration, which was to constitute a predominant portion of the artist's *oeuvre*. There may be a tendency in some circles to think of the painter and printmaker as artists, the illustrator as artisan. Such distinctions did not exist in Hokusai's time, nor have they any validity today. A single painting or print may, indeed, be more important (and certainly more expensive) than any single book-illustration; but when the total book is judged, it may well be considered a major work and of greater interest than the independent print or painting.

Of course, in reproduction it is almost impossible to

evaluate the merits of the original, and the viewer's impression may be revised, even reversed; the painting reduced to miniature size is lacking in power; the print, perhaps only halved in size, may retain much of its grandeur; the book-illustration will profit from being shown in full size, but then lose the context of the total volume and its place in the full series.

Suffice it to say that Hokusai fulfilled three major roles as an artist: painter, print-designer and illustrator; but he considered none of these any more important or prestigious than the other. Indeed, he probably enjoyed the painstaking, miniature work of book-illustration most of all, for—aside from his physical pleasure in the creative act itself—it provided the greatest variety and range of action for the artist, and also reached the largest audience.

Yet in turning to the books themselves, it must be admitted that, for this early period at least, the medium was hardly an impressive one. For, as is only natural for an inexperienced commercial artist, Hokusai's early work is not in the format of the grand picture-books, but in the more journeyman tasks of illustration for the light novelettes popular at the time: mainly *kibyōshi* (didactic tales) and *sharé-hon* (Yoshiwara stories)—the latter with only limited illustration. Perhaps the most striking feature of the popular literature of this period is the preponderance of the 'picture-novelette', in which the entire work (usually comprised of two or three slim volumes of ten pages each) consisted of illustrations with the text—including the characters' conversation—inserted within each plate. This format had derived from the earlier picture-scroll, and formed the nucleus of children's fiction from the later seventeenth century, only in Hokusai's time developing into a form of adult literature as well. Because of the intimate relation between text and plate, the early examples occasionally featured the authors' own illustrations and sometimes—as in Hokusai's case—the rather amateur text of the artist. However, by the 1780s a separate class of semi-professional authors had taken over much of the field, led by the great Santō Kyōden, who himself had started out as an ukiyo-e artist of great distinction, but evidently found authorship more lucrative and to his taste.[4]

It is of particular interest that in several of these books the texts are by Hokusai as well: an indication that, whatever formal schooling he enjoyed, he had also developed into something of a *bunjin* or literatus, albeit in the comic, plebeian tradition. Naturally these *kibyōshi* tend to feature a greater freedom of expression than was possible for the artist in illustrating other authors' texts.

But despite his best efforts the young Hokusai failed to achieve any great literary acclaim; he could not, in the end, equal the work of his contemporary, Kyōden. Nevertheless, it was not long before the artist's strength in book-illustration came to be generally recognized, and his name began to appear not only in the novelettes of Kyōden himself, but in the work of his celebrated follower Kyokutei Bakin as well. Hokusai's collaboration with Bakin was to last many years, continuing into the new age of popular fiction with the *yomi-hon* 'Gothic novels' of the coming generation.

Given the limited general interest of the medium, our plates on this theme will necessarily be few and fragmentary. More than any other form of Japanese art, these little booklets must be enjoyed directly and at leisure, and that includes reading the witty texts that adorn each page.

The majority of Hokusai's early books are in the *kibyōshi* or 'Yellow Cover' genre, inexpensively produced light fiction, the equivalent of our 'pulp novels'. The earliest of these date from 1780, and being most often published at the season of New Year, they would have been designed the previous autumn when the artist was only 19. One characteristic example is the tableau of our Plate 9, which shows the climax of the story: the hero Banzuiin Chōbei, unmasking the deceit of the clerk Jinkurō, throws him down and out. Despite the rough engraving, printing and paper, throughout these primitively charming 'Yellow

9 Dramatic Tableau. Illustration from the *kibyōshi* novelette *The Love-mound of Meguro*; *chūbon*-size, 1780. Signed Katsukawa Shunrō. (For other early Hokusai books see Appendix, Fig. 171 ff. For book sizes see also p. 298.)

10 Warrior breaking out of Prison. Illustration from the *kibyōshi* novelette *The Earlier Pre-Taiheiki. Chūbon*-size, 1786. Signed Shunrō.

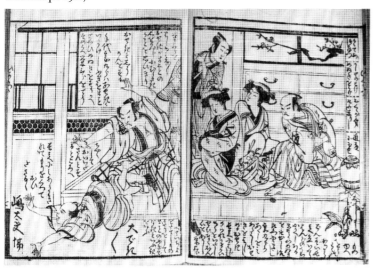

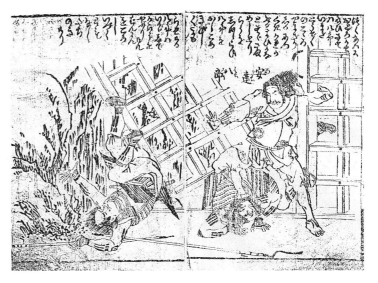

11 Geisha and Lover. Illustration from the *sharé-hon* novelette *Views of Fukagawa*. *Chūbon*-size, 1782. Signed Shunrō.

12 *Below* Young Lovers with Voyeur. Illustration from the collection of risqué stories *Erotica: Groping in the Dark*. *Chūbon*-size, 1782. Signed Katsu Shunrō; the text is also probably by Hokusai. (For other early shunga examples, see Figs. 230, 231.)

Books' one finds intriguing hints of Hokusai's later development. The 'Jailbreak' scene of Plate 10, for instance, forms an interesting precursor to the more famous samurai tableaux of our Plates 101, 319 ff.

Another related genre was the *sharé-hon* or 'Books of Élan', devoted to witty tales of the Yoshiwara (and occasionally of the lesser pleasure-quarters). Here the sparse illustrations are only an adjunct to the texts, but they therefore tend to be more concentrated in composition. Typical of Hokusai's early work in this field is Plate 11 from the *Fukagawa haiken* (Views of Fukagawa) of 1782. As in all these youthful efforts one perceives a sure sense of composition—though the designs lack really significant innovations.

Hokusai continued his work in these popular genres for two full decades, his style gradually becoming more mature and less indebted to that of his mentor Shunshō. These later efforts will be discussed in a subsequent chapter.

While on the book theme it must be added that one of the ukiyo-e artist's standard commissions was *shunga* ('Spring Pictures'), that category of Japanese art devoted to the erotic. Hokusai's early experiments in this difficult genre date from his Shunrō Period, and feature a careful transmission of the Shunshō style in this medium, as well as a painstaking attention to anatomical detail that was to

13 The Kabuki-actor Hanshirō IV in the Role of the Tea-house Courtesan Kashiku. *Hosoban*-size print; Eighth Month, 1779. (Among Hokusai's earliest known works—designed at the age of 19—the print is signed with the artist's first *nom d'artiste* 'Katsukawa Shunrō'. For other early Hokusai actor-prints see Appendix, Fig. 1 ff.)

14 *Right* Lady Walking in Snow. Pillar-print; *c.* late 1780s. Though toned with age, the print is preserved in its original, simple kakemono mounting. (Signed Katsu Shunrō. The verse is unsigned but in the hand of Hokusai's mentor Shunshō. For another early Hokusai print in this format see Fig. 5.)

15 Matron with Lover. Detail from a small *yoko-bon* shunga volume, title lost; *c.* 1789. Signed Gankō—thought to be a Hokusai pen-name. (See also Fig. 231.)

serve the artist in good stead during later years (Plates 12 and 15).

A page of book-illustration—usually incorporating the text around and about the design—was not necessarily any easier to compose than a more impressive large print. And it should be pointed out that the artist's early production of prints was far exceeded by the thousand and more pages of book-illustration designed during the same period. These consisted of some 46 works in the *kibyōshi* genre (in total at least 110 slim volumes, with over 660 illustrations, most double-page); four Kabuki booklets; four Yoshiwara and other *sharé-hon*; two comic *hanashi-bon*; three shunga books; and several miscellaneous works. The Appendix, Books, Nos. 1–53, provides a full listing of the artist's illustrated books from this Shunrō Period.

But though they form a treasure-house for the Hokusai specialist and are well worthy of more detailed attention, these early books can really only be savoured by holding the originals in one's hands, by grasping the intimate relation of text and illustration—a feat no longer easy, even for the native art-scholar, so great have been the changes in language, script and orthography in the intervening two hundred years. Hokusai's total production of well over two hundred prints and at least sixty books during these years was no mean achievement for an apprentice. But for a seasoned artist of 34 with a full 15 years of experience it was not particularly notable, averaging about 14 prints and four books annually. Clearly Hokusai's immense talents were not being fully utilized, and it is likely that much of his time was being spent on studio work—for example, the backgrounds of designs to be signed by senior con-frères. This was surely one reason for the artist's eventual departure from the Katsukawa atelier.

The young Hokusai thus experienced a full and varied period of apprenticeship; and managed to encompass in his work not only the actor-prints that formed the bread-and-butter of his school, but also a multitude of other ukiyo-e subjects and formats that were to serve him in good stead when he chose, shortly, to set out on his own. But although Hokusai's *oeuvre* grows increasingly skilled in execution during these fifteen years, the number of real masterpieces is small. His few outstanding works are rare commissions on untypical themes—and the artist had to experience the impending, difficult period of breaking with the past before he could discover his true *métier*.

When three decades ago James Michener, later to become friend and collaborator, wrote in his perceptive *Floating World* of the first half of Hokusai's career '. . . in 1817 an impoverished artist already in his mid-forties and lacking fame . . .', in addition to remarking the error in dates (either '1807' or 'mid-fifties'), I chided him thus in an early review-article:

> There is, I hope, no need to cite the vast quantity of Hokusai's work, dating from about 1780, and much of it already famous by the end of the eighteenth century. . . . Mr. Michener has chosen Hokusai as an example of 'late development', and has accordingly let his judgement be governed by this *idée fixe*. . . .[5]

But perhaps we both were right: it is simply a question of how one evaluates these first twenty years (of which the final, crucial five will be the subject of the next chapter) against the total of the artist's seventy-year career. Certainly many will wonder, with Michener, why Hokusai did not express his undoubted genius more graphically during his first decade and a half.

NOTES

1 This famous Bashō haiku is essentially didactic in nature—reflecting the Confucian precept 'Speak not ill of others, nor well of one's self'—but, in typical ukiyo-e fashion, it is here interpreted in purely sensual, imagist terms.
2 The *megane-e/nozoki-e* 'peep-pictures' had several practical functions: as well as being laid flat under a special optical viewer, they could also be mounted on paper lanterns, with tiny apertures cut or punched out for moon/stars/lamps/lighted windows and the like.
3 The original title of the print—*Hyaku-monogatari* (One Hundred Tales)—refers to the folk-custom of villagers gathering together at night and telling a series of ghost tales while gradually extinguishing the lamps: at the end of this ceremony the actual ghosts were said to appear. Hokusai's tableau presumably depicts the ending of one such seance. For some of the other supernatural scenes referred to, see Plates 96–103, 277, 282.
4 For my translation (and illustration) of a typical *kibyōshi*—Kyōden's famed *Edo-umare uwaki-no-kabayaki* of 1785—see *La Chant de l'Oreiller*, Geneva, 1973 (English version, *Song of the Pillow*, in press).
5 See *Harvard Journal of Asiatic Studies*, XX, 1/2 (June 1957), pp. 330–57.

IV
Independence,
Hard Times, Rebirth

1

LITTLE is known of Hokusai's personal life during his formative years, but Japan itself was in something of a turmoil. The Temmei Famines of 1783–7, when the artist was in his teens, followed upon severely inclement weather and massive crop failures, causing widespread unrest, looting, starvation and, not unnaturally, curtailment of many publishing and other cultural schemes.

The subsequent—and consequent—Kansei Reforms of 1787–93 (while Hokusai was still in the Shunshō atelier), in attempting to root out the corruption and laxity of the previous Tanuma Regime and to enforce austerity and morality, essayed, with only moderate success, to limit the range and quality of ukiyo-e publication. It was, for example, from these reforms that in 1790 the Censorship System was decreed for publications: the *kiwame* (censor's) seal being required on all commercial prints as a sign that they had been approved. And though the townsmen were too clever and resilient to obey any more than the superficial form of such edicts, there was nevertheless a clouding of the unsuppressed vitality of the previous age, reflected, perhaps, in the fashion for svelte, attenuated figures in the prints of the ensuing decade.

It is of no little interest that the Kansei Reforms failed in the end because of strong opposition from the Shōgun's own retainers, especially from the influential ladies of his harem, those wealthy and redoubtable authoritarian women who formed such a critical portion of the audience for ukiyo-e, and particularly for the actor-prints and erotica.

Hokusai reached maturity just at the time of these government reforms—both of Temmei and Kansei. Having no political aspirations he doubtless, like most Edoites, obeyed the letter of the law while taking all liberties that would not catch the eye of the feudal government's numerous 'spies'. However, the pressure to conform was strong throughout this period, and Hokusai (with his early contemporary Shiba Kōkan) stands out as an example of an Edo artist who, by strength of will and character, was able to remain aloof. Other ukiyo-e artists—Harumachi, Kyōden, Utamaro, Kuniyoshi, not to mention the publisher Tsutaya—suffered government prosecution, but that was for specific offences of satirizing the authorities; whereas it could be said that Hokusai's whole life represented a silent protest against bureaucracy and the oppression of feudal conventions.

As for the artist's private life at this time, all we can say is that, to judge from the ages of his several children, he must have married in his mid-20s. Indeed, it was possibly under the calming influence of family life that his designs from this period turned from prints of actors and girls to historical and landscape subjects, especially to *uki-e* (those semi-

historical landscapes using Occidental-influenced perspective techniques) and to prints of children. The artist's book-illustrations and texts also turned away from Kabuki and Yoshiwara themes in favour of historical and didactic subjects.

When the master Katsukawa Shunshō died early in 1793 at the age of 66 there were, naturally, repercussions in the atelier, so long under his steadying influence and meticulous tutelage.[1] The senior disciple Shunkō was already 50 and still active but—possibly due to the paralysis of his right arm a few years earlier—evidently chose to take an honorary position and let his younger confrère Shun-ei take over nominal leadership of the studio. Shun-ei was several years younger than Hokusai; but in his actual achievements, and potential, in the narrow field of actor-prints, he probably ranked after Shunkō in the hierarchy of pupils (the very talented Shunjō having died several years before). But where did this leave Hokusai, already 32 and highly ambitious? His position was secure enough, but there was no very appealing future in sight.

There are tales that the elder Shunkō once publicly criticized a poster-painting done by Hokusai; possibly it had been commissioned outside the studio and Shunkō may have been critical of that aspect rather than of the execution of the painting itself. The young Hokusai was—to judge from what we know of his later character—by nature stubborn, proud, individualistic and somewhat conceited. Whatever the actual circumstances, Hokusai's extant work in the two years following his teacher's death is minimal, mainly occasional novelettes and *surimono* greeting-cards; possibly his best efforts were expended in the field of painting—like the poster, now lost. It is also in occasional prints of this period that we find him sometimes dropping the school name and substituting 'Kusamura': perhaps an indication of his gradual divorce from the Katsukawa School (Fig. 7).

Lifetime employment has always been a Japanese ideal and it comes as something of a surprise to find Hokusai in 1795—his fifteenth year under the Katsukawa School—completely abandoning the *nom d'artiste* 'Shunrō'. According to one account, Hokusai was expelled from the School in that year. The details are unclear but it is thought that he had been secretly studying under the rival, neo-classical Kanō School. His purpose was, of course, to expand his repertory, to experience more in the *painting* medium than was possible within the confines of a print-studio (and one limited mainly to Kabuki themes, at that). At the same time, there is the story that his impulse to stray afield lay in his resentment of the criticisms, such as that cited above, from Shunkō. As Hokusai is said to have commented in later life, 'What really motivated the development of my artistic style

16 *Opposite Sumō* Wrestlers in the Ring. *Aiban*-size print; *c.* late 1780s. Signed Katsu Shunrō. (For another early Hokusai *sumō*-print, see Fig. 9.)

17 *Above* Haunted House. *Ōban*-size print; *c.* 1790. (For reference to other Hokusai *uki-e* see Plate 8.)

was the embarrassment I suffered at Shunkō's hands.' And indeed, after the death of Shunshō, the atelier and workshop may well have been the scene of numerous rivalries, from which Hokusai doubtless felt it would be best to remove himself.

Although it is customary to think of Hokusai's period of apprenticeship as representing a curtailment in the development of his talents, the benign influence of the great Shunshō must not be lightly dismissed: under his aegis Hokusai was able to master the predominant ukiyo-e styles of the age, to grasp the powerful, detailed yet flamboyantly realistic manner of the theatrical print. This long and severe period of discipline may well have been the catalyst that created the master that we know today. Nevertheless, after well over a decade of restricted activity, it was natural that a vital and creative artist like Hokusai should wish to strike out on his own: to explore other subjects, other styles— even beyond the bounds of the ukiyo-e school. Such was not, however, the norm in a feudal society, with its strong traditions of lord and vassal, master and pupil, senior disciple and junior apprentice. Whatever the circumstances of

Hokusai's birth and adoption, he was never wealthy, never adequately patronized. Estrangement from the Katsukawa School was therefore a milestone in his career: stimulating and full of potential—both for success and disaster.

The reasons for this break with security, with the past, lay surely in Hokusai's insatiable thirst for knowledge, regardless of the consequences. And the consequences were, indeed, sometimes drastic, entailing a loss of all those privileges, perquisites, patronage and services available only to a member of an established atelier. Hokusai had no easy time; for a while he was even compelled to eke out a precarious living as a pedlar of condiments and calendars about the streets of Edo. These years were also marked by a period of dissolute behaviour as he sought an outlet for his energies and artistic frustrations.

Furthermore, in the year 1794 his young wife died, leaving a small son and two daughters. However, Hokusai was never a man to keep house for himself, and after the customary year or two he remarried, with the subsequent birth of three daughters (including the famed O-Ei, who was to care for her father in his old age), and then a son. This was clearly a period of change and crisis both in Hokusai's life and in his career.

But whatever the artist's personal problems, his painting-studies were surprisingly extensive during this, his first taste of independence. Indeed, it is impossible to understand the later Hokusai without comprehending the background of his wide and tenacious studies in all the art-forms of his age. This background is thus not of mere academic interest but crucial in explaining the essence of Hokusai's art. He is said, for example, to have studied with the plebeian artist Tsutsumi Tōrin III, nominally a follower of Kōrin and of the Sesshū classical forms, but actually master of a very heterogeneous style by this time. Tōrin was known for his delicate book-plates and large *ema* (votary-panels offered to Shintō shrines), as well as for banners, lamp-designs and other such decorative piece-work that fell to the lot of the *machi-eshi* or 'town painter'. Stylistically he was noted for his sinuous brushstroke and imaginative employment of colouring, and it was these features that must have attracted Hokusai, whose powers of expression had been severely delimited within the confines of the Katsukawa print-school.

In his new freedom Hokusai was not to be restrained by any one style, and he also studied the gracefully traditional Tosa School of painting—especially its Edo branch, the Sumiyoshi School. He was likewise attracted to the Occidental-style experiments of Shiba Kōkan (whose personality and style resemble those of Hokusai in more ways than one). He studied too the techniques of the academic Kanō School, which, with its foundation in the massive forms of classical Chinese painting, was to constitute one of the essential bases of his mature style. (However, the story that Hokusai entered the School of Kanō Yūsen—1778–1815— and was later expelled for insubordination, may be questioned: for Yūsen was only 16 at the time.)

It was probably at this period that Hokusai commenced his study of Chinese painting (which influence was to become more central to his style a generation later); the Nanga, literati-style of landscape also received his attention. Other possible influences were the Kyōto non-conformist painters Jakuchū and Shōhaku: the former, a master of two styles, one a mixture of Kōrin-plus-Ming decoratism, the other a bold but decorative manner of *sumi-e* monochrome painting. Shōhaku was the supreme master of dynamic *sumi-e* painting, of the type Hokusai was later to exploit in his Outdoor Painting Exhibitions.

The influence of Kyōto was strong in Edo at this period, and the development in the Old Capital of the naturalistic school of Ōkyo could hardly have escaped the attention of such an eager and eclectic student as Hokusai. Indeed, though there were no formal museums at this period, artists and collectors often held private exhibitions of antique and modern paintings, as did the larger temples and shrines; thus an artist could well have had very intimate contact with such stimuli.

From the evidence of his later picture-books, Hokusai also studied the abundant and near-encyclopedic book-illustrations of Shumboku and Sō-Shiseki, as well as the topographical guides of Kyokkō, and the Chinese painters' manuals (*The Ten-bamboo Studio* and *Mustard-seed Garden*, both available in Japanese reprints): these, however, served more as reference books on subject-matter than as truly stylistic influences.

All these kaleidoscopically varied styles and schools of Far Eastern painting in the later eighteenth century fuelled Hokusai's passion for new knowledge, new skills, new achievement: a passion—even mania—that was to char-

acterize his career and, indeed, form a major element of his genius (so much in contrast to his placid and unprepossessing follower Hiroshige).

Where the ukiyo-e pioneers of the earlier generations— Matabei, Moronobu, Sukenobu, Masanobu, even Shunshō—had been versed in *painting*, there was indeed a tendency in Hokusai's time for the ukiyo-e artist to neglect this basic study and turn immediately to the more popular and stylish medium of the print and illustration. Probably Hokusai—if only subconsciously—perceived that both for his own development and for that of ukiyo-e itself, a broadening of the artist's base was now necessary, a return to basic studies in the essentials of Far Eastern art.

2

Such studies took not only time and great effort, but required funds, both for materials and for tuition from older masters. With his official Katsukawa School standing gone, Hokusai had to rely on the fickle world of part-time commercial art: commissions were scarce and emolument depended on the whims of patron or publisher. But despite these tribulations Hokusai managed, in the mid–1790s, gradually to evolve a style all his own, to create an artistic world which was soon to become, for his contemporaries, the 'Sōri Style'—after the name he employed from 1794 to 1798.

There are still all too many gaps in our knowledge of the artist at this crucial juncture: are the pen-names 'Kusamura Shunrō', 'Hyakurin Sōri' and 'Tawaraya Sōri' certainly identifiable with Hokusai, even for this limited period? Is the hypothesis tenable that Hokusai once used the pseudonyms 'Mari' and 'Gankō'? How many of the posthumously recorded anecdotes—the Kanō School episode, the altercation with Shunkō, etc.—are actually true? How can one explain the unsigned *kibyōshi* novelettes in Hokusai-style during 1794–7? For these and other enigmas there is simply no factual evidence. But whatever the pains and perils of independence, for Hokusai this was a necessary stage in the development of a new *métier*, a new style better suited to express the artist's vision of the 'fleeting, floating world'.

One further artistic connection which must be mentioned here is that of Hokusai with the Tawaraya School, a branch of the Sumiyoshi and nominally artistic descendant of the famed, early seventeenth-century Kyōto master Sōtatsu.[2] Hokusai's actual contact with this sub-school was hardly profound, and his studies there only one of many such, but possibly because of some personal relationship he found himself 'adopted' into the atelier, with the new name Tawaraya Sōri—a most unusual case of a plebeian artist assuming a prestigious non-ukiyo-e name (and rank). The artistic surname was soon forgotten, but under the name Sōri, Hokusai was to establish a new style of ukiyo-e design, aptly suited to this Golden Age of genre art (currently led by Utamaro, with such notable followers as Eishi, Eishō and Chōki).

By the New Year's season of 1795 Hokusai was issuing occasional prints under the sobriquet Sōri: some indication that he had already made a name for his fresh, distinctive style. This was the beginning of Hokusai's notorious practice of adopting a new *nom de plume* with every change in style or circumstance (his two childhood names do not count, as this change was a standard custom in Old Japan).[3]

Despite its complexity the study of Hokusai's various names in this coming decade is a fascinating one, as they are often the only manifest guides we have to the artist's thinking. Indeed, of the thirty or more alternative names that Hokusai employed during his seventy-year career, about half were passing fancies. Most were used with the previous name for some time, so as not to confuse his public (though, due to the artist's drastic break with the Katsukawa School, this is not true of the first, Shunrō-Sōri transition); and in the end, only about six of these pseudonyms were really of great significance.

However, Hokusai did not change his art-names solely out of caprice. In most cases the change was made to indicate an innovation in style, a new start—even though the intent and result may have been more apparent to the artist than they are to us today. But for this reason, Hokusai's various names do offer a useful guide to the student in tracing the chronology of Hokusai's vast *oeuvre*. Without these obvious keys to dating, the student would have to become an expert in all the artist's calligraphic and stylistic mutations over these seven decades.

The complex problem of the artist's names and their re-use by his pupils in the years from late 1798 on has yet to be fully resolved. It would seem that the *surimono*, books and prints of this period signed Tawaraya Sōri and Hishikawa Sōri are by Hokusai's pupil Sōji, who received the name Sōri [III] from his master late in the year 1798. Though quite adept, the *surimono* and book-illustrations of Sōri III (who was a relation of the Tawaraya family) may generally be distinguished by the doll-like, pinched or lifeless faces and figures, and by a lack of suppleness in the general designs. (The same might be said of the early work of another pupil, Shinsai, who was, however, a much more skilled artist.) The problem is complicated by the fact that exact dating of the prints is not always possible; furthermore, a really skilled engraver, one who was familiar with Hokusai's style, could 'touch up' the work of a pupil to make it look much like that of the master himself. Fortunately, such latter occurrences are rare, and a long acquaintance with Hokusai's genuine *oeuvre* will usually serve to distinguish the work of pupils (not to mention that of copyists and forgers: see Plate 37).

Around 1785–94, while still in the Katsukawa School, the artist also used the alternative pen-name Gumbatei. The 'Gumbatei prints' are characterized by a rougher, less polished style than was usual for Hokusai at this time. This unfinished quality could have been the fault of an unskilled engraver, or perhaps the result of the artist's own unsettled state of mind. The designs could have been made as unauthorized side-jobs, with the artist concerned at the possibility of censure from the *maître*. In the absence of solid records of the time, we simply cannot know.

Hokusai's occasional *noms de plume* for his literary efforts and erotica are more readily comprehended (see the list of these in the Appendix); but problems arise immediately with the artist's earliest major change of *nom d'artiste*, from Shunrō to Sōri in late 1794.

The first question concerns the pseudonym 'Kusamura Shunrō', which appears on prints at the end of the artist's Shunrō Period around 1794. Stylistically, these rare prints could pass for early Hokusai, if one makes allowance for the variations in line that might be attributable to an unaccustomed engraver. And the name Kusamura ('Thicket') might indeed be interpreted as implying the artist's distancing himself from the Katsukawa atelier. But Kusamura Shunrō could also just possibly be an early, talented pupil of Hokusai; and indeed, later in the same year 1794 we do find Hokusai bequeathing his 'Shunrō' art-name to an anonymous pupil who became, in effect, 'Shunrō II'—though his actual prints are signed 'Shunro'; and, if undated or undatable, these can be distinguished from those of the master only by variations in signature and style.

It is significant that Hokusai should have passed on his first *nom d'artiste* (but not, of course, the Katsukawa part, which was proprietary to the School) to a pupil so shortly after leaving the atelier. From this we may surmise that the artist had already achieved a name of some value on the commercial market, and had also risen to a rank warranting the taking of a private disciple. This was, indeed, only the first of many such 'name-sales'—each involving a certain contribution on the part of the pupil, a welcome supplement to the artist's meagre income. But, like many of Hokusai's numerous pupils, this new 'Shunrō II' never developed into a significant artist; in fact, his work—mainly *hosoban* actor–prints—is so little known or studied that it tends to be confused with the less distinguished *oeuvre* of Hokusai himself. (The said Shunrō II is better known by his alternative name Toyomaru, so the problem only occurs for a few years of his work.)

Hokusai's next name, Sōri, had previously been used by the founder of the school (d. 1782), so that Hokusai actually became, as we have seen, 'Sōri II', even though the dynastic notation was hardly if ever used (the seal is different, however—Kanchi vs. Genchi). Hokusai employed the name from 1795 (or late 1794/5) to late 1798 but there are variations even within this period—Hyakurin Sōri vs. Tawaraya Sōri—which are questioned by some scholars.

Then, late in 1798, Hokusai suddenly bequeathed this name to a skilled pupil, Sōji, who became Sōri III but again, with no such numerical distinction included in his signatures. Sōri III/Sōji is clearly a weaker and less sure artist than Hokusai, but at the hands of a master engraver his work in the delicate *surimono* genre is adequate, sometimes inspired, and has again often been confused with Hokusai's. And the situation is further complicated by the obvious problem that Hokusai, already a popular artist by 1799, could not always so wilfully abandon his established name; probably at the request of publishers and patrons, he continued to cite the former name for some time, usually in a form such as 'Hokusai, formerly Sōri', but sometimes with the old name used alone. Whether this represents the publication of an earlier sketch, or the demand of a publisher/patron, we cannot know. The lack of solid records combined with the problem of the intervention of the engraver often means that the only one who could answer our questions would be Hokusai himself.

One other, less controversial, pen-name of the artist for this period should also be mentioned: Kakō. A stylish variation of the epistolary expression *sōrō-beku*, 'thus be it', it is employed occasionally in the years 1798–1811 on a few of Hokusai's most impressive prints (among other media), and is therefore well known to collectors.

The reader may well inquire, at this point, as to when the artist finally arrived at the name *Hokusai*, by which he is known throughout the world. In fact, this alternative name first appeared late in the year 1796 and was used up to 1819, a relatively long time for Hokusai. It was, indeed, the name by which he was known to his later contemporaries. For some time the artist also added to it the previous *nom d'artiste* Sōri. The chronological order of usage is thus, generally: Sōri, Hokusai Sōri, 'Sōri, changed to Hokusai', and 'Hokusai, the former Sōri'.

Even after he moved on to other names (Taito, Iitsu, Manji, etc.), commercial considerations dictated that 'Hokusai' be included as part of the signatures to his published works, even to the titles of his guidebooks for artists, such as the famous *Hokusai manga* (the fifteen volumes of which extended from 1814 until well after the artist's death).

'Hokusai', incidentally, means 'North Studio', a reference not to the location of the artist's atelier but an abbreviation of *Hokutosai* or *Hokushinsai*, meaning 'North-star Studio'. It derives from the artist's fervent belief in the deity Myōken (famed for his miraculous deeds), whose principal temple was located at Yanagishima in Hokusai's native district of Honjo. 'St Myōken' was, in effect, an incarnation of *Hokushin*, the North Star—central among the Seven Stars of *Hokuto*, the Polar Constellation (i.e. Ursa Minor). Myōken, 'Shining Eye of all the Gods', was one of the special deities of the Nichiren Sect of Buddhism noted for its proselytizing fervour even today. Hokusai's attraction to this, the most fervent sect of Buddhism, was no coincidence (and indeed he thus entered the company of several other noted painters, not to mention many samurai and other men of active disposition). His choice of the North Star as his patron-saint was also appropriately symbolic: setting himself a firm yet unreachable goal he spent his life in one continuous effort to achieve it.

Other of the artist's later *noms de plume* such as Taito—likewise one of the Seven Polar Stars—also derive from this astronomical connection. Even Hokusai's childhood name Tokitarō (and the later pen-name Tokimasa) is taken from his birth in the Year of the Dragon (*tatsu/toki*), 1760, all of these reflecting a belief in the influence of cosmology/astrology that was practically universal at the time.

It may be surmised that even during Hokusai's lifetime these frequent name-changes were confusing to his contemporaries, if not to his intimates, and that he made them for reasons that were sometimes merely wilfully eccentric. They may, for that matter, even have impeded his burning ambition to make a reputation for himself. In this, we may well perceive a stubbornness, a single-minded independence that bordered on the self-destructive.

Hokusai's restless nature was not limited to name-changes but extended to the more troublesome matter of lodgings and residences as well. The artist himself confessed to having moved house at least 93 times; indeed, a contemporary directory lists him as 'address uncertain'.

Even Hokusai's later collaborator, the renowned novelist Bakin, appears to have been exasperated by these quirks, writing: 'So far as moving residence and changing name goes, I have never heard of anyone so fickle as this man.' Obviously the Master was never satisfied with his current situation, whether artistic or geographical.

NOTES

1 Actually, Shunshō retired from active print-designing after 1786, devoting himself thereafter to painting-consignments—while still maintaining a watchful eye over the Katsukawa atelier.
2 Sōtatsu was the founder of the Tosa-derived, native school of decorative painting later to be consolidated by Kōrin.
3 I must comment that, while the controversies that surround the authentication of Hokusai's paintings strike at the very essence of art studies, the elaborate quibbling among Hokusai specialists and collectors over the artist's varied pen-names must impress the outsider as slightly ridiculous. Suppose, for example, that a collector has long treasured a book or print signed 'Sōri', only to find that this is not Sōri II (Hokusai) but Sōri III (a noted pupil). He now feels cheated—by some dealer or auction-house—whereas he was actually deceived only by his own eyes and imagination: the print is perfectly genuine and exactly the same print it was before, but its charm is gone. To be sure, a first-rate Sōri III print is less valuable than a third-rate Hokusai: though both are, in the end, only second-rate prints. But this is, surely, only a problem of the marketplace—of the capricious whims of collectors—not of art criticism.

V
On Wings of Song (1):
The *Kyōka* Movement
and Hokusai's
Surimono-prints

1

THE LONG-AWAITED independence had come at last for Hokusai. He was now free to design and paint what he pleased. But, who would pay for it? In order to make a living he had to find a market for his art. And though his first two years were difficult ones, fortunately a new market was evolving and expanding at just this juncture with the elaborately designed anthologies of that form of light poetry known as *kyōka*—'mad-verse'—and the *surimono* greeting-prints that were their adjunct. These *kyōka* books had reached an early peak with the work of the artist-writer Kyōden in the previous decade, and in the 1790s developed into some of the most sumptuous volumes of book-illustration known in Japanese art. The plates were full-page colour prints, many of which, removed from their bindings, grace the collections of museums today. A brief account of this literary genus may be useful here.

The *kyōka* literary form itself was an ancient one—comprised of 31 syllables after the manner of classical *waka* and quite distinct from the shorter, more modern *senryū*, satirical epigrams in haiku format—allusion, word-plays and parody being a feature of Japanese verse from early times. With the eighteenth century, however, the *kyōka* genre saw a sudden resurgence in popularity: first in the Kyōto-Ōsaka region, but with the 1770s in Edo as well, where its witty, satirical nature struck a responsive chord that soon made this genus the favourite one of poets and poetasters (though aficionados of *waka*, haiku and *senryū* of course remained). These devotees of light verse were not by any means limited to the townsmen; indeed, because of its parodic nature the genre required an intimate grounding in the classics, and many of the leaders of the *Kyōka* Movement were actually lesser samurai, often alienated by the rampant corruption of the current Tanuma Administration. Thus the *Kyōka* Movement profited from a mixing of classes, and wealth, that was denied many of the cultural media of feudal Japan. The parallel here with the earlier fashion among the upper classes for elaborate *surimono* in the mid-1760s under Harunobu will be readily apparent.

Before long, *kyōka* readings and contests came to be held regularly. *Kyōka* clubs were formed and, the participants being of some means, the results were published, both as verse anthologies—sometimes lavishly illustrated—and in the sumptuous greeting-cards known as *surimono*. Because these were privately published they were nominally free of government censorship, and were employed primarily as exchange-gifts among these affluent poets. The *surimono*

were even the subject of special exchange parties, in which each participant passed round copies of his own production for judging and comment. Thus among the addicts of this hobby, effort and expense were not spared: printing and paper were of the highest quality, and the accompanying designs—on the theme of the verses—were often commissioned from the leading ukiyo-e artists of the day.

Such *surimono* were necessarily of limited circulation, but the elaborate *kyōka-bon*—'mad-verse-books'—though not cheap, were commercially available to the lesser poetasters and amateurs who thronged about the leading poets. At the peak of the movement towards the end of the eighteenth century, well over a hundred *kyōka* books and literally hundreds of *surimono* were produced each year, forming a major source of income for both publishers and artists. One of the plebeian poets, Hamabe-no-Kurohito, was himself the noted Edo bookseller Mikawaya (1717–91), who soon combined business with pleasure by issuing these privately printed *surimono* on commission, and then selling extra copies to general poetry fans. The more popular poets were remunerated for such sales, and some even made a fair living from these activities, as well as from teaching versification, and judging in the numerous poetry-contests.

It may be surmised that freedom from government censorship played a certain role in the immense popularity of *surimono* and in their widespread production. Even the *Kyōka* Movement, however, could not escape the current political conditions. With the Kansei Reforms of the late 1780s, many of the samurai poets were obliged to return to their neglected, official duties. The influence of plebeian versifiers consequently increased, and the tone of satire and parody was somewhat curtailed, for a time at least.

It must be admitted that the taste for Hokusai's early illustrations and *surimono* is a somewhat rarefied one; they cannot, at first glance, compete with the artist's more powerful and richly hued prints of his later years. The two species represent entirely different worlds and quite variant generations: indeed, a very different Hokusai. Now 35, the artist was well into maturity and one may conclude that at his best in the later 1790s he fully equalled the achievements of his leading contemporaries in the Japanese print. Indeed, if he had died in 1805 at the age of 45 Hokusai would certainly be remembered as the equal of Eishi, Chōki, Toyokuni, Kunimasa, if not quite of the great Utamaro (who was ten years Hokusai's senior and died in 1806). This first decade of his independence can be designated his first golden age, for it was then that the artist first explored his own capabilites and celebrated the full range of the Floating World of old Japan, in a *belle époque* that was never to be realized again.

2

The deluxe, privately issued *surimono*, coexistent and parallel with the *kyōka* verse-anthologies, were another facet of the same cultural activity. Commissioned by the more affluent poets at holiday times and other special occasions, they served as elegant poetry greeting-cards and announcements and must surely rank among the most delicate and transitory art forms ever produced. As casual prints, designed by major artists but circulated to only a limited circle of aficionados, many of them were lost or destroyed within a month of publication. Given their ephemeral nature, the wonder is that so many *surimono* have survived: there is at least one example from perhaps half of those originally published. Most survived quite by accident; but some were pasted into souvenir albums by the original recipients, only to be dispersed again in the late nineteenth century, when Western collectors discovered their charm.

Surimono (the word means simply 'printed items') are not of any single size or shape, but vary from tiny greeting-cards through postcard and double-postcard size and were generally printed on heavy but pliable hand-made paper. The even larger sizes—up to twice the width of this book, and usually on thinner and softer paper—frequently included an announcement of a musical recital, poetry–meeting, memorial or obituary, often with the text printed on the lower half of the same large sheet of paper.

There were also erotic *surimono*, usually miniature and produced in sets of twelve (for the months of the year), enclosed in a tasteful, decorated wrapper (sometimes, in a little wooden box with the title on the cover). These were issued both for the amusement of dilettantes and as accoutrements for a bride's (or groom's) trousseau—a pioneer form of artistic sex-manual.

There were, in short, *surimono* for practically every occasion. They encompassed the functions of the greeting-card and formal announcement or invitation today, but each was designed by a noted artist, woodblock-printed by hand, and issued in a very limited edition: 50, 100, 200 at the most, and hardly ever to be reprinted. (Very rarely, the most popular *surimono* designs were reissued in commercial editions, with original verses deleted and with less elegant printing and paper.)

These, the most ephemeral examples of ukiyo-e art, are also, alas, the most difficult to reproduce: for not only has the original delicate colouring often faded, but the special effects (embossing, as well as printing in gold, silver, bronze, mica) are truly three-dimensional, and defy the best efforts of the modern photographer and printer.

Surimono lie a trifle off the mainstream of ukiyo-e: their subjects—in harmony with their refined patrons—tend to revert to classical themes and still-life, rather than showing actual scenes of the vibrantly fleeting, floating world. Their audience, too, was hardly a proletarian one, consist-ing of the cultured classes who could afford such elegant playthings. (One must note, however, that increasingly from this period—the 1790s on—the subject-matter of ukiyo-e will be gradually extending its range far beyond the actual Floating World, to include all kinds of subjects that were often alien to the traditional art.)[1]

While one may for convenience think of the *surimono* as elegant greeting-cards and announcements, they were actually more than this. They served, for example, as 'first editions' for the leading poets of the time. Furthermore, they also represented the first editions of significant prints. Their literary and artistic importance should therefore not be undervalued.

Many of the *surimono* were issued on a seasonal or festive occasion. The most prominent of these was of course New Year, and *surimono* were normally designed and printed in the preceding month or two. There was, as it happened, a government monopoly on the publication of calendars, and many of the New Year's *surimono* slyly evaded that law by including somewhere in the design little code-like markings, to indicate the Long or Short Months of the coming lunar year. Such specialized *surimono* were generally of smaller format and were termed *egoyomi*—'picture-calendars'. Their production had played a major role in the development of the colour-print under Harunobu a generation earlier.

The fascination of these calendar-prints thus combines literary interest with beauty of design and printing, and—for those with sharp eyes and analytical minds—the challenge to search out and decipher the tiny calendrical notations that are often worked into the design like a kind of artistic crossword-puzzle.

A related type is the *saitan*, or 'New-Year's-Morning' *surimono*, more literally a greeting-card. Here there are no calendrical markings but the Year will be indicated by means of the Zodiacal Sign—rat/ox/tiger/hare/dragon/snake/horse/goat/monkey/cock/dog/boar—and sometimes in a separate notation as well.

In all these types and formats the most prominent element is the artist's attempt to illustrate the verses in the most *chic* and stylish manner possible. The obvious and realistic are eschewed, and the complex allusions are deliberately half-concealed. At the same time, that typically ukiyo-e device of *mitate* or pastiche is frequent—the equivalent of parody in the verses themselves.

The over-refined and subtly sophisticated charms of the *surimono* were quite forgotten in the generations following their production. Even today in Japan they are valued mainly by scholars for their verses by noted poets, and for their signed and dated, though casual, pieces by famous ukiyo-e artists. At their best, however, *surimono* are a delightful genus of miniaturistic art, every tiny detail contributing to the whole. But often they may seem to the outsider merely pretty pieces of aged paper, justified only by the skill of the engraver and the art of the paper-maker.

Surimono have attracted a small but passionate following among Occidental collectors for their charm, wit and jewel-like, consummate craftsmanship. The student of ukiyo-e must be grateful for the attention and care paid to *surimono* in the West for, whatever their relative importance, the artists are those we know so well from the larger prints, books and paintings. Furthermore, these ephemeral bits of paper are often exactly datable and, as is the case with Hokusai, sometimes throw light upon an artist's development which is not known from any other extant source.

Because they are the least understood of all the varieties of ukiyo-e prints, we have spent some time on the background of the *surimono*, but our prime concern here is with Hokusai's intimate relation to this miniature art. Indeed, he followed fast in the steps of Kyōden, Shumman, Shigemasa and other pioneers of the 1780s, but made a name for himself in this genre with surprising ease. Probably his long training in the field of actor-prints (the smallish, narrow *hosoban* designs of delicate execution and colouring, not to be confused with the later, massive productions of Sharaku and Toyokuni) made him ideally suited to transfer his talents to the new medium. In fact, in the limited but affluent circle of *kyōka/surimono* aficionados he became quite a celebrity. Hokusai was also, it will be remembered, something of an amateur novelist himself, in the comic vein. It was natural therefore that he should become an occasional versifier as well, if only to maintain close contact with the literary groups that commissioned and financed these elaborate publishing projects. His preeminence in this specialized field can be surmised from a light verse in the rival *senryū* vein, published in the *Yanagi-taru* anthology of 1811:

> *Hokusai da-ne to / surimono wo / bachi de yose*
> 'It must be Hokusai', the geisha exclaimed,
> lifting a *surimono*
> with her samisen-plectrum

Although there has yet to be a comprehensive survey of Hokusai's work in the *surimono* genre, at least from the year 1795 it was a primary source of income for the artist. The Appendix lists well over a hundred such series-prints from his long career, not counting the far greater number of miscellaneous single prints that have fortuitously survived (see p. 280 ff.).

3

Hokusai's production in the *surimono* genre did not begin with his independence in 1795: there exist several examples, usually minor, from his later Shunrō Period.[2] But though none of these early *surimono* is very remarkable, some are indeed charming and their existence does indicate that Hokusai, even while in the Katsukawa atelier, had begun to develop some reputation in non-Kabuki assignments. The artist's more important work in *surimono* dates, however, only from the mid-1790s, and this is true likewise of his *oeuvre* in the related genres of *kyōka* books and albums (which will be the subject of the following chapters). The *surimono* genre proved particularly adapted to Hokusai's detailed, precise style—which was sometimes glossed over by the exigencies of commercial printing projects.

As we have noted, many of these *surimono* are readily datable, particularly those issued as New Year cards and carrying an annotation of the zodiacal connection. The Year of the Ox, for example, fell every twelve years in the Japanese almanac, and it is usually possible on the basis of the artist's style to tell whether such cards were for 1793, 1805 or 1817. The current fashions depicted, and even the manner of printing and pigmentation, also provide vital clues as to date.

Astonishingly, these colourful little slips of printed paper often conceal a veritable encyclopedia of Japanese lore, an explanation of which would take up far more space than the original print. *Surimono* are not always this complex, but they do tend to combine literature, legend and history in a manner drawn—sometimes strained—to the limits of elliptical allusion. To view them only for their consummate printing and design is, at the least, to miss the point for which they were originally issued.

Hokusai's *surimono* of this decade (not to mention the succeeding ones) are too numerous to cite in detail, and we can only provide a few examples. Comment on these plates must also be brief, so our selection is of the rather less complex themes, and of subjects readily appreciable without immersion in Japanese life and legend. It must be confessed, however, that the subjects presented here are not necessarily typical. Many *surimono* are simply too delicately printed—or the colours too faded—to be reproduced meaningfully, and my own taste in this medium is for ukiyo-e subjects, rather than still-lifes and classical themes.

Hokusai's work in this genre dates back, as we have seen, to his early Shunrō Period. The miniature *egoyomi*, by their nature, are hardly likely to harbour major works (the following example is only 9.5 × 13.8 cm/3¾ × 5½ in). Indeed, such smaller *surimono* are often of interest mainly in tracing the artist's early development. By coincidence, our first example (Plate 18) appeared at the start of the same lunar year as the death of Hokusai's mentor Shunshō.

Here we view a teacher, at right, explaining to his young samurai-pupil a calligraphic conundrum which incorpo-

18 Pupil and Teacher. Small *surimono*-print; *egoyomi* (picture-calendar) for the year 1792. Signed Shunrō.

rates the calendar-data of the year Kansei IV/1792.[3] Now Kansei IV was the Year of the Rat: and this well-known conundrum-limerick takes advantage of the fact that Japanese ideographs can be pronounced in several ways. The character most usually read *ko* (child) can also be rendered *shi* or *-ji* (the Chinese-style reading), as well as *ne* (short for *nezumi*, as in *ne-no-toshi*, The Year of the Rat). Thus the three basic readings *ko / shi-ji / ne* are combined phonetically to form the words *neko* (cat) and *shishi* (lion), and hence utilized to read the twelve identical characters as:

Neko-no-ko no koneko
shishi-no-ko no kojishi

—which comes out (more or less) in English:

The cat's kid is a kitten
the lion's kid is a cub

19 Chinese Princess at Toilette. Small *surimono*—size of original: 5½ × 6¾ in / 13.6 × 17.1 cm; calendar for the year 1798. Signed Sōri. For other miniature *surimono* of this period, see Fig. 17 ff.

And it will be noted that the sizes of the characters are further varied: the larger ones representing the Long Months—of thirty days each—II/III/V/VI/VIII/X/XII. (Such calendar-prints are not always precise. Here, the fact that there was an additional, intercalary Fourth Month that year is not noted on the actual 'kakemono', as thirteen characters would not have fitted neatly with the well-known limerick.) The conversation between teacher and pupil explains the conundrum, and on the screen at right are mounted a fan depicting the rice-bales of Daikoku (god of wealth, often shown with rats eating his abundant rice-supply), and paintings of snake and monkey-trainer (representing the symbols of certain key days in the recurrent zodiacal cycle), with the numbers of their calendrical details.

The print is not an artistically important one, but will serve to represent both the fad for hidden, overly complex calendar-markings, and more significantly, the beginning of that delicate style of figure-depiction that was to characterize Hokusai's work in the decade and a half of his first period of independence.

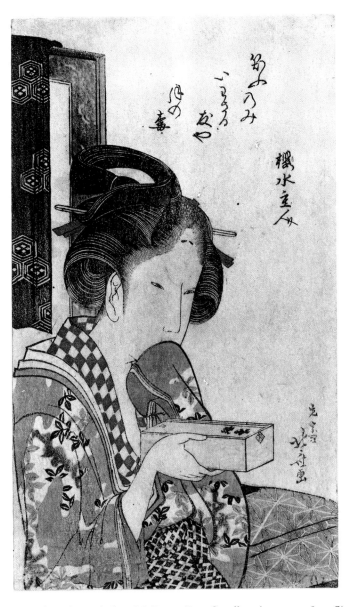

21 *Above* Girl folding Cloth. Small *surimono*, 1799. Signed Sōri, changed to Hokusai. (For the series, see Appendix, Prints, No. 35.)

22 *Below* Girl weighing Coins. Small *surimono*; calendar for the year 1800. Unsigned. (See Appendix, Prints, No. 40.) (Note: the seal at lower right was added by the auction house which handled the sale of the famed Vever Collection: a practice hardly to be encouraged.)

20 *Above* Court-lady with Secret Box. Small *surimono*, *c.* 1800. Signed Hokusai, the former Sōri. (See Appendix, Prints, No. 42.)

Of slightly larger size but considerably greater aesthetic value is the charming *surimono* of Plate 19. Here we view a Chinese princess—probably Yang Kuei-fei—at toilette, bent over a washbowl and wiping her face and torso with a hand-towel. This is a calendar-print for the Year of the Horse (which may here be pinpointed, on stylistic grounds, as Kansei X/1798); on the side of the washbasin may be discerned the Short Months of that year: I/IV/VI/VII/IX/X. In a typical conceit, this 'greeting-card' is fashioned as though it were the wrapper for the powdered soap that the girl is seen using.[4]

With the more typically ukiyo-e calendar-print of Plate 21, we catch the artist in the midst of (as the inscription reads) 'Changing from Sōri to Hokusai'. The subject is again a young woman, but here Japanese and seen folding a silk cloth with the aid of her teeth. Two *kyōka* verses appear at left, and the year is cited in the large calligraphy on the screen at right: 'Beauty of the Year of the Goat'— i.e. Kansei XI/1799.

Of perhaps a year later—and the signature now 'Hokusai, formerly Sōri'—is a set of tiny portraits which, for their insight into female psychology, are a little reminiscent of Utamaro. Plate 20, for example, portrays a lady of the Edo Court. She holds her kimono-sleeve to her face in an expression of partly feigned modesty; grasped in her hand is a box containing a tortoise-shell dildo-phallus, one of the secret pleasures among the neglected women of the Shōgun's seraglio. (With several hundred such ladies-in-waiting—many there for purely political reasons—meetings with the Lord and master were usually infrequent at best; and some Shōguns preferred boys anyway.) The refined but insinuating haiku-verse reads:

One can but smile at
that Silent Companion:
plum-blossoms by moonlight.[5]

From about the same year dates another interesting *suri-*

mono set on the 'Four Classes' (samurai/peasant/artisan/merchant—in that descending order of importance, so far as the ruling-class was concerned in feudal Japan). Plate 22 illustrates the merchant class with a girl shown weighing silver coins. The shop-sign (and the ledger on the floor) cleverly conceals the Short Months of the year Kansei XII/1800: II/III/IV/VI/VIII/X/XII (which had an extra, intercalary Fourth Month).

An even more elaborate set of *surimono* is the pastiche *Seven Sages of the Bamboo Grove*, of which three are shown in Plate 23. From left to right we see a matron at leisure (with shaven eyebrows) reading a *jōruri* theatre-text; a young woman in travelling-garb perusing a love-letter; and a servant-girl with saké, on whose apron appear the zodiac letters for the Year of the Monkey, Kansei XII/1800. On each of the prints will be found two verses by members of the Shōfūdai poetry-group that commissioned the series. Not only is the signature now 'Hokusai' alone, but it is notable also just how far the Master has progressed in figure-depiction: gone are the echoes of his Kiyonaga and

23 Three Beauties. From a set of eight small *surimono*, 1800. Signed Hokusai. (For others in this set, see Fig. 28.)

24 Beauty in Mirror. Small *surimono*—size of original: 2½ in / 6 cm wide (detail); *c.* late 1790s. Unsigned.

Shunshō imitations, and we discover the 39-year-old artist for the first time achieving a distinctive style of his own.

In the miscellaneous Hokusai work of this period there are also intriguing little prints that, in their present state, are difficult to identify. The 'Mirrored Beauty' of Plate 24, for example, is clearly in the Hokusai style of the late 1790s, but what was its original purpose? The shape is obviously intended to imitate the appearance of a hand-mirror (with attached cover, printed on the same sheet of

25 Girls on New-Year's Morning. Long-*surimono*, dated 1796. Signed Sōri. (For others in this format, see also Fig. 20 ff.)

paper). But was it part of a *surimono*, with *kyōka* text appearing on a separate sheet of paper on the reverse, now lost; or one from a set of miniature portraits originally enclosed in a wrapper; or could it be the front of an actual wrapper for a miniature shunga set? Like the similar curious examples of our later Plate 209, one can only admire and surmise, pending discovery of an integral specimen.

We may now turn from the miniature to the larger formats of *surimono*. These tended (in this period, at least) to average some 20 × 50 cm/8 × 20 in in size, and there was a good reason for the elongated format: originally, each of these prints was part of a larger, squarish sheet of paper, the other half of which comprised the announcement (of concerts, recitals, name-accession parties and the like) that formed the real purpose of the publication. In former days, at least, Western collectors tended to consider this text-appendage unsightly and discarded it; and even in the artist's time, there was probably a tendency to cut off and keep the pretty picture, when clearing out a chest-of-drawers. (For a rare example of the original format, see Fig. 22.)

Here, provided with a truly wide-screen size and format, the artist suddenly blossoms as a master of the landscape-with-figures, which was a natural subject for this long, horizontal shape. In Plate 25, for example, Hokusai's svelte and attenuated figures are depicted in an idyllic setting: one girl sweeps up fallen pine-needles, one carries the 'first water' of the New Year, the other attends to a caged bush-warbler. Behind them appear other symbols of the New Year: a pine-tree, and fragrant plum-blossoms. The signature is simply 'Sōri', and the inscription at right clarifies this as a publication of Kansei VIII/1796, the Year of the Dragon. (The artist, it will be recalled, was born three 'cycles' earlier in the Dragon Year 1760.) The print features Hokusai's characteristically frail figures of this period, harking back to the pioneer of two generations earlier, Harunobu, but probably more directly influenced by the work of Shumman and Utamaro, as well as of Hokusai's own mentor Tōrin.

Less poetically conceived, but of interest in relation to

26 *Above* River Scene. Long-*surimono*, 1799. Signed Hokusai, the former Sōri, 'on travels'.

27 *Below* Shellfish-gatherers. Long-*surimono*, *c.* 1798. Signed Sōri.

28 *Bottom* Moon-viewing at Geisha House. Long-*surimono*, *c.* 1799. Signed Sōri, changed to Hokusai.

Hokusai's development as a landscape-artist, is the curious *surimono*-print of 1799, shown in Plate 26. Here we glimpse a transitional stage in the traditional landscape as influenced by the pseudo-Occidental 'perspective-print'. The various elements are not yet well integrated and it will, in fact, be at least a generation before the artist effects

29 *Top* Outing at Enoshima. Long-*surimono*, early 1800s. Signed Gakyōjin Hokusai. (Note the typically dynamic balance of Fuji against the inverted triangle of the hands at left.)

30 *Above* Travellers at Tea-house. Long-*surimono*, 1804 (the printed text cites only 'Seventh Month', but one extant specimen bears the manuscript notation 'Bunka I/1804, Year of the Rat'; there is also a version with alternative text, printed separately, dated 'Sixth Month'—see Fig. 22; this was the season for the Summer Pilgrimages to Ōyama). Signed Gakyōjin Hokusai.

his major step in creating the fully realized landscape-print.

The scene depicted is of cargo-boats on a wide river; at the far bank will be seen a lumber-yard and warehouses. But is this really (as is customarily assumed) the Sumida River? In the first place, there is the problem of the lone cormorant at right; except in parodies, ukiyo-e details are predominantly conventional: cormorants tend to go with the Naraga and Nagae Rivers (near Gifu and Kiso-Gōto): and a different water-bird is associated with the Sumida, *miyako-dori* (the oyster-catcher).[6] Moreover, looking at the signature, we see that it reads, 'Hokusai, formerly Sōri, *sketched on travels*'. Just what the locale is, and its relation to

the artist's hitherto unknown travels at this early period, must be left to scholars to discover. (This design, interestingly enough, proved surprisingly popular, being re-issued, with a new announcement attached, in 1804; and again, in foreshortened, *ōban* format—with the pines cut off and a snowy night sky added for a quite different effect.)

Important Hokusai 'long-*surimono*' of this period abound, for, as we have seen, he was by the late 1790s the most popular artist of Edo in this one genre (which was rather eschewed by, for example, the great Utamaro—probably for good commercial reasons). Justly famous is the 'Shellfish-gatherers' of Plate 27, in which graceful women and sinuous men are seen on a beach at low tide, with Mt Fuji in the far distance. The composition is strongly influenced by Western perspective-techniques (on which see Chapter IX). Hokusai has here effectively employed exotic Occidental theory to produce an integrated design and a masterful work of art.

The large *surimono* were not solely concerned with the outdoor world of nature, to the exclusion of the Floating World. But coming suddenly upon a print like Plate 28, one may experience a slight sense of claustrophobia after the artist's exuberant attention to the beauties of *plein-air*. 'Moon-viewing at Geisha House' vividly evokes the exotic atmosphere of the Yoshiwara: the elegantly bedecked courtesans were in truth 'caged birds' in a strange, closed world.

From about the turn of the century, Hokusai in his signatures adopted the prefix *Gakyōjin* ('Man Mad with Painting'), as we see in the long-*surimono* of Plate 29. The scene is a favourite resort of Edoites, the shrine-island of Enoshima (a peninsula at low tide, as here), with Mt Fuji towering in the distance. The relation of foreground and background is again ambiguous, but in the details of the main figures (the mother playing a finger-game with the children) we glimpse that concern with individual humanity that was to prove the artist's trademark.

An even more complex composition is the famous 'Travellers at Tea-house' of Plate 30 (the design is ostensibly a decorative adjunct to a programme for a musical recital). Again the background is not well conceived (the ill-perspectived boats, especially), but the dramatic—almost Kabuki-like—tableau of travellers and waitress more than compensates for this fault. One first observes that these varied figures are by no means mannequins: nearly all of them are engaged in some characteristic activity: from the girl reclining at far left, to the waitress (having just served tea to a pilgrim to the Ōyama Shrine, ceremonial blade on his back), the boy sipping his tea, the traveller holding his hat, and the pack-driver re-doing his baggage; even the girl astride the pack-horse straddles the encumbered beast in her own peculiar manner.

With this print we have reached the year 1804, when the artist was at the peak of his powers for this early period. Before proceeding to the surprising developments of the next generation we must turn back a decade, and recapitulate Hokusai's other varied achievements in those further, lovely genres of this golden age: *kyōka* albums and picture-books, and yet more beauties of the Floating World.

NOTES

1 This insistence on distinguishing between *surimono* and commercially issued prints may perhaps puzzle the layman who has never handled the originals; the difference is not only one of quality of engraving, printing and paper, but lies also in the nature of the design itself: *surimono* are in essence decorative adjuncts to poetry-texts and calendars. That the power of the design is often sufficient to overcome this handicap is one of the wonders of Japanese art. As the *Ukiyo-e ruikō*—a record of the time—states, 'What is valued in *surimono* is their lack of resemblance to the usual colour-prints [*nishiki-e*].'

2 It must be remembered that Hokusai passed on the name Shunrō to a pupil in 1794; and some Shunrō II *surimono*, as well as other prints, have been mistakenly given to Hokusai.

3 As noted above, dating correspondences are only approximate. In this case, the Fourth Year of the Kansei Era ran, in the Gregorian calendar, from 24 January 1792 to 10 February of the following year, 1793. As it happens, this includes the confusing month of Shunshō's death—see note on p. 10.

4 There is also the view that this is the actual soap-wrapper, rather than a true *surimono*; but this would then raise the problem of why the calendar-markings are included. The original Yang Kuei-fei, by the way, was supposedly quite plump—reflecting the feminine ideals of the underfed T'ang Dynasty. The ukiyo-e artist, of course, depicted such historical beauties entirely after the ideals of his own time.

5 Although the box is clearly labelled (*on-kata*, 'august dildo'), and bears the 'four-eyed' crest of the famed Edo sex-implement shop Yotsumeya, not surprisingly the true nature of this subject has been lost on cataloguers unfamiliar with the intimate details of Edo life. See, for example, L. Binyon, *Catalogue of the Japanese and Chinese Woodcuts in the British Museum*, 1916, p. 307: M. Forrer, *Hokusai—The Serial Graphics*, 1974, p. 15; and F. Tōgasaki, *Art of the Surimono*, 1979, p. 164.

6 In late actor-prints, however, the location may be that of a noted Kabuki play on the cormorant-fishing theme, set on the Ishiwa River in Kaga Province (a theme deriving from the medieval Noh play *Ugai* [The Cormorant-Fisherman]).

VI
On Wings of Song (2):
Hokusai's *Kyōka*
Albums

As WE HAVE SEEN, *kyōka-bon*—'mad-verse books'—
were primarily lyric anthologies, paid for by the contributors, many of whom came from the provinces as well as
from Edo. The plates and illustrations which are their principal charm today were often merely ornamental, and
sometimes quite unrelated to the text. Indeed, the most
effective *kyōka* book-plates tend to be those that are purely
decorative in intent, whereas in the more integrated
volumes of text and illustration, the latter may be less independently impressive, even though the volume itself is a
more unified work of book-art.

The *kyōka* volumes were basically of two types: the *orihon-*
album bound in 'accordion-style', in which a full-sized print

was folded at centre and tipped in, and the more customary
tōji-bon book in which the two halves of the illustration were
printed on different sheets of paper for binding. In the
albums, the verses were usually printed on separate sheets,
while in the picture-books, the verse often appeared within
the illustration itself. In either case, the nominal purpose of
the volume was to publish the new poetry of the time: a
feature largely lost on collectors and art-lovers today, even
in Japan. We may be grateful that the poets and poetasters
of that age had the means and the taste to support such a
sumptuous and refined variety of publication, for among
these volumes will be found some of the acknowledged
masterpieces of book-art.

It is not, alas, possible to show here more than a fragment of
Hokusai's work in this lovely genre of the album. One must
lift out (as some barbaric collectors have done literally in the
past) a sample plate for illustration, leaving the remaining

31 *Below* Travellers at Enoshima. Album-plate from *The Willow-
branch*, 1797. (Note that such album-plates often show wear due to
having been folded at centre, as here.) (For other *kyōka* albums,
signatures and bibliographical data, see Appendix, Books, No. 60 ff.)

text and illustrations (sometimes the work of other leading artists of the time) unseen. And once having isolated the plate, one will perceive that a curious transformation occurs: when viewed in the original album, folded at the centre, the plate formed a perfect composition, but when it is stretched out one is struck by a certain consequent over-elongation, and by a flatness, even emptiness at the centre of the design. Whether consciously planned or not (and I have not seen this point made before, even in Japan), the double-page book-plate is almost three-dimensional in quality: rather like a Japanese folding screen, which like-wise suffers from being flattened against a wall.

Three years after his independence Hokusai had already become a frequent contributor to this genre, but this did not necessarily mean that he monopolized the entire volume. For the sake of variety some of the most elaborate *kyōka* albums featured an anthology of artists, as well as of poets.

One of Hokusai's earliest known plates of this type appears in the album *Yomo-no-haru* (Spring All Over), a collaborative work with illustrations also by Masayoshi, Kyōden, and several non-ukiyo-e artists. Hokusai's con-tribution is a masterful scene of a festively decorated ferry-boat on a river at New Year, loaded with travellers and even, in a characteristic Hokusai touch, a diminutive horse, doubtless miniaturized the better to fit into the design, if not the boat (Plate 32).

Equally typical of these elegant poetry-albums is *Yanagi-no-ito* (The Willow-branch) of 1797, featuring plates by Eishi and Shigemasa, as well as the non-ukiyo-e masters Rinshō and Tōrin (the latter, it will be remembered, for a time one of Hokusai's mentors). The Hokusai design is one of his most famous, and is again signed 'Hokusai Sōri' (Plate 31). We see a breathtaking New-Year's view of the seacoast at Enoshima, with Mt Fuji in the distance, and the beginning of the characteristic 'Hokusai waves' in the foreground: Kōrin-cum-Occidental elements that will be discussed in a later chapter. The figures represent a pedlar with his wares, and two women travellers talking to local children. Dis-mounted from the album, the design displays a certain emptiness at the centre; nevertheless, it ranks among the major album-plates of the period. It is also interesting as one of the artist's first—and not completely successful—attempts to create the 'landscape-with-figure' print that

was to form, over a generation later, one of his major con-tributions to world art.

A more complicated—and therefore less striking—plate appears in the album *Sandara-kasumi* (Mists of Sandara) of the same year (Plate 34). Sandara was one of the pseudonyms of a noted poet whose verse and editorship the volume celebrates. Hokusai's contribution in this case is in collaboration with Shigemasa and Ittei, and must be judged more interesting for its parts than as a whole. There is again an ambiguity between figures and landscape that characterizes much of his work at this transitional stage.

The year after, a quite different and even more notable *kyōka* album was issued under the very same title, again celebrating the poet Sandara. This later *Sandara-kasumi* of 1798 included artistic contributions by Shigemasa and Set-tan, but Hokusai's complex yet well-ordered plate is surely the high point of the album, and even of his total *oeuvre* in this format (Plate 35). At a rustic tea-house before looming Mt Fuji, a stylish traveller, blooming plum-branch stuck jauntily in his baggage, pauses for a smoke and cup of tea, the latter proffered by a lovely girl in a sombre kimono with a vivid sash. Inside the house an old man (a favourite 'representative' of the artist in such designs, even in his youth) is engaged in making ivory *netsuke*, assisted by a girl and an older woman, who turns the lathe. Within the room is seen a small screen with mounted paintings/*surimono* and—in a deft touch of informality—a pair of *geta* (wooden clogs) lie in partial disarray on the threshold-stone. The season is early spring, symbolized by the snow-clad Mt Fuji and the plum-blossoms (those at lower-right still buds), as well as, probably, by the high-shaven foreheads of the women—a coiffure-style of the time known colloquially as *Fuji-bitai*, 'Fuji-forehead'.

Yet another striking *kyōka* album of 1798 (remembering, of course, that the actual design, engraving and printing usually were accomplished during the previous winter) is *Hatsu-wakana* (First Young Herbs), the print being signed 'Sōri changed to Hokusai' (Plate 33). In harmony with the book's title, a child and his young mother are depicted greeting the New Year's dawn, the latter interrupted in plucking the traditional 'New Herbs' for the first repast of the year. Here the artist has dispensed with complex ele-ments in the middle distance, much to the advantage of the composition.

Possibly Hokusai's most evocative album-plate of this period—if not his whole career—appears in the anthology *Otoko-dōka* (Men's Dance of Spring), also of 1798. The artist-collaborators are Shigemasa, Tōrin, Utamaro, Eiji and Eishi, and the signature is 'Hokusai Sōri' (Plate 36). The bucolic scene probably depicts a shrine-precinct near Edo at New Year. The stylish women stand out in striking contrast to the rustic setting, just as the ukiyo-e mood of the graceful figures contrasts with the traditional landscape style—re-sembling that of Hokusai's mentor Tōrin—of the back-ground. But unlike some of the previous examples, land-scape and figures are perfectly integrated: the composition is a most satisfying one of curved stream and bridge, con-trasted with the V-shaped mass of lovely figures. Moreover (though the design is more laterally spaced than would be the case with an independent print), there is no emptiness

32 Ferryboat. Album-plate from *Spring All Over*, 1796.

33 New Year's Dawn. Album-plate from *First Young Herbs*, 1798 (left edge trimmed).

in the central area even when the album-plate is flattened out. To me, this tableau represents Hokusai's masterpiece in the realm of book-illustration.

However, Hokusai's album- and book-plates of this period were not always so successful. He was still experimenting in an attempt to find his own style and to integrate the standard elements of genre depiction into his new vision of the landscape-with-figures. But from about the year 1797, this vision becomes increasingly clarified and masterful. His work was published alongside the great names of his day, and Hokusai himself was gradually acclaimed as their equal.

As we have seen, the season of the New Year was the favourite time to issue these deluxe editions, and thus spring (which in the lunar calendar began in the chilly month of February) is a frequent theme. These luxurious albums were sometimes published quite privately—with no copies at all available commercially—and this special class is called *kubari-bon*, 'gift-books'. This genre included anthologies not only of *kyōka*, but of variant verse-forms such as haiku, as well as other cultural contents. Surely one of Hokusai's most delicately attuned productions in this

genre is *Haru-no-miyabi* (Elegance of Spring) of *c*. 1798. The slim volume includes only two plates, but both rank among the artist's most evocative (Plate 40).

In effect, such plates represented *surimono*-prints bound into album-form, though the compositions—almost demanding to be folded at the centre—were of course designed for this specific purpose. In the tableau shown here, three girls in festive kimono are seen aboard a shallow boat in an eddy. The girl at left poles the craft, her body bent in that sharp angle characteristic of Hokusai's figures (though harking back to Harunobu and Sukenobu). Another girl beckons and the third strives to break a branch from the flowering plum-tree at right.

With both albums and *surimono* one is quite soon confronted with the problem of what to do with unsigned and undated works. The prudent scholar will doubtless prefer to limit his examples to signed and dated, well-known prints and books, yet in so doing he will be forced to neglect many of the masterpieces in these formats. Approximate dating—based on a lengthy study of the artist's stylistic mutations for each period—is not such a problem: an error of a year or two is seldom crucial to one's main argument. But to mix in the unsigned work of pupils (some of whom were very good) with the Master is less forgivable. Yet for some simple figure-designs, the intervention of the

34 *Opposite top* Rustic Scene. Album-plate from *Mists of Sandara*, 1797.

35 *Opposite bottom* Mountain Tea-house. Album-plate from *Mists of Sandara*, 1798.

36 *Above* Rustic Scene. Album-plate from *Men's Dance of Spring*, 1798.

woodblock-carver might well make it difficult to distinguish the skilled work of a pupil. With the more fully realized prints, however, it becomes easier to detect the slightly inept line, the vaguely awkward figure, the ill-integrated background that often characterize the work of disciples and imitators. And if a striking print or plate is—after careful study—concluded 'good enough to be Hokusai', that may be reason enough to accept it, at least for the present. One is reminded here of the confident words of the modern potter Shōji Hamada, regarding such unsigned works: 'In the future, my failures will be ascribed to pupils, and their masterpieces, to me.'

A case in point is the lovely—but as yet unidentified—album-plate of Plate 41.[1] The scene is full of the youthful naïvety of the artist at this period. Indeed, the figures are not all that different from those of the previous example; what renders the tableau outstanding is its effectively printed background, illustrating the traditional theme of *Yoru-no-ume*, 'Night Plum-blossoms'. Here is evoked a special world rather reminiscent of Hokusai's confrère Chōki of the same period: a dreamlike atmosphere that typifies the essence of ukiyo-e.

How had Hokusai managed to progress so quickly from his conventional and stilted work of the Katsukawa School? The answer can only be that the artist had long prepared for this giant step; and when he took it, all his pent-up energies

were released, to create (not overnight, but within a year or two) the fresh and new 'Hokusai/Sōri' style.

One well-known album-sheet of the period (Plate 37) serves to illustrate a problem of Hokusai studies. Signed only 'Sōri', it has long been considered one of Hokusai's minor masterpieces. Recent research reveals, however, that one of the poets of the anthology, Sōyōan Hoshinori, only took up the former pen-name in the Fifth Month of 1802. Thus publication was probably New Year of 1803 and the artist not Sōri II (Hokusai) but his gifted pupil Sōri III. This remains, withal, a notable book-plate: and a useful reminder of the role of engraver and printer in the quality of an ukiyo-e print.

Not only did Hokusai collaborate with other artists in the verse-anthologies, but in one, he even provided a frontispiece to a *tour-de-force* album by the noted ukiyo-e master Eishi, who was four years his senior and the scion of an influential samurai family. The book is *Nishiki-zuri onna sanjū-rokkasen* (Brocade-prints of the Thirty-six Poetesses), prepared in 1798 and published in 1801. Here, to Eishi's elegant portraits of these lady poets, Hokusai has contributed a frontispiece-plate that both complements the portraits and adds a strikingly fresh touch of his own (Plate 38).

We view a small bridge before the grounds of a large mansion. In the foreground, a group of lesser nobles and their servants depart on an expedition (the young scion on one servant's back). And, in a typical Hokusai touch, three plump little peasant boys, neglecting their task of gathering spring herbs, look on in glee, their rotundity in sharp contrast with the refined but effete courtiers. These urchins represent not only the real, plebeian world, but also the

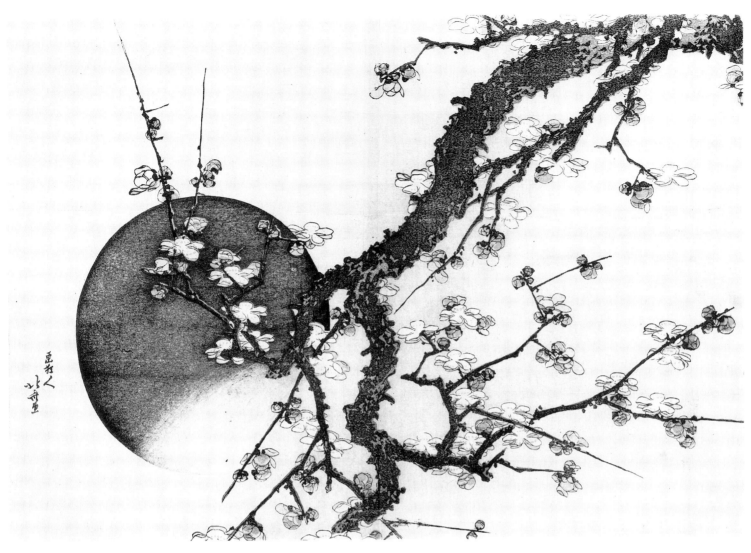

37 *Opposite top* Sōri II or III?: Comic Noh Dancers. Album-plate from *The First Moon*, c. 1803 (?).

38 *Opposite bottom* Courtiers and Urchins. Frontispiece-plate from *Brocade-prints of the Thirty-six Poetesses*, 1801.

39 *Above* Plum-tree and Moon. Album-plate from *Fuji in Spring*, 1803. (See also Plate 43.)

viewpoint of the artist himself: ever an amused onlooker at the rarefied society of the upper classes, which he could never enter (and probably did not much care to anyway). Thus while the subjects of a commercial artist were dicated to him, it is in such asides as this that we glimpse the true Hokusai—and, perhaps, his most significant and deep-seated contribution to Japanese art.

This was indeed a decade of splendours. Among the loveliest *kyōka* albums of this period must also be numbered *Miyako-dori* (Birds of the Capital) of 1802. The delicate, almost tactile printing utilizes a peculiarly grainy texture at times reminiscent of *fuki-bokashi* stencil-printing, and lends a strikingly plastic effect and mood to the six designs. From this example (Plate 42) it may be perceived how essentially hand-created were these limited editions: each with a personality all its own, dependent not only on artist (and poet), but equally on the anonymous master-artisans who effected the consummate engraving, printing and (it must not be forgotten) papermaking.

The scene shown here is the famed Sazaidō or 'Turban-shell Tower' past the artist's birthplace east of Edo, which Hokusai was to depict again three decades later in his *Thirty-six Views of Fuji* (Fig. 70). It was the custom for worshippers to offer prayers to the '500 Saints' enshrined there, and then mount the steep spiral staircase in order to view Mt Fuji from afar: a neat amalgamation of Buddhism and more primitive nature-worship. At the left a boy (with kite on his back) drops sheets of tissue-paper from the three-storeyed temple-tower as his elder sister watches; a man points to some famous sight as a courtesan follows his lead. At the lower right an old man (probably representing the artist) rests against the tower, wearied from the climb; and in the distance stretches a misty swamp, a forest, and the lumber-yards of Fukagawa. The season is that of *higan*, the Buddhist memorial festival in late spring.

The last of these sumptuous albums to be detailed here is *Haru-no-Fuji* (Fuji in Spring) of 1803, which contains only three plates—all by Hokusai. Of particular interest is the 'still-life' (if that is the proper term) of Plate 39, in which the flowering, arched branch of an aged plum-tree is pictured against the full moon of early spring. This is a powerful composition in which the two protagonists (traditionally 'old friends' in Japanese art) are depicted in close communion (though, in fact, separated by a distance of some quarter of a million miles). The design is a notable precursor of the

40 *Top* Girls Boating. Album-plate from *Elegance of Spring, c.* 1798.

41 *Above* Girls gathering Night Plum-blossoms. Album-plate (or trimmed long-*surimono*), *c.* 1798. Unsigned. (The signature at lower centre is that of the engraver.)

many later *surimono*-prints—by Hokusai and others—on this theme; but in one way it excels them, for the artist was free to fill the full frame, without concern for the inevitable addition of *kyōka* verses (which, in this album, were printed on separate pages). The plate likewise preludes the artist's two major series of Flower Prints of a generation later (Plates 280–1, 283, 286), but in mood and sense of intimacy, at least, it surely surpasses them. One further plate from this striking album may be illustrated—this time a colour detail in order to show more vividly the precise and complex printing methods of the genre (Plate 43).

As to why these lovely, ephemeral albums flourished most brilliantly only in these brief years, the answer must obviously await more detailed research on the activities of the *kyōka* clubs—and their financial resources—during this period. But even with poets, artists and funds readily available, it may be surmised that the death of the great and imaginative publisher Tsutaya Jūzaburō in mid-1797—and the oppressive nature of current government sumptuary-edicts—must have cast a pall over such elegant pursuits.

No one really knows how many of these albums Hokusai contributed to. Perhaps a dozen are extant for these years—some in lone, unique examples—but an equal number may well have been lost to us forever.

NOTE

1 Although this important design is generally assumed to derive from a lost and otherwise unknown album, there is just the possibility that it might originally have been an independent *surimono*, trimmed and then folded at centre; i.e. the size, 19.1 × 36.2 cm / 7½ × 14¼ in, could represent either an album-plate, slightly trimmed from the customary 25 × 38 cm / 9¾ × 15 in; or a long-*surimono*—with the usual horizontal dimensions of 50 cm-plus / 19¾ in considerably trimmed at right, thereby losing the signature—which might, indeed, form a more natural composition.

42 *Top* Temple-tower View. Detail of album-plate from *Birds of the Capital*, 1802. (For locations, see also Fig. 70.)

43 Girls gathering Spring Herbs. Detail from *Fuji in Spring*, 1803. (See also Plate 39.)

VII
On Wings of Song (3):
Hokusai's *Kyōka*
Picture-books

THE DISTINCTION between the *kyōka* album and the *kyōka* book may seem only a superficial one, but in the album format each plate was printed on a separate, two-page sheet, bound in accordion-fashion, and generally a much higher quality of heavy, soft but relatively stiff paper was used. Also, the pigments were somewhat different and more luxurious, the engraving and printing techniques usually of a higher standard. The albums constituted, in effect, a set of specialized *surimono*-prints, planned and arranged in order, for binding.

With the books in more conventional form, two pages were printed on one sheet; but this was then folded—the printing outwards—for binding by sewing together the open sides, with the folded sides to the front (often with title and pagination recorded at the edge of this 'turnover'). The paper, though handmade and resilient, was generally thinner and harder than that of the albums and prints, and the woodblock-printing featured an outline more precise, less subtle in flavour. Since facing pages were printed separately, care had to be taken to match the colours; and the separation at the centre of the design may seem an obstruction to some viewers. The albums were generally limited editions, seldom reissued, whereas the books were usually planned for a more popular market, and hence often reprinted, sometimes decades after the original edition, with stronger, even garish colours, typical of the later age. This is by no means to disparage the book versus the album, however. The latter genre, indeed, is often too pretty, too delicate, whereas the picture-book (and the illustrated book as well) offers more solid fare.

Even with the albums, a majority were printed in monochrome, although inevitably the more impressive chromatic examples are selected for illustration. This was true of the books as well, and our first example of this genus falls in that category. It is one of several works which, though perhaps seeming a trifle austere, are of great importance in tracing the artist's development in these crucial years. The tableau shown here is of special interest in that it displays the entrance to a leading Edo bookshop (Plate 44).

It will be recalled that Japanese publishers were usually their own booksellers, and here we see the shop of the famous Tsutaya Jūzaburō, at Tōri-abura-chō in the heart of Edo. Many such publishers' shops were located here, not far from the Kabuki district: convenient for gathering both theatrical information and customers. Tsutaya ('Ivy Shop') was the patron-publisher of most of the great names of ukiyo-e in this Golden Age, not only Hokusai but also Kyōden, Utamaro, Sharaku, Chōki. It must be added, however, that when Kyōden's Yoshiwara novelettes were

banned by the government in 1791 (not for moral reasons but for their controversial—almost anti-establishment—texts), their publisher Tsutaya had both of his shops closed down for six months, and half his property confiscated by the authorities, a shock from which he never quite recovered. The event cast a shadow over plebeian publication in general. After his death in the year 1797 the shop-name and tradition were carried on by two successors, but never with quite the same energy, creativity and *élan*.

In Hokusai's plate a figure probably depicting the founder of the firm, Tsutaya Jūzaburō I, is shown seated quietly in the rear, at far left; since he had died over a year before this volume was prepared, the portrait must be assumed a memorial one. At lower left, addressing the proprietor, is a

44 Shop of the Edo Publisher Tsutaya. Illustration from *Dances of the East*, 1799. (See also Plate 45.)

rustic samurai (two swords at sash) and his servant; at right, artisan-clerks prepare books for binding. On a shelf towards the rear are displayed newly published prints and books (the prints seen stacked on the front mats are the so-called *shita-uri*, 'floor-sales', consisting of lower-quality items and outdated actor-prints); on the outer wall at right can be seen boards with current book-titles inscribed (including an announcement of Hokusai's forthcoming *Tōto meisho-ichiran*). In front of the store is a pylon with the shop's symbol—Mt Fuji and *tsuta* (ivy)-leaves—name and address, and the large characters 'Wholesaler in *Beni-e*': an interesting reminder that at this period, the newly fashionable 'brocade-prints' (*nishiki-e*) still retained their original name, 'rose-prints'. This Hokusai plate is really too detailed to succeed as an artistic design, yet in it we can sense the artist's painstaking devotion to a subject that comprised, in effect, the centre of his life.

The remaining illustrations of this book, *Azuma-asobi* (Dances of the East—i.e. Edo) of 1799, feature other notable scenes of Edo life and trades, including a passing view of the 'Nagasaki House' where Dutch commercial emissaries were housed—and largely confined—located near Nihonbashi in the centre of Edo (Plate 45). As is shown in Hokusai's illustration, both adults and children would wait for hours at the side-street from which the windows of this hostel were visible, and when a foreigner came into view a great shout would arise, as at the sighting of a great whale, or of a baby panda at the zoo.

Interestingly, Hokusai may actually have had contact with the foreigners depicted here; certainly, his direct relation to the Occident dates from many decades before his rediscovery in Europe with the 1860s. According to the account in *Koga bikō* (written in the late 1840s), in about 1797–8 the Dutch *Kapitan* (and Emissary to Edo) commissioned a pair of handscrolls from him 'to show the full life, from birth to death and in all situations, of Japanese men and Japanese women. . . .' At the same time, the Mission's physician also commissioned a similar work. When completed, the Emissary gladly paid the artist's fee—150 pieces of gold—but the physician, claiming he was low on funds, demanded that the fee be cut in half. The proud artist refused, and took the latter scrolls back with him, telling his wife, 'Even though there is no market for these at home, it would be a national disgrace to accede to such an unreasonable demand.'[1] Hokusai is said also to have received subsequent commissions from such emissaries from Europe, though details are unclear until his famous productions of 1826 for Dr von Siebold, to be examined later.

In this volume one is immediately reminded of the 1790 picture-book of similar title by Utamaro: but whereas the earlier work is based on the traditional Far-Eastern perspective of the overhead view, in his landscape-plates Hokusai takes a new approach—dividing sky and earth at centre—in the new-found technique he had derived, probably, from his studies in Occidental art (see Chapter XI). The plates are, however, essentially decorative in intent and bear little relation to the text of this important *kyōka* anthology. Significantly enough, the special interest of Hokusai's detailed illustrations was soon recognized, and most of these—without the original verses—were reissued a year or so later, with colour-blocks added to the plates (as in the second tableau shown here). Not unexpectedly, the result is hardly the equal of Hokusai's productions in which colour-printing was planned from the outset. Nevertheless, this re-issue is a clear indication of the artist's rising fame as an illustrator, and of the increasing popular interest in his work, quite unrelated to the *kyōka* boom.

Artistically of far greater importance is Hokusai's two-volume picture-book of the following year, *Tōto meisho ichiran* (Famous Views of the Eastern Capital). Here we find a fully integrated picture-book of Edo life, consummately printed in delicate yet striking colours and featuring Hokusai's best work of this period. It should be noted that the effect of the Japanese picture-book is a cumulative one, of many delightful images indelibly inscribed in the viewer's subconscious memory. And further, one tends to focus on the more attractive details of the illustrations. Thus, rather than reduce the size of the double-page plates, I have sometimes, as here, chosen to concentrate attention on the most vital segment of an illustration. Indeed, reduced in size, many of Hokusai's book-illustrations may seem a bit cluttered in design, a fault not apparent in the original.

We commence, then, with a detail from an evocative Yoshiwara scene (Plate 46), in which three eminent courtesans—the fashion models of their day—appear dressed in the pure white robes of the late summer *hassaku* festival, which featured their formal procession through the pleasure quarter. One senses here a naïvety, a sensitivity to the feelings of others, that is often lacking in the magnificent beauties of the great Utamaro (who, however, knew the Yoshiwara far better than did Hokusai). The fully realized background represented a great advance in ukiyo-e technique over that of the previous generations, and is an innovation that goes back to Hokusai's early mentor Kiyonaga.

In this detail (shown here about twice the original size) we can also see something of the technical fascination of the ukiyo-e print: the soft yet sinuous quality of the engraving, printing and paper, the vegetable (rather than mineral) hues with an incredible intricacy of design and pigmentation—employing only a limited number of woodblocks—the decorative flatness of dimension and perspective (here, rather emphasized by the telephoto detail); and withal, the masterful placement of figures in a complex and artful design.

Other images from this remarkable book command attention but there is space here for only two. Plate 47 displays an unusual, rear view of the Kabuki stage, probably depicting a *Hangonkō* drama. Three actors are seen in the midst of their performance before a motley audience, with even the stage-props—smoking brazier and flying pigeons—delineated in full. In this realistic, deglamorized view of the actual stage, one may perhaps sense the artist's feeling of relief at being freed from the conventions of Kabuki depiction that had so constrained him in his early career. A photographer could only marvel at Hokusai's consummately positioned 'camera-angle' on this scene, and envy the artist's freedom to encompass the entirety of a playhouse within a single book-plate.

One example of a full, double-page tableau is shown in

Plate 50, 'Sumida River', an excellent combination of figure-print and landscape. A madame and geisha, kimonos blown by the winds of dusk, are sending off a client at a ferry-wharf. The design is not perhaps 'complete' enough to stand as an independent print, but viewed in the context of the total volume it comprises a memorable tableau, in which the artist has moved away from his early experiments in perspective-technique to a more integrated concept of landscape and figure.

In all these volumes, the inevitable *kyōka* verses appear prominently at the top of each plate. And it must be admitted that the demands for space of the poets (who, it will be remembered, both commissioned and paid for the more

45 *Right* 'Nagasaki House' in Edo. Illustration from *Dances of the East*, 1799—shown here in the edition of 1802, with colour-blocks added. (See also Plate 44 and Fig. 174. For bibliographical note see Appendix, Books, Nos. 76 and 85.)

46 *Below* Scene in the Yoshiwara. Detail from *Famous Views of the Eastern Capital*, 1800. (See also Plates 47 and 50.)

47 *Opposite top* At the Kabuki Theatre. Detail from *Famous Views of the Eastern Capital*, 1800. (See also Plates 46 and 50.)

48 *Opposite bottom left* Geisha-house Madam at Leisure with Child. Detail from *Songs of Itako*, 1802. (See also Plate 55.) (Note the format of the Japanese book—and the reading habits that explain why mint specimens of ukiyo-e works are rare.)

49 *Opposite bottom right* Poet in Masquerade. Detail from *Humorous Verses on the Isuzu River*, 1802. (See also Fig. 177.)

50 *Top* On the Sumida River. Illustration from *Famous Views of the Eastern Capital*, 1800. (See also Plates 46 and 47.)

51 *Above* Geisha in Snow. Illustration from *Three Loves*, c. 1805.

52 *Opposite* Geisha and Madam. Enlarged detail from *Mountain upon Mountain*, 1804. (See also Plates 56 and 59, Fig. 181.) (Note that in this specimen the 'grey block' is slightly off register, shading the woman's hand at right.)

luxurious albums and books) sometimes interfered with the artist's treatment of a theme. In that sense, the commercially published picture-books often manage better to integrate the verses than do the privately issued volumes.

This Hokusai *tour de force* of stylish Edo views proved quite popular, soon being reprinted under the revised title *Tōto shōkei ichiran* (Fine Views of the Eastern Capital). Of this edition there were several later printings in the following decades, with increasingly garish colouring. Yet even such inferior re-issues were similarly hand-printed, some two hundred copies being the limit that the woodblocks—which had then to be dried out—would sustain per printing. Thus at the time total sales of several thousand were considered phenomenal. Indeed, editions of Japanese books rather resembled those in the West at the time: specialized works were issued only in a few hundred copies, more popular works in the thousands, with the figure 10,000 or above representing a kind of 'best-seller'. It may also be surmised that by Hokusai's time Japan was one of the more literate nations on earth—literacy rates averaging up to fifty percent for men and a third that for women, and much higher in the cities. Hokusai doubtless had his aficionados in both the highest and lowest levels of Edo society; but his principal audience was the affluent middle class: the more successful shopkeepers and salesmen, the

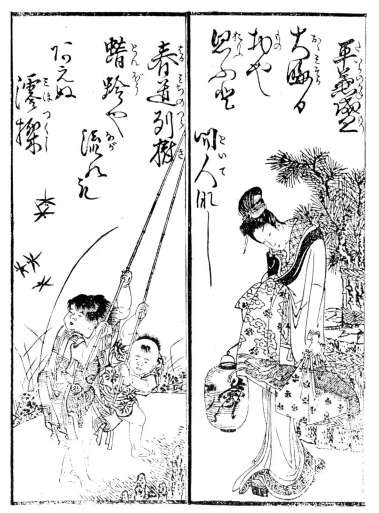

senior artisans, and (it must not be forgotten) the lower-ranking samurai—and their ladies—who formed such a large proportion of the eastern capital's population.

Besides these handsome colour-printed picture-books, the artist was ever busy at other lesser, and therefore today neglected works in black and white—often revealing surprising facets of his artistry. Mention should thus be made in passing of such interesting monochrome books-with-verse as *San-ai-shū* (Three Loves) of 1801 (Plate 51), and *Ogura hyakku* (Verses after the *Hundred Poems*) of 1803. The latter volume features yet another poetic form, the more realistic *kyōku* or 'mad haiku' and the verses are integrated into vertical designs run two to a page. For the book-lover, at least, such little cameos may well offer pleasure not inferior to that of the more impressive works in colour. And the artist, too, was often freer in these less sumptuous books to depict the actual world about him, rather than the dream-world of the literary societies. In the two samples shown here (Plate 53), we view at left two little boys chasing after summer dragonflies; and at right a tradesman's wife forlornly returning from a frugal year-end shopping expedition. The plates represent a vivid contrast in mood and circumstance, but both reflect sharply the realities of plebeian life.

Further in this realistic vein is yet another neglected

53 Children Playing/Woman Shopping. Illustrations from *Verses after the Hundred Poems*, 1803.

54 *Below* Front of Kabuki Theatre. Illustration from *The Twittering of Birds*, 1805. (See also Fig. 183.)

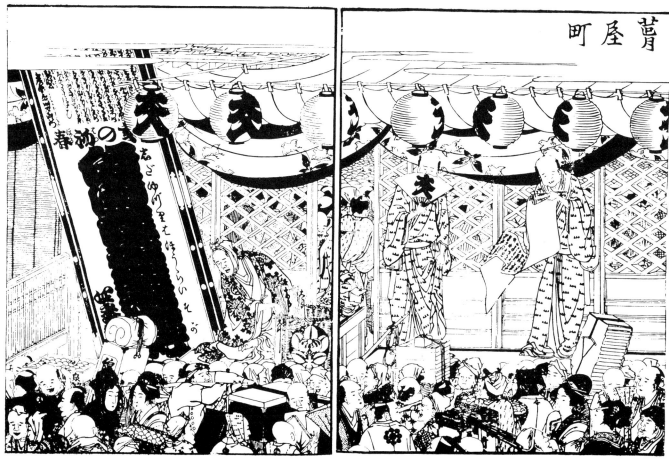

55 Geisha in Boat. Illustration from *Songs of Itako*, 1802. (See also Plate 48 and Fig. 178.)

monochrome work of the period, *Momo-saezuri* (The Twittering of Birds) of 1805 (Plate 54). The style of the designs seems to come from a somewhat earlier period than the date of publication; and in fact the theatrical poster in this tableau cites 'New Year, Year of the Wild Boar', i.e. 1803. It is also well to remember that with an anthology like this, contributed to mainly by provincial poets, the illustrations tend to be more detailed, documentary and even didactic than would be the case if the audience (and purchasers) were mainly sophisticated Edoites.

The volume forms a kind of sequel to the earlier *Dances of the East*, featuring *kyōka*-verses with interesting—and quite detailed—illustrations of Edo customs. Plate 54, for example, offers a striking glimpse of what it was really like in the crowded theatre district: 'you are there', so to speak. The designs were—rather unusually—later reprinted as independent *ōban* prints; see the landscape of our Plate 82. Besides such verse anthologies the artist was also very soon to begin the extensive illustration of lengthy novels, which will be the subject of a later chapter.

Returning to Hokusai's coloured picture-books, the diminutive *Itako zekku-shū* (Songs of Itako) of 1802 features less forceful, almost languid illustrations, but is interesting in several respects. First, its texts are in the rare *kyōshi* form, 'mad odes' in pseudo-Chinese style, parodying the popular ditties of Itako (a pleasure-area far north-east of Edo) that form the title and basis of the book; secondly, there is the mystery of why the illustrations are unsigned. The author of the verses, Karamaro—a noted Confucian scholar—wrote a generation later in his memoirs: 'This collection was issued at the urging of the publisher Tsutaya, who had the artist Hokusai provide the illustrations of beautiful women. . . . It proved popular enough, but the authorities found its colourful beauty too much like shunga [erotica] and banned it. . . .' The illustrations are, indeed, rather languorously decadent, though hardly enough to warrant banning. And any voluptuousness is much diluted by Hokusai's innocuous style of this period. The government intervention was possibly a fortuitous piece of bureaucracy (perhaps they objected to the employment of classical Chinese for amorous songs?), in the midst of the sporadic Reform Movement of the time. In any event, though small in size, *Songs of Itako* includes some of Hokusai's most satisfying illustrations of the period (Plates 48 and 55).

Less pictorially appealing, but significant in the artist's development, is his *Ehon Chūshingura* (Picture-book of the Loyal Retainers) of the same year, 1802. The artist spoke often of his mother being a descendant of one of the samurai of this famous incident—'The Revenge of the Forty-seven *Rōnin*'—and this popular theme was to absorb him in several series of prints from this period on. The illustrations themselves are workmanlike compositions, offering an integrated sequence of the vendetta; but, perhaps necessarily, they lack the inventive imagination that characterizes Hokusai's more important picture-books of this remarkable decade (Plate 57). At the same time, the book may be taken as a harbinger of the coming period, when the artist was to expend much of his energies on even more specialized types of book-illustration, sometimes almost to the detriment of his development as a creative artist.

Following the lead of Kyōden a generation earlier, is a *kyōka* anthology of 1802, *Isuzugawa kyōka-guruma* (Humorous verses of the Isuzu River), featuring on each page stylish pastiche portraits of the poets themselves. Hokusai's designs may seem a trifle static today, but they must really be appreciated in the context of the comic verses and the imaginative and witty depictions of actual versifiers. Plate 49 is a portrait of Matsuri Wataru, by profession a hairdresser in the Kanda district of Edo. He is depicted imitating a Kabuki actor, with nobleman's cap in hand.

Another interesting volume of comic portraits is *Kyōka sanjū-rokkasen* (Thirty-six Poets of *Kyōka*) of c. 1804–5, each design again cleverly combining creative portraiture with adroit allusion both to the profession of the versifier and to the actual verse which is included (Plate 58).[2]

A charming, and far more important, *kyōka* picture-book from this period is the famed *Yama-mata-yama* (Mountain upon Mountain) of 1804, in which the plates take precedence over the verses. The title refers to the hilly Yama-no-te areas of Edo, the delights of which are celebrated in the plates and verses. Hokusai's illustrations are stylish depictions of the refined customs of the leisured classes, to which the *kyōka* poets themselves belonged (Plate 52). At times, the modern viewer may again feel that the balance and impact of the compositions are somewhat weakened by the artist's purposeful accommodation of much upper space to fit the verses in—though this is more apparent from dismembered plates than when viewing the original (Plate 59).

Like many of these picture-books, this set of three volumes was originally issued with a strikingly designed wrapper, which has fortunately been preserved (Plate 56). Depicted is Yama-uba, the legendary 'Mountain-Woman', and her boisterous son Kintoki (whom we have already met in Plate 5), with the publisher Tsutaya recorded at lower right. The analogy of the jacket-design with the book-title and subject is not merely from the 'mountain' connection, but even more from the 'mountain-roving' (*Yama-uba no yama-meguri*) theme associated with the Yama-uba legend, which is here transposed to the concept of 'Roaming the Hills of Edo'.[3] (There was a fashion at the time for depictions of this odd pair, often with semi-erotic connotations—of which Utamaro's prints on the subject are justly famous.)

Such idyllic scenes as one finds in *Mountain upon Mountain* do not, of course, correspond to the manner in which the average Japanese lived; nor are they very pertinent to the actual life of Hokusai himself, who was nearly always in straitened circumstances. This contrast between the artist's life and his subject-matter is, indeed, a dichotomy one often senses in ukiyo-e. It was only rarely that these plebeian artists (to their contemporaries, mere artisans) could actually savour the pleasures of the Floating World that they depicted with such charm; and if they did, it was generally in their final years of success. Many, including Hokusai himself, never tasted such pleasures.

The final major picture-book of this, Hokusai's first real flowering, is *Sumida-gawa ryōgan-ichiran* (Views of Both Banks of the Sumida River) of c. 1804–05. This three-volume set constitutes, in effect, a continuous panorama of scenes along the bank of the great river that ran through the centre of Edo, and still subtly dominates modern Tokyo. Thus, although each double-page plate is independent and complete, it also runs integrally into the next scene, just like the traditional Japanese picture-scroll. It should be added that the albums/scrolls of similar title by the earlier artist Rosui, published in 1781, consisted of uninspired panoramas of the entire length of both river-banks. They were of limited interest and circulation, but formed the inspiration for Hokusai's more creatively visualized treatment of this majestic theme. Unlike his predecessor, however, Hokusai evokes not only the far bank of the river, but also the varied life on the near side—an innovation which, with its complexity of creative insight and visual impact, makes all the difference. (One is also reminded of certain formal Chinese handscrolls depicting life along the great rivers.)

Hokusai's three volumes treat the famous river in its full sequence of seasons, times and aspects, as seen from the western, Edo bank, running up to its northern extremity, and ending with supplementary views of the Yoshiwara and its environs. The centre of focus is not the landscape, however, but the vibrant life of the middle and lower classes on the nearer shore: the river as it actually appeared to the people who lived there. Such a varied and integrated set of picture-books is hardly susceptible to ready sampling. We can only pluck out a detail plus one longer, six-page view to demonstrate the artist's overall conception (Plates 60 and 61).

Perhaps the most striking single plate of the set is that entitled 'Squall at New Willow-Bridge' (Plate 60 and the right third of Plate 61). Here we view a motley group of passers-by, reacting variously to the sudden shower: in the right half, three frail women shelter under two large umbrellas; at centre two porters are running with makeshift coverings; and at left, a pedlar with rain-hat stoically carries his wares. The figures hurry barefoot—having removed their sandals to avoid splashing their clothing. On the other, far side of the river are seen the varied warehouses and other waterfront buildings of the Honjo-Fukagawa District (the artist's birthplace). This bridge lay at the mouth of the lesser, Kanda River and—in one of the

56 Yama-uba and Kintoki. Wrapper for *Mountain upon Mountain*, 1804. (See also Plates 52 and 59.) (In classical Japanese prints the delicate, vegetable blue is a fugitive colour, often fading, as here, to beige or mauve.)

minor mysteries of ukiyo-e—the subtitle and verse speak of a 'rainbow' that appears nowhere in the picture. Readers acquainted with the artist's late-contemporary Hiroshige will recall here the latter's masterpiece 'Evening Squall at Great-Bridge' (Plate 62), of just a half-century later (which print impressed Van Gogh so much that he copied it in oils). The similarity of theme and details is unlikely to be coincidental.

Taking a closer look at the left-hand scene of our panorama (Plate 61), one perceives also that the tableau bears interesting affinities with Hokusai's more famous print 'Sunset over Ryōgoku Bridge' of nearly thirty years later (Plate 251 and page 194). The artist had still a long road to travel before reaching this final mastery, but that road is strewn with little gems which, if not so perfect as the later masterpieces, often prove more intimately compelling in their youthful naïvety.[4]

Compared with earlier picture-books—those of Kiyonaga and Utamaro, for example—Hokusai's figures are more lively, more full of movement: not just figures *in* a landscape but figures-with-landscape. This new harmony of figure and background is found in enhanced form first in the Master's *Famous Views of the Eastern Capital* of 1800, perhaps reaching its culmination in the *Songs of Itako* of two years later; already by the *Sumida River* volumes of c. 1804–05, however, the artist's manner reverts to that intellectualized conception of man and landscape on equal terms which was, clearly, closer to his true nature.

It is worth observing that these *kyōka*-books helped to reawaken Edoites to the beauties of their own environment—providing fresh views and insights to scenes that had, through familiarity, come to breed something near contempt. In addition to this, Hokusai contributed his own innate love for and fascination with humanity, both real and abstract. Such concerns lay, to be sure, at the heart of ukiyo-e as a genre: but all too many of the artists—riding on the wave of popular fashion—tended to lose touch with the common mass of people. In this respect Hokusai's faults were also his strengths: with the coming generation we shall see him gradually losing his veneer of sophistication and reverting to his inborn, earthy nature. But it is this very touch of the earth that distinguishes Hokusai from his contemporaries even during the years that he was trying to emulate them.

57 *Above* Mother and Daughter on Journey. Illustration from *The Loyal Retainers*, 1802. (See also Fig. 179.)

58 *Opposite top* Poet and Poetess. Illustrations from *Thirty-six Poets of Kyōka*, c. 1804–5. (See also Fig. 186.)

59 *Opposite bottom* Girls catching Fireflies. Illustration from *Mountain upon Mountain*, 1804. (See also Plates 52 and 56.)

The delicate, poetic, even sentimental side of the artist's nature may be a revelation to some readers. We may conclude that Hokusai's style at the turn of the century was—under the influence of the *Kyōka* Movement—distilled and sublimated: its rarefied beauty heightened by the very conflicts that stirred his subconscious.

NOTES

1 This may well be the same Dutch official as that recorded as later dying en route to Edo in 1798, being buried at the Tennenji temple in Kakegawa.
2 In photographing this particular book, I have dispensed with the usual pressure-plate in an attempt to convey something of the bookish, three-dimensional quality of the original. Such is possible only with a volume that, by the nature of its binding and the resiliency of its paper, lies naturally flat—but not too flat.
3 An alternative view on the interpretation of this title, by M. Forrer, will be found in the catalogue *Hokusai and his School* (1982), p. 177. This interpretation seems to me farfetched. (The main source for this expression is the Chikamatsu drama *Komochi Yama-uba* of 1712—which itself derives from the early

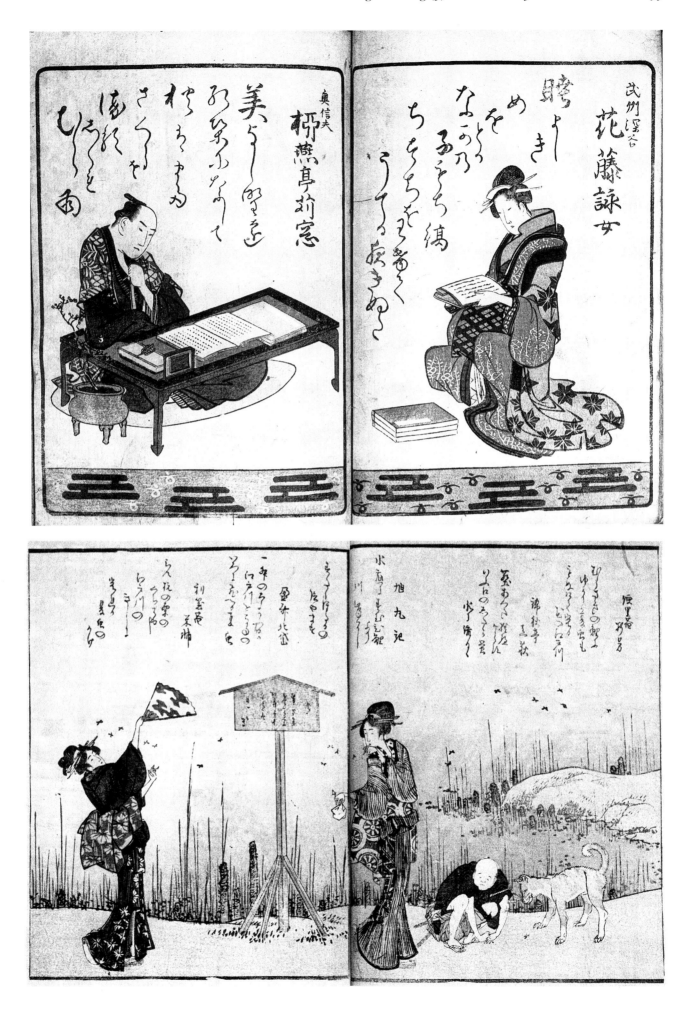

Noh play *Yama-uba*, with its resounding lines, *Yama-mata-yama ni yama-meguri, yama-mata-yama ni yama-meguri shite....*) Note also that the subtitle '*Kyōka*' often appears at head of title for such verse-anthologies; for simplification this—and the similar '*Ehon*' (picture-book)—have usually been omitted here. Thus in this case the full title is *Ehon kyōka: Yama-mata-yama*—which form must be remembered when using the indices of technically oriented book-catalogues.

4 Just as I completed the manuscript for this chapter the original woodblocks for Hokusai's three main picture-books of this period were rediscovered in the storerooms of the Museum of Fine Arts in Boston, acquired in Japan by the Museum's patron W. S. Bigelow in 1889. These were subsequently exhibited in Japan, together with complete, new printings by the Adachi Institute. Although the fresh pulls from the original—but necessarily worn—blocks were inevitably disappointing (not only because of the modern pigments but even more because of the modern paper), the exhibition did offer interesting new insights even for the specialist. The first such insight came in viewing the cut-out montage of the *Sumida River* volumes spread along a full wall, revealing how impressive a picture-scroll Hokusai's original concept effected. The second came with the exhibition of new pulls from the different colour-blocks, the sample of the 'water-block' of our Plate 60, for example, revealing the figures in white relief against a pale blue, graded background: a strikingly independent silhouette reminiscent of Greek pottery and artistically frosted glass, withal 'modern' in more ways than one. (On this important discovery—and some of the bibliographic implications—see the excellent catalogue *Boston de mitsukatta Hokusai-ten*, Tōkyō, 1987.)

60 *Opposite* Squall at New Willow-Bridge. Detail from *Views of Both Banks of the Sumida River, c. 1804–05.* (The number inscribed at left is that of a noted rental shop of these oiled-paper umbrellas.) (For full view see right panel of Plate 61; also see Fig. 185.)

61 *Below* River Panorama. Three consecutive spreads from *Views of Both Banks of the Sumida River, c. 1804–05.* (See also Plate 60 and Fig. 185. Mottling in sky is due to soil on original. In other examples water is rendered in pale blue and there are colour variations.)

62 *Right* Hiroshige: Evening Squall at Great Bridge. *Ōban*-size print, 1857.

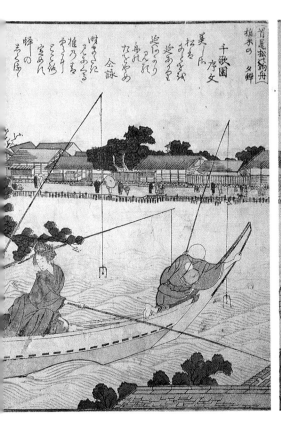
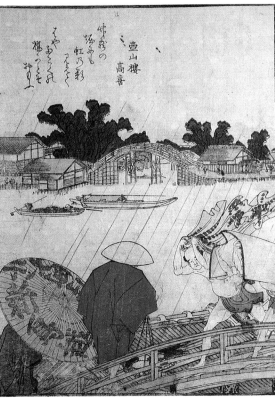

VIII
Vying with Utamaro:
Further Beauties
of the Floating World

1

THE DECADE 1796–1805 witnessed a prodigious out-pouring of Hokusai's pent-up energies. Indeed, the critic's first problem is how to effect some kind of organization of this mass of prints and books.

One cannot, of course, expect a commercial artist to de-vise a limited style or contrive a single speciality when he must cater to the varied demands of clients in a fast-changing world. Hokusai, perhaps more than any other ukiyo-e artist, tended to stretch his potential to its very limits, to take on each and every commission whether it represented his forte or not. It is surprising that although there were failures, so many of these bold experiments resulted in fresh masterpieces, and a few yielded contribu-tions that were to mark a peak of the era, and sometimes even lead the way to the coming generation.

Having detailed Hokusai's work in the *surimono* greeting-cards, the *kyōka* books and albums, we can now turn to the remaining category of his work in this period, the commer-cially published print. And of this genus the first and most striking category is that of the *bijin-ga* or figure-design, comprised principally of paeans to female beauty, but also including depictions of famous pairs of lovers.

Because of his training and background in the rather austere actor-prints of the Katsukawa School and, perhaps, because of a certain inherent awkwardness in that genre, Hokusai's early work in female depiction had been hardly outstanding. It consisted mainly, as we have seen, of de-rivative designs in the Kiyonaga tradition. With his in-dependence in the later 1790s, however, Hokusai was induced to try his hand at many different genres, and his work in *bijin-ga* involved him in an attempt to emulate the glamorous achievements of the great Utamaro.

Sustained success in such a venture was hardly within the scope of Hokusai's powers: after all, Utamaro was one of the 'Five Great Names' of ukiyo-e, quite the equal of Hokusai in native genius, and surpassing him in this one speciality, at least. But though the younger artist was, in effect, working in a genre rather beyond his particular forte and outside his natural inclinations, the results were unique and curiously attractive, even to his contem-poraries, who dubbed this the 'Sōri Style', after Hokusai's principal *nom de plume* of the period.

The Sōri Style, as we have already seen in the discussions on *surimono* and books, featured frail, attenuated figures with stylized, rather pinched faces. Indeed, Hokusai's new concept of feminine beauty (and, as well, the monosexual male) entailed a strong element of the *shibui*—the austere and astringent, almost anti-erotic and ethereal—that re-minds one somehow of the relation of Bunchō to Harunobu

in the ukiyo-e prints of over a generation earlier. Thus, of the masters who worked under Utamaro's great shadow in this decade—Eishi, Eishō, Eiri, Chōki et al.—Hokusai's peculiar vision of female beauty is surely unique, if not suited to all tastes (Plates 63–66, 68).

Unlike the calendar-prints and books, Hokusai's com-mercially issued *bijin-ga* are difficult to date exactly. They probably spanned the years just before the turn of the century—the end of that Golden Age of ukiyo-e, the Kansei Period (1789–1801). Rather curiously, the artist's signature on most of these prints is not Sōri but 'Kakō'. We do not know just what this capricious *nom de plume* meant for Hokusai, but clearly the resultant art represented a new facet to his many-sided genius.

Among the most intimately charming prints of this period is Hokusai's series of genre scenes in the smaller *chūban* format (Plates 63–65). While revealing the influence of those powerful masters Kiyonaga and Utamaro—and of his own mentor Tōrin—the younger artist here manages to create a style that is completely his own: frail figures which convey well that profoundly moving convention, derived from the Kabuki tradition, of loving couples almost too delicate to survive the winds of chance.

Hokusai's principal work in this vein is known as the 'Eight Views of Star-crossed Lovers' series, of which some six prints have so far been found. These designs all feature ill-fated romantic couples, without specific series-title but with the protagonists' names recorded in detail, plus the seasonal/temporal designation which goes back to the classical 'Eight Views of Lake Biwa' theme, of which the series forms a pastiche.

Although these prints are devoted to tableaux famous from the Kabuki and *jōruri* (puppet) theatre—mainly works by the great Chikamatsu—Hokusai's approach is directed to the human elements, and there is nothing of the stage here. Whether the series was completed or not is unclear (completion sometimes depended more on the publisher's financial situation than on artistic quality or even critical acclaim); but some of the designs, at least, proved popular enough to warrant later reprinting, with the captions omit-ted. Yet even in the first issue, the prints of this notable series are not quite up to the technical quality of Hokusai's other works of the same period, possibly an indication that the anonymous publisher was not of first rank. Such con-siderations are not, of course, directly related to the ideal of Hokusai's art; but in the originals they tend to detract some-what from the artistic effect—a reminder of how much the ukiyo-e master was dependent on the combined efforts of publisher, engraver and printer for the success of the final print.

The best-known design of this neglected series is that depicting the Yoshiwara courtesan Azuma and her young lover Yogorō (Plate 65)—the seasonal subtitle being *Zansetsu* (Lingering Snow). The lovers are seen ensconced upon a bench before a barred window (a reminder that the courtesans were not permitted much freedom of movement), with a snowy landscape beyond. The pliant human forms are contrasted with the geometrical and architectural details, and the natural glories of the background—from which the 'geisha-houses' and their quarter were so inexorably shut off—seem as though from a quite different world. The young man sits nonchalantly enough, as his sweetheart leans over him in a languorous eroticism that is the more effective for its subdued expression, its mood of restrained passion. One senses here most poignantly the

voluptuous and yet hopeless flavour of the Yoshiwara, which had been expressed all too well by the balladeer of *Ake-garasu* (Dawn Raven) in the preceding generation:[1]

Silent the spring rain: dozing
and softly aroused, lost and dishevelled
through love, the courtesan Urazato is reflecting:
'By what strange affinity
did I love him so from the first meeting!—love for him
filling my whole body, an unbearable
passion and longing'. Hidden from others' view
by the protective bedding, reluctantly
the lovers rise and she
coifs and coifs his rumpled sidelock. . . .

Another striking design (Plate 63) depicts the tragic lovers O-Ume and Kumenosuke (the latter shown adjusting his sweetheart's sash on a mountain path at Kōya-san). The monosexual figures are portrayed in an effective, triangular composition in contrast to the rigid cryptomeria trees. The remaining prints of this series are less patently dramatic, owing much of their poignancy to literary overtones that will be perceived only by the initiated; but this is ever a problem of Japanese art, in which there so often exists a complex layer of meanings beyond the superficial charm and decorative beauty.

Thus in the tableau of the disreputable 'Yosaku and Koman: towards Dusk' (Plate 64), we see only a stylish but plebeian young couple resting at a mountain tea-house.

63 *Below left* 'The Lovers O-Ume and Kumenosuke: The Vesper Bell'. Small-*chūban*-size; late 1790s. Signed Kakō. From a series on the theme of 'Eight Views of Star-crossed Lovers' (for others see Plates 64, 65 and Figs. 26, 27.)

64 *Below right* 'The Lovers Yosaku and Koman: Towards Dusk'. (From the same series as Plate 63.)

65 *Overleaf left* 'The Lovers Azuma and Yogorō: Lingering Snow'. (From the same series as Plate 63.)

66 *Overleaf right* Girls at their Toilette. *Ōban*-size; late 1790s. Signed Kakō. From the series *Seven Stylish Foibles* (see also Plate 68).

The design marks the beginnings of that fascination with composition that will later become Hokusai's trademark. The figures are placed in a curiously parallel, diagonal position—emphasized by the L-shaped benches—the twin pines complementing the couple at middle-ground, and the stable mass of clouded Mt Fuji filling out the background. The lovers touch each other affectionately but not erotically, gazing forward like wide-eyed children. But the scene is brought into sharp relief when we remember that they are fleeing from their fate on the short journey to their likely death.

Just how much the ukiyo-e artist was dependent on his publishers will be apparent when we record that Hokusai's major series of this period—the famous *Fūryū nakute nana-kuse*[2] (Seven Stylish Foibles)—was cancelled after only two designs had been published (Plates 66, 68). The two known designs are among the most elegantly printed works of the time and—combining rarity, great beauty, and a major artist—among the most valuable of all Japanese prints. Not unexpectedly, the publisher was the great Tsutaya, patron of most of the major ukiyo-e artists of the day. Although Hokusai's prints seem to have been issued a year or more after Tsutaya's death, the series was probably planned some time before that, but then curtailed in the wake of his demise. Whatever the circumstances, the two extant prints mark a pinnacle of Hokusai's work in the genre, a level of quality that quite equals the best of such eminent contemporaries as Utamaro, Chōki and Sharaku; and it is one of the minor tragedies of ukiyo-e that the artist was never permitted to complete this major series, and extend his range in such impressive *bijin-ga*. Had the publisher survived, Hokusai's career, and the course of the figure-print, might have been different.

Turning to Hokusai's actual prints, in Plate 66 we view two young women of the pleasure quarter at toilette. The girl at left has just washed her hair, which hangs over her shoulders and chest; in her mouth she sucks a shrill-toned *hōzuki* (ground-cherry). The girl at right has almost completed her coiffure (in the *Shimada*-style) and is applying rouge before a hand-held mirror. Both display that vapid self-absorption that is sometimes noticeable in women prettying themselves. The elongated faces and foreheads, and the supple, boneless fingers, are typical of Hokusai's ideal of femininity at this period: very different from the sinuous and powerful figures of his later work. The bold dashes of colour form a striking, semi-circular visual pattern, the flat background lending an opulent final touch in a composition somehow reminiscent of the masterpieces of Sharaku.

It is well to remember, though, that certain delicate colours in Japanese classical prints are more fugitive than others: thus even in this fine example the blue of the *shibori*-robe is faded/oxidized to mauve, and the pink was almost certainly a stronger colour when the print was first issued, nearly two centuries ago. (Compare the colouring scheme of the following plate, from the same series, where the pigments are remarkably well preserved.)

Even more justly famous is the magnificent print of Plate 68. We see here a mother and daughter of the upper classes, possibly even ladies of the the Shōgun's court, on an outing with large parasol and inlaid telescope, into which the maiden squints. In this daringly bold telephoto view, Hokusai displays his early mastery of the figure-print in a composition reminiscent of his contemporary Chōki. The print is enhanced by dramatic and original use of colouring, including a strikingly modern background half in yellow and half in mica.

As with the previous design, only three examples of this masterpiece are known to be extant. A comparison of this near-pristine specimen with the similar, better-known but faded impressions (in the Ikenaga and Grabhorn collections) graphically reveals the fugitive nature of the vegetable colouring employed in Japanese prints through the early nineteenth century: the cobalt-blue parasol has faded to light grey, the purple robe to brown, the red to pink, the brown of the telescope to light orange; mustard has turned to light yellow and pink to light saffron, and the opulent mica ground is omitted in these later issues. As in the previous plate, the keyblock is again printed in grey and the deeper blacks are rendered by a separate woodblock employing a lacquer-like pigment; at upper left will be seen the excess margin of the print, which was normally trimmed off. Even from these brief comments something may perhaps be perceived of the problems inherent in the collection, description and preservation of classical Japanese prints: the collector or critic may, unwittingly, be admiring mutated colouring that represents but a shadow of the original; the collector or curator who puts such prints on permanent display may quite literally see his investment fade before his very eyes.[3]

Other, lesser *bijin-ga* series could be cited for this period (for example, *Noroma-kyōgen*—Comic Interludes—of Plate 67, which is much influenced by Utamaro), but they are all both rare and uncompleted: possibly an indication that they were not too popular even in the artist's day. Though Hokusai succeeded very well in emulating the great Utamaro he could hardly supplant the latter in the popular mind. Thus these brief experiments remain today but a hint of what might have been, had publishing circumstances permitted: and Hokusai's more extensive achievement in the figure-print must be sought, rather, in the smaller formats of *surimono* and illustration, already discussed.

It is worth enquiring at this point how Hokusai managed to develop this new style of figure-depiction during the brief years after his break with the Katsukawa school. His assiduous private study of the most popular ukiyo-e masters of the time was clearly important: Utamaro's early, more delicate style was obviously a model. The similarly graceful yet effete figures of Eishi and Chōki come even more to mind, but it must be remembered that these artists were themselves only developing their characteristic styles at this period. Thus, while Hokusai's delicate ideal of beauty may be said to evolve from one facet of the great Utamaro, it represents both an epitome of the taste of the times and a distillation of the artist's own fancy during the 1790s. We shall, to be sure, discover a quite different Hokusai a generation later; but it cannot be denied that, during the period of his immersion in the stylish *Kyōka* Movement, he managed perfectly to create an ele-

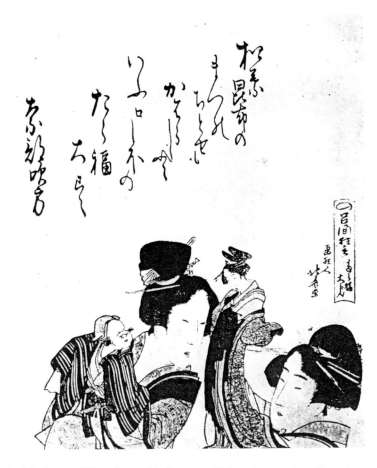

松昆虫の
まろ
かろく
口本
ろく福
なら
ちら
東弥喝

67 Mother and Daughter with Puppets. *Koban*-size; *c.* 1800. Signed Gakyōjin Hokusai. From the series *Comic Interludes*.

gant world of modish figures, imbued with wit and *élan*. Hokusai was patently an artist of many styles, even many personalities. The fact that his later, craggy, more earthy and realistic face is yet hidden in this, the beginning of his middle period, in no way detracts from the inherent strength of his art.

It may be assumed that the artist—not to mention his long-suffering family—was now enjoying a little more prosperity than had been the case after his break with the Katsukawa School. However, remuneration was most often in the form of gratuities rather than fixed payment; and Hokusai was never one to pay much attention to his own surroundings or his own finances, so absorbed was he in his art. Indeed, this was the characteristic spirit of the Edoite—in which (unlike the case in the older cultures of Ōsaka and even Kyōto) the aim of life tended to be the pleasureful spending of money rather than merely its acquisition and hoarding. This attitude may well have been a reflection of the special nature of Edo society: fully half the population of this huge metropolis was comprised of the samurai class—into which the *plebs* could never aspire to enter. They turned, therefore, to light-hearted hedonism as a natural outlet for their pent-up energies: but a hedonsim often restrained and refined by a strong sense of style and *élan*—of which ukiyo-e was not the only, but certainly the most obvious, manifestation.

2

There is a great gap between the magnificent figure-work of the plates discussed above and the lesser prints with which we shall round out this chapter. Yet the essential beauty is the same, and to the novice student and collector, at least, it may be difficult to comprehend why, for example, at an auction the print of Plate 68 would fetch at least a thousand times that of our next Plate 69. It is in the nature of collectors to covet popular art-objects, thereby widening the differences between major and minor works of the same artist and period. This is, of course, an advantage for the modest collector, who is still able to acquire lesser but worthwhile examples of the artist's work.

Hokusai's remaining figure-prints of this period fall mainly in the realm of nominally topographical works: principally, his several different series on the 'Fifty-three Stations of the Tōkaidō' (Plates 69–74).

The immediate stimulus for such series was not the inspiration of the artist but the demands of the publishers. And this demand was itself the result of the new boom for travel—and travel-related publications such as maps and guidebooks—in the later eighteenth century. With the beginning of the nineteenth century popular interest spread to the world of prints as well. However, the market was not yet ready for the enormous development in the landscape-print that we shall witness three decades later (see Chapters XVII–XIX). Rather was the focus in this preliminary period on the more miniature formats, of roughly postcard and double-postcard size.

Such miniature prints represent, in effect, a commercialization of the *surimono* genre: interest is turned from the verse and its seasonal theme to the locality and the specific, genre subject, brought down to the level of the plebeian consumer, so to speak. The sumptuous printing, paper and pigments are likewise replaced by more practical techniques and materials, permitting wider circulation at a fraction of the price. It must be added that with such themes, the division between 'figure-prints' and 'landscapes-with-figures' is sometimes a tenuous one. The latter category will be discussed at greater length in the ensuing chapter.

Hokusai's production in this genre was large, and only three such series—all devoted to the Tōkaidō Highway between Edo/Tōkyō and Kyōto—can be detailed here (for further data see Appendix, Prints, Nos. 51, 64, 76, 76a–c, 100). They all date from the first years of the nineteenth century, differ only marginally in style, but—in the originals at least—may be readily differentiated by size, format and titling.

The earliest is probably the series of 54 small, horizontal designs with neither margins nor series-titles. (Note that the more renowned, later series on this theme usually comprised 55 prints—the 53 stages plus the starting- and end-points—but in these earlier examples the number varies.) The name of the posting-station appears in semi-*gyōsho* (cursive calligraphy) and each print is signed 'Hokusai *ga*' (= *pinxit*). Many of the scenes represent a compromise between landscape and figure, but some of the best tend to emphasize the charms of the ladies (of the

68 *Opposite* Lady and Maiden on an Outing. *Ōban*-size; late 1790s. Signed Kakō. From the same series as Plate 66.

69 *Above* 'Fuchū': Women at their Toilette. *Koban* print (shown here about double size), early 1800s. Signed Hokusai. From an untitled Tōkaidō series (see also Plates 70–71, Fig. 31.)

night or otherwise) at the post-stations *en route*.

In the design of Plate 69, 'Fuchū', for example (the word means merely 'Provincial Capital', in this case Shizuoka), we view two women of the town at toilette, seated between mirror-stand and brazier. The tableau is surprisingly reminiscent of our Plate 66, and even though the level of society depicted is rather different, there is little hint of the sordid conditions of such tea-house girls and harlots. To the artist they are in essence, and in effect, fairy princesses. Enlarged to *ōban*-size and printed more sumptuously, this design would instantly become a 'major Hokusai print'.

With 'Kakegawa' from the same series we turn to another phase of Hokusai's development, the genre scene. Plate 71 shows two travelling entertainers: the young man is tapping out a tune on the set of gongs tied about his waist, as his older companion beats the drum. Two onlookers watch, but another turns away. The young dan-

70 'Hara': Foreign Emissaries by Mt Fuji. *Koban*-size; early 1800s. Signed Hokusai. From the same series as Plate 69.

71 'Kakegawa': Roadside Entertainers. *Koban* print (shown here about double size), early 1800s. Unsigned. From the same series as Plate 69.

cer seems to be appealing to the spectators, even as his mallets impel him in the opposite direction. On the straw mat spread over the ground will be seen small coins, probably placed there by the entertainers themselves—a hint as often as not snubbed by unfeeling onlookers. Hokusai's design can hardly be termed a masterpiece even of a miniaturistic kind: the dancer's feet are not well done and the traveller at left is insufficiently integrated, but the strength of the young lad's intent head and torso compels us, somehow, to retain his image in our minds.

In passing, mention may also be made of 'Hara' in this series, showing three foreign emissaries (probably one of the missions from Nagasaki) led by a pack-horse driver (Plate 70). It is a less effective design than the previous two, but remarkable for proving how early the artist had evolved his own special 'view' of Mt Fuji. From a comparison with our later Plate 225 it will be apparent that—had the audience and medium permitted—some approximation of Hokusai's landscape masterpieces of three decades later could well have appeared now.

Another notable miniature Tōkaidō series dates from slightly later, one of the prints bearing the date 'New Year 1804' (Plates 72 and 73). Here, the bibliographical details are more complex. Basically, these 59 small horizontal prints feature a framed margin, a cartouche with the station-name in *kaisho* (squarish calligraphy), and below it, in two columns, the artist's signature (generally, Gakyōjin Hokusai *ga*), and the name and distance of the following post-stage. In the first edition, however, eight of the prints consist of double-length panoramas, rather in *surimono* manner. In the more usually seen late editions the size is unified by replacement of these long prints by smaller, standard ones, the work of Hokusai's pupil (and son-in-law) Yanagawa Shigenobu, whose surname appears on them. After Hokusai's death the later version was even printed in book form, as 'Old Hokusai's Guide to the Road', and many of the loose plates one sees today are from the latter reprint. At least one edition also includes verses in certain of the designs.

More important, of course, are the prints themselves. That of Plate 72, 'Goyū', follows in the tradition of the artist's *surimono* figure-prints, again showing a tea-house girl of this famous, bawdy post-station, serenely arranging her coiffure. The background simply but effectively positions the painted screen in the room and plum-blossoms outside the window: the two pivot around the lovely, frail girl and the ponderous, lacquered mirror-stand. Again, there is no hint of the more sordid aspects of her life as a rustic 'lady of the night'.

With 'Numazu' (Plate 73) from the same series we turn to a more everyday theme that was to form something of a trademark for the artist (compare Plates 38, 53 and 208 for example): two rustic boys are shown walking past, nonchalantly neglecting their task of sweeping up leaves. In the background snow-clad Mt Fuji looms faintly through a clump of pine trees. Within its severe limitations, this may well be one of Hokusai's more perfect prints.

The final such series to be cited here is in the larger vertical-*chūban* format, and bears the title *Tōkaidō gojūsan-tsugi* (Fifty-three Stations of the Tōkaidō). The name of each post-stage is given at top centre in modified *reisho* (seal-script calligraphy). These prints (56 in number, plus wrapper) are rather less intimately charming than the two smaller series just mentioned. They are also later in date, *c.* 1806, when the artist's style was beginning to evolve into another, less graceful but more massive phase; and they are unsigned, except for the first edition of the final scene, and the wrapper for the set.

One example from this series must suffice, the bucolic 'Fujisawa' (Plate 74). Viewed dispassionately the print is a not too successful attempt to combine distant landscape and foreground figures, being somehow detached and re-

72 *Above* 'Goyu': Tea-house Girl at Mirror. *Koban*-size; 1804. Signed Gakyōjin Hokusai. From an untitled Tōkaidō series (see also Plate 73).

73 *Below* 'Numazu': Boys gathering Leaves. *Koban* print (shown here about double size); 1804. Signed Gakyōjin Hokusai. From the same series as Plate 72 (see also Fig. 37).

ふ
藤

さは
澤

東海道
五十三次
七

mote from its subject. But, as is often the case with Japanese prints, in the original the viewer tends to get absorbed in the tasteful colouring, the events depicted, even to lose his critical faculties (especially if he feels a certain empathy with the oxen and other beasts of burden, which the artist brings so effectively to life).

The first known record of Hokusai's actual travels over the Tōkaidō date only from the year 1812, well after these Highway and other early travel-series were published. We do not know much of the artist's actual life in this middle period, yet his emphasis on figures, and the rather detached quality of the landscapes themselves, suggest perhaps that the scenes were products of the artist's imagination, rather than based on actual sketches and experience. This was, to be sure, the normal custom among Japanese commercial artists: no publisher could afford to send them on an expedition to sketch the actual scenes; and thus they had little choice but to depend on pictorial maps and guidebooks, supplemented by their own related experiences and fertile imaginations.

We commenced this chapter with the artist vying with that master of female portraiture, Utamaro. It is only fitting that we end it with Hokusai, despite several masterpieces in the Utamaro vein, coming to the realization that this stylish genre of *bijin-ga* was neither his true forte nor part of his own intrinsic nature. We must now seek out the roots of an achievement that was, nearly thirty years later, to elevate his art to its very pinnacle.

74 'Fujisawa': at the Seashore. *Chūban*-size; *c*. mid-1800s. Unsigned. From the *Fifty-three Stations of the Tōkaidō* (see also Fig. 42).

NOTES

1 By 'all too well' I refer to the fact that such *Shinnai* ballads had to be banned from the Yoshiwara in the nineteenth century: their plaintive tales were inciting too many love-suicides on the part of star-crossed courtesans and their lovers. (The translation is of the opening lines only. My fascination with this marvellously decadent ballad derives from early studies of the samisen repertoire, and sections of my translation appeared in Oliver Statler's *Shimoda Story* of 1969; publication of a full translation is also planned.)
2 The title derives from a proverb, *nakute-nanakuse atte-yaguse*—roughly the equivalent of 'Every man has his quirks', or even, of Buffon's famous aphor-

ism, 'The style is the man himself'. There is, incidentally, an Utamaro print-series of about the same time with related title, consisting of bust-portraits of single beauties. I have been able to discover only three designs extant, but these bear no relation to Hokusai's series other than the title.
3 I do not recall prior mention of the point, but it is interesting to note the prevalence of tableaux featuring 'Mother and Daughter' combinations in this period (Plates 52, 57, 67, 68). The upper-class 'Older-woman/Younger-woman' theme obviously appealed to one element of the print and book audience. In view of the importance, and buying power, of the Edo 'Court ladies'—whether of the Shōgun's or the daimyōs' seraglios—there may well be veiled, or even subconscious, erotic implications.

IX
Topographic Exotica
and Figures
in a Landscape

1

BEFORE we move on to the next period of Hokusai's *oeuvre*, we must turn, in this final chapter on his first Golden Age, to that neglected portion of his early work that deals with the landscape, and only incidentally with the striving humanity that forms its natural and integral component. It is now time to show how the Master's distinctive landscape style actually evolved, and to what extent he was truly influenced by Occidental art. Indeed, in this chapter I hope to reveal a hitherto unknown Hokusai, a voracious student struggling with an alien and only partially understood art-form, which he may never actually have mastered, but which exerted a most profound effect on all the most typical work of his later maturity. As I have written elsewhere,

> Hokusai's great landscapes . . . represent, in a sense, the final assimilation and culmination of Occidental concepts in traditional Japanese art. This hidden perspective has contributed immeasurably to making Hokusai, with Hiroshige, the best loved of Japanese print artists. This subtle Western influence echoes somewhere in the modern viewer's mind as a thing not so wholly alien.[1]

We have already seen in Chapter II how the artist—in his

75 'The Seashore at Enoshima'. *Chūban surimono*, dated New Year 1799.

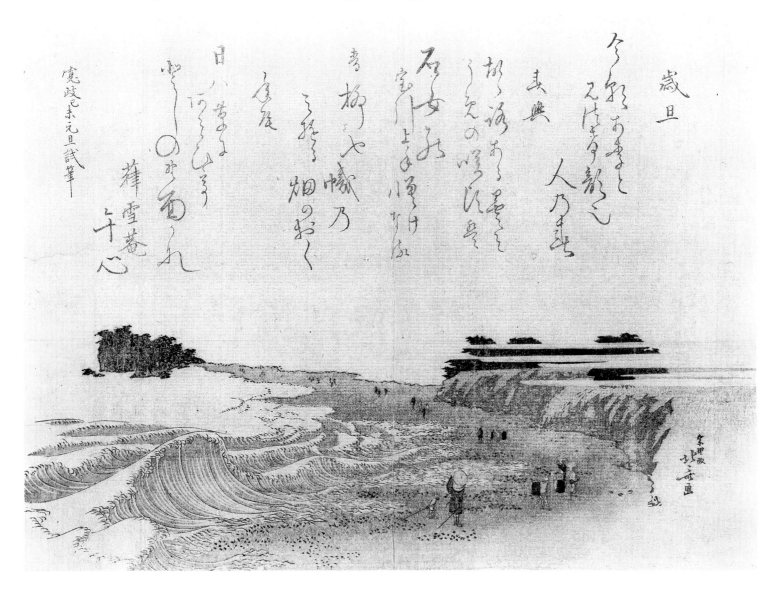

passion for a complete knowledge of painting—turned not only to the tremendous variety and scope of traditional Japanese art, but also to the range of Occidental art that was now being imported. Experiments in the Western technique of copperplate engraving were being made by Kōkan and Denzen, and there were also many adaptations of the Western viewpoint to the native woodblock-print tradition: picture-books by, for example, Sō-Shiseki, Chūryō and Masayoshi. All of these were almost certainly known to Hokusai, who carried on an avid search for as much of this exotic material as he could lay hands on.

With so many varied if fragmentary sources of this new knowledge, it is difficult to specify exact influences on Hokusai's early work; but the results were to come to a remarkable climax in several series of woodblock-prints dating from shortly after the turn of the century. There are even examples of such exotic experiments in the artist's *surimono*-prints. One of the earliest is that dated New Year's Day, 1799 (signed 'Sōri changed to Hokusai'), and shown in Plate 75. One notes here a strange mixture of East and West: the prominent haiku verses float above a landscape which combines traditional composition with hints of Western perspective, plus copperplate-*cum*-Genji clouds, and Occidental-*cum*-Kōrin waves (the latter having already appeared two years earlier, see Plate 31). Yet to the Japanese intelligentsia of the time, the incongruities that we perceive today were quite overlooked. This fascination with the West was the exact equivalent of the uncritical enthusiasm for *Japonisme* that was to captivate European artists some three generations later. Indeed, ukiyo-e itself was once the focal-point of this ardent and rather blind infatuation. As Edmond de Goncourt wrote in 1867: 'Why does a Japanese gateway charm me and please my eye when all the architectural lines of Greece seem to my eye tedious? As for people who pretend to feel the beauties of both these arts, my conviction is that they feel absolutely nothing.'

This digression may help in understanding Hokusai's absorption for a time in things Occidental—though his interest, while limited to art and science, was probably more profound than that of most of his contemporaries. The artist's more concentrated efforts in this exotic manner were to come in some five or six series of remarkable landscape prints to which we now turn.

Although these early Hokusai prints are well enough known to specialists, when approached in detail they present many evident problems: for example, in what years were they actually published? Who were the publishers? In what form did they originally appear? What was the immediate stimulus for their publication? Why are they often unsigned? Why are they so rare?

To few of these questions do we have any concrete answers. We can only surmise from general stylistic and technical considerations that these prints were produced a little after the turn of the century; that they may originally have been issued in sets, with wrappers bearing the name of artist and publisher; and that they may have been commissioned by specialized patrons for a particular purpose (for example, a group of intelligentsia devoted to *rangaku*,

'Dutch Studies'). Yet this is but guesswork: all we know is that several groups of such prints exist, all carefully designed and excellently printed, often with only a few designs of each series extant today. It is more than likely that a good many others have not survived. Admitting, therefore, how little we actually know of their background, we can only turn our attention to the prints themselves.

The enthusiasm for travel and topographical art—and literature—at this period has already been noted; indeed, the travel boom formed the basis for all publication in the landscape genre during the final century of ukiyo-e. It is not too hard, therefore, to imagine that some publisher (and group of patrons) should have been inspired to produce 'something different': Edo landscapes in the *Europeénaiserie* manner, one might say. To be sure, the *uki-e* (perspective-print) pioneer Toyoharu had, in the 1780s, designed occasional woodblock prints after the manner of European etchings, usually depicting foreign scenes; but such exotica had, with the actual copperplate prints of Kōkan in the same decade, been of limited circulation and only minimal influence. Revival of this tradition was, thus, one sure way to produce something both bizarre and controversial. Yet this time, too, popular interest was limited: the more plebeian print-buyers simply could not feel any personal identity with such 'outlandish' prints. It was not until some three generations later that Japanese artists in Occidental style, having sharpened their skills in study abroad, were to come into their own—in a land which was itself then embracing Western civilization *en masse*.

The first such Hokusai series to be mentioned is of the small *koban* format, comprising the *Edo hakkei* (Eight Views of Edo), Plate 76. The actual designs, though woodblock-printed, are in direct *dōban* (copperplate-print) style, and while the artist's mastery of perspective technique is a trifle faulty, the result is, nevertheless, far superior to most of the vapid and dowdy depictions of Japanese scenes by early Western artists. Perhaps more interesting than the tableaux themselves are the details: lateral strata of clouds, receding lines and the like, which were, just thirty years

76 'Suruga-chō'. *Koban* miniature-print, *c.* early 1800s. From the series *Eight Views of Edo*. (For the full series, see Fig. 32.)

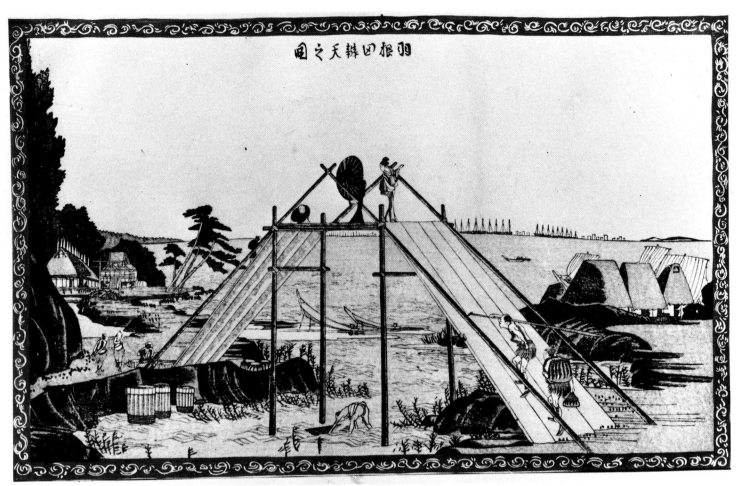

羽根田辨天之図

77 'Benten Shrine at Haneda'. *Aiban*-size, *c.* early 1800s. From an untitled series in Occidental style. (See also Plates 78 and 88, Figs. 34, 35.)

later, to be more successfully integrated into the artist's more mature prints on similar themes. (One may fruitfully compare, for example, this 'Suruga-chō' view with the same scene of the artist's famous *Fuji* series, Fig. 69.)

The tiny prints themselves show only the name of the site; but in this case the original wrapper to the set has miraculously survived and includes, apart from the main title, the artist's name, 'Hokusai *sensei zu*' (By the *maître* Hokusai), the publisher, and the prominent subtitle *Oranda ekagami* (Dutch-style Mirror-pictures), well conveying the exotic appeal the set was aiming at. The small tableaux are enclosed in foreign-style 'frames'; the colouring, unusually, emphasizes sepia; and some effort is made at imitating the effects of oil painting in the selection of pigments and their application. Such smaller prints are said sometimes to have been engraved from blocks cut across the grain, again in imitation of Western technique. As the subtitle and decorative design imply, this series may well originally have been intended for use in some kind of optical viewer. At the same time, such commercially issued miniatures were often employed for incidental decoration—pasted on screens or decorated boxes—which will explain why they are rare, and the original wrappers or envelopes usually lost.

Of the same type is a later and less notable series on the 'Eight Views of Lake Biwa: in *Dōban*' (Appendix, Fig. 48). This set is less obviously in Occidental style, and to judge

from the censor's seal seems to have been published a decade later, *c.* 1811: an indication of the continuing demand for such home-grown exotica. The series bears the subtitle '*Dōban*' (Copperplate Prints), but these prints are not, of course, *dōban*, only imitations. The technique is basically that of the earlier *uki-e*, with cosmetic touches of the Occidental. Yet this was enough for the populace of the time; as always with the Japanese, it was only a modicum of the exotic that was craved: and genuine copperplate prints would not have sold at all.

Far more impressive in composition and technique is the *aiban*-size series with decorated margins, of which five prints are known. All feature a colour-scheme of sepia-related tones, after the manner of copperplate prints (Plates 77–78). General title, artist and publisher are not recorded on the prints, although they may well have been included on the original wrapper, now lost. Each of the prints represents a fresh but withal undramatic tableau of scenes in and about Edo, as for instance 'The Benten Shrine at Haneda'. (Haneda was at that time a quiet fishing village far beyond the limits of Edo, and noted only for its Shrine to the goddess Benten.) The print shows a curiously tilted plank-bridge that would be readily navigable only to wild goats (Plate 77): the purpose of the distortion is, obviously, to satisfy the artist's fancy for an unusual approach in a bizarre composition. The actual shrine of the title is relegated to a diminutive, perspectived detail at far left, balanced by the rounded fishermen's huts and the sailboats at far right. All these elements feature block-gradation in Western style, with an oddly curved horizon

78 'The Sumida Seen from Azuma Bridge'. *Aiban*-size, *c.* early 1800s. From the same series as Plate 77.

in the distance (this was in line with Galileo's hypothesis—only recently introduced into Japan—that the earth was round). But the centre of the print is obviously the precariously tilted bridge and its curious wayfarers: shrine pilgrims and returning fishermen. The student of Hokusai will be happy to discover some familiar figures: for the ladies at top, see Plate 68, and for the basket-fisherman under the bridge, Plate 36; while the design itself recalls the famous 'Cooper and Fuji' of over a generation later (Fig. 60).

'The Sumida seen from Azuma Bridge' of Plate 78 is also of interest. The modern viewer will perhaps first be struck by the incongruities of the design: Kōrin-style waves and trees, with stolid bridge at left, depicted in more or less Japanese manner (though with somewhat uncertain touches of perspective); but houses and embankment done in a curiously decorative Occidental style (while reminiscent at the same time of the rounded contours of a Sōtatsu-Kōrin stationery-box). The employment of traditional woodblock *bokashi* (gradation) to express the three-dimensional effect of Western shading is done so effectively that even the specialist may have trouble distinguishing East from West here. The clash of perspective effect is almost vertiginous: one rolls about with the boatman on the unsettling surface of the turbulent river, uncertain where to rest one's eye, only saved, at last, by the

strength of the firm pillars at left. The print obviously raises more compositional questions than it solves, but in this it may be taken as a vivid reflection of Hokusai's own early and uncertain dabblings with the dangers of only half-assimilated Occidental concepts.

For the student of Hokusai, however, surely the most fascinating of this series is the 'View of Hommoku off Kanagawa' (Plate 88). Here we find a composition in which the artist is at last able to exploit his emerging powers as a designer. The huge, improbable wave effectively dominates the tableau; the details at right are somewhat ambiguous, but the imperilled boat at centre enables us to identify immediately with the boatman in this little contest between man and Nature. And, of course, the concept is that which, three decades later, the artist was to refine into one of his crowning achievements, the 'Great Wave' (Plate 247).

Similar in general appearance but lacking place-names, and in the large-*koban* format, is the further landscape series of Plate 79, of which four designs are known. Here, however, though the decorated frame is similar, the artist's name appears at top right in a curious imitation of Occidental calligraphy—the Japanese *hiragana* syllabary run on its side as it were: 'Ho-ku-sa-i *u-tsu-su*' (= *pinxit*). These rare prints are delicately and sumptuously printed, and the designs, too, are rather in the privately printed *surimono* style: lacking in dominant forms and bold compositions—an arrangement which gives the *kyōka* verses the principal role. These tableaux are also notable

79 *Top left* Enoshima and Fuji. Large-*koban* size, *c*. early 1800s. From an untitled *surimono* series in Occidental style.

80 *Top right* View of Kanazawa. Large-*koban*-size *surimono*, *c*. early 1800s.

81 *Above* 'Cargo-boat passing through Waves'. *Chūban*-size, *c*. mid-1800s. From an untitled series in Occidental style (decorative margins trimmed). (See Plates 89 and 92, Figs. 40, 41; Prints, No. 87.)

for their omission of the customary keyblock outlines of ukiyo-e, relying primarily on colour-masses: a technique that, as noted in the previous series, goes back as much to the Sōtatsu-Kōrin tradition of Hokusai's early studies as it does to influences from Western art. The result makes full employment of the potential of the woodblock technique, and is surprisingly modern in effect.

Also of interest is a probable series of similar—and possibly related—prints in *surimono* style, the *Kanazawa hakkei* (Eight Views of Kanazawa), which refers to a famous scenic area near Yokohama, not to the western Province of that name. The example shown (Plate 80) amalgamates several exotic features—chiaroscuro-shaded landscape elements, *dōban*-style figures, houses and frame, Chinese-derived bridge—yet still forms an essentially Japanese landscape.[2]

Last, and most significant of all, is the *chūban*-size series of Plates 81, 89 and 92, of which five designs are extant. Here, likewise, the artist's signature appears in lateral syllabary, but it is accompanied by the title of each print. In this series, Hokusai is at last able to express his true creative energies in this essentially alien medium. In particular, 'Jūnisō Shrine at Yotsuya' and 'Ushigafuchi at Kudan' (Plates 89, 92) represent a startling integration of Occidental techniques into the tradition of classical Japanese painting. But all the designs are minor masterpieces of unified, bold composition, and demonstrate the artist's superb control of massive forms.

It will be noted that instead of the sepia tones of the earlier series, we find an emphasis on the more evocative yellow. In the 'Yotsuya' scene (Plate 89), for example, with waterfall and distant thunderclouds, the rich colouring is

perfectly matched to this rare view of the desolate suburbs of Edo. Perhaps the most curious feature of the print is its subject—or rather, the relative lack of one. For this was hardly a 'scenic wonder' of Edo or a theme that would sell on its own merits. It must simply have caught the artist's fancy and he sketched it in a strongly exotic manner. It is no wonder that, at the time, the print failed to find buyers. Only today, indeed, has the intrinsic interest of such rare Hokusai prints come to be re-evaluated, with the advantage of aftersight—of fresh, modern eyes.

Even more striking in its creative approach to landscape is the 'Ushigafuchi at Kudan' scene (Plate 92), where the centre of focus is placed, unusually, at the edge of the composition, and the colour-blocks themselves are employed as massive, almost abstract forms, without the usual reliance on the keyblock. The design also features the un-Japanese depiction of *reflections* on the surface of the water—and summer clouds in Western style. ('Ushigafuchi' means 'Ox Chasm', and the site is so-named because an ox-cart laden with coins once fell into its depths and had to be abandoned—the ox-cart, not the coins. What happened to the bullock is unrecorded.)

The first issue of the design features, as here, shadows cast by the figures: a phenomenon quite absent from traditional Japanese art. They are omitted from the second edition, probably because shadows were too 'busy' a detail for the taste of the times.[3] Such *chūban*, medium-sized print-series were usually engraved and printed two on the

82 View of Edo with Fuji. *Ōban*-size print, *c*. 1806. (See also Fig. 183, and Appendix, Books, No. 117.)

83 Shellfish-gatherers. *Ōban*-size print in *surimono* style, *c.* mid-1800s. Unsigned. (See Appendix, Prints, No. 108; Figs. 44–6.)

same woodblock (a technique known as *nichō-gake*), and then divided after printing. This was the case with the present design and 'Fuji from Takahashi' (Fig. 40). Such 'pairs' naturally sport rather similar colour-schemes and pigments. (The latter tableau also, incidentally, bears interesting comparison with the 'Mannen Bridge' scene of Hokusai's more famous *Fuji* series, Fig. 56.)

The masterful prints of this rare series exhibit no trace of that compositional awkwardness and lack of East-West integration that we saw in the prior examples. It is, indeed, difficult to comprehend how the artist could have produced them at just the same period as the previous prints; flouting the customary chronology, I feel tempted to date them to, at the least, a few years later.

There is yet another predecessor to the 'Great Wave' in the 'Cargo-boat passing through Waves' (Plate 81), from the same series. The design is both unified and compelling, though (this time—compared to Plate 88—the composition reversed) the ancillary boat at left is again, doubtless on purpose, ambiguous; and the overwhelmingly decorative quality of the massive waves tends to lull our senses into disregarding the potential perils of the situation.

As suggested above, Hokusai was fully prepared at this

period to create a new genre, the Japanese landscape-print. What made him cease these increasingly effective experiments in Occidental style? The answer cannot be merely a long-term lack of patronage or acclaim, as further extensions in this manner were to be carried out two decades later by such followers as Shinsai, Hokuju and Kunitora. However, there was, for a while at least, a disheartening lack of enthusiasm from the print-buying public; and by the time the genre gained greater popularity the Master had, as always, simply moved on to other things.

But although Hokusai's specialized work in Western style ended here, it was this effective amalgamation of three major elements—Japanese/Chinese/Occidental—that will characterize the art of his later career, and, indeed, render him the most universal of Asian artists. Hokusai is one of the most complex of all painters. The great *Fuji* series did not by any means spring forth miraculous and *deus ex machina* twenty years later. Every line, every concept, every colour mass is somewhere presaged in the master's work of this fascinating, but little understood, previous generation.

2

This is not the end of our discussion of Hokusai's landscape work in this period, for he also experimented in related themes more in the ukiyo-e tradition. They were extensions, so to speak, of his *surimono* and of his illustra-tions in the commercial-print medium, but again limited in scope and popular acclaim.

Many of these prints consisted of updated versions of the topographical 'perspective-prints' we saw in Plate 8. They are skilfully designed but basically dull, and reveal little of the artist's individuality or powers of expression. Most probably, they conformed to the commission of the publisher for a series of designs, 'in conventional style'. Curiously, these late productions—around 1810—are not the *uki-e* that they are cited to be: they make hardly any use of perspective techniques. Clearly, the term was simply employed by the publisher as a sales phrase, and meant something more like 'bird's-eye views'.

Less characteristic of Hokusai's perspective-prints is the view of Mt Fuji from Edo, of Plate 82. Typically for this genre, the original title is 'Suruga Bluff and Waterway'; in other words this is a standard Edo view, with the Sacred Mountain and the landscape only incidental. It is this ambiguous approach that distinguishes such *uki-e* from Hokusai's later *chefs d'oeuvre*: here, neither the foreground nor the distant view is given adequate attention, and we are left with a feeling of dissatisfaction. It was to be a full two decades before the artist was to achieve his mastery of—indeed, actually to *create*—the Japanese landscape print. We glimpse in this example not so much the seeds of that achievement as the conventions from which he had to break before he could discover a new vision: a focusing on vivid details and dynamic composition that was to direct our attention to the essentials of a scene. (Curiously enough this print represents a revised version of an earlier Hokusai book-illustration—from the work we illustrated in Plate 54—shown in Fig. 183. At the centre of the print will be discerned the 'seam' left after joining the two woodblocks of the book-pages together. Such re-use of book-blocks for prints—with new colour-blocks added—is rather rare, the reverse being more common.)

More artistically significant are Hokusai's series of *ōban* landscapes likewise issued in the mid-1800s, but featuring more creative designs, rather in *surimono* style. 'A View of Mt Fuji' (Plate 93) is known in two editions—one bearing the alternative title 'Eight Views of Fuji', implying that a series was planned. Since no other designs seem extant today, it is likely that lack of sales forced it to be retitled as an independent print. The foreground figures are more pleasing than those of Hokusai's later works, but the mid-dle ground is ineptly handled and the relation between Mt Fuji and the figures is also ambiguous: we do not really know which is meant to be the centre of focus. In such early experiments Hokusai had still to master that integra-tion of elements which was to characterize his later, more famous landscapes (Plates 247 and 251, for example). Furthermore, the demand for such prints had not yet reached its peak, which severely limited the artist's mar-ket, and hence the motivation to produce more.

From the same period and perhaps of greater pictorial interest is the 'Shellfish Gatherers' of Plate 83, which effec-tively combines two frail beauties with the more raucous activities of the male participants. (Note, however, the curious intrusion of half-digested perspective technique in

the middle-ground dwelling at left.)

It should be added that there is a close relationship be-tween these *ōban* landscapes and Hokusai's 'long-*surimono*' prints of the same period—though in most cases this has yet to be fully clarified. It was very easy for a publisher to foreshorten such *surimono* and print them, with additional sky area, in the more squarish *ōban* format for a commer-cial edition. Such *ōban* prints are often unsigned: possibly an indication that the signature was at the edge of the *surimono* and hence trimmed off when foreshortened. (The fact that the earlier versions of some of these prints have yet to be discovered may be another indication that, at least for this early period, extant *surimono* number only a fraction of those originally published—a fearsome rate of attrition.) This conversion happened, for example, with the early masterpiece of Plate 83, which though in *ōban* format features the refinements of engraving and printing more often associated with private editions—and, in fact, is known in an earlier *surimono* version.

The print is also of similar subject-matter (though rather different flavour) to the *surimono* we saw in Plate 27. But whatever its derivation, the print offers a striking example of Hokusai's successful integration of the traditional land-scape with Occidental-derived perspective techniques; and as always with this master, it is the essential humanity of the conception that remains in the mind's eye long after the memory of the specific locale is forgotten.

Of this group of fresh but Japanese-style landscapes, perhaps most evocative of all is the 'Evening-cool at Ryōgoku' (Plate 94). It is sealed with Hokusai's new sub-sidiary pseudonym, Gakyōjin ('Man Mad with Painting'), and is, for the period, a masterful study of the subtle inter-play of light and shadow at dusk, with effective contrasts of black and yellow-orange. In this view at Tatekawa—a branch of the Sumida, famed for its lumber-yards—we see a bridge at left, three frail females at right, and in between them, two boisterous boys balanced precariously on logs. Beyond the figures loom the silhouettes of boats, shoreline and lumber-yards, as fireworks light the sky. The details are thus readily enough explained, but not the beginning of that mastery of overall mood and integrated composi-tion that was to prove Hokusai's principal contribution to the landscape print. Again we must deplore the fact that the conditions of the market-place did not permit the artist to explore this genre at length. Only a full generation later, when he was quite another man, far more powerful in artistic conception and realization, did he return to this theme; but he was never able to recapture this lovely figure-style of his middle years.

It will by now be apparent that the distinction between 'pure landscape', 'landscape-with-figures', and 'figures-in-a-landscape' is never sharp in Hokusai's works: the same series—whether historical, genre or topographical in nominal subject-matter—may well include all three cate-gories. Thus we end this account of Hokusai's early land-scape work with a review of his treatment of that famed literary-historical theme, the *Chūshingura*: the stirring account of the Vendetta of the Forty-seven *Rōnin*, which

84 Night Attack of the Forty-seven *Rōnin*. *Ōban* triptych, *c.* late 1780s. Signed Shunrō.

comprised a major theme of Japanese theatre, fiction and popular legend alike.

We have already noted that Hokusai himself claimed some blood-relation to one of the participants in the affair, which had caused a sensation a century earlier. The details of the vendetta and its Kabuki elaborations may be briefly characterized here as an aid to following the sequence of events in each of Hokusai's several series of *Chūshingura* prints and books—our illustrations to which are also indicated.

Chūshingura [The Treasury of Loyal Retainers]: This famous Kabuki drama was first staged as a puppet-play in 1748 but was soon adapted for the Kabuki stage. It represented the most popular of all Japanese plays, being regularly performed every year. (An English rendering was made by John Masefield under the title *The Faithful*.) The drama is based on actual events of the years 1701 to 1703. The Twelve Acts of the *Chūshingura* [*Chūshingura jūni-dan*] are entitled (with considerable variations):

Act I: *Tsurugaoka shinzen* [Before the Shrine at Tsurugaoka (Kamakura)]: After insulting his Ceremonial Aide, Lord Momonoi, the evil Minister Moronao makes improper advances to the Lady Kaoyo—wife of his other Aide, the Lord Enya-hangan—but is rebuffed.

Act II: *Momonoi no yashiki* [At Momonoi's Mansion]: The young lovers Rikiya and Ko-Nami—son and daughter of the lieutenants to the Ceremonial Aides—meet briefly; Momonoi vows to take no more insults from the evil Moronao.

Act III: *Kamakura denchū Ashikaga-yakata monzen-no-ba* [In the Palace at Kamakura; before the Gate of the Ashikaga Palace]: Momonoi's chief retainer Honzō secretly bribes the villain Moronao in order to save his master; the evil Moronao vents his frustration on his other Aide, Enya-hangan, provoking the latter to draw his sword in the Palace, a capital offence. [Fig.

179; Fig. 30 (the latter illustrating yet another subplot: Kampei trouncing some villains outside the Palace)]

Act IV: *Hangan seppuku* [The Suicide of (Enya-) Hangan]: Enya-hangan is sentenced to *harakiri*, which he performs valiantly, while waiting anxiously for the arrival of his trusted chief retainer (and father of Rikiya), Yuranosuke—who appears as his master is dying and solemnly vows to take revenge on the evil Moronao. Yuranosuke and his forty-six companions are now *rōnin*—'wave-men'—samurai without lord, fief, or emolument.

Act V: *Yoichibei ōshi* [The Murder of Yoichibei]: Kampei, one of the forty-seven *rōnin*, has retreated to the country, staying with the parents of his wife, O-Karu, who (unknown to him) has been sold as a courtesan to raise funds so that he can join the other *rōnin* in their vendetta. O-Karu's father Yoichibei is robbed of the funds and murdered on the way home; in the dark Kampei, who is out hunting, accidentally shoots the robber and retrieves the money. [Plate 87]

Act VI: *Kampei Sumika* [At the Dwelling of Kampei]: O-Karu, on the point of being taken away by the brothel-mistress, is stopped by Kampei's return home. Kampei mistakenly assumes that, in the darkness, he has killed his wife's father (whose body has been discovered) and commits *harakiri*, but before he dies, he is exonerated.

Act VII: *Ichiriki ageya (chaya)* [At the Ichiriki Courtesan/Geisha-house]: In Kyōto the leader of the *rōnin*, Yuranosuke, has apparently given himself to dissipation: in reality a disguise to conceal his vendetta-scheme. Receiving a letter of encouragement from the Lady Kaoyo, he is spied upon by Kudayū, a minion of the evil Moronao, and by O-Karu, now a courtesan. Yuranosuke adroitly disposes of the spy. [Fig. 5]

Act VIII: *Tōkaidō michiyuki* [Poetic Journey along the Tōkaidō]: A lyrical interlude—the bridal-journey of Ko-Nami to Kyōto, to marry her lover Rikiya (Yuranosuke's son). [Plates 57, 85]

Act IX: *Yamashina-bessō (kankyo)* [The Villa at Yamashina]: Yuranosuke returns home from the pleasure-quarter. Ko-Nami arrives with her mother but they are treated coldly, for it was her

新板浮繪忠臣藏八段目 可候画
板元 下谷地信佛所 伊勢屋利兵衛板

85 *Above* Journey of Bride and Mother. *Aiban*-size, *c.*-late 1790s. From a *Chūshingura* series. (The composition is geographically reversed, possibly in imitation of copperplate technique. For bibliographical details, see Appendix, Prints, No. 32.)

86 *Opposite* Amakawaya confronting the *Rōnin. Chūban* print (shown here enlarged), *c.* early 1800s. (See also Fig. 30.) From a *Chūshingura* series. (For another, rarer *chūban* series on this theme, see Appendix, Prints, No. 50a.)

father Honzō who had restrained the *rōnin's* master in his attempt to kill Moronao. Honzō appears, disguised as a *komusō*-minstrel—and provokes Rikiya to stab him, thus expiating his offence and making the marriage possible again.

Act X: *Amakawaya sumika* [At the Dwelling of Amakawaya]: Amakawaya Gihei, a valiant merchant of Sakai, has been secretly supplying the forty-seven *rōnin* with arms, but is apparently discovered by the police (actually they are Yuranosuke's men, who wish to test Gihei's loyalty). [Plate 86]

Act XI: *Gishi yo-uchi* [The Night Attack of the Loyal Samurai]: At last the *rōnin* attack Moronao's mansion in Edo on a snowy night near the end of the year. The Act is comprised of stylized sword-fights, ending in the death and beheading of the villain Moronao. [Plates 95, 84]

Act XII: *Sengakuji hikiage* [The Withdrawal to Sengaku Temple]: The triumphant *rōnin* attach Moronao's head to a halberd and march to the temple of Sengakuji (South of Edo, see map on p. 6) to report their success to Enya-hangan's shade, and then immolate themselves in a mass *harakiri* rite.

Among Hokusai's earliest treatments of this tortuous yet

stirring theme are pastiches in his *kibyōshi*—'yellow back'—picture-novelettes of the years 1790–94; there are also two *share-hon*—Yoshiwara novelettes—1801–2 (see Appendix, Books, Nos. 34, 51, 93, 94); and we have already noted his skilled picture-book of 1802 on the theme (Plate 57). In the print-field, likewise, Hokusai commenced work on this subject early: including one of the more elaborate prints of his early Shunrō Period, a triptych featuring the final 'Night Attack' scene, in a complex panorama incorporating both human interest and comic relief (Plate 84). Reduced to monochrome the triptych—like most of those by this artist—will probably seem confused. This may be due in part to the complex subject-matter, but even more to the Master's striving to include so much action and movement within a single tableau.

The artist began his more extended and comprehensive treatment of this theme in the late 1790s, employing the *nom d'artiste* Kakō. This preliminary series consisted of eleven *aiban* prints (following the principal acts of the Kabuki play), and was entitled *Shimpan uki-e Chūshingura* (New *Chūshingura* Perspective-pictures). Plate 85 shows one typical scene from Act VIII. It comprises a curious mélange of varied landscape planes, basically in the traditional *uki-e* manner; only the distant clouds are in exotic 'Dutch-style'. The protagonists—Ko-Nami and her mother journeying to Kyōto to prepare for her ill-fated nuptials—are relegated to the lower-left foreground. The series forms, in effect, a re-creation of the stage-tableau, with figures but a minor part of the composition: there is little

87 *Above* The Murder of Yoichibei. *Ōban*-size print, 1806. From a *Chūshingura* series. Unsigned. (See also Plate 95 and for bibliographical details, Appendix, Prints, No. 98.)

88 *Opposite top* 'View of Hommoku off Kanagawa'. *Aiban*-size, *c.* early 1800s. From the same series as Plates 77 and 78.

89 *Opposite below* 'Jūnisō Shrine at Yotsuya'. *Chūban*-size, *c.* mid-1800s. From the same series as Plate 81.

attempt to pictorialize the more dramatic elements of the actual events.

Following minor, miniature series on the theme—and occasional *surimono*—the artist's next significant *Chūshingura* series dates from the early 1800s. It bears the signature 'Hokusai' and comprises twelve prints (including the terminal scene, often omitted), in the medium-sized *chūban* format. The series title is *Kana-dehon Chūshingura* (The Syllabary *Chūshingura*). The most impressive print of the set is that of Act X: Amakawaya confronting the *Rōnin* at his shop near Ōsaka (Plate 86). Despite the diminutive size of the print itself, the method of depiction is dynamic and dramatic, well suited to the theatrical theme.

After further *chūban* and miniature series of the same period, the artist's next and most definitive treatment of this perennial theme dates from 1806, just at the time his figure-style was changing from svelte beauties to more robust forms. The title is the same as that for the previous series, but the set of eleven *ōban* prints is, for unknown

reasons, unsigned, though in Hokusai's unmistakable style. (We do not usually know the cause for such unsigned commissions: there may have been an overall wrapper, now lost; sometimes there were contractual problems; or the publisher may even have wanted to place emphasis on the subject rather than on the artist.) Here, Hokusai's approach is not to take a distant view nor a close-up, but to employ what would be, in photographic terms, a 'standard' lens. The main elements of each composition are tightly compressed, and there is not even a frame to confine the action.

In the first scene shown here (Plate 87, from Act V), the bizarre beauty of the night landscape almost overpowers the horrendous and tragic events which, though only a subplot to the play, have always been considered among the most moving. In the foreground we see the brigand murdering Kampei's father-in-law. Kampei himself is shown in an apologetic pose in the far background as the boar (object of his ill-fated hunting-expedition) runs wildly towards an ominous Buddhist tombstone.

Our second scene from this remarkable (and rather neglected) series comes from the climactic Act XI (Plate 95). The perseverance of the forty-seven *Rōnin* is repaid; they attack the enemy's stronghold (east of Ryōgoku—see map, Plate 1) and at long last achieve vengeance against the villainous Lord Kira who caused their lord's disgrace and death. As part of a literary/Kabuki series, the print is

essentially an illustration, but it ranks among Hokusai's masterpieces in this genre. One notes first of all the artist's enhanced feeling for composition: the dynamic line from the attack leaders on the black ladder to the forty-odd followers forms a dramatic, crooked arrow, which is then counterbalanced by the more stolid, almost zigzag line of the gate and rooftops. The powerful figure of the one-man battering-ram at left is worthy of a print in itself, and the force of his action seems almost to reverberate against the coiled columns of his comrades. This essentially dynamic approach to figure depiction comprised, I suspect, something quite new in Japanese art (though influenced by the traditions of Kabuki). It was certainly to form the basis for Hokusai's work in the coming generation and, through his pupils and followers, serve as an example for the masses of *musha-e* ('warrior-prints') that were later to be issued from the studio of Kuniyoshi and a host of other, lesser artists. The effective employment of completely realized backgrounds takes full advantage of the printer's skill in near three-dimensional effects. In this print, for example, to place one's hand over the distant view of the Sumida River is not only to deprive the print of its geographical setting, but also to rob it of the special flavour that was, a generation later, to distinguish the artist's emergence as the master supreme of the landscape-print. (In this unusual specimen, note the use of the mineral-pigment *tan* [red oxide of lead]—a throwback to the powerful colouring-schemes of the more 'Primitive' period of ukiyo-e.)

It may be instructive to compare the artist's earlier depiction of the same Kabuki Act in Plate 84, done in his 'late Shunrō' period, nearly two decades earlier. The triptych is certainly 'interesting' enough in detail (and particularly so for the Master's original audience, who could recall with pleasure the names and stories of each and every character depicted). With the later print (Plate 95), however, the bedlam and confusion are gone and it will be obvious that Hokusai has now mastered the art of group composition, and come to the realization that simplification is the key to dynamic effect. This is a basic truth that was to illuminate all of his work for the final five decades of his long career.

In briefly tracing Hokusai's devotion to the *Chūshingura* theme in this decade, we have also followed his development from a prosaic exponent of historical pictography to a major figure in the development of the historical and landscape print. Within the space of one chapter, we have discovered Hokusai as a master of both the semi-traditional 'landscape-with-figures' and the exotic, new 'Dutch Style', based on a fragmentary yet instinctive mastery of Occidental art principles. Such incongruity and contradiction lie at the foundations of Japanese art in the nineteenth century, and continue to this day. Hokusai was great enough to absorb the West and, eventually, to make it his own: few subsequent artists have enjoyed the same success.

Well-known masterpieces alone do not, of course, serve to present a full view of an artist's *oeuvre*. I have, quite naturally in these chapters, emphasized Hokusai's more notable productions of this Golden Decade, *c.* 1796–1806. The Appendix will indicate that his output was prolific, with a total of at least seventy different books and albums to his credit, and literally hundreds of *surimono* and other prints, including many lesser masterpieces. Among these were further *kibyōshi*, including some with the text by the artist himself—indicating that Hokusai had not given up his literary aspirations. One may be cited here for its intriguing glimpse of the 'Sōri Style', even within the limitations of the 'yellow-back' novelette (Plate 90), and also for its final page, in which the author-artist pays ingratiating respect to his publisher Tsutaya, with a self-portrait in which he characteristically portrays himself as a generation older than he actually was at the time (Plate 91). Indeed, this exaggeration of his own longevity represented but one of the Master's manifest idiosyncrasies. Already now, in his mid-40s, he was beginning to call himself 'Old Hokusai' in his signatures, even changing his pen-name Gakyōjin—'Man Mad with Painting'—to Gakyō-rōjin—'Old Man Mad with Painting'. In this foible one senses not only a desire prematurely to present himself as an established 'grey eminence', but also the beginning of a strong tendency to distance himself from the frenetic world of fashion and sophistication that was the milieu of the traditional ukiyo-e artist.

90 Prodigal Daughter bathing with Gold Coins. Detail from *The Tactical Treatise of General Oven. Kibyōshi* novelette, 1800. (See also Appendix, Fig. 175.)

NOTES

1 *Masters of the Japanese Print: Their World and Their Work*, 1962, p. 256. Note, incidentally, that the Japanese taste for things European goes back even to the sixteenth and seventeenth centuries—first, in the 'Portuguese Fad' during the Momoyama Period (1568–1615); then again, with the later seventeenth century: the leading novelist of the age was nicknamed *Oranda Saikaku*, 'Dutch Saikaku', for his 'outlandish', avant-garde style; and his own mentor, the poet Sōin, has an intriguing haiku comparing 'Dutch letters / with the flight of wild geese'. (See my: 'The Foreign Image in Japanese Art', in the journal *Asia Scene*, 1966–68; 'Japanese Genre Painting in Western Style', in *Ukiyo-e* No. 56, 1974; and *Saikaku: Novelist of the Japanese Renaissance*, 1958.)

2 At the time of writing, only one print from this presumed series is known to be extant. There is, however, an *Ōmi hakkei*—'Eight Views of Lake Biwa'—set by Hokusai's pupil Shinsai which includes an imitation of this design; and the remainder of the set may well reflect Hokusai's lost original. Although the verses added to Hokusai's print refer specifically to the 'Eight Views of Kanazawa', it is just possible that the design was originally part of a lost Hokusai 'Lake Biwa' series—here adapted to an alternative use. This hypothesis—which is a new and possibly wild one—would account for the unseemly mixing of verse and birds in the sky, and (for a long-time resident of the Lake Biwa area) the greater resemblance to the actual Bridge of Seta than to Kanazawa.

3 Kuniyoshi aficionados will be immediately struck by the influence this print must have exerted, a generation later, on such masterpieces as 'Kasumigaseki' (in effect, a close-up of the figures and cart at lower right: moved to the top of the slope, complete with their shadows). See my 'Hokusai's Exotic Decade', in the journal *Andon*, in press.

91 Self-portrait as an Old Man. Terminal detail from the same book as Plate 90.

92 *Overleaf top left* 'Ushigafuchi at Kudan'. *Chūban*-size, *c*. mid-1800s. From the same series as Plates 81 and 89.

93 *Overleaf bottom left* 'View of Mt Fuji'. *Ōban*-size, *c*. mid-1800s. (See Appendix, Prints, No. 96.)

94 *Overleaf top right* 'Evening-cool at Ryōgoku'. *Ōban*-size, *c*. mid-1800s. Unsigned. Sealed: Gakyōjin. (See Appendix, Prints, No. 108.)

95 *Overleaf bottom right* Night Attack of the Forty-seven *Rōnin*. *Ōban*-size print, 1806. From the same series as Plate 87. (Publisher's seal, lower right: Tsuruya Kinsuke, whose abbreviated name [Tsuru-Kin] is also given in the *kana*-syllabary nameplates of four of the *rōnin* at lower right.)

X
The Chinese/
Gothic Connection:
Hokusai's *Yomi-hon*
Illustrations

1

WHY SHOULD Hokusai forswear the lovely and impressive prints and albums of his first flourishing, and immerse himself so wholeheartedly in the detailed, miniaturistic work of 'Gothic' book-illustration? There are several reasons for his turning away, around the year 1806, from the traditional ukiyo-e subjects.

First, this was the year that the great Utamaro died: an event which, though not necessarily decisive in itself, surely hastened the already visible decline in the figure-print, for he was the driving force in the entire range of *bijin-ga* during this golden age. Secondly, there was the intrinsic nature of Hokusai himself: he had never considered himself a specialist in the figure-print, and though he produced some major works, and numerous important picture-books, he never felt this to be his true *métier*; nor did he, approaching middle age, really feel any great affinity with the Floating World that formed the inseparable background of ukiyo-e. Thirdly—and perhaps most important of all for a struggling commercial artist—income from the more painstaking and austere work of book-illustration was more reliable and paid just as well as (if not better than) the more impressive commissions. It was therefore clearly a combination of the market-place and the artist's own natural inclinations that led him gradually to divorce himself from the more flamboyant aspects of the Floating World.

Interestingly, the artist's very style was to be affected by this change in subject-matter, audience, and approach: his figure-work soon loses the frail charm of the 'Sōri Manner', being replaced by more monumental—if less lovely—depictions. In this, he was but reflecting his intensive studies in that great source of Japanese civilization, China, and it was the tradition of Chinese painting, both classical and modern, that would prove most pertinent in the next stage of his work, the illustrations to the 'Gothic Novels' that had suddenly come into tremendous popularity with the early 1800s. As a memoir by his important follower Eisen cites:

> In the late 1790s the Chinese Manner became all the rage in Edo. . . . Calling this the 'Hokusai Style', he painted ukiyo-e with the brushstrokes of Ming painting. Hokusai is the founder of that manner of Japanese painting modelled on ancient and modern Chinese styles. Even his fellow artists were impressed by the bizarre nature of his style; naturally it enjoyed a great fad among the populace as well.

Aside from a stronger, more formal (but harder and less pliant) sense of composition, it is from this Chinese connection that the artist derived his characteristically nervous, zigzag lines, claw-like waves, moss-dotted rocks. Indeed, this Continental influence obviously struck a responsive chord in his subconscious, and the rediscovery of Chinese painting formed the major element in the artist's stylistic mutations of this period. This new 'Hokusai Style' was to form our standard, set image of the man, and to characterize his art of the final four decades.

The voluminous works of fiction to which the artist now turned so wholeheartedly were called in Japanese *yomi-hon*, simply 'reading-books'. Although most often abundantly illustrated, they were distinguished from the *e-hon*, 'picture-books', where the text was minimal, and from the *kibyōshi*, 'yellow-backs', where the fictional texts also tended to be somewhat abridged, being printed within the actual illustrations.

The content of the *yomi-hon* ranged from native historical vendetta and supernatural tales, to adaptations of novels imported from China. The emphasis is mostly on the plot, the action, not on the development of character. For lack of a better term we can only dub these books 'Gothic novels'; in fact, they match very well R. L. Stevenson's apt description: 'That conjunction of the grotesque . . . with passionate contortion and horror, so characteristic of Gothic art.'

Despite (or perhaps in compensation for) their melodramatic, terrifying, and sometimes sadistic contents, these novels reflected the superficial morality of the concept *kanzen chōaku* ('reward good/punish evil'). Yet often they submitted 'The Good' to all kinds of painful indignities, even foul death, with the happy ending sometimes achieved only by the heirs—or the shades—of the poor victims. Nevertheless, these works are filled with fantastic and wonderful images that provided new stimulus to the artist's fervid imagination. Hokusai always revelled in being different from others, and this new medium provided him with a grand opportunity to express his varied powers.

As we noted in Chapter I, such sets of fiction were most often distributed by the lending bookshops, for which Hokusai had himself acted as salesman in his teens. It is, in fact, for this reason that they are relatively rare today. Sets which have survived are often worn or defaced, and are generally found in late editions with the strength of the original woodblocks much impaired.[1]

But why did this type of escapist, fantasizing, terrorizing—yet withal didactic and moralizing—fiction flourish just at this period? The answer may be found first of all in the social and political conditions of the time. As we have already seen, in the Kansei Reforms of the 1790s the central government had attempted to control and regulate all the vigour and *élan* that had characterized the first Golden Decade of the 1780s. Government directives had, in effect, emasculated the 'yellow-backs': their backbone of *chic* and parody was expunged, and in their place the ideals of conservative Confucian morality were inserted. But purely didactic and moralizing stories soon proved of little intrinsic interest, and the novelists increasingly enlivened their tales with the supernatural, the fantastic, the terrifying, the violent—even the voyeuristic and sadistic. To the modern mind, the results may well seem more objectionable than the fashionable wit and satire that they replaced: but not so to the stuffily moralistic censors of the feudal bureaucracy.

Just how much government interference and guidance affected cultural taste and movements at this time is difficult to measure. To some degree, the citizens of Edo were perhaps themselves ready for a reaction against the excesses of the previous generation. But certainly the Age of Bunka ('Culture' or 'Civilization'), from 1804 to 1818, marked a quite new era in Japanese life and art; and the changes in the work of Hokusai, a most sensitive and responsive barometer, were perhaps among the most remarkable and clearly evident.

The *yomi-hon* had existed for at least a generation, principally in the form of translations or adaptations of lengthy, classical Chinese historical and supernatural fiction, and the elaborate plots were clothed with a veneer of Confucian ethics. With the early 1800s, however, the same themes were converted *en masse* to Japanese customs and settings: sometimes, they were simply adaptations of the lurid Kabuki dramas that were also the rage of the time. Indeed, these plays and the colourful prints (mainly by Toyokuni) that celebrated them were inseparable. So, too, during the period 1806–12 were the *yomi-hon* novels and their complex illustrations, which were almost the monopoly of Hokusai. It was only natural therefore that he should have formed a team with the doyen of these novelists, Kyokutei Bakin (1767–1848), the two masters collaborating in fully 18 different books.

These lengthy works of fiction appeared in a quite different format from their equivalents in the West. In the first place, they were usually issued in sets of five slim volumes. If these proved popular, sequel after sequel might well appear—a development hardly envisioned by author or illustrator at the beginning of the project. The volumes also sported hard (though pliable) covers and were larger in size, and with far better printing and paper, than the earlier 'yellow-backs'.

The frontispieces to each series might well be printed in subdued colours, but the illustrations—several to each fascicle—were either in monochrome or, at the most, black and shades of pale grey. The original author generally provided his professional illustrator with roughly sketched suggestions for each plate; and—because of their voluminous nature—both text and illustrations were customarily copied by skilled copyists for the final manuscript. This was then pasted, face-down, on woodblocks for carving and subsequent printing. The illustrations are therefore often somewhat removed from the artist's originals, both the copyist and the engraver having subtly added their own influence—as well as quelling something of the artist's verve and vigour. With lesser artists the results could be rather dull and static. Hokusai, however, was a powerful master of design well able to surmount these considerable obstacles.

Inevitably, the *yomi-hon* illustrations represent a special taste, their effects much dependent upon the content, implications and aftertaste of the tales to which they form such an intimate conjunct. The fancy of the times demanded elaborate settings and absolute authenticity in each and every historical detail: it was not just a matter of the artist dashing off a series of imaginative sketches. But though difficult and time-consuming, such work was evidently well remunerated. Indeed, the novelist Bakin sometimes complained of the artist's high fees—though it is unclear how Hokusai actually spent the money, as he was habitually low on funds.

Unlike most of his ukiyo-e confrères, Hokusai was well suited to this type of detailed work, having been apprenticed as an engraver himself and completed a dozen years of meticulous work on actor-prints of the Katsukawa School. Moreover, his interests were truly encyclopedic. Both by training and inclination Hokusai was the ideal man for the job, and indeed, he practically dominated the field throughout the Bunka Era—with occasional such work even in his later years.

Hokusai's first *yomi-hon* date from towards the end of the period we have already discussed—1803–4. These early and experimental volumes were followed by a veritable flood: one in 1805 (Plate 96), three in 1806, seven in 1807 (Plates 97, 100, 101), eleven in the peak year 1808, comprising over 450 separate illustrations (Plate 98), six in 1809 (Plates 99, 102–103), three each in 1810 and 1811, and two in 1812. From the latter year the artist became, as we shall see, preoccupied with other work, but even then he continued to illustrate *yomi-hon*: three each in 1813/15, with others scattered through the years 1819, 1820, 1822, 1828, 1835, 1841; and even in 1844, 1845, and 1846 when, already in his mid-80s, he was still able to do minute and detailed work beyond the powers of most younger men (Plate 331). Some of these novels in their sequels spanned a number of years: the famous *Shimpen Suiko-gaden* (The New Illustrated *Suihuchuan*) comprising a total of 61 fascicles in six series over the years 1805–38.[2] (See also Fig. 184 ff.)

Of these 48 or more sets of different novels, over a third were done in collaboration with Bakin, with whom the artist even resided for a time. Both men were strong individualists, confident of their art, and it was only natural that they should often disagree on the details of Hokusai's illustrations. The story goes that their relationship (inevitably reminiscent of that between Cézanne and Zola) more than once broke up in quarrels. But by this time Hokusai's pictures were so vital to the success of the books that other, more complaisant novelists had to be employed to complete the projects. Eventually the publisher managed, with great effort, to mend the two men's difference. It is significant that Bakin, in his letters and diaries, complains of Hokusai's insistence on his own way of arranging a design—'sometimes seeming to rearrange my suggestions just to be contrary'. However, the novelist then adds, almost grudgingly, 'But there is no other artist to match him'. And Hokusai himself had the same begrudging view of Bakin and of their turbulent—but in the end, mutually fruitful—relationship.

Despite his didactic, even scholarly nature, Bakin was himself an eminently creative writer, expending great energy in an attempt to fill the gaps of documentation with his historical novels. In this effort he found a worthy illustrator in Hokusai (seven years his senior), who spared no pains to create fresh depictions of scenes which no other Japanese artist had ever attempted before. Perhaps surprisingly, Bakin owed much of his own expansion of creative horizons to the prodding influence of his demon illustrator (an element that, I suspect, has been neglected by Japanese scholars of Bakin, though of course it is difficult to gauge exactly).

Both men, however, in their concentration on realistically re-creating the complex details of history, inevitably suffered from the restraints thus imposed. With Hokusai, the result is clear even in the brief period of his first novels of 1803–7. As the figures become gradually more monumental and the designs more majestic—features both emulating and competing with the accompanying heroic texts—so do the graceful, pliant charms of his earlier work gradually disappear. One need only compare the artist's last major picture-book (Plate 60) with an early *yomi-hon* (Plate 96), and then the latter with another similar illustration of only four years later (Plate 103). Indeed, it is almost as though one were viewing a different artist, a different man. It is more than just a change of subject-matter. What appears here must be another facet of the original Hokusai, perhaps his true nature, which had been so long suppressed by intensive training and by commissions to depict the *chic* but frivolous Floating World: a milieu that was not, in the end, to the artist's real taste.

One may also mention again the influence of the stylized and fantastic Kabuki drama on both the *yomi-hon* texts and their very illustrations. The figures to Hokusai's plates often seem to be posing as though for the *mié* (climactic posturing) of a bombastic theatrical tableau, and very probably the readers of the time, in their mind's eye, actually translated the fantastic and exaggerated actions of

96 Haunted Couple (detail). Illustration from *Young Brocade of Edo. Yomi-hon* by Shigeru, 1805. (For a complete listing of Hokusai's *yomi-hon* see Appendix, Books, No. 112 ff., and Fig. 184 ff.)

97 The Suicide of Lady Hatsuhana. Illustration from *Plum-and-Willow on the Sumida River*. *Yomi-hon* by Bakin, 1807. (Such plates often include a caption summarizing the action.) (See also Fig. 191.)

each novel—and its illustrations—to the conventions of the stage.[3]

2

Hokusai's first *yomi-hon* illustrations were published at just the same time as some of his major picture-books (Plates 52–60 above). Our Plate 96, from *Azuma futaba-nishiki* (Young Brocade of Edo) of 1805, shows a representative early *yomi-hon* and a typical subject: the manifestation of a dreadful ghost, intent on wreaking vengeance on his two murderers. Here, the dastardly couple are depicted beside the mosquito-netting of their boudoir as the disembodied shade attacks the sword-wielding husband. Not entirely by coincidence, the Buddhist lantern at left duplicates that of the artist's famous 'O-Iwa' print of three decades later (Plate 277). Although rendered melodramatically, the composition and style are to a large extent reflections of Hokusai's genre works of the same period.

Within a year or two the artist had already developed his more fully integrated style of *yomi-hon* illustration, which we glimpse in Plate 97, from *Sumida-gawa bairyū-shinsho* (Plum-and-Willow on the Sumida River) of 1807. Here we view the dramatic scene where the Lady Hatsuhana, learning of her warrior husband's death in battle, drowns herself in Lake Ōsawa, leaving her four-year-old daughter, Princess Hannyo, to the care of a wet-nurse. The composition is typically and uniquely Hokusai's in its emphasis on the strong attraction between mother, nurse and frightened child. The sense of action is further intensified by the startled water-fowl, not only the birds depicted prominently at left, but also those half-concealed in the foliage at lower right.

One of the problems of Hokusai's *yomi-hon* illustrations lies in the almost excessive complexity of the designs. Even more than was the case with the simpler and less labyrinthine early illustrations, one is tempted to concentrate on details for examples: the full, double-page plates are often too tightly packed with complex information to withstand reduction in size and loss of the sharply edged woodblock-printing via modern reproduction, whereas in the originals, one can peer closely and the woodcut will reveal more details than the eye can absorb. This is not entirely the fault of the artist: one cannot really expect him to make of each and every design a dramatic poster, fully appreciable from afar; nor was that what his audience wanted. Yet although each element of these plates is effective enough in itself, the result seldom equals the artist's major work even in book-illustration (see Plate 61 for example). Perhaps the subjects are simply too tortuous; perhaps this was the best that the times would permit. There is no ready answer to the question of why Hokusai's *yomi-hon* illustrations are in the end not entirely satisfying.

The early *yomi-hon* book-plates feature the same frail yet sinuous, dream-like beauties that we have seen in the albums and *surimono*, but now in a setting of melodrama in which the figures stand out against an increasingly complex background. This method of depiction was necessitated in part by the involved story-telling needs of the medium, and in part by the demands of the audience. But there was also one facet of the artist's own personality which drew him in this direction. Clearly his fondness for

the baroque, sometimes rococo approach to a design, in which the bizarre, even grotesque, is emphasized, and every bit of space filled with intricate interrelated details, occasionally led him to forget one prime quality of most Japanese art: that 'less is more'.

It is sometimes difficult to comprehend that we are looking at the same frail females we so admired in the picture-books and albums of just the same period. Here, the story has become the artist's theme and the figures inevitably suffer from the change of focus. In the end, one must conclude that Hokusai's masterful plates are, quite literally, designed in intimate conjunction with the texts, and lose too much when viewed purely as works of graphic art. In this sense they are the victims of their own destiny: being essentially indivisible from their own contexts, they remain profoundly parochial. The student who would understand them must do as Hokusai's own audience did—read the novel as he views the pictures.

Just how quickly the artist was progressing in these brief years will be apparent from yet another example of that favourite of the Gothic novel, the revenge-scene, from *Shimoyo-no-hoshi* (Stars on a Frosty Night) of 1808 (Plate 98).[4] Here the villain Ihyōe, having murdered his ugly wife O-Sawa out of love for the beautiful O-Hana, is beset by his wife's foul apparition, which appears as head and arms only, grasping the treacherous husband's sword in an

98 *Below* Haunted Couple. Illustration from *Stars on a Frosty Night*. *Yomi-hon* by Tanehiko, 1808.

99 *Opposite top* Family Quarrel. Illustration from *The Craftsman from Hida*. *Yomi-hon* by Rokujuen, 1809.

100 *Opposite bottom* Samurai and Giant Spider. Illustration from *Snow in the Garden. Yomi-hon* by Bakin, 1807. (See also Fig. 190.)

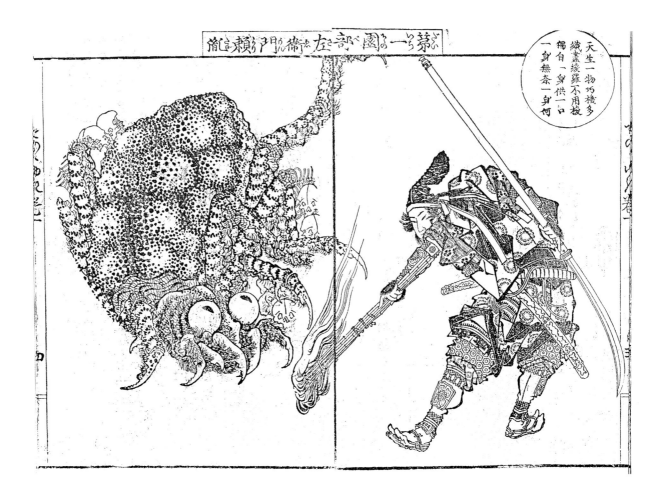

almost adoring manner. The flames of her passion swirl in the direction of her rival like vengeful snakes (the serpentine shape assumed, indeed, by her own under-sash at left).

Compared to Plate 96 this is quite a new approach to the supernatural. The composition is dramatic, the figures eminently human; moreover, a most effective application of special *sumi* tones is employed for the background. But perhaps most impressive of all is the essentially *endearing* quality of the participants. Despite their dastardly deed one feels a hint of sympathy (or at least commiseration) for the beleaguered couple; and the vengeful ghost is touchingly human in her inability to suppress lingering affection for her treacherous mate. It is in such human gestures, which the artist manages to insert even in the most horrific scenes, that Hokusai goes a step beyond the actual novelist—adding that element of characterization which is so often lacking in fantastic fiction. And again, one wonders if Japanese scholars of the *yomi-hon* as a literary genre have ever sufficiently considered the important role of the artist in fleshing out, even orchestrating, the structure of these books.

The critic may tend to select such strikingly dramatic, supernatural tableaux from these volumes, but it is well to remember that the bulk of their content is of quieter scenes, conveying crucial but less fantastic turns in the plot. Thus in Plate 99, from *Hida-no-takumi monogatari* (The Craftsman from Hida) of 1809, at lower right we view the maiden Murasaki who, having fallen in love with the scion of her family's dire enemy, weeps at the remonstrations of her enraged father. The design features a fairly straightforward composition, much enhanced by the effective employment of decorative background.

At the same time as these genre-centred melodramatic scenes, Hokusai began also to develop his skills in the dramatic depiction of epic and heroic tableaux. In Plate 100, from the novel *Sono-no-yuki* (Snow in the Garden) of 1807, one notes immediately the heightened sense of drama and dynamic composition which replaces the weaker, more graceful postures of his earlier *Chūshingura* scenes, for example (Plates 77, 86). The confrontation of the warrior Yoritane and the Giant Spider in its cave is (once one accepts its fantastic nature) an effective design, enhanced by the attention to decorative detail, such as the intricate armour, spidery patterns and the flaming torch. Here we discover the elements (harking back to the ukiyo-e pioneer Moronobu) which will characterize Hokusai's own more famous work in this genre a generation later, and which

101 Samurai and Attackers. Illustration from *Strange Tales of the Crescent Moon. Yomi-hon* by Bakin, Series I, 1807. (See also Figs. 188–9.)[5]

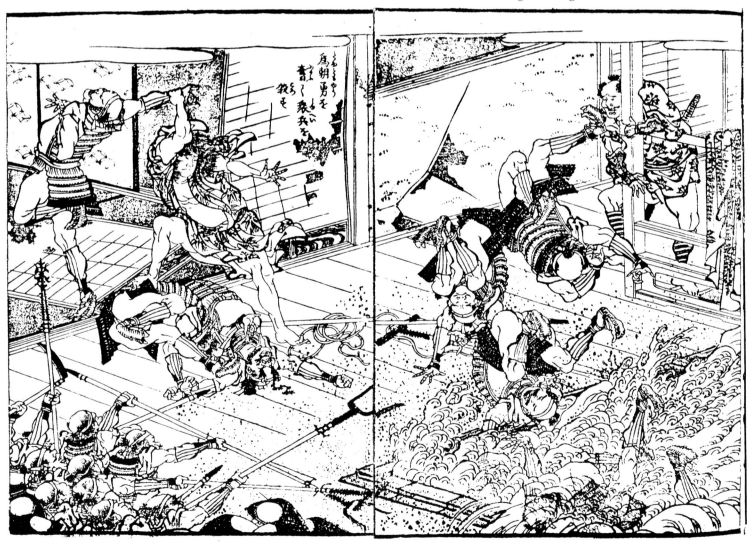

102 Boudoir Carnage. Illustration from *The Chūshingura: a Sequel.*
Yomi-hon by Emba, 1809.

formed the pattern for such worthy followers as
Kuniyoshi.

These frontispiece-plates tend to follow the impressive
manner of the picture-books, and it is well to counter-
balance this illustration with a more typical heroic tableau
of the same period (Plate 101). The famous *Chinsetsu
yumihari-zuki* (Strange Tales of the Crescent Moon) was
published in five series over the period 1807–11, and represents a historical novel of grand scale, taking the redoubtable hero overseas as far as the Ryūkyū Islands. The
powerful scene shown here displays the protagonist
Tametomo, surprised while bathing, yet still managing to
subdue a small army of his enemies. To this traditional
samurai/*chambara* battle-scene the artist adds his special
touch: the hero himself is a bundle of muscles, a personi-
fication of manly power; the assailants are hurled one after
another into the steaming water, its splashing drops filling
out the blank spaces of the flooring, just as the partitions
and walls fill out the background. Every inch of the tableau
is taken up with action and movement; this was something
quite new not only in book-illustration, but in Japanese art
itself.[6]

As we have already seen, among Hokusai's most

effective—or, at least, most effectively reproduced—book-
plates are those which employ the *sumi-tsubushi* technique
of black backgrounds. Here the artist is freed from his
propensity for rococo detail and can concentrate more on
the foreground elements. Our Plate 102 from the novel
Kanadehon gonichi-no-bunshō (The *Chūshingura*: a Sequel) of
1809 catches the eye immediately, even though one may
not readily comprehend the exact subject-matter. Indeed,
the scene is surprisingly pleasant and decorative, and it is
only on close examination (or on reading the text) that one
perceives the macabre details: books and utensils scattered
about, old grandmother Ikuyo lying bloodily murdered
under the mosquito-netting, her little grandson Bunnosuke fallen lifeless at centre, his virtuous mother, the
widowed Saeda—breasts bared—pinned down by the
nonchalant ruffian at right; their bedroom clouded with
the smoke of the brazier (rendered in *dōban*, chiaroscuro
style). The whole frame is filled yet there are no extraneous elements; when compared with the previous
plates one notes a welcome emphasis on a close-up
approach, enhancing the horror of a night attack on the
boudoir of these innocent victims of outrage.[7]

One further example of this more lurid type of Gothic
novel must suffice to affirm Hokusai's increasingly developed powers in these years. Plate 103 is from *Yume-no-
ukihashi* (The Bridge of Love-dreams), also of 1809, and

103 Haunted Couple. Illustration from *The Bridge of Love-dreams.*
Yomi-hon by Tōei, 1809.

surely ranks among the artist's masterpieces in this neglected genre. In this scene once again the ebony background most effectively limns the figures and foreground
elements. Although (reading the novel) one may feel sympathy for the revengeful passion of the blind masseur
Awaichi—his ghost depicted here with Occidental-style
shading—the force of Hokusai's brush turns our sympathies even more to his murderers, and especially to the
unfaithful wife O-Ushi, attempting to flee the bedroom but
magnetically drawn back by the ghastly demon (or by her
own conscience).

From the relatively simple, almost naive, essentially
ukiyo-e scene of our earlier Plate 96 to the masterful,
almost 'modern' mood of this forceful tableau is a
tremendous step for a mere four years in the artist's life.
There was not, one must submit, much further that Hokusai could go in this medium: he had stretched the miniature format of book-illustration to its very limits—
succeeding, now and then, in producing major works of
art within a severely restricted space and unpromising
medium.

Such scenes of the terrifying and supernatural are
among the most impressive of Hokusai's illustrations in
this period, a subject to be raised to even greater heights
over a generation later in the famous 'Ghost Prints' (Plates
277, 282). Equally chilling—though, perhaps luckily, we
have no space to reproduce them here—are the numerous
scenes of torture and bloody death that fill the pages of the
yomi-hon: a special taste that was to be revived by the
artists Kuniyoshi, E-Kin and Yoshitoshi in a later, equally
repressed age.

Whether this predilection for the violent and cruel mirrors Hokusai's own personality is difficult to say. He was,
after all, only illustrating the works of others, and catering
to the general taste of the times. And he invariably includes evocative, even poetic elements, often irrelevant to
the literary texts, that tend to dull the absolute horror of
such scenes. Yet one does have the feeling that Hokusai
relished the opportunity to explore every facet of experience, both human and inhuman, through his art.

Having described something of the background of these
melodramatic tableaux, one is left with the thorny question: how great is art if it has to be explained? This is
perhaps the fate of book-illustration in general, but it con-

stitutes a particularly decisive problem in Hokusai's *yomi-hon* plates, which represent an intricately intertwined amalgam of literature, legend, art, no one quite separable from the other.

A sober judgement of these varied pictures—totalling at least 1500 separate tableaux—is hardly easy. While not, of course, all of equal interest, the Master's illustrations are surprisingly uniform in quality, if not in imagination. There are no great failures: and indeed, to turn from Hokusai's work to that of even his best emulators (for example, his pupils Hokuba, Shigenobu, Taito II, as well as Toyohiro and Toyokuni) is immediately to sense a loss of power, skill and inspiration. Thus, while the subjects and style are not well suited to modern taste, the actual illustrations form a significant portion of Hokusai's *oeuvre*, and may well be re-valued by another generation.

Hokusai's *yomi-hon* represent perhaps the most concentrated essence of the artist's genius: but of these hundreds and hundreds of plates depicting fantastic themes, few in themselves have much interest for us today. This contradiction is difficult to explain logically, and one can only repeat that the pictures are essentially inseparable from the books which they grace, and that these archaic novels are, in effect, inaccessible to the modern reader.

Yet it might well be claimed that, whatever the limitations of the medium, Hokusai was one of the most creative illustrators the world has known: not only does he convey with reasonable fidelity the main action of the novel, but he also manages to expand and even enrich the content and nuances of the original works of literature. This feature alone would ensure Hokusai of very high ranking in this most difficult branch of graphic art.

As we have commented before, Hokusai was essentially a commercial artist and perforce followed the demands of the times, and of his own livelihood. In the end, it is simply unreasonable of us to wish that he might have continued forever with his graceful beauties of the turn of the century. Had he done so, his genius might simply have become stunted and his work repetitive. This decade of intensive work in 'Gothic' illustration formed—like an earlier decade under the Katsukawa atelier—the necessary

groundwork for Hokusai's later mastery in the consummate albums and sketchbooks, and his final triumph in the *Fuji* series. In fact, his 'Gothic' illustrations of around the year 1809 constitute a kind of turning-point in the artist's style; and after this the fragile grace of his earlier years appears only in fleeting reflections.

Hokusai himself must have recognized this as a major crossroads: in 1811—after a dozen or more years of rather steady use—he changed his art-name to 'Taito' ('Polar Star'), bequeathing 'Hokusai' to a minor pupil. And in the following year he travelled to distant Nagoya, beginning yet another and quite different phase of his life and work.

NOTES

1 To a surprising degree, Western appreciation of ukiyo-e has depended on the fastidious taste of early French collectors—sometimes rarefied, sometimes parochial—who rather neglected such Hokusai genres as *yomi-hon* and *kibyōshi*: being rare, not particularly impressive, and seldom found in the pristine condition that these aesthetes demanded. (High standards of condition are all well and good for wealthy collectors, but hardly vital for the student who would grasp the total *oeuvre* of the artist.)

2 The title of this famous Chinese novel is literally 'Tales of the Water-margin'—best-known in the West from Pearl Buck's free translation under the title *All Men are Brothers*. For Hokusai's later treatment of this perennial theme see Plates 234–236.

3 In fact, this is one easy method of attempting to enjoy these complex scenes even today: to imagine one's favourite Kabuki actor in each role, to apply their poses and mannerisms to each scene, each bit of action.

(Several of these Hokusai *yomi-hon* were so successful that they themselves were even adapted to the stage: to the Ōsaka *jōruri* in 1808–9, as well as to an Edo Kabuki production of 1814. See Appendix, Books, Nos. 134 and 173.)

4 It will be perceived that the titles of many of these novels are most poetic and evocative, irrespective of their melodramatic or bizarre contents. The actual novel in this case, though published only in 1808, was completed two years earlier, in 1806. A really specialized study of Hokusai's illustration would of course entail a more detailed investigation into the exact months of execution—here, sometime in 1807. This novel is thought, incidentally, to have formed the inspiration for the famous Kabuki drama of 1825, *Yotsuya kaidan*, featuring the vengeful ghost of O-Iwa—the specific subject of Hokusai's later print masterpiece of Plate 277.

5 Although this composition is complete in itself, there is actually a third, preparatory page of illustration on the reverse of the right plate.

6 Compare, for example, Hokusai's own rather similar scene of two decades earlier in Plate 10.

7 While not wishing to give away the full denouement, I will at least reveal that in the next scene, the shade of Saeda's dead husband Bungo appears and—with the help of the benevolent god Jizō—restores Grandmother Ikuyo and little Bunnosuke to life, routing the evil bandits. One can obviously never tell what is going to happen next in these breathtaking novels—except that everything will turn out right in the end. (Note, incidentally, that in an alternative edition the dark background is omitted from this plate, rather reducing the dramatic impact of the tableau: see illustration *left*.)

Left Boudoir Carnage. Alternative version of Plate 102.

XI
Hokusai's Middle Years
and the Labyrinth
of Painting

1

HOKUSAI'S artistic activities in the first quarter of the nineteenth century covered such a wide variety of genres and media that a truly integrated account is well-nigh impossible. In the preceding chapter we detailed something of his 'Gothic novels' and in subsequent ones we shall turn to further picture-books, prints and erotica. The present chapters will attempt to survey Hokusai's paintings, and his multiple series of printed 'sketchbooks for artists'. But first we must discuss briefly the several fragments of biographical data that have come down to us. Exact dating is often difficult, however, and any attempt to relate such events to specific facets of the artist's work can be perilous.

What meagre data we possess regarding Hokusai's personal life at this time comes largely from incidental references in his books and in the diaries of associates; yet even so, it is rather more plentiful than that available for most of his confrères of the plebeian Ukiyo-e School. Thus it seems likely that during the 1780s Hokusai lived for a time in Kodemma-chō (towards the centre of Edo); and from the end of 1790 in Katsushika (on the eastern outskirts of town); then in the mid-1790s in Asakusa, and later Hayashi-chō (Honjo) and the Ueno area. It may be added that Hokusai's studies of this period were not confined to art in the limited sense of the word: he expended great effort in comprehending, for example, the complexities of Buddhist philosophy and iconography; and is said even to have briefly apprenticed himself to a bone-setter, in order to increase his knowledge of anatomy.

Of the artist's children by his first marriage one daughter, O-Miyo, married her father's pupil Shigenobu, in about 1808 at the age of 19, but was divorced several years later, returning to her parent's home. O-Miyo died in her 20s and her only child was subsequently taken in by old Hokusai; the artist doted on the boy, but he later proved an incorrigible delinquent and a constant source of trouble to his grandfather.

Hokusai's own son Tominosuke is said to have been

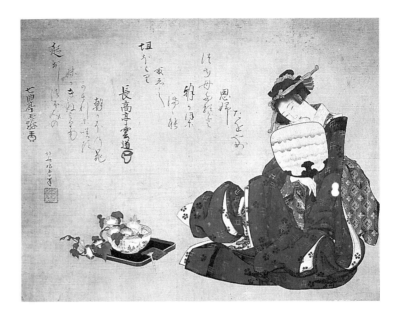

107 O-Tatsu (Hokusai's daughter): Maiden and Morning-glories. Kakemono in colours on silk; mid-1810s. 13½ × 17¾ in / 34 × 45 cm. Signed Ms. Tatsu, Hokusai's Daughter.

adopted as heir by the influential Nakajima Family (official mirror-makers to the Shōgun, and already mentioned in connection with the artist's own close relationship with them), but died young, about 1812.

Hokusai's other early daughter, O-Tatsu (or O-Tetsu), also died in her 20s—life expectancy was low in this age—but left at least one admirable painting in her father's style, which indicates that she was an artist of great promise (Plate 107). This delightful work depicts a maiden, summer fan in hand, silently contemplating an arrangement of morning-glories in an Imari bowl.

Due in part to his painstaking efforts—and notable success—in the illustration of popular fiction, Hokusai seems to have enjoyed a rare period of prosperity for a time. In 1808 he moved to a new house in Honjo (his birthplace, and frequent site of residence), and even held a Painting Party to celebrate the event. The loss of his son provoked not only an emotional crisis but also an economic one, for as adopted heir to an influential family he had been instrumental in obtaining a certain stipend for Hokusai, which terminated at his death.

After the death of his first wife in the mid-1790s, Hokusai had remarried, siring a son and at least three daughters. The son was later adopted (as was the occasional custom in non-affluent plebeian families), first by a Honjo merchant, and subsequently by a minor government official, later

104 *Opposite top* Flying Swallows. Detail of a fan-painting in light colours on micaed paper; *c.* 1807. *c.* 13¾ in / 35 cm wide. Signed Hokusai.

105 *Opposite bottom left* Dancing Monkey. Small kakemono in light colours on paper, *c.* early 1810s. 14½ × 10 in / 37 × 25 cm.

106 *Opposite bottom right* Courtesan with Fan. Kakemono in light colours on paper (centre panel of a triptych); *c.* 1805. 38½ × 11 in / 98 × 28 cm. Signed Gakyōjin Hokusai.

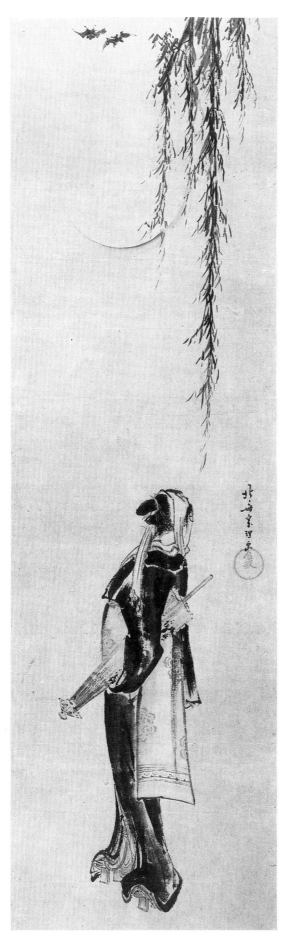

108 Street-walker in Moonlight under Willow. Kakemono in light
colours on paper; style of late 1790s. 39½ × 11 in / 100 × 28 cm.
Signed Hokusai Sōri.

109 Maiden under Willow. Kakemono in colours on silk; style of
early 1800s. 33 × 10 in / 84 × 25 cm. Signed Gakyōjin Hokusai.

110 Courtesan as Goddess on Lion. Fan-painting in light colours on micaed paper; *c.* 1799. *c.* 13¾ in / 35 cm wide. Signed Fusenkyo Hokusai.

taking over the government post himself.

The third of these later daughters, O-Ei, was to be most significant in relation to the artist's life. In about 1818 she married the minor painter Tōmei (pupil of Hokusai's own teacher Tōrin), but she proved of a rather masculine, domineering nature—'she could paint but not sew', it was commented—and eventually, nearly a decade later, was divorced. On the death of her mother (Hokusai's second wife) she returned home to live with her father. O-Ei was a distinguished artist herself, assisting Hokusai in his work as well as ministering to him in his old age (see Plate 128). (After her father's death her idiosyncrasies became more pronounced and O-Ei left Edo for distant Kanazawa on the Japan Sea, where she died at the age of 66.)

In the summer of 1828, Hokusai's life was further complicated by the death of his second wife. The Master was then 68, afflicted intermittently with palsy, troubled by his profligate grandson, but indomitable in his work. Indeed— as we shall see in a later chapter—it was during this most turbulent period of his family life that Hokusai produced some of his greatest masterpieces.

Yet though these sketchy family details might well fire the imagination of the novelist or playwright (and indeed there are several Japanese novels/plays/films about Hokusai), they do not themselves shed much light on the artist's progress in his career—other than to indicate that he had many distractions, not too much peace of mind, and only rarely enjoyed any degree of economic security. However, these conditions may have provided as much a stimulus as they did a distraction.

To these personal details may be added a few other biographical facts rather more related to Hokusai's art, includ-

ing his first Public Painting Exhibition, at Edo in 1804. It may seem curious that we have not, in this account, hitherto made more detailed reference to the artist's work in painting; but few early paintings are extant, and problems of authenticity inherent in this field are immensely complex. Here we will speak mainly of stylistic trends, of selected examples, and of the paintings recorded in contemporary accounts.

Even during Hokusai's lifetime there were a multitude of pupils, copyists and forgers of his paintings, and the forgers' work continues to this day. In fact, it is surprising that there are so few absolutely genuine Hokusai paintings extant; and the fact that none of these has been subjected to intensive scholarly study makes an authoritative survey impossible at this stage of our knowledge. We know from the contemporary records that Hokusai did execute paintings practically from his earliest years; and since several of the extant works do match his style of this period it may be useful to illustrate a few—without pretending that any final word is yet possible on them.[1]

The 'Streetwalker' of Plate 108 shows a rear view of one of the Edo 'ladies of the night' strolling in moonlight under a willow-tree, auspicious bats circling at top. The signature is Hokusai Sōri and the seal Tokimasa—matching Hokusai's illustrations and *surimono* of the period *c.* 1797. The subject-matter may seem a trifle odd to the casual observer but in fact, at this period there prevailed a fashion for ukiyo-e depictions—perhaps in commiseration for those portrayed—of this, the lowest class of harlot (see also Plate 118). It might be thought that for both artists and art-connoisseurs of the time, there was a seeming suspension of the critical, if not moral, faculties: they had not the least objection to picking the objects of aesthetic idealization from the very gutter. But though the moralizing school of art critics tends to view this as 'a debauched age and an immoral art', to me it seems, rather, evidence of a commendable, new and humanistic outlook in which class, caste, position, profession, destiny and karma bore no relation to the intrinsic value of a human being. When this painting is examined with a critical eye, it must also be remarked that both brushstrokes and signature are a trifle weak: but are we to interpret this as merely an indication that the artist was yet to develop real confidence in painting?

Much the same can be said of Plate 109, a rather similar tableau but depicting a maiden of quality. It is painted on silk, with a consequently greater attention to detail than was possible in the previous, more sketch-like example on paper. In the details of tree and foliage we may detect evidence of Hokusai's studies in the Continental styles, especially that of the later Chinese painters such as Shen Nan-p'in, and of the Chinese-derived Sō-Shiseki school. Like all too many ukiyo-e paintings, however, the pigments appear to have been retouched: the three-dimensional effects seen on the parasol, for example, may well be the result of later restoration; and such paintings often provide disappointing surprises when subjected to the cold eye of infra-red/X-ray scanning. The signature reads *Gakyōjin* Hokusai and the style, too, dates from a few years after the previous example.

Perhaps more enjoyable—at least for those who appreciate small things—may be such fan-paintings by Hokusai as that in Plate 110. Here an exalted but winsome courtesan is shown seated on a grumpy *shishi* (mythical lion); she is depicted as the deity Monju in a pastiche on a well-known Buddhist theme. (The title could almost be rendered as 'Beauty and the Beast', though *shishi* are too human to be truly beastly.) The miniature format of the fan—which was often put to use, folded and mounted on ribs by connoisseurs of the time—was well suited to Hokusai's genius for complex compositions within cramped spaces, and this is one of his early masterpieces. It bears not only the signature Hokusai but also the rare pseudonym Fusenkyo ('Unsullied').

Faced with some of the more impressive paintings ascribed to Hokusai for the subsequent period, the first quarter of the nineteenth century, one can only say that they are expertly done, but often do not seem to capture the spontaneous spirit of the artist that we glimpse even in his prints and books (Plates 117, 120). Was Hokusai really so inhibited when carrying out such more luxurious commissions from patrons of eminence? The method of painting is so formal and detailed that it sometimes requires careful study to distinguish the hand of the master from the early copyist, the restorer from the original painter.

With the early nineteenth century Hokusai, now in his mid-40s, came into his own as a painter, and several outstanding examples are extant from this period (as well as a large number of copies and forgeries). To me, he is at his best in the more impromptu-style work in light colours on paper, rather than in the more formal paintings in heavy colours on silk which, though impressive enough (and

111 Courtesan and Flying Cuckoo. Kakemono in light colours on paper; early 1800s. 35 × 11 in / 89 × 28 cm. Signed Hokusai.

114 *Above* Courtesan by Fence. Fan-painting in light colours on micaed paper; *c.* 1805. *c.* 13¾ in / 35 cm wide. Signed Gakyōjin Hokusai.

115 *Right* Fuji and Pine-tree. Kakemono in *sumi* and light colours on silk; *c.* mid-1800s. *c.* 13¾ × 19½ in / 35 × 50 cm. Signed Hokusai (with Tokimasa seal); inscription by Bunrai-an.

sulted in very elaborate forgeries.[6]

Hokusai's sketches and smaller *sumi-e*, ink-paintings, are yet another matter. The problems of authentication remain, and for the print-drawings are complicated by the normal stages in the development of a design: artist's first draft; more careful drawing; 'block copy'—tracing made from the artist's original sketch for use by the engraver (the latter two often done by pupil or professional copyist). But these works appear in smaller and more intimate formats, and with their impromptu, less mannered brushwork they have long been treasured in the West. Indeed, in the opinion of some critics they are to be ranked alongside the drawings of Leonardo or Rembrandt.

In viewing traditional Japanese painting one must remember that the technique was, in effect, that of watercolour or gouache applied on the scale of Western oil-painting. The most important requirement of this technique is that the design be firmly embedded in the artist's mind before he ever sets brush to silk or paper: there is no room for uncertainty or correction. Naturally enough, this factor severely limited the degree of experimentation possible during the actual painting; in his apprentice years an artist had to practice each and every stroke a thousand times in preparation for final mastery. At their best, the resulting impromptu-appearing works were, in effect, the distillation of the painter's entire range of experience: an instantaneous explosion of concentrated powers that might be compared to the tense climax of a *jūdō* or *sumō* match, in which success or failure is decided in a few brief seconds.

116 Raven flying against the Dawn Sun. Painting in light colours on paper; *c.* 1810. 10 × 14 in / 25 × 36 cm. Signed Hokusai.

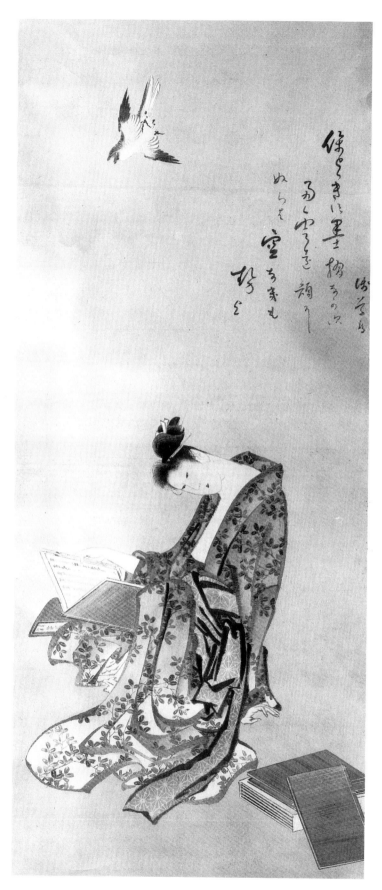

Coming to the 1810s we reach what many would consider the high peak of Hokusai's work in painting. This is, of course, very much a matter of taste, and if I differ on the matter it is not to deny the impressive quality of these works, and their important place in the artist's *oeuvre*.

Beginning, as usual, with the Master's more abbreviated work on paper, one finds very few extant examples. That of Plate 117 (unsigned but clearly in the artist's style) is a familiar theme, but this time it is a matron who, in *déshabillé*, thumbs through a large book as a cuckoo flies above. The painting is skilled enough, but in the angular lines of face, neck and hand one looks in vain for the lissom beauties of a decade earlier.

Most of Hokusai's paintings from this period are on silk, rather rough in texture, and carefully executed in heavy colours. Such a medium and its obligatory techniques naturally placed great constraints on an artist of Hokusai's temperament; and one must assume that his commissions specified this kind of work.

Commencing with the smaller formats on silk, we first note an interesting contribution to a painting-album by various ukiyo-e masters of the time—including Utamaro, Eishi, Toyokuni I, Kunisada and Hokusai's own pupil Hokuba. Hokusai's work (Plate 118) is an unconventional depiction of a *funa-manjū* or boat-harlot, one of the ladies-of-the-night who plied their trade on small boats along the Sumida River (and, in case anyone wondered, under bridges when it rained or snowed). The scene depicted is, indeed, of winter; and the young woman, her head hooded from the cold, is seen warming her vital parts at a charcoal-brazier in the boat. Although the pose is somehow reminiscent of shunga-scenes, the tableau is essentially non-erotic; there is even a certain pathos in the chilly scene, and the hooded bust recalls the Goddess of Mercy, Kannon, here sacrificing herself to mankind's lusts.

Turning to the larger kakemono, all on silk, we come first to one of Hokusai's acknowledged masterpieces of the period, the 'Tipsy Beauty' of Plate 119, in which a lovely girl—probably of the pleasure quarter—rests upon a lac-

117 *Above* Woman and Flying Cuckoo. Kakemono in colours on paper; *c.* early 1810s. 45¾ × 19¾ in / 116 × 50 cm. Unsigned (verse by Asakusa-an).

118 *Right* Boat-harlot. Album-painting in heavy colours on silk; *c.* mid-1810s. 9½ × 11¾ in / 24 × 30 cm. Signed Hokusai.

quered samisen-box, a saké-cup visible on the *tatami*. Although the figure's proportions are near-monumental the total effect is one of an intimacy rare in the Hokusai of this date. Perhaps the informal subject-matter—a drunken girl—permitted the artist to infuse more humanity into the design than was customary in his standard works in the formal painting manner.

More typical of this genre is the famous 'Beauty in the Snow', which many would consider Hokusai's *chef-d'oeuvre* in *bijin-ga* painting (Plate 120). Here, however, the female charms are rather overpowered by the elegant but bulky robes and umbrella; and the solidly rooted triangular composition is striking without being entirely enjoyable. Already we are approaching the end of the 1810s, and the artist's gradual divorce from such themes of the Floating World of feminine beauty. (In viewing such elaborate bedizenment one is reminded of the words of the famed Ōsaka courtesan Naoe, in her protest to the author-

ities at the time of the Kansei Reforms: 'Our world is different from the ordinary world. . . . If we were to dress ourselves like ordinary girls, how on earth could we manage to attract lovers!'[7])

Notable group-scenes also make their appearance in this decade, for example the unusual composition of Plate 121. Here we see a traditional theme: the Courtesan of Eguchi making her appearance to the monk Saigyō, as though an avatar of the Buddhist god Fugen bestride an elephant. (Although the paintings are unrelated, the subject forms a pair in Buddhist iconography with that of Plate 110.) The full design is a little awkward in composition, and would have been improved by skilful employment of effective background features, but the detail shown is typical of Hokusai's best *bijin-ga* of this period. This work is in the miniature *shikishi* (poetry-card) format, and though our detail here is rather larger than the original, yet it retains its full brilliance: vivid testimony to the truth of Hokusai's legendary exhibition of 'painting two sparrows on a grain of rice'.

Far more effective as an overall composition is the

119 Tipsy Beauty (detail). Kakemono in heavy colours on silk; *c*. mid-1810s. 10½ × 12¾ in / 26.5 × 32 cm. Signed Katsushika Hokusai.

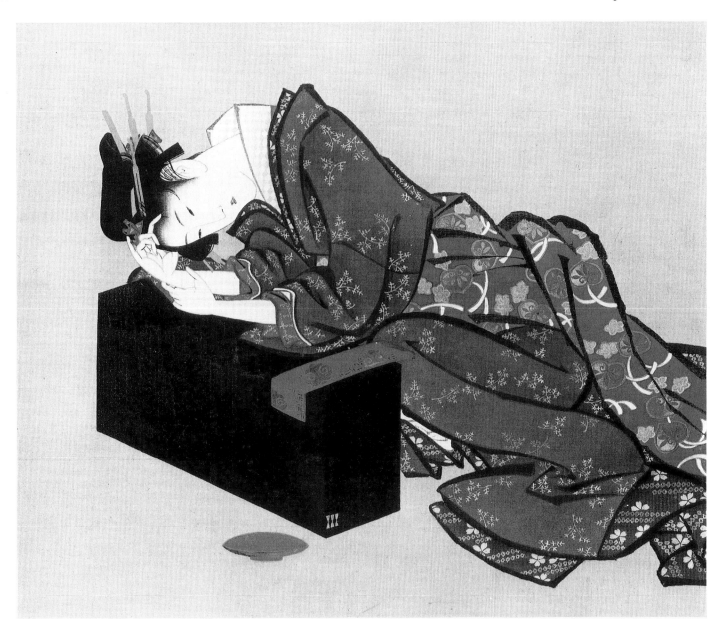

Hokusai of this period: the figures robust and monumental, yet still retaining traces of the human delicacy of his earlier work. The tableau bears interesting comparison with similar scenes already shown: the prints of Plates 27, 83 for example.

In the West, Hokusai's most famous painting of this period will be the 'Tametomo and Devils' of Plate 124. In earlier viewings of this work—in the 1950s and '60s—I must admit that I had my reservations about its authenticity. Now, however, I tend to think the garish colouring and essentially awkward figures are evidence simply of the artist's over-absorption in the Chinese style at this period (when he was, it will be remembered, immersed in *yomi-hon* illustration). The painting is basically a book-

120 *Left* Elegant Beauty in Snow (detail). Kakemono in heavy colours on silk; *c.* late 1810s. 39 × 13¾ in / 99.5 × 35 cm. Signed Taito, formerly Hokusai.

121 *Below* Courtesan as Goddess on Elephant (detail). *Shikishi* miniature, mounted as kakemono, in heavy colours on silk; *c.* early 1810s. 10½ × 8¼ in / 27 × 21 cm. Signed Katsushika Hokusai.

group-scene of Plate 122, which ranks among the artist's major figure-paintings. Four young women—probably geisha—are examining new kimono material for possible purchase, seated in front of an older woman with a pipe. Again, the master's lively brushwork is visibly impeded by the recalcitrant intermediary of rough silken ground and body-colours: to Japanese connoisseurs and patrons, always the medium *par excellence* in its gorgeous, almost baroque effects; but hardly the ideal one for Hokusai.

Equally famous, and perhaps even more successful, is the rather large tableau 'Shell-gathers' of Plate 123. The setting is the seashore at Izu, with Mt Fuji in the far distance. The background is somewhat reminiscent of Hokusai's pioneer predecessor in Occidental-style painting, Shiba Kōkan; and the middle-distance elements are again a trifle ambiguous. But the foreground is typically

122 *Top* Five Women. Kakemono in heavy colours on silk; *c.* mid-1810s. 15¾ × 31 in / 40 × 79 cm. Signed Katsushika Hokusai; the verse is by Sankyū, a minor poetaster.

123 *Above* Shellfish-gatherers at Seashore. Kakemono in heavy colours on silk; *c.* mid-1810s. 21¼ × 34 in / 54 × 86 cm. Signed Katsushika Hokusai.

124 Tametomo and the Devils. Kakemono in heavy colours on silk;
1811–12. 23¼ × 32¼ in / 59 × 82 cm. Signed Katsushika Hokusai
Taito.

illustration enlarged to panel size. It features the legendary
bowman Tametomo (whom we saw in Plate 101), his giant
bow being unsuccessfully drawn by four inhabitants of the
Isle of Devils, to which the hero had been exiled. (This
famous scene is, of course, illustrated in the original
novel—see Fig. 189—though it is hardly one of the more
notable plates.)

To me, at least, the painting is more interesting for its
details—the vividly flying birds, the decorative waves, the
masterful pine-tree—than for the central theme. But it is a
work of historical importance, enhanced by the inscription
of Hokusai's collaborator Bakin. The latter records elsewhere that just such a painting was commissioned by the
publisher Hirabayashi, to commemorate the completion of
the lengthy and many-volumed novel treating this theme,
in the year 1810. (The inscription, at least, is dated from
the end of the lunar year 1811—which would fall in 1812 in
the Gregorian calendar.)

Hokusai's achievement in the field of painting was not
limited to figure-work but extended also to nature-
subjects, such as the impressive, large composition of
'Carp and Turtles' shown in Plate 125. Providing further
evidence of the artist's wide studies in naturalistic painting
styles, the method of depiction is first of all reminiscent of
the Inaba School of painters, particularly Tōrei (who had
died only a few years before), and his mentors Ōkyo and
Sō-Shiseki. To this essentially Chinese-derived influence
are added Hokusai's characteristic, anthropomorphic eyes
and the decoratively placed seaweed, in a curiously lifelike
yet withal surrealistic tableau. (The subjects will reappear
later in famous prints of the Master, see Plates 152, 287,
and Fig. 99.) As often happens with Hokusai's animals,
the nature of the expressions makes us wonder if this is a

parody of certain human characteristics—or simply a kind
of self-portraiture. (Although this peculiar type of viewpoint was practically inimitable, it surely influenced the
more overt animal/fish parodies of Kuniyoshi, a generation later.)

The inscription, by the artist himself, is of particular interest. Dated Fourth Month of 1813, it records that the
painting is dedicated to a disciple, to whom is herewith
bequeathed the Master's seal of the time. The pupil's name
is not cited, but the reference must be to Hokumei, who
later employed this curious device on his (or her) own
works. The seal bears the legend *Kimō dasoku* ('Hair on a
tortoise, legs on a serpent', a Zen-type nonsense conundrum which could, I suppose, be freely translated as
'Don't ask silly questions').[8]

From the same period dates the lively sketch of a dancing monkey shown in Plate 105. But this is not only a
simple depiction of a trained monkey. For—just as in Hindu mythology—these little creatures were considered
messengers of the gods; and from the details of Shintō cap
and festooned exorcism-staff, this most probably represents the Monkey Dance customarily performed at the
Hie-gongen Shrine on Monkey Day of the Fourth Month.

The last to be mentioned of Hokusai's nature-studies in
this period is a remarkable set of paintings originally done
for a pair of small sliding-doors. The left-hand panel (Plate
126) features a rare subject for ukiyo-e (and, alas, a bird
practically extinct today), the Japanese stork, while the
right-hand panel features the more customary cranes, all
in full flight. The style of depiction is more graceful and
natural than that of the previous 'Carp and Turtles'. The
panels do not, however, attempt to achieve overly graceful, decorative patterns: and I suspect that this was because Hokusai wanted to reflect the true characters of
these essentially ungainly birds. In this we may glimpse
something of the artist's view of realism: getting at the
heart of things.

125 *Above* Carp and Turtles. Kakemono in heavy colours on silk; dated 1813. 11 × 36¼ in / 28 × 92 cm. Signed Hokusai.

126 *Right* Flying Storks and Cranes (detail). Painting in heavy colours on silk, originally mounted on two sliding-doors (now remounted as a screen); *c.* 1810. 61½ × 10 in / 156 × 25 cm. Signed Hokusai.

NOTES

1 It should be noted that *kakemono*, 'hanging-scroll' paintings, often feature large blank spaces at top and, to a lesser extent, bottom. These are of compositional significance when the painting is seen as it should be, in a *tokonoma*-alcove and the viewer is seated in a low, leisurely position on the *tatami*-mats. For our purposes here, however, enlargement of detail has been deemed more important than showing the full frame for kakemono. In our captions the notation 'detail' thus refers to more drastic cropping of the design—where significant elements are omitted. In the first example below, background elements are important and cropping has been minimal. With Plate 109, however, the top quarter of the original is blank, and has been deleted here.

2 I have just noticed that this work was included in the *Catalogue* of the first and only great exhibition of Hokusai paintings, that held at Tōkyō in 1900. The English catalogue, by the pioneer connoisseur of the time, Ernest Fenollosa, is a masterpiece both of soaring erudition and resounding prose—such as the description of the colours in the sash here: 'These greens are strangely got; the ground a mere breath of olive, shot with light robin's egg clouds, small leaves in sage green, and birds in claret brown. . . .'

3 This painting, incidentally—derived from a Japanese collection—is unlikely to have been known in Europe; nevertheless it bears interesting affinities to Van Gogh's drawing 'Flying Swallows' (see fig. *right*; No. 58 in the 1951 Amsterdam catalogue *Rembrandt/Hokusai/Van Gogh*). It has always been my contention that, whether in literature or art, such coincidental resemblances are far more intriguing than strictly 'comparative' influences—a view that has never been accorded any welcome in academic circles. (On this theme see my 'Saikaku and Boccaccio: The Novella in Japan and Italy', in *Monumenta Nipponica* Vol. XV (1959–60), pp. 87–118; reprinted in my *Studies in Edo Literature*, Tōkyō, in press. Predictably, this paper was originally rejected by the journal *Comparative Literature*, on the grounds of being 'insufficiently comparative'.)

One may also fruitfully compare this fan-painting with the master's more decorative treatment of the same subject, twenty years later, in our Plate 227.

4 One student of ornithology has proposed that the subject is a *yotaka* or nightjar, rather than a raven or crow. But it must be pointed out that such subjects tend to follow traditional lines in Japanese art, even when the approach is unconventional. Thus 'Dawn Raven' was a standard theme of art (and of the ballad, as we saw in Chapter VIII); and a 'nightjar' would probably be depicted only in a book on Rare Birds. The scientist should probably not try to analyse ukiyo-e too literally: Hokusai, in creating an individualistic raven might, by chance, make it look like some other bird that he had never seen. (On the 'nightjar' problem see the journal *Andon* No. 10, 1983.)

5 Naturally the brocade mounting of the kakemono became, to some Japanese eyes, almost as important as the painting itself; and even today the more discriminating native collectors may spend large sums on remounting a painting with antique brocades that match both the painting and the room in which it is intended for hanging.

6 Until the (unlikely) day when someone devises a computer that can confidently determine both exact age and absolute authenticity in such paintings, the question of Hokusai forgeries is likely to remain a very complex field (cf. my articles cited at end of Bibliography, p. 316).

8 This interesting seal has customarily been misread by Western scholars—for example, J. Hillier cites it as 'Kishutsu Kisoku' (*The Art of Hokusai in Book Illustration*, 1980, pp. 269, 272, 274), and the specialized catalogue *Hokusai and his School* (Haarlem, 1982, p. 16) gives it as 'Kinshu dasoku'. (Regarding Hokumei, see Appendix, p. 312.)

Vincent van Gogh, *Flying Swallows*. Drawing.

XII
Teacher without School:
the Artist as Showman

1

WHATEVER the problems of painting-authentication, we are on firmer historical ground when we turn to the artist's paintings for public exhibition which were deemed worthy of recording—and sometimes copying—by his contemporaries, even though the originals are not always extant. For example, it is recorded that, in the Second Month of 1799, the Master prepared both a framed *ema* panel and a group of impressive votive-lantern-paintings for the Mimeguri Shrine, to much popular acclaim. This was particularly important to the artist at this juncture as he had recently changed his name, from Sōri to Hokusai. There were likewise, in 1806, designs for brocade curtains made for a village in rather distant Kai Province, featuring Dragon and Tiger portrayals. These works are now lost, but others are still preserved. Of historical importance—but woeful condition—is the large *ema*, or votary shrine-painting on wood, a detail of which is shown in Plate 127. As is customary in such framed panels, the subject is a traditional one: a famed hunting-party at Mt Fuji, held by the Shōgun Yoritomo in the year 1193. The most exciting episode is that depicted here: the valiant samurai Nitan no Shirō subduing a wild boar single-handed (a theme to appear later in *Hokusai gakyō* and *Fugaku hyakkei*). The panel is dated Sixth Month of 1806, and was painted by the artist during an extended journey through Kazusa (Chiba), for the Hie Shrine in Kisarazu (across Edo Bay), which still treasures the work.[1] Like most shrine votary-tablets this was left open to the elements and hence the pigments are much damaged. But the wild boar in the foreground is said to have been defaced intentionally by a village boy, who became terrified at the animal's fierce gaze.[2]

Another large painting still extant is the 'Cherry-blossoms' panel done for the Chōsen-in Temple (in distant Chichibu) in the Third Month of 1812. It was also in the Tenth Month of the same year that the artist executed his famous 'Nagoya Daruma', to be discussed below. Before that, however, we must look at the first of the artist's elaborate Public Exhibitions of his painting skills: a feat perhaps commonplace enough today, but hardly so in Japan of the early nineteenth century (for an early copy see Plate 129).

This grand event took place in the spacious grounds of the Gokokuji, a temple on the northern outskirts of Edo, at festival-time in the Fourth Month of 1804, the artist being now 44 years of age. Before an admiring crowd Hokusai himself painted, in *sumi*, the bust-portrait of the Zen Saint Daruma on a giant expanse of composite paper some 170 *tatami*-mats in size (i.e. nearly 350 square metres). The pigment was prepared in a saké-cask; for brush the artist used a reed broom. At first, the puzzled onlookers thought he was painting a landscape; it was only when some of them clambered up on the Temple roof that they could perceive that it was a half-length portrait of the Buddhist patriarch: '. . . the mouth large enough that a horse could walk in, eyes bigger than a man: the spectators entirely awed at his astonishing feat. . . .'[3]

In this showy exhibition of his skills we can glimpse something of the artist's qualities—and quirks—that we have only hinted at up to now: a massive ego, a fervent ambition, a desire for popular acclaim, even a certain exhibitionist tendency. These are all qualities we tend to condone—even expect—in geniuses, providing their art comes up to the level of their egos.

This was not, indeed, to be the last of such public feats: we shall soon come to the artist's similar exploit in Nagoya; before that, in a Honjo piazza he once created a Jumbo Horse; at the Ekōin, a temple east of Edo (the exact years are uncertain), he went even further by contrasting his skills—at first painting a huge figure of the God of Luck, Hotei, and then drawing a sketch of two sparrows on a grain of rice, 'which one could barely make out with the naked eye'.[4]

Although there are records of rather large 'exhibition paintings' before this (e.g. by the eighteenth-century monks Kokan and Hakuin, as well as Keiho and his great pupil Shōhaku), these were of sizes suitable for display in a temple-hall; and such monumental outdoor exhibitions seem to have been Hokusai's invention. This was, to be sure, an age of immense and insatiable *curiosity*—on the part of both scholars and the masses; and such feats by the artist must be seen as one facet of this love for new things, and for spectacle.[5]

Various stories have come down of other impressive (if less gargantuan) Hokusai exploits: executing paintings rendered upside-down, or with odd objects in lieu of brush—fingers, flasks, boxes, even chicken-eggs, for instance—and there is at least one known example of his painting in the curious *gyakuhitsu* technique, in which the bamboo *handle* of the brush is employed for 'stick-painting'. Another story, probably from the 1830s, tells how Hokusai was summoned, together with the classical master Tani Bunchō, before the august Shōgun. After Bunchō had executed a formal design, Hokusai strode up, and on a large expanse of Chinese-style paper painted a decorative background of blue water. Then, magician-like, he produced a cock from its cage, swiftly dabbed its claws with vermilion and had it dash crowing across the paper, the artist proclaiming, 'Maple-leaves on the Tatsuta River!' Whether all such anecdotes are true or not, they do reveal what Hokusai's contemporaries—and possibly the artist himself—thought he was capable of.

2

We have already followed the Master in his various name-changes nearly to the end of the eighteenth century—most notably that to 'Hokusai' around 1796. To these must now be added the pseudonym Tokimasa (also pronounced Tatsumasa), which was employed from 1799 to at least 1810, particularly in books. Its first part refers, as we have seen, to the 'Dragon' of the artist's birth-year, and echoes his early name Tokitarō.[6]

Even more significant is the *nom d'artiste* 'Gakyōjin'—Man Mad with Painting—of 1799–1808 (and with variations thereafter). In this we first discover the Master declaring his own eccentricity, his passion for his art. There had been manic artists before him, but seldom had they made their mania so public. Several other *noms de plume* are noted in the Appendix, but one deserves special notice, 'Fusenkyo', which was first used briefly in 1799, possibly in *c*. 1808, and taken up again in 1822. This compound has two meanings, the first and most profound, 'Unsullied by one's surroundings', combining a Taoist concept ('Live in the mundane world, yet remain detached from it') with the Buddhist 'lotus flowering amidst the mud'. But besides this, there is a more typically Edoite interpretation: 'unattached to one's abode'—the latter concept ideally matched to Hokusai's well-known penchant for moving residences.

To these early aliases must now be added Taito, Raishin and Raito. Taito was employed from about 1810 up to 1820 and, as we have seen, was derived from the artist's fervent belief in St Myōken—God of the North Star—being an abbreviation of Taihokuto, one of the Seven Polar Stars. The names Raishin and Raito (Lightning Star), possibly original creations of the artist, are said to derive from an incident when Hokusai was struck by lightning (not directly, but close enough for him to be hurled into a roadside paddy) while on a pilgrimage to the Myōken Buddhist temple. The names Taito and Raishin will be especially familiar to book-collectors, as they appear in the artist's most famous sketch-series, the *Manga*. The *nom d'artiste* Taito is tricky, however, for Hokusai passed it on to a pupil late in 1819. The latter proved to be a very good painter and illustrator, and though we today call him 'Taito II', his actual works are usually signed simply 'Taito'. They may be distinguished from those of the Master by a certain weakness of design, concept and brush-stroke, but in the case of undated sketches have often been mistaken for the work of Hokusai.

The prefaces to two notable sketchbooks to be discussed below—*The Quick Guide to Drawing*, Series I and II—seem to be in Hokusai's own handwriting and feature the curious *noms de plume* Kyōrian Bainen and Tengudō Nettetsu. Possibly the artist's impulse to write the prefaces arose from a feeling that the literati usually called upon for such tasks could not really comprehend the intent of these complex and innovative works (the equivalent of a writer today preparing his own jacket-blurbs). Such 'one-time' pseudonyms may be passed over as curious foibles, but to the collector and student many of Hokusai's aliases provide a vital key to dating the artist's work—and distinguishing it from his pupils'—during these years. (For a

127 Samurai quelling Wild Boar by Mt Fuji. Detail of a large *ema*-panel in heavy colours on wood; dated 1806. 54¾ × 71 in / 139 × 180 cm. Signed Gakyō*jin* Hokusai, 'on travels'.

detailed listing see Appendix, 'Hokusai's Signatures and Art-names', p. 278.)

We know all too little of Hokusai's earlier pupils—Shunrō II, Sōri III, Shinsai and the like—other than that they sometimes succeeded to his previous art-names. With the 1800s, however, Hokusai was able at last to establish himself as a popular leader of the ukiyo-e movement; indeed, he formed an effective rival to the school of Toyokuni (which had largely taken over the figure-print after the passing of Utamaro).

Attracted by his eccentric, innovative style, Hokusai's new pupils came from all walks of life: of the more notable ones Hokuba, for example, was a retired government official, and Hokkei had been a fishmonger. Other significant disciples of this period were Shigenobu (who, as we have seen, married one of Hokusai's daughters), Hokutai and Hokusū—as well as the Master's own daughter O-Ei. This

128 O-Ei (Hokusai's daughter): Musical Trio. Kakemono in colours
on silk; *c.* early 1810s. 18½ × 26¼ in / 47 × 67 cm. Signed Ōi, 'Miss
Tipsy' ['Ei-jo'—a play on words with her name, O-ei (flourishing),
and *ei*, inebriated].

was only the beginning of a long line of pupils—major and
minor but most now forgotten—the total eventually to
reach some three hundred in number. (For detailed listing
see Appendix, 'Hokusai's Pupils and Followers'.) In 1811
one of these disciples (the proprietor of a Yoshiwara tea-
house) even succeeded to the august name 'Hokusai',
though he never produced any work of note. By this time,
however, that *nom d'artiste* had become so firmly associated with the Master that he was, in effect, obliged to
identify most of his subsequent, wilful pseudonyms with
the prefix *saki-no-Hokusai* — 'Formerly Hokusai'. Even he
could not escape the fact that people tend to identify
names with the objects that they represent.

The restless and ever-ambitious artist, now well into
middle age, soon perceived the limitations of the 'direct
disciple' system. His strategy in seeking to extend his influence and spread his fame was to commence a series of
woodblock-printed 'guides for artists', with which he
hoped to make his name renowned throughout the land
and to establish the Hokusai Style as the standard of 'modern art'. In this he was to succeed to a surprising degree;

yet—with the uncertain tuition/royalty system of the
time—none of this acclaim was to make his life much
easier.

It may be added that though we speak of 'ukiyo-e
schools' these were, in fact, of many varieties: ranging
from rather large studios such as those of the Katsukawa
(Shunshō) and Utagawa (Toyokuni) to informal gatherings
of interested pupils and amateurs. In Hokusai's case,
though he loved to teach, by his own nature he was never
one to organize a formal 'atelier'. He taught—over his 55-
year career after independence—some 150 known pupils,
and undoubtedly an even larger number who neither published nor left signed paintings. Few of these could have
been live-in apprentices; most presumably visited the
Master regularly, but others—including those from out-
lying areas like Nagoya—received only occasional instruction by correspondence, and rare visits. The exception to
this would, of course, be Hokusai's own daughters (who
deserve, indeed, a separate study of their own), and particularly O-Ei, whose art-name was Ōi—a homonym for
'Hey', the Master's customary manner of summoning her.[7]
Definitive paintings by O-Ei are rare, which may well support the view that she was preoccupied in anonymously
assisting her father in his *oeuvre*. The 'Musical Trio' of Plate
128 is one of her few genuine, known works. In this intricate composition we view two girls and a woman intently

performing on *koto*, *kokyū* and samisen. The style is clearly patterned after her father's, but there is a noticeable lack of interrelation among the participants and a more detached, less intensely individualistic manner than one finds in the Master himself. (The signature includes the notation 'Miss Tipsy'—which may reveal one facet of O-Ei's personality; but such a carefully executed painting on silk was unlikely to have been finished in a day, and the notation presumably indicates the artist's mental state at the time of completion—or, more likely, a general fondness for drink.)

The Hokusai School may well have been not only the largest in Japanese art-history under a single master, but also unique in making wide use of the modern techniques of mass education: printed texts, after-hours instruction, correspondence courses, advertising and self-publicity stunts.

3

Although Hokusai was obviously fond of travel—part of his passion for actually seeing things before he tried to paint them—we possess no diaries or notes and must infer his activities from stray references in rare letters or book-colophons. From these it is clear that he travelled widely in the regions of Edo (Tōkyō) and Ōsaka, as well as in the adjacent Provinces north and west of Edo, and particularly those surrounding Mt Fuji. The radius of this area may span only 700 kilometres or so, but when it is remembered that these journeys were by foot and that it took, for example, up to two weeks from Edo to Ōsaka, the artist's penchant for travel may perhaps be better appreciated. Travel is, indeed, all too easy for us today and—through forsaking the experiences en route—has lost much of its meaning. In old Japan a journey by horse or palanquin was pretty much the privilege of the samurai or the nobility, and the plebeian not only went by foot, but required besides introductions, a kind of 'internal passport' to cross the several government barrier-stations along the way. Hokusai's journeys, comparable to 'expeditions' today, were probably undertaken alone, or sometimes with a pupil or two.

Of all these varied sites in East and West Japan, however, two were most significant for Hokusai—both over a week's journey from Edo by foot—the first, Nagoya to the West, and the other (in later years), Obusé in the mountains of Shinano. The Nagoya connection was to prove, indeed, a most important one in relation to the artist's work, both for the network of influential disciples he cultivated there, and for his strong connection with the major publisher Eirakuya, who was headquartered in Nagoya (with a branch in Edo).

The stimulus for Hokusai's first sojourn in Nagoya, in 1812, seems to have been an invitation from his pupil Bokusen—a samurai of the local Owari Fief—who had earlier studied with Utamaro in Edo. The artist stayed a full six months with Bokusen and developed a varied circle of pupils so that Nagoya became, in effect, a veritable centre of Hokusai popularity. It was at this time, indeed, that the first volume of the famed *Hokusai manga* was con-

ceived and published.

The immediate purpose of Hokusai's second long sojourn in Nagoya, some five years later, from the early spring of 1817, was preparation of further volumes to the *Manga*; for one of the two principal publishers of these sketchbooks was the leading house of Eirakuya. It was also during this stay that the Master produced the sketches for several other 'artists'-guides' of the late 1810s. Towards the end of his visit, moreover, Hokusai—with the support, if not instigation, of his publisher—planned and carried out yet another of those prodigious outdoor Jumbo Painting Exhibitions, which was to do more to impress his name on the public than any of his more worthy works would ever do.

This event—again the execution of a huge Daruma mural—occurred in the grounds of the Nishikakesho, a Nishi-Honganji temple-branch on the outskirts of this samurai capital. Rather in contrast with the results in blasé Edo, the Exhibition proved a major attraction in the provincial capital, and was recorded in several manuscripts, broadsheets and other publications of the time. It was performed before an audience of hundreds, consuming a full afternoon and several buckets of *sumi* and other pigments: after which the giant sketch (here, some 240 square metres in area) was raised on a platform for all to see—a viewing repeated the following day. Like all such public displays, this great mural is now lost, but there are several contemporary, much-reduced copies and prints that attest to the impression it made on Hokusai's spectators.[8] There is a tendency to see a self-portrait in any of the Master's old men; but it is amusing to find here that even the Buddhist patriarch has aged more than a decade since the earlier giant mural of 1804 (Plate 129).

The artist's popularity in Nagoya was such that the

129 The Zen Patriarch Daruma. Painting in *sumi* on paper. A reduced copy, *ōban* size, of Hokusai's grand Edo mural of 1804.

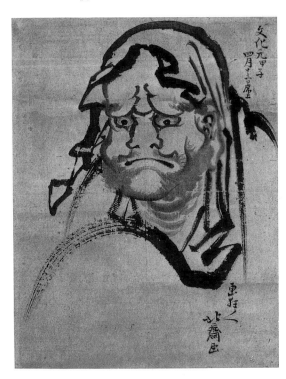

painting was featured in *surimono*-prints, and a ditty was even composed on the Exhibition theme combining the measurements of the Great Daruma ('eyes, six-feet wide') with the calendric 'short-months' of the year 1817. Made up entirely of puns, the doggerel is quite untranslatable—consisting mainly of homophonetic numbers that convey the idea:

> Hokusai / beautifully drew / the Daruma / but the short-month was / a bit foreshortened at the base

Acclaimed thus in verse and song, it might well be thought that Hokusai would rest on his laurels, and perhaps degenerate into a 'celebrity'. This was not his nature, however. He revelled in publicity but in his heart well knew that even if some considered him 'the greatest' that was not enough: he had yet to satisfy the ultimate critic, himself—and life was all too short to permit the leisure of basking in past accomplishments.

The results of Hokusai's long, first Nagoya sojourn were not only the acquisition of greater fame and further disciples, plus an influential new publisher, but also an enhanced awareness of the differing styles of painting then flourishing in *Western* Japan—the source of most Edo culture—especially of the Maruyama-Shijō school, and of Ōsaka/Nagoya ukiyo-e. And by the same token, the artist in effect gave up his lead in the illustration of popular novels: such painstaking work simply required more time and extended concentration than a 'popular artist' could possibly spare. Patronage and fawning disciples obviously provided him with as good an income as he had enjoyed in Edo, with less hard work and greater, more direct acclaim. Possibly it was this personal element—a more intimate feeding of the artist's ego, if you like—that turned Hokusai from his solitary work of book-illustration to the more satisfying world of the art-manual.

The elaborate public exhibition in Nagoya was undoubtedly arranged and financed by the publisher Eirakuya as a publicity stunt; and indeed, it helped make Hokusai's name renowned throughout West Japan—and surely was one factor in increasing the sales of the *Manga* and other 'guides for artists', accounting to some degree for the large numbers of these volumes extant even today. Characteristically, a Hokusai letter to the publisher written some ten days after the event expresses his fervent wish for a loan; and there is evidence that, towards the end of the year, the artist travelled from Nagoya as far west as Ōsaka, Ise, Kii and Yoshino.

Having thus established something of the background of Hokusai's life and ambitions at this period—his increasing attention to the publication and dissemination of the Hokusai Style—it is with no little interest that we turn to his first attempts to convert the traditional text-and-picture-book into the manual-for-artists. Amazingly, he managed to make the books both commercially attractive and yet true to his own lights and style.

4

To a degree perhaps difficult to comprehend today, sketching and painting were among the most passionately favoured hobbies of the Japanese in the Edo Period—perhaps rivalled only by amateur versification. Manuals for painters in the classical style—sometimes derived from Chinese sources—had flourished from the mid-eighteenth century, first in Kyōto and Ōsaka, but with the end of the century in Edo as well, with the innovative work of Masayoshi. Such volumes formed one of the staples of commercial publication, though they are collected by connoisseurs today simply for their great beauty, the original, practical function quite neglected. Hokusai—and his publishers—thus took up a traditional, popular genre and adapted it to the more modern world of ukiyo-e: but an ukiyo-e that was to become increasingly removed from the traditional Floating World of courtesans and actors, following both the taste of the times and the influence from the amateur painters who formed the principal market.

The Master's 'sketchbooks' consisted, in effect, of plate after plate of woodblock-printed pictures issued with a clear practical aim: to provide detailed guides for amateur painters (as well as artisans), both in subject-matter and in method of depiction. In addition there was a more general, educational market for such picture-books—in an age when schooling was often informal—as well as an influential class of impulse buyers, who simply bought these little volumes because they were so intrinsically fascinating.

With an artist as prolific and multifaceted as Hokusai it is no easy task to organize a reasonably detailed discussion of his work: and this is particularly true of his book-illustration, which covers the full seven decades from 1780 to 1849. We have already said something of the early illustrated novelettes, and somewhat more of the magnificent picture-books and albums of Hokusai's early to middle period, and of his varied plates to the 'Gothic novels' of the following decade. What remains to be discussed here of the Master's middle period—c. 1810–30—is the vast treasure-house of less luxuriously printed picture-books and artists' primers, genres in which Hokusai continued to publish almost to the day he died. For simplicity these three decades of illustration will be consolidated in four chapters, with only the artist's culminating *Hundred Views of Fuji* given separate, later treatment. This rather summary discussion of these hundreds of kaleidoscopically fascinating volumes must be justified not only on grounds of space limitation, but also because in the first place they are often miniaturistic in nature, interesting more to artists and collectors than to the general reader; secondly, considerable space has been given to them in the Appendix (and Figs. 193–229); and finally, we are fortunate in having a readily available monograph on aspects of the subject (Jack Hillier's *The Art of Hokusai in Book Illustration*, 1980).

Even to the specialist the sheer number and variety of Hokusai's 'sketchbooks' can be confusing. Indeed, some aficionados in Japan simply term all these hundreds of varied volumes 'Hokusai *manga*': a commendable way of clearing the mind and concentrating on more important things. However, some more detailed description of the more significant of these multiple series of similar-sounding books will I hope be useful here.

Since a good part of Hokusai's reputation rests on such printed 'sketchbooks' it is with no little interest that we seek out his earliest work in this genre. So far as I have been able to discover, this is represented by a rare set of two small books issued separately during the year 1810—just as the artist was in the midst of his major work in the illustration of fiction. The facetious title of these slim volumes is *Ono-ga-Bakamura mudaji-ezukushi* (Foolish Ono's Nonsense Picture-Dictionary). (The title includes a pun on the name of the famous ninth-century scholar and statesman Ono-no-Takamura who, in legend at least, was renowned for his adroit use of word-plays.) The publisher was Tsutaya Jūzaburō II—son and successor of Hokusai's early patron.[9]

Because of the pictographic nature of Sino-Japanese characters, there had long been a minor artistic tradition of adapting them to playful pictures. Hokusai—and his literary collaborator in the books, Sensō—carried this kind of parlour-game one step further by compiling a guide for amateur artists in which each design is formed of a series of simple lines and curves, more or less resembling calligraphic letters, and with the order of suggested execution

clearly cited. By this method the novice student—even a child—could form a recognizable drawing while employing the familiar brushstrokes of calligraphy: an excellent mnemonic device which also skilfully utilizes the previously acquired, inherent skills of the learner.

These volumes are significant not only as the first clear evidence of Hokusai's penchant for didactic education in art, but also for the Master's passion for analysis of the elements of design: a feature that was to characterize much of his book-work in the coming decades, and prove a deciding factor in the artist's style itself. One cannot but suspect that Hokusai got hints of this approach from the fragments of scientific knowledge that were gradually entering Japan from the Occident. As we have seen, he had avidly studied Western perspective techniques, as well as the principles of copperplate printing and even Western anatomical texts. This analytical approach is not typically Japanese; future research may well be able further to clarify the Master's role as one of the 'Renaissance men' of this Japanese Age of Enlightenment (on which theme see the discussion below).

Given the nature of the subject one does not expect to

130 Mouse and Sacred Jewels. Plate from *Foolish Ono's Nonsense Picture-Dictionary*, Series I, 1810. (See also Plate 131.)

131 Flying Bats. Plate from *Foolish Ono's Nonsense Picture-Dictionary*, Series II, *c.* 1810. (See also Plate 130, and Books, No. 159.)

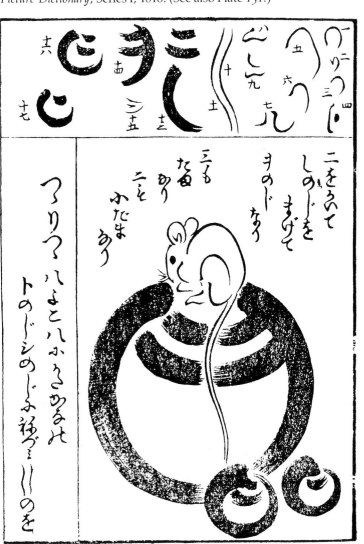

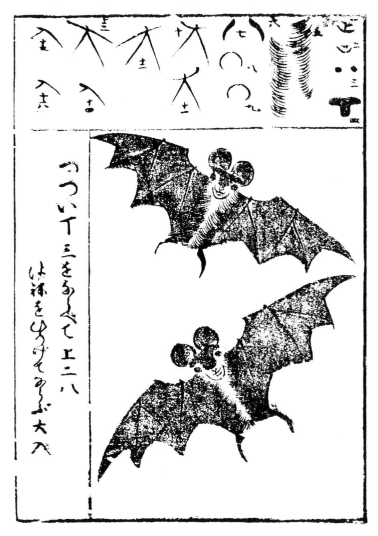

find masterpieces of art in these little volumes. Indeed, for their enjoyment one really needs to know written Japanese. Two typical examples must suffice, therefore, and even here we have not space for a full translation and explanation (though this would, I feel sure, fascinate anyone engaged in art-education).

Plate 130 shows a mouse perched upon the Sacred Jewels of Hotei, the God of Plenty (who is thus suggested, but not actually depicted). The directions in the upper column are numbered, top-to-bottom/left-to-right, beginning with the mouse's ears. Each of the strokes is related to a Chinese character or a letter of the Japanese *kana* syllabary—seventeen in all, to complete the design. The explanation within the picture gives details on executing the Jewels, and at the left is a limerick including mnemonic notes on the order of sketching. One can well imagine the art-novice of the time assiduously but silently reciting these lines as he impressed his friends with such an 'impromptu picture'.

The plate of 'Flying Bats' (Plate 131)—another lucky symbol in Japan—is more pictorially interesting and involves a more complex combination of elements: all effective memory-devices, even though sometimes only remotely related to actual calligraphic forms. Unlike many such didactic models, the design succeeds in stirring the imagination as well as serving a practical function. There could indeed be no more effective introduction to the techniques of Japanese painting than this 'Nonsense Picture-dictionary'.

Rather surprisingly, these two little books did not sell all that well, and hence are little known today, even to Hokusai specialists. Perhaps the concepts were too unusual for immediate popularity; perhaps the publisher (no match for his great father) neglected publicity and promotion. These volumes remain, thus, an esoteric curiosity—yet a vital first start in the artist's feverish activities as an art-teacher in the coming years. (The colophon to the First Series includes the publisher's 'Catalogue of Katsushika Hokusai Taito Picture-books'—the present two series, plus three other volumes, 'intended for the novice who would master the art of sketching': but of these latter, only the first title seems actually to have been published.)

Whereas Hokusai's first drawing-manual bordered somewhat on the party-game and tended to strain for its effects, his next production in this line focused on the very essence of design. This was the more prosaically titled *Ryakuga haya-oshie* (Quick Guide to Drawing)—the First Series appearing two years later, in 1812.[10]

In this small volume we are treated not only to more naturally designed sketches by the artist, but are also shown the principles behind them. The volume is, in effect, a popular but artistically valid treatise on geometrical analysis and stereometric diagramming—the proposition being that most pictures can be broken up into circles and squares. Nominally, at least, Hokusai takes his theme from an elliptical phrase in the Confucian classic *Meng-tze* (Mencius): 'Without compass or ruler, even the sage cannot draw a perfect circle or square.' But to this the artist adds something of his knowledge of Occidental art and—East and West fused in his brain—goes on to create a brilliant adaptation that belongs to neither world, but to the Master's own special universe.

It was, I think, Cézanne who expounded something similar two generations later; and it seems likely that Hokusai himself derived the basic idea from abroad—e.g. certain Dutch painting-manuals of the mid-seventeenth century—but indirectly, perhaps through the excerpts in Chūryō's *Kōmō zatsuwa* (Discussions on Europe) of 1787. Once the concept entered Hokusai's head, however, it underwent all kinds of transformations, so that the result is a work of real creativity and, I suspect, far ahead of its time, both in theory and practice.

But though the concept was not original with Hokusai, it proved ideally suited to the characteristic method of design which he was gradually evolving in these his middle years. And at the same time it provided a meaningful guide for the fledgling artist. Thus, while the preceding manual had taught the novice to draw by adapting the familiar strokes of calligraphy, the new textbook went a giant step further and taught the beginner to grasp the dynamics of a subject before he let the concept find expression on paper. This was very much like the sculptor's feeling of releasing the statue from its hiding-place within the block of wood or stone; and indeed, Hokusai's deft analyses of his own designs may sometimes strikingly resemble modern sculpture (Plate 132).

In this masterful pair of plates we see at right a traditional subject, the classical poet Su Tung-p'o riding his donkey in the snow (a theme later to make a famous large colour-print, Plate 273). To the contemporary eye, however, more striking will be the artist's analysis of his own work: a Don Quixote-like pair under a pine-tree to end all pine-trees. One cannot but exclaim, on viewing this remarkable Hokusai book, 'How modern!'—and this, in the sense that already in the early nineteenth century Hokusai somehow managed to foresee significant artistic movements that we tend to think of as belonging exclusively to our own times.

Unlike most drawing manuals, this one is surprisingly *inspirational*. One has the feeling that with a little practice one could, by adopting this basic method, acquire something of the essence of Far Eastern painting; and somehow grasp the sinews and *élan* that form the foundations of any drawing of note.

This fascinating little volume is indeed full of surprises, but one further example must suffice. Plate 133 shows a design of a horse and two bulls, all seated, each subject shown with its pair on the opposite page but arranged in rather asymmetrical order. The Western reader will most likely think that Far Eastern *sumi-e* painting itself is reduced to its basic elements. It may come as something of a shock therefore to see the masterful (but traditional) horse at left converted into a truly cubist Pegasus at right. This

132 *Opposite top* Poet on Donkey in Snow. Plate from *Quick Guide to Drawing*, Series I, 1812. (See also Plates 133–5 and Fig. 193.)

133 *Opposite bottom* Horse and Two Bulls. Plate from *Quick Guide to Drawing*, Series I, 1812. (See also Plates 132, 134–5.)

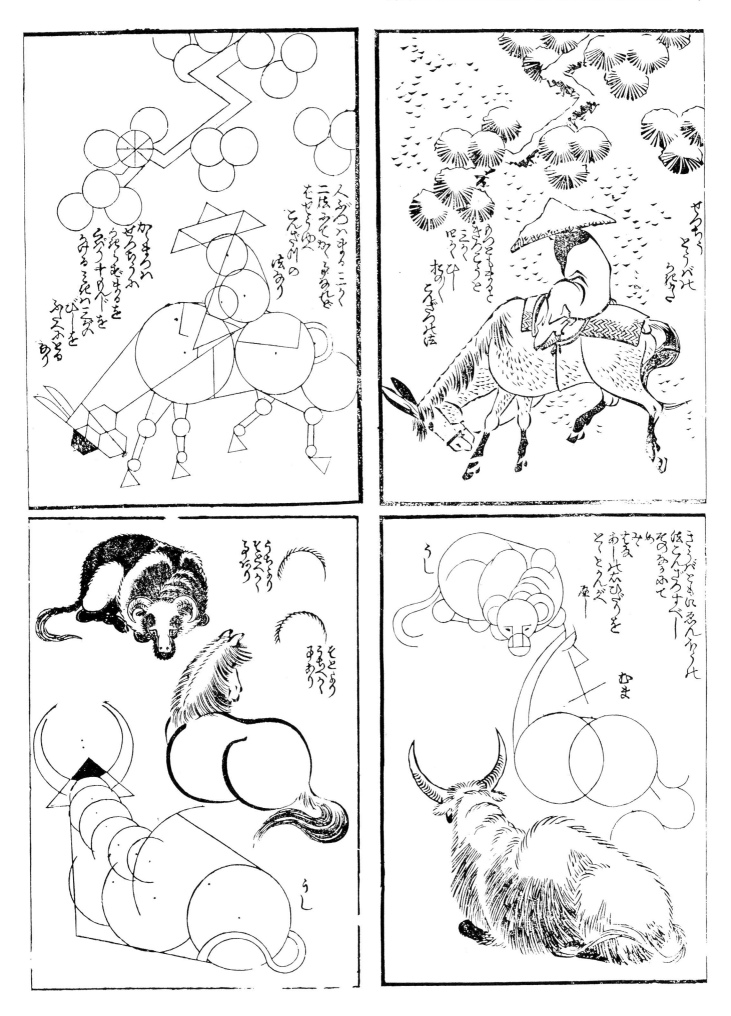

is, indeed, the very essence of a plump, seated horse; and though one cannot, of course, praise things simply because they are 'modern', one can (particularly after reading accounts of the prices fetched by modern art) suspect that Hokusai is sorely undervalued today—as he was in his own time.[11] He was in truth a master endowed with both genius and ambition, yet he lacked those more vital requirements for success: patron, publicity, connections, diplomacy, gallery, museum.

The texts accompanying the plates shown here serve mainly to identify the subjects and elaborate on the best methods of depicting them. Obviously one of the special interests of the volume will be, after studying it, to see to what degree the theory finds application in Hokusai's own great prints of a generation later (and how skilfully the method is concealed). I turn from this remarkable little volume only with regret; and if I leave the reader with a feeling of insatiability it is on purpose: each one of Hokusai's two hundred and more such books deserves at least a week of undisturbed reflection, a little monograph for itself. Every study of this prodigious artist is doomed, from its inception, to remain incomplete.

Series II to the same *Quick Guide to Drawing* appeared two years later, c. 1814, and, if less 'modern' in approach,

avoids the perils inherent in most sequels: repeating and diluting the same subject. Here, rather, the artist goes back to the method of his first such art-manual, reverting to the theme of drawing as a derivation of calligraphy. Unlike the earlier book, which seemed directed more to children and party-dilettantes, the actual sketches are more serious, fully conceived designs, even while fragmentary. Though only a minor sketch, Plate 134 will show this method clearly: the outlines of the figure form the very name of the subject, *Ka-ga-mi-ya*—'mirror-maker' (which, it will be recalled, was the profession of Hokusai's adopted family).

More significant is the example of Plate 135, in which one sees at right a typical depiction of an ukiyo-e courtesan, and at left the essence of the design as reduced to calligraphic forms. (For a similar composition rendered in more monumental size, see the painting of our prior Plate 120.) The text perforce (this being a publication directed to the market-place) summarizes the strokes and/or calligraphic elements in a limerick ('She grasps a thousand men's hearts. . . .'); but we can today perceive in such 'party-games' the vision of a true artist. His talents—albeit bent to commercial needs and sometimes apparently perverted—shine forth with his message like some lotus flowering from a muddy pond.

134 'Mirror-maker'—*ka-ga-mi-ya*—the word appearing at upper left, then adapted to form the actual sketch. Plate from *Quick Guide to Drawing*, Series II, c. 1814. (See also Plate 135.)

135 Yoshiwara Courtesan, with calligraphic outline and final design. Plate from *Quick Guide to Drawing*, Series II, c. 1814. (See also Plate 134 and Fig. 197.)

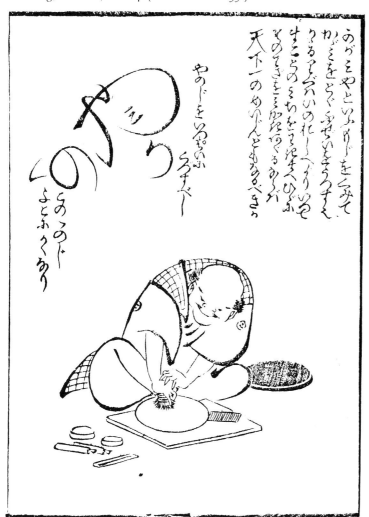

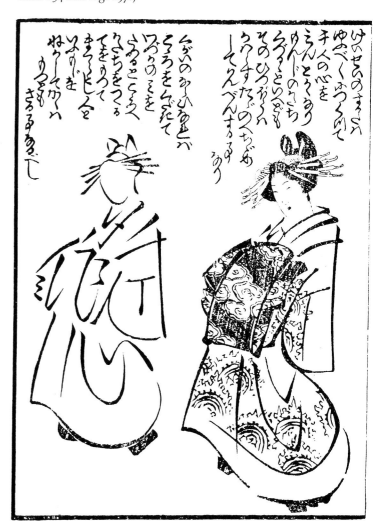

Unlike its predecessor, the *Quick Guide to Drawing* pair was an immediate success, running into several editions (the bibliography is complex; see our reference under Appendix, Books, No. 171). The fact that this—and most of Hokusai's subsequent 'sketchbooks'—remained popular, and in print, on through the end of the century (and even today, for that matter) is a striking indication of the artist's inherent powers and long-lasting appeal. Normally, changing fads and fashions were the deadly enemy of the ukiyo-e artist, who could only hope in vain for acclaim in succeeding generations (even if he desired such).

But whatever the intrinsic interest of these scattered early art-manuals, it is to their logical conclusion in the *Hokusai manga* that we must now turn for the essence of his work in this genre—and the basis for much of his later fame.

NOTES

1 It will be recalled that this was right after the period when Hokusai stayed several months with the novelist Bakin; just what happened to the artist's family during these sojourns is unclear.
2 Although I have not been able to trace any extant originals, there is evidence that Hokusai did many other varieties of functional art work (aside from the decorated envelopes and wrappers cited in the Appendix, pp. 287 and 292). Besides painting lanterns, festive banners and curtains, he even (according to an advertisement appended to a novel of 1823) was commissioned by the publisher Eijudō to paint sets of porcelain saké cups with miniature scenes of Edo depicted on them.
3 One should not normally cite the efforts of film-producers as evidence of anything, but in this case it may be worth noting that, for the Japanese movie *Hokusai manga* of 1981, such a scene was re-created at a Kamakura temple—joining 100 sheets of *tatami*-sized Japanese paper (i.e., each *c.* 1 × 2 m/3 × 6 ft.), and using some 4.5 litres of *sumi*-ink. This effort was repeated twice: once, to film the actor in the actual (and overly-theatrical) painting-performance—the result hardly very artistic or even very coherent; and once by a professional artist working over a period of two days to produce the final result: some indication that Hokusai's feat was not as easy as it sounds. I may add that this film attempts to augment the drama of Hokusai's famous 'Diving-girl and Octopus' scene—our Plate 205—by having the artist sketch it from the life and practically on his death-bed, rather than in his late 50s. This is probably more valid evidence of the director's lifelong obsession with sex (Kaneto Shindō—who was 69 himself at the time) than of Hokusai's.
4 Hokusai continued this type of exhibition painting even in later years. A giant painting of the Chinese warrior Shōki on horseback (*c.* 23½ × 13 ft/7.2 × 4 m), signed *zen*-Hokusai Iitsu, is said to have been extant up to the time of the Kantō Earthquake of 1923.
5 One is inevitably reminded of this kind of showmanship in Japanese *literature*, during that other 'golden age' of Genroku in the later seventeenth century; for example, the novelist-poet Saikaku's feat of composing over 20,000 haiku verses in a single session. (On this theme, see my doctoral dissertation *Saikaku: Novelist of the Japanese Renaissance*, Ann Arbor, 1958.) This was, one should add, an age in which public 'exhibitions' flourished: for example the giant straw/wickerwork dolls of legendary figures displayed at the Asakusa fairgrounds in 1820—the designs for the figures being prepared by Hokusai himself (and commemorated in prints).
6 Due to the characteristic ambiguity and/or pliability of the Japanese language, these ideograms can be read either Tokimasa or Tatsumasa—as well as, in Chinese style, Shinsei—'Dragon Star' (the second part being written with the character for 'government', which in ancient China was closely

The Zen Patriarch Daruma. Large-*ōban* broadsheet, after a reduced copy of Hokusai's great Nagoya mural of 1817.

connected with astrology). The reading 'Toki' was more frequent in artists' names—Kitao Tokinobu, for example—and I have here adopted the former reading in analogy with Hokusai's childhood name: written with different characters and *only* readable as 'Tokitarō'. (By the same analogy, the name of Hokusai's daughter—and pupil—might be read 'O-Toki' rather than 'O-Tatsu'; but the latter reading seems more suitable for a girl's name.)
7 Note, incidentally, that 'Ōi' is not only a homonym for 'Hey' but the characters also convey the meaning 'Follow Iitsu'—i.e. 'Obey Father'—and therefore this *nom d'artiste* probably dates only from the year that Hokusai adopted that name, 1819. [N.B. I once published (*Ukiyo-e* Nos. 52 and 72) three paintings then in my collection signed with an alternative second-character for 'Ōi' ('Follow the Meaning' rather than 'Follow Iitsu')—as possibly early works by Hokusai's daughter. This was purely a random hypothesis, however, and (as noted in *Ukiyo-e* No. 89, p. 128) conclusive evidence has yet to be discovered. Thus this second 'Ōi' (with the alternative name Gidō) may well but represent yet another lesser Hokusai pupil.]
8 One of these is reproduced *above*.
9 The direct inspiration for these volumes was probably Harumachi's *kibyōshi* novelette of 1783, *Sato-no-Bakamura mudaji-zukushi* (Foolish Ono's Yoshiwara Useless Word-plays), also published by Tsutaya.
10 The title is written with the characters *Haya-shinan*, but the preferred reading *Haya-oshie* is indicated in rubrics. In the publishers' advertisements, however, the more standard reading *shinan* also appears. Such variations are frequent in Edo texts, and do not affect the meaning—or translation—of titles; but they will naturally be confusing to students working only from romanized data.
11 Certainly, to a Japanese today there is no greater praise than for something to be called 'modern'. I also recall the sentiments expressed by an American reviewer of my earlier book, *Images from the Floating World*: 'All those delicate maidens wound in yards of silk ... all those macho warriors ... all those wistful, fading landscapes. You begin to yearn for a skyscraper or two.' I must confess to living in a different world from all these 'modern' people.

XIII
To an Unseen
Audience: Hokusai's
Sketchbooks for Artists

1

IT MAY SEEM curious to the Western reader that such great artistic and publishing efforts should have been directed at aspiring artists, who were surely only a minor group and mostly impecunious. On the contrary, amateurs with some interest in painting formed a good portion of the publishers' market, and a relatively affluent one at that. This phenomenon goes back first to the fact that Japanese characters were not only written with the same basic brush as *sumi-e* painting, but even employed many of the same basic strokes. Thus painting—or at least, brush-drawing—came relatively naturally to anyone who could write even the simple *kana*-syllabary.[1]

It may be recalled that in the eleventh-century *Tale of Genji*, Prince Niou dashed off some shunga sketches to console his distant sweetheart, the Princess Ukifune; Japanese novelists often did the preliminary illustrations for their own books (even today many make sketches of reference material rather than take photographs). The tradition of the *e-nikki* or 'picture-diary' was a long one even among non-artists; and the ability to make a quick impromptu sketch at a social party or literary gathering was much prized, and probably came easier to many than such related 'performances' as amateur musicianship, songs, or joke-telling.[2] My point is that the quite general demand for painting-manuals from the 1790s, like the accompanying rage for *kyōka*-versification, had very little to do with formal 'art-students'. Rather, such manuals catered to a very wide circle of dilettantes and dabblers: as well as to casual purchasers who, like many buyers of 'how-to' books, doubtless engaged in wishful thinking that the mere possession of one would augment their talents.

Yet having explained this background, how really pertinent is it to Hokusai himself? Certainly he was pleased that his books sold and that further commissions kept him busy and relatively affluent; but I suspect that he maintained a purposely blind eye to this social aspect of the painting-manual. He put his best efforts into every work, quite irrespective of the market—and his true eye was not only on his own fame, but also on that small coterie of disciples who, he hoped, would carry his style on for posterity.

It must be said that whereas the painter had mainly to contend with the taste (or lack of it) of his patrons, the print-artist had also to cope with the vagaries of his engravers (or more correctly, his woodblock-carvers). The latter were skilled professionals but not always objective craftsmen. Thus they sometimes—perhaps even at the publishers' urging—let their own view of popular taste intrude

in their work. Hokusai himself complains of this problem in a famous letter to a publisher and his engraver (see p. 242). And, of course, there were cases where a master perfectionist such as Hokusai could not necessarily demand the services of his favourite artisans. Thus in another letter, of 1835, the artist pleads:

> For the Engraver please get Mr Egawa Tomekichi of Asakusa Umamichi . . . by which, I refer to the fact that both the *Manga* and the *Chinese Verses*, though well-engraved, yet suffered from a lack of unity in the figures and the heads. On the other hand, the *Hundred Views of Fuji* [done by Egawa], from Series I through Series III, had not a single error. . . .

In fact Hokusai was in the practice of writing long letters to his publishers/printers regarding all such details in the production of his work—not only the all-important woodblock-carving, but even the finest points of printing such as *bokashi* (gradation). Thus he writes in one letter, 'As for the actual printing, the *fuki-bokashi* ['wiped-shading'] was fine for the first two hundred or so copies, but hardly so for the later issues. . . .' (It is my own sad experience—I must comment as an author of sorts—that such pleas often fall on deaf ears when commercial considerations are at conflict with the creator's ideals.)

As we have seen, in Hokusai's time planning, production, printing, publishing and sales were all handled by the same shop, though the actual writing/sketching/engraving and hand-printing were subcontracted to semi-independent writers, artists, block-carvers and printers. Thus the publisher was able to maintain strict control over all stages of bookmaking, and keep an eye on sales—a situation possible today only in private editions, if even then. There was also a very intimate contact between publisher and author/artist, the latter (as with the younger Kyōden and Utamaro) sometimes even boarding with the publisher. On the other hand, emolument was minimal and dependent on the arbitrary will of the publisher. When sales went well or when a potentially valuable author/artist seemed in danger of starving—or of going elsewhere—the pay would go up.

Would-be purchasers might visit the actual publisher's shop to examine the books and prints, which were displayed on racks, with advertisements hung on the walls. The larger publishers sometimes had branches (like Tsutaya at the Yoshiwara, which was in fact his original headquarters); itinerant pedlars handled routine sales. Moreover, especially with novels, hundreds of lending-bookstores flourished, their wares carried about by fledgling salesmen, which task, as we have already noted, was the young Hokusai's first known employment. (For views of two of the leading Edo publishers' premises, see our Plates 44 and 232; and for a somewhat imaginative rendering of the Chinese equivalent, Fig. 212.) Having thus set the scene, we may turn with perhaps greater understanding to that seminal work of Hokusai's later career, the *Manga*.

2

Even a cursory reading of the *Hokusai manga*—fifteen volumes of nearly four thousand different plates—may take one most of a day because so many of the designs are so intrinsically interesting. The labelled ones evoke images of the sages and scoundrels of history and legend; those unlabelled usually identify themselves readily enough, but a few treat of obscure Chinese and Buddhist subjects, the details of which do not come so easily to mind. Sometimes one tiny detail will require a full minute to savour; other pages one flips past with no flicker of interest at all (unless perhaps to remark, 'This man's concerns are really encyclopedic!'). And after this experience one wonders: how much of the real Hokusai has one caught here? is this really the essential man? where are the promises of major works of art so pregnant in his *oeuvre* around the turn of the century?

If there is any subject that deserves a book rather than a sub-chapter it is the *Manga* or 'Random Sketches'.[3] Here we can give only a brief survey of this fascinating source. But however superficial, some attempt must be made to describe and evaluate this vast, and sometimes ill-digested, mine of Hokusai material.

The impetus for the *Hokusai manga* lay, as we have already seen, in the artist's first visit to distant Nagoya, from the autumn of the year 1812. During his half-year sojourn there Hokusai taught many new pupils, some of them quite affluent. It was at their behest that he, gladly enough, allowed his random, sample sketches to be edited and copied for publication by the Nagoya firm of Eirakuya. (With Series II, publication was shared with Kakumaruya in Edo, though the blocks were later bought by Eirakuya, who issued the reprints most commonly found today.) To this chance origin may be traced the haphazard nature of the sketches themselves: had they been commissioned from the beginning, doubtless several series on more unified themes would have resulted—as was the case with the two earlier sketchbooks just discussed. (Indeed, from Series IV there is a greater tendency to systematize the themes treated, if not the method of depiction.)

But this random quality represents the very essence of this massive series—almost the epitome of the artist himself, at least as teacher. We view here, in effect, the instruction-materials of a great but rather disorganized *guru*, throwing off sketch after sketch like so many random yet brilliant ideas: it being left entirely to the disciple to make sense of them, to put them into some kind of order. In short, one looks in vain for any overall rhyme or reason to the *Manga*: these are indeed 'random sketches' and what unity they possess comes solely from their creator

himself, and from the writhing, vibrant mass of Nature and humanity that he manages to compress into each volume.

In contrast to the exaggerated and supernatural tone of the artist's *yomi-hon* illustrations, which immediately preceded the *Manga*, the emphasis here is on common humanity: displayed in uncommon attitudes but with warm, if detached affection. And it is not only humans but also birds, animals, fishes—even rocks and mountains—that take on an aura of humanity under Hokusai's magic touch. This is, indeed, the essence of his style: that each element in a design must be *alive*. It is no wonder that none of his hordes of pupils and emulators was able fully to ignite this spark of life in each and every stroke of the brush. As the *kyōka* poet Shokusanjin wrote in the preface to *Manga* Series III:

> It is easy to paint demons and deities that no one has seen, but difficult to paint ordinary people near at hand.... All that the Master sees, all that he imagines, all these—in full form and full spirit—issue without fail from his lively brush. And these are things from daily life; one cannot fake them—they appear before our very eyes, they take us by surprise.

With such picture-books as the *Manga*, the spirit of Far Eastern painting—as opposed to the special, closed world of ukiyo-e—became for the first time readily accessible to the plebeian classes of Japan. They immediately took Hokusai as their very own: a recognition that, in one form or another, has continued to this day.

As we have seen, the figure-design lay at the basis of Hokusai's *oeuvre* from the very beginning: actor-prints, genre picture-books, novels and novelettes which treated the figures of drama, legend, fantasy and the Floating World. In the *Manga*, however, the artist's attention turns more and more to plebeian life, to his own world rather than that of current fashion; and with this, his primary audience changes as well. Although sequels to this series ran on even after the artist's death, the first ten volumes, published between 1814 and 1819, form the basic canon, and it is these that will be discussed in this chapter.

The sheer variety of Hokusai's world (and not only that in the *Manga*) brings up the interesting question of how much he was indebted for this plethora to the very limitations and freedoms of Far Eastern painting, where figure-sketching was hardly ever done from an actual model. Japanese artists of course *looked* at people as a guide to sketching—and some of them doubtless looked hard. But when it came to the final painting they largely relied on the images they had stored in their minds. Hokusai, in particular, was a very master of this method.[4]

I have no wish to count the number of sketched figures in the *Manga* volumes, but they certainly run into the tens of thousands and to sketch even a portion of these from the life would have been an impossible feat. Thus, in a sense, it may well have been the 'idealized' nature of Japanese drawing that permitted completion of a massive work such as the *Manga*, where the theme is really nothing more or less than the artist's eye, his vision of the Universe.

A few samples of the Master's sketches will serve to display his considerable talents as well as the necessary

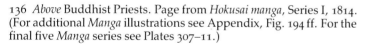

136 *Above* Buddhist Priests. Page from *Hokusai manga*, Series I, 1814. (For additional *Manga* illustrations see Appendix, Fig. 194 ff. For the final five *Manga* series see Plates 307–11.)

137 *Above right* Night Scenes. Page from *Hokusai manga*, Series I, 1814.

limitations of this miniature form—the actual figures are often only an inch high. But from the outset it must be emphasized that the *Manga* forms a veritable encyclopedia of Far Eastern life, history, legend and material civilization: often it would quite literally require a full page of text to explain a leaf of sketches that Hokusai probably dashed off in a few minutes. In the limited space available I would, frankly, rather show more art at the expense of less commentary.

Plate 136, for example, is obviously on the theme of Buddhist monks—on pilgrimage, inscribing a tomb-marker, aged abbot and grovelling acolytes, row of priests in cacophonous recitation of *sutra* as they hammer at their gongs; and, at the bottom, a monkish procession followed by porters with viands. The artist's viewpoint is a trifle satirical but not bitterly so, and would probably not greatly offend the subjects themselves, even if they perceived the humorous approach to their own solemn ceremonies. We see the priesthood as rather vain and self-centred, but no more so than humanity in general.

Plate 137 (from the same *Manga* Series I of 1814) takes us to yet another world, that of plebeian life and especially women. The setting is night, with a noodle-seller at upper left, a lantern-bearer at centre, and in the lower half of the design, a public-bathhouse scene—the proprietor's face buried in a book, as women of the lower classes undress and enjoy a steaming bath. One must not expect in such scenes any kind of unified composition: each figure or group exists quite for its own sake and any interrelation is coincidental. Nevertheless, there is often a certain pleasing pattern to the placement of the various elements, and this is about the most that one can expect in the way of overall composition: these books are, after all, meant as a guide to aspiring artists. And here, too, Hokusai's approach is typically semi-humorous: the individuals are eminently human though completely absorbed in their own private activities.

The exception to this lack of compositional unity occurs when, as in Plate 139, one page is limited to two clearly defined groups. Here, for example, the road-scene at top is of snow, whereas that at bottom is of rain; yet the two different situations fuse into a coincidentally unified view of passers-by as seen in two different seasons but under related circumstances. The page forms, indeed, a pair of attractive patterns, humanity all the more human for being faceless.

With the later series of the *Manga*, fragmentary views sometimes give way to overall ones, as in Plate 138—showing a comprehensive tableau of farm-work. Despite its scope, however, the scene resists transformation into a landscape: the artist persistently maintains his focus on the figures, and the background elements serve only as an incidental setting. Each fragment seems, indeed, as though intended for transformation into an independent painting—by the aspiring artists who formed the Master's principal audience. Such Hokusai tableaux must really be savoured at leisure: it is, for example, only on careful study that one discovers the reason for the contented look of the cow at right—and her reluctance to go out to the fields: she is nursing two little, whitish calves. (Interestingly enough, in this Series III will also be found a pictorial treatise on Occidental perspective.)

With Plate 140 (also from Series III of 1815) we note employment of a rather different technique, using a more cursive form of depiction, for figures, birds and animals. As always, we catch happy glimpses of little details that evoke famous Hokusai prints or paintings: the cooper, for example (who had first made his appearance in a *surimono* at the turn of the century), was to appear some fifteen years later in an impressive *Fuji* print (Fig. 60). Yet it would be a mistake to treat the *Manga* only as a harbinger

of greater things to come: in its total, it may confidently stand as a major work in its own right.

The legendary, too, takes prominent place in this series, as in Plate 141 (from Series VI of 1817) featuring the Buddhist guardian-deity Bareki, shown in a vertical, two-page spread. This warrior *par excellence* is conveniently equipped with fully six arms, and thus able not only to sharpen his two swords and rein in his fierce steed, but also to guard a fledgling wagtail and a baby monkey in his other hands—all at the same time. We note here, it may be added, further development of those nervous, wavy lines that are to characterize Hokusai's style from this middle-late period. Plate 142 from Series VIII—engraved in 1818 but published in the spring of the following year, 1819—is devoted to fat people, depicted humorously but not cruelly: they have their own pleasures and *raisons d'être* (and even their cats are fat). The next, Series IX, tends to excel in more impressive, larger figure-compositions, such as that of Plate 143, depicting the famous strong lady O-Kane, who could stop a wild stallion dead in its tracks by one stomp of her foot (this is also the subject of a derivative colour-print by Hokusai's follower Kuniyoshi).[5] And from the same powerful series is the samurai horseman of

138 Farm-work. Double-page from *Hokusai manga*, Series III, 1815.

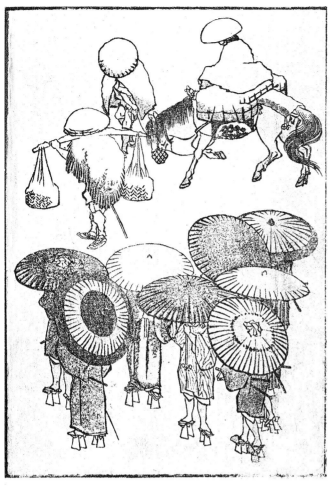

139 *Above left* Figures in Snow and Rain. Page from *Hokusai manga*, Series I, 1814. (A design that influenced Manet and Renoir.)

140 *Above* Miscellany. Page from *Hokusai manga*, Series III, 1815.

141 *Left* The God Bareki. Page from *Hokusai manga*, Series VI, 1817.

142 *Opposite top* Fat People. Double-page from *Hokusai manga*, Series VIII, 1818/19.

143 *Opposite bottom* Strong-Woman. Double-page from *Hokusai manga*, Series IX, 1819.

Plate 144: 'so swift that he was able to capture the god of Thunder'. In Plate 145 we find two Chinese legends combined in one tableau: the cruel fox-witch Dakki (Ta Chi) at left; the monkey-warrior Son-Gokū (Sun Wu-K'ung) at right, creating an illusion of supporting armies from his sleight of hand. A more thoughtful portrait is that of Plate 146 from Series X of 1819 depicting the fallen monk Seigen, gone mad for love of the maiden Sakura ('Cherry'), whose flowered robe is seen draped on his shoulder as cherry-petals fall from the sky.

We must now turn from this survey of the figure-work (albeit the most significant theme of the *Manga*), to look at the scenes of nature and human artefacts, commencing with Plates 147 and 148 from the First Series. Both the 'Trees' and the 'Houses' are obviously designed as guides to artists; indeed they are reminiscent of plates from earlier, classical painting-manuals. But examined more

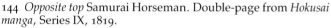

144 *Opposite top* Samurai Horseman. Double-page from *Hokusai manga*, Series IX, 1819.

145 *Opposite bottom* Fox-witch and Magic Monkey. Double-page from *Hokusai manga*, Series IX, 1819.

146 *Above* Apostate Monk. Page from *Hokusai manga*, Series X, 1819.

147 *Above right* Varieties of Trees. Page from *Hokusai manga*, Series I, 1814.

148 *Right* Types of Buildings. Page from *Hokusai manga*, Series I, 1814.

closely, one perceives that the individual characteristics of each tree, each dwelling, endow them with an identity all their own: these are not merely the forms of things, but their very personalities.

The famous 'Incoming Waves'/'Receding Waves' of Plate 149 (Series II, 1815) is again meant simply as a guide to amateur artists, yet succeeds even more in grasping the essence—almost, the soul—of the sea's solemn and studied movements. It is doubtful whether Hokusai's contemporaries recognized the fact, but seldom, if ever, has a manual on any subject featured fine art of this level of quality.

Bridges and boats, too, receive their due in Series IV (Plates 150, 151). Again, the practical function of the volume is surpassed by the Master's grasp of essentials: the scattered, unrelated elements are unified by the deeply imbedded impression that the images held in the artist's

mind before he ever set them to paper.

Animals and birds achieve their proper place in the *Manga* as early as Series I (Plate 153), and further in Series IV (Plate 154) and VII (Plate 152). Here again, their individual features are grasped by the artist with sure touch, and with attention to that near-human view of animal life that characterizes Hokusai's peculiar approach from this period on. Sometimes the very foliage assumes a personality of its own, as in the 'Akita Butterbur'—a kind of rhubarb, depicted in somewhat exaggerated size—of Plate 155. Here, it is the humans who seem like dolls, as the plants stoutly thrive and flourish in the driving rain.

It may be added that although the *Manga*—like many of Hokusai's copybooks for artists—includes some tinting

149 *Opposite top* 'Incoming waves/Receding waves'. Double-page from *Hokusai manga*, Series II, 1815.

150 *Opposite bottom left* Types of Bridges. Page from *Hokusai manga*, Series IV, 1816.

151 *Opposite bottom right* Types of Boats. Page from *Hokusai manga*, Series IV, 1816. (Compare the boat pattern in 'Tsukuda Island' of the *Fuji* Series, Fig. 62.)

152 *Right* 'Turtles in Sayama Pond'. Page from *Hokusai manga*, Series VII, 1817.

153 *Below* Various Birds. Page from *Hokusai manga*, Series I, 1814.

154 *Below right* Animals of the Zodiac. Page from *Hokusai manga*, Series IV, 1816.

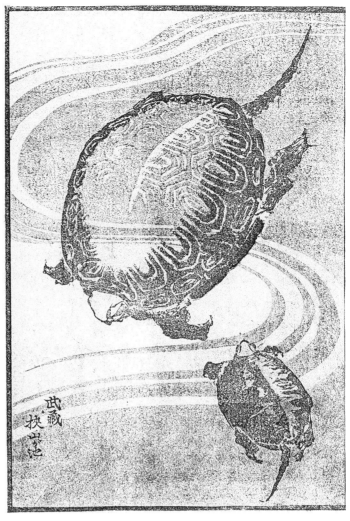

155 *Opposite top* 'Butterbur Plants in Akita'. Double-page from *Hokusai manga*, Series VII, 1817.

156 *Opposite bottom* Landscapes: Spring and Winter. Double-page from *Hokusai manga*, Series II, 1815. (Note that in such Japanese books the left and right pages are hand-printed separately, and therefore may vary in pigmentation, as here.)

157 *Above* Lakeside Fuji. Double-page from *Hokusai manga*, Series V, 1816.

(usually light grey and beige), the plates are almost equally effective in monochrome reproduction; indeed, the presence of the antique, softly pliant handmade Japanese paper is often more crucial to the success of the originals. There are occasional pages, however, where the subject demands colour, for example the delicately tinted 'Cherry-blossoms' of our Plate 182, in which the luxuriant flowers are shown close up, in shades of pink and yellow, with the aged tree-trunk itself placed at rear. At the same time, the design reveals again the almost lyrical, Romantic side of the artist's nature, and serves to refute critics who have termed the *Manga* a great 'debauch of sketches'.

For last we have reserved mention of the more fully developed landscape scenes in the *Manga*. These reach, in truth, a surprisingly advanced level of realization, considering the 'sketchy' nature of the anthology. In Series II, for example (Plate 156), two quite different scenes and seasons are combined on the same spread: plovers flying past

a bent willow, and boats moored by a snow-covered port. One could, I suppose, wish that each tableau had been given its own, more fully realized spread; yet so far as art-manuals go, one cannot imagine any better example to illustrate the varying moods of landscape—one raucous and active, the other mute and passive.

With the 'Lakeside Fuji' of Series V (Plate 157) the *Manga* begins to escape the bounds of the painting-manual and approach that of the picture-album (subject of our next chapter). The date is 1816, more than a decade before the commencement of the great *Fuji* prints; and, as we shall have occasion to repeat later, there was really nothing to stop Hokusai from producing his great landscape-prints from this period: only the absence as yet of a commercial market.

Presaging the major works of Plates 247 and 300 is the 'Maelstrom of Awa' of Series VII (Plate 158). The design is perhaps too decorative to stand as an independent composition, yet shows clearly the early stages of Hokusai's development as the 'Artist of Water' (he was of course the artist of many other things as well, and such popular epithets may be misleading, even self-defeating in their limitations). More cartoon-like is another wave-scene, of Series III, the 'Ship-ghosts', in which the shades of drowned seamen ride merrily over the crest of a bounding, surrealistic wave (Plate 159).

Matters of taste loom large in any selection or appreciation of such a potpourri as the *Manga*, and my own

158 *Above* 'The Maelstrom of Awa'. Double-page from *Hokusai manga*, Series VII, 1817.

159 *Left* 'Ship-ghosts'. Page from *Hokusai manga*, Series III, 1815.

favourite of the set, the snow-scene of Plate 160 in Series IX, may well seem lacklustre to the casual viewer. In the centre of a vast panorama of Ancient China a great army of troops progresses in a prolonged S-curve through the barren, snow-covered wastes under a leaden sky. This represents—as the brief caption informs us—the army of the warlord Duke Huan, who, reaching an impasse in his conquests, consulted with his horse. Unmoved by fleeting dreams of glory, the aged beast promptly turned about and headed home, speedily followed by the all-too-willing troops. To me, at least, this scene represents a minor masterpiece of literarily evocative landscape-with-figures, neither element dominating and the real protagonist, a diminutive old horse, personifying the invisible longings of most men for peace. This simple episode—and Hokusai's masterful design—may indeed illustrate one of the earliest recorded examples of horse sense.

For Hokusai's contemporaries these volumes surely provided fresh insight into the time-honoured events and

160 Returning Army. Double-page from *Hokusai manga*, Series IX, 1819.

legends of antiquity, as well as a fast-paced, kaleidoscopic view of everyday life. Yet their true importance tended to remain obscured by their practical function, and recognition came only much later, and a full continent removed.

This is not the place to detail the profound effect that Hokusai and his 'sketchbooks' had upon the intellectuals of the West from the later nineteenth century. Nevertheless, a few quotations may be of interest; and if they occasionally seem naive to us today, it must be remembered that these were the remarks of pioneers who had stumbled onto something as surprising—and vastly complex—as the ruins of Angkor Wat. Thus William Rossetti, for example, writing in 1863 of the 'Hoxai *Manga*' (at the time, the romanization of the Master's name was yet unsettled) observed:

> It assuredly belongs in various respects to the greatest order of art practised in our day in any country in the world. It has a daringness of conception, an almost fiercely tenacious grasp of its subject, a majesty of designing power and sweep of line, and clenching hold upon the imagination. . . . [One hopes that viewers of these books] may come to recognize their superior-

ity, in some respects, to anything which contemporary European art has to show us.

Such paeans were repeated by the artists and critics of the time (there were exceptions, Swinburne, for example), culminating in the rather excessive effusions of James McNeill Whistler in 1885: '. . . the story of the beautiful is already complete—hewn in the marbles of the Parthenon—and broidered, with the birds, upon the fan of Hokusai—at the foot of Fusiyama.' And although it is much outdated on facts, the American poet A.D. Ficke's *Chats on Japanese Prints* (1915) offers an intriguing comparison here: 'In this work Hokusai stands beside Harunobu exactly as Whitman stands beside Keats—a more interesting mind but a far less perfect artist.'

This, then, is the *Hokusai manga*—well known by name but, I suspect, really very little understood. It represents, in fact, a motley and panoramic encyclopedia of Far Eastern life and legend, providing not only a guide to the student of art and culture but even surprising insights into the nature of man and his environment. There could be no better introduction to the roots of Japanese culture than this set of little volumes.

Taken as a whole the *Manga* volumes constitute—as I have suggested above—an important body of art-work. Their diminutive size and the process of woodblock carv-

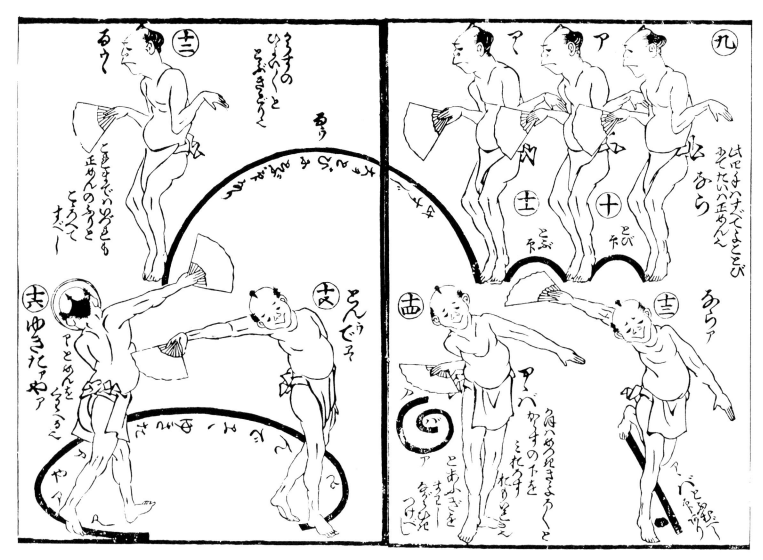

161 Dance-steps. From *Teach Yourself the Dance*, 1815. (For another example from this book, see Fig. 200.)

ing and printing were not ideally suited to such fluent and essentially delicate, impromptu sketches, but had the original drawings come down to us today, they might rank equal to those of Leonardo and Michelangelo.

3

After the *tour de force* of the *Manga* it might seem that Hokusai's other 'practical' manuals of this decade would come as something of an anti-climax; in fact, there are several books at least of equal interest—if less comprehensive in scope—and some that are among the artist's best works of the period.

As an indication that the Master took on practically any kind of assignment, we may mention in passing the *Odori hitori-geiko* (Teach Yourself the Dance) of *c.* 1815. This charming little volume features fully diagrammed details of a Kabuki dance by the great Danjurō VII, as well as other solo dances for men, in a series of double-page illustrations such as that of Plate 161. Here a male dancer—half-naked for clarity of leg and arm movements—progresses from upper right to left in a series of skips and

jumps, then to lower right, then left, for a group of fan-movements. The designs are hardly great art but reveal one further aspect of the Master's perception of figure-drawing: the ability to grasp, amidst the ceaseless flow of movement, the 'decisive moment'. The book, in effect, combines instruction in amateur Kabuki dancing with the drawing-manual.

From the following year 1816, which saw publication of Series IV and V of the *Manga* as well, dates one of Hokusai's most careful expositions on the art of painting. This is the *Santei gafu* (Painting in Three Aspects). In this work (which has generally been misunderstood in the West) the artist attempts to apply the three standard styles of calligraphy—formal, informal and cursive—to painting; and the subjects themselves are seen from three different points of view. Each design is thus provided with a symbol—square/diabolo/circle—to indicate which style, or view-point, is depicted.

At initial glance the intent of the volume is not all that apparent. In the first place, the format—two designs to a page—means that the 'three aspects' are often not visible at the same time (this problem, at least, is easily resolved here by adjusting the photographs); and furthermore, the order of 'aspects' is sometimes confusingly varied; the artist often avoids overly clear-cut application of his theory, and he seems to have gone out of his way to avoid

162 Landscapes Formal/Semi-formal/Cursive. From *Painting in Three Aspects*, 1816. (See also Plates 163–165, Fig. 201.)

163 Waves Formal/Semi-formal/Cursive. From *Painting in Three Aspects*, 1816. (In the original, 'Semi-formal' appears on separate page and first in order.)

repetition. Few of the designs are of exactly the same subject, so that meaningful comparison often requires concentration—which was probably Hokusai's exact intention.

The method will be apparent from Plate 162, where we view first a landscape with overhanging cliff, rather static

and very much in the classic Chinese style—as practised by Sesshū and the early Kanō masters in Japan from the fifteenth century. In the next, semi-formal version of a similar scene all of the forms are rendered more fluent, the clouded sky further enhancing the sense of movement. With the final, cursive version the scene becomes more

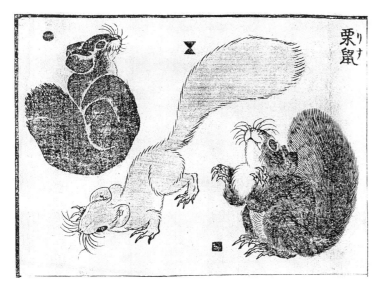

164 Squirrels (right to left) Formal/Semi-formal/Cursive. From *Painting in Three Aspects*, 1816.

165 Lions Formal/Formal/Semi-formal/Semi-formal/Cursive. From *Painting in Three Aspects*, 1816. (Order is right to left.)

typically Japanese, the cliff a single, massive unity, the sailing-boats more impressionistic (some half-concealed at right). And both sea and sky are now rendered in washes, the emphasis being on mood rather than on detail.

With Plate 163, Waves alone receive special attention, ranging from the detailed, tenacious fingers we tend to associate with Hokusai (see Plate 247) through more attenuated forms, on down to decorative designs that resemble the *sumi-nagashi* ink-patterns of Japanese hand-made papers. The method is applied to animals as well, first in the 'Squirrels' of Plate 164, later in the '*Shishi*'—mythical lions, one of the artist's favourite subjects—of Plate 165. The latter appear, in fact, in five different poses: two formal, two semi-formal, with the final, cursive one reduced (or sublimated) to an impressionistic mass in whose sentient face one can, perhaps, see something of Hokusai himself.

In a sense, this little volume signals a return to the theme of the Master's first art-manual: that painting and calligraphy are one. This concept represents one of the essential features of Far Eastern painting—here presented in a graphic form in which many of the diminutive examples are themselves minor masterpieces of creative art.

One is sorely tempted to pass over some of Hokusai's more miniaturistic art-manuals of this prolific decade, yet once the eyes are focused on them it is difficult to turn one's gaze away. In viewing Plate 166, for example (like many of these, shown here over half-size), one immediately recalls the Master's famed public performance of drawing two sparrows on a grain of rice. That feat alone is, of course, more a sign of good eyesight than of genius; but when one looks closely at these faceless little figures, one soon perceives that something of the essence of great art lies here—only waiting to be expanded, amplified, defined.

The example is from *Ehon hayabiki* (The Quick Pictorial-Dictionary) of 1817, a sequel to the *Quick Guide to Drawing*, already discussed. This little volume (of which a sequel appeared two years later) is arranged in the order of the

Japanese syllabary, with all sorts of unrelated figures packed into each and every page, in 'alphabetical' order. Again, even one such leaf would require some pages to explicate: the plate of the syllable '*i*', for instance, runs from such unexpected subjects as *iki-hotoke* (living Buddha) at upper right through the bloodcurdling *ike-nie* (sacrificial victim) below it, to the *ichinen* ghost and exorcist at the end. In between, one glimpses priests, peasants, travellers, profligates, drinker and tattooer, weaver, grinder, newly-weds—the artist's selection providing ample evidence of his taste for the bizarre, as well as his vivid powers of total recall.

At the risk of straining the reader's attention—and eyes—I must add one other tableau (Plate 167), a page for the syllable '*ne*'. It shows: unequal combatants, priest and congregation, the rice-levy, a boudoir, night-watchman, clerk, rat-catching, talking in one's sleep, nun at prayer, preparing for bed, giant radish, rice-pounding and prayer-procession (the preponderance of 'sleep' and 'prayer' themes coming from the compounds of *ne* and *nen*). Again each minuscule sketch represents a complete tableau, a little world in itself. To understand Hokusai without knowing his books is clearly an impossibility; and this diminutive volume of tiny miniatures, so representative of his special genius, may be cited, without exaggeration, as comprising some of his best work.

As Hokusai had demonstrated so forcefully in public, if he could paint a giant Daruma he was also a master of the near-microscopic. To this latter talent he again turned in the production of a quite different kind of book, the three-volume *Imayō sekkin hinagata* (Models of Modern Combs and Pipes) of 1822–3, devoted to two important accessories of Japanese life and artisanship: the elaborately carved or lacquered combs and hairpins, and the delicately chased or inlaid boles and handles of smoking-pipes—the designs flattened out for easy reference.[6]

But unlike the case with the previous book, the practical function is here a clear impediment to the artist's freedom: miniaturism alone he could conquer, but the need to shape each minuscule tableau onto the tiny frame of a handcomb or pipe-stem—and make the designs detailed enough to satisfy skilled artisans—was clearly a superhuman assignment. Indeed, our attention here is drawn not so much to the pictures themselves as to their implications for Hokusai's later, major prints. Thus in the designs of Plate 168 we cannot really overcome the impression that these are, after all, only comb-designs: yet at the same instant we can perceive in them the seeds of such masterpieces as, for example, Plates 245 and 248. In the 'Waves' of Plate 170, likewise, we sense the limitations imposed by the practical function, while seeing in our mind's eye other, greater Hokusai waves, both before and after (Plates 81, 247, 300).

Yet having said this, we chance upon the compelling

166 The Syllable *I*. From *The Quick Pictorial-Dictionary*, 1817.

167 The Syllable *NE*. From *The Quick Pictorial-Dictionary*, 1817.

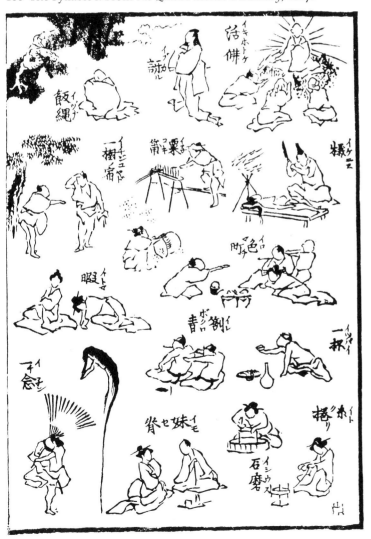

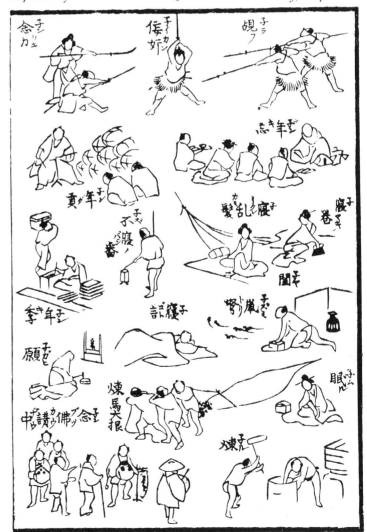

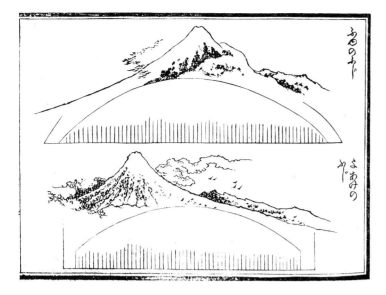

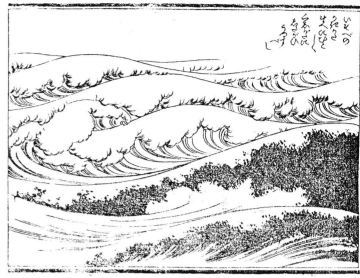

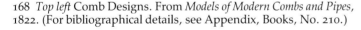

168 *Top left* Comb Designs. From *Models of Modern Combs and Pipes*, 1822. (For bibliographical details, see Appendix, Books, No. 210.)

169 *Above* Comb Designs. From *Models of Modern Combs and Pipes*, 1822.

170 *Top right* Comb Designs. From *Models of Modern Combs and Pipes*, 1822.

171 *Right* Pipe Design. From *Models of Modern Combs and Pipes*, 1823.

animal-designs of Plate 169, and in the final volume the charming little urchin of Plate 171—the latter (the subject of which appeared earlier in the *Hokusai gashiki* of 1819) intended as a model for the pipe-artisan—and discover, as we did in the previous miniature book, the very essence of the subject, and of Hokusai himself. Here will be found, then, a treasureful guide to the decorative themes of Japanese arts and crafts, as well as a key to many of the ideas that the artist was to amplify in his later great prints. Not only the *Fuji* landscapes, but also the various 'Flowers' series are presaged here; and even the remarkable 'Spaniel' of our Plate 278 may be glimpsed among the lively animals of one of the tableaux just cited.

The reader may perhaps find it disheartening that an obviously major artist should have to spend a quarter of his life working on handbooks for craftsmen and dilettantes. But the Master enjoyed such difficult and didactic assignments, doubtless boasting in his heart that only he could accomplish them. And true to his expectations, the results were indeed edifying and enormously influential on the development of Japanese arts and crafts in the nineteenth century. It is hard, therefore, to say that the artist might better have spent his time on works of more 'fine' art. In any case, the pay was the same (if not better), and the distinction between arts and crafts hardly existed then: there was only the line drawn between plebeian artists (ukiyo-e or other) and privileged artists (who worked for the samurai or court nobility).

Hokusai's other volumes of an eminently practical nature deserve further study, but I can mention only one more here, the *Shingata komon-chō* (New Models for Kimono-patterns) of 1824. The main illustrations feature page after page of carefully and creatively designed geometric patterns—yet another facet of the artist's personality. The closing scene of a master-dyer at work is both striking and poignant—even if one does not stop to consider the implied occupational hazards (Plate 172). (We note, incidentally, the artist's new pen-name of this period in the signature at lower right: *Iitsu*—'Become One'—a reference to the Master having entered his sixtieth year in 1819. At this age the Japanese believed that human beings began a new cycle of existence.)

As the last of these educational manuals I have reserved space for my own favourite. Published in 1823 but probably originating from Hokusai's Nagoya sojourn of six years earlier, this is the *Ippitsu gafu* (Drawings at One Stroke).[7]

We have followed the artist's progress, in his analysis of sketching/painting (in the Far East, much the same thing), from drawing as an extension of calligraphy, through geometric forms as the basis for composition, on to an exposition of the categories of painting in terms of calligraphic styles. Hokusai's final step in this process was to find the essence of graphic art in the line, *ippitsu*, the single brushstroke.

172 Dyer at Work. From *New Models for Kimono-patterns*, 1824.

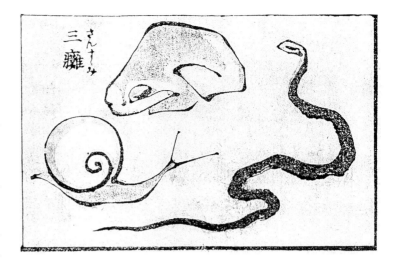

173 Toad, Snail, Snake. From *Drawings at One Stroke*, 1823.

Of course this term is a euphemism, for—except in simple Zen circles and the forced compositions of party-games—few complete designs are really feasible with a single, uninterrupted line. The artist's aim, however, is to show that the essential elements of a design may be defined with a minimum number of strokes, and are often the better for it.

The concept itself was an ancient one in Far Eastern art; indeed, it was one of the bases of *sumi-e* painting. The technique had appeared in the Edo picture-books of Kitao Masayoshi, as well as in the work of the Nagoya master Niwa Kagen (an intimate of the great Taiga in the eighteenth century), Hokusai's direct inspiration.

With Hokusai, however, the method was not only applied with encyclopedic comprehensiveness, but in masterful designs, many of which may stand as independent works of art quite divorced from their didactic intent. Examined closely, the volume contains hardly a dull plate and—unlike the case with many of the artist's books—even the fastidious critic may choose examples practically at random.

The 'Wild Geese' of Plate 183 takes a prosaic enough subject and raises it to art of real quality. The essence of the goose—its cavalier, self-satisfied attitude, its sinuous neck and awkward head—is effectively captured with calligraphic strokes that leave one wondering if any artist could hope to surpass them. The same may be said of the even more lowly subjects of Plate 173. And though the volume reproduces very well in monochrome, one example (Plate 183) at least may be shown in the original, subdued colouring (which was to be echoed some generations later in the work of artists as disparate as Mary Cassatt and Yamamoto Kanae).

With the landscape genre, this abbreviated technique was rather more common—even conventionalized—and though Hokusai's contribution forms an effective study in planes and structures, it is mainly of interest in relation to his later *Fuji* prints (Plate 174). Yet when he turns to a more original theme, as in Plate 175, the artist evokes a powerful mood of moonlit silhouettes that far exceeds the practical needs of any mere painting-manual. The original caption—'Each stroke must create an actual object'—

174 Lakeside Landscape. From *Drawings at One Stroke*, 1823.

175 Birds by Moonlight. From *Drawings at One Stroke*, 1823.

though it well expresses the nature of the volume, seems somehow redundant in the face of such an overwhelming, living example.

To me, however, the most fascinating plates of the volume are those that depict—nay, reveal—the essence of the human form. In my one example (Plate 176), the theme is taken from the life of the Yoshiwara courtesans, but it is a rather different world from that depicted in the vivid colour-prints of the period (see Plate 28 for example): instead, we are treated to a medley of *forms*, orchestrated like a minor work of music. Here, too, commentary is redundant: at upper right we see four courtesans, presumably engaged in public promenade but depicted with an intimacy that makes us know them all the more for their being only suggested. Below this group we view two palanquin-bearers, and a hooded gallant alighting on his way to a house of assignation. The left-side plate is of indoor scenes, at top, again four courtesans, this time seated 'on display' to prospective clients. Below them is a party-scene in the Yoshiwara: two courtesans and three servants watch the performance of a monkey-trainer and his charge. But such antiquarian details are not really that important; unless I am very wrong, one can perceive here the very essence of figure-painting, and of art itself: the reduction of forms—and impressions—to their essentials, the render-

ing of reality as a crystallization of experience.

The plates themselves speak better than any commentary could and, like all the books of this chapter, this little volume was appreciated by the student artists of the time and ran to many editions. Yet how well they were able to emulate it seems problematical, for the very simplicity of the *ippitsu* technique demands great technical competence and absolute sureness of intent and aim.

The book represents, to be sure, a rather different Hokusai from his usual image (though, indeed, there are all too many Hokusais to be effectively comprehended in a brief monograph). One can but regret that he did not—or, for commercial reasons, could not—apply this method more extensively to his more impressive work in painting, prints and illustration.

With this volume, in fact, we find a Hokusai who has, purposely or not, come to exceed and overcome the bounds of his medium. And this may serve as a fitting introduction to the more elaborate albums for painters that form the subject of our next chapter.

NOTES

1 Though I have attempted no real survey, it may just be that Japan had—and may still have—more potential artists, or at least more potential producers of

176 Yoshiwara Scenes. Two pages from *Drawings at One Stroke*, 1823. (Original size of each page: 9 × 6¼ in / 22.8 × 15.8 cm.)

artistic graffiti, than any other nation on the earth. (I should perhaps qualify the 'and may still have', for I recall now the comments of writer-friends that, for speed and convenience converting to word-processors, they have found themselves not only gradually forgetting how to write Japanese characters, but also losing the complexly sensitive tactile nerves that seem to go along with this difficult system of writing.)

2 I had one Tōkyō friend, back in the early 1950s, whose only artistic accomplishments were, at parties, to (1) write legible calligraphy in mirror-reverse on the back of translucent paper; and (2) have a serving-maid or geisha hold a similar sheet of paper on which he would, in four seconds flat and to the girl's feigned horror, draw a huge, throbbing *sumi-e* phallus.

I must add one further personal note here, and that concerns a visit at the same period to the atelier of the artist who probably qualifies as the 'last of the ukiyo-e masters'. This was Seiu Itō (1880–1961), who was indeed distantly related to Hokusai. I was particularly impressed by the essentially *visual* responses of the man: on practically every subject I brought up about old Edo he immediately dashed off an impromptu sketch—often with an accompanying caption—that was practically ready for the printer. I went home with a handful of sketches—including a large shunga drawing which he 'dedicated' to me—only marginally related to my research topic, a dissertation on the novelist Saikaku: but with the strong impression that this is what it must have been like to know old Hokusai.

3 In fact, James Michener has done just such a volume, *The Hokusai Sketchbooks* (assistance on which, back in 1957, was indeed my first essay at ukiyo-e studies): yet even that work only begins to scratch the surface.

4 As an aside I may add that Japanese films—whether on Hokusai or Utamaro—love to feature prolonged scenes of nude sketching: but this is simply from an ignorance of traditional art, and a desire to attract audiences who would not otherwise attend an 'art' film.

5 See colour-plate 190 in my *Images from the Floating World*.

6 Not unexpectedly, Hokusai's designs were adapted by artisans for implements other than those nominally intended. I have seen, for example, several *tsuba* (bronze sword-guards) of the later Edo Period which adapt the Master's smoking-pipe sketches; and a more extensive survey would probably reveal his widespread influence on subsequent craftwork design. One pupil, Issoku, actually became in later life a leading artisan of sword-furniture (see Appendix, page 313).

7 Although Hokusai had nominally bequeathed his name 'Taito' to a pupil late in 1819, this *nom d'artiste* appears on fully three of the plates as well as on the wrappers to the volume; and it thus seems likely that the book was commenced at the time of his second visit to Nagoya, even though—for unknown reasons—not published until some years later. But for an alternative view on this problem, see Appendix (under Books, No. 211). It is, indeed, often assumed that the dates listed for Hokusai's art-names are absolute, but this is not necessarily the case. For example (as will be noted later) a directory of as late as 1836 lists 'Taito' among the Master's names; and evidence of that name appearing in the *Ippitsu gafu* would indicate that—in Nagoya at least, site of the Great Daruma Painting Exhibition—it was not so easy for the artist to effect such name-changes, either vis-à-vis publishers or in the popular mind. (One notes, incidentally [Appendix, Books, No. 178], that Hokusai's name remained unchanged in the Nagoya editions of the *Manga*—series I to X, 1814–19—whereas the Edo editions employed his more recent *noms d'artiste*.)

XIV
Artist without Gallery: Hokusai's Later Picture-books

1

IT WILL BE recalled that the more lyric and poetic qualities of Hokusai's complex personality reached a peak of expression in his picture-books, albums and *surimono*-prints around the turn of the eighteenth century. Within a decade he had turned to other, less idyllic themes and styles and, in a sense, it was his follower Hiroshige who was to revive these earlier approaches a generation later. But this was all part and parcel of Hokusai's restless nature: to create and evolve—with great effort—new subjects, new themes, new styles, new approaches and then, after carrying them to what he considered their most fruitful limits, going on in search of new worlds to conquer. Thus, no one style was really brought to its conclusion, nor exploited to its final demise. By the same token, the artist's 'image' is all too diverse and many-faceted: he refuses to rest in a single mould or even several; and his true nature is far more difficult to grasp than is the case with Hiroshige—or most of his other confrères of the Ukiyo-e School.

In an earlier chapter we left Hokusai's major genre picture-books with that masterpiece *Both Banks of the Sumida River* (Plates 60, 61) to turn to the quite different world of the artist's work in illustrated novels and manuals for painters. We may now turn back to his *oeuvre* of the latter period—again in the medium of picture-books, but with a quite new and different approach to the subject: one in fact often far removed from the stylishly traditional world of ukiyo-e.

177 *Below left* Wild Goose in Flight. Plate from *Lone Haiku Verses*, c. 1805. (For bibliographical data on this chapter, see p. 302 ff.)

178 *Below* Plum-tree in Bloom. From *First Hundred Verses at Horikawa*, c. 1811.

179 *Opposite top* Travellers in Snow. Frontispiece to *Strange Tales of Northern Echigo*, 1813.

180 *Opposite bottom* Landscape in Snow. From *Hokusai's Album from Life*, c. 1814. (See also Plate 187 and Books, No. 179.)

Hokusai's work in this neo-classical manner began about the time of his first 'Gothic novels' and these changes in subject and style were probably indicative of mutations in the artist's psychology: a longing, with middle age, for a position of greater respect, greater fame—even greater respectability—than was possible among the myriad plebeian artists of the Floating World. There was also perhaps a certain fatigue with the clamorous milieu of the fashionable ukiyo-e master. In short, the artist, reaching his mid-40s and already beginning to sign his works 'Old Hokusai' (at that time 50 was considered the 'standard' of longevity), had concluded that his talents required a new direction and a new milieu to explore, preferably one that was more stable, more prestigious and more attuned to his own true nature.

Hokusai's experimentation with neo-classical themes had been apparent early in his *surimono* greeting-cards and a few de luxe albums, but their first notable appearance in his general book-illustration may be seen in Plate 177. This came out in the anthology *Hitori hokku* (Lone Haiku Verses) of *c.* 1805. The book itself is unusual, featuring an anthology not only of poets but also of artists: most of them of the literati and other semi-classical schools. Hokusai was prob-

ably at pains to make his contribution match the sedate and neo-classical setting, and such associations—such recognition in non-ukiyo-e fields—surely helped direct the artist towards more classical themes from this period.

The illustration shown here—a masterful design of a wild goose descending above flowers—reveals the beginnings of that anthropomorphic attitude towards birds and animals that was to prove one of Hokusai's trademarks. Another anthology, *Horikawa tarō hyakushu* (First Hundred Verses at Horikawa), this time of *kyōka*, reveals a similar facet of Hokusai's new absorption in the neo-classical. The aged plum-tree of Plate 178 is at once a harbinger of the artist's later style, while retaining vestiges of his youthful *élan*.

Yet another excellent illustration of this period appears in the *Hokuetsu kidan* (Strange Tales of Northern Echigo) of 1813, the year after Hokusai's sojourn in Nagoya. Though usually classified as *yomi-hon*, this work is actually not a novel but a collection of curious legends characteristic of the Echigo region of north-west Japan. The frontispiece shown here (Plate 179) reveals a most effective combination of traditional beauty and Occidental-derived perspective: the foreground figures dominate the scene, but the distant snowscape and travellers add a depth of visual connotation that represents, again, a rare new contribution to the vocabulary of Japanese art. The printer's adept employment of 'lowering'—the hand-pressed, soft and grainy gradation

181 Rain Scene. From *The Hokusai Painting Style*, 1819. (See also Plates 184–186, and Fig. 208.)

182 Cherry-blossoms and Aged Tree-trunk. Page from *Hokusai manga*, Series II, 1815.

183 Wild Geese. From *Drawings at One Stroke*, 1823.

outlines—produces a rich effect of three dimensionality that raises the result far above our usual concept of book-illustration. The strong sense of dramatic design that lies at the basis of all Hokusai's *oeuvre* is well displayed; the faces of the anonymous figures in the foreground are doubtless deliberately concealed: man, beast and Nature are thus accorded equal status in a picture where the design itself becomes the central theme.

2

Shortly after this, in the year 1814 (which also saw the first volume of the *Manga*), Hokusai began in earnest the production of a series of major picture-books. These consisted of 'collections' of finished sketches and paintings on traditional themes. But though the subjects were generally standard ones, the artist's viewpoint and mode of depiction were not: the Master's approach revealing a freshness of insight and an originality of conception that must have startled his contemporaries, and no doubt enraged traditionalists. The nominal intent of these books was again to provide models for fledgeling artists; so far as Hokusai himself was concerned, however, they provided an ideal gallery, museum even, for his fertile mind to fill with the

varied products of his brush. Whereas the art-manuals of our previous chapter taught the details and techniques of painting, these woodblock-printed picture-books collected the final result and were, as the Master himself must secretly have hoped, an ideal way to bequeath the Hokusai Style to posterity.

The first and one of the most important of these picture-books is *Hokusai shashin-gafu* (Hokusai's Album from Life). Unusually for this genre, it is printed and bound in album-format, with each double-page plate on a separate sheet of high-quality, soft paper. The preface is dated Spring of 1814 and it seems likely that the volume was privately printed later in the same year (the first commercial edition appearing in 1819). The title includes the word *shashin*—literally, 'depicting reality'—used today for 'photography', but in older Japanese (most often pronounced *shō-utsushi*) the word implied 'sketching from the life', which was, as we have seen, hardly the customary technique of academic painters, who copied their masters rather than reality. This book features more complex printing than many such albums, and Hokusai's fifteen plates are, indeed, taken from life, both human and natural. To the modern viewer (depending of course on taste), some of the depictions may seem excessively realistic and rather

184 *Opposite top* Sumō Bout. From *The Hokusai Painting Style*, 1819.

185 *Opposite bottom* Eagle amid Blossoms. From *The Hokusai Painting Style*, 1819.

186 *Above* Birds above Reeds. From *The Hokusai Painting Style*, 1819.

lacking in mood. They represented, however, a startling innovation for most of Hokusai's audience, combining the artist's mastery of form with his studies in Western perspective, and featuring his eccentric and sometimes bizarre approach to traditional themes.

In Plate 187, for example, we find a standard subject—a pheasant in autumn—but the large bird is crowded to the right of the design, looking down introspectively, and with its own tracks used to represent the traditional setting of fallen maple-leaves. Remarkably, however, the design manages to remain balanced.

There is only one landscape in the album (Plate 180), a masterful depiction of a lakeside mansion and a distant, snow-clad mountain (not Fuji). The design effectively balances two major forces of Nature—mountain and giant pine-tree—with man represented only by his relatively puny contributions. The composition integrates a modicum of Occidental perspective in the relation of tree and mountain; but the middle ground is typically Far Eastern in its disregard of relative sizes between the boats and buildings. Withal, it is an effective design (enhanced by the lowering sky) and one regrets that the artist did not find opportunity to enlarge it into a major work of painting. Indeed, one's most lasting impression of this important album is that these are impressive paintings forcefully reduced to book-size: hardly adequate compensation for this great master's lack of gallery, museum—or adequate patronage.

Less grand in scale but of equal interest to the Hokusai student is a volume of smaller designs first published *c*. 1818 under the title *Hokusai gakyō* (Mirror of Designs by Hokusai). The original version in monochrome was soon followed by an edition with colour-blocks added, retitled *Shūga ichiran* (Excellent Pictures at a Glance), by which title it is best known in the West.

This little volume might well be considered a luxurious appendage to the *Manga* (which was already in its eighth series by this year). But though the actual tableaux are small (and usually printed as two horizontals to a double-spread), the concepts and execution are more finished than is customary in the 'sketchbooks', and rather than fragments, the illustrations might better be viewed as sections of a hand-scroll, portraying all variety of contemporary life and legend.

The 'Bacchanalian Revelry' of Plate 188, for example (as with most of these plates the title is mine), vividly depicts a stylish orgy of the *shōjō*, the mischievous Japanese gods of saké. The 'Ox-herd' of Plate 189 is a quieter scene of rustic life—ox fording a stream as a cow-boy follows over a rickety bridge, each in his own way—but equally satis-

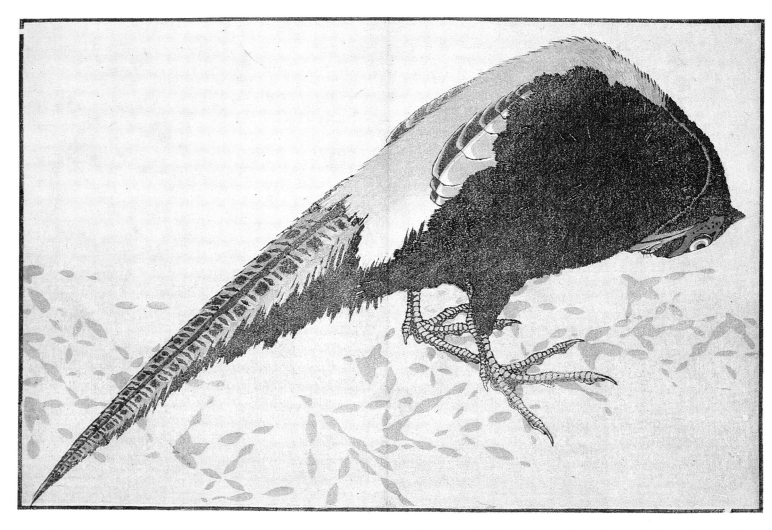

187 Pheasant in Autumn. From *Hokusai's Album from Life*, c. 1814.
(See also Plate 180.)

fying in its own right. When compared to Hokusai's large
picture-books this diminutive volume will tend to be overlooked, partly because of its complex format; for this
reason I have chosen, perhaps controversially, to illustrate
each tableau as a separate plate.

One indication of Hokusai's popularity at this time is the
curious picture-book and verse-anthology *Hyōsui kiga*
(Strange Pictures by Chance Encounter), also of 1818,
which was, in fact, a revamped edition of an 1803 book of
Kabuki landscapes by the Ōsaka master Ryūkōsai. Single
figures by Hokusai were now added here and there, by
insertions into the old woodblocks, to replace the figures
of Ryūkōsai. It is odd that the Master should have agreed
to such a patched-up production; the publisher's aim was,
obviously, to produce a 'new book' by the cheapest possible method. Perhaps Hokusai felt some special affinity to
the other artist (who had died in 1816); or more likely, he
was under some special obligation to the publishers (who
included Eirakuya of Nagoya). The book is cited not so
much for its own sake as to suggest the likelihood of many
other such compromises for a commercial artist without
independent income (Fig. 205).

With the *Hokusai gashiki* of 1819 we return to the independent picture-book. As the title indicates—'The Hokusai Painting Style'—the professed aim of the volume is the
display of the Master's designs as a guide to amateur
painters, who obviously represented an important market
for the publishers of the time, with Hokusai as one of their
leading lights.

This largish volume (25.7 × 18.3 cm/10 × 7.2 in) includes
a number of important designs and one's choice must be
dictated as much by variety as by intrinsic quality. The
'Rain Scene' of Plate 181, for example, represents a powerful genre tableau: a 'snapshot' which any photographer
might envy. The figures are typical of the artist's work
from the 1810s and on—more solid and muscular than
those of a decade earlier, though less exaggeratedly so
than in his later work. We can perceive here Hokusai's
significant mastery of figures in groups: separate yet none
the less interacting, whatever their distance apart. The
artist employs a variety of brushstrokes within the same
design, and the effect is an unobtrusive enriching of the
elements contributing to the total composition. Looking
more closely, we see that the composition itself is vaguely
oval, with black tree and woman with parasol balancing
each side. The middle area may seem a trifle vapid, but
one must remember that to an illustrator of Hokusai's long
experience, allowance for the central cleavage of the
Japanese book came as second nature; and when we flat-
ten out the book for photography—and reduce the centre
margins—we lose something of the three-dimensional
quality of the original.[1]

188 *Top* Bacchanalian Revelry. From *Mirror of Designs by Hokusai*, 1818/19. (The youthful gods of saké are seen joyously carousing beside an open wine-keg.) (Plates 188–9 are shown in the retitled, colour-printed edition: *Excellent Pictures at a Glance*.)

189 *Above* 'Ox-herd'. From *Mirror of Designs by Hokusai*, 1818/19.

An even more elaborate display of muscles appears in the 'Sumō Bout' of Plate 184, in which two hairy wrestlers entwine in combat before a small sea of contestants, and a mountain—probably Fuji—towers across the bay. As is often the case with Hokusai, a touch of comic relief is included: in this case, the humorously intent referee. With the 'Eagle' of Plate 185, the artist succeeds in raising the traditional 'flower-and-bird' print to monumental impressiveness. Gone is the sweetly decorative flavour of Ming painting; here, not only is the great, soulful bird of heroic proportions, but even the foliage tends to assume a Hokusai-like quality of its own.

My own favourite of the volume is the less pretentious 'Birds above Reeds' of Plate 186. It is a *tour de force* of complex ornithology: a mass-portrait that one is hardly likely to view in nature, but one in which there is surprisingly little of the posed, the artful or the unnatural. The plate effectively amalgamates the artist's studies in the decorative qualities of Kōrin, the naturalistic methods of Ming/Ch'ing painting and of Ōkyo, and the realism of the West to achieve a style that is none of these, but only authentic Hokusai.

This impressive volume must rank among the Master's principal works. For the busy viewer who finds the *Manga* too diminutive and varied to be enjoyed at length, it may serve as an ideal introduction to Hokusai's powers of design at their peak.

From the succeeding year dates the last of these printed 'galleries' of Hokusai's paintings, the *Ryōbi shahitsu* (Elegant Brushstrokes) of 1820. This work is best known in the Occident under the title of its second edition, *Hokusai soga* (Designs by Hokusai). As with several of these picture-books, early versions exist in both monochrome and with light colours added. Often, the more economical version was issued first, and then the elaborate one when popular-

190 *Opposite top* 'Figures in Snow'. From *Elegant Brushstrokes*, 1820.

191 *Opposite bottom* 'Snow-thawed Stream'. From *Elegant Brushstrokes*, 1820. (See also Figs. 210–212.)

192 *Above* 'Snowy Night'. From *Elegant Brushstrokes*, 1820. (See Fig. 213 and Books, No. 203.)

ity so warranted. It is, however, sometimes difficult to choose one version over the other. Strong designs may seem more dramatic in black and white; landscapes may sometimes be enhanced by the addition of cloud-forms and flat washes of colour.

If anything, the designs to this volume are more carefully planned and executed than most of their fellows, and the engraving and printing are also of the highest order. Plate 190, for example, shows another oval-shaped composition in which the snow-clad umbrellas at left and right neatly balance—even, anchor—the varied elements of the design.

In the bucolic scene of Plate 191, we find featured a more complex, S-shaped composition, which dispenses with distracting background. (If there seems to be a plethora of water-buffaloes here—see also Plates 74, 189, 285, 313—I must plead that [1] these huge and cumbersome beasts often lend themselves to effective compositions; and [2] I like water-buffaloes.)

And, coming less than a decade before the world-famed *Fuji* prints, it is interesting to view the earlier landscape masterpiece of Plate 192. Within the limits of book-illustration, this is probably about as far as the landscape could evolve. The design is impeccable, and the inclusion of the peasant and his little son, trudging home on this snowy night, adds a human warmth without becoming artificial or sentimental. (In a characteristic Hokusai touch, the child's smallness is subtly emphasized by his wearing a man-sized rain-cap.)

With these impressive picture-books of the later 1810s, Hokusai succeeds not only in displaying the technical bravura of his fully mature style for aspiring artists of his time, but also manages to provide us with an impressive gallery of his *oeuvre*. He has with these entrancing volumes at last reached a stage of mastery that will prepare him for the overwhelming task of creating the full-blown Japanese landscape-print of a decade later. But in the meanwhile the artist had still much other meaningful work to do.

NOTE

1 I do not, however, favour reproducing such plates with the centre space left to the caprice of the original bookbinder, which may vary with each edition; so long as the design is continuous, I prefer to reduce this gap to a uniform minimum.

XV
Robust Beauties
and Erotic Dreams

1

IF I HAVE given the impression that, with the 1810s, Hokusai had entirely given up depiction of the Floating World that is hardly correct. We have already seen that a certain portion even of his more classically oriented illustrations had featured the contemporary milieu of Edo life. It is the purpose of this chapter to seek out more actively his less positive but continuing contribution in this period to that key genre of ukiyo-e, *bijin-ga*: fair beauties, mostly of the current world—and to that closely related form, *shunga*.

We have observed that Hokusai, from about the year 1806, became engrossed in the detailed illustration of 'Gothic novels'. This experience—plus the increasing influence of Chinese classical painting—led gradually to a change of style, resulting in more powerful and monumental figures, but a loss of the willowy grace of his earlier work in the ukiyo-e manner. There are, however, a couple of years—1806–8—where the two contrasting styles seem to merge or, rather, struggle for domination. Thus in the intriguing cover to a theatre-booklet of 1808, we can see both something of the pliant grace of the earlier Hokusai, and the beginnings of that harder, less graceful style of his coming middle period (Plate 193).

In the Master's attempt of the year before—evidently unsuccessful—to return to the medium of the actor-print after a fifteen-year absence, we can clearly detect the baleful influence of the predominant Toyokuni school of Kabuki portrayal (Plate 194). Indeed, these few and rare actor-prints seem almost dowdy: rather resembling the way early

193 *Below left* Cover to *A Medley of Caps*, X/1808. A theatre-booklet by Bakin, issued in Edo to commemorate the *jōruri* dramatization in Ōsaka of a popular *yomi-hon* of earlier the same year by Bakin and Hokusai, *A Dream of Nanka* (see Appendix, Books, Nos. 141/145). (Unusually the names of calligrapher and engraver are recorded, at lower right.)

194 *Below* Kabuki Actor in Female Role (Ronosuke as Komume, wife of the gambler and thief Yoshibei). *Ōban*-size print, Third Month, 1807. (See Prints, No. 104.)

Occidental artists depicted the kimono (and it may even be that Hokusai was momentarily attracted to this Western ineptitude—as conveyed in the etchings of Kōkan and Denzen—in depicting phenomena only half-understood).

More graceful, but still difficult truly to love, is the famous set of the 'Six Poets' in which, reminiscent of the artist's early drawing-manuals, the poets' names are skilfully concealed in the calligraphic folds of their kimonos (Plate 197). And reflecting Hokusai's current work in the *yomi-hon* genre—and the continuing enthusiasm for Chinese/Gothic themes—the artist in 1807 produced a pair of impressive diptychs on the fantastically horrid subject of 'The Cruelties of Dakki' (the Chinese witch and despot Ta Chi of our *Manga* Plate 145). Probably the better of these is the scene in which the fearsome female (concubine of the ill-fated Shang Emperor) watches as her lieutenant presses his sword to the throat of a small boy, in preparation to behead him. I reproduce here only the left panel of the set, showing her other frustrated victims, not so much to suppress the sadistic subject as because the individual panels are far more effective than the whole (Plate 198).

195 *Left* Festive Dancers. Pillar-print, *c.* 1810. This is an unusual example of a *surimono*-type *hashira-e*, with extra paper at top for a series of verse-inscriptions, here omitted (total size: 44½ × 5½ in / 113 × 14 cm). (See prints, No. 119.)

196 *Below* Exotic Beauty. Medium-small *surimono*-print, *c.* 1807.

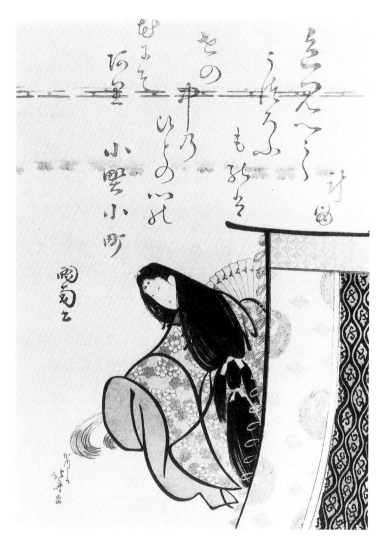

197 The Poetess Komachi. *Ōban*-size print, *c*. 1810. (See Prints, No. 118.) (The rebus here may be deciphered thus. *Ono-no* appears at left, in the *kana* syllabary: *o[wo]* at shoulder and sleeve; *no* at sleeve-edge; *-no* beneath it, upside down. *Komachi* is shown in *Kanji* characters at right: *Ko* at right shoulder; *-machi* [abridged] in the T-shaped *kichō*-screen.)

Perhaps Hokusai's most ambitious print-design of this transitional period is a pentaptych—composed of five vertical *ōban* prints—featuring the interior of a Yoshiwara house of assignation. With over a dozen figures crowded into each panel it is difficult to achieve any unity of composition in the overall tableau. However, even in this cluttered scene the artist makes an attempt to develop some kind of design: viz. the snake-like, zigzag line from ovens to figures to the stairs at the rear. But there is just too much detail involved for him to effect a really dynamic composition—and this is even more true of the complete tableau of five panels. Nevertheless, in the details will be found some of the artist's best figure-work of the time. And again, a single panel will be most meaningful in the space available here (Plate 199).[1] But possibly the Master's most successful large print of this middle period is one in the unusual *hashira-e* format, depicting dancers in the summer *Bon* Festival: an impressive column in which the seven figures are compressed into the narrow format as though onto a totem-pole (Plate 195).

As always, Hokusai's *surimono* must really be treated separately from his general prints, not only because of their diminutive size and de luxe, private issuance, but because the result of these factors is such a difference in effect and mood, if not in importance. One interesting *surimono* from this transitional period is the 'Exotic Beauty' of Plate 196. Stylistically this smallish print would seem to belong to the end of Hokusai's first major sequence of figure-prints. The girl's face retains much of the graceful beauty of the early 1800s, but in the strong jawbone and muscular hands we see the beginning of the next period in Hokusai's development: increasingly powerful, indeed monumental figures, but with a loss of the delicately poetic charms of the previous decade. The date of about 1807 suggested by the style is supported by literary evidence: for the *kyōka*-poet featured here had changed to another pen-name by 1808.

The subject is that strange mixture of the native and the foreign that has always intrigued Japanese artists (and similarly, but in reverse, was reflected in the *Japonisme* of Whistler and Monet): a Japanese beauty depicted in exotic

198 Frustrated Victims of Dakki. Left-hand panel of an *ōban* diptych. Seal-date at lower left for the year 1807. (See also Fig. 43.)

199 Foyer and Kitchen of a Yoshiwara Salon. Right panel of an *ōban* pentaptych, *c.* early 1810s. (For the full scene see p. 170.)

200 Courtesan and Maidservant. Detail of an *aiban surimono*, *c.* early 1810s.

dress and hairstyle, playing a *charumera* horn (an import of the Portuguese *charamela*) as though in a parade. Such masquerade-parades were actually conducted by the Yoshiwara geisha, in imitation of the processions of the Embassies to Edo from Korea and Okinawa.[2] The issuance of such prints need not, however, have coincided with an actual Mission (such as took place, for example, in 1796, 1798 and 1806); exotic subjects were often invoked for quite incidental reasons.

More important so far as our artist goes is the question of why this significant change starts taking place in Hokusai's figure-work at just this time. It is usually assumed that the 'Chinese Connection' and the artist's increasing absorption in the illustration of Chinese-derived, historical novels led to a change in his style: replacing the youthful dream-world with a more detailed, realistic, formal and neo-classical manner. This is indeed probably the case. At the same time, one may also be tempted to look deeper into Hokusai's own personality. For fifteen years he had

laboured in the Katsukawa School of formalized actor-prints; in the following decade he found his freedom and plunged wholeheartedly into the modish *Kyōka* Movement—essentially, an idealized world of over-civilized and effete versifiers. Is it not just possible that the artist, now entering his late 40s, had come to realize that the chic world of the poetasters and Yoshiwara 'gallants' was not for him? With middle-age, the charms of the Floating World had perhaps begun to fade, and he may have sensed that his own true nature was really of a different and more earthy, painstaking and *shibui* kind. Whatever the answer, a combination of natural bent and new publishing opportunities was to produce quite a different Hokusai in the coming generation.

Despite the decline in intimacy the technical quality of

201, 202 *Overleaf top* Monkey-business: discreet and indiscreet versions. Small *surimono* with flip-up device. From a calendar-print series, datable to 1812. (Size of original: 4¾ × 3½ in / 12.3 × 8.8 cm.) (For additional shunga calendar-prints see Figs. 232–3.)

203, 204 *Overleaf bottom* Sailing, Sailing. From the same series as Plates 201–2.

205 *Overleaf far top right* Diving-girl violated by Octopi. Plate from *Pining for Love*, 1814.

206 *Overleaf far bottom right* Lad with Ladies. Plate from *The Gods of Intercourse*, 1821.

these little gems remains excellent; most *surimono* can be enlarged to several times their original size and yet retain every fine detail. Such is the case with the minor masterpiece shown next (Plate 200), in which only a quarter of the print is displayed, in about twice the size of the original. We see a high-ranking Yoshiwara courtesan and her little maidservant, dressed in all their finery (note the elaborate comb and hairpins, the subject of Hokusai's artisan-manual of Plates 168–70). Yet despite the impeccable design and immaculate printing, there is something missing: gone is the sense of intimacy, of mood, of female frailty. The figures are not exactly Rubenesque, but—allowing for taste—we may again find it a trifle difficult to love them.

Another charming *surimono* (Plate 207) includes, on the furniture door, not only the artist's new *Iitsu* signature (cited above as commemorating his sixtieth year), but also *Fusenkyo*—'Unsullied'—already discussed. The subject is an indoor scene featuring a young gidayū (*jōruri*) chantress, and is interesting not only for the near-vertiginous medley of nervous patterns that catches our eye, but also because it graphically illustrates the format of Japanese *books*, seen

207 *Left* Chantress with Drama-text. *Chūban surimono, c.* early 1820s.

208 *Below* Boys at Play. Detail of a *chūban surimono*, 1821. (See also Fig. 52.)

209 *Above left* Geisha and Farm-girl. Pair of small *surimono*, c. mid-1810s.

210 *Left* Distraught Heroine. Plate from *Mixed Verses on Jōruri*, 1815.

211 *Above* Blind Minstrel. Detail from *Mixed Verses on Jōruri*, 1815. (See bibliographical note under Books, No. 181.)

or, at least, in full size and in colour. There are also delightful genre scenes such as that of Plate 208. In this detail we glimpse five little boys absorbed in play beside two large parasols set out to dry. As always, this artist's mischievous urchins are irresistible (though one is inevitably reminded of the Master's later problems with his own delinquent grandson). The print is from the noted series *Genroku-kasen-gai-awase* (Genroku Poetry Shell-Game) of 1821, comprised of 36 different designs. The nominal subject of the series is various poems on shell-themes. Naturally, adroit word-plays predominate in the verses, in which the artist joins: in the example given, by illustrating the *katashi-gai* ('one-legged', or univalve shell) with two boys shown hopping on one leg while another two look for a lost sandal. The signatures to these prints include, incidentally, yet another new Hokusai pen-name: Getchi-*rōjin*—'Moon-mad Old-man'—which may be derived from the West, as the concept lunar → lunatic does not seem native to Japan.

One real curiosity of this period—reminiscent of our earlier Plate 24—is the pair of little prints shown in Plate 209. They take the shape of a miniature hand-mirror, and with the covers lifted reveal portraits of fair women, with verses on the rear of the lids. These belong to that unique

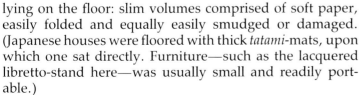

lying on the floor: slim volumes comprised of soft paper, easily folded and equally easily smudged or damaged. (Japanese houses were floored with thick *tatami*-mats, upon which one sat directly. Furniture—such as the lacquered libretto-stand here—was usually small and readily portable.)

Hokusai's *surimono* were not by any means limited to fair women: there are an equal number of still-lifes (see p. 289, No. 107 ff.), which are of course best viewed in the originals

212 *Overleaf top left* Girl after Rape. Plate from *The Gods of Intercourse*, 1821. (For additional shunga books, see Fig. 236 ff.)

213 *Overleaf bottom left* Young Lovers. Plate from *The Jewelled Merkin*, c. 1820.

214 *Overleaf top right* Furtive Lovers. *Ōban*-size plate from *Models of Loving Couples*, early 1810s. (See also Fig. 234.)

215 *Overleaf bottom right* Festive Lovers. *Ōban*-size plate from *Models of Loving Couples*, early 1810s.

variety of game-prints called *shikake-e*, usually featuring a flip-up device, of which we shall see more in a subsequent section on erotica (which function, indeed, the present examples may originally have performed: e.g. with vulva 'portraits' depicted on a separate sheet, now lost).

We have already covered most of Hokusai's book-illustration of these years, but mention must be made of one unusual theatre-book devoted entirely to figure-designs. This is the *Jōruri zekku* (Mixed Verses on *Jōruri*) of 1815 (Plates 210, 211). Each page illustrates a separate scene from the exceedingly popular puppet-drama; but the figures themselves are quite alive and human, and represent some of the artist's best *bijin-ga* of the period—commanding, yet still graceful.[3] The texts to the volume feature an unusual combination: at the top of each page is the original Japanese version of a famous excerpt from the play (in typically rounded, *Kanteiryū* calligraphy), but within the picture-frame this text is condensed and freely interpreted in classical Chinese (this, the work of Bokusen). Such an odd combination goes back to the mixed form of Chinese/Japanese poetry as featured in the classical *Wakan rōei*, and had appeared a decade before in the Master's own *Songs of Itako* (Plate 55), which may well have been the immediate inspiration of this book. From this period Hokusai's famous 'nervous line' becomes most noticeable: commencing first in the naturally crinkly lines of kimono-collars and similarly crêped material, but later extending to many other details of the artist's style as well.

Lastly for the genre of the figure-print comes the *comic*, which, as we have seen from the *Manga*, was one of the Master's fortes and one strong element of his personality (as it was of most Edoites). Hokusai's principal prints in this category (which are rather after the manner of classical cartoons, of the *Toba-e* and the eighteenth-century cartoonist Jichōsai) come in two series of medium and smaller sizes. The former is the more sophisticated, as in the notable Kabuki parody of Plate 216. Here we view a sad and melodramatic *michiyuki* scene, in which two ill-starred lovers attempt to escape their destiny in a journey that will end in fulfilment of a suicide pact. Now as any Kabuki-goer will know, one can either take the performance seriously—with all its bathos and stylized exaggeration—or not. The artist here chooses to take a critical view, perhaps in rebellion against his earlier decade of more serious actor-prints. Thus the rather dowdy lovers are shown posturing in a languorous pose that may prompt the cynic to exclaim, 'Get on with the suicide!', as the chanters at rear lustily proclaim the denouement, mouths strained wide open. The print forms a striking contrast with the artist's evocative, romantic treatment of such themes only a decade earlier (Plates 63–65).

The smaller of these comic series is not of the same artistic quality but the designs are amusing, and rich material for the study of Japanese humour. Thus in our Plate 217 we view an octopus as master of a shop, being offered tea by his servant as he tries to figure out an account of stringed coins on the abacus—evidently confused by some of his own surplus arms. Such scenes will find re-creation later in the work of Kuniyoshi, Kyōsai and Yoshitoshi; and indeed, this odd couple will make their own reappearance in

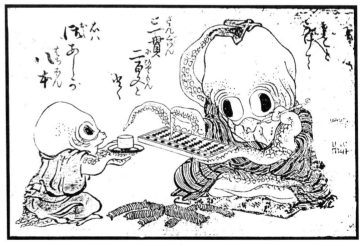

216 *Top* Kabuki Parody. *Chūban*-size print, *c.* mid-1810s. (For another of this series see Fig. 50.)

217 *Above* The Calculating Octopus. Small-*chūban* print, *c.* mid-1810s.

an even more famous tableau of Hokusai's shunga—to which we may now turn directly.

2

To those who know my prior work it may seem a trifle odd that I should feel perplexed at how to treat Hokusai's erotica. After all, I have studied the subject for thirty years; I also issued the first unexpurgated study of shunga (including Hokusai) back in 1968—and even suffered banning by the Japanese police for a massive yet inoffensive *expur*gated study of shunga two years later. The problem, then, is not so much a paucity of material as a plethora—plus the cavil of one moralistic reviewer of my *Images from the Floating World*, charging that I might have overemphasized shunga in order to increase sales (whereas in fact the publisher of the *German* edition complained that the illustrations were 'not meaty enough'!).[4]

In the end, however, such decisions on balance must be strictly objective: as a modern book, shunga must be shown, and uncut, even though the result may lead to banning in many countries (including present-day Japan); examples must be chosen solely on the basis of artistic quality, not sensationalism; and the number must be limited to their actual proportion of, and importance to, the artist's most meaningful *oeuvre* (with, in this case, greater detail to follow in a future monograph devoted to this subject alone). Yet even so, the problem remains that Hokusai's erotica comprises fully a dozen important books and albums, and a brief sub-chapter is hardly enough to do them justice.

We have already cited something of the Master's early work in shunga illustration, executed in a style closely patterned on that of his teacher Shunshō. Unlike his later erotica, these works are often signed; indeed, without his signature they would be difficult to distinguish from the work of several fellow-pupils in the Shunshō School (Plates 12, 15). There next follows a gap of about a decade, after which we begin to discover specimens of unsigned erotica in the Hokusai style, in the miniature-*surimono* format. (The presence or absence of signatures on shunga most often reflects government policy: the genus was never banned for Western-style moralistic reasons, but was sometimes the victim of general anti-decadent 'Reforms', such as we have already cited in Chapters IV and X.)

These diminutive, private editions for the connoisseurs of the time were originally issued in sets of twelve prints, enclosed in wrappers or envelopes—usually now lost—which included the title of the set, often the date, and sometimes even the pseudonym of the artist. One of the earliest of these delicate little prints—of which at least two hundred are known—datable to the year 1805, is illustrated in Plate 218. The scene is at Ushi-gozen, the 'Ox Shrine' at Mimeguri across the Sumida River. The protagonists are depicted in Hokusai's typically frail and graceful style of this period: indeed, although they seem to be very adequately equipped in primary sex characteristics, one almost fears for their health after such strenuous activities on a cold winter evening. This is obviously a 'calendar-print', for the short months of the year 1805 are inscribed on the lantern at lower right, which in fact matches the setting, as 1805 was the Year of the Ox.

Some of these miniature shunga feature an ingenious flip-up device in which a separately printed little flap is pasted to the print, providing both discreet and indiscreet versions of the same design. This flap was, however, often

218 Lovers at Ox Shrine. Small *surimono*, datable to 1805.

lost—or removed by unsubtle aficionados. Such may well be the case with the above specimen; but it is *not* with the rarely intact but somewhat later examples shown in Plates 201–204, both closed and opened.

It will be obvious that this kind of 'play-print' (adult toys, so to speak) is not susceptible to easy reproduction, and the tactile joy of flipping must be left to the reader's imagination. I will merely add that this device—termed *shikake-e* or 'trick-picture', and sometimes a feature of later shunga books as well—is always most ingeniously contrived (and provides vivid evidence that Japanese dexterity in export markets should not have been so unexpected).

It does not seem to me that shunga require much erudite commentary (and the texts that appear on many of them are seldom of a quality equal to the art). The scenes depicted here are (Plates 201–202) a New Year's monkey-trainer and his charge, resting before a window where hooded lovers furtively rendezvous; and (Plates 203–204) a river-scene with boatman on roof and lovers under it, as the New Year's sun rises in the background. Like many *surimono*, these sets of little prints often served as stylish New Year cards, and several of the present set bear the calendar-markings for 1812—the Year of the Monkey. These appear, for example, on the trainer's skirt, indicated by the number of petals in the floral decorations; and the

219 *Above* Street Encounter. *Ōban*-size plate from *Brocade of the East*, early 1810s. (See also Fig. 235.)

220 *Opposite top* Attempt at Rape. *Ōban*-size plate from *Brocade of the East*, early 1810s.

221 *Opposite bottom* Diving-girl with Lover. *Ōban*-size plate from *The Adonis Plant, c.* 1820. (See also Fig. 238.)

cyclical character for the year (*jin*) is shown on the bundle at lower left. Likewise, the pattern on the boatman's cloak comprises the character *saru*, 'monkey', which also appears on the lantern within the boat. I cannot claim that these minuscule calendar-prints (sometimes, only one of the set includes the actual date) are important works of art: merely that they are of higher quality, more enjoyable and creative than most of the greeting-cards one sees these days.

Such colourful little adult toys cater to people's latent voyeurism and delight in games. They are not ostentatiously erotic and, in fact, one can imagine children enjoying them as much as adults (and getting pleasurably educated in the process). With a set of these playful gems in hand, one is all too readily transported to another and more leisurely age, when the erotic was merely one of humanity's natural pleasures.

It must be commented that the influence of the woodblock-carver increases in proportion to the miniaturization of a tableau. In the absence of signature, with such

tiny prints (smaller than a postcard) absolute authentication of the artist is not easy. To weed out the works of pupils (Sōri III and Shinsai for the early ones, Hokusai II, Taito II and Eisen for the later) is no simple task, even for the specialist.

With most of Hokusai's shunga *books*, however—to which we now turn—there is rather more certainty of authorship. And like most of the artist's more impressive erotica these are clustered together in the years *c.* 1814–21. The Master was now in his mid-50s: perhaps his own sexual powers declining; or perhaps simply experiencing a rejuvenation of youthful passion; but above all, no doubt, stimulated by the flood of erotic publishing commissions that characterized this particular age of Edo culture.

The first such datable book is *Kinoe-no-komatsu* ('Pining for Love', to attempt an equivalent English pun) of 1814. Like all of the later Hokusai shunga books, it was issued in three slim volumes with five or so double-page colour-plates to each fascicle. As is customary, the text takes the form of a novelette recounting the erotic adventures of various heroes and heroines. The complicated plots—and Hokusai's probable involvement in their composition—must form the subject for a later study (he was fond, for example, of vividly employed erotic onomatopoeia); we can here only cite a few characteristic illustrations.

Plate 222 shows two lovers beside a *kotatsu* or covered-brazier (on which the girl rests her arm). The figure-composition is an unusually simple, diagonal one, but the complexity of clothing patterns combines with the busy

text to create a somewhat jumbled impression at first glance. (The original Japanese viewer probably turned to the text first and simultaneously absorbed the illustration, without ever trying to differentiate the two.)

The *pièce de résistance* of the set is the famous scene of 'Diving-girl and Octopi' (Plate 205). Hokusai's own mentor Shunshō had produced notable shunga illustrations of diving-girls subjected to seduction and rape at human hands as well as bestial, and Hokusai carried this concept to its pinnacle in this remarkable scene. On the right, a large octopus ravishes the girl with adroit cunnilingus, while a smaller octopus (his son?) assists earnestly at the left. Yet however bizarre the concept, the effect is neither comic nor pornographic; in this fantasy of a passionate shell-diver, we discover a new facet of Hokusai's genius and a consummate work of erotic art.[5]

Not unexpectedly, this masterful shunga design caused something of a sensation in Europe when it first became known. Edmond de Goncourt wrote of it as 'A terrifying plate . . . the nude form of a woman, swooning with pleasure. . . .' and J.-K. Huysmans' paean of 1889 also goes to some length:

The most beautiful Japanese erotic print that I know is truly frightening: it is of a Japanese woman mounted by an octopus; with its tentacles, the horrible beast sucks the tips of her breasts and rummages in her mouth, while its head drinks from her lower parts. The almost superhuman expression of agony and sorrow—which convulses this long, graceful female figure with aquiline nose—and the hysterical joy—which emanates at the same time from her forehead, from those eyes closed as in death—are admirable.

Understandably, there are certain misconceptions in Huysmans' lurid prose; and the 'terrifying' scene that thrilled these two connoisseurs would in more sophisticated circles today likely draw but a jaded yawn. In any case, despite its fame this is but one plate of many in these little volumes, albeit the most unusual.

It is important to emphasize that there had been no tradition of nude art in the Far East. The naked form appeared only incidentally: in scenes of disaster and pillage, or of bathing, for example, but with hardly any erotic connotations; and in shunga, where the situations were erotic but the nudity was not. (To be sure, at periods of government 'Reforms' semi-nude depictions sometimes flourished briefly in ukiyo-e, as compensation for the bans.) Nor was there any long tradition of sketching from the life—and none at all of the nude *per se*. Thus—not

222 Lovers by *Kotatsu*. Plate from *Pining for Love*, 1814.

having studied anatomy or the originals in any systematic manner—the Japanese artist was at a disadvantage in attempting to depict the human form; and Hokusai was certainly one of the pioneers in this category, as he was in many others. Indeed, this opportunity to attempt a new genre, a new approach to the human form, may well have been one of his principal stimuli to such elaborate erotic productions. There was, in fact, no particular stigma—social or legal—attached to erotic art at the time, nor to the artists who produced it. This was but another assignment. Yet with Hokusai, each new commission meant a chance to explore new worlds of graphic meaning, well above and beyond the requirements of the particular task in hand.

The artist's other major work in the shunga book will be found in *Mampuku wagōjin* (The Gods of Intercourse), datable to 1821. The printing is (at least in the early editions) of the finest quality and the illustrations, too, are uniformly excellent. Unlike the previous work, this one features a number of multiple scenes: double pairs of couples, onlookers and the like. The technique had appeared earlier in classical shunga scrolls, and Hokusai adapts it to fill each frame to the limit in complex compositions.[6]

Such a scene is that of Plate 206, where the young hero pleasures a matron at right, as another plays with herself at left. Again the combination of kimono-patterns and minuscule calligraphy will doubtless seem too busy for the Western viewer: the fault of the medium, not the artist. From the same volume, Plate 212 features one of the heroines of the novelette, lying exhausted at the roadside after being violently raped. The tableau is not all that different from the 'Diving-girl', and conveys a curious sense of quietude following outrage.

Two lesser shunga books of the period in Hokusai's style are *Tsuma-gasane* (Overlapping Skirts), of which an attempted rape scene is shown in Plate 223; and *Tama-* *katzura* (The Jewelled Merkin), of which a scene of young lovers will be found in Plate 213. Both books are a trifle weak in authority of style (and the second smacks a bit of Eisen, who sometimes imitated Hokusai at this period); but given the intervention of the woodblock-carver they cannot, for the present, be so readily removed from the Hokusai canon.

The Master's remaining—and more major—shunga *oeuvre* are in the album format: sets of twelve prints, usually in the larger, *ōban* size, plus brief texts. Bound in accordian-fashion, the plates are easily dismounted and many are thus scattered through the collections of the world.

The most famous of these albums is *Tsuhi-no-hinagata* (Models of Loving Couples), dating from the early 1810s. The signature Shishoku Gankō appearing on one of the prints is thought to represent a temporary Hokusai pseudonym, though exact verification is not possible. Each plate of the album is filled with the forms of amorous couples; the compositions, enhanced by bold yet tasteful colouring, are often striking, with the texts (comprising the participants' conversation) rather less obtrusive than in the smaller books.

The furtive rendezvous is a frequent theme in shunga, and serves to heighten the emotional impact of the situation (and one is curiously reminded of works by Huysmans in this connection). In Plate 214, for example, we glimpse a lover's secret, hurried visit to his love: he looks furtively to the left; she has just come from the bath after washing her long hair. The undulating waves of kimono-pattern, flesh and hair echo the urgency of the occasion; and again, the larger format permits more simplification of

223 Attempted Rape. Plate from *Overlapping Skirts*, c. 1820.

224 Matron with Lover. *Ōban*-size plate from *Plovers above the Waves*, *c.* 1820.

225 *Opposite top* Massive Lovers. *Chūban*-size plate from *The Lusty God of Nuptials*, 1822. (See also Fig. 242.)

226 *Opposite bottom* Massive Lovers. *Chūban*-size plate from *The Lusty God of Nuptials*, 1822.

composition than was found in the books.

With Plate 215 the frame is filled even more tightly, as a geisha and her secret lover meet at festival-time—he sporting a half-opened fan and cape, regalia for performance of the Lion Dance. The tension of the situation is well expressed by the girl's passionate kiss (in Japan, reserved for intimate contact only), and in the strategic placement of the man's hand. (The reader unfamiliar with the Orient may require time to differentiate the participants' various appendages, but it is worth the effort.) As is customary in shunga, the sex organs are depicted in exaggerated size: an artistic device that is perhaps a vestige of ancient phallic worship, perhaps symbolic of the protagonists' highly aroused state.

Another major album of the same period, unsigned but in Hokusai's distinctive style, is the *Azuma nishiki* (Brocade of the East).[7] Plate 219 again shows a furtive meeting—this time, on the street, as the hooded lover urgently accosts his receptive love, partly hidden by an umbrella. Scenes of rape are very common in shunga; Plate 220, for example, shows a matron being accosted by an insistent admirer. (The frequent appearance of matrons may well reflect one

important—and affluent—portion of the shunga audience: ladies-in-waiting, whether of the *daimyō*-lords or of the Shōgun's harem.) In expressing the forceful interrelation of the couple, the artist employs a kind of inverted S-curve that effectively leads the action back to where it started from.

From the late 1810s the Master's shunga style turns even more to massive figures and monumental compositions: filling—and sometimes reaching beyond—the frame of the print. His major work of this later period is popularly known, from the pattern on its decorated box, as *Namichidori* (Plovers above the Waves). This significant production exists in several editions, but the earliest is probably that issued under the title *Fukujusō* (The Adonis Plant—a New Year's symbol). In Plate 221 we view a Junoesque diving-girl (her basket of shellfish at left), mounted by her equally monumental lover. The pair form a massive union that somehow reminds one of the artist's 'Sumō Wrestlers' of more than three decades earlier (Plate 16).

In the better-known and more luxuriant edition of this album—*Plovers above the Waves*—the woodblocks are recarved and the text is deleted, being replaced by an opulent background of mica-dust; hand-colouring is added here and there, and the vulva details are also hand-applied (whether by artist or assistant is unclear). This de luxe edition is shown in Plate 224—the protagonists appearing more like a Rock of Gibraltar than slaves of passion. In this album, also, we find touches of the comic—characteristic both of Hokusai and of Japanese erotica in general—as in the scene of the maladroit attempted rape of a maiden by

her father's clumsy clerk (Fig. 240).

Smaller in size and dating from somewhat later, 1822, the *En-musubi Izumo-no-sugi* (The Lusty God of Nuptials) is again characteristic of Hokusai's final stage of shunga production.[8] The participants are rendered in increasingly massive fashion, as though sculpted from blocks of wood or marble, and here Hokusai foreshadows one of the trends of modern sculpture, while admittedly considerably reducing the passionate content of his shunga.[9] Plates 225 and 226 are typical of this curious, terminal development in the artist's style of nude depiction, in which the erotic element tends to get lost in the block-like mass of the entwined figures.

One may well re-inquire here as to what drove Hokusai to such increasing extremes in the depiction of sex at this period? Obviously, the commissions were there: ukiyo-e artists did not paint just for fun, nor publish for their own amusement. But there is more to this remarkable interval of erotic activity than a simple job to be done. One thinks here, inevitably, of Picasso (who was, incidentally, an avid collector of Japanese shunga), and of his similar burst of erotic energy in his later years; and, without wishing to go any further into psychoanalysis than I have already, I think it will be clear that, at least, one of the keys to Hokusai's personality is to be found in his shunga of this surprising decade. Scholars who shy from this difficult theme will do so only at the risk of missing half their man.

New Year in a Yoshiwara Salon. *Ōban* pentaptych, *c.* early 1810s.

NOTES

1 The full pentaptych is reproduced *below left*.
2 There is a famed set of seven prints by Utamaro, from the late 1790s, showing the full 'Korean Parade'—with several of the geisha blowing the same imported horns; and Toyohiro produced a similar series on the Ryūkyū theme. In view of the fact that a Ryūkyū Mission did visit Edo in XI/1806, a date of I/1807 seems very probable for such a 'New Year's Card'.
3 The monochrome edition of I/1815 is not only the best known but also the most effective in reproduction, and hence has been used in our first plates rather than the possibly earlier, block-coloured edition of *c.* 1814–15—which has fewer plates and is entitled *Ehon chōsei-den* (Picture-book of Longevity-Hall). It should also be remembered that publication was sometimes rather later than the artist's date of execution; from the fact of collaboration here by the Nagoya patron-pupil Bokusen, it may well be that the plan for this volume derived from Hokusai's lengthy stay there in 1812. Such discrepancies between dates of production and publication constitute one of the many problems in exact Hokusai dating and stylistic studies.
4 Indeed, that edition proved far less successful than the American, British and French ones. For the review, see the incurably casuistical Prof. David Waterhouse in *Impressions*, No. 6, 1981 (and my rejoinder in the following issue), whose viewpoint—common enough some generations ago—is that ukiyo-e is immoral and that Japan possessed: '. . . one of the bawdiest societies the world has known. . . . To maintain a doctrine of art for art's sake is intellectually dishonest . . . but even if one decides to condemn Edo morals, it does not follow that the prints are negligible as art. Indeed, if there is immoral art, it is historically false to ignore it. . . . If, as I believe he should, the student of history of art asks himself *why* he is interested in a particular art-form, he may find that a full and honest answer impinges on his system of moral values. . . .' (For an even earlier exchange on the subject of Japan's 'relative bawdiness' see my 'Floating-world Morals vs. Ukiyo-e Scholarship', in *Ukiyo-e Art* No. 12 (1966), and the Waterhouse rejoinder in the following issue.)
5 See fig. *bottom left* for the Shunshō, and Plate 217 for an earlier view of this briny pair. One is also reminded of Utamaro's famous underwater scene of 1788, showing *kappa*-devils ravishing a diving-girl.
6 On such predecessors, see my *Erotica Japonica: Masterworks of Shunga Painting*, New York and London, forthcoming.

7 In later reissues, plates from this work are often found bound in with those of the previous set; I am happy here to be able to clarify the original title and format, for the first time.
8 The convoluted title refers to the fact that such books were often included in a bride's trousseau, for instructional purposes; on this subject, see again my *Erotica Japonica* (note 6). This is the rarest of Hokusai's later shunga works, and our plates probably represent its first unexpurgated publication in modern times (for bibliographical data, see Appendix, Erotica, No. 18). I might add that the title is written with extremely complex characters that would be quite unreadable without rubrics. There is also a further play on words in that *Izumo-no-sugi*—'Cryptomerias of Izumo', the God of Marriage—also implies *itsumo-no-suki*—'forever horny'.
9 It might well be asked why Hokusai himself did not attempt sculpture. The answer is simple: in Japan, sculpture worthy of the name was entirely for religious purposes—mainly Buddhist, some Shintō—and probably the only other area open to the plebeian artisan (aside from architectural decoration) was in such practical miniatures as *netsuke*: in which genus, in fact, there is considerable erotica.

Style of Shunshō: Diving-girl and Amorous Octopus. Plate from the shunga book *Yōkyoku iro-bangumi* (Noh Erotica), 1781.

XVI
Gestation Period:
Hokusai in the 1820s

FOLLOWING the frenetic decade of the 1810s—dramatic illustrations, bold paintings, startling shunga—it must come as something of an anticlimax to examine the Master's *oeuvre* of the intermediate half-decade *c.* 1823–8. Hokusai was, after all, in his mid-60s and intermittently afflicted with palsy (which he boasted of having cured himself, with Chinese medicines)—though health does not seem to have been a major problem. Doubtless considerations of the market-place loomed largest in the activities of a commercial artist. The next generation of Hokusai scholars will have to dig more deeply into the year-by-year details of Edo (and Nagoya/Ōsaka/Kyōto) publishing—fads, tastes, prosperity, bankruptcies—as well as into the social life of the times, in order to get a clearer picture of their man. But any artist so active deserves a period of reflection and gestation before the next great creation; and our book itself may well profit from a brief chapter less replete with masterpieces and superlatives.

Of Hokusai's book-illustration we saw that around the year 1820 his work reached a peak in the artistically unified albums for painters; the final, monumental erotica came at this juncture likewise, as well as some notable *surimono*

227 Swallows flying amid Wisteria. Plate from the anthology *Illustrated Verses on Flowers-and-Birds*, 1828. (For bibliographical data on this chapter see Appendix, Books, No. 205 ff.)

228 Bee on Wild-rose. Plate from *The Lotus-pedestal,* verse-anthology, 1826.

229 *Above* Scene in a Nagasaki Geisha-house. Plate from *Fashionable Edo Cookery*, Series IV of 1835. (See also Fig. 217.)

series. The latter were followed by many further sets of these privately issued little prints—particularly in the still-life genre—but this not being a *catalogue raisonné* I have neither the space nor the intention of detailing such abundant productions of secondary importance (but see the

Appendix sub Figs. 53 ff.).

In the book-field, too, major works for this time are rare—and in any case I have already cited the volumes of 1822–4 in Chapter XIII. Furthermore, Hokusai's main *oeuvre* was in lesser *kyōka* anthologies and in miscellaneous books that did not give full scope to his talents. It is probably worth re-emphasizing here that the commercial artist really had very little say regarding the medium in which his work appeared: the effort involved in a small monochrome illustration and in an elaborate, polychrome album-plate was not all that different as far as the print-designer was concerned. Though he did not know it, Hokusai's future fame lay very much in the hands of his publisher, who—his eye on immediate sales—was the one who decided the quality and elaborateness of printing, and the artisans best suited to effect the desired product.

It is thus almost by accident that a few major book-plates do appear, even in this low-keyed decade; and they are principally from volumes in which the illustrations feature the same mixed collaboration as the verse-anthologies themselves. Perhaps Hokusai's best-known illustration of the period is that from the *kyōka* volume *Renge-dai* (The Lotus-pedestal) of 1826 (a commemorative volume, hence the Buddhist ring to the title). The design (Plate 228) is rather reminiscent of Utamaro's famous *Insect Book* of 1788; and we look in vain here for the powerful flower-work we shall find in the Hokusai prints of but a few years later. Compared to the masterpieces of even a generation earlier this example serves mainly to show how far the *kyōka*-books had declined in vigour, if not in quality.

Of greater visual interest are the illustrations in *Kachō-gasan uta-awase* (Illustrated Verses on Flowers-and-Birds), which appeared in 1828. Plate 227, for example, is surprisingly decorative—the placement and motion of forms taking precedence over emphasis on the artist's individuality—possibly under the influence of such collaborators of the time as the great Kōrin School painter Hōitsu. In the more practical category of 'how-to' books we may cite the *Edo-ryūkō ryōri-tsū* (Fashionable Edo Cookery) of 1822 (with a sequel in 1835). Hokusai's earlier plate will be found later (Fig. 217), but for more prominent illustration here I have chosen, both for its design and its content, one from the sequel. Plate 229 provides an intimate view of Maruyama, the pleasure quarter of distant Nagasaki, showing food being served to a Chinese member of the Trade Mission. One can readily imagine Dr Von Siebold—who figures later in this chapter—in his place.

The mid-1820s indeed mark a low point in ukiyo-e publication: the reasons were probably economic and social rather than artistic (although, by coincidence perhaps, the leader of the Kabuki-print school, Toyokuni I, had died in 1825). It is, in fact, only towards the end of the decade that Hokusai returned to his usual level of productivity. Thus one may find of greater aesthetic interest that other little volume of practical function, *Bonga hitori-geiko* (Teach Yourself Sand-painting) of 1828; its frontispiece is of value in tracing the artist's *bijin-ga* style in this transitional period (Plate 230).

From the same year dates yet another guide for craftsmen; but even more significant is the masterly *Ehon Teikin-*

230 *Top* Girls making Sand-paintings. Plate from *Teach Yourself Sand-painting*, 1828.

231 *Above* Street Scene. Plate from *Illustrated Home Precepts*, Series I of 1828. (Text at top of each page has been omitted.)

ōrai (Illustrated Home Precepts), with two sequels in later years. The illustrations bear little relation to the classic, moralistic text, and are the better for it. The most interesting are those that provide vignettes of Edo life, such as Plate 231. Here we view a tiny panorama replete with bell-ringing visionary, lion-dancer, Buddhist sculptor, bitch with pups, *sumō*-wrestler, Bishop and acolytes—each panel squeezed into postcard-size. And if only for its subject, we must also include a view of the shop-front of Nishimuraya Eijudō, the leading Edo print and book publisher (Plate 232).

With the year 1829 comes the charming *Ressen gazō-shū* (Portraits of the Immortals); Plate 233 shows one of those quaint genii of Chinese legend, Gama-sennin, here de-

picted as a plump 'Toad Boy', playing with his magic pet. During this year, rather surprisingly, the artist also returns to the painstaking (and eye-straining) work of *yomi-hon* illustration, in a sequel to the *Suiko-gaden* series (which he had commenced back in 1805—see p. 302). Of greater visual appeal is his picture-book on the same theme, *Suikoden yūshi-no-ezukushi* (Heroes of the *Suihuchuan*), also of 1829. (These publications obviously reflect a resurgence of popularity for this classic of Oriental heroics.) Some readers may feel they have had a surfeit of macho Chinese warriors by this time; but in the more striking designs to this set, the artist for a moment transcends the formal scenario of this novel to transmit something of its stirring *spirit* (Plate 234). And special mention must be made of one uncharacteristically titillating detail from the novel, for it is fortunately known also in the artist's preliminary drawing as well (Plates 235, 236).

Even more provocative, and probably also from this period (though the earliest dated edition is of 1844), is the

232 *Top* Shop of the Edo publisher Eijudō. From the same book as Plate 231. (See also Fig. 218.)

233 *Above* Immortal with Pet Toad. Plate from *Portraits of the Immortals*, 1829.

striking work on famous women of Japanese history and legend, *Onna Imagawa* (The Women's Precepts). In this interesting volume we find examples surprisingly close to Hokusai's erotica of a decade earlier, such as Plate 237. Indeed, in this voluptuous view of a lady relaxing after the bath, her yielding form and fluent robes contrasting with the geometrical background, one may well perceive a more moving and evocative eroticism than one feels in much of the artist's final and more monumental shunga.

A *kyōka*-anthology on a related theme is *Onna-ichidai eiga-shū* (Lives of Flourishing Women) of 1831. Compared to the previous plate, the style of figure-depiction seems rather stiff and unpliant; this, however, is more likely to be the fault of the engraver than of the artist (Plate 238). And again, it is well to recall that, unlike the case with the sketches or paintings, we are here viewing the artist at least one degree removed. Nevertheless, with old age (he was now over seventy) Hokusai's figures do tend to become less supple and, therefore, less human and lovable—contrasting sharply with the more loose and evocative figures of his middle years. When to this feature is added the increasingly precise but hard and unpliant techniques of later ukiyo-e engraving and printing, it is not strange if some observers wonder if it is really the same artist involved in these so strikingly different generations of production.

For the artist's more significant print *oeuvre* one must await the coming decade. But there are in the mid-1820s interesting smaller prints that tend to bridge the gap between the miscellaneous, random tableaux of the *Manga* and the masterful, integrated landscape-with-figures of the *Fuji* prints: for example, the series of twelve miniatures known as *Daidō zui* (Scenes on the Road) of *c.* 1825. In the Fishmarket Scene of Plate 239, the striking integration of figures rather overpowers the diminutive print (only 12 × 20 cm/4.7 × 7.8 in) giving one the impression of viewing something far more monumental, even mural-like. And again one becomes suddenly conscious of the ukiyo-e artist as captive of his medium: the same print, enlarged to *ōban* size and printed with the quality of the *Fuji* series, would today command the fervid attention of print-collectors the world over; whereas few of them know, much less covet, this rare series. Yet the concept, the Platonic ideal involved, is hardly all that different.

The Master's lesser prints of this period will be cited in the Appendix (Figs. 52 ff.), but at least one further example should be shown here: that in the small, narrow *tanzaku* format, into which *Manga*-like genre subjects are adroitly squeezed. In the example of Plate 240 we glimpse the artist's customary grasp of the 'decisive moment' in a flowing situation. And among Hokusai's more interesting *suri-mono* of this time is one that might be interpreted as a kind of 'imaginative self-portrait'. This is the 'Fisherman Resting' of Plate 241. The design itself is not specifically signed but at the end of the poems at top will be seen a variant version of the artist's late pen-name *Manji* (the Buddhist 'Swastika'), which he used first in *senryū* verses from the year 1821. The lower-right inscription, recording only 'Both painting and verse', has sometimes been mistranslated as implying 'Self-portrait', but there is, of course, no harm in seeing some-

234 *Top* Chinese Merlin and Pet. Plate from *Heroes of the 'Suihuchuan'*, 1829. (See also Fig. 219.)

235 *Above* Attempted Rape and Rescuers. From the same book as Plate 234.

thing of the artist in any such evocative and reflective portraits, whoever the actual subject.

Other Hokusai biographical data from this interval would include notice of such oddities as the designs for floats in a sideshow at the Asakusa entertainment quarter in 1820, the death of an unidentified daughter in 1821, a probable period of residence with the painter Tōrin in 1822, and the divorce of his eldest daughter O-Miyo (from the disciple Shigenobu, whom Hokusai had made his adopted son). The Master continued his hobby of *senryū* composition (these satirical verses being published regularly in the anthologies of the time). In 1828 the artist's second wife died. Hokusai was now 68, his delinquent grandson causing him all kinds of trouble, even being unsuccessfully returned once to his father Shigenobu in 1830. And Hokusai himself seems (not for the first or last time) to have been in financial straits: unwilling to lower his fees, yet not able to get sufficient work. At least half of the artist's book-production of this period was done in collaboration. And in this connection it is important to cite an extant publisher's advertisement of the year 1823, which not only announces several Hokusai picture-books that were never published, but also offers 'Original painting-albums by the Master Iitsu'. Clearly the art-publishing world was not thriving if

236 Attempted Rape. Preparatory sketch for detail of Plate 235. *Sumi* and pentimenti on paper, 11¾ × 12½ in / 29.8 × 31.5 cm. Unsigned (the seal is that of an early collector). (In Japanese drawings, corrective lines are most often done in light *sumi* on small, overlaid sheets of paper; at other times, revisions are made directly on the sketch, either in *sumi* or in *shu*, vermilion, as in this plate.) (Note: due to the large size, this sketch may represent the drawing for a proposed painting on the same theme.)

the Master was reduced to preparing original sketch-albums to eke out a living. But although the new idea of selling an artist's manuscript-sketch-albums *en masse*—and actually advertising them in print—might seem the height of commercialism, we must not think that such a consideration worried Hokusai. He was, after all, a professional artist and had to work to live (in Japan there was no tradition of the artist starving in a garret). Moreover, he seems to have had a passion for spreading both his fame and his artistic style. The following quotation is taken verbatim from the publisher Eijudō's advertisement, which appeared at the end of *Models of Modern Combs and Pipes* of 1823:

MAITRE IITSU PAINTING ALBUMS

THESE ARE NOT ENGRAVED ON WOODBLOCKS, BUT THE ORIGINAL PAINTINGS OF THE MASTER IITSU, FORMERLY HOKUSAI. EVEN THOUGH ONE MIGHT BE A PERSON LIVING IN A DISTANT PROVINCE, IF ONE BUT BUYS AND STUDIES FROM THIS ALBUM, IT IS THE SAME AS HAVING ENROLLED IN THE MASTER'S STUDIO.

One can well imagine the effect that such an advertisement might have had on aspiring artists in the 'Provinces' (indeed, some readers may well feel—as I myself do—a certain twinge of regret at having been born a century and a half too late): and the only wonder is that Hokusai was not deluged with orders. The scarcity of such albums suggests that they were too expensive for the average amateur; and, of course, most of the extant albums were broken up around the turn of the last century, when Hokusai became popular among Western collectors.

It must here be remarked that undisputed Hokusai *paintings* of this period are surprisingly rare. For the coming 1830s this scarcity is readily explicable by the Master's major efforts in the *print* genre: not only the great *Fuji* series but dozens upon dozens of other important works. As for much of the preceding decade, however, the 1820s

seem to have been a period of gestation, of intense but scattered efforts mainly in book-illustration, *surimono* and miscellaneous prints: all presumably limited by a decline of publishing prosperity. One of the few unquestioned paintings of this era that I have seen is the thoughtful 'Wandering Soothsayer' of Plate 242. Dated New Year of 1827, this is a depiction—in the snow—of an itinerant priest-pedlar of versified, fortune-telling 'charms'. It probably refers to the noted Noh drama *Uta-ura*, in which the protagonist is just such a wandering diviner, long separated from his family, sometimes half in trance. One is attracted here by the masterful depiction of face, hand, and divination-bow: but in the overly massive attention to robe, feet and clogs, we perceive an incongruity rather typical of ukiyo-e in this transitional, 'decadent' age—an era characterized by mass feelings of restlessness and the need for change.

For this period there are also occasional 'avant-garde' paintings (reminiscent of some of the startling experiments of the Kyōto masters Shōhaku and Rosetsu in the later

237 Lady relaxing after Summer Bath. Detail of plate from *Women's Precepts*, c. late 1820s (?). (See note to Books, No. 229.)

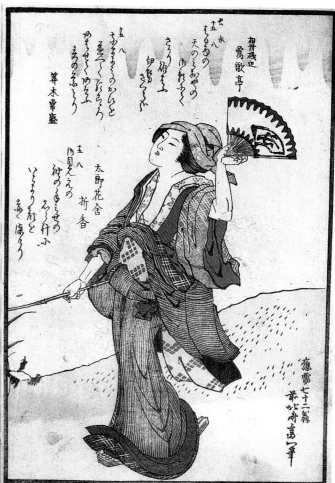

238 *Opposite top* Tipsy Women on Picnic. Plate from *Lives of Flourishing Women*, 1831.

239 Fishmarket Scene. Small, *koban* print from the series *New Scenes on the Road*, *c*. 1825. (See Prints, No. 136.)

240 *Left* Roof-tilers at Work. *Tanzaku*-size print, *c*. 1830. (See also Prints, No. 140.)

241 Fisherman Resting. *Chūban surimono*-print, *c*. 1830. (It has not been noted before but, interestingly enough, not only is the verse at left by Hokusai (signed 'Manji'), but that at right bears an elliptical signature resembling that in our Plate 128—and would then be by Hokusai's own daughter, O-Ei.)

eighteenth century), such as the 'Great Waterspout' of Plate 243. Here, in effect, the movement and action quite literally *become* the subject. One is struck not only by the Master's grasp of the essentials of composition and effective design—the rhythmic line, the impeccable spacing— but also by the willingness to take chances with fresh viewpoints, bizarre concepts.

One other curious—and not characteristically Hokusai—painting of this decade is the 'Crabs' of Plate 244. Here we see depicted in incredible detail a variety of crustaceans, large and small, against a background of aquatic plants. The stylishly scientific—yet somehow surrealistic—approach goes back to the pseudo-Ming experiments of Jakuchū (with something of Ōkyo as well) in the previous century. Though the scene is underwater, the briny protagonists are delineated sharply and with traces of Occidental influence in the shading. Perhaps the painting reveals most of all that Hokusai could, when so commanded, handle practically any kind of assignment.[1]

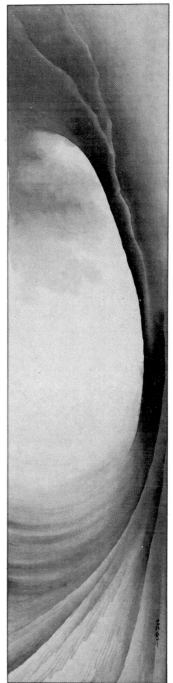

242 *Opposite left* Wandering Soothsayer. Painting in light colours on paper; dated 1827. 49 × 19½ in / 124 × 50 cm. Signed Hokusai Iitsu.

243 *Opposite top right* Great Waterspout. Kakemono in light colours on silk; *c.* 1819. 49 × 12 in / 124 × 30 cm. Signed Katsushika Taito.

244 *Opposite bottom right* All kinds of Crabs. Kakemono in colours on silk; *c.* late 1820s. 19 × 23½ in / 48 × 60 cm. Signed Hokusai, changed to Iitsu.

In addition there is interesting evidence—and this, from *abroad*—that Hokusai did many other paintings in this decade. However, these may no longer be extant in the originals.

As we have noted earlier, Japan had been deliberately closed off from foreign intercourse since the 1620s, the Shōgun permitting only limited trade-delegations from China, Korea, Okinawa and Holland. The Dutch Connection was tolerated in the belief that this Protestant merchant-power would devote itself to pragmatic business rather than emulate the conquistatorial designs of the Catholic powers. And this was indeed the case: the Dutch Mission remained content, aside from occasional tribute-journeys to distant Edo, to remain holed up on the man-made island of Deshima, in Nagasaki Harbour. (Wives were usually banned, but the local courtesans were given free entry, so that it was not exactly a hardship post; indeed, there are frequent shunga depictions of the hyper-active Dutchmen.)

To this Mission in the year 1823 came the German-Dutch physician Philipp-Franz von Siebold. He remained in Japan until 1830, but his later activities were curtailed by imprisonment, then exile, for having gathered geographical data and maps (a banned activity for a government morbidly fearful of foreign intervention). From practically the day of his arrival this remarkable man set out to record and collect everything he could about the 'Hermit Nation'. Von Siebold's voluminous compendium *Nippon* was, alas, never completed (for example the proposed sections on art), but seven parts were published between the years 1832 and 1858, and the illustrations include several re-workings of Hokusai's *Fuji* prints and *Manga* plates. More pertinent to our theme is the fact that this erudite physician was familiar with our artist's name, even referring to the *Manga* volumes as 'a collection of sketches put out by the yet living court-painter *Hoksai* in Edo, who in spirit as well as in taste excels all others of the kind'. It is somewhat doubtful whether Von Siebold actually met the artist (his use of the term 'court-painter' certainly indicates that he was unaware of Hokusai's plebeian status), but during his sojourn in Edo in 1826 he did commission from him a set of paintings depicting genre scenes of the samurai capital. Whether the actual 'Hokusai Paintings' still preserved in the Siebold Collection are the originals, or copies, is a matter of scholarly debate.[2] But it is clear that even in this relatively quiet decade leading up to the celebrated *Fuji* prints, the master was a much-sought-after painter of renown in Edo, and must have done considerable other, notable work that has not survived the fires, earthquakes and other disasters that so often ravaged that fragilely constructed, sprawling metropolis.

NOTES

1 A related tableau appears in the *Hokusai gashiki* of 1819.
2 See my 'Hokusai's Dutch Connection Revisited'. In the journal *Andon*, in press; reprinted in *Studies in Edo Art*.

XVII
Landscape Peak:
The *Thirty-six*
Views of Fuji (1)

1

HOKUSAI was an eminently *commercial* artist, perhaps the greatest the world has known. He was therefore strongly and inevitably influenced by his market, by sales conditions, by popular fashions and, most of all, by his publishers' actual commissions.

Most artists have, of course, patrons, supporters, clients, dealers, who often influence the direction of their work. For the ukiyo-e print-designer, however, the publishers were normally his only contact with the sales-market, and their influence was not only predominant but often total. As good luck would have it, the Edo publishers were men of taste and—if they were not overly generous to their artists—the direction they gave to the development of the ukiyo-e print was an overwhelmingly favourable one. The audience for this 'floating-world art' was likewise enthusiastic and receptive, generally following the major publishers' leads in matters of taste: though it was not always that apparent just who led whom.

We find Hokusai now approaching 70, long past retirement point for most men in his age, having achieved a full career as painter, print-designer and, above all, book-illustrator: but, somehow, not having arrived at the pinnacle of his potential.

The reason for this may be found largely in Hokusai's market: following the death of Utamaro in 1806, the genre of *bijin-ga*—depictions of female beauty—had gradually declined and the actor-print had risen to principal place in popular interest. This change in fashion was caused and directed mainly by the great burst of popularity for the Kabuki theatre itself in the first quarter of the century.

As in his youth Hokusai could, of course, have done capable work in the world of Kabuki-art; but this was evidently not to his taste: the essentially journalistic nature of such commissions, necessitating daily association with actors, playwrights and theatre-managers, probably did not suit his way of life. And thus Kabuki depiction became something of a monopoly of the rival Utagawa School of ukiyo-e masters, with Toyokuni I as the dominating figure.

Hokusai therefore tended to devote himself to the detailed work of book-illustration and specialized *surimono* miniatures—both fields which he enjoyed, in which he excelled, and which provided an adequate living, even if the results were not so impressive as the large prints. (It must be remembered, however, that the size and grandeur of the artist's production did not much affect his income or even his fame at the time.)

Had Hokusai died approaching his seventieth year he would be remembered as an important artist during two different generations of ukiyo-e development; and, if the discussion were limited to book-illustrators, he would surely rank only after Moronobu (pioneer of ukiyo-e in the later seventeenth century) as the master of this field.

Hokusai, however, did not die but went on to a 'second life', to a new period of feverish artistic activity that was, in the end, to bring him to the acme of acclaim in his own land and—from a generation after his death—a recognition abroad such as has never been accorded to an Asian artist before or after.

Long life alone was not what brought this acclaim to Hokusai: it was, rather, the sudden surge of popular interest in the landscape-print, that swelled up and reached a peak in the early 1830s.

Hokusai had already designed excellent, occasional landscape-prints from around the turn of the century, and this field was clearly one of his potential fortes. We have already detailed the background that lay behind Hokusai's new and final assault on the landscape-print: his experiments—from fully three decades earlier—with Western-style scenes and with the pseudo-Occidental 'perspective-prints', as well as with more native-style, miniature series of book-illustrations and Tōkaidō prints, plus numerous larger landscape-prints and *surimono* that constituted bold attempts to create a new genre. But all of these efforts stopped short of their mark: for the popular audience was not yet there, nor were the publishers ready to pioneer a new field of action. By the late 1820s, however, the time had become ripe and the ageing but untiring Hokusai was ready and willing to take this opportunity to widen the horizons of ukiyo-e, to infuse new life into this multifaceted artistic creature of the times. Thus it was only as the artist approached the final phase of his career that this hitherto minor genre revived and, suddenly, expanded into major proportions.

The social background for this phenomenon lay in the widespread growth of interest in travel itself. The Japanese had, from the early seventeenth century, been prohibited from voyage abroad; and travel within Japan itself was subject to severe restrictions. But with the nineteenth century came a general weakening of government authority and the rise of inherent plebeian power, and these restraints were relaxed. For the first time the possibilities of nation-wide travel were opened up to the commoners of Edo and other regions.

At first, guidebooks, maps, travel-fiction, picture-books, and such lesser print-series as those Hokusai himself had issued early in the century, served such needs. In the later 1820s, however, the boom in travel began to reach a peak; around the year 1830, for example, it is recorded that annually the Ise Shrines alone—hundreds of miles away from the urban centres—received over a million pilgrims: most of them travelling by foot and taking some weeks for the journey. Travel was, nominally, most often related to pilgrimages to famous shrines and temples; but the impulse was only partly religious: the scenic views, the inns and pleasure quarters en route were surely as much an attraction as the destinations themselves. So great was the fever for distant excursions that neighbourhood associations even set up lotteries, with the poorer citizens pooling their funds for a chance at the lucky number.

And, a traveller having spent the best part of a month on the road (or, having missed out on the lottery and being forced to pine impatiently at home), it was only natural that souvenirs of the places visited, or dreamed of, should likewise achieve an acme of popularity. The result was a plethora of pictorial guidebooks and, most important as far as our particular subject goes, *prints*. This fashion was the deciding factor in raising Hokusai's art to its final, crowning achievement.

One tends to think of Hokusai as an all-round artist; indeed, there are few if any areas of painting and drawing that he did not cultivate at one time or another. Yet no master, however great, is equally talented in all fields. Moreover, with an artist of Hokusai's long life and frenetic career, one will find inevitable mutations in taste, interest, style, and even in skill in a given subject. Hokusai's *bijin-ga* figure-prints marked one early culmination of his career; but before a decade had passed he was deeply into his 'Chinese Period'—and even had he wished, he could hardly have repeated his earlier success in, for example, the depiction of delicate female beauty. An artist's development is continuous (with, to be sure, sudden bursts of inspiration or slumps) and he can never really go back to an earlier phase of his development.

Thus Hokusai's middle period in the first quarter of the nineteenth century featured notable work in figure-design, but increasingly less delicate in execution, and most often expressed through the media of illustration and sketch-books, rather than in more monumental forms (except, that is, for his rare paintings). The landscape genre ideally suited the next stage of Hokusai's development, and the explosion of the market afforded him the opportunity to give free reign to this inherent talent, which was only waiting to be reawakened.

Perhaps luckily, with a market still rather limited, there was as yet no one to challenge him. Toyokuni I and II, Kunisada, Kuniyoshi, Eisen and others were to experiment briefly with the new genre in this period, but then go back to their own specialities. And the young Hiroshige was still waiting in the wings: soon to be stimulated by the old master to take his own place on the ukiyo-e landscape stage.

But what were the first fruits of this fortunate coincidence of demand and available talent? As fate would have it, the initial result—the outpouring of all the artist's suppressed energies in the field—was to prove the major work of his career: perhaps the greatest single achievement of the Japanese print.

2

It would be difficult to speak of the Japanese landscape without mentioning the towering, majestic mountain Fuji. Indeed, it has become one of the underlying symbols of Japan. But to the natives, Mt Fuji (*Fuji-san*—sometimes misread abroad as 'Fujiyama') has long been more than just a landmark. The Japanese—like many ancient peoples—were sun-worshippers. Indeed, the Sun-goddess Amaterasu is considered the first ancestor of the Imperial dynasty. And it was the radiant summit of Mt Fuji that first caught the rays of the dawn sun, in magical times of old just as today.

First formed from three separate eruptions in the pre-historic period, this huge (3776 metres/12,000 ft high, with a base some 30 kilometres/18 miles wide), symmetrical, semi-active volcano—dormant since 1707—was from early times an object of primitive worship. The ancient Shintō cults eventually merged with the Buddhist mountain-worshipping sect Shugendō to develop an extensive system of Fuji/Asama (Sengen) subsidiary shrines that was finally to cover the entire nation. Nearly every Province had its own 'Provincial Fuji'—a local mountain vaguely resembling the Sacred Peak; and the Fuji-*kō* associations in each hamlet or ward were ever active in arranging pilgrimages to Mt Fuji itself, and related activities at the hundreds of local subsidiary shrines—these often featuring a mound of earth and stone, called *Fuji-zuka*, in emulation of the Sacred Mountain and serving as an alternative object of worship. (Included were even artificial hills of some elevation, such as one raised at Waseda in 1779, and two at Meguro in 1812 and 1829.) This 'Fuji Religion' was but one of many such strange popular phenomena in this uncertain *fin-de-siècle* age; and, naturally, such Fuji-worshippers were, along with print-lovers and amateur artists, among the prime purchasers of Hokusai's new series. For the more affluent, these prints may even have partly taken the place of the simple printed charms that worshippers brought back from their pilgrimages to the mountain itself, functioning as 'Fuji-talismans'.

This obsession with Mt Fuji thus spread to the art-world as well. The Sacred Mountain had occasionally appeared in scroll-paintings as early as the eleventh century, and by the fifteenth century had become a standard subject for painters—first of the Yamato-e, Tosa, Sesshū and Kanō classical schools—but most often as the adjunct to some travel-narrative: the *Tales of Ise*, the wanderings of St Ippen or the poet Saigyō, the *Soga Tales* and, later, the *Chūshin-gura* drama. With the eighteenth century Fuji became a theme even for such Nanga literati masters as Taigadō (one of whose painting-seals bears the proud inscription, 'Climbed Mt Fuji, 1748'). Contemporary with Taigadō was the dilettante painter Minsetsu, another devotee, whose sketchbook *Hyaku-Fuji* (The Hundred Fujis) was published in 1771 and featured the mountain in all manner of times, milieux and seasons. Minsetsu's actual sketches are only records of famous scenic views, quite lacking in artistic power; but the *idea* he innovated may well have been a direct inspiration for Hokusai, who at last brought vigorous artistic focus on the mountain in all its aspects.[1]

Like many of his contemporaries Hokusai, too, was a Fuji-worshipper, and he had evidently nurtured the concept of a 'Fuji Series' for some years. In Series III of his *Models of Modern Combs and Pipes* of 1823 appeared the announcement for a picture-book to be entitled *Fugaku hattai* (Eight Aspects of Mt Fuji). This work seems never to have been published, nor is the manuscript extant, but the advertisement (possibly by the artist himself) cites full details, which I shall translate literally, to retain the elliptical, almost stream-of-consciousness qualities:

EIGHT ASPECTS OF MT FUJI

THE FOUR SEASONS / WEATHER CLEAR AND RAINY / WIND-SNOW-MIST—/ DULY FOLLOWING THE SUBLIME CREATIONS OF HEAVEN: / ALL THE VARIATIONS OF SCENIC BEAUTY / CAUGHT ON THE ARTIST'S BRUSH-TIP....

This blurb represents in effect an ideal description of the subsequent major print-series *Thirty-six Views of Mt Fuji*. Seldom has self-laudatory, advance publicity justified itself so completely.

In the First Series of this illustrated guide for craftsmen in comb and smoking-pipe designs eight Fuji illustrations are included for employment on decorated combs: in a sense, they are the direct predecessors of the later *Fuji* series (Plate 168).

Hokusai liked to call himself 'Gakyōjin' or 'Gakyō-rōjin' (The Old Man Mad with Painting), and although this was something of an affectation, he could be so single-minded as to seem mad in the eyes of more ordinary and temperate contemporaries, and a reputation for eccentricity certainly gave him an excuse to indulge in his inspirations without interruption or overt criticism.

Hokusai's fixation with the 'Fuji Theme' may seem itself a kind of madness, but—and most pertinent to our theme—it provided an ideal focus of attention for a landscape artist. Indeed, if there is one work that made Hokusai's name, both in Japan and abroad, it must be this monumental print-series *Fugaku sanjū-rokkei—Thirty-six views of Mt Fuji*—issued between 1830 and 1832 and, with a supplementary group of ten prints, totalling 46 designs in all.

Here, for the first time, the total splendour of the Sacred Mountain was revealed in full detail and in a readily accessible medium. Here one could view Mt Fuji from each of the surrounding Provinces, and even from the sea and the sky, in all its moods and aspects: most of them quite inaccessible to the ordinary traveller. And there was not only the mountain itself, but an infinite variety of settings: the wild sea, sparkling dawn, raging thunderstorm, abandoned windstorm, still snowscape; breathtaking views from under bridges, gates, trees and platforms, from over roofs, caravans, lumber-yards, paddies, plantations, hills, cliffs, hamlets, lakes, rivers, bays, bridges, canals and promontories. And all with the vibrantly colourful life of Old Japan displayed in full pageant in the foreground:

each scene a distillation of Hokusai's long years of experiment at obtaining the utmost compositional power from a given design.

The *Fuji* series thus represents an amalgamation and a bringing to perfection of all the artist's earlier works which, despite their own intrinsic interest, could also be interpreted as 'preparatory sketches' for this major production. The great mountain is seen here, indeed, as the noble protagonist of a set of scenes—even episodes—in an epic novel which almost comprehends the totality of Man's universe since its creation. It is no wonder that these prints astounded Hokusai's contemporaries, as they have viewers ever since, both at home and in distant lands where Japan is only a vision, formed largely by these very images from this artist's magic brush.

With many of Hokusai's prints, dating is largely a matter of educated guesswork. With the *Fuji* series we can with reasonable certainty set the date at the years 1830–2.[2] First, we have the publisher Eijudō's advertisement, appearing in the back of the novel *Shōhon-jidate* (Kabuki Tales), published at the New Year's season of 1831, which may be translated as follows:

The Thirty-six Views of Mt Fuji / By Venerable Iitsu, formerly called Hokusai / single-sheet prints, in *aizuri* technique / one scene on each sheet, now in the process of publication / these pictures show Fuji's form in each of its different locations and shapes / for example, its form at Shichiri Beach, or its aspect as seen from Tsukuda Island /—all, in their infinite variety, for the edification of those who would master the art of landscape painting / thus, if engraving proceeds apace, the result will likely exceed a hundred scenes /—not just limited to thirty-six

From this advertisement it will be apparent that by the autumn of 1830 (when the above text must have been engraved) the *Fuji* series was already proceeding apace, its success even inducing the publisher to contemplate supplements totalling some three times the original plan.[3]

Other interesting items of information gleaned here include the fact that the series was, at least at this intermediate stage, characterized as *aizuri*—that is, a special category of print in which the colour Prussian blue predominated; and, that a good part of the public for the series consisted of amateur painters (who, indeed, had always constituted Hokusai's prime market with his picture-books). As a matter of common sense, one may surmise that a certain part of the planned 'Thirty-six Views' had already been published—and acclaimed—by the time of this advertisement.

Prussian blue, I may add, seems to have been employed experimentally from the 1790s but was widely imported only from about the year 1829.[4] The use of this pigment (called in Japanese *berorin*, i.e. 'Berlin' blue, from the place of manufacture) began with privately issued *surimono*-prints, and was then extended to fan-prints (mainly by the artist Eisen). The fashion soon spread to figure-prints as well and, within a year or so, to the landscape, in Hokusai's new series. For the aficionado of the earlier Japanese print, it may be difficult to understand why this 'foreign', mineral colour should so suddenly usurp the place of the delicate and lovely blue pigments that had been favoured hitherto—in, for instance, the prints of Harunobu and Utamaro. The first reason for its adoption was simply the characteristic Japanese love for new things, and their near worship of imported goods. At the same time, the native, vegetable dyes were often fugitive, and blue was particularly susceptible to fading. (Today, indeed, collectors and museums often refuse to lend their early prints for extended exhibition, for this very reason.)

Furthermore, in the stricter sense of the term *aizuri*, only nine or ten of the *Fuji* scenes would qualify as predominantly in blue (including the two cited in the advertisement itself). It may well be that the blurb was merely exploiting a popular expression; and that the publisher saw fit to add other, subdued colours at will—or as the subject dictated—for variety. Certainly all the early impressions of the first 36 designs are characteristically printed with dark blue for the key-block, that is, the basic lines, the title and signature. It is only with the supplementary ten designs that the key-block is inked in the customary black, and the colouring accordingly rendered more bright: a sign, probably, that the *aizuri* fad had waned. (These later designs are known colloquially as *Ura-Fuji*—The Rear Fuji—though they do not necessarily feature scenes from the back of the mountain. Only one print, 'Minobu-gawa', actually includes the term *ura-Fuji* in the original title; and the phrase may be taken simply as implying 'Supplementary'.) Thus so far as pigments went, convenience and fashion took immediate precedence over traditional forms of beauty: a process that has continued to this day in all aspects of Japanese life.

This simple innovation of pigments not only affected the total colour-scheme of Hokusai's series, but also serves as a handy key to dating its commencement, probably a year or so subsequent, some time in 1830. This surmise assumes, however, that the *Fuji* series was already at the planning stage before the rage for Prussian blue began. If, however—as is not impossible—the publisher's immediate impulse for the series was to *cater* to this sudden artistic fashion, then it would be reasonable to assume that simple preparation, block-carving and printing ran near to the end of the year, and actual publication may have begun with the New Year's season of 1831.

In the absence of further contemporary documents, more exact dating is difficult—nor is it all that vital for our purposes. It would seem that some months had passed—and a dozen or so prints issued—between commencement of publication and issuance of the advertisement of early 1831.[5]

The advertisement for the *Fuji* series appeared in novels from the same publisher in 1832 and 1833, in the latter year accompanied by notice of Hokusai's new *Waterfalls* series (to be discussed below). With the year 1834, the blurb is revised, integrating the *Waterfalls* into the *Fuji* notice and adding a further new Hokusai series, the *Bridges*, as well as announcement of a *chūban*, *Flower-and-bird* series. Finally, in 1835, notice is added of yet another major series, *The Hundred Poems*, rounding out Hokusai's print-work of this period and summarizing his tremendous achievement of over one hundred major designs in the brief space of four years.

As for the completion of the initial series of 36 *Fuji* prints, here, too, we have a convenient publisher's notice—this appearing within the print itself. On 'Tatekawa in Honjo' (Fig. 83) we find the publisher's name and address, and the notation, 'Our New Publication, *Thirty-six Fujis*—Now in stock'—presumably indicating that this represents the first of the supplementary series. The latter print cannot be dated precisely, but from other considerations we may assume the *Fuji* series to have terminated in about 1832. Although the publisher's advertisement—translated above—continued to appear for several years, it probably post-dated termination of the series. Furthermore, publishing fashions, and Hokusai's own restless nature, make it unlikely that the project would have extended much more than these two years. Indeed, by 1833 Hokusai was already hard at work on a related, alternative project, the major picture-book *One Hundred Views of Mt Fuji*. This, one senses, was even closer to his heart, with its more detailed and didactic attention to the needs of the amateur painters who formed his 'fan club'.

In all, therefore, 46 striking *Fuji* prints had been issued: but the publisher's, and artist's, dream of 'over a hundred prints' was never to be fulfilled.

It would be convenient if we could somehow reconstruct the original order of issuance of this important series. Japanese scholars have made attempts at this, based upon correspondence of the artist's signatures and other incidental data, and our order in the Appendix, Prints, pp. 288–91 follows this tentative scheme. But the problem is not a simple one. Hokusai was a complex artist and did not necessarily standardize his methods and techniques in any consistent manner. All we can say for sure is that the 'Shichiri' and 'Tsukuda' prints (Figs. 62, 63), hardly among the more outstanding designs, are mentioned in the publisher's advertisement and hence belong to the first part of the series. Beyond that, the problem is wide open.

Among Hokusai's hidden (or subconscious) aims in the series was surely the idea of challenging the rival Utagawa School of ukiyo-e designers, whose speciality was the figure-print, whether actor, warrior, or fair beauty. This aim of publicizing the Hokusai School will be apparent from the blurb's phrase 'for the edification of those who would master the art of landscape painting', as well as from other evidence of the period (see, for example, Hokusai's letter to another publisher, quoted in Chapter XXII). At the same time, Hokusai may also have aimed at adding the 'pure' landscape genre to the ukiyo-e repertory, just as it had always reigned supreme in Far Eastern painting itself. Whether or not this was his intention, he succeeded resoundingly in this herculean task.

Today the collector would probably like to think of the artist contemplating each design intently at leisure, possibly after a formal tea ceremony and a session of *zazen*. But that was certainly not Hokusai's nature, nor that of his publishers. The artist probably had only a day to prepare each design: he had to produce the initial sketch, confirm

245 Mt Fuji at Dawn. *Ōban*-size print from the series *Thirty-six Views of Mt Fuji (Fugaku sanjū-rokkei)*, early 1830s. Signed Hokusai *aratame* [changed to] Iitsu *hitsu [pinxit]*. For detailed listing and illustration of the complete set of *Fuji* prints—with more exact translations of the original titles—see Appendix, pp. 288–291.

that it did not duplicate previous ones, and check the details of landscape and costume. After approval by the publisher he then perhaps enjoyed a day to make the final draft for the woodblock-carver, carefully filling in all details and further improving the design. This final sketch was then pasted, face down, on a well-planed cherry-block by the woodblock artisan and the outlines carved with the greatest possible speed. After this proofs were dispatched to the publisher who, as time and inclination allowed, consulted with the artist on colouring schemes, ever watching the deadline to get a print out—to meet some particular need, financial, fashionable or seasonal. This process consumed perhaps a month; if it took much longer the publisher's funds might run out or the current fad might wither.

To the print-collector or curator, of course, it will be mind-boggling just to think of all those pristine first impressions of the 'Red Fuji' and 'Great Wave' scattered about the parlours of wide Edo like so many $100,000 bills, so to speak, eventually to be defaced by children, scratched by cats, chewed by dogs and mice, finally to be discarded like so much trash. But this was the inescapable nature and fate of a popular art like ukiyo-e. Indeed, considering these perils—and the all-too-frequent fires, floods and earthquakes—it is a wonder that so many prints survived to delight us in modern times.

Today, we have a natural tendency to regard each of these prints as a separate entity, an independent work of art. But it is well to remember that the artist considered them as a *series*, almost as a set of unified illustrations, its purpose—as cited in the original blurb—to reveal the 'full face' of the Sacred Mountain, from every likely angle, in every possible condition and mood. The unifying factor in all this, the protagonist, is towering Mt Fuji, within which Hokusai himself resides.

In the *Fuji* series Hokusai was at last able to combine the many elements he had mastered from both Oriental and Western painting, to express his total philosophy of art. No longer was the landscape merely a copying of traditional forms, or simply a subjective expression of the artist's state of mind—an exclusive medium for the delectation of the nobility or of connoisseurs. It became not only a possession of the more affluent masses, but also, in Hokusai's hands, a subject to be analysed and dissected into *forms*—lines, squares, circles, triangles—and then, recreated in the artist's own image. Hokusai's transformation of the landscape genre extended even to colouring. In the *Fuji* series he usually eschews bright colours, not only because of the *aizuri* fashion, but also as though to express supreme confidence in his own strength of line and perfection of composition. In all this he was not, of course, completely without fault, but at his best he probably came as near to perfection as any artist before or after him.

However, it is only proper to add that the faults of the *Fuji* series are those of Hokusai himself: an overt avoidance of the natural and obvious, a constant striving for the spectacular and unusual, a desire to be different at any artistic cost. The artist wanted to gain attention and to create a new and successful art form, but in the process, it must be admitted, something was lost of the former intimacy and ethereal charm of the Japanese print. It is futile, however, to long for the more delicate beauties of Utamaro, or much more of Harunobu: a new age had arrived and Hokusai was its master and, for a time at least, its idol.

Yet even in his near failures Hokusai cannot be faulted for trying. The *Manga*-like, overly prominent foreground elements of 'Fujimigahara' and 'In the Tōtōmi Mountains' (Figs. 60 and 67) are initially striking yet only superficially so; but without such middling attempts, there would very likely have been no 'Great Wave'.[6]

The reader interested in Japanese travel and geography may like to refer to available maps regarding the approximate locations from which Fuji is viewed in each print of Hokusai's series. It will be seen that some thirteen views are from within Edo itself, another four are from the suburbs, three are from the eastern Provinces (Kazusa two, Hitachi one), eighteen from the Tōkaidō Highway (even as far away as Nagoya), seven from Kai Province in the north, and the final print from the summit itself. Hokusai was a great traveller, and probably visited many or most of the sites indicated. He was first of all an artist, however, and was quite prepared to improve upon nature. A too literal attempt to identify each and every *Fuji* site must therefore be doomed to failure, and this applies to ukiyo-e prints in general, if not to all of Japanese traditional art. Realistic topographical detail was not what art-lovers demanded nor what the artist cared to provide.

Fuji was inseparable from the mind of Edo, and Hokusai depicts it as a constant, impassive but friendly observer of the busy life of the Eastern capital. What the mountain was to the people, the citizens were to Mt Fuji: in this may be sensed something of the Japanese animism of prehistoric times. There was even a famous, and untypically sentimental, *senryū*-epigram that went:

'At least half / belongs to Edo: / The snows of Mt Fuji'.

It was, indeed, of this very period that Hokusai spoke in the colophon to a subsequent picture-book: 'In my seventy-third year I finally apprehended something of the true quality of birds, animals, insects, fishes, and of the vital nature of grasses and trees....'

Having described the background and realization of the *Thirty-six Views of Mt Fuji* we may turn now to a discussion of certain specific masterpieces of the series (Plates 245–259).

NOTES

1 The concept of the Sacred Mountain described from certain special vantage-points goes back even earlier, to the 'Eight Views of Fuji' verses of a sixteenth-century Zen monk—the idea being picked up by the classical painter Kanō Tanyū in the middle of the following century. Aside from Minsetsu's book, cited above, mention might also be made of such publications as Masayoshi's *Hyaku-Fuji* print-series in *chūban*-size of the 1780s, Kyokkō's *Sansui-kikan* of 1800–2 (which was an important source for Hiroshige), and Tani Bunchō's *Meisan zufu* of 1804; but these references serve more to indicate the gradually increasing interest in Fuji (and mountain) themes than any specific influence on Hokusai's actual compositions. It should be added that Hokusai himself had early planned an *Eight Views of Fuji* series, though only one design is known (Plate 93). There is also a pictorial *wrapper* extant for a series of twelve medium-sized prints which shows an impressive view of Fuji—reminiscent of our own Plate 248: see appended figure *below left*. For some incidental early Hokusai depictions of the Sacred Mountain see also Plates 64, 73, 74, 76, 79, 129 and Figs. 37, 40, 43, 184.
2 Earlier writers have tended to date the series to '*c*. 1823–9', this going back to the studies of the Japanese pioneer Usui Kojima. For a full discussion of the problems, see my 'On the Dating of Hokusai's *Fuji*', in the journal *Andon*, No. 23 (1987). (The traditional dating of the Fuji series as 'from 1823' doubtless derives from the coincidental advertisement for an 'Eight Views of Fuji' series, appearing in the book illustrated in our Plate 168.)
3 Solid evidence that the blurb was engraved several months earlier is seen in the colophon date of the *Kabuki Tales* itself: 'New Year's, Bunsei XIV [1831]'. Actually, the Bunsei Period changed to the Tempō Period with the Tenth lunar Month of Bunsei XIII and never really achieved a 'fourteenth year'. As often happened, the publisher did not deem the error important enough to correct; or it may be that a good part of the edition was already printed by this time, in preparation for sales from the beginning of the new year.

One problem which, so far as I know, has not hitherto been noted is the original *reading* of Hokusai's title. The *Fugaku sanjū-rokkei* series itself makes no indication of the preferred pronunciation of the Chinese characters, but the advertisements of 1831 ff. bear the following clear *furigana* (phonetic-rubric) reading: *Fuji sanjū-rokukei*. Now *rokukei* is merely a phonetic variant of the less formal *rokkei*; but what of *Fuji* vs. *Fugaku*? It should first be noted that *Fugaku* is a literary form of the more native *Fuji*. But there was a fashion—in the mid and later Edo Period—of writing formal, Chinese-derived symbolic characters but reading them in Japanese style. This would be something like our spelling a word in French but purposely pronouncing it in the plain English equivalent—e.g. *repertoire*/repertory. It is likely, however, that Hokusai's contemporaries pronounced the characters as written, *Fugaku*. And indeed, the reading '*Fuji*' may only have represented a playful exhibition of *élan* on the part of the artist or copywriter. Thus I have retained the customary formal reading, pending the discovery of further contemporary evidence. (For further comment on this general theme see my '*Essays on Japanese Art*: Some Reflections', in *Andon*, No. 10, 1983, p. 23, and also Appendix, Books, No. 239.)
4 The reference to earlier experiments should perhaps be qualified to read: 'Prussian blue (or a similar-appearing, permanent mineral blue)'. That is, my comments are based purely on visual observation, not on chemical analysis.
5 One further possible guide to dating might be found in the evidence of Hokusai material brought back to Holland in 1830 by the Deshima physician Ph. F. Von Siebold—and still preserved in the National Museum of Ethnology, Leiden (see above, Chapter XVI). Whether the Hokusai-style paintings of this Collection are actually by the Master or not, some of them do relate to compositions in the *Fuji* print-series (or perhaps to even earlier designs on the same themes, now lost?).
6 In such abridgement of middle ground and dramatic emphasis on prominent, sometimes even distorted foreground elements, one may surmise the likely influence of the noted Akita painters in Western style, Shozan and Naotake, who worked mainly in the 1770s, when Hokusai was in his teens.

Mount Fuji. Wrapper for a series of 12 *aiban* (?) prints, *c*. late 1810s(?)

XVIII
Landscape Peak:
The *Thirty-six*
Views of Fuji (2)

WE MAY COMMENCE our description of this, Hokusai's most celebrated print-series, with the design bearing the title *Gaifū kaisei* (South-wind, Clear-dawn)—the only abstract title of the series—but known affectionately to every Japanese schoolchild as *Aka-Fuji* (The Red Fuji).

In this essentially symphonic print of Fuji at dawn (Plate 245), the eye is led gradually up the left slope of the sacred mountain—huge trees reduced to shrubbery by the distance—up past the treeline to a brick-red peak, and on to the autumnal summit which displays the first light snows of the coming winter. The mountain itself is divided into four planes—dark and light green, dark and light sienna—the dark masses spaced far apart, the light areas adjoining, two basic colour-planes rather like the geological plates of two continents welded firmly together.

The background to Hokusai's design consists only of the cerulean sky, with strata after strata of cirrocumulus clouds spaced across like ice floes or (as the Japanese have it) a school of small fish. As though representing the clear silence that reigns briefly before a typhoon, the sky is shaded gradually from light to dark, with an uppermost band of dark blue to 'fix' the composition. In essence, there is only one line to the design, and three basic colours; but seldom have such magnificent artistic results been obtained with such economy. The result is one of the few perfect prints and Hokusai's acknowledged masterpiece: a startlingly direct glimpse of Nature at its most superb.

Note, too, the typically Japanese love of asymmetry, in which it is left to the viewer to fill in the missing elements that the ordered mind requires. As much is left unsaid as is actually shown, and one thus actively collaborates with the artist in 'completing' the scene. It is difficult for us today to comprehend the effect this great print must have had on Western painters when they first viewed it a century or more ago. But it could be said that in the 'Red Fuji' may be found the seeds of Impressionism, Post-Impressionism and abstractionism—in fact, much of what is 'modern' in modern art.

As we have observed, many artists had depicted Mt Fuji before, but it was Hokusai who made this dormant volcano into a worldwide symbol of ukiyo-e and of Japan itself. Yet this inspired print was produced with a minimum number of four (or at the most five) woodblocks and only eight printing-stages: the shading effects are the result of colour manipulation by hand before printing; the patterns on the mountain mirror the natural grain of the cherrywood itself.

Early impressions of this famous print tend to be less strongly coloured, and the *bokashi*-shading narrower in width at the mountain-base—the result being less dramatic

in effect than the bolder, more standard 'improved' version. Several alternative colour schemes exist; there is even a rare state with the mountain white and blue, rather than brown; here, only the upper strata of clouds are visible, and a part of the sky is printed in brown (Plate 246).

Although Hokusai chose not to make use of the full resources of the complex 'Brocade-print' technique, he has succeeded in producing a masterwork by reducing the design to its essentials, concentrating, so to speak, his whole art on this one print. Quite literally the Mountain is Hokusai, the Artist is Mt Fuji. We have accused Hokusai of lacking discrimination; but here, with his tremendous powers under full control, we confront the perfection he could achieve when truly inspired.

Of equal renown is the print entitled *Kanagawa-oki namiura* (Under the Wave Off Kanagawa), known colloquially as 'The Great Wave' (Plate 247). Here, as in much of the series, Mt Fuji looms only as a distant, immobile but majestic spectator and focal-point: the protagonist is clearly the mammoth wave seen soaring up at left, octopus-fingers grasping at the sky and downwards towards the three boats and the diminutive sailors who cling tenaciously to their crafts amid the tumult. Such a searchingly dramatic depiction is probably the fruit of actual observation and experience during the artist's travels (possibly some by sea), to the Miura and Bōsō peninsulas near the mouth of Edo Bay.

Note that the waves are not one, each is possessed of its own distinctive personality: the grandly towering master-wave (in form echoing the snow-clad mountain), the fast-breaking, more gentle wave before it, the powerful, undulating swells at right—the flying foam. Indeed, for this one brief moment it seems almost as though there is a

246 *Overleaf top left* Mt Fuji at Dawn. Late edition of Plate 245 with variant colouring. (As with all late impressions of most of this series, key-block is printed in black rather than Prussian blue; note also the uppermost cloud-formations, not visible in the earlier versions.)

247 *Overleaf bottom left* 'Beneath the Wave off Kanagawa'. From the series *Thirty-six Views of Mt Fuji*, early 1830s. For further details see Plate 245, p. 186.

248 *Overleaf top right* Mt Fuji in Thunderstorm. From the series *Thirty-six Views of Mt Fuji*, early 1830s. For further details see Plate 245; and for alternative editions, Plates 249–250.

249 *Overleaf bottom right* Mt Fuji in Thunderstorm. Later impression of Plate 248 with variant colouring.

greater volume of water towering in the sky than remains in the whole wide ocean below. In this simple-appearing but highly complex and unconventional design the plastic forms of the waves swell and interact before our very eyes, a drama of Nature that man can only view in wonder, and never hope to control or even influence.

As with the best prints of this series the colour scheme is simple: white and shades of blue for waves and mountain (employing only three colour-blocks), blue-grey shaded sky (whether at dawn or at dusk), with only touches of accent on the boats, and angry yellowish cloud-patterns to consolidate the sky area.

Although it perhaps does not quite achieve the absolute perfection of the 'Red Fuji', Hokusai's 'Great Wave' represents one of his acknowledged masterworks, vividly contrasting majestic Nature with diminutive mankind. While this splendid design represents, in a sense, the culmination of the artist's 'circle-and-triangle' theory of composition (see Plates 132–3), the influence of Western perspective technique also looms large. Where the Japanese artists of a generation or two earlier would have had to present a telephoto view, with the wave hardly reaching the height of the mountain, Hokusai is able to leap into the turbulent sea, to project us into the midst of the action with a low, wide-angle close-up in which Mt Fuji is reduced to a focal element of the background. The print is so strongly decorative in design that we almost tend to overlook the human element—three cargo-boats with their oarsmen clinging on for dear life as the sea batters them at will. (The boats, by the way, are the oshiokuri, which hauled cargoes of fresh fish and vegetables from Izu and Awa to the metropolis Edo.)

Interestingly enough, Hokusai had experimented with very similar scenes in his early 'perspective-prints' (see Plates 81, 88); and a further key to his development will be found in the much-neglected yomi-hon illustrations—the 'Harakiri amid Waves' of Fig. 188, for example. But only now, some two decades later, did he succeed in combining Western art notions with native tradition to finalize his concept of the landscape-print.[1]

One curious bit of datable evidence exists to prove how well this print—and Hokusai's great series—was known. At the time of extensive flood-damage from Mt Fuji in the late spring of 1834, the 'Great Wave' design was pirated—adapted to a kawaraban broadsheet reporting this event in Edo. The surreptitious publisher cleverly twisted the intent of Hokusai's design to imply floods from the mountain, rather than waves far at sea. This was to prove, indeed, only the first of many pastiches of Hokusai's magnificent concept—none, however, even reaching to his foothills in artistic worth. Though we have no specific record of contemporary reactions to Hokusai's Fuji series, it will be obvious that its more memorable designs very quickly became the standard for depictions of the Sacred Mountain—and its watery surroundings.[2]

It was this 'Great Wave' more than any other Japanese print that astounded and delighted artists in Paris around the close of the nineteenth century. Debussy, too, is said to have used it as his inspiration for the orchestral piece La Mer; and Rilke for the verse series Der Berg. Equally great as works of art, the 'Red Fuji' and the 'Great Wave' will affect the viewer in different ways: for those who prefer a human element with which to identify, 'The Great Wave' will prove most compelling; for others, to whom Nature alone suffices, the 'Red Fuji' may well linger longest in the mind's eye.

While featuring much the same design as the 'Red Fuji', in Sanka-hakuu (Thunderstorm beneath the Summit) Hokusai makes a conscious effort at variety, complexity, innovation: the result is a fascinating design but one surely on a lower level of importance (Plate 248).

To his contemporaries, of course, the inclusion of storm and calm in the same scene, the Western-influenced cloud-forms and the dramatic, stylized lightning-pattern must have lent an exotic flavour to the print. Today these elements may tend to seem more quaint than innovative, and in the end detract from the majesty of the main subject—Mt Fuji at dusk.

In a sense this dramatic scene harks back to a very old and traditional subject of Japanese painting: Mt Fuji towering majestically above the clouds, with a magic dragon seen ascending in the sky towards its sacred summit. Such themes appear in the Manga sketches, the Hundred Views (Plate 298), as well as in one of the artist's last known paintings (Plate 358). In this remarkable print, has not the Master substituted for this wonderful beast the equally awesome apparition of lightning? In fact, the two are probably but different avatars of the same natural/supernatural phenomenon.

Yet though not quite on the same artistic level as the 'Red Fuji' and the 'Great Wave', this striking Hokusai landscape reveals a compelling contrast: the sacred mountain rising calm and untroubled above the turbulent thunderstorm that belabours its lower reaches with lightning. In this print Fuji is seen from quite a different angle—from the rear side—with lower mountains in the background and conventionalized thunderclouds in the distant sky. This and the 'Red Fuji' are the only prints in the series in which the entire mountain is shown in close-up, quite dominating the design.

Today, of course, it is easy enough to view mountains and storms from all possible angles; but in the artist's time there were no aircraft to carry him where he would, only in his ever-active mind was he free to travel at will.

Three alternative 'states' are known for this print: in the first, the lightning design is different, of narrower lines (indeed, being the less forceful version this may well represent the earlier one). In yet another, definitely later edition, a grove of pine-trees is interpolated across the lower part of the design; these are presumably not in Hokusai's hand and clearly represent a subsequent publisher's attempt to liven up a classic print (Plates 249 and 250). In the rare specimen illustrated here in Plate 248, the pub-

250 *Opposite top* Mt Fuji in Thunderstorm. Late alternative state of Plate 248 with added trees. (See also p. 288, Nos. 3/3a.)

251 *Opposite bottom* 'Sunset over Ryōgoku Bridge'. From the series *Thirty-six Views of Mt Fuji*, early 1830s. For further details see Plate 245.

lisher has neglected to trim the excess right and lower margins, providing an interesting insight into the techniques of the Japanese woodblock printer.

After these three designs, critical opinion tends to diverge on which are the major secondary prints of Hokusai's great series. In viewing the originals a sharp, fine impression of a lesser print will often look superior to a late, blurred impression of a major design: this is the nature of the classical Japanese woodblock print, in which the condition of the 'living' blocks and the skill of the individual printer play such an important part in the final result.

The following comments thus follow my own tentative and very personal order of ranking, and the reader is invited to view the full series in Plates 245–259 and Figs. 56–91 (pp. 288–291), to make his own discoveries and choice of favourites.

Not far below these three famous designs must rank 'Sunset over Ryōgoku Bridge' (Plate 251). As a depiction of the 'floating world' of mankind—as opposed to the solitary world of Nature—it is certainly one of Hokusai's major prints. In this essentially orchestral tableau the scene is dusk on the Sumida River, the foreground dominated by a small ferryboat, with a boatman plying his oar at left, a traveller napping at right, and in the boat itself a variety of wayfarers—including tradesman, bird-catcher, pedlar (the mark of the publisher Eijudō on his pack), masseur, samurai—one man washing his hand-towel in the river. For the main part the figures are deliberately depicted facing away from the viewer, so as not to detract from the distant landscape beyond; and just as the bird-catcher provides an accent with his long pole piercing the sunset sky, so does the busy boatman represent the viewer, taking a brief pause from his labours to enjoy this magic scene. At left, too, a woman does her laundry from a houseboat. One cannot but marvel at Hokusai's success in introducing such predominant foreground elements without intruding in the least upon the lovely landscape—the total effect enhanced by the pleasing, gentle, lateral S-curve of both foreground and background, accentuated by the surging river. Further into the middle ground are seen the impressionistically hued forms of other boats, as well as the great bridge itself, houses and trees, with the deep blue form of Mt Fuji looming in the far distance. The heaving waters (quite deep at this point), and the dark sky-band at top, may well indicate that the artist intended to depict the stillness before a storm, or the quiet after a squall has lifted.

The print is redolent of the still air of dusk, the river in ceaseless motion and Fuji in dark blue silhouette. Notable also is the dynamic positioning of curves in the composition (bridge and foreground wavelets), the intriguing chain of circles (from laundry via oar and bird-pole on to parasol and rain-hats) with angular Fuji as the eventual focal-point. In a masterful manner the vertical pole serves as a slashing line to identify the centre of focus—the brooding mountain—not by pointing towards it but by serving as stopper for the powerful receding lines of the bridge: binding together, as it were, the multiple strata of sky, shore, river and boat. The composition provides, indeed, a most pleasant exercise for the roving eye, curving from house to bridge to Fuji, on to boat-prow and towering pole down to trailing towel, and up again to the motley humanity that is ever Hokusai's central theme—then once again to the distantly looming mountain.

This ferry ran, incidentally, from the Ommaya Embankment of Asakusa to Honjo; townsmen paid two pence, samurai rode free. The Ommaya ('Official-stables') Embankment was at one time the site of the Shōgun's Stables, which gives its name likewise to the ferry-crossing of Hokusai's print. The area was famed for its views of Mt Fuji across the wide Sumida River, and the crossing was also known, appropriately enough, as 'Fuji-view Ferry'.[3]

The scene is typically Edo—Hokusai's home and the principal market-place for his prints. We have no record of contemporary comment, but I suspect that this design was just as evocative to Hokusai's audience as it is to us today: equally to those of us who have lived by this very river as to those who know it only through the lovely prints.

Depending upon earliness and quality of 'impression' the design expresses several moods. In the first issue, as here, not only is the engraving sharper but the potentially stormy atmosphere hangs over the print like a cloud itself. Even in early impressions, however, the width of the black sky-band may vary, and the depth of the greens likewise, changing the mood of the scene considerably. In later issues the black band in the sky becomes blue, and the print is rendered as a bland yet picturesque tableau, far more suited to the casual print-collector.

It is of some interest to compare the composition of this magnificent print with those of the same artist a generation earlier: the rather similar Ryōgoku scene of our Plate 94 comes immediately to mind. Perhaps more revealing, however, are the tableaux of his famous picture-book *Views of the Sumida River*. The boating scene of our previous Plate 61, for example, features a typical sense of Oriental perspective; looking closely we perceive that the foreground roofs and the boat are really on the same plane, and that the background elements of Western-derived perspective are somewhat out of harmony with the main elements. In its own context the design is, however, a most effective one. Coming back to the rather similar composition of Hokusai's later years (Plate 251), it will be seen that all elements are far more adroitly integrated; yet the layout is still not scientifically realistic: in a photograph, for example, the boat would be flattened out and lose its three-dimensional effect, but this is the very element that makes the print so striking. And in the end, one must abandon such attempts to view Hokusai—or any other such master—with scientific objectivity. Logic and science are not the artist's concerns; and to reduce an ukiyo-e print to the Western norm is simply to destroy it.

'Mt Fuji from Kajikazawa' (Plates 252 and 253) is for me the most evocative print of the *Fuji* series, not only for its masterful design and mood, but for the intimate interaction between man and Nature that is revealed. Place a hand over either of these figures and you will perceive how integrated is the design, how essential is each element, including the rocky promontory, the turbulent waves, the mid-ground of mists, and the fisherman's net-lines which reflect the rightward slope of Mt Fuji with the sunset sky looming at top. In a typical Hokusai device, the triangular form of the Sacred Mountain is mirrored in the foreground figures, rock and lines: but we do not consciously realize this so much as feel its powerful influence on the total composition.

As with most of Hokusai's best designs, this represents a simple setting simply organized: against the nebulous background a determined fisherman stands on a sharp and perilous promontory, his taut net cast in the rain-swollen, writhing river—man and Nature actually *connected* by the frail fishing-lines—while his little son (tending the fish-basket) adds a touch of pathos to the scene. It is this sense of commiseration that renders the print unique in the series. One subconsciously senses here the harshness of the life depicted: few indeed must be the opportunities for this humble rustic to stand back and enjoy the abstract beauties of Nature. If he enjoyed them once it would have been in his wide-eyed youth, represented here by his own small, seated son.

Kajikazawa (Bullhead Marsh) lies near the head of the Fuji River, far in the mountains of Kai Province. Although it was on a minor highway from Kōfu to Minobuyama, few of Hokusai's Edo contemporaries would have known the actual site of his sketch. The visitor to the spot today will assume the natural forces seen in Hokusai's print to be much exaggerated, for the Fuji River has been entirely subdued in modern times by dams and hydroelectric plants. In Hokusai's day, however, the river was often violent, and on its banks may yet be seen memorial stones to those who perished in its torrents.

Although the basically blue mood is retained, as in many Japanese prints there are variations in colouring from one impression to another of this design; some versions include a pink or saffron-coloured band in the sky and yellow or yellow-green on the rocks to the lower left (as though struck by a shaft of sunlight), and the fisherman's robe may be coloured red; but the earlier issues tend to limit the colouring entirely to shades of blue, as in our first plate. With such prints, the collector or curator will often have to face the problem of deciding whether to keep the version that appeals to him personally, or that which the experts (and auction houses) cite as 'early, rare and valuable'.

'Mt Fuji from Mishima Pass' (Plate 254) is the Japanese print that first captivated me and some four decades later it still charms—its human touch remains memorable even though it may well not be a major work of art.

Mt Fuji is seen from the top of Mishima Pass, north-west of Hakone; the mountain flank, split into three colour bands, is shown in summer, bedecked with decorative clouds. The centre of interest is not, however, the distant view, but the three travellers in the foreground who, expressing their childlike wonder at an ancient cryptomeria tree, are trying to measure it, to encircle it in their co-operative embrace. Hokusai has succeeded admirably in expressing the feeling of freedom and exuberance experi-

enced after climbing a rugged mountain pass, and at last reaching a summit of breathtaking splendour.

But can a humorous print be great? This is the first question that faces the critic on viewing a Hokusai design such as this. The gargantuan tree is magnificent, Mt Fuji, shaded in two hues at top and bottom, impeccably placed; but in lieu of further impressive natural elements we are shown, rather, three plebeian travellers (plus four lesser figures) and, like many of Hokusai's humans, they are depicted in vaguely comic manner, hardly adding anything of majesty or grandeur to the scene. These humorous, humble beings are nevertheless vital to the artist's concept, they fit the scene perfectly: but in the end, one must conclude that they tend to reduce Nature to man's own diminutive level, and hence one must, regretfully, relegate this print to secondary class. Such criticism does not, however, lessen one's pleasure in the least.

The curious clouds over the mountain top are called in Japanese *kasagumo* ('cap-clouds') and in former times were thought to represent wandering human souls. Here, the shape is somehow reminiscent of the *nobori-ryū* ('Ascending Dragon') said to dwell near the summit of Mt Fuji (see Plates 298 and 357). Perhaps unconsciously, the artist arranges the accompanying clouds after the manner of traditional themes.

Hokusai had also depicted Mishima Pass in the *Manga* sketchbooks (see Fig. 203), and later he included it in the *Hundred Views of Mt Fuji*. But the three tableaux differ so much in detail that at least two of the views must have been largely figments of the artist's fertile imagination.[4]

'Hodogaya on the Tōkaidō' (Plate 255) resembles 'Ryōgoku' (Plate 251) in its emphasis on foreground figures—in this case, varied travellers along the Tōkaidō Highway: palanquin-rider and bearers at left, pack-horse driver and rider at centre (the seal of the publisher Eijudō is partly visible on the saddle-blanket), *komusō* Zen-minstrel at right—a neat summary of the principal forms of land-transportation in old Japan, with each figure displaying the variety of pose that is typical of Hokusai's method. A row of craggy, ageing pines dominates the middle ground, their individualistic foliage adding a lively, decorative accent to the composition. In the distance, beyond fields, houses and foothills, rises Mt Fuji: with this artist's characteristic attention to reality, one senses imperceptibly that

252 *Overleaf top left* 'Mt Fuji from Kajikazawa'. From the series *Thirty-six Views of Mt Fuji*, early 1830s. For further details see Plate 245. (Note variation in summit detail and colouring when compared with Plate 253.)

253 *Overleaf bottom left* 'Mt Fuji from Kajikazawa'. Later impression of Plate 252, with variant colouring.

254 *Overleaf top right* 'Mt Fuji from Mishima Pass'. From the series *Thirty-six Views of Mt Fuji*, early 1830s. For further details see Plate 245.

255 *Overleaf bottom right* 'Hodogaya on the Tōkaidō'. From the series *Thirty-six Views of Mt Fuji*, early 1830s. For further details see Plate 245.

256 'Hodogaya'. Small print from a Hokusai *Tōkaidō* series of the early 1800s (shown here about double size). For others of this early series see Plates 70, 71. (Note the absence of dramatic sharpness of focus when the design is compared with the work of Hokusai's final maturity in Plate 255.)

the season is late spring, and that the half-melted snow represents the south slope of the mountain. This striking design may be taken as typical of the many prints in the series that feature prominent foreground figures: they are invariably interesting and picturesque but are generally lacking in the grandeur of the scenes previously described.

Hodogaya lay on the Tōkaidō Highway, only three stations from Edo, just at the border of Musashi and Sagami Provinces. It featured the infamous Shinano Slope, seen to the right of Hokusai's design, and obviously the palanquin-bearers of this print are resting up after having traversed its rocky terrain. In former times the main Japanese highways were all planted with rows of pines, which afforded shade and shelter to the traveller and served as barricades in time of war.[5]

Behind such magnificent *Fuji* prints lay, of course, the experience of earlier prints, sketches and books. There is,

for example, a similar horseman in the *Manga* sketchbooks, Series I (1814—Plate 139). And it is even more revealing to compare the artist's treatment of the same 'Hodogaya' in his miniature *Tōkaidō* series of three full decades earlier, the image of which surely lay imbedded in his brain even if not consciously recognized (Plate 256). One is impressed here by the difference between great landscape and quaint pictorialism, and what really matters is the culmination of the artist's work on these themes, as seen in this final *Fuji* print. As for Hokusai's followers, it may not be too far-fetched to suggest that Hiroshige got the idea for his great *Tōkaidō* series of a year or two later from just such a print as this.

'The Cushion-pine at Aoyama' (Plate 257) is also one of the 'average' prints of the *Fuji* series. There is nothing particularly spectacular or dramatic about it; it is simply a masterful design of a rather prosaic scene. The view is of the noted garden of the Ryūganji temple in Edo, with its famed 'Cushion-pine'. The elongated branches (some thirteen metres in width) are supported by stilts and flow over the design from right to left, the rotund pine contrasting with the svelte form of the distant eminence. At lower right we see picnickers by a stone lantern, and at lower left—a typical Hokusai touch—the legs of a gardener. Beyond the garden, past temple and foothills, looms the sacred peak, majestic Fuji; the middle distance is concealed by haze.

Almost paternally overlooked by Mt Fuji, the protagonist of the print is clearly the marvellous 'Cushion-pine', each branch of which is executed with the artist's full energies. And in the end, the success of the print will depend upon whether the viewer shares the artist's fascination with massed foliage and aged pine-trees.

This peculiar technique of depicting pine-branches with rounded ends probably goes back to the eighteenth-century Nanga painter Taigadō, and before him to earlier Chinese masters. It is an interesting sidelight on Hokusai's method to note that this garden (near the present Harajuku) was almost equally famed for a single tall and aged, partly truncated pine that stood beside the stone lantern of this tableau. To have included this impressive relic would have put it in direct competition with Mt Fuji for vertical dominance of the scene; so the artist simply omitted it entirely. Not only that, but the cleft seen at the summit of the mountain is not visible from this location. Though Hokusai knew these details well enough, he had no compunctions about adapting them to his total scheme.

Yet another of the secondary prints of the *Fuji* series may be cited, 'Senju in Musashi Province'—a view from the northern suburb of Edo, with the Arakawa River in the middle distance (Plate 258). The design well reveals Hokusai's strengths and weaknesses: the ageing, slightly dejected pack-horse represents one of the Master's minor masterpieces of evocative detail, the figures—carp-fishermen and farmer—are intrinsically interesting, the compositional details (triangles of horse and weighted bridle reflecting the form of the mountain) intriguing, the landscape impeccable; but did the artist really have to emphasize that wooden framework intruding so prominently at right? Doubtless this particular site indeed featured such a *suimon* or flood-gate; doubtless the Master was taken by its angular shape, its contrast with the luxurious landscape and distant, stolid Fuji; doubtless he included it so prominently in order to make his picture 'different'. Yet one cannot but feel that the design would be better without it—or, including it but smaller, with the whole composition tightened up.[6] One cannot, though, really second-guess an artist: Hokusai is long gone, and we can only admire the harmonious colouring, savour the artist's obvious sympathy with the overworked animal—and regretfully drop the print to second rank.

As noted above, with the supplementary ten prints of the *Fuji* series the key-block is printed in black rather than blue, and engraving, printing and colouring tend to be of a harder, more precise nature. The artist's mode of depiction, too, waxes more detailed, with a tendency to geometrical forms and compositions. These features reflect the general change in ukiyo-e tastes with the 1830s as well as, doubtless, the artist's own ageing. There are no world-class prints in this later group but all display a continuing mastery of effective composition, and the 'Kanaya on the Tōkaidō' scene is of more than passing interest (Plate 259).

This striking depiction of travellers fording the Ōi River harks back to Hokusai's earlier studies in the decorative, Kōrin style and forms a most pleasing tableau—with its rhythmic patterns of colour dramatically reflecting the parallel movements of man and nature.

It would not be difficult to provide detailed commentary on the 36 remaining designs of Hokusai's monumental series: the compositions are impeccable, the customs fascinating, the locations of interest both to traveller and geographer. But we would not, in the end, know much more about the artist than I have outlined above; hence I shall leave such matters to the summary catalogue at the end of this volume.

Suffice it to say that within these brief three years were produced a significant proportion of the masterpieces of the Japanese print. With the *Fuji* series both Hokusai and the ukiyo-e landscape simultaneously reached their peak: and the populace of Edo learned, for the first time, really to *see* this majestic eminence.

NOTES

1 Yet another predecessor to the 'Great Wave' will be found in a Hokusai illustration of 1813, in vol. IV of *Hokuetsu kidan*, where a shipwrecked sailor spies a Ghost Ship, amid similar great waves.
2 To speak in more detail, from the night of the seventh day of the Fourth Month of 1834, following volcanic tremors and a rainstorm, snowslides and floods from melting snow poured down from the Fifth Stage of the great mountain, with much resultant loss of life. The broadsheet in question is far more artistically interesting than most such, and with good reason: the foreground—with tiny figures seen floundering in the waves—is clearly modelled on Hokusai's 'Great Wave' of some two years earlier (with the image reversed), only the mountain being rendered in more realistic form; and further details seem to have been lifted from the 'Hōei Eruption' plate of the artist's *One Hundred Views of Mt Fuji*, the first volume of which was issued early in the same year, 1834 (see Plate 293).
3 Native scholars do not appear to have noticed this, but the print's original title may not be strictly accurate: the view is ostensibly *towards* Ommaya Embankment, not from it—for the artist must have been standing at Honjo, on the eastern bank of the Sumida. Since this area was Hokusai's birthplace he is unlikely to have made an error (though a copyist or engraver might have). Possibly the illogical title was intentional and the design was 'flipped', after the exotic manner of copperplate etchings—as was the case with our previous Plate 85. But the matter is also complicated by evidence that, in popular usage, the eastern ferry-landing seems to have been, by association, nicknamed 'The Stables' as well. Note, incidentally, that an interesting predecessor of this scene will be found in the 1803 *surimono* series noted on p. 283, No. 68.
    I may add that Japanese writers usually identify the centre figure of Hokusai's print as 'a fisherman with pole'. But both from costume and common sense this figure must be either a *torisashi* or an *esashi*: the first was a professional bird-catcher who catered mainly to pedlars who sold live birds for 'release' (*hōshō*) by pious Buddhists; the *esashi* provided live food for the falcons of the feudal lords. In either case, sticky lime was placed on the pole-top to trap the unfortunate, wild creatures. (A bird-catcher also appears in the rather similar 'Ommaya' scene of Hokusai's early *Sumida River* picture–book—see our Plate 61, left side—as well as in the *Manga*, Series III.)
4 The human figures are also presaged in an intriguing plate of the *Manga*, Series VII (1817), in which travellers clamber up a giant gingko tree in Chiba, to view a natural altar to a pair of Shinto deities (see fig. *overleaf, bottom right*).
5 Today one finds traces of such rows of pines only at a few areas that have been designated for preservation; clearly, all things traditional in Japan must be considered as endangered species.
6 Compare the similarly obtrusive wooden sign of Plate 59—which is, however, more adroitly handled.

257 *Opposite top* 'The Cushion-pine of Aoyama'. From the series *Thirty-six Views of Mt Fuji*, early 1830s. For further details see Plate 245.

258 *Opposite bottom* 'Senju in Musashi Province'. From the series *Thirty-six Views of Mt Fuji*, early 1830s. For further details see Plate 245.

259 *Above* 'Kanaya on the Tōkaidō'. From the series *Thirty-six Views of Mt Fuji*, early 1830s. For further details see Plate 245.

Right Travellers Mounting a Gingko Tree, from *Manga* Series VII, 1817.

XIX
Hokusai's
Golden Decade (1):
Further Landscapes

IN THE WEST, at least, Hokusai has a reputation as 'The Artist Preeminent of *Water*': and indeed, 'The Great Wave' (Plate 247) is alone sufficient in dramatic power and later influence to justify that acclaim. The Master's nervous line, his sinuous brushstroke and intuitive feeling for movement made him an ideal artist to depict the ever-changing form of turbulent bodies of water.

By the same token—even in his *Gashiki* and *Soga* albums—he does not quite equal his follower Hiroshige in the depiction of *rain*: perhaps the flat, parallel lines of driving rain matched and contrasted with the latter artist's more placid genius. With Hokusai, a dramatic rainstorm would have required the equivalent of roaring dragons within the raindrops—a concept less suited to the landscape genre than to scenes of fable and the supernatural.

Rushing bodies of water played an integral part in Hokusai's great *Fuji* series, usually in a role subservient to the more solid landscape. Only in the 'Great Wave' does water become the main protagonist. With his next print-series, however, the artist turned to water itself as his principal subject. If not the equal of the *Fuji* series, *The Waterfalls* is unique—for the first time in the colour-print bringing focus on the variety possible within such a difficult theme. (The subject is not so unrelated to the preceding *Fuji* theme as one might think, for great or wonderful waterfalls had a special significance in ancient Japanese Nature-worship. Indeed, one of the most famous of medieval Japanese religious paintings is the '*Waterfall of Nachi*'—late thirteenth century—in which this 'source of life' takes on strong Shintō connotations, becoming, in effect, an object of worship in itself.)

To judge from the advertisement already cited, *The Waterfalls* began to appear in 1833, the year after the *Fuji* print-set had reached its termination. The latter started out, it will be recalled, as a proposed series of 36 prints, later extended to 46, but never reaching the publisher's and artist's dream of 'A Hundred Prints, by popular demand'. The audience for the popular prints was, indeed, a fickle one: the time had come to change the subject, if not the technique. The answer came in series after series of masterful landscape prints, the most monumental being *The Waterfalls*, of which a total of eight designs was issued during the years 1833–4.

The formal title was *Shokoku taki-meguri* (A Tour of Japanese Waterfalls). This new set of *ōban* prints employed, naturally enough, the *vertical* format best suited to the subject.

Needless to relate, few waterfalls provide a dramatic focus of visual grandeur; much of their appeal lies in sound, spray, movement and atmosphere—features difficult for any artist, even Hokusai, to re-create with unfailing verve and intensity in a varied set of eight prints. And unlike Mt Fuji, each famous waterfall had to be viewed close-up if its distinctive features were to be depicted effectively—as Hokusai's public surely demanded. The series thus posed severe problems.

The artist's approach was basically a naturalistic one: each waterfall is shown in characteristic detail, usually filling the frame of the print, with less forceful human figures delineated viewing—or utilizing—the turbulent waters. Rather by coincidence, then, the most dramatic of the series are those prints depicting the waterfalls with the most bizarre, graceful or unified natural shapes, and those which the artist had been able to sketch in person. However, the set is notable throughout for its effective modelling—varied blues, browns, yellows, greens—within a limited palette of colours.

One of the most compelling in the series is 'Amida Waterfall on the Kiso Highway' (Plate 260), so named because its 'haloed' head was thought to resemble that of the Buddha Amida. The decoratively flowing river accumulates at a perfectly rounded gorge, then empties abruptly into a seemingly bottomless chasm. Both river and fall are depicted in the decorative Kōrin-school style (which the artist had studied intensively over thirty years earlier). The surrounding landscape is in the characteristic Hokusai Style—the grassy cliffs at top standing like poised waves (or even, like playful *shishi*-lions), the craggy cliffs asymmetrically balanced at right and left (a scraggly pine-tree barely managing to survive), and a human touch added by two men picnicking at left, as their little servant tends a cooking-fire.

The artist has chosen colouring that is both simple and dramatic, the waters in varying shades of blue, the cliffs in green and yellow. Of the series, this is the only print which—with its compelling, keyhole-like design—remains striking even when viewed across a room. But it should be remembered that the Japanese print was originally designed to be savoured when held intimately in the hands, not viewed from afar. (This is one reason why the Master's world-rank designs did not really sell much better than his lesser prints during his own lifetime.) And the critic may well have to choose a different design for each of his purposes: poster, exhibition, book-cover, illustration, or hand-viewing of the original.[1]

If 'Amida' is the most compelling of the series, the 'Horse-washing Falls' is probably the most lively and effective in composition (Plate 261). This waterfall takes its name from a famous episode of medieval history, when the tragic, twelfth-century hero Yoshitsune bathed his favourite mount at this spot in the mountains of Yoshino. Here we view a relatively restrained cascade with two pack-horse drivers washing their beast at its foot; typically Hokusai is the Z-shaped composition—the potential force of the torrent hinted at by snow-white foam and spray. The print combines dramatic composition with scenic grandeur, accompanied by a slightly humorous, human touch that conveys an intimacy—a close identification with Nature—unequalled in the series.

Each of the remaining six prints of *The Waterfalls* reveals similar charms when viewed in close-up and in the originals; but it will suffice here to say that Hokusai succeeded splendidly in his unique approach to a difficult theme: albeit without producing a masterpiece to rank with the best of the *Fuji* series.

Following *Mt Fuji* and *The Waterfalls* the next logical subject in Hokusai's suite of landscape subjects was *The Bridges*, which, indeed, appeared shortly after, in 1834. The full title was *Shokoku meikyō kiran* (Rare Views of Famous Japanese Bridges), under which eleven prints were issued. Aside from appearance in an 1834 advertisement, one of this series may also be dated from other sources. The Tempōzan view (Fig. 145) features a man-made hill only completed in the spring of 1831—from the reclaimed silt of the adjacent Aji River (near Ōsaka). Since its tiny bridges were neither famous nor particularly remarkable, the print was obviously appended to the series to take advantage of the enthusiasm for Tempōzan prints in the period *c.* 1831–5. Hokusai made no special trip to sketch the scene, and his signature includes the specific notation, 'after an Ōsaka design'.

Although it was the new fashion for landscape-prints that made such widespread publication of Hokusai's several great series commercially feasible, as we have seen the Master had been making plans from at least a decade earlier. For example, in his oft-quoted book *Models of Modern Combs and Pipes* of 1823 he announced a proposed print series, *Hyakkyō ichiran* (Views of One Hundred Bridges). Indeed, both artist and publisher, a decade later, probably had that goal in mind. But being practical they settled on a less ambitious title lest—as actually proved the case—the market could not absorb more than a dozen or so designs on this particular theme. (Just at this period, as well, the publisher Eijudō suffered financial problems that may well have curtailed several such Hokusai series as this one.)

Like most of Hokusai's landscape-series the general level of quality is high in *The Bridges*, both in design and printing (on a par, say, with the average scenes of the *Fuji* series): but again, obviously world-class masterpieces are lacking, and there is a tendency (seen also in the concluding *Fuji* prints) to over-emphasize geometrical forms. It is not easy, therefore, to choose designs for discussion and illustration: one tends to fall back upon individual taste, personal associations, and the availability of first impressions in fine condition.

Pictorially speaking, the snowscape 'Pontoon-bridge at Sano' is surely the most striking of the series (Plate 264).

Under a lowering, greyish sky we view the ancient pontoon-bridge of Sano in north-east Japan. From the bridge-warden's hut and scraggly pine at right the eye is led in an S-curve to the precarious-seeming bridge with horseman and pack-driver, preceded by two caped travellers, and two diminutive figures on the far shore—the design leading on to the distant line of trees and mountains. The Toné River itself breaks wavelets against the wave-bowed bridge; and then we suddenly notice two further travellers in centre-foreground, one going, one coming.

But that is all. In one's mind the beauty of the colouring remains but—somehow—little impression of the grandeur of Nature that one feels in the best of Hokusai's work. A masterly sense of design raises the print above the merely picturesque, yet the effect is perilously close to that of the Master's younger contemporary Hiroshige, who was just beginning his landscape work at this time. The junior artist almost certainly took his initial inspiration from such Hokusai designs: simplifying them, and adding his own special mood. And while there is little evidence of the influence working backwards, it cannot be denied that Hiroshige's sudden popularity at this point would have changed the *publishers'* concept of what kind of prints would sell best, and the *printing-effects* best suited to current taste.

Although it is likely that Hokusai had sketched most of the actual sites of the great *Fuji* series, that was not the case of such distant scenes as this one. Indeed, his caption adds the notation 'Ancient View', indicating that this fragile pontoon-bridge, famous in early verse, was no longer extant. With this essentially earthy artist one senses that—from just such detached, abstracted qualities—with care one might be able to distinguish the imagined views from those he had actually experienced.

With *The Bridges* one gets the feeling that the artist might have succeeded better if he had placed more emphasis on humanity than on the structural features and background. This will be apparent from a glimpse at one other notable print in the series, 'Suspension-bridge between Hida and Etchū' (Plate 265). Here the human figures, though diminutive, are in such apparent peril—emphasized by the nonchalant flight of wild birds and the ominous dark peak—that one identifies immediately with them. Thus drawn personally into the setting one savours more directly the striking beauty—and the stark reality—of peasant life in the harsh mountains of north-west Japan. The landscape itself would make an effective print, but to this is added the characteristically Hokusai element of parlous humanity. Woodsman and wife are, indeed, placed at a critical juncture in the composition—balanced by the looming, cobalt mountain; they have just reached the bottom of the bridge's swaying incline, but as any climber knows it is the following, easier stage that is the most dangerous. The perspective features an odd mixture of Eastern and Western, doubtless to retain the clear focus on the figures, which would

260 *Overleaf left* 'Amida Waterfall on the Kiso Highway'. *Ōban*-size print from *The Waterfalls, c.* 1833. (See also Plate 261.)

261 *Overleaf right* 'The Horse-washing Falls'. *Ōban* print from *The Waterfalls, c.* 1833. (See also Plate 260 and Figs. 100–105.)

群橋多少長江卧
繞機連續漸峯礬
珍重厂畍勁圖裏
有來傾作覊旅情
景壽

262 'The Hundred Bridges'. Topographical map, double-*ōban* size, *c*. early-mid 1830s. Sealed: Hokusai *aratame* Iitsu. (Later reprinted under the title *Shokoku meikyō ichiran*—'View of Famous Japanese Bridges'—with text and seal removed.)

have been much diminished had they been depicted in realistic, receding perspective—not scientifically logical yet none the less effective. (Two primary 'states' of this print are known: in the later version the right flank of the central mountain is deleted. There is also an even later edition of the series—perhaps posthumous—trimmed and with blank margins added after the manner of Hiroshige's prints.)

In looking again at the designs of this series I see that my choice combines compositional and psychological effects: both prints feature a bold curve towards the centre of the design, and both display human beings at a potentially dangerous—or at least, dramatic—point in that curve. With the remaining scenes (Figs. 137–145) the result may be masterful landscapes but the figures are only incidental, decorative adjuncts. It is not without reason that I have characterized Hokusai's forte as 'humanity by design'.

But why, one may well ask, did the artist fail to expand on the mastery of landscape grandeur that he had achieved in the best of the *Fuji* series? One can only suspect the influence of his audience: fellow-artists and connoisseurs may have admired the magnificence of the 'Great Wave' and 'Fuji at Dawn', but the average print-buyer was far more interested in the subject-matter than in the perfection of design. Indeed, to judge from the quantity of extant examples today (and hence the numbers originally sold), major prints were hardly more popular than the lesser designs of the same series. Thus although the critic must, on the one hand, occasionally try to view these works through the eyes of Hokusai's contemporaries, he will, in the end, inevitably accept the advantage of historical hindsight. Only now, perhaps—a century and more after Hokusai's death—can we really appreciate the essence of this great, if much-flawed artist.

But though the Master was, for purely commercial reasons, unable to complete the *Bridges* series there is interesting evidence of his continued fascination with the subject. This appears in his inscription to the large 'Hundred Bridges' topographical map illustrated in our Plate 262.[2] Hokusai's vision is almost Coleridge-like in breadth:

One year in late autumn while sitting in meditation a picture appeared most vividly before my eyes. It was a landscape in which rose bridge after bridge, each one connected to the roads between and no paths obscure at all. Counting the bridges, their number exceeded a hundred. . . . Indeed, what shall I call this magic Land? . . .

Hokusai's varied landscape work in these brief few years represents an embarrassment of riches. In the standard horizontal *ōban* format, for example, we find the evocative set of three prints of *c*. 1832 entitled *Setsu-gekka* (Snow/Moon/Blossoms) depicting variously a Snowscape by the Sumida River, Moonlight on the Yodo River (near Ōsaka) and Flowering Cherries at Yoshino (near Nara). The 'Snow' view (Plate 263) is at Mukōjima, looking north-east along the Sumida from an imaginary elevation. At the lower right is seen a small shrine, the Umewaka Jinja, dedicated to a little boy who was kidnapped and died here in ancient times.[3]

More exotic in theme is another set of *ōban* prints dating from *c*. 1833, entitled *Ryūkyū hakkei* (Eight Views of Ryūkyū). Hokusai had never visited Okinawa (which was, in fact, still a semi-independent Kingdom at this period), and the views are taken entirely from an earlier topography of Chinese authorship, reprinted in Edo in 1831.

263 'Snowscape by the Sumida River'. *Ōban* print from the series *Snow/Moon/Blossoms*, *c*. 1832. (See also Figs. 95–96.)

Inevitably, the prints end up as illustrations rather than personally experienced, dramatic views (Plate 266).

In its detachment from the subject, its pictorialism and prettiness, its lack of the smell of the earth, the print is again dangerously close to Hiroshige, or even to *bonseki*—miniature landscapes fashioned from sand and pebbles. (It may seem curious that public taste should have reached, even briefly, to scenes of such an unknown and unvisitable 'Shangri-La'. But like many such depictions of Okinawa in ukiyo-e—see Plate 196—the immediate stimulus to publication was the Mission to Edo of a large Ryūkyū Court Embassy: two hundred strong and parading about the city in flowing Chinese-style garb, in the Tenth Month of 1832.)

Also from the years 1833–4 dates one of Hokusai's most unusual, masterful and least-known sets: the ten medium-sized *chūban* prints entitled *Chie-no-umi* (Oceans of Wisdom). Here varied scenes of commercial fishing are presented against dramatic river- and seascapes: a vital subject of Japanese life and landscape, necessarily neglected in the earlier scenes of mountains, waterfalls, bridges. Like many such sets, this one was never completed, but the existence of Hokusai's original sketches or proofs for over a dozen other designs proves that this termination was the publisher's, not the artist's, decision, based of course on purely commercial considerations. The strikingly avant-

garde quality of most of the designs was clearly ahead of its time and did not appeal to the Edo populace (indeed, the remarkable nature of this series is—partly because of its rarity—only now coming to be recognized). Such was the plight of the ukiyo-e artist, customarily at the mercy of a fickle public.

Noticeable in this rare and neglected series is a modicum of influence from Western oil-painting: for example in the striking colour-tones—yellows, greens, reds, with extensive employment of *kakeawase* overprinting—and especially in the un-Japanese use of massive black pigment, as well as the dynamically realistic approach to the subject (though there is no overt employment of perspective effect, as was found in Hokusai's earlier experiments). To the specialist the most striking element of the series may be the curiously softened—almost blurred—technique of block-carving, with a purposeful avoidance of strong black lines in the key-block. In part, this rough texture may go

back to the publisher, Moriya Jihei, whose engravers were (according to Bakin) known for their rather unsophisticated technique. And doubtless a professional like Hokusai to some degree adapted his designs to suit the artisans of each particular publisher. One's impression of this series is that something of the *surimono* technique has here been applied to commercial printing—with an exotic oil-painting effect thrown in for good measure. By the same token the series—with its tangible, almost three-dimensional qualities—is hardly amenable to very effective reproduction.

The most readily appreciable scene of *Oceans of Wisdom* is certainly 'Whaling off Gotō', with its neatly patterned harbour and boats—only the great whale depicted in dramatic ebony (Plate 267). The frothing waves about the trapped whale reflect the great beast's form, as do the concentric rings of water-patterns that stretch out to the arch of waiting boats and on to the surrounding hills (with look-out hut at upper right); again, the strongly decorative quality is an indication that this is a product of the imagination rather than of personal experience.[4]

More evocative is the close-up of 'Fishing by Torchlight, Kai Province' in which the nocturnal tableau is almost Kabuki-like in its decorative intensity (Plate 268). Again, 'Basket-fishing in the Kinu River' (Plate 270) effects an even more dramatic juxtaposition of landscape, seascape and man—and bears interesting comparison with

264 *Opposite top* 'Pontoon-bridge at Sano'. *Ōban* print from *The Bridges*, c. 1834. (See also Plate 265 and Figs. 137–145.) (A vainglorious collector's seals appear by signature and publisher's seal.)

265 *Opposite bottom* 'Suspension-bridge between Hida and Etchū'. *Ōban* print from *The Bridges*, c. 1834. (See also Plate 264.)

266 *Below* 'Voice of the Lake at Rinkai'. *Ōban* print from *Eight Views of Ryūkyū*, c. 1833. (See also Figs. 107–113.)

267 *Opposite top* 'Whaling off Gotō'. *Chūban*-size print from *Oceans of Wisdom*, c. 1833–4. (See also Plates 268–70 and Figs. 122–127.)

268 *Opposite bottom* 'Fishing by Torchlight, Kai Province'. *Chūban* print from *Oceans of Wisdom*, c. 1833–4. (See also Plate 267.)

269 *Above* 'Chōshi in Shimōsa Province'. *Chūban* print from *Oceans of Wisdom*, c. 1833–4. (See also Plate 267.)

'Kanaya' in the *Fuji* series (Plate 259). We perceive in this diminutive space a heroic attempt to achieve a maximum of *reality* within the confines of the woodblock colour-print: the brick-red embankment appears almost a thing alive; and the old fisherman is not just an idle spectator but represents the ageing artist himself.

But—though difficult to reproduce, even if by woodcut—most striking of all in the original is 'Chōshi in Shimōsa Province' (Plate 269).[5] Despite the print's smallish size, we are impelled as though by a maelstrom, drawn into a kind of nautical roller-coaster ride. The main feature of the series is that it tends to spotlight the fishermen rather than the landscape; and this print is, in effect, a closer view of the wretched sailors we knew so well under the towering 'Great Wave' (Plate 245). I doubt that any

post-Creation ocean was ever quite this turbulent—gargantuan masses swirling in variant directions in spite of the huge promontory at right. But Hokusai's message is certainly not one of disaster or despair: but rather one of triumph, of man eking out his living despite the forces of Nature and always managing, like the artist himself, to survive and come back for more.

It should perhaps be emphasized that though colour is employed in this series largely for its dramatic impact—and is a long stage removed both from reality and from traditional usage—this was not from any conscious effort on the artist's part to be outrageous. Hokusai was simply expressing his instinctive reaction to certain subjects—in certain sublime moments of inspiration. The fact that he was by nature stubborn, uncompromising, anti-conventional, ambitious and dedicated to his art did not in any way engender the creative process: these factors only provided the necessary background and environment for it to find concrete expression.

In *Oceans of Wisdom* we discover Hokusai engaged in a penetrating search for the plastic, basic forms of land-scape, with a near-total disregard for the commercial re-quirements of the landscape print: the picturesque, the

270 *Top* 'Basket-fishing in the Kinu River'. *Chūban* print from *Oceans of Wisdom*, c. 1833–4. (See also Plate 267.)

271 *Above* 'Snow at Shinagawa'. *Koban*-size print from *Fine Views of Snow/Moon/Flowers*, c. 1832–3. (See Appendix, Prints, No. 149.)

pleasant and sentimental, the familiar and readily enjoyable. In all this, there would seem to be no better characterization of the artist than 'intractably avant-garde'.

Even smaller in format but of surprising quality is the *koban* set of nine prints known as *Shōkei setsu-gekka* (Fine Views of Snow/Moon/Flowers) of *c.* 1832–3. In 'Snow at Shinagawa' (Plate 271), one is struck by the remarkable plasticity of forms that creates a near three-dimensional effect rare in such small format. One may indeed wonder that an important work should have been relegated to such a diminutive size; but this was entirely a matter for the publisher's decision. Such sets of miniatures (about 12 × 16 cm/4.7 × 6 in) were popular not only for children's diversion and education, but also for mounting in albums and on screens. In this case, certainly, the publisher got more than he bargained for. The originals suffer, however, from the printer's lavish employment of the red 'haze-strata' that enjoyed something of a vogue in this period. The blood-coloured, conventional clouds tend to dominate the compositions, and can only be compared to the excesses of some Hindu or Chinese festivals or of certain psychedelic/luminescent colourists today.

From this period also date several other small prints,

which feature landscapes and nature subjects in a rather cursive manner, and with employment of a minimum of colours. The effect is almost one of direct transfer of the artist's sketches to the print medium, without the intermediation of the engraver (Plate 272).

Again from the years *c.* 1833–4 we find that impressive series of ten, extra-large *naga-ōban* panel-prints entitled *Shiika shashin-kyō* (A Mirror of Chinese/Japanese Verse).

Today when viewing Hokusai's prints at an exhibition there is a tendency to be impressed by size. When the originals are held in the hands, however (ideally, unencumbered even by mats or frames), one may regret the loss of intimacy in these large 'panel-prints', and even have difficulty in focusing on the total design at one glance. When reduced to a book-plate, one's impression will again be different. Such is the inevitable fate of the Japanese print, which, in a sense, can only be fully appreciated by those with constant access to the originals. Indeed, the specialist is rather at a disadvantage here: he must, for the moment, look at these admittedly magnificent prints not as curator, collector or scholar, but as, so to speak, a simple gallery-viewer.

The 'panel-print'—of varying dimensions—was patterned on, and generally mounted as, the kakemono or 'hanging-scroll' format of traditional Japanese art. It was intended primarily to be seen from a distance rather than held in the hands. The interest was thus similar to that of a small poster. From this viewpoint, the most impressive design of this series is surely the 'Chinese Poet in Snow', which depicts a gentleman on horseback—probably the Sung literatus Su Tung-p'o—with a servant in a snowy, lakeside landscape (Plate 273). The design suffers somewhat from a lack of integration between the figures and the snowscape; but for this larger format it ranks, nevertheless, as one of Hokusai's masterpieces. (Of the series, this is the only print lacking indication of the specific subject—possibly evidence that it was the design first issued.)

Less impressive but better integrated as a design is 'Nakamaro in China', depicting the classical Japanese poet on a balcony in moonlight, beneath a pine-tree, yearning for his native land (Plate 274). Others of the series are perhaps of equal interest, but with some ('Tsuraki', for example) the principal figure sometimes gets lost in the landscape; and in others (such as 'Sei-Shōnagon') the design tends to represent more an illustration than an independent print (Figs. 135, 136).

One noteworthy feature of *A Mirror of Chinese/Japanese Verse* is the mixing of customary Hokusai artistic techniques with a certain poetic lyricism and pictorialism, which were obviously meant to match not only the tone of the subject but also the tastes of the new audience for such prints, who were fast coming under the spell of the more romantic and lyrical Hiroshige. One cannot, indeed, very well imagine the stubborn old Hokusai acquiescing to the Hiroshige boom; yet he knew in his heart that the times had changed—and his art had to change with them, if it was to remain publishable. In this situation he was worlds removed from the stereotyped image of the dedicated painter in the West: happily ensconced in an attic-atelier,

sustained by self-faith and a patron or two. None the less, as in much of Hokusai's later work, this series reflects a rather didactic, realistic, historical and semi-Chinese approach that detracts from the artistic effect of the design. And one must conclude, in the end, that the artist did not really employ this larger, 'panel' format to the best of his abilities or to the limits of the medium.

Hokusai's only other significant landscape-series towards the middle of this eventful decade is the set of eight fan-prints entitled *Shōkei kiran* (Rare Views of Famous Landscapes), of about 1834–5. This series is stylistically somewhat reminiscent of the remarkable *Oceans of Wisdom*, but with a predominant employment of *aizuri* (indigo) colouring technique, and with the necessary adjustments of composition attendant on the fan format. There seems, indeed, to be an as yet unexplained relationship between these two series. Possibly lack of sales induced the publisher to convert some of the unpublished *Oceans* sketches to fan format; possibly the fan series was originally planned as a sequel to the *Oceans*, in *chūban* size.

Typical of the series is 'At Suwa Lake in Shinano' (Plate 275). In its lateral composition—empty at centre and with opening for handle at bottom—the print shows clearly the practical constraints of the rounded fan format. But probably the most remarkable of the set is that depicting Mt Myōgi, with pilgrims perched precariously on one of the

272 Landscape by Moonlight. Small-*chūban* print (trimmed) from an untitled *aizuri* series, 1831. (See Appendix, Prints, No. 142.)

273 Chinese Poet in Snow. *Naga-ōban*-size print from *A Mirror of Chinese/Japanese Verse, c.* 1833–4. (See also Plate 274 and Figs. 128–36.)

274 The Poet Nakamaro in China. *Naga-ōban* print from *A Mirror of Chinese/Japanese Verse, c.* 1833–4. (See also Plate 273.) (In this early impression the grain of the woodblock is sharply visible at centre.)

275 'At Suwa Lake in Shinano'. Fan-print from the series *Rare Views of Famous Landscapes*, c. 1834–5. (See also Plate 276 and Fig. 155.)

fantastically jagged peaks. It is a scene dramatically divorced from reality (Plate 276). In this rare and striking series the landscape, while reduced to a format resembling the miniature blue of Delft ware, opens up a surprisingly wide horizon to the mind's eye.

It must be added that the exact dating of such Hokusai prints of the mid-1830s is still unsettled, even in Japan. In the absence of historical records one can only judge from the stronger colouring and the more precise techniques of engraving prevalent from the middle of the decade, and from certain minute changes in the artist's style—hardly a very exact guide with this period and subject.

The above account is not, of course, the full story of Hokusai's remarkable landscape output in the early 1830s: there are miniature highway scenes and views of Edo and, even, a large 'Highway Backgammon' design, plus the wide variety of flower-and-bird, ghost and other prints which will be the subject of the next chapter. And though one may discover here only a half-dozen prints clearly of world rank, there can be few artists who have published such a prodigious quantity of high-quality *oeuvre* in such a short span of time—and at the age of 70 or more.

NOTES

1 As a kind of afterthought on this famous print I should add that (as was also the case with Hokusai himself) one of my specialities is shunga, and I should therefore normally try to avoid seeking erotic allusions in a seemingly 'straight' landscape print. But Hokusai himself was a past master of the erotic (see Chapter XV) and it is difficult to deny the possible phallic implications of this 'Amida Waterfall and its Source'. Indeed, in several of the contemporary shunga books there are 'close-up' plates of phallus and vulva that come very close to the basic elements of Hokusai's design. In addition, I once published (*Ukiyo-e*, No. 82, 1980) a shunga plate by the ukiyo-e pioneer Moronobu which bears a curious resemblance (see fig. *overleaf, bottom*). With these two artists, of course, we may be dealing with subconscious forces—the Boat in Moronobu, the Fall in Hokusai, both straining towards the Source: but with artists who had designed literally hundreds of masterful erotic prints I tend to feel the implications are there, whether consciously intended or not. (To the conventions of shunga may be added, indeed, the naturalistic function of Japanese phallic worship. *Linga* and *yoni* natural stones—very much resembling Hokusai's Fall and Source—were quite normally set up as objects of worship by barren wives and bordello-owners; and waterfalls themselves had mystic male-female connotations in Old Japan.)

2 Another interesting variation on this theme may be seen in the *Manga*, Series XI, 1833; and a related 'Seven Bridges at One Glance' will be found in Series II of *Fugaku hyakkei* the following year, 1834. Whereas in the West bridges are used metaphorically to express connection and linkage, in Japan

276 'On Mt Myōgi'. Fan-print from the series *Rare Views of Famous Landscapes*, c. 1834–5. (See also Plate 275.)

they tend to be associated with dreams, and with the uncertainty and transience of life and love: see, for example, the 'Bridge of Dreams' chapter in the 11th-century *Tale of Genji*, and the 'Gothic' novel illustrated by Hokusai himself, *The Bridge of Love-dreams* (Plate 103).

This print is sometimes assumed to correspond to the 'Hundred Bridges' advertisement in the 1823 book shown in Plate 168. However, the blurb specifically cites 'scenes of the *Edo* region' (which I further interpret as representing a *series* rather than a single print); and moreover, the style and colouring of our Plate 262 seem to date from the later decade.
3 The artist would have been standing near the Mokuboji, a Buddhist temple erected in the dead boy's memory. The water in the foreground with boat is an inlet of the river; in the distance is Sekiya Village, which appears in a notable *Fuji* print (Fig. 79). Note that this lonely scene is depicted also in the artist's miniature set *Shōkei setsu-gekka* of the same period.
4 An earlier whaling scene will be found in the *Hokusai gafu* of 1820. Several published depictions of whaling would have been readily available for the artist's reference—e.g. Mitsunobu's *Nihon sankai meisan-zue* of 1754 (reprinted in 1797), and Shiba Kōkan's *Saiyū ryotan* of 1794.
5 Interestingly enough, a kind of predecessor of this tableau may be found in one of Hokusai's early *yomi-hon* illustrations, the dramatic 'Harakiri amid Waves' of 1810 (Fig. 188). (Compare also our *Manga* sketch of Plate 158, as well as the early *Tōkaidō* miniature of Fig. 38.)

Left Moronobu: Love-making by the River. Plate from the shunga book *Makura-e daizen* (The Pillow-Picture Compendium), 1682.

XX
Hokusai's
Golden Decade (2):
Ghosts and Flowers;
The Hundred Poems

1

PERHAPS HOKUSAI'S most unusual productions of this frenetic half-decade of print activity in the early 1830s were his 'Ghost Prints', a species hitherto met with mainly as an adjunct to depiction of supernatural Kabuki tableaux. Behind the creation of such prints and tales featuring wrongs and their revenge may be surmised the rising tide of indignation on the part of the masses at government corruption: a contempt for authority that was to be expressed even more openly in satirical prints by younger artists such as Kuniyoshi.

The Master's approach was characteristically bizarre and dramatic. The five striking prints of his *Hyaku-monogatari* (Ghost Tales) of *c.* 1831 are all based on traditional Japanese supernatural tales, but each design comprises a haunting detail plucked out and enlarged—and featuring occasional touches of black humour. The set represents, in a sense, the culmination and distillation of Hokusai's long experience in the illustration of the 'Gothic novels' of his earlier years. (The title, literally 'The Hundred Tales', refers to a traditional practice of villagers gathering together at night to tell a series of ghost stories. As each tale was told, one candle from the hundred lamps was extinguished; and with the death of the final lamp, an apparition would issue forth. Hokusai's early print of Plate 17 may well depict the ending of one such seance.)

My own favourite of this series of smallish *chūban* prints is the 'Ghost of O-Iwa' (Plate 277). O-Iwa was the tragic heroine of the Kabuki ghost tale *Yotsuya kaidan*; cruelly murdered by her husband, she came back from the grave to wreak bloody vengeance. Here we see her dismembered visage metamorphosed into the smouldering Buddhist lantern offered to her spirit on All Souls' Night, when her vile widower visits the cemetery with his new wife. On the gaping lantern appears the Buddhist invocation '*Namu Amida-butsu* (Hail to Amitabha Buddha), *zokumyō Iwa-jo* (secular name: Ms. Iwa)'. On O-Iwa's forehead is an approximation of a sacred Sanskrit letter. The title is placed on the upper right: *O-Iwa-san / Hyaku-monogatari*. There can be few more terrifying depictions of the supernatural; and even the viewer unfamiliar with the bloody details of Tsuruya Namboku's famous play might be a trifle shaken were this inspired apparition suddenly to appear at a bedroom window.[1]

Equally startling (if on a somewhat lower artistic level) is the scene of Plate 282 showing the semi-skeletonized ghost of Kohada Koheiji—an itinerant actor who was drowned by his wife's lover—peering intently over the boudoir mosquito-net at his widow and his murderer. The smoke-streams (presumably issuing from the mosquito-repellent beside the bedding and depositing unlikely soot on the edge of the netting) are transformed into the ghost of Koheiji himself, who diabolically retains the skin and hair on the back of his emaciated skull. The green and cobalt colouring adroitly evokes the scene of Koheiji's cruel murder by drowning, in similar murky waters.

In Koheiji's macabre skeleton one can glimpse not only fine art but also evidence of Hokusai's long attention to the details of human anatomy. Other artists perforce turned to medical texts for such data, but Hokusai had from his early years nurtured a fervent interest in the medical and other scientific knowledge newly imported from abroad; as we have seen he had even studied for a time with a traditional bone-setter. Thus he could the more readily combine reasonable scientific accuracy with the impulse of his artistic intentions. Prolonged effort and intense study are not, of course, the final key to artistic achievement; yet there can be few artists, East or West, who have expended such energy on acquiring the manifest details of their craft. But though a delightful print (at least, for those who enjoy this kind of thing), 'Koheiji' does not quite rank with the masterpiece 'O-Iwa' either in composition or in conception; and the slightly comic flavour of the design detracts from its effectiveness in a theme that, by definition, must be totally haunting.

The remaining three scenes of this remarkable series are less dramatic, if equally chilling once one knows the bloody tales of ghastly vengeance that they represent (Figs. 92–94).

Nothing could be more tranquillizing than to turn from *The Ghosts* to Hokusai's several series of *kacho-ga* (flower-and-

277 *Overleaf left* 'The Ghost of O-Iwa'. *Chūban*-size print from *Ghost Tales*, *c.* 1831. (See also Plate 282 and Fig. 92 ff.)

278 *Overleaf top right* Japanese Spaniel. Fan-print, datable to 1833. (For other such Hokusai fan prints see Plates 288–9 and Appendix, Nos. 150 and 151.)

279 *Overleaf bottom right* Porters in Landscape. *Ōban* print from *The Hundred Poems*, *c.* 1835–6. (See also Plates 284–5, 291, Figs. 157–66.)

bird pictures) of the same period. The latter genre was an ancient one in Far Eastern painting, but it was Hokusai who first developed it as a major, independent *print* subject—as distinct from its appearance in the *surimono* greeting-prints, where the design was always but an adjunct to the verse or announcement.

The 'flower-and-bird' theme, which also includes insects, fish, reptiles and animals in natural or still-life settings, had been a predominant one in Ming (as well as Korean) painting, quantities of which were imported into Japan in the two centuries before Hokusai, together with several itinerant Chinese artists in the flesh. And though the original Chinese paintings were not too widely available, Japanese copies, or variations on them, were abundant, as well as woodblock-printed textbooks containing reproductions. The latter were at first of Chinese origin—notably the *Ten Bamboo Studio* and *The Mustard-seed Garden*—but with the mid-eighteenth century these classics came to be reproduced, and expanded upon, by Japanese publishers and artists.

So far as the independently issued ukiyo-e print went, the flower-and-bird theme had occasionally been featured in the work of such early masters as Kiyomasu and Shigenaga; it even achieved a certain general recognition in the later 1760s with Harunobu and Koryūsai, followed by the *surimono* of Shumman—and of the younger Hokusai himself—as well as the albums of Masayoshi and Utamaro. But the form reached its culmination—in scale, popularity and achievement—with Hokusai, to be concluded by the graceful work of Hiroshige in the ensuing decade.

Further comment may be in order here regarding this specialized genre, also known as *kachō-e* and, with the somewhat wider connotation of 'nature art', *kachō-fūgetsu*—(flower-and-bird/wind-and-moon). These categories are different from the Western still-life or *nature morte* not only in content but in that the painter's aim is not so much to display his skills as to express his own subjective, emotive feelings towards nature, his instinctive reactions to natural phenomena. Much effort is devoted to conveying the essence, the inner spirit of the subject, whether alive or inanimate. Nature is thus seen as a reflection of man, and the latter's aim is to identify—even become one with—nature.

Over the centuries, certain conventional combinations of elements had come to be associated in Far Eastern art—plum-blossom and moon, pine and crane, cloud and dragon, dragon and tiger, withered tree and raven, and dozens of others. Employment of such familiar combinations permitted a far greater range of connotations within a simple design, because the whole background of Eastern poetry and literary associations could be called upon by this elementary device. Most of these time-honoured combinations of subject found expression in Hokusai's *oeuvre*—often only in minor *Manga* sketches, but sometimes in major works as well—now and then mutated either in form or connotations to suit the Master's peculiar talent and taste. Naturally, Hokusai's strongly individualistic—even bizarre and outlandish—approach to such themes had both merits and perils: the general populace of novelty-loving Edoites admired him as an eccentric genius; but the average art-patron tended to prefer something more conven-

tional—less controversial—to hang in his sedate parlour. This has ever been the problem for innovative and unconventional artists, and one reason why their general recognition, whatever their talents, must often await the changing judgement of a future generation.

Yet while recognizing the artist's considerable creative achievement here, I personally (though fond enough of birds and flowers and their depiction in *painting*) do not find Hokusai's style of his later years most suited to this theme. And this is particularly true in the *print* medium, where his realistic, unpliant and Chinese-derived manner often conflicts with the softness and pliability of the original subject. In this genre, at least, I feel he is surpassed by the achievement of the more evocative and romantic Hiroshige. This is, however, much a matter of taste, and some collectors and connoisseurs value Hokusai's *kachō-ga* almost as much as his landscapes. (This may be partly due to their rarity, which again attests to their low popular appeal even during the artist's lifetime—acclaim not having sufficed to justify the publisher issuing later printings.)

Be that as it may, this genre is, nevertheless, perhaps the most readily appreciable to the novice of Far Eastern art: the subjects are familiar ones and no background in the complexity of Oriental lore is needed to enjoy them.

The best known of Hokusai's prints in this category is probably the untitled, horizontal *ōban* series of *c*. 1833–4—known in the West as the 'Large Flowers'—of which ten prints are recorded. And, as noted above, 'flower-and-bird' is a wide generic category, in which flowers and plants are usually the centre of attention, with birds, butterflies, dragonflies and even toads and lizards serving mainly as decorative accents to the composition.

Hokusai's approach is to take a close-up view of some striking flower or plant, filling the frame and employing bold patterns of contrasting leaf and flower. The subject itself tends, however, to limit the exercise of the artist's dramatic powers and there are few acknowledged masterpieces in the series. Yet one cannot but admire the consistently masterful handling of a theme so difficult to render dynamically within the limitations of the print format. Hokusai's feat is not only to depict flowers as essentially alive (which they certainly are) but also, to a degree, as sentient and keenly sensitive to their environment (which fact is often forgotten).

The first example illustrated here is an effective floral print, but one cannot but feel that the design would have come more to life had the artist been permitted to place greater emphasis on the little tree-frog, almost lost in the dew-drenched foliage at lower centre (Plate 280). Most likely, the series was issued for the delight of flower-fanciers, which placed severe constraints on the artist's range of activity.

Even more striking in its own way is the 'Poppies' of Plate 281, in which the ungainly flower is presented as a sentient

280 *Opposite top* Morning-glories. *Ōban*-size print from the 'Large Flowers' series, *c*. 1833–4. (See also Plate 281 and Figs. 114–21.)

281 *Opposite bottom* Poppies. *Ōban* print from the 'Large Flowers' series, *c*. 1833–4. (See also Plate 280.)

282 *Below* 'The Ghost of Koheiji'. *Chūban* print from *Ghost Tales*, c. 1831. (See also Plate 277.)

283 *Right* Bullfinch and Weeping Cherry. *Chūban*-size print from the 'Small Flowers' series, c. 1834. (See also Plate 286 and Figs. 147–54.)

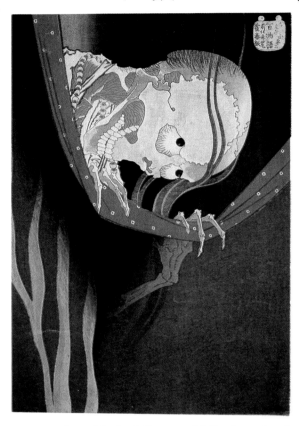

creature in a kind of Dance of Life, bent by the wind and enslaved to the sun—yet poignantly alive and possessed of its own graceful, pliant character and rhythmic personality. Short of resorting to caricature, this is about as 'human' as simple flora can get. The personification/anthropomorphosis is achieved without overt preciosity or cloying cuteness—indeed, the casual observer may see here only a simple branch of flower-stalks and leaves, arranged in a quaintly Oriental manner. For the artist, the composition doubtless represented a natural placement of floral curves arrayed against unseen natural forces; for us, comparison with his 'Great Wave' is inevitable (Plate 247). In these simple yet most sentient flowers the artist projects a vision rather than a record—and with an intensity that is surprisingly like that he expended just a decade earlier on erotic themes.

Perhaps more successful within such severe limitations is the *chūban* 'Small Flowers' series of about 1834, of which ten designs are also known.[2] Here, the emphasis is reversed and the wild birds of each design are given a more central position in the composition. With his smaller 'flowerprints' Hokusai was less strictly bound by tradition and public taste. He could not, however, let his imagination range too far afield: this was not a ready medium for the humorous, the grotesque or the overly dramatic. Thus the artist vented his powers on the creation of bold patterns and compelling compositions, treated from an objective rather than a subjective point of view; and—considering the

limitations of the genre—he succeeded very well.

With 'Bullfinch and Weeping Cherry' (Plate 283) composition is—as always with Hokusai—the keystone, and here it is accompanied by a most precise rendering of natural forms. Characteristically, the bird is an individualized creation, perhaps too humanized to be very lovable. (The bullfinch, incidentally, has the unfortunate—albeit gourmet—habit of eating up the buds of flowering trees; it is hardly welcomed in Japan at cherry-blossom time.) At the upper right of the print is seen the name of the bird (*uso*) and the flower (*shidare-zakura*), and a poem by Raiman: 'A single bird comes out / drenched by the dew: / the morning cherry blooms.' Such verses often refer obliquely to the human world—here, for example, to the picture of a young man returning at dawn from a night of love in the Yoshiwara.

The printing and colour of this smaller series, too, are more careful and gorgeous than the *ōban* set, coming close to the standards of *surimono* limited editions. Such prints are, of course, not unrelated to *surimono* taste; but besides being commercially issued, they feature more dynamic designs, as well as Hokusai's typically sharp powers of observation—creating a very different dramatic effect, which would have been quite out of tune with *surimono*. At

284 *Opposite top* Women Divers. *Ōban* print from *The Hundred Poems*, c. 1835–6. (For other data see Plate 279.)

285 *Opposite bottom* Bull and Parasol. *Ōban* print from *The Hundred Poems*, c. 1835–6. (See also Plate 279.)

the same time, Hokusai's strong indebtedness to Ming painting is obvious: though the artist has added his characteristically anthropomorphic birds (and even flowers)—and, in the print shown in Plate 283, a very effective employment of the newly imported pigment Prussian blue (which happily obscures the rather obtrusive text). In the less successful designs, however, there is a tendency for decorative conventionalization to clash with Hokusai's dramatic vision. In 'Wagtail and Wisteria' (Plate 286), for example, the frail flowers are rendered impressively vital and the bird is masterfully drawn. (One notes with a smile that though no Japanese wagtail ever sported such an elongated tail as this, Hokusai has drawn it out to just the ideally critical point in the composition.) Yet the print itself, owing in part to the white background and dominant verse, barely escapes the bounds of the botanical textbook, or the decorative title-page. While this series may be praised as gem-like and opulently decorative, it never really reaches the level of the classical Chinese/Korean/Japanese *kachō-ga* that were its inspiration; nor does it even begin to come near the artist's own work in the field of *painting*.

It is indeed interesting to note Hokusai's very different approach to the standard *kachō-ga* themes in his painting and in his prints—reflecting not only two aspects of his own artistic personality but also the influence of the different mediums, and the varying types of audience to which these forms were directed (see Plates 104, 125–6, 347).

Of these two famous print-series it may be said that whereas the 'Small Flowers' was precise and gem-like, much indebted to the legacy of painting, it is in the 'Large Flowers' that Hokusai was best able to express his natural reactions to the themes, and in the flowers themselves, something of his empathy towards all living creatures.

More impressive, both in size and grandeur, is Hokusai's extra-large, *naga-ōban* flower-and-bird series of *c.* 1832–3, of which five designs are known. (Unlike the landscape and ghost prints, none of these *kachō-ga* series bears any title on the originals.) As with all such designs in the larger formats, these prints were probably intended for mounting as plebeian kakemono—hence the predominance of felicitous scenes: cranes and tortoises, for example, being standard symbols of longevity. The subjects and their treatment tend therefore to be limited by the traditional tastes of the audience, and Hokusai's distinctive personality is rather obscured, revealed mainly in the anthropomorphic touches to the birds, fish, tortoises or whatever.

With a format here enlarged almost to panel-size, the artist is able better to employ his talent for dramatic composition, to utilize his painterly skills. In accord with the kakemono function, the treatment and most of the sub-

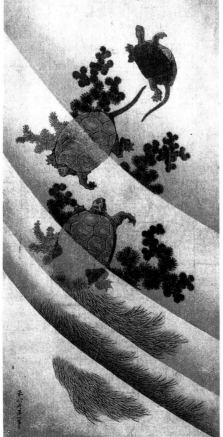

286 *Above left* Wagtail and Wisteria. *Chūban* print from the 'Small Flowers' series, *c.* 1834. (See also Plate 283.)

287 *Left* Swimming Tortoises. *Naga-ōban*-size print from an untitled series, early to mid-1830s. (See also Figs. 97, 98.)

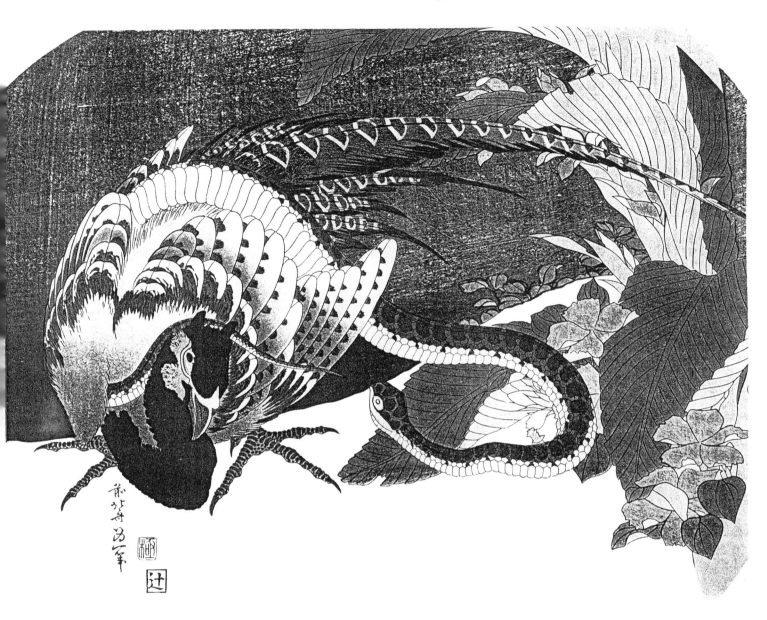

288 Pheasant and Snake. Fan-print, *c.* 1834. (Compare the 1820
album-plate of our Fig. 210.)

jects are traditional ones—falcon/carp/cranes/horses—but
in one print at least the artist is able to escape these con-
straining bounds. In 'Swimming Tortoises' (Plate 287), the
composition is divided into planes by the overlay of water-
patterns, a device derived from Chinese painting but
rather rare in conventional Japanese art. Here, these
charming creatures are individualized but not anthropo-
morphized (the most ancient one at bottom depicted in
traditional manner, with trailing appendage of marine
algae); and with the adolescent turtle at top, one can identify with the joy of a creature ungainly on land but completely free in its natural, underwater habitat. The design
could even be seen as a kind of parable: an inspiration for
those individuals prevented—either physically or
mentally—from swimming through life as freely as they
might wish.

Curiously enough, for Hokusai's most successful *kachō-
ga* designs of this period one must turn to the ephemeral
fan format. The *uchiwa-e* or 'fan-print' (of large-*chūban* or

aiban size) was intended for mounting on the bamboo ribs
of rounded summer fans; because of this practical function
they were normally 'consumed', and thus comparatively
few survive today.

The subjects in the fan genre tend to be more intrinsically interesting, often less traditional or conventional, and
the printing of the highest quality. Knowing that they
would be widely seen and used (albeit soon worn out),
Hokusai took special care in their execution, treating each
design as a separate creation rather than as part of a series.
Perhaps, also, the very limitations of the format—with
rounded edges and blank for the handle at bottom—add
to the concentrated effectiveness of the *uchiwa-e* medium.

For special attention my natural choice falls inevitably
on the deceptively charming 'Japanese Spaniel' of Plate
278. This curious little creature, the *chin*, was first imported to Japan in the Muromachi Period—*c.* fifteenth
century—and because of its somewhat ambiguous appearance was also known as 'cat-dog' or 'puppy-cat'. The subject is one more apt to appear 'cute' than artistic—and
indeed the print is almost irresistible in its colourful,
dreamlike world: the background enhanced, moreover, by
the unconventional setting of nettles and dandelions. Like

the contemporaneous *Ryūkyū Views*, the print reflects the current fashion for things foreign, and forms a kind of paean to exotic fantasy.

Hokusai's mature treatment of animals and birds is nearly always distinguished by the peculiar quality of the eyes: piercing, glaring, almost accusing—and this design is no exception. Certain small dogs do, indeed, sometimes have a wild, almost insane expression, as if they were about to bite one (as they sometimes do). Hokusai has both captured this expression and rendered it haunting by the simple printing device of 'transparency': the blue of the eyes is printed from the same woodblock as the azure background, lending an almost psychedelic quality to the mood of the tableau. A point hitherto neglected is that Hokusai bears interesting affinities with the later eighteenth-century Kyōto 'eccentric painters' Jakuchū and Shōhaku. The latter, in particular, may well have influenced the younger Hokusai with his stubborn individualism, and his vision of all creatures on this earth as slightly mad.

289 Group Portrait: Chickens. Fan-print, datable to 1835.

Another striking flower-and-bird print in fan format is the 'Pheasant and Snake' of Plate 288. The subject is potentially macabre: a pheasant squats before an azure ground with a plantain-lily at right, as a serpent wraps its tail about the bird's body. Surprisingly, however, the print is neither repellent nor frightening, even to bird-lovers. We know that birds and animals may sometimes give up when trapped or hypnotized by a natural enemy: but here, the effect is of two creatures merely playing; and our impression is, rather, of the colourful forces of nature, the resources of the Japanese woodblock-printer, and the supremacy in design and concept of the artist, Hokusai. (There is yet another dimension to this miniature drama. For, in Japan at least, the pheasant is known for its unique, and only, method of defence when captured by a snake: to narrow its body to the utmost and then, when the serpent has tightly entwined itself, to spread its wings and, with all its life-energy, to desperately attempt to break the snake in two.)

Of equal interest in this format—if a less compelling theme—is the 'Group Portrait: Chickens' of Plate 289.[3] Each of these cocks and hens is an individual, each por-

trayal showing one aspect of the bird's natural expression: most often alert and watchful but sometimes napping, the whole covey compressed into the severe limitations of a summer fan. It is a tribute to the artist's skill that within this mass of seven barnyard fowl one can sense the individuality, the fighting spirit of the humble chicken. The composition is surprisingly similar to that of the 'Women Divers' of a few years later (Plate 284). All things considered, 'The Chickens' is probably a more perfect print. It may be added that the number seven was an auspicious one for Japanese art-subjects—the Seven Gods of Luck, the Seven Kabuki Roles, the Seven Komachis—and here the lowly chicken is elevated by the artist to the sublime level of the Seven Sages of the Bamboo Grove. In this complex, near-three-dimensional composition, the primary colours project from the receding background; and one cannot but be fascinated by the varied, individualistic character expressed in each recalcitrant bird. They are, one might say, a composite self-portrait of Hokusai himself: living mostly by instinct, vulnerable yet unbowed.

In effect, these flower-and-bird prints represented an attempt to translate the miniaturistic designs of Hokusai's earlier *Sketchbooks* to the print form. Within these severe limits, they are indeed successful though their objective rendering of nature was not ideally suited to Hokusai's genius, nor compatible with the production of major works of art in this specialized genre.

The variety of Hokusai's subject-matter is often amazing, and we must briefly mention his rare warrior-prints of this period—of which five are known. Here he seems briefly to be challenging the position of his younger contemporary Kuniyoshi, the acknowledged master of this genre. Our example (Plate 290) is the famous combat between the samurai Kagemasa (known in Kabuki as 'Shibaraku'), who dispatched his enemy Yasunori in spite of being shot by an arrow in his right eye. Kagemasa appears above his overturned opponent, with the fateful arrow in his mailed hand. The print comprises a riotous pattern of medieval arms and armour, in which the participants, like the figures of Japanese tattoos, retain their identity only with effort. Hokusai's design is certainly impressive—albeit tending to the decorative rather than the heroic: almost an essay in the handling of *form* unrelated to life (on which, compare his *shunga* of a decade earlier, Plates 221, 224–6). But the artist seems to have realized the limitations of the subject so far as the independent print went. His best work in this field is surely in book-illustration, especially in his three volumes of around 1836, where the essentially illustrative nature of the historical warrior genre is rendered in scene after scene of heroic tableaux (Plates 319–23).

Many, if not most, of Hokusai's important print-series were, as we have seen, terminated before completion; and it may be useful to look further into the reasons for this. The publishers were all established firms and the artist himself, though at times intractable, could not really afford to be temperamental. With the remarkable *Oceans of Wisdom* series, we even possess most of the completed, but unpublished, designs. Cancellation of such series must therefore have been a consequence of purely commercial

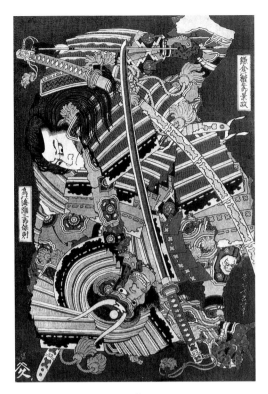

290 Samurai Combat. *Ōban*-size, *c.* 1834. (See also Fig. 146.)

considerations: namely the lack of continued sales on these particular, extended themes. The problem was not so much the absence of an affluent audience as its fickle nature.

Quality prints had, moreover, to be prepared carefully and by hand: designed/copied/engraved—each sheet of high-quality paper then went through a complex process of separate hand-printing for each colour-effect. With the first run of two hundred prints, the publisher might get back his investment in the design and woodblocks, but it required at least one more printing before he was making any kind of profit. And even then, the cost of hand-printing remained constant, however well the subsequent issues sold.

The solid audience of Hokusai aficionados accounted for distribution of the first printing; but for commercial success a wider public was needed—and, therefore, a subject and style of depiction that had a general appeal. With the mid-1830s (making allowance for concurrent famine and crisis conditions, to be discussed shortly) it was the more pliable and Romantic Hiroshige who came gradually to meet this popular taste.

Aside from his *Manga* sketchbooks, the output of the unyielding Hokusai was never able to match the best-selling records of his young rival, whose prints, whether major or not, were sometimes issued in totals of 10,000 or more over the last decades of the Edo Period. Popularity is not, of course, synonymous with artistic quality; and there is a far greater quantity of worthless hack-work in Hiroshige's *oeuvre* than we find in Hokusai's. Still, the latter was a commercial artist and his inspiration was naturally influenced by the moods of his audience. Yet he never gave up: when the popular print market moved to

Hiroshige the older artist simply went back to book-illustration, to specialized *surimono* prints and to paintings. The goading need to design, to sketch, to paint was ever there, even to his dying day.

And it may be well to clarify here what is meant by a 'relatively affluent audience'. Today even a lesser print from the more important Hokusai landscape series—in first impression and fine state—may be in the £5,000/$8,000 range, and the possession of any extensive, complete series will require a small fortune. In the Edo Period, however, the same print tended to cost rather less than a hand-printed woodblock reproduction would today—the equivalent of £18/$30 or so—and thus was theoretically within the reach of anyone with a good job and few bad habits. Even so, probably only an avid and wealthy aficionado would buy up every design in too extended a series.

The early 1830s formed a kind of watershed in the progress of ukiyo-e as a popular art. On viewing the originals one will immediately note a difference in quality between the prints of Hokusai and Hiroshige: the former tend to be printed on softer paper, with softer lines and less harsh colours; and there is likewise a pliant, more handmade quality to Hokusai's prints which is difficult to express in words. Such technical mutations in woodblock printing and styles were probably the result of adaptations designed to meet popular taste; but they surely posed a major problem to Hokusai and his publishers. And in the end, rather than change his style to meet the new printing techniques—fresh-appearing but not of optimum quality—the artist chose largely to give up the popular print field to his younger rival. For Hokusai's final major print-series of the decade, however, more ominous and more general social and economic conditions were to prove a crucial factor—to a discussion of which we will turn shortly.

In all, this was a prodigious half-decade for Hokusai. During the brief period of 1830–4 he had not only produced a hundred or more important woodblock prints, but also firmly established both the landscape and the flower-and-bird genres in the firmament of ukiyo-e. But for this ever-changing, ever-moving artist such achievements were but past history. He was already planning, dreaming of new goals, greater efforts: for many of which life was to prove all too short, fate not too accommodating.

2

If the first years of the 1830s were such a golden age in the development not only of Hokusai's art but also of ukiyo-e prints in general, how is one to explain the sudden decline after the middle of the decade? For the answer to this question we must momentarily turn our attention away from the artist and towards social and economic conditions in Japan.

As fate would have it, Hokusai's final 'golden decade' was cut off just at its peak with the year 1836, the time of the notorious 'Tempō Famines'. Following fast upon a generation of great prosperity, severely inclement weather plagued the countryside, reducing crops to less than half the normal yield; prices doubled; famine and near-famine reigned—the worst such conditions since the infamous Temmei Crisis of 1782. Amidst all this unrest occurred, the next year, the Ōshio Rice Rebellion in Ōsaka, as well as local riots and looting. With the consequent economic inflation, even the print-buying middle classes could not but be affected, and with them the publishers, who had to abandon or postpone most of their ambitious projects. Hokusai's departure from Edo to Uraga, and his other peregrinations of this period, clearly reflect his need to eke out an existence in the less-affected rural areas.

Eventually the nation recovered and cultural life returned somewhat to normal: to be subdued again by the Tempō Reforms of 1841, in which the government sought (not for the first time) to regulate life and culture by a series of sumptuary-edicts aimed at quelling the ebullient spirit of plebeian culture, including ukiyo-e.

For Hokusai, too, this was a turbulent period. Never much concerned about financial matters, he lived from day to day on what the publishers deigned to pay him, and on what little tuition fees his pupils cared to contribute. The years from early 1836 to 1839 thus form a kind of vacuum in Hokusai's publishing career—though he did receive income from occasional painting assignments. In one of the Master's few publications of this period—an 1838 sequel to the *Suiko-gaden* novel—we find the notations 'painted on sickbed'. And the next year his bad luck culminated in an Edo fire in which he lost not only his house and meagre possessions, but also his vast stock—'a cartload full'—of sketches. (It is such disasters—certainly one of the more significant losses in the history of Japanese art—that make it difficult to attempt any meaningful estimate of Hokusai's total original *oeuvre*. The early critic Goncourt conservatively estimated some 35,000 designs extant; but we have no idea of how many further thousands perished even in the above 'cartful'.)

A case in point for the dire artistic effects of this crisis-period is Hokusai's last important print-series, commenced in 1835 just when the Famines were beginning to increase in severity. This was the *Hyakunin-isshu uba-ga-etoki* (*The Hundred Poems*: Explained by the Nurse). Throughout the prints of this series (which was first announced in the publisher's advertisement of 1835) will be noted the distinctive Hokusai *nom d'artiste*—one of his last—*Manji*. This is pronounced in Japanese to signify 'Universal Letters', but written with the Buddhist swastika: a symbol of the Boundless Light issuing from the breast of the Buddha of the Future. As we have seen, Hokusai had used this as a pen-name in *senryū*-verses and occasional *oeuvre* from earlier in the century, but took it as his principal pseudonym during the final years 1830–49.

While obviously planned as a *tour-de-force* depiction of the full hundred verses of this famous classical anthology, only 28 prints seem actually to have been issued—though the artist's original drawings (or block-copies of them) for some 62 more are also extant.

The Hundred Poems was by far the best known of all Japanese verse anthologies, being the subject of numerous early books and commentaries. Even more important, it was the theme of the most popular of all New Year's games. In this diversion the first and second parts of a verse were prepared on separate cards and, when the opening line of each poem was read off by a reciter, the contestants scrambled about to find the matching verse amid the cards strewn over the *tatami*-mats. Thus these hundred poems were known by heart to a surprising majority of the literate Japanese populace—all potential purchasers of literary and art work on this special theme.

But whereas the early books and prints had limited their illustrations to portraits of the hundred poets (sometimes against a simple landscape-background as implied in each verse), with Hokusai the theme is considerably extended. His approach is an impressionistic—sometimes even wilful—one. The designs are entirely free renderings, frequently inspired by association rather than by conventional usage; and often far removed in concept from the originals. Indeed, in the absence of the verses (printed in a cartouche at the upper corner of each design) it would be most difficult even for a literary expert to match each poem and print.

This avant-garde feature was, of course, a startling innovation for Hokusai's audience: a delight to his fans, but presumably an offence to traditionalists. And in the end, it may partly have been the latter's lack of enthusiasm that curtailed the series after less than a third had been completed—and prevented its continuation even after the Tempō Crisis was over.

As for the content of *The Hundred Poems* itself, here again we find a great variety of fascinating designs, but few of world class. From a contemporary Japanese point of view, of course, the prime interest was in the all-too-famous verse, and in how skilfully/wittily/evocatively it was illustrated. For the modern viewer, however—even in Japan— such considerations are of only tertiary interest and one must focus on the design purely as a work of art.

From the outset it must be noted that there is a hard-edged quality to the engraving and printing of this series that tends to detract from its mood. This technical feature is closely related to the changing taste in woodblock prints noted above, but it also coincides with a certain lack of pliability, almost ungainliness, in figure-depiction that is characteristic of Hokusai's final years. The designs are often more effective where the figures play a less than dominant role in the composition.

Typical of the contradictions found in such late work of Hokusai's is the 'Porters in Landscape' of Plate 279. The tableau is a curious mixture of evocative landscape and ungainly human figures. We view here a scene at daybreak on the Nihon Embankment leading to the Yoshiwara. Palanquin-bearers—in their haste knocking over a lantern at centre—hurry to take their lovelorn, hidden passengers home, as peasants carry tea-leaves in the foreground. The picture is a mélange of *Manga* subjects against a truly remarkable background. But the two major elements are not really integrated and, though one may marvel at the Master's bold attempt at 'stop motion' and his pre-photographic grasp of the 'decisive moment', the result is somehow unsatisfying either as landscape or genre scene.

A rather more successful example would be the famous 'Women Divers' (Plate 284). Here the lively scene and intrinsic interest of the subject—diving for abalone at Ise —tend to offset the rather unpliant delineation of the figures. As with much of the series, however, there is a certain ambiguity: is it the figures or the landscape which is the subject? This ambiguity sometimes deprives the scenes of a firm and dramatic centre of focus.

A similar problem exists in the 'Bull and Parasol' of Plate 285, perhaps my favourite of the series, in which the huge and powerful bull strikes a neat balance against the two frail ladies behind the parasol: and the receding, misty landscape—at Ōsaka Bay—obscures most of the unnecessary detail. (All such convenient print-titles are, I must note, of my own creation: the originals cite only the name of the classical poet—here, Prince Motoyoshi—with the actual verse in full.) The print's elliptical and suggestive qualities (all too rare in this series) are indeed its strong points. There is a Japanese proverb that expresses this sentiment beautifully: *Yome tōme kasa-no-uchi*: 'Viewed at night/at a distance/behind a parasol.' (Only partly by fortuitous coincidence, the first word is also a homophone for 'bride'.) So far as the landscape-print goes, to these ideal viewing conditions may be added: In rain/snow/mist/ moonlight. It may be of interest to refer back to Hokusai's rather similar design of thirty years before, one of his earlier experiments at the landscape-with-figures, to see just how far he had come. (Plate 74).

One final example must suffice to represent this interesting—if occasionally monotonous—series. In Plate 291 we see a characteristic scene of Edo: the Sumida River on a summer evening with pleasure-boats in the background and what is the equivalent of a 'fast-food' boat in the foreground. The details are splendid, the printing excellent, the design impeccable: but the elements do not interrelate or integrate. One need only compare the very similar *Fuji* 'Ryōgoku' scene of Plate 251 to perceive how in but a few years the change in printing techniques—and the artist's own loss of suppleness—has converted a potential masterpiece into a merely striking tableau.

As noted earlier the designs of this series are not literal interpretations of the famous verses but imaginative ones, with—typical of Hokusai—graphically bold, free pastiches on the themes. Thus in our Plate 284 the final line of the verse, *ama no tsuribune* ('fishing-vessels of the fishermen'), is wittily reinterpreted as another word pronounced *ama* ('diving-girls'); and in Plate 285 the poet's anguished love-plaint is presumably mirrored in the struggling herdsman and his recalcitrant bull. (Sometimes the treatment is even more farfetched, as with the 'pheasant's long tail' of one poem being interpreted as a winding trail of smoke—Fig. 157; and in our Plate 291 the 'clouded moon' of the classical verse may well be represented by the round soup-bowl being rinsed in the river—each a kind of pictorial conundrum.) But though the landscapes themselves are impeccable, as in much of the Master's late figure-work there is a certain awkwardness, a puppet-like quality that doubtless hints that even he could not forever escape the ravages of old age.

The interesting, but hypothetical, question remains of

291 On the Sumida River. *Ōban* print from *The Hundred Poems*,
c. 1835–6 (horizon line tilted in original). (See also Plate 279.)

how truly baleful were the effects of the Tempō Famines
on Hokusai's *oeuvre*? To aficionados, of course, every
minor jotting of the Master is a treasure; to the outsider,
the loss of a few dozen prints may not seem all that crucial.
Indeed, to judge from the unpublished sketches for *The
Hundred Poems* the designs were characteristic of the series
and of Hokusai's final period: at the least, draughtsmanlike and interesting, clever modern pastiches on the
themes of classical poetry. But most important, is there a
potential 'Great Wave' or 'Red Fuji' to be found lurking in
these unpublished drawings? The answer is 'No', though
there are certainly many designs that would rank among
the artist's minor masterpieces. Yet even aside from the
loss of the theoretical completion of *The Hundred Poems* set,
what of Hokusai's other potential works, left uncreated
during the crisis years 1836–9? Here we may best view
Hokusai as a dedicated but ageing human being, rather
than simply as a commercial artist. He was faced, in effect,
with a near-total loss of his market for three vital years of
his life. Just how crucial those years were could only be
known to the Master himself: aged 76 and still straining at
the bit to prove that he could, in the end, 'become a great
artist'.

In the space of this brief decade Hokusai developed the
landscape and flower-and-bird print as major genres of
Japanese art. In a total of over two hundred glowing prints
he re-created the beauties of Japanese nature in his own
image, producing several masterpieces of world art. The
artist was already approaching his ninth decade, however;
and though he may have continued stubbornly to refuse to
surrender to old age, it was, inevitably, affecting his style;
and the tastes of the times, too, were tending to pass him
by.

NOTES

1 For earlier Hokusai treatment of related themes see Plates 17, 96, 98. The
second example is of particular relevance as it features a similar Buddhist
lantern; while the third depicts a literary predecessor of the same 'O-Iwa'
ghost-tale. The dating of this series, incidentally, is based on the inscription of
the *Shūnen* design—Fig. 94—which refers to the change to the Tempō Era, and
thus was probably published early in 1831.
2 In the 1834 advertisement—from the same publisher, Eijudō—they are
termed *shikishi-e*, rather than *chūban*—a pertinent reminder that the latter
print-size was derived from the *shikishi*, 'poem-card' format of classical
Japanese verse and miniature-painting.
3 The small round seal at lower left indicates the 'Year of the Goat', which I
interpret as implying 1835. Japanese authorities (Narazaki, Kikuchi, Nagata et
al.) tend to construe this as referring to the preceding or following cyclical
years, 1823 or 1847, which seems to me erroneous, both in relation to style and
to printing technique.

XXI
Graphic Summitry:
The *Hundred Views*
of Fuji

1

ONE MIGHT THINK that Hokusai, having issued a full 46 grand prints on the *Fuji* theme, would have satisfied his thirst for the subject. For him, however, the significance of the Sacred Mountain can only be compared to the nude in Western art: a perennial motif of undying interest, its depths never to be fully plumbed.

It must be stressed that for this master, completeness and/or perfection were anathema; invention, creation, incessant change provided the principal spice of life. This did not mean a frivolous flitting from one theme to another: he could be tenaciously persistent towards a motif that possessed him—indeed, the artist took his greatest pleasure in attempting a fresh and bizarre approach to classical art-themes, attacking again and again the same subject from different angles and with new concepts: both to prove his own worth as an artist and, undeniably, to startle his audience.

The landscape-print had at this juncture at last come into its own, artistically and commercially. And the *Fuji* theme itself was central to Hokusai's concept of landscape—as it was to much of his audience, for reasons religious and magical as well as traditional and artistic. Thus although the artist treated a variety of other landscape subjects in this period, the *Fuji* motif was clearly never far from his heart.

Hokusai had therefore by no means exhausted his muse, and it will be recalled that he, and his publisher, had contemplated a full hundred prints on the *Fuji* theme. Had sales and longevity but permitted, he could probably have continued the theme forever. This was not the destiny of commercial publication, however, and this great series ended well before the artist had begun to assuage his enthusiasm for the Sacred Mountain.

Though Hokusai turned to other landscape and floral subjects he had not given up the *Fuji* obsession: what was not possible in the large print, he would accomplish in the smaller world of book-illustration, whose aficionados could always be counted on to support such off-beat projects. Thus in the Third Month of 1834 he published the first volume of his *Fugaku hyakkei*: 'The Hundred Views of Fuji'.[1]

This was, by the native calendar, the Fifth Year of the Tempō—'Heavenly-peace'—Era, which had commenced with a resurgence of the popular arts, was to falter with the Tempō Famines of 1836 on, and found the same plebeian culture curtailed with the austere Tempō Reforms of 1841, which caused an economic depression without any decrease in commodity prices.

For Hokusai, however, this was a zenith of his feverish activity. He was already well into his 70s, but during the years 1833–5 was to produce not only the several series of further magnificent landscapes and flower prints that formed the subject of the previous chapters, but also one of the world masterpieces of book-illustration.

The Hundred Views of Fuji is comprised of three volumes in *hanshi-bon* format (22.7 × 15.5 cm/8.9 × 6 in—slightly larger in the later issues). The prefaces are by leading literati of the time, with signed colophon and publication data at the end of the first two volumes. The First Series appeared in 1834 and the second in 1835; as fate would have it, the Third Series was scheduled for 1836, which, with the Tempō Famines, was the worst year in memory both for Japan and for publisher/artist alike. It was no wonder that publishers (and many others) curtailed most ventures and cultural activities, to wait out the crisis.

The exact date of publication for the Third Series is not known, but it appeared (in part, at least, because of the financial problems of the Edo publisher Nishimuraya Yohachi) in the provincial capital Nagoya, and probably only in the 1840s when the nation was at peace again, although the key-blocks seem already to have been engraved in 1835.

Economic conditions had already been worsening by the year 1834, and thus four different publishers co-operated in producing the first two volumes of the set: three in Edo, and Eirakuya in Nagoya. They put much stock in the work, as preliminary advertisements of the year before show:

> Despite the Venerable Hokusai's numerous publications and their wide popularity, they have never really satisfied the Master.... In these volumes, however, the Master has travelled the Provinces, sought out strange scenes and fine views ... encompassing their true forms in these rare miniatures.... As the Master himself recounts, 'The true essence of my art lies in these albums.'

From such remarks it will be clear not only that the series bore a special significance for the artist himself, but also that there was an active public for such landscape volumes, even above and beyond the limited circle of Hokusai fans, harking back to the long tradition of amateur landscape painting in the Far East, and—in this case—to the special class of 'Fuji Worshippers' as well. Thus, from the method of numbering—I/II/III, rather than the more delimiting *jō–chū–ge* (first/middle/final)—it may be surmised that both artist and publisher might have envisioned at least four volumes (which would have then totalled one hundred 'leaves'—though well over a hundred actual plates): and possibly more, had popular demand warranted.

292 Dust-jacket to *The Hundred Views of Fuji*, Series I, 1834. (See also Plates 293–306, 359, and for other examples from this chapter, and bibliographical details, Figs. 222–225.)

Certainly, for the artist himself this theme was a practically inexhaustible source of inspiration.

This is hardly the place for a detailed bibliographical study of the *Fuji*—or any of Hokusai's other masterful books: suffice it to say that the first impressions, done under the artist's supervision, are rare. They feature, for Series I and II, salmon-pink, landscape-embossed covers with falcon-feather design on the title-slips; the printing is in black and two shades of grey, on soft, heavy white paper; the wrappers (a kind of dust-jacket) feature a design of a tethered falcon, with the artist's full signature and 'Fuji' seal appearing at left, the whole graced by Hokusai's elegant, archaic-style calligraphy—the equivalent of our own copperplate handwriting—Plate 292. (The tableau reflects the well-known folk belief expressed in the proverb: 'One—Fuji, two—falcon, three—eggplant'—traditionally good omens to dream of on New Year's dawn; the 'eggplant' motif appears on the title-page.) With later editions the title-slips are undecorated and the covers are generally either grey, red, black or yellow. The paper may be thinner and light blue may replace the grey pigments; more troublesome printing-effects may be omitted, but sometimes a mauve-coloured block is added; and later still,

some of the woodblocks are recut. Aside from modern reprints the most commonly seen edition is that dated December 1875—with yellow or black covers—which is largely from the original blocks and, though somewhat weak in effect, still worthy of appreciation.

In the colophon to both Series I and II of the early editions appears Hokusai's oft-quoted autobiographical note:

> From my sixth year I have had a passion for sketching the form of things. From about the age of fifty I produced a number of designs, yet of all I drew prior to my seventieth year there is truly nothing of any great note. In my seventy-third year I finally apprehended something of the true quality of birds, animals, insects, fishes, and of the vital nature of grasses and trees. Therefore in my eightieth year I shall have made some progress, in my ninetieth I shall have penetrated even further the deeper meaning of things, in my hundredth year I shall have become truly marvellous, and at one hundred and ten each dot, each line shall surely possess a life of its own. I only beg that gentlemen of sufficiently long life take care to note the truth of my words.

The engraving to this set (or, more strictly, the woodblock-carving) was supervised by Hokusai's favourite, Egawa Tomikichi, with each individual engraver's name cited on the edge of every page. Although the turnover-title of the first volume appends the subtitle 'Series I', this is omitted from the title-slip: possibly the publishers were not yet confident of success as a *series*. The advertisement at the back of the book features—in addition to the announcement of Series II and III of the set—an ambitious list of eleven proposed volumes in the *Hundred Views* vein: Bridges, Flowers, Magicians, various Cartoons and Sketches, Fishermen, Moonlight Views, Horses and Bulls, Peasants, Birds and Animals, etc.—none of which, however, was to see the light of day.

Coming to the Second Series, the same colophon is employed—but with all three *Fuji* volumes cited (rather as though already on sale), and with Hokusai's age changed from '74th Year' to '75th', the publication date being revised to 1835. In addition a flyleaf, printed in blue, is appended, advertising three series of Hokusai *manuscript* albums on sale (such as are discussed in Chapter XVI).

Of the Third Series, appearing in Nagoya and much delayed in publication, determination of the first issue is more difficult, though it is possibly the edition with orange-red embossed covers and title in dark blue, with colophon citing the Nagoya publisher Eirakuya and its Edo branch. Perplexingly, the Preface to this Third Series speaks of 'the ninety-yeared Hokusai, his eyesight sharp as a young lad's. . . .' Taken literally, this would place publication at the year of the Master's death, 1849—i.e. some fourteen years after the designs were made and the initial blocks engraved. But the expression might mean merely 'most venerable'—coincidentally matching Hokusai's age at death. (It must again be recalled that, by traditional Japanese calculation, a child was in his first year at birth, hence exact translation of ages involves subtle problems.[2])

In Series III the engraver's name, Egawa Sentarō, appears solely in the margin of the final plate; and there is no date or signature in the colophon—Hokusai's name being cited only in the Preface. From their rather crude nature, the woodblocks for the grey areas seem to have been engraved in Nagoya, and under the supervision of the artist's pupils, rather than of the Master himself.

The above data will necessarily seem a trifle dull for the general reader, yet all too sketchy for the collector or curator trying to evaluate his own specimen of the original. It is provided here as a hint at the typically complex delights that await the bibliophile in a study of Hokusai's illustrated books.[3]

Unlike some earlier Hokusai works, individual plates of this series come out reasonably well in reproduction. True, one misses the soft, pliant quality of the handmade, matte paper, the peculiarly rugged, three-dimensional texture of the woodblock printing, the vivid, penetrating ebony of the *sumi* ink: but the originals are, fortunately, only in black and greys, and the magnificent designs of a calibre to surmount such losses. At the same time, the art-lover or collector who is able both to appreciate this handmade quality and to focus his attention on the miniaturistic book-format will discover in such Hokusai volumes a completely satisfying world in itself, and—at least in the later editions of the 1870s—at a price only a fraction of that fetched by even the lesser of Hokusai's landscape-prints.

It will be recalled that Hokusai's younger rival Hiroshige had issued his popular *Fifty-three Stations of the Tōkaidō* in 1833–4, and that Hokusai's own *Fuji* print-series had also terminated by then. The boom in landscape prints—and travel books—was thus at its peak, the older Master himself stimulated to even greater efforts. Having somewhat appeased his desire to present Mt Fuji in large scale, Hokusai now turned to the more intimate format of the picture-book, within which he could enjoy even greater freedom in depicting all sorts of strange, striking and even bizarre angles of the Sacred Mountain. As we have seen, the artist had been planning such a work from at least a decade earlier; and the miniatures of his *Models of Modern Combs and Pipes* volumes of 1822–3 are graphic evidence of how long this theme had been on his mind (Plate 168). Although Hokusai's artistic viewpoints are uniquely his own, he had at least one predecessor for this work: the earlier, academic artist Minsetsu's *Hyaku-Fuji* (The Hundred Fujis) of 1771, a rather pedestrian tome of monochrome illustrations, but notable as the first attempt to depict the mountain in a great variety of situations. Hokusai rather assiduously avoided emulation of this work but he obviously knew it, and from it presumably derived the basic idea for his own production on the theme. Indeed, Minsetsu was a semi-amateur artist of the same Katsushika quarter of Edo as Hokusai; and his book was published just at the time the latter was first indulging his 'mania for sketching'.

Having said this much of the background and bibliography of Hokusai's famed series, we may turn to the actual content of this, one of the most masterfully unified of all Japanese books.

2

The first of Hokusai's *Hundred Fuji* series commences with a cloud-borne vision of Princess Konohana-sakuya, the deity of the Sacred Mountain; followed by the mystical emergence of the volcano itself in the Fifth Year of the Emperor Kōrei (traditionally 286 BC); and then, an impressive depiction of the first mountain-priest to make it his abode, 'St Ubasoku' (*En-no-gyōja*). These introductory plates not only set the legendary background of the subject, but also provide a necessary element for one important portion of Hokusai's public, the avid Mt Fuji pilgrims and worshippers.

For the remainder of the volume depictions are freer in concept and show the mountain in more contemporary settings, aside from the dynamic scene of the eruption in the year Hōei IV (late 1707)—a stroboscopic instant of frozen action—in which was created the hump still known today as Mt Hōei (Plate 293). In this volume we find, too, masterful landscape scenes reminiscent of the best of Hokusai's previous *print* series—for example the 'Tuji at Dawn' of Plate 294, which, with a little imagination, one can readily envision as a larger print of world rank. (I make this remark mainly for print aficionados; for the book-collector the difference is only one of size and medium, not of intrinsic quality.)

One discovers also in this volume full evidence of Hokusai's characteristic concern with humorous humanity—an element rather more restrained in the larger print series (Plates 295 and 296). The theme of the set might well be characterized as motley humanity against the leitmotif of Mt Fuji: man ever implied—whether as participant or spectator—even when not specifically depicted. Indeed, humanity forms the core of Hokusai's work whatever the medium he is working in.

It is all too easy to skim through these familiar volumes and stop only at the two or three acknowledged masterpieces. In the aforementioned Plate 295, for example, close scrutiny reveals that the very paddies are alive in this deceptively placid scene—in which Fuji takes second place not only to humanity, but also to sentient vegetation. In the careful, methodically creative attention to the rice-plants (literally thousands of them), one glimpses again that painstaking attention to detail that remained with the artist until his dying day and, cumulatively, contributes so much to his achievement. Other evocative scenes hark back to the artist's more famous earlier prints, but they are always creative extensions on a common theme, never imitation or repetition. Compare Plate 296 with the 'Kajikazawa' of Plate 252, for example. (This design illustrates Hokusai's method of combining traditional Far Eastern landscape-perspective—foreground/centre-ground/

293 *Overleaf top left* 'The Emergence of Mt Hōei'. From *The Hundred Views of Fuji*, Series I, 1834.

294 *Overleaf bottom left* 'Fuji at Dawn'. From *The Hundred Views of Fuji*, Series I, 1834.

295 *Overleaf top right* 'Fuji at Harvest-time'. From *The Hundred Views of Fuji*, Series I, 1834.

296 *Overleaf bottom right* 'Fuji with Reeds and Rafts'. From *The Hundred Views of Fuji*, Series I, 1834.

297 *Opposite top* 'Fuji on Rice-paddy'. From *The Hundred Views of Fuji*, Series I, 1834. The title alludes to a play-on-words from classical verse: *tanomo no kari* [wild geese on the paddy-surface] and *tanomu no kari* [beseeching the wild geese].

298 *Opposite bottom* 'Dragon and Fuji'. From *The Hundred Views of Fuji*, Series II, 1835.

299 *Above* Dragon and Fuji. Preliminary drawing for Plate 298, 1834–5. (Tree-branch at right is unrelated bit of graffiti but cloud detail at upper left indicates a pattern to be followed throughout the design.)

distance—with his own interpretation of Occidental perspective: the result always interesting, if not without faults and ambiguities of its own.)

To me, at least, the most successful plates are those that seek not to emulate large tableaux but, instead, focus on more limited themes ideally suited to the book format. Plate 297 for instance represents a striking concept that would doubtless prove too pretty a conceit for a major print, but which is here concentrated by the very restraints of book-illustration. So overpowering is the composition that we only sense subconsciously the artist's detailed mastery—the triangular balance, for example, of crying geese at left, right, bottom. This design may also be counted among Hokusai's most successful attempts at the bizarre: the huge reflection of Fuji is placed so perfectly in the composition that we have not the wits to wonder how it could possibly get there.

With the Master's Second Series the *Fuji* theme is extended to even more dramatic visions, probably encompassing the major designs of the series. The legendary 'Dragon and Fuji' was a standard theme of classical Japanese art, but Hokusai here brings these two strange entities—one mythical, one geographic—into a dynamic proximity, a kind of divine dialogue, in which one is hard-pressed to say which of the two is the more alive (Plate 298). A glance at the artist's preliminary drawing for this

illustration (Plate 299) reveals both the manner in which the dragon was added on a separate overlay of thin paper, and how extraneous elements were deleted for the final design.

In Plate 300 attention is turned from the Mountain to the Sea, in what is probably Hokusai's masterpiece on this theme. The depiction of water not only surpasses that of the more famous 'Great Wave' (Plate 247), but adds to it a breathtaking concept straight out of a Japanese magician's repertoire: the plovers do not simply dart about the waves, they are actually *created* from them.[4] Here, too, the concept is all too pretty for a formal, framed print; yet it constitutes a book-plate that one returns to again and again, with undiminished pleasure. Indeed it is only with leisurely reflection that we perceive the similarity of subject-matter with the 'Great Wave', so skilfully has the design been adapted to the smaller, more intimate book form; and in place of the struggling boatmen we find the delighted plovers—free to go anywhere they please, yet purposely frequenting a site perilous to all but birds and fish.

Less perfect but another landscape masterpiece is the 'Thunderstorm at Dusk' (Plate 301), of which we are for-

300 *Overleaf top left* 'Fuji at Sea'. From *The Hundred Views of Fuji*, Series II, 1835. (Note that every edition of this famous work differs in details of hand-printing; here, the photograph has been printed rather darker than usual, to bring out the greyish details of the wave-trough at left.)

301 *Overleaf bottom left* 'Thunderstorm at Dusk'. From *The Hundred Views of Fuji*, Series II, 1835.

302 *Overleaf top right* 'Thunderstorm at Dusk'. Artist's preliminary sketch for Plate 301; 1834–5.

303 *Overleaf bottom right* 'Fuji in Snowstorm'. From *The Hundred Views of Fuji*, Series III, *c.* 1840s.

304 *Above left* 'Fuji through Spider's Web'. From *The Hundred Views of Fuji*, Series III, *c.* 1840s.

305 *Above* 'Fuji and Local Shower'. From *The Hundred Views of Fuji*, Series III, *c.* 1840s. (Umbrella at right bears the legend 'Series III'.)

306 *Left* 'Fuji through Fisherman's Net'. From *The Hundred Views of Fuji*, Series III, *c.* 1840s. (Note that here, again, an even darker printing of the photograph would be necessary to bring into relief the full outline of the mountain behind the net.)

tunate enough to possess Hokusai's original sketch as well (Plate 302). Here, too, the hamlet is sharply illumined as though in a stroboscopic instant. Many such designs could easily have been included in the great print-series of a few years earlier. It is interesting to compare the present tableau with Plate 248: the addition of rustic village and temple creates an entirely new print, in which the interaction of nature and man is superbly balanced. Here it is the rugged yet delicate chiaroscuro of the lowering sky and rainclouds that remain in the mind's eye: a forceful reminder that even with such a simple near-monochrome bookplate there is truly no substitute for viewing the original.

Series III of the *Fuji* volumes tends to depict more specific aspects of the mountain, and suffers somewhat from the delayed nature of its publication: the grey blocks were probably added by the Nagoya publisher, without the artist's direct supervision. Yet this volume too has its share of minor masterpieces—'Fuji in Snow-storm', for example (Plate 303): but again, the delicate texture of the hand-printing will be largely lost in reproduction. (In Japan this phenomenon is called *botan-yuki*, 'peony-snow', though the view is never quite so transparent as the one that Hokusai depicts.)

For some reason, in this third volume a majority of the designs are rendered as single-plate verticals, and are therefore rather diminished in effect. In their elegant camouflage of the principal subject, 'Fuji through Spider's Web' and 'Fuji through Fisherman's Net' (Plates 304 and 306) will delight *surimono/netsuke* collectors, as well as photographers and graphic designers, but cannot escape the bounds of miniaturism. The former plate is rather characteristically Japanese in the decoratively humanistic touch of showing not a struggling insect trapped in the web, but a graceful maple leaf. And, continuing a bit further *à la Japonaise*, one is even drawn into the fascinating question of what the spider's reaction is to this giant 'catch': will he not be momentarily lulled into thinking he has, in one fell swoop, acquired enough food to last the entire winter? (The latter design, incidentally, was later to be imitated by the print-masters Kuniyoshi and Kunisada.)

Perhaps the most evocative page of this final volume is the 'Fuji and Local Shower' of Plate 305, but here too the subject deserves the more spacious dimensions of the horizontal format. The scene is reminiscent of one *Manga* page of two decades earlier—our Plate 139; it is less 'sketchy' perhaps, but hardly rises to the level of the major designs of the first and second volumes of the *Fuji* series.

In fact, it may well be that this third volume had to compress within itself the better designs of a proposed Series IV, which was never to see independent publication. (Indeed, whereas Series I and II feature 31 and 30 scenes respectively, Series III comprises 41 tableaux—within the same limitation of 25 leaves/50 pages.)

3

The influence of Hokusai's *Hundred Views of Fuji* on modern Western art has been considerable, both from the originals (of which literally dozens of sets are treasured in the cultural centres of the world) and from the reproductions, as well as from a detailed commentary issued in London in 1880. Plates from the set had appeared in Europe even earlier, beginning with a Paris publication of 1861.

In Japan itself—aside from Hokusai's actual pupils and followers—the *Hundred Views of Fuji* exerted influence in more subtle ways. Certain landscapes of Hiroshige (two in the *Hundred Views of Edo*, for example) obviously derive their inspiration from Hokusai; but in a sense the old Master had simply lived too long to remain a fresh source of inspiration for his contemporaries and rivals.

However, it need not be assumed that the striking and bizarre quality of Hokusai's method was lost on his contemporaries, or dismissed simply as curious or outlandish. When Hiroshige prepared his own small picture-book *Fuji-mi hyakuzu* (One Hundred Fuji-views) of 1857 he specifically noted in the Preface,

> Old Hokusai's *Hundred Views of Fuji* ... displays the Master's customary genius ... his power of brushstroke, his emphasis

on variety of composition: yet with Fuji often as but a decorative adjunct. My own designs are different—the scene just as it lay before my eyes. . . .

As with all of Hokusai's work in his maturity, we perceive in this book a conscious attempt—sometimes an *over*working—to re-create the Universe in his own image. Thus Mt Fuji is displayed from every conceivable angle, but with the Master's greatest effort expended on milking each design of all possible graphic nuances, in order to impress the viewer with the uniqueness of his conception. Herein lies Hokusai's strength and brilliance, if also his undeniable faults of often overstraining for effect, of sometimes achieving little more than decorative preciosity. Yet the masterpieces indubitably remain.

Of the 102 views completed of Hokusai's *Fuji* illustrations, the art-lover will surely discover other gems, other striking insights into the nature of graphic design. The plates reproduced here represent only a scattered personal selection (see also Figs. 222–226). In the end, such picture-books must be taken into the hands, perused at leisure, cast aside and taken up yet again. Only after repeated viewing does one begin to comprehend the artist's total concept.

Yet whatever one's favourite scenes, whatever one's opinion of Hokusai himself, it must surely be concluded that the *Hundred Views of Fuji* is among the most successful of all picture-books, a crowning achievement to Hokusai's career in that lovely, much-neglected genre.

NOTES

1 Regarding the possible alternative reading of the title, *Fuji hyakkei*, see our Note 4 to Chapter XVII and Appendix, Books, No. 239.
2 Popular writings on Hokusai often mistake his ages and sometimes, even scholars do: cf. M. Forrer's Ph.D. dissertation *Eirakuya Tōshirō: Publisher at Nagoya* (1985, p. 173): 'Hokusai died, in 1849, at the age of ninety. . . .'
3 For a lengthy—but excessively complex—bibliographical note on *Fugaku hyakkei* see M. Forrer's *Eirakuya Tōshirō*, op. cit., pp. 170–7. As with much of this scholar's work, the more important matters are quite obscured by indiscriminate attention to extraneous detail.
4 One is reminded of the words of a great Indian conjuror, 'Magic is born not on the stage but in the minds of the spectators.' The above analogy was taken, incidentally, from actual performances seen in traditional Japanese magic shows; but I note now that Hokusai in the *Manga* Series X (1819) devotes two pages to actual magic tricks—including one of 'producing waves from the palms of the hands' (see appended illustration *below*). (But without plovers: a feat easier for the artist than the magician; a few pages later, however, one discovers a series on more legendary wizards, including a scene of herons produced from sheets of paper.)

XXII
The Unending Dream:
Hokusai's Final Years

1

IN DEALING with an artist whose work is known in great detail but whose life is rather obscure, it is difficult to decide where to insert the meagre facts that are confirmable. Thus to recapitulate the decade after the appearance of the great *Fuji* print-series: during the 1830s the Master continued his eccentric, periodical movements of residence (often 'lodgings' would be a more appropriate word). As of the year 1834 these totalled 56 in number—by Hokusai's own account—the final total coming to 93 different dwellings by the end, in 1849. Many of the districts are known by name (mainly from letters, as well as from the diaries of associates), and several are indicated on our map (Plate 1). Naturally enough, they tend to cluster in the 'downtown' quarters of Hokusai's own birth: the north and east areas bordering the Sumida River: Asakusa, Honjo and Fuka-gawa.[1] There is also the theory that these changes of res-idence had a practical function, for the Master hated cleaning house (and his daughter O-Ei probably took after him). Thus moving was often the easiest way not only to change the environment, but also to obtain more sanitary lodgings. Towards the end, indeed, Hokusai seems to have taken a certain pride in his own eccentricities, aiming for example at 'a hundred different residences before I die'—though he fell short of that mark.

Hokusai's desultory publication of, often ribald, even erotic *senryū* verses—his principal literary efforts of the time—continued. Their composition usually took place, in fact, at social gatherings of poetasters. The pen-names of Hokusai's later years may best be relegated to the Appendix (pp. 278–9); but following the pervasive *Manji* (which appears mainly in the form of the Buddhist swastika-symbol), several purposely inartistic pseudonyms were used now and then, as though the artist were denying his earlier pretensions to stylish sophistication and returning to his plebeian, almost rustic, origins.

Towards the end of 1832, Hokusai's notable disciple (and son-in-law) Shigenobu died, at 45. He was, it will be re-membered, the father of that delinquent grandchild; and though divorced from Hokusai's daughter he had remained the artist's adopted son.

In addition to the major print-series already cited, there were occasional *surimono* and other lesser prints, as well as minor illustrations—often in collaboration with younger artists (including Kuniyoshi, Kuninao, Kunisada). And as we have seen there are various printed announcements of several Hokusai book and print-series that were never actually published, partly because of the financial problems of the major publisher Eijudō, and partly because of the after-effects of the 'Tempō Disasters'.

From this period there is evidence of further travels—to Sagami, Izu, Chiba, even distant Shinano—and an ex-tended period of residence—almost self-imposed exile—at Kurihama/Uraga, far south of Edo (the fishing-village and transportation centre, of easy access to Edo, which was, a generation later, willy-nilly to host Commodore Perry of the US Navy). Such long sojourns were presum-ably undertaken to escape the problems and inflationary costs of life in the metropolis during this period of turmoil; they probably depended upon the assistance of pupils or lesser patrons, though the exact details are unknown. To judge from a letter of 1836, Hokusai occasionally returned incognito to Edo: perhaps an indication that he wished to avoid troublesome social contacts or, more likely, creditors.

As there are no known personal scandals involving Hokusai, it is difficult to explain these covert moves of his mid-70s, other than to attribute them to problems caused by his delinquent grandson. In such a closed and restricted society as Old Japan, the Master probably had to take full responsibility—both moral and financial—for the recalci-trant lad's misdeeds. In a letter to his publisher of about 1834, the artist speaks of at last getting 'that rascal' married off and set up as a fishmonger—this was followed by the usual appeal for necessary funds.

In general, the artist's extant letters concern the usual problems of the freelance artist/writer: details of work, pro-testations of poverty, and appeals for advance-payments. One letter of 1836—to the publisher Sūzambō in Edo—reveals fascinating details of the Master's never-ending passion for perfection; and his continuing problems, de-spite his age and standing, in maintaining the Hokusai Style against the encroachments of fickle ukiyo-e fashions. The paragraph in question is worth translating, but I must necessarily reproduce the original as well: however, this is not the artist's manuscript (now lost), but a tracing that appeared in the first and only Hokusai biography, pub-lished in 1893 (to be viewed from right to left—see page 265):

> Memo for the engraver, Master Sugita:
>   Regarding figure-work, please engrave: eyes like this, with-out lower eyelid . . .
> noses like these. . . .
> Utagawa-style noses are like *this* . . .
> but *mine* are to be cut thus. . . .
> *This* type [three sample eyes, one nose, in Toyokuni-style], I quite realize, is now all the rage; but personally, I can't stand it! . . . .[2]

In full spring of the same year, Hokusai moved back briefly to Edo, to a site at Fukagawa (near the Mannen, 'Eternal' Bridge of Fig. 56). And it is from this period that, in the *Jimmei-roku* directory of prominent Edoites, he is listed with his names in full—'Hokusai: alias Taito, Raishin, Iitsu Gakyōjin and Katsushika Hokusai', but with the added notation, 'Residence uncertain'.

With the year 1839 the artist was back in his home-quarter Honjo; but as we have seen it was, alas, in one of these residences that he met his first major disaster: a conflagration that destroyed not only his home but all of his sketches and reference-materials.

2

One might well wonder what more might be accomplished by an ageing Master who had essayed—and nearly completed—so many grand projects after the age of 70. Hokusai was quite literally insatiable, however; for him, work itself had a kind of metabolic function; it renewed his energies in a way that rest or holiday never could.

It will be recalled that we left the *Hokusai manga* at Series X, with the year 1819 (Plate 146; Fig. 209), but with so many other projects on hand it was to be more than a dozen years before the artist, at his publisher's prodding,

took up the theme again. Series XI, though undated, must have appeared about 1833 and Series XII, which is dated, in 1834. Presumably these publications took advantage of the Master's renewed fame with his *Fuji* and other major print-series of the immediately preceding years.

The first problem with all of the later *Manga* series is their actual date of composition: for, being collections of random sketches, these compilations may well have included earlier drawings as well as those newly prepared for the volume in question. Doubtless an intensive study would enable one to sort out these complexities; for our own purposes it will suffice to illustrate a few examples of the last five series here, to round out our discussion.

Among the more notable design techniques we remark in the later series is the integrated inclusion of several dramatic scenes on one double-spread. That of Plate 307, for example, is obviously on the theme of the supernatural: at the bottom, three figures are seen grouped around the Magic Box of Urashima Tarō, which (in the Japanese version of Pandora's Box and Rip Van Winkle) has just been opened, with disastrous results. In contrast, the upper scenes are only pseudo-horrific: a man drawing his sword, scared by two cemetery-lanterns; and another man, frightened out of his wits by a devilish, falling kite

307 Fantastics. Plate from *Hokusai manga*, Series XI, *c.* 1833. (For other examples, see below and Fig. 221.)

and its weighted lines. Once one recognizes the subjects, such complex tableaux become surprisingly lucid.

In Plate 308 Hokusai reveals his continuing mastery of animal subjects, in a scene illustrating the old Chinese saying, 'Fortune is divined by cry of cock and dog'. As is typical with this artist, one may be captivated most by an incidental detail: here, the sturdy little puppy, howling away with his elders though not knowing the slightest reason why.

The two details of Plate 309 feature the Master's Juno-esque ladies of his later years: in the public bathhouse, at right, and at leisure on the left. And with his usual attention to intriguing, minor touches, the artist arouses our human interest as well as our artistic admiration: in, for example, the curiosity-consumed little boy crouched on the bathhouse floor (what indeed is he playing with under that dropped girdle?), and the guiltily satisfied dog making off with a delicious fresh fish-dinner.

308 *Left* Cock crowing/Dogs barking. From the same book as Plate 307.

309 *Below* Women at Leisure/Bathhouse Scene. Details from *Hokusai manga*, Series XII, 1834. (See Books, No. 238.)

310 *Opposite top* Farm Scene. Plate from *Hokusai manga*, Series XIII, 1849. (See Books, No. 265.)

311 *Opposite bottom* Recalcitrant Donkey. Plate from *Hokusai manga*, Series XIV; posthumous, *c.* early 1850s. (See Books, No. 269.)

Just about this time, it will be remembered, the Tempō Famines intervened, interrupting publishing as well as many other cultural and social activities. Thus the *Manga* was only to be resumed a decade and a half later: Series XIII appearing the year of the artist's death, 1849; Series XIV a few years later; and the final Series XV well into the succeeding Meiji Era, in 1878.

With these posthumous works a second problem arises, for the hand of copyist and editor looms large. Plate 310 is certainly an impressive tableau of farm-life (preparing *kampyō*—dried-gourd—a favourite *sushi* ingredient); but it is obviously one long step removed from the Master's direct brushstrokes. Plate 311, likewise, is not wholly Hokusai, yet it forms an intriguing composition with bold, sweeping lines, and ludicrous jackass (the nominal subject of the plate) depicted amidst a dramatically enchanting landscape. With the later posthumous volumes one also finds much re-use of earlier Hokusai book-plates; but there are some striking compositions, such as that in Plate 316, where a street-scene showing a fight among six blind masseurs is combined with that of a hawk flying off with a succulent bonito, as the deliveryman (having dropped his basket) belatedly attempts to draw his sword: these derived from the *Hokusai gakyō* of 1818. Purists will doubtless claim that the essence of the *Manga* lies in the first ten series and that is doubtless true. But for the general reader, Hokusai's compelling designs will continue to appeal, despite having been subjected to much revision and recopying.

The sheer quantity of the Master's picture-books is such that half of them could be skipped over and no one but the specialist would ever notice. It happens, however, that Hokusai's books of this late period are the most commonly found today, not only because they represent the standard work of his best-known years, but also because they remained popular and hence were reprinted widely on through the end of the century. Thus both for collectors and for those who would see the whole artist, it will be useful to make at least passing reference to several of them here.

Continental subjects loom large in Hokusai's later work, reflecting not only his own tastes but also those of his audience. One typical volume on the superficially unpromising theme of the Chinese classics is *Ehon Chūkyō* ('The Canon of Loyalty' Illustrated) of 1834, which, how-

312 *Top left* Scene with Wild Geese. Plate from *'Chinese Verses'* *Illustrated*—series of 1836. (For another of the series and bibliographical note see Fig. 220.)

313 *Centre left* Chinese General and Retainer. Plate from *'The Canon of Loyalty' Illustrated*, 1834. (For the books of this chapter see Appendix, Books, No. 236 ff.)

314 *Bottom left* Chinese Beauty. Detail from *'The Thousand Letters' Illustrated*, 1835–6.

315 *Opposite top* Rustic Chinese Scene. Plate from *'The Canon of Filial Piety' Illustrated*, 1834.

316 *Opposite bottom* Comic Figures. Plate from *Hokusai manga*, Series XV; posthumous, 1878.

風下の天狗

ever, has its share of impressive illustrations (Plate 313). From this year, likewise, comes the educational text *Ehon Kōkyō* ('The Canon of Filial Piety' Illustrated) seen in Plate 315. In line with the content the scenes are nominally classical Chinese, but the figures are very much of the contemporary world, as is the seemingly lovelorn ox (or perhaps he is absorbed in the ecstasy of a good back-scratch). On reading the text, one finds that this is a sermon on being kind to animals. Another neglected volume is the *Ehon Senjimon* ('The Thousand Letters' Illustrated) of 1835–6, featuring illustrations of Chinese and Japanese genre scenes, including the introspective study of an exotic beauty shown in Plate 314. And though superficially perhaps the least interesting of Hokusai's books, *Tōshisen ehon* ('Chinese Verses' Illustrated) of 1833/6 has its share of fine scenes. The 'Wild Geese' of Plate 312—shown flying before a Chinese procession—is reminiscent of several earlier examples of this charming and dynamically decorative

317 *Left* Mythical Lions. Plate from *New Designs for Craftsmen*, 1836. (See also Plate 318, and for bibliographical note, Books, No. 246.)

318 *Below* Travellers at Boat-bridge. Plate from *New Designs for Craftsmen*, 1836.

319 *Opposite top* Warrior with magic Mirror battling Serpent-witch. Plate from *Warriors Illustrated: China and Japan*, 1836. (See also Plate 320 and Fig. 227.)

320 *Opposite bottom* Magic Lion routing Army. Plate from *Warriors Illustrated: China and Japan*, 1836.

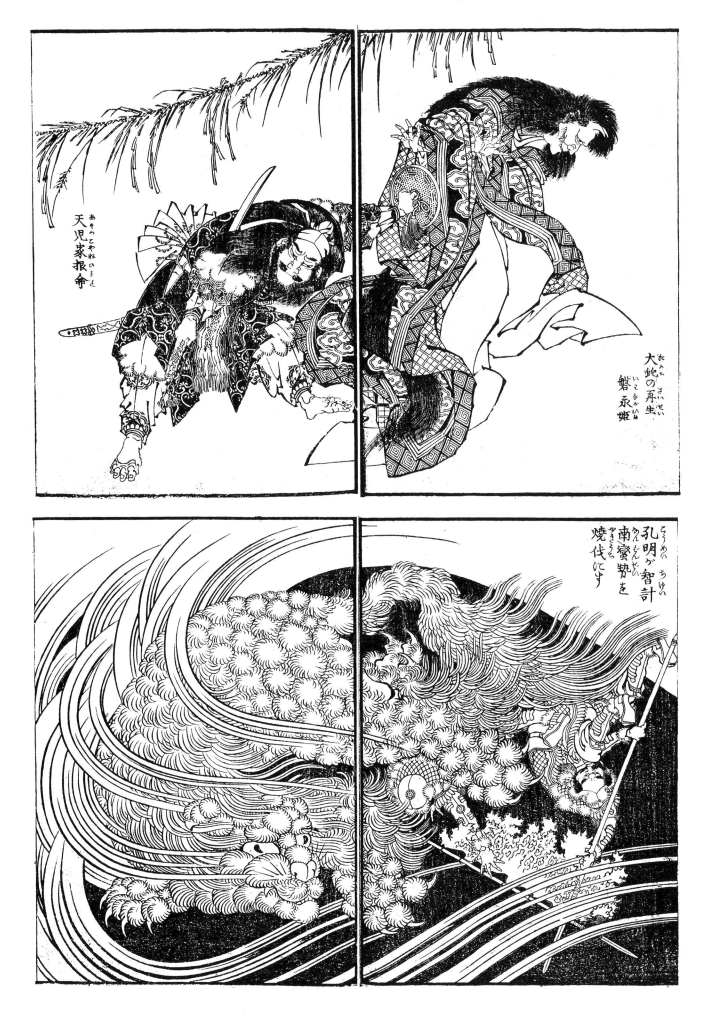

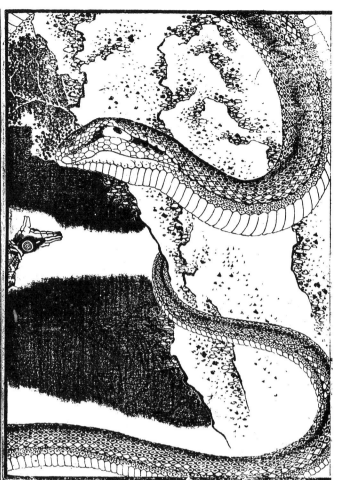

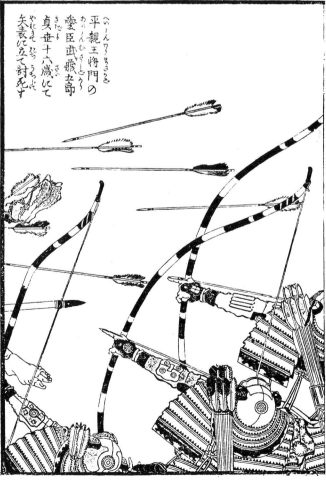

subject (Plates 97, 297). The treatment is typically the Master's in its dramatic and impressionistic attention to a detail that is only incidental to the original verse. One can well imagine literal-minded, conservative purchasers of the time complaining that what they wanted was the actual verses illustrated, not Hokusai's wilful interpretation of them. And in fact, only two of the series were actually published with the artist's work.

Designed for practical uses is another intriguing book of the latter year: *Shoshoku-ehon shin-hinagata* (New Designs for Craftsmen). The volume is filled with imaginative designs that far exceed the usual limitations of the avowed purpose: a guidebook for master-carpenters (whose work covered sculpture, architecture and engineering as well as carpentry—'Renaissance men' in their own way). The *shishi*-lions of Plate 317 are doubtless included only as guides to architectural decoration, but become works of art in their own right (in a subject dear to the artist's heart), and provide amusing self-portraits as well. And the 'Boat-

bridge' of Plate 318, while well illustrating the principles of bridge-building—and the use of roped casks as a makeshift boat—also gives an evocative genre view of peasants and priest: the latter's little acolyte adding that touch of engaging *élan* that we have come to expect of the Master even in such technical treatises.

Also in 1836 Hokusai prepared his extensive and famed trilogy of 'Warrior Books'. Plate 319 from the *Wakan ehon-sakigake* (*Warriors Illustrated: China and Japan*) shows a pre-historic samurai with sword in one hand and Divine Mirror in the other at battle with the Snake Witch. One notes, almost imperceptibly, the effective placement of the *shimenawa*, Sacred Shrine-rope: it not only adds its own mystical implications, but also physically binds the composition together. Even more bold and startling is the sweeping design of Plate 320, in which we view the Magic Strategy (embodied in a huge *shishi*) of General K'ung-ming devastating the Barbarian Hordes, effectively symbolized by a single warrior.

From the second of this trilogy, *Ehon Musashi-abumi* (The Stirrups of Musashi) I take yet another supernatural scene (Plate 321): General Tokimasa receiving Divine Inspiration from the Giant Serpent. (The enormous snake, though fearsome enough, sports that unique Hokusai look of supercilious embarrassment.)

Some of the artist's most impressive warrior-designs appear in the final volume of the trilogy, *Ehon wakan-no-homare* (*Heroes of China and Japan Illustrated*). Publication seems to have been held up by the Tempō Famines, and

321 *Opposite top* Warrior and Snake-apparition. Plate from *The Stirrups of Musashi*, 1836.

322 *Opposite bottom* Young Warrior receiving Enemy Arrows. Plate from *Heroes of China and Japan Illustrated*, c. 1836/50. (See also Plate 323; on the dating, see Appendix, Books, No. 245.)

323 *Below* Chinese Warrior repulsing Sea-demon. Plate from *Heroes of China and Japan Illustrated*, c. 1836/50.

the book may well have been published only over a decade later. Plate 322 is a tableau in the *yomi-hon* tradition; even without knowing the historical details one can admire the heroic young protagonist, alone and surrounded by the enemy, but dying like a man (Musashi Sadayo was in fact only 15 at the time of his death in battle).

One of the finest of all Hokusai's heroic designs—the more effective for its masterful re-creation of the essentially unknowable—is (to give the full title) 'Cheng Chih-lung Repelling the Sea-Demon on the Lotus Sea', also from the final volume (Plate 323). The combination of Chinese warrior and European arquebus is arresting enough in itself, but what raises this illustration far above the ordinary are the marvellously delineated 'Phantom Clouds' that loom so ominously above the magic, wild sea. (One can almost visualize Old Hokusai himself in this defiant figure, at times plagued by palsy but steadfastly refusing to submit to Providence's attempt to limit his human existence to a mere 75 years.)

It might here be queried as to whether such heroic tableaux are really ukiyo-e; and also, just why they were so popular at the time. The *musha-e* or warrior-print had, indeed, been a standard theme of ukiyo-e from its inception; in effect, the latter represented a school of 'modern, genre art', not necessarily limited in subject to the Floating World of courtesans and fair young men. Thus a good part of the content of ukiyo-e consists of traditional, even conventional and classical, subjects, but treated in an up-to-date manner. With Hokusai and the nineteenth century, of course, the influence of Chinese art came to loom large, and the style of depiction often tended to adopt the techniques of classical Far Eastern art. (When the 'flower-and-bird' theme becomes the subject, the line between ukiyo-e and the traditional styles becomes an even finer one.)

As for the resurgence in popularity of heroic subjects, this had come at the beginning of the century, first in the *yomi-hon* novels and their illustrations—often on Chinese themes—followed by the prints and picture-books. It was, in fact, already two centuries since the last major battles in the unification of Japan: the samurai, though tending to become effete, looked back in nostalgia on the brave deeds of their forebears; and the commoners, too, thrilled to tales of that bold adventure so denied them in their regimented daily life.

During the aftermath of the Famine Years, 1837–40, publication remained at a low ebb, with only a few Hokusai works appearing, and these usually of a practical nature. Such was the case with the *Nikkōzan-shi* (A Guide to Nikkō) of 1837, with its impressive, four-page landscape, of which half is shown in Plate 324. One can well visualize this

327 Saint despatching Villain to Hades. Double-page plate from *The Life of Sakyamuni Illustrated*, 1841. (See also Fig. 228.)

magnificent design reworked as a large print-triptych, in the manner of Hiroshige's later panoramas.

Educational texts, too, remained popular even in these difficult times. Generally speaking, they were vernacular versions of the Chinese classics. Such, for example, is the *Wakan inshitsu-den* (Divine Providence in China and Japan) of 1840, where the artist features not only Continental themes but also native ones (Plate 325). Compared to the Master's earlier days the style of figure depiction tends to be stiff and unpliant. We cannot escape the fact that we are dealing not only with an artist of 80, but also with a changing taste in engraving and printing methods—a move towards the precise and realistic, away from the pliant, atmospheric and evocative.

Likewise in an educational vein is the little pictorial dictionary *Nagashira musha-burui* (Warriors Classified) of 1841. In a typical tableau (Plate 326) we discover a full half dozen minuscule heroes cavorting about in a space not much bigger than a postcard, strong evidence that the artist's eyesight—and sense of design—was flagging hardly at all.

Perhaps most amazing for this period is the old Master's return to the complex and detailed work of *yomi-hon* illus-

324 *Opposite top* Landscape at Nikkō. Plate from *A Guide to Nikkō*, 1837.

325 *Opposite left* Street-scene. Plate from *Divine Providence in China and Japan*, 1840.

326 *Opposite right* Heroes of Eld. Page from *Warriors Classified*, 1841. (See also Plate 336.)

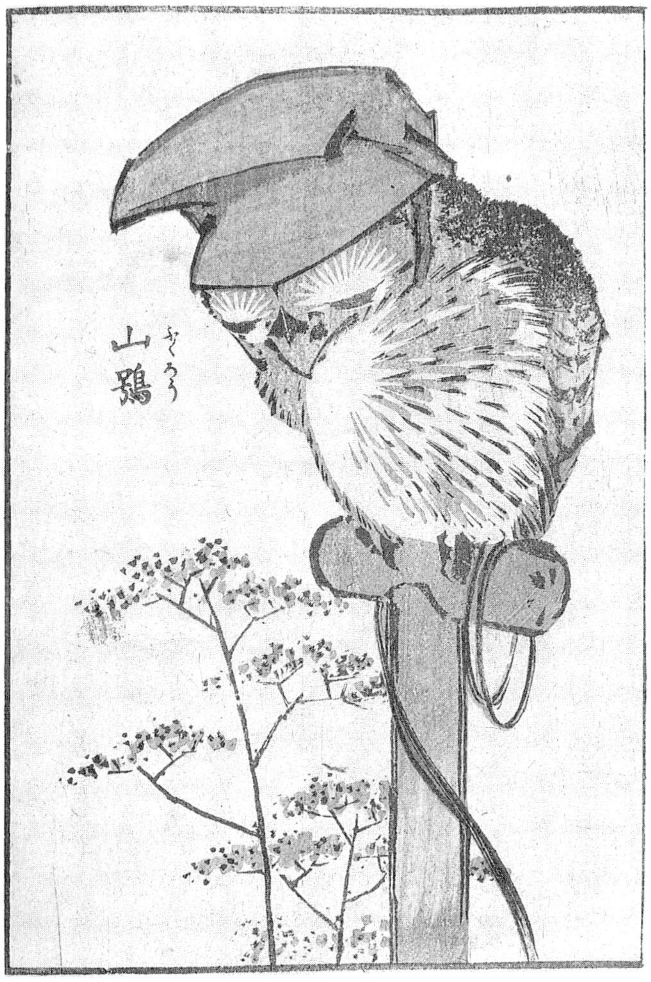

tration. This found fruition first in the *Shaka goichidaiki-zue* (Life of Sakyamuni Illustrated) of 1840. In this account of the historical Buddha we find scene after scene of powerful designs: lacking, of course, in the supple forms of the early works, but sometimes almost sculptural in their massive intensity (Plate 327).

But quite untypical of this period is the impressive picture-book *Manji-ō sōhitsu gafu* (Old Manji's Cursive Album). Although only published in 1843, the preface is dated 1832 and the illustrations seem likewise to date from the earlier decade. Yet in spite of the bibliographical complexities, several of the designs are most charming. The little 'Owl' of Plate 328 is justly famous: blinded by daylight, the bird is a kind of parable on people 'out of their element'. Some of us, too, never tire of Hokusai's *shishi*-lions; this one (Plate 329), depicted in the rain, has an uncharacteristically dappled coat. And in the 'Late-winter Landscape' of Plate 330, we see a vivid application of the 'semi-cursive' style to a panorama in which the individu-

328 *Left* 'Pet Owl'. Plate from *Old Manji's Cursive Album*, 1843 [1832]. (See also Plates 329–30 and Appendix, Books, No. 254.)

329 *Below* 'Lion in Rain'. Plate from *Old Manji's Cursive Album*, 1843 [1832]. (See also Plates 328, 330.)

330 *Opposite top* 'Late-winter Landscape'. Plate from *Old Manji's Cursive Album*, 1843 [1832]. (See also Plates 328–9.)

331 *Opposite bottom* Chinese Ship. Plate from *The Wars of Han and Ch'u*, 1843.

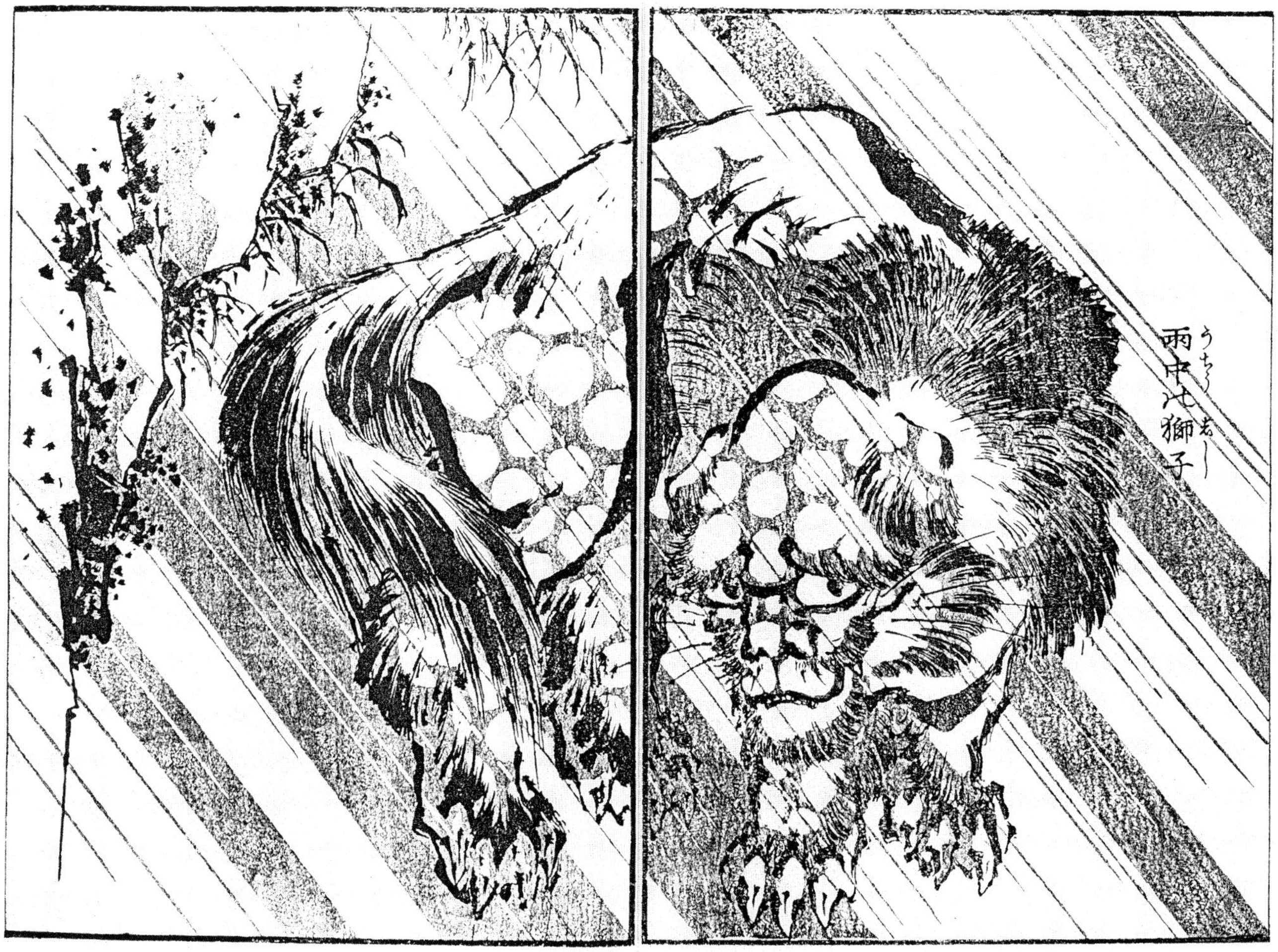

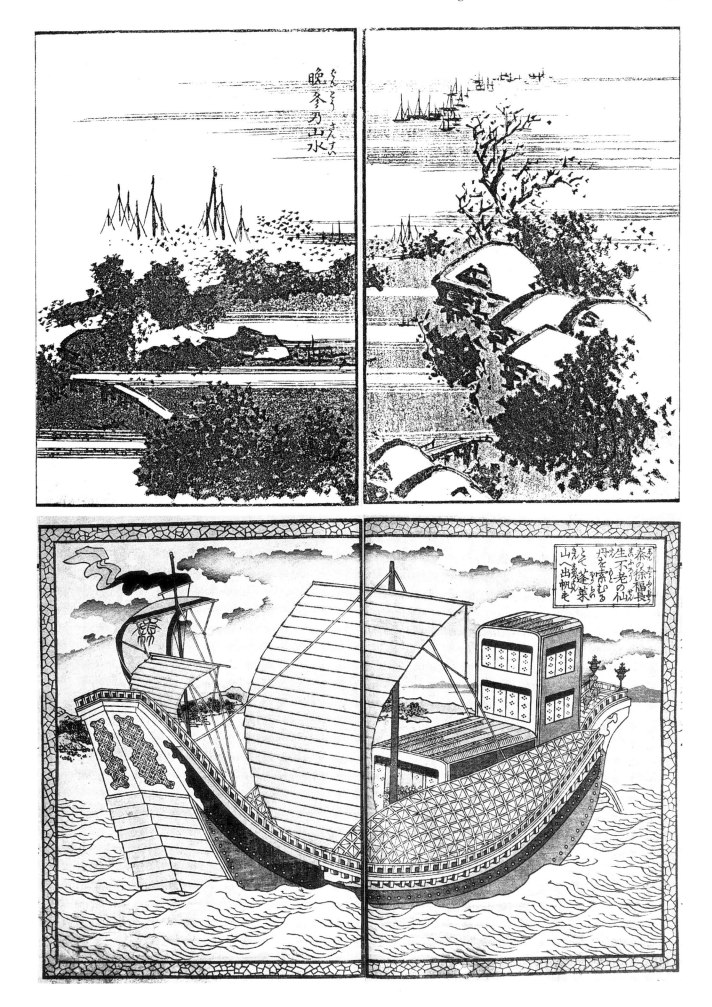

332, 333 *Above* Pair of Shōjō breaking up New-Year Rice-cake. Small *surimono*, with trial proof; 1844. Signed Manji, in eighty-fifth year. (For the subject, see also Plate 188.)

334, 335 *Right* Children at Music and Dance (design for a tobacco pipe-holder). Original drawing, and copy for engraver; *c.* 1830s.

ally fascinating elements are always subservient to the whole.

In the *Ehon Kan-So gundan* (The Wars of Han and Ch'u) of 1843–5 we find Hokusai essaying another complex *yomi-hon* novel. The excessively architectural, and oddly pers-pectived, 'Chinese Junk' of Plate 331 will certainly not appeal to all tastes; yet one cannot but admire an artist, now in his mid-80s, quite literally living up to his pen-name Gakyō-*rōjin*, 'Old Man Mad with Painting'.

I have hinted at the gradual and subtle changes that took place in ukiyo-e engraving and printing techniques during the first half of the nineteenth century. To judge from the results at least, the effect was a greater precision of tech-nique and draughtsmanship, but with a loss of the softer and more evocative line and colour of the 'classical' period. This increasing emphasis on sharp and objective realism was of course a general trend of the times, but for a sensi-tive and eminently professional artist like Hokusai, the needs of publisher, engraver and printer tended to be re-flected swiftly in his style—in spite of his age and natural stubbornness in other matters. This is not, however, to imply that the Master's basic sketches were all that dif-ferent from those of his earlier years, and a few examples may be of interest.

There exists a miniature album (about 11 × 8 cm/4¼ × 3 in) of Hokusai sketches and sample proofs/plates, gathered together and annotated by an anonymous pupil, which is most instructive regarding some of the essential processes of ukiyo-e production. For example, we discover here not only one of Hokusai's last known *surimono*—done in his eighty-fifth year—but also the printer's proof for the same print (Plates 332, 333). In effect, the proof to the key-block is pretty much what a monochrome book-plate would be like. In the final *surimono*, however, the same

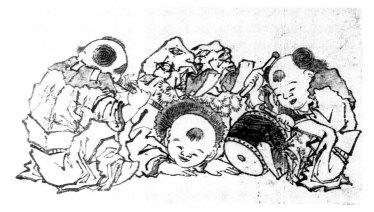

vital block is pigmented in delicate grey and the emphasis is transferred to the colour-blocks—in particular, that ren-dered with black, lacquer-like pigments. Both specimens are, of course, far removed from Hokusai's original sketch (now lost), and for such we must turn to other examples in the same, diminutive album.

Plates 334, 335 show at top the Master's original drawing of little boys at play; and below it, the final version made for the engraver. The initial sketch is alive with the artist's inspiration; the copy—whether done by the Master or a skilled pupil—is merely expert, no longer infused with life. And the same can be said for the preliminary sketch and its printed version of Plates 337, 338. The book repre-sented is one of Hokusai's last, and hardly a significant one; yet even in the drawings for such a didactic and un-promising volume there will be discovered a vitality, a sureness of brushwork that is largely cancelled out by the intervention of the overly meticulous woodblock-carver (at least in this late period). The remainder of this intriguing album collects a variety of further Hokusai preliminary sketches for miniature works that seem often to have remained unpublished. Those of Plate 336, for example, were obviously intended for one of the little 'pictorial dictionaries'. And indeed, on more careful examination one discovers at right the Master's drawing for a portion of our earlier Plate 326: the warrior Tadanobu routing the enemy with a heavy *goban* chessboard. Here the free and impromptu quality of the tiny sketch is rather successfully translated to the print medium, but there is still something missing: that 'shock of recognition' when one confronts the artist face to face in an original drawing or painting.

I hope this brief aside may serve to illuminate a problem met throughout ukiyo-e: in the prints and illustrations one does not really meet the artist 'in the flesh', but only his drawings as reproduced by skilled engraver and consummate printer. With many artists of unsure brushstroke the final prints are often, in effect, greater works of art than the designs; with an assured master like Hokusai—and particularly during the period of decline in printing *élan*—the reverse may well be the case.

It would certainly have been no surprise if Hokusai from his mid-70s should have faltered in energy if not in imagination. But the fact is that what books he did in this late period were good ones; and many of his best paintings

date from his 80s. Thus the scarcity of his publications from the mid-1830s seems, rather, to derive from the general problems of Japanese publishing at this time.

We have already taken note of the Tempō Famines of 1833–6, during which inclement weather and crop-failures combined to cause widespread inflation, unrest, and, in certain Provinces, death from starvation running into tens of thousands. In reaction to these various crises both the local and central feudal governments undertook various counter-measures, culminating in the famed Tempō Reforms of 1841–3. These included attempts to improve fiscal policies and food-production, as well as to strengthen defence capacities (foreign ships were already clamouring for access to Japanese ports, and there was a general mood of crisis in diplomacy). Moreover—and most related to our theme—there was a strong attempt to regulate and even abolish 'luxuries', among which were included ukiyo-e, and popular publication in general.

Indeed, as early as 1833, 1838 and 1840 there had been

336 *Right* Bandit-Assassin hiding under Ox-skin; Warriors Fighting. Preliminary drawings for book-illustrations; *c.* 1840.

337, 338 *Below* Domestic Scenes. Preliminary drawings and corresponding printed versions for the miniature picture-book *Kijin Hyakunin-isshu* (The 'Hundred Poems' by Eccentrics), published posthumously in 1852. (See Books, No. 268.)

sumptuary-edicts urging the 'return to former standards of frugality and propriety' (with, as usual, the qualification, 'Of course, such regulations do not apply to items for Official Use'). To have followed the letter of the law would have meant the end of ukiyo-e, for practically all the most popular subjects and techniques of the prints—depictions of women and courtesans (not to mention shunga), Kabuki-actors, as well as extended print-series and elaborate colouring—were either restricted or banned outright.

In some cases, the restrictions were complied with in form if not in spirit: for example, publishers—and artists—resorted to the *aizuri-e* or 'indigo-print', in which great effort was expended to produce gorgeous prints solely in shades of blue. And extended series of landscape and historical prints, often with women or actors included in 'insets', or other clever subterfuges, were published. There followed, too, the natural spread of satirical prints pointing ridicule at the Reforms, and at the bureaucrats themselves (for which, as we have seen, the leading figure-print artist Kuniyoshi was penalized in 1843).

Had such sumptuary-edicts been concentrated only on

ukiyo-e they might have succeeded; but the government policy was aimed at all aspects of Japanese life and its amenities, both plebeian and upper-class, and in the end it failed for lack of support from practically all levels. But though its main perpetrator Lord Tadakuni, Chief of the Shōgun's Councillors, was relieved of office in the spring of 1843, the residue of the Tempō Reforms continued in one way or another to poison Japanese life during the remaining two and a half decades of the Edo Period. Certainly for Hokusai, lost forever was the opportunity finally to prove that he 'could become a great artist'—at least, so far as published results went.

3

But what of Hokusai's *paintings* in this final decade or so? It is often stated (incorrectly, as we have shown above) that the artist devoted his final years mainly to this medium. Yet certainly it is a fact that during the publishing crisis from the mid-1830s a freelance artist had a better chance of selling paintings than book-designs. But it must also be added that this represents the very period for which copies and forgeries most abound—and not only for the usual commercial reasons: paintings and calligraphy by great elders were always treasured in Old Japan, and were thought to possess a talisman-like magic. Thus the Mas-

339 Playful Lion. Painting in *sumi* on paper, dated New Year's Day, 1843. 9 × 12¼ in / 23 × 31 cm. From the sketch-album *Daily Exorcism*, 1842–3. Colophon signed: Gakyō-*rōjin* Manji, in Eighty-eighth Year.

340 Playful Lion. Painting in *sumi* on paper, from the same album as Plate 339, dated Sixth Month, Sixth Day. (Average size, *c.* 9½ × 13¼ in / 24 × 34 cm.)

ter's works of his 80s were in sufficient demand during his own lifetime that skilled copies were made, for sale in the Provinces and elsewhere, and the practice continued through the remainder of the century, when indiscriminate collectors from the West became the prime market for such 'Hokusai' paintings.

With the proviso, then, that research is still at a pioneer stage, let us take a look at some of the Master's representative paintings in this final stage of his career.

Perhaps the most charming of all Hokusai's extant painting *oeuvre* are to be found in the vast series of daily sketches he made over the years 1842–3. The subject had long been a favourite of the artist: the ebullient and playful *shishi*—the demon-quelling mythical lion derived from China and still celebrated throughout much of East and Southeast Asia (indeed, the best preparation for an appreciation of Hokusai's work might be a careful viewing of the

gaily prancing Balinese *Barong* dance).[3] Being done for his own pleasure the paintings—all in *sumi*—are very personal; yet like most serious artists, even in such facetious work Hokusai also maintains a veiled eye for posterity.

The exact number of these original *shishi* sketches is not known (sometimes, two or three days' work is included on one sheet), but at least 220 seem to be extant today. The artist's avowed purpose in this daily regimen was to create a powerful talisman against illness, a prayer for long life— and, perhaps, an appeal for magical relief from the problems caused by his delinquent grandson. The major group—86 of these 600 or more sketches—was gathered together by Hokusai's daughter O-Ei, for presentation to a samurai-patron from distant Shinano in 1847, two years before the artist's death. The title given to this manuscript was *Nisshin joma* (Daily Exorcisms). In the terminal-note, added at the time of presentation, the Master describes himself as then in his eighty-eighth year, and includes a note on his formula for long life: a potent recipe consisting of *longan* ('Dragon-eye' evergreen-fruit), white sugar, and a gallon of strong potato-whiskey—'to be left standing in a

341 Lion in Rain. From the same album as Plate 339, dated Fourth Month, Fourth Day.

well-sealed jug for sixty days, after which, two cups each to be taken morning and evening, without fail.'

As might be expected of such an extended daily exercise, the drawings are not all of equal quality or interest: some are repetitive, some a bit uninspired, others are rather too contrived, even coy. But at their best these *Daily Exorcisms* represent the essence of Hokusai's genius as a painter in his later years; and even at their least inspired, they are an epitome of his uneven genius.

In his *shihitsu* or 'First sketch of the New Year' (a customary rite for Japanese artists) of 1843, for example, we find the Master—and his protagonist—infused with effervescent energy (Plate 339). Though of venerable age the mythical beast leaps about like a young puppy, overjoyed simply at being alive. Not unnaturally, one may be tempted to see here not only a frisky lion but also the artist himself, aged 83 yet still feeling his oats (not all of the time, to be sure, but on certain days and at certain times).

The technique is basically that of the classical Kanō masters: swift and fluid brushstrokes with hardly a pause in between. Although this is a fully realized *sumi-e* painting, it probably entailed only about sixty seconds of uninterrupted concentration. Indeed, the inscription may have consumed almost the same effort, being executed in con-

trasting, formal *reisho*-style calligraphy. Needless to say, such impromptu sketches are very difficult to forge: though a serious copy by a major pupil might well resemble the original in all but expression and indefinable 'style'.

Far more fluent and cursive is another 'Playful Lion' (Plate 340). Like the previous example, it could be considered a striking manifestation of the 'cursive and informal styles' (as detailed in the earlier Hokusai text-book of Plate 166). Here the same beast, amidst the same frenetic action, is rendered in great washes of the flattened brush—the hind legs blurred as one might expect in a photograph. Only the head is depicted in greater detail: a device familiar in 'blur-photography', but rare in classical art. The calligraphy, too, is ideally matched to the design, a kind of semi-formal *gyōsho* variation on the seal-style *reisho* (if there is any such category). (Hokusai's calligraphy, though individualistic and expert, would probably not, by classical Japanese or Chinese standards, be considered very refined. Like his art itself, this 'handwriting' reflects the energetic, earthy nature of the man, rather than the literati goal of sublime idealism.)

Old men of 83 do not usually go out uncovered in driving rain, but in Plate 341 we view a lion doing just that, and enjoying the experience to the full. The masterful lines of the drizzle (drawn with the broad *haké*-brush but, of course, without recourse to ruler) lend a special flavour to this sketch; and the date—May in the modern calendar—assures us that the beast is in no danger of catching cold or distemper.

Hokusai's sketches of this series are not exclusively of the mythical *shishi*, but also include revealing tableaux of the *shishi-mai* lion-dancer, a feature of Japanese festive occasions. In the example of Plate 342 the roles are strangely ambiguous: is this a man become a *shishi*; or a *shishi* imagining he is a man? For the snarling mongrel dog, at least, the situation is clearly one of confrontation and—tail between legs in preparation for flight—he barks, literally with his entire body.

With the 'Standing Lion' of Plate 344, the roles are even more complex, perhaps inexplicable. And while not one of the major designs of the set, it is my own favourite. Indeed, it might be said that this curious *shishi*, depicted standing on its hind legs, is for all the world the same posturing creature we saw in *Teach Yourself the Dance* (Plate 161). The inscription reads: 'Doubtless, you've heard tell of the famous *Lion King* of West India? That's me!' To my mind this is the Hokusai self-portrait *par excellence*: humorous yet a bit sly, complex yet childlike, legendary but very modern, vain yet self-depreciating, and intensely human.[4]

Hokusai's later kakemono paintings form a unique category, and were obviously intended for a special type of patron. Gone are the gorgeously robust beauties of his middle to late years. In their place we find a succession of bold figures from history and legend, together with rare animals, rendered in a monumental, stylized and rather exaggerated manner not suited to all tastes. One favourite subject was the heroes of ancient China, as depicted in, for example, the *Three Kingdoms* novel. The subject of the painting shown here (Plate 345) is the heroic General Chang Fei (assassinated in AD 220), shown standing in the

342 Mongrel and Lion-dancer. From the same album as Plate 339, dated Fourth Month, Eighth Day.

snow, spear in hand and reed-cap raised, preparing to meet the enemy single-handed. The composition is impressive and impeccable; it is clearly a display-piece and one should not therefore expect the intimate charm or fierce individuality of Hokusai's earlier periods. It dates from the artist's eighty-fourth year. (Indeed it is interesting to note that most of these late works include the Master's age: as we have seen, in Japan longevity was both prized and honoured—calligraphy by elders even being displayed as a kind of decorative talisman.)

Of Hokusai's other late paintings, one must note also the biographically interesting 'Daikoku' of Plate 343, though only a sketch. Here the traditional God of Prosperity is depicted, as usual, seated on bales of rice, but his Bag of Plenty forms a veritable halo behind him. The painting commemorates Hokusai's entry into his eighty-fifth year and is dated New Year of 1844, with the unusual notation, 'Born in the Ninth Month of 1760, the Year of the Dragon'. This may, indeed, be the only extant evidence of the month of Hokusai's birth; and—with a painting later to be mentioned—reconfirms the year of birth as well (otherwise known only by counting back from his datable ages).

It is often assumed that various of the artist's sketches of independent-looking elders are 'self-portraits'; but in the illustrated letter of Plate 346 we indeed view Hokusai as he saw himself in his late years: wrinkled, active, a bit cantankerous, but withal a reasonable man. The letter accompanied a group of earlier sketches sent to a publisher, and is signed 'In eighty-third year, Hachiemon' (the latter being the unartistic, rustic name the Master affected in some of his later works).

More famous is the preparatory drawing depicting the Old Man walking with a stick, shown in Plate 348. Though untitled, this is said to derive from the collection of Hokusai's late pupil Isai. It is a thoughtful portrayal of the infirmities of old age, reflecting the artist's perception that more important than problems of the flesh are matters of the mind.

Of more general interest are Hokusai's impressive paintings of fierce eagles in this final stage of his *oeuvre*. Perhaps the finest of these is that shown in Plate 347. Here, in a seemingly incongruous combination, a huge and strikingly individualistic eagle peers up at the sky, positioned by a rocky rivulet, an elegantly blooming cherry-tree behind. The magnificent bird—doubtless glowering at some flying prey—is most effectively contrasted with the evocative, subtly gradated setting. And again, one seems to glimpse the soul of the artist himself in this cranky, defiant, essentially lonely great beast.

The theme was a favourite of Hokusai's at this period (indeed, the technique corresponds rather closely to that

343 The God Daikoku. Kakemono in *sumi* on paper; 1844. Size and present whereabouts uncertain. Signed Gakyō-*rōjin* Manji, in eighty-fifth year, with full date and birthdate.

344 *Below* Lion introducing Self. From the same album as Plate 339, dated Twelfth Month, Twentieth Day.

345 *Right* General Chang Fei. Kakemono in heavy colours on silk; 1843. 52¼ × 17¼ in / 133 × 44 cm. Signed Gakyō-*rōjin* Manji, in eighty-fourth year.

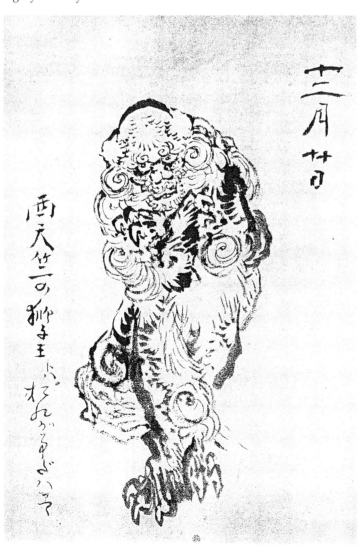

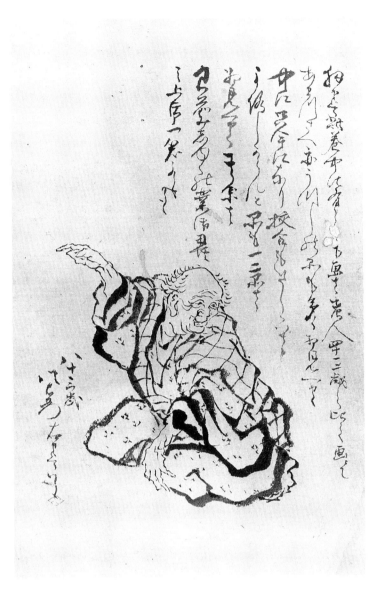

346 Self-portrait. Detail from an illustrated letter, *sumi* on paper; 1842. 10½ in / 27 cm high. Signed Hachiemon, in 83rd year.

347 *Right* Eagle with Cherry-blossoms. Kakemono in heavy colours on silk; 1843. 38 × 18 in / 97 × 46 cm. Signed Manji, in eighty-fourth year.

of the painting-manual of Plate 352), and at least three other examples are known. One is of the same date, featuring a similar bird but against a less well-realized background; one other is from four years later, showing a rather less impressive eagle but against the background of a snowstorm. (The question that must be asked is does the lesser quality of the two latter paintings represent merely a temporary decline in the artist's powers—or the hand of a skilled, early copyist?[5])

Whether in the precise and exacting task of book-illustration, or in the nerve-attuned, concentrated work of sketching or painting, it will be seen that the 1840s formed a surprisingly active and productive decade for Old Hokusai. But whatever the strength of his brushstroke, whatever the vitality of his aspirations, there was to be a limit even to his protestations against Fate.

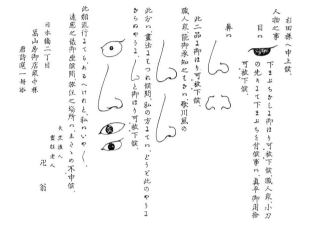

Memo to the Engraver Sugita. From a letter to the publisher Sūzambō, dated I/17/1836. (Reprinted from K. Iijima, *Katsushika Hokusai den*, 1893.)

NOTES

1 I might add the personal note that, though I was not yet studying Hokusai, it was to these very areas that I was most attracted during my early years in Tokyo, 1950–7: they most embodied whatever was left of the essence of old Edo. Once, indeed, I went to inspect lodgings that happened to overlook the Master's grave at Nagazumi-chō in Asakusa—being warned, however, that the area was not of very good reputation. My final choice of residence was the old quarter of Umamichi, a mile to the north-east—which turned out to be Hokusai's next-to-last residence and barely a stone's throw from the Matsuchiyama temple-grounds where the Master breathed his last.
2 The tracing of Hokusai's memo is shown below.
3 The sketches were done one each morning—discarded, the story goes, only to be picked up and preserved by Hokusai's daughter O-Ei. Aside from various book-illustrations of *shishi* (Plates 165, 231, 234, 317, 320, 329, 354) there is also a noted, large kakemono-painting on this theme of the following year, 1844. It is not, however, as effective as these impromptu original sketches.
4 The above 'identification' was written simply on intuition, but I have since noticed that Hokusai, in the letter of early 1836 translated above, also facetiously signs himself *Tenjiku-rōnin Gakyō-rōjin Manji-ō*—'Manji the Old Man Mad with Painting, Unemployed-Samurai from India'. For a Japanese of this period, of course, 'India' was merely a fabulous, unknown country—the equivalent of Shangri-La or Xanadu, or Japan itself to Europeans of the time.
5 On these works see my 'Labyrinth or Hornet's Nest? A Note on Hokusai's Paintings'. In the journal *Andon*, in press: reprinted in *Studies in Edo Art*, in press.

348 *Opposite* Self-portrait. Preliminary sketch in *sumi* with *pentimenti*; *c.* mid-1840s. Unsigned.

XXIII
Conclusion:
Old Man Mad
with Painting

1

LET ME AGAIN pick up some of the meagre threads of biographical data as they pertain to this final period. These are given but briefly, for detail is usually lacking; to fill them out further would often require the novelist's touch.

In 1844 (at the age of 84) Hokusai's name is seen on a printed broadsheet of 'Famous Elders'. And in 1845 the Master appeared (with Bakin, among others—including imagined portraits) as one of the many 'odd geniuses' in the book *Nihon kijin-den* (Tales of Japanese Eccentrics), illustrated by Kuniyoshi. In the same year Hokusai painted a remarkable, large *ema*-panel depicting the lusty god Susanoō and the Vanquished Demons.[1] Dated 'In 86th year', this was dedicated to the Ushijima Shrine at Mimeguri (but was lost in the Great Kantō Earthquake of 1923). Two *ema*-panels depicting tableaux of the Immortals are also known, executed for the Kiyoyasu Fudōin temple. More than once in this period the artist is cited as still able to do the most detailed work without benefit of eyeglasses, and as daily walking long distances, back unbent; but then, in a Hokusai letter of 1846 appears the note, 'My ailment has returned, and I am unable to walk': presumably a reference to the palsy of the prior decade.

There is a well-known sketch showing Hokusai's private life at this time, done at a later date by a disciple, Tsuyuki Iitsu II (d. 1893). In it (Plate 349) we see the artist at right, huddled under a quilt, assiduously painting away on the floor-mat as his ageing daughter O-Ei looks on. The notice on the wall reads, 'Absolutely no commissions for albums or fan-paintings. . . .', presumably indicating Hokusai's desire to concentrate his efforts on more important works. Installed in a fruit-box at left may be seen a small figure of St Nichiren, the Master's guardian-deity. The drawing is described as 'Hokusai's Temporary Lodgings', but in a sense that was true of every place he ever lived.

We have already made passing reference to several Hokusai pupils of note: for the early period, Sōri III and Shinsai, for the middle and later years, Hokuju, Taito II, Bokusen, Hokuba, Hokkei, Shigenobu, O-Ei. Each of these interesting artists deserves separate study. But of special significance in relation to the Master's later years was a patron—and amateur artist—living at Obusé, far off in the mountains of Shinano. This was the local luminary Takai Kōzan (1806–83), a wealthy scholar and poet. At Kōzan's invitation Hokusai paid him several lengthy visits in the years 1842–5. (In 1848 he had to decline another invitation because he was by then unable to walk.)

Various episodes have come down to us regarding Hokusai's sojourns in Obusé, but his principal documented

works of art there seem to consist of a set of four panels executed in 1844–5. Painted on wood, each nearly a metre square, these impressive paintings were commissioned for the ceilings of festival-floats: for the East Quarter, designs of 'Phoenix and Dragon' in 1844; for the Upper Quarter, the 'Angry Waves' of 1845. It will be seen from the example shown (Plate 350) that the Master has surpassed himself yet again in the dynamic depiction of *water*: these waves are not only dramatic and compelling but also very definitely *alive*; and beyond them looms a kind of water-tunnel reminiscent of the 'Great Waterspout' of our earlier Plate 243.

These panels are all executed in the heavy body-colours and poster-style of the *ema* shrine-panels, with touches,

349 Tsuyuki Iitsu II: Hokusai's Lodgings of the mid-1840s. Sketch in *sumi* on paper, 1880s. 10 × 6¾ in / 25 × 17 cm.

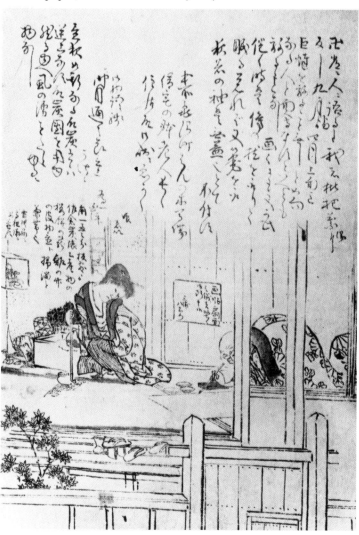

even, of Occidental influence. They are essentially architectural decorations, rococo works best viewed *in situ*. But though they tend to lack a central focal-point they are impressive compositions; and in the 'Angry Waves' panels the artist comes close to equalling the great Kōrin's earlier and more famous *oeuvre* on this difficult theme.

In the details of these large and complex late works one may well discern the assistance of pupils—for example O-Ei, who accompanied her father on his visits to Kōzan; and indeed the Wave panels are surrounded by elaborately painted frames said to have been added by Kōzan himself, after Hokusai's designs.

The Obusé Village collections (there are both Hokusai and Kōzan museums) preserve several other items of direct Hokusai provenance. These include his letters to Kōzan, such as that shown in Plate 351. At the end of this missive (which is concerned with colouring details of the 'Phoenix Panel', just discussed) the artist concludes with the lines (a word-play on 'Ukiyo-e'):

Ah! never quite what one had hoped!
The Floating World
—Pictures

and then depicts himself as a dancing ghost with sleeping cat, in a tableau poignantly reminiscent of the Master's 'Final Verse' (p. 272).

2

In his mid-80s Hokusai, amazingly, managed not only to overcome his failing health, but also to maintain his spirits, his determination, and above all his overriding ambition to 'become a great painter'. (The latter tends, indeed, to be the aim of all artists, even when they claim that money is their goal.) But when we search through our carefully collected lists of the artist's published *oeuvre* in the 1840s, we look in vain for work of major importance. However, this does not mean that the artist in Hokusai was dead; only that the Master had become far less publishable commercially. It will be remembered that ukiyo-e, though the most distinguished of all commercial arts, was always in the end a business. And Hokusai had become, in effect, a 'great grey eminence', revered by former pupils and friends, but viewed as out of date and past his prime.

This was not, however, Hokusai's view: age was but relative and his heart and mind were just as full of the 'passion to depict the form of things' as they had been in his childhood. All that was lacking was sufficient patronage—and, perhaps, a more nutritious diet.

There is one important exception to this dearth of notable late Hokusai publications, and that is the two small volumes entitled *Ehon saishiki-tsū* (On the Use of Colouring), which appeared from the New Year of 1848 (sequels were planned but never realized).

The reader may well ask why an artist—aged, impoverished, bedridden and largely forgotten—would suddenly start preparing a comprehensive manual on the art of painting? There was, to be sure, strong support from the publishers (attendant on the artist's *beiju* or 'eighty-eighth

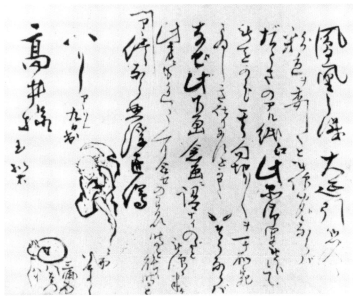

350 *Top* Angry Waves. Large panel in heavy colours on wood; 1845. 37¾ in / 96 cm square. Unsigned. (In line with the Oriental love of symmetrical pairing, this set of panels is categorized as 'Masculine Waves' and 'Feminine Waves', the latter shown here. The designs are based on a *Suikoden* episode.)

351 *Above* Illustrated letter to Takai Kōzan. Dated only 'Eighth Month, Ninth Day' (*c.* 1843). Signed Miuraya Hachiemon.

year' celebration). But most of all it was the Master's own burning passion to complete his appointed task: to give final and detailed clarification of the Hokusai Style. Despite his infirmities, the artist was unconquered in all that really mattered.

Thus in 1847 in his eighty-eighth year Hokusai turned to what would be his last significant book. Here he would, for all posterity, transcribe the didactic yet febrile details of his artistic style, so that the Hokusai Method should be passed on correctly to future generations. All of the material 'secrets' of the Master's art will be found here: the preparation of pigments, the basic brush technique, the necessary technical terminology, plus full examples (in monochrome) of flower-and-bird work, fishes, animals, landscape details and even geometrical patterns. Not only does the text (including some rudiments of Occidental oil-painting) provide fertile ground for future Hokusai students, but the illustrations themselves are often minor masterpieces, in no way inferior to the artist's best work of the preceding decade.

Though not typical of the book's subjects, it will none the less be instructive to reproduce the sole figure-design (Plate 352). We view yet again the ever-fascinating contrast of 'cursive' and 'formal' styles of brushwork, here cited for the variant methods of colouring to be employed. And in Plate 354 we see another of the Master's impressive *shishi*-lions—cavorting, evidently, about the sky in an exuberant freedom of physical movement that was, by now, denied to the artist himself. The design is filled out with the most detailed comment on possible variations in colouring and painting technique.

The eminently practical purpose of this book sometimes comes as something of a shock when, after absorbing the artistic mastery of a design like the 'Eagle' of Plate 353, for example, we discover in the text the prosaic directions, 'First one delineates the entire outline in light *sumi*, then adds the yellow....' At the risk of appearing sentimental, I must admit to a feeling of sadness that such a noble print should have been published only in an ephemeral 'colouring-book'. The same design—with only a little more effort—would have made a major painting (such as Plate 347). For the Master, however, it was all the same: the *ideal* of the concept lay in the same source, and it was only a question of which medium was demanded of the moment: he was all his life a commercial artist and proud of it. Furthermore, he was here able to address posterity in a manner far more likely to survive than could be the case with a single, impressive painting for a rich patron.

On the Use of Colouring may to the casual viewer appear prosaic, but on closer acquaintance with their contents these volumes leave the impression of the Master having summoned all his resources for this final effort. Here will be found abundant details of the Hokusai Style: missing only is the secret of his energy and spirit that so dynamically gave sentient life to every line that he drew.

352 Figure of a Seated Man. Page from *On the Use of Colouring*, 1848. (See also below.)

353 Eagle on Rock. Page from *On the Use of Colouring*, 1848.

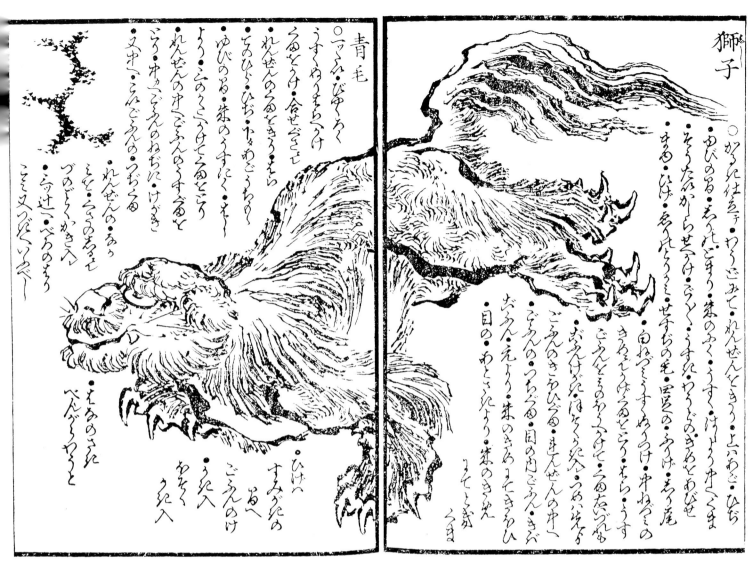

354 Playful Lion. Page from *On the Use of Colouring*, 1848.

Although his publishing commissions were indeed few, Hokusai was not entirely abandoned. Aside from the ministrations of his daughter O-Ei, he did have occasional patronage for his paintings, several of which are extant today. The problems in authenticating them have been mentioned before, and suffice it to say that some of these dated late works seem genuine and worthy of our attention.

Of a similar theme to our Plate 345 (but more evocatively executed) is the painting shown in Plate 355. Another *Three Kingdoms*—but this time, opposing—Chinese general, Ts'ao Ts'ao, is shown on a boat's prow with halberd in hand under moonlight, as crows and magpies fly over the distant hills. The scene (celebrated in a famous verse by this tyrant warlord) is that of the night before his portentous—and disastrous—attack on Red Cliff. Painted in the artist's eighty-eighth year, this late masterpiece is reminiscent of scenes from the *Mirror of Chinese/Japanese Verse* print-series (Figs. 128 ff.), and clearly shows that even at this advanced age he had lost none of his mastery either of composition or of detailed brushwork and colouring.

Among Hokusai's most strikingly unusual paintings of his last years is, curiously, a religious one. The Master was—like most of his contemporaries—a fervent believer in Buddhism, particularly that of the proselytizing Nichiren Sect (see p. 24). He portrayed St Nichiren several times: one early, formal portrait-painting, the books of Appendix, Books, Nos. 5, 175; and various scenes in the *Manga*—as well as *Fuji* and fan prints of Minobu River (site of the Sect's head temple in Fig. 88); the artist also treasured an image of the Saint in his late years (Plate 349).

In the remarkable painting of Plate 356, we view St Nichiren, his robes blown by wind and cloud, suspended in mid-air above cowering parishioners, himself unconcerned by the sudden appearance of a protective, seven-headed Dragon during the course of his sermon on the Lotus Sutra. (It will be recalled that Hokusai was born in the Year of the Dragon and that his patron-saint Myōken even rode a great Dragon; he had many reasons, apart from artistic ones, to be fond of this mythical creature.) For a religious painting—commissioned by a distant Nichiren temple—the work is extraordinarily creative: the passive Saint and the fierce, many-faced Dragon are impressive enough, but the decoratively forceful pattern of the fearful congregation lends the design a human flavour that is difficult to forget. (One notes here, incidentally, the em-

355 *Above* Warlord Ts'ao Ts'ao. Kakemono in heavy colours on silk; 1847. 45¼ × 13¼ in / 115 × 34 cm. Signed Manji, in eighty-eighth year.

356 *Right* St Nichiren in Sermon. Kakemono in colours on paper; 1847. 52 × 23¼ in / 132 × 59 cm. Signed Old Manji, in eighty-eighth year.

ployment of the artist's *Hyaku*—'One-hundred'—seal: a talisman for long life, which he had carved especially for his eighty-eighth year, in Japan a particularly auspicious birthday.)

From the Master's final, ninetieth year dates the remark-

357 *Opposite left* Tiger in Rain. Kakemono in colours on paper; 1849. 48 × 16¾ in / 122 × 42.5 cm. Signed Old Manji, in ninetieth year.

358 *Opposite right* Dragon above Mt Fuji. Kakemono in shades of *sumi* on silk. New Year, 1849. 37½ × 14 in / 95 × 36 cm. Signed Old Manji, in ninetieth year, with full date and artist's birthdate.

able 'Tiger in Rain' of Plate 357. These beasts were not native to Japan and hence became creatures of the imagination—much like dragons and *shishi*-lions. Hokusai's tiger is surprisingly true to life and one cannot but marvel at its magnificent realization at a juncture so close to the end.[2]

Though he prayed for immortality—if only to perfect his art—Hokusai may well have seen the end coming. As was customary for the New Year, he painted a theme of good omen. Dated 'Dragon-day, New Year 1849', the subject was indeed an auspicious Dragon, rising in a dark cloud above towering Mt Fuji (Plate 358). The colophon is unusually detailed, giving not only the date of painting, the artist's age and signature, but also the notation: 'Born in 1760, the Year of the Dragon'. For this artist, the style of depiction is tractable, almost meek; he is, for a change, not trying to impress an audience but only to satisfy himself. No longer does the Master pretend to be the equal of the Sacred Mountain: at best, looking closely, we see him in the aged and slightly weakened Dragon, writhing about the sky, uncertain whether to go or to remain.

3

The year 1848 brought the death of Hokusai's old collaborator, the novelist Bakin, and of Keisai Eisen, whose early works had, three decades before, offered skilled imitations of the Hokusai Style. In the same year the Master moved from his old quarter of Honjo, across the Sumida River to Asakusa—first to Tamachi, then to Umamichi and finally to a tenement on the grounds of the Henjōin temple at Matsuchiyama, far behind the great Asakusa Kannon. Here he was to remain a full year—something of a record for Hokusai, but there was good reason for this lapse in the urge to move on.

His last paintings were from the New Year season of 1849; after that he fell ill and by the early spring was permanently confined to bed (by which, of course, I mean a thin mattress laid upon the *tatami*-mats: a somewhat cold arrangement in winter-time).

Though the end was near Hokusai could be jocular, writing to a friend,

> King Emma of Hades is very old . . . and having built himself a pretty little house in the country has asked me to go and paint a kakemono for him. I shall be obliged to leave shortly and when I go, shall take my drawing materials with me. I expect to have a nice little place on a corner of Inferno Road. . . . Happy to see you if you ever pass that way . . .

A record of this juncture states: 'The Master became ill and medicines had no effect. After this the doctor said to his daughter O-Ei, "It's old age; medical art is of no avail." Hokusai's pupils and friends gathered, and watched over him without fail.'

On his deathbed Hokusai is said to have pleaded once again for more time to prove himself: 'If Heaven will grant me but ten more years of life', and after a pause to gain his breath he sighed, 'with even five more years . . . I could become a true artist.' Man has, indeed, many reasons for not wanting to die; but for any dedicated person the dread

is that he will go before he has realized his full potential. Hokusai's thoughts as he was about to close those keen eyes forever were not on the hereafter, but very much on the present world.

It was the practice of Japanese of literary bent to write a *jisei* or 'farewell verse' on their deathbeds; and some ageing poetasters probably worried about its composition long before the time came. Hokusai's verse was characteristically playful and unsuited to the solemn occasion.

Hitodama de / yuku kisanji ya / natsu no hara

Though doubtless only as a ghost,
yet evenings spritely will I tread:
the Summer Moor!

The Master died on the eighteenth day of the Fourth Month, 10 May 1849 in the Western calendar. O-Ei dispatched notices and the funeral was held the very next day, with contributions from pupils and old friends. The record continues,

> The coffin was plain enough, but in the funeral procession there were to be seen fine samurai as well as commoners, one hundred in all. The denizens of this run-down quarter had never in their lives seen a plebeian funeral attended by samurai in full regalia, and were beside themselves with envy.

4

Of Hokusai's personal habits we have only occasional glimpses. Accustomed to hard work, he rose early and continued painting until well after dark. This was the customary regimen of his long, productive career. Throughout his adult life he took hardly a day of rest, and his wants were frugal: a modicum of alcohol (he had a dislike of smoking and even of mosquito-repellent fumes), consumption only of the lower grades of tea, a love of *Daifuku-mochi* rice-cakes, and of a bowl of noodle-soup before retiring for the night.

With a lifetime of hard work, and always a current roster of dozens of pupils, one may well wonder why Hokusai found himself so often destitute. In the first place, as we have seen, the ukiyo-e commercial artist was generally ill-paid, depending on nominal remuneration which might or might not be supplemented if publications sold well. And even the taking of pupils involved no standard emolument; nor would the Master stoop to fixing 'tuition rates'. But a more basic reason for the artist's difficulties lay in his own lack of concern with financial matters, which was probably shared by his family members—wives in earlier times, daughter in the later years. Thus in periods of relative prosperity, his income was all spent; in other times the Master suffered silently. This was, after all, the ingrained philosophy of the hedonistic, native Edoite.[3]

If he felt insulted or even slighted the Master could be irascible: when the Kabuki-actor Baikō III came to request a painting (of a ghost—to commemorate a famous stage-role), this celebrated female impersonator found Hokusai's lodgings too untidy and had a rug brought from his palanquin to spread on the floor, only to be thrown out by the indignant artist. On another occasion an order for a set of screens from the exalted Daimyō of distant Tsugaru some-how offended the Master and was forthwith rejected—though the samurai-messenger had every right to cut down a cheeky commoner on the spot.

In the absence of more detailed, contemporary accounts of Hokusai's character and personality we must, to some degree, resort to conjecture. As we have noted, and as the artist himself confided to a visitor the year before his death, he had, during the seventy years of his adult life, moved house some 93 times: occasionally, only staying in one place a month or two. Moving itself is generally a troublesome task for most householders; one may, at the least, surmise here Hokusai's constant dissatisfaction with his surroundings, and with his current position, whether artistic or geographical; and as well, the burden that such habits must have represented for his family.

So far as the wilderness of *noms d'artiste* goes, we are happy to accept—even applaud—the artist's early change on leaving the Katsukawa School after fifteen years. But what is one to say of the series of name-changes (bewildering even to specialists) that bestrew the path of ukiyo-e studies in the ensuing years—a total of two dozen serious pen-names, plus several more temporary. One can only conclude that the artist was basically unsettled, that he insatiably craved variety, that he was self-centred almost to the point of mania, believing that every mutation of style required a new name to celebrate it. And in the same vein, he was quite oblivious to the practical requirements of a commercial artist: a standard style, an established name and atelier.

Hokusai was convinced that his own artistic styles were sufficiently unique to be readily recognizable whatever the signature; and that the world would follow all his caprices and beat a path to his door regardless of the obstacles that he set up. To some degree he was right. Despite his reputation for personal eccentricity he was known as a reliable commercial artist, always doing a professional job promptly and at about the going rates (Bakin sometimes complained of his illustrator's high fees—but this was surely a result of the Master's conviction of the superior quality of his work, and not from any desire for money itself). Yet at the same time, his quirks and mutations could not but prove a disadvantage in the daily market-place of art-commissions—and the social intercourse that this often involved. But this is not to deny an artist the right to his own personality, however troublesome it may have seemed to his associates and family. Just as 'The style is the man himself', so is the personality the style. To remove Hokusai's craggy character from his work would reduce it to bland, jejune eccentricity; and in the end we must accept it as part and parcel of the art itself. In all this, Hokusai represented a kind of epitome of his times: a restless age of political, social and economic uncertainty, in which the Master's eccentricities were surely better understood and condoned than they would have been in any age before or after.

For Hokusai, change and experiment were the essence of art, as of life: self-satisfaction and complacency, the greatest enemies. One of his lesser pseudonyms expresses this feeling perfectly: *Fusenkyo*—literally, 'remain unsullied';

but also, 'never settle down'. It might be said that variety and pride were the spice of Hokusai's life and work, the fountainhead of his creativity. Possessed of near-barbaric energy and passionate nerves, he was not—unlike his late-contemporary Hiroshige—given to weakening of style with old age. His was an independent, unbridled, even brash personality, forever seeking friendship and approval, yet ever alone.

Hokusai had never sought wealth nor ever managed to acquire it: that was the stuff of lucky tradesmen. Primarily, he required an outlet for his art; and that, largely, he achieved—as well as no little acclaim during his lifetime, although neither the fame nor the fortune was as great as the artist might have wished. Yet in spite of the manifest problems of his life there is no sign of cynicism or bitter satire in Hokusai's work, or even of disappointment or dejection. Once he took brush in hand he became instantly the master of a special universe, quite divorced from humdrum daily activity. The artistic figures constantly teeming in his mind, forever demanding expression, constituted, quite simply, his world. If one had to summarize Hokusai's art in a phrase, I suppose it might be: optimistic humanity illumined by design.

We have detailed something of Hokusai's popular reception during his lifetime: the limited and somewhat specialized acclaim of his early to middle years, the more widespread fame of his 50s and 60s, and its peaking in his 70s with the *Fuji* prints. But what of the more critical assessment of the artist by his social superiors of the upper classes, both in his own time and in the following generation? This point is well expressed in J. Hillier's perceptive, and still eminently readable, *Hokusai* of 1955.

> 'That classic perfection of touch,' wrote Morrison [*The Painters of Japan*, 1911], 'the glory of the ancient painters of China and Japan, that lofty quality which the European eye recognizes so slowly, and commonly not at all—this final perfection was not Hokusai's.' But this is as unreasonable as a complaint that Turner and Constable lack the touch of Titian or Rubens.

Hokusai is Hokusai and we can only study and enjoy, not re-create or improve him. I have purposely avoided any temptation here to glorify the Master for his influence on Occidental art—which seems to me rather irrelevant to the artist himself—but it is worth noting that it was this very plebeian, almost rustic quality that was to form one of the idealized images of Western *Japonisme*. As Van Gogh wrote to his brother from Arles in 1888, 'Here my life will become more and more like a Japanese painter's, living close to nature like a petty tradesman.' And later '. . . . One's sight changes; you see things with an eye more Japanese, you feel colour differently. The Japanese draw quickly, very quickly, like a lightning flash, because their nerves are finer, their feeling simpler.'

Even in this day and age there is still a certain degree of class consciousness in art-appreciation. Thus a collector or curator might, having spent a huge sum of money on a painting or print, prefer to speak of his acquisition as the work of a 'samurai court-artist' rather than as that of a former fishmonger (as was the case with Hokusai's major pupil Hokkei)—or, of the illegitimate son of a mirror-grinder (as was likely the case with Hokusai). But in art how much does caste or class really matter? To be sure, an artist of (or even for) the nobility will probably be the master of a refined—and very traditional—style. But most often he will by the same token be lacking in originality, vigour, genius—and the courage to experiment: all the qualities that we value most in an artist today.

In the *Hundred Views of Fuji*, there is a rather poignant scene which I have not dwelt on earlier (Plate 359). It is not, in truth, one of the most successful landscapes of Hokusai's great book—the placement of pine-tree and shrine can hardly be called adroit—but here it is the subject that compels us. Looking closely, we find an eminent artist, two brushes in his right hand, seated on a cushion placed upon the grass, eagerly sketching the Sacred Mountain, and accompanied by obsequious attendants: a porter at left unpacks the artist's gear, as a pupil opens a parcel and an attendant warms saké in a kettle at right. An idyllic scene and the immediate suspicion arises, is this not a self-portrait of Hokusai himself? Earlier and more romantic critics have in fact always assumed this to be the case. My own reaction is more complex: a self-portrait? yes and no. One can, indeed, imagine the Master, now ensconced in his frugal and unkempt Edo tenement, attended only by his irascible daughter, deliciously savouring the imagery of such honour and glory, which, in this life at least, was to find fruition only in his dreams. But perhaps Hokusai rather saw himself in that gaunt white heron perched on a pole at upper right, surveying the fine landscape in splendid loneliness.

Nowadays we tend to think of education as implying schooling. The words are not synonymous, however, and Hokusai was one of those rare individuals to whom—like Shakespeare—life itself was the greatest educator. From his youth he learned trades—bookselling, woodblock-carving—as well as mastering Japanese and Chinese prose; next he apprenticed himself to a series of artistic masters, who successively stimulated his talents but did not really satisfy his thirst for ideal technique and knowledge. And, while producing series after series of commercial prints, *surimono* and books, he still continued to study. From his late 30s there was no one left to teach him in Japan, so he turned first to the rare imported European engravings, ingeniously adapting Western technique to native themes; and after that, to the great source of Far Eastern civilization, China, which was to provide one dominant element of his later style. With his late 40s he was to find that for further inspiration he had no choice but to look further into his own subconscious; and it is from this period that, it might be said, the real Hokusai first emerges.

He was not of course the only major Japanese painter of the time; but after Utamaro's death in 1806, Hokusai had no equal in the ukiyo-e ranks. And of the more traditional schools, such artists as Tani Bunchō, Gyokudō, Goshun, Hōitsu were really in a world apart, one which Hokusai had studied for a time but found too far removed from everyday life to satisfy him for long. As any artist (or writer) knows, it is work itself which is the greatest teacher.

Thus Hokusai had no compunction about working continuously, and he gladly took on each and every commission that came his way: not only the more glamorous prints and paintings, but also literary greeting-cards, pictorial-maps, advertisements, and a vast variety of books—the illustrations ranging from genre scenes and shunga to cookbooks and novels—plus a mass of hand-books for all manner of artists and artisans. And he continued to study until the day he died, ever dissatisfied with his own manifestly magnificent achievements.

There had long been a tradition in the Far East of the artist—and writer/poet—seeking a higher reality than the common world, an ideal of which one strove to evoke the essentials, the essence, in one's work: landscapes of the mind. While this concept remained one of the keys to Hokusai's composition and to his general approach, he was different from his predecessors in failing to remain satisfied with this idealized universe, but insisting on a constant return to the actual, everyday world of commonplace humanity. Furthermore, in his restless curiosity he conceived of this world as volatile and inconstant, ever moving—in a perpetual state of flux. As in a kaleidoscope, no one moment could ever be truly 'decisive': only by consistently concentrated effort and activity could the artist hope to record enough such moments to, in the end, comprise a valid picture of the universe. In this sense, an evaluation of Hokusai must involve not single masterpieces but many. Despite his own expressed striving for 'a perfect line, a perfect dot', in effect he viewed the world as an ever-expanding succession of images that even an artistic life of seventy years was not sufficient to capture in full.

Unlike the case in much of Western art, Japanese painters tended to take extreme pride in their artistic lineage; and the standard of judgement was how well one preserved one's tradition, not how widely one deviated from it. Hokusai was brought up in such a tradition—indeed, as we have seen, he mastered several artistic lineages. But he was never happy to rest on these laurels; in the end, he could never be true to any tradition other than that which he had fashioned himself.

Hokusai seems to have possessed a peculiar genius, a near-demonic passion, for identifying himself not only with Nature, but also with inanimate objects—waves, clouds, mountains and even rocks—which become, through his magic brush, sentiently alive. Eminently an artist of *instinct*, he literally seizes his subjects and moulds them into his own vital and dynamic image. In this re-creation of Nature in his own likeness Hokusai was quintessentially Japanese: a race most lyrically in love with Nature—yet a Nature transformed inexorably by man's art, whether in *bonsai, bonkei, ikebana, netsuke* or colour-prints. Perhaps paradoxically, Hokusai's approach is at the same time an intellectualized one, requiring some concentrated thought to appreciate fully; likewise, his use of colouring is more symbolic or decorative than a medium for the evocation of mood. In all these facets he contrasts strongly with the gentle, lyrical and sentimentally Romantic Hiroshige, whose more natural—and less tiring—manner appealed more to plebeian audiences in the final decades of the Edo Period.

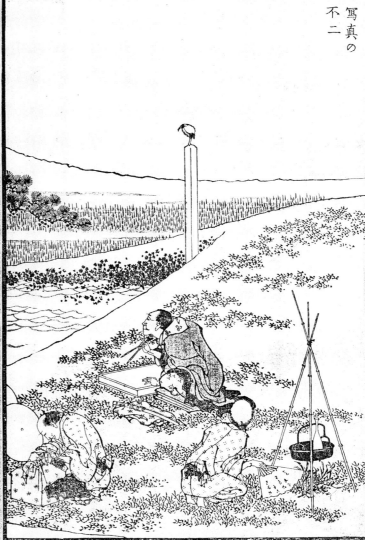

寫真の不二

359 Eminent artist sketching Mt Fuji. Illustration from *One Hundred Views of Fuji*, Series II, 1835.

Although Hokusai knew nothing of Western philosophy, for this artist—by pure instinct—man was the measure of all things: he dealt with that most universal of values, the common currency of humanity. Even in his more ethereal landscapes there is always the smell of mankind and on closer examination we invariably discover him to be re-creating Nature in his own craggy and quirkish, intensely human image.

Hokusai was, like most dedicated, possessed artists, passionately concerned with his 'image' and with the continuance of his hard-won style through the work of pupils. These were the spurs that led him to the extravagant public exhibitions of Jumbo Painting, to the expenditure of great effort on the printed 'sketchbooks for artists', and that impelled him to take on each and every assignment. Yet strangely enough, overwork did not (as was the case with Hiroshige) result in hack-work but rather led to an expansion of the Master's consciousness and creative powers. Goaded on by such vain yet unworldly ambitions, he was forever seeking goals that seemed to move further away with each effort, like ever-receding stars in the night.

Hokusai was so sure of his own powers, and mission, that in his eighty-seventh year he wrote to an Osaka publisher, 'If you hear rumours that the Old Man has died before the age of one hundred, don't give them credence.' And as we have seen, in his late years he even employed an art-seal with the character *Hyaku*—'One Hundred'. As he wrote in his last important book, *On the Use of Colouring* (1848): 'From my ninetieth year I shall again change my style and at the age of one hundred I shall revolutionize the art world. . . .' There have surely been greater braggarts in the world of art than Hokusai, but few who have so nearly matched their boasts.

From the strength and quality of his late paintings it will be clear that the artist in Hokusai was by no means burnt out: he was simply lacking the wide and responsive audience that he had enjoyed during his first six decades. But what could the Master have achieved further had he lived, as he so fervently desired, to one hundred or more? We cannot know, but most likely his output would have resembled that of his final decade: slightly old-fashioned yet vividly conceived paintings that transcend the decadent age in which he spent his final years; scenes of ethereal landscape and mythical creatures—scenes that had been pent-up in his mind's eye ever since childhood, only waiting to be conjured up and re-created in still another display of verve and vigour far beyond his years. Hokusai did indeed arouse the awe of his contemporaries, but for his amazing longevity. That final artistic recognition that he so craved was long in coming: and when it did come, it was to be in yet another hemisphere—a continent of strangers speaking alien tongues, sometimes praising him for sterling qualities that even he knew not.

Hokusai had become a legend in his own lifetime—a legend quite divorced from the gaunt old man, stubborn and lonely, eking out his final years in the company of his equally headstrong, ageing daughter. When he died it was as though a lone, towering cryptomeria had fallen in the forest of Japanese art. Other, lesser masters may have attempted to fill the gaping space, but in vain. And within another generation Japan itself was to begin to lose its roots, to become something quite different from that Floating World that has been described in these pages.

It is worth repeating yet again that ukiyo-e was an essentially commercial art, its existence dependent on sales rather than on patronage. Publishers did not widely publicize themselves, partly through fear of government regulation, but they did tend to develop a 'star-system', even though the artists were not under formal contract to any one house. The ukiyo-e masters themselves had good opportunity for self-publicity, although only a few of the more ambitious took advantage of this. (The early artist Okumura Masanobu was fond of pointing out his print innovations at the head of his signatures; Utamaro occasionally complained in his prints of imitators, adding to his signature 'The Real Thing'; and the artist-novelist Kyōden sometimes included publicity for his tobacconist-shop.)

But it was Hokusai who carried this self-advertisement to its extreme in Japanese art: he might deprecate his own earlier work, but he was none the less convinced that it was better than anyone else's. Such shades of megalomania are common, possibly even necessary, in dedicated geniuses; and, indeed, a self-effacing talent in any field is liable to get lost in the crowd unless it has powerful patrons or sponsors. The public tends to be fascinated by strength of personality in an artist, who may sometimes find himself transmogrified into a showman, to the deterioration of his art. Hokusai's publicity campaigns occurred, however, in his middle years, when his style and character were well formed; and the stimulus of artistic pageantry, admiring public and idolizing pupils does not seem to have been a deterrent to his continued, further development. Usually, of course, the self-publicizing artist is forgotten with his retirement or death, to be revived some decades later if his intrinsic merit so warrants. With the Japanese system of artistic schools and publications, Hokusai could hardly be forgotten, for many of his hundreds of pupils lived on into the following generation; and his published guidebooks for artists formed the most voluminous body of work available on any genre of Japanese art.

And just at the time that Hokusai should have been forgotten, the 1870s, when ukiyo-e and native traditions in general were being abandoned in favour of Occidental art techniques and photography, he was suddenly rediscovered in an unexpected place: by the artists and connoisseurs of Europe and America. By the turn of the century, native collectors, scholars and critics had also reclaimed Hokusai, partly from that characteristic Japanese 'complex' to emulate and copy foreign trends, but also from the intrinsic interest of his art and personality.

This 'Hokusai Boom' has continued in modern Japan, though interrupted by the militaristic years when ukiyo-e in general was condemned as 'decadent'; and curtailed by the economic woes of the post-war decade. But with the 1960s the enthusiasm for Hokusai was renewed again: including not only scholarly studies (always fragmentary in nature, for the artist is really too big for a 'definitive' work), but also novels, plays and films on the theme of his life. There was increasing recognition as well of his importance as a creative graphic-designer, with consequent influence on modern artists, both studio and commercial.

How can one really judge an artist's stature? Even for ukiyo-e I should be hard-pressed to rank the top masters. There are artists—for example Sugimura, Bunchō, Chōki, even Sharaku—who produced great prints but whose *oeuvre* is most uneven; other artists—Moronobu, Masanobu, Harunobu, Kiyonaga, Utamaro, Hiroshige—are equally great masters: but only Hokusai remains firmly embedded in the public consciousness.

To the critic who has studied each of the dozens of major painters, print- and book-artists of Japan since the eleventh century, the current idolization of Hokusai may seem a trifle exaggerated. Is he really on a level with Sesshū, Eitoku, Moronobu, Kōrin, Buson, Taiga, Ōkyo, Utamaro and Tessai, for example? This is a moot and endlessly debatable point, and a similar comparison with the master painters of Europe or continental Asia would prove equally inconclusive.

What can be stated is that Hokusai was, as he himself claimed, an artistic genius of the first water, worthy to rank with the top dozen artists of any other nation in any period. He worked in such disparate forms and media that it would not, frankly, occur to me to try to compare him with, for example, Leonardo or Rembrandt; but others—better qualified—have done so and, in the end, such comparisons may even be stimulating in intellectual terms, forcing us to ask: What is the essence of great art, of great artists?[4]

I am not myself given to philosophic abstractions, but can none the less envisage that at a certain level of connoisseurship a critic might indeed grasp an abstract essence of quality that transcends nations and even artistic media. Like Hokusai, I look forward to that happy day when 'each dot, each line shall surely possess a life of its own'.

Hokusai's production was extravagant in more than one respect. During his lifetime he painted well over thirty thousand designs, an average of at least one work for every day of his long artistic life. That favourite pen-name of his later years, 'Old Man Mad with Painting', typifies his nature: he seems quite literally to have devoted his life to art.

Anyone examining this artist's total *oeuvre* may well receive an impression of over-abundant production, of indiscriminate energy and too little selectivity. The difficult task of the critic, then, is to be discriminating where Hokusai was not and to attempt to assess the cream of his work rather than its totality, which despite its high level of draughtsmanship and variety, tends to obscure rather than illumine the Master's undoubted genius. His primary greatness obviously lies in the rare figure-prints, illustrations and paintings of his middle years and in the *Fuji* landscapes of the eighth decade of his life. Judging from these alone, Hokusai stands out as a master of two unique styles: either is sufficient to place him in the first rank of ukiyo-e artists.

Whether one can forgive Hokusai his lack of discrimination is another matter; the best Japanese critics long relegated him to secondary rank for this fault and have only changed their views under the influence of foreign opinion. The Master's work is so full of humanity as almost to obscure the true quality of his artistic talent. One has the strong feeling that he would not understand why we call certain of his works marvellous creations of beauty and others simply products of competent draughtsmanship. It was as though, indeed, his art had become indistinguishable from life itself.

Commonplace humanity is the essential element of Hokusai's theme, but design is the keystone of his artistry. His human figures may sometimes distract from the total effect, but his sense of proportion never fails. It is this, coupled with his bold visions of nature, that has made him the favourite of modern artists and amateurs alike.

It is only fitting that the most striking individual figure in the Ukiyo-e School should have been almost the last and that Hokusai, who epitomized the total range of Far Eastern art and combined with it all he could learn of Western painting and prints, should have been the major figure in the introduction of Japanese art to the Occidental world. To his own countrymen Hokusai seemed only a prodigious eccentric, but to Westerners of the late nineteenth century he appeared as an overpowering genius. Perhaps he was both. In any case Hokusai was the first Japanese artist to combine the two worlds successfully into an artistic whole: he formed the necessary bridge between Eastern and Western tastes. It is a pity that this goal was never again attained by any artist of equal genius.

The importance of an artist lies not only in the sum of his extant works but also in the abstract quality of his vision: the degree to which he sees the world with original, fresh eyes, how much he shows us things in a way that we should never have thought of before. This concept is expressed in homely, concrete terms in a haiku-verse by the early modern novelist Kafū Nagai:

Mono-hoshi ni / Fuji ya ogamu / Hokusai-ki

Through the laundry-poles
Mt Fuji! Homage on
Hokusai's anniversary

There are, quite probably, greater painters in Japanese art than Hokusai. He compels us, however, with some strange force stronger than simple art. We sense in this master, above all, an impassioned curiosity, a lust and respect for life—both his own and that of his subjects. As Hokusai himself wrote in his final manual for artists, 'Learning this, discerning that, if one cannot express the difference between the quick and the dead, one should not paint.' It is through being so intensely personal that he becomes, at the same time, so eminently universal.

NOTES

1 *Susanoō and the Vanquished Demons* is reproduced *below*.
2 Supposedly the first real tiger was imported for a Ryōgoku circus-sideshow in 1860 (a decade after Hokusai's death)—and the beast is celebrated in several Yokohama Prints of that year. The matter is complicated by the fact that the Japanese customarily confused tigers and leopards, assuming the latter to represent the female of the same species. (From early times, pictorial representations of the tiger were believed to ward off smallpox and cholera.)
3 There are anecdotes that Hokusai simply disdained money—handing over envelopes of painting-fees to tradesmen without even examining them.
4 I refer in the above first to that remarkable Amsterdam exhibition of 1951, 'Rembrandt, Hokusai, Van Gogh', which was, logically enough, confined to the *drawings* of these masters. (To exhibit oil-paintings and kakemono side-by-side would be about like comparing eagle and falcon—as to which is the 'finer bird'.) Secondly I refer to an interesting correspondence with the eminent Dutch scholar L. H. van der Tweel, who wrote to me (19 September 1983) of this exhibit and of his own friend and mentor, the great art-scholar M. M. van Dantzig: 'It may interest you that Van Dantzig once told me about an exhibition "Rembrandt, Hokusai, Van Gogh"; that to his own astonishment the *quality* of the works was in the same order. Actually this is why a Japanese artist and Leonardo may be (but need not be) "brothers under the skin...."'

Susanoō and the Vanquished Demons. Large *ema*-panel in heavy colours on wood, 1845. 110¼ × 47¼in / 280 × 120 cm. Signed *zen*-Hokusai Manji, in eighty-sixth year. (Susanoō was the rambunctious guardian-deity of the Ushijima 'Ox shrine' at Mimeguri—for which Hokusai had done several paintings [and which formed, as well, the setting for the amorous endeavours of our Plate 218].)

Appendix
An Illustrated
Hokusai Handbook

It is hardly an exaggeration to remark that no one—not even the artist himself—has ever really studied the originals of Hokusai's complete works.

This great mass of artistic material comprises several thousand individual prints of various sizes, and over 300 different book titles (most of these including dozens of separate illustrations, for a total of many thousands of plates). In addition, the artist's original paintings and sketches must also have numbered in the tens of thousands, though most are today lost (and even of those early works that remain, there rages much controversy on problems of authenticity).

The present preliminary guide to Hokusai's published *oeuvre* follows the general plan of my 'Illustrated Dictionary of Ukiyo-e' (appended to *Images from the Floating World*, 1978), but has been greatly emended and amplified on the basis of

subsequent research. It is concerned primarily with the Hokusai prints and books (including shunga) that I have been able to examine personally over the past three and a half decades. But for the convenience of students, I have included reference to works seen only in facsimile or photographs, as well as certain items (these cited in brackets) ascribed to Hokusai by earlier cataloguers. Research on so prolific yet unexplored an artist involves almost constant discoveries. Even during the period between submission and final proofing of this book, significant new finds have been made—principally in hitherto unknown Japanese collections—and these have been included here by means of sub-numbers (a, b etc).

For a fuller understanding of this complex artist there is a pressing need for a true *catalogue raisonné* of Hokusai's vast production: prints, books,

shunga, paintings, sketches. Such a complex compendium is rather beyond the scope of the private scholar; but I am happy to report that a beginning has recently been made (though, alas, only for the relatively simple *prints*) by the Center for the Study of Japanese Woodblock Prints.

The following data represent, thus, but a modest compendium of material gathered willy-nilly over the years in the midst of other, more pressing tasks. It is presented here for the express purpose of criticism and correction by future students, who may train their supercomputers (and presumably their minds as well) on certain specific problems: while, it is hoped, retaining an overall view of that craggy Master who, somewhere, surely views our puny efforts with no small amusement.

I

Hokusai's Signatures
and Art-names

Typical Hokusai Signatures (in chronological order)

Katsu · kawa Shun · rō *ga*   Katsu Shun · rō *ga*   Shun · rō *ga*   Ka · kō *ga*   Hoku · sai *ga*

Ho · ku · sa · i *e · ga · ku* (in *kana*)   Ga · kyō · *jin* Hoku · sai · *sha*   Ga · kyō · rō · *jin* Hoku · sai   *zen · [saki · no ·]* Hoku · sai I · itsu *hitsu*   Hoku · sai *aratame* I · itsu *hitsu*

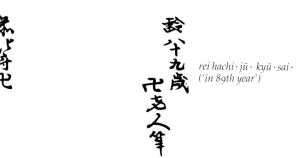

rei hachi · jū · kyū · sai
('in 89th year')

zen · [saki · no ·] Hoku · sai Manji   Manji · rō · *jin hitsu*

**Hokusai's Principal Art-names
and the approximate periods of their use**

The exact dating of Hokusai's various art-names differs with each writer on the subject, and indeed every year new discoveries are made which necessitate slight revisions in chronology. The following list, for example, incorporates at least two dozen refinements or additions when compared with that in my own 'Illustrated Dictionary of Ukiyo-e' (appended to *Images from the Floating World*, 1978), p. 255. For the first time, detailed citations have been attempted for various combinations of names: these are mainly for the purpose of amplification by future students. Most figures are based on dated books and datable prints (particularly *surimono*): both categories tended to be published at the New Year Season— early February in the Gregorian calendar—but obviously the new name was most probably adopted a month or two before that, towards the end of the preceding year. Due to the multiple readings possible with Sino-Japanese characters, notes have been included regarding certain alternatives [in brackets], with references to where these are discussed in the text proper, as well as to Plates (and a few Figs.) where the actual signatures are illustrated—these being the ultimate source in any study of Hokusai's multifarious names. (N.B. Several of these *noms d'artiste* were later used by Hokusai's disciples as well; for these, see Index, and list given under each entry in the Appendix, 'Hokusai's Pupils and Followers'.)

Tokitarō: childhood name and occasionally employed in later writing and illustration (pp. 7, 24; Plate 91, Fig. 182)
Shunrō: 1779–late 1794 (often preceded by School-name Katsukawa [sometimes abridged as 'Katsu']; see text, pp. 9, 23, Plates 2–8, 11, 13, 14, 16–18, 84
Mari/Mari-ko: c. 1780–82 (hypothetical pseudonym)
Korewasai: 1781–82
Gyobutsu: 1782
Gumbatei: 1785–94 (the name is sometimes

written with a character—[*kuni*]—read *kun/kum-*: and therefore *Kumbatei* may have been the more usual reading at the time) (pp. 14, 23)
Shishoku Gankō: c. 1788–mid 1810s (thought to be a pseudonym used by Hokusai for erotica; also used by Utamaro, and later by Eisen; see Plate 15)
Kusamura Shunrō: 1793–94 (identity with Hokusai questioned) (p. 23; Fig. 7)
Sōri [II]: late 1794–late 1798 (see text, pp. 22–24, Plates 19, 25, 27, 37 [= **III**]; in an 1840 novel by Shunsui, reference is made to this name with the alternative reading *Shūri*)
Hyakurin Sōri: 1795–98—(questioned)
Tawaraya Sōri II [III or IV]: 1796—(questioned) (pp. 22–23)
Hokusai Sōri: 1796–99 (Plates 31, 32, 34–36, 108)
Hokusai: late 1796–1819 (following death of Hokusai II c. 1826, the Master occasionally employs name 'Hokusai', without prefix 'former' (pp. 23–24, Plates 23, 51, 69, 70, 79–82, 86, 92, 104, 105, 111, 112, 115, 116, 118, 125, 126, 194, 198, 216, 256)
Kakō: 1798–1811 (pp. 24, 58, Plates 63–66, 68, 85, 91)
Fusenkyo/Fusenkyo Hokusai: 1799–1800, c. 1808– 9, 1822 (p. 111, Plate 110)
Sōri *aratame* [changed to] Hokusai: early 1799 (p. 24, Plates 21, 26, 28, 33, 75, Figs. 17, 18)
Sōri *aratame* Hokusai Tokimasa: 1799
saki-no [former] Sōri Hokusai: 1799–1800 (Plate 20)
Tokimasa [Tatsumasa/Shinsei]: 1799–1810 (pp. 24, 111, and on the various readings, see Note 4, p. 119; for *seals*, see Plates 108, 109, 114, 115)
Gakyōjin: 1799–1808 (pp. 34, 111, Plate 94)
Gakyōjin Hokusai: 1800–06 (p. 34, Plates 29, 30, 38, 39, 67, 72, 73, 106, 109, 113, 114, 129)
Tōyō Hokusai: 1800
Senzankō: 1800–
Katsushika-*rōfu* [aged peasant]: c. 1805 (Fig. 25)
Kintaisha: 1805–09
Kyūkyūshin: 1805
Gakyō-*rōjin* [elder]: 1805–06, 1834–49 (p. 83, Plates 177, 195)
Katsushika: 1806–24 (p. 6)
Katsushika Hokusai: c. 1807–c. 1822 (Plates 122,

123, 178, 193, 196–7, 199)
Katsushika-*rōfu* Gakyōjin Hokusai: c. 1808
Katsushika Hokusai Tokimasa: 1810–
Taito: 1810–20 (pp. 24, 111)
Katsushika Hokusai Taito: c. 1810–20 (Plate 124)
Katsushika Taito: c. 1810–20
Kyōrian Bainen: 1812 (p. 111)
Raishin: 1812–15 (p. 111)
Raito: 1812–15 (p. 111)
Tengudō Nettetsu: 1814 (p. 111)
Hokusai *aratame* Taito: 1814–20 (p. 111)
Hokusai *aratame* Katsushika Taito: 1814–20
zen-[*saki-no-*] Hokusai Taito: 1815–20 (Plate 120)
Hokusai *aratame* Iitsu: 1820–c. 1830 (Plate 233, Fig. 54)
Katsushika Hokusai Taito: c. 1810–20 (Plate 124)
Katsushika *zen*-Hokusai Taito: 1819
Hokusai *aratame* Iitsu Katsushika: 1820
Hokusai *aratame* Katsushika Iitsu: 1820
Katsushika Iitsu: 1820
saki-no Hokusai Iitsu: 1820
Iitsu: 1820–34 (p. 139, Plates 228, 230)
Getchi-*rōjin*: 1821–28 (p. 162, Plate 227, Fig. 52)
saki no [*zen*] Hokusai Iitsu: 1821–35 (Plates 172, 238, 251–255, 259–261, 263–271, 273, 274, 280, 281, 283, 286–289)
Fusenkyo/Fusenkyo Iitsu: 1821, 1828 (p. 111, Plate 207, Figs. 53, 55, 168)
Manji: 1821–23, 1830–49 (pp. 174, 228, Plates 241 (verse), 332–333, 347, 355–358)
Getchi-*rōjin* Iitsu: 1822–28 (Plate 227, Fig. 52)
Katsushika *no oyaji* [old man] Iitsu: 1824
Katsushika-*rōfu* Iitsu: 1824
Hokusai Iitsu: 1827 (Plate 242)
Katsushika *zen*-Hokusai Iitsu: c. late 1820s
zen-Hokusai: c. 1830–32 (Plates 240, 272, 277, 282)
Tsuchimochi [Down-to-earth] Nizaburō: 1834
zen-Hokusai Manji: c. 1834–36 (Plates 275, 276, 279, 284, 285, 291)
Hyakushō [Peasant] Hachiemon: 1834–46
Miuraya Hachiemon: 1834–46 (Plate 351)
Hachiemon: 1834–46 (Plate 346)
Gakyō-*rōjin* Manji: 1834–49 (Plates 292, 324, 343, 345)
Manji-*rōjin* [elder]: 1844–48
Fujiwara Iitsu: 1847–49

II

Hokusai's Prints and Print-series

This list of over 160 different print-series attempts to be reasonably complete so far as present scholarship permits. For the hundreds of non-serial, miscellaneous single-sheet prints, however, only a limited number of titled prints, plus general categories of special significance have been selected, including, where space allows, sample illustration. In a sense, however, the plates and figures of this book represent much of the best of Hokusai in the print field, at least; and with such a prolific and long-lived artist, a true *catalogue raisonné* would probably be of only specialized interest for his prints—though fascinating enough for original paintings and sketches (if limited to genuine items!).

The more important works are marked with an asterisk. Dates are often only approximate ('1800s' refers to the period c. 1801–9). Where not recorded, prints are unsigned. Generalized titles appear in roman rather than italic type. At the end of each of the series-entries is a number referring to M. Forrer's pioneer *Hokusai: A Guide to the Serial*

Graphics (1974), in which more detailed listings may usually be found; where significant correction of Forrer has been necessary, a note to that effect has often been included, for the reference of future students. It will be noted that several dozen of these series are cited as *F–x*— 'not in Forrer': it is my sincere hope that researchers who follow will unearth an equal number 'not in Lane'.

PRINT-SIZES: these follow traditional Japanese measurements (which are based on divisions of standard, handmade paper sizes), and are only approximate, varying with period and even publisher; for other print-terms, see Index. Where not otherwise noted, format is *horizontal*. In signatures, the suffixes *ga* / *hitsu (fude)* / *sha (utsusu)* / *zu* / *egaku* = *pinxit*, 'painted by'.

koban: small-size prints, ranging from 12 × 9 to 'large-*koban*' of 19 × 13 cm / 4¾ × 3½ to 7½ × 5 in. (Some authors, including Forrer [see his Nos. 7

and 8, for example, which are of similar size but cited, respectively, as *chūban* and *koban*], tend to confuse the larger *koban* with the smaller *chūban*; for these, I have coined the terms 'large-*koban*' and 'small-*chūban*'.
chūban: medium-size prints, 29 × 22 to 25 × 18 cm / 11½ × 8½ to 9½ × 7 in; also, small-*chūban*, 23 × 16 cm / 9 × 6¼ in; and *shikishi-ban* ('poem-cards')/*kakuban* ('square prints'), 22 × 19 to 25 × 18 cm / 8½ × 7½ to 10 × 7 in.
hosoban: medium-size narrow prints, 33 × 15 to 47 × 16 cm / 13 × 6 to 18½ × 6¼ in (often found in diptych/triptych sets).
tanzaku-ban: narrower 'poetry-slips', 25 × 12 to 39 × 8 and 33 × 15 cm / 15¼ × 3 to 10 × 4¾ and 13 × 6 in; also, larger formats, 39 × 13 and 39 × 17 cm / 15¼ × 5 and 15¼ × 6¾ in.
aiban: intermediate-size prints, 34 × 22 cm / 13¼ × 8½ in.
uchiwa-e: 'fan-prints', generally of *aiban* or large-*chūban* size, but often cut down for practical use, mounted on bamboo frame.
ōban: the standard, larger print format, 36 × 25 to

39 × 27 cm / 14 × 9¾ to 15¼ × 10½ in (sometimes found in diptych/triptych, or even more extended sets).
naga-ōban/nagaban: 'long-prints', 47 × 17 to 52 × 25 cm / 18½ × 6¾ to 20½ × 9¾ in.
long-surimono: larger gift- or announcement-prints, 19 × 50 cm / 7½ × 19½ in (usually originally issued in double this size, including verses or announcement-text).
hashira-e: 'pillar-prints', 77 × 13 cm / 30¼ × 5 in.
kakemono-e: 'scroll-prints', 76 × 23 cm / 30 × 9 in.
bai-aiban: 'double-*aiban*', 31 × 43 cm / 12 × 17 in.
bai-ōban/dai-ōban: 'double-*ōban*', 38 × 50 to 39 × 54 cm / 15 × 19½ to 15¼ × 21¼ in.
tate-banko: cut-out 'assemblage' prints (usually *ōban* size, in a series).

1 ACTOR PRINTS—*HOSOBAN*

Over 100 untitled early Hokusai actor-prints are known from the years **1780** through **1794**, in vertical *hosoban*-size, usually comprising parts of triptychs (also, a few *sumō* prints)
Signatures: Shunrō, Katsu Shunrō, Katsukawa Shunrō
(A useful summary of this category appears in Izawa, K.: 'Katsukawa Shunrō no yakusha-e kōshō', in *Ukiyo-e Art*, No. 79, 1983; the surmised roles and dating require, however, careful re-study)
▶ Plates 2, 3, 13; Figs. 1–4

Fig. 1   Fig. 2

Fig. 3 *(left)*
Fig. 4 *(above)*

2 FIGURE PRINTS—*CHŪBAN*

Over 45 untitled early Hokusai figure-prints are known for the years *c.* **1782** through **1794** in vertical *chūban*-size, depicting genre scenes, children and warriors
Signatures: Shunrō, Katsu Shunrō, Katsukawa Shunrō

3 FIGURE PRINTS—*ŌBAN*

Some 16 untitled early Hokusai figure-prints are

Fig. 5 *(left)*
Fig. 6 *(above)*

known for the years *c.* **1782** through **1794** in vertical *ōban*-size, depicting genre scenes, children, warriors, Gods of Luck
Signatures: Shunrō, Katsu Shunrō, Katsukawa Shunrō
▶ Plate 5

4 PILLAR PRINTS

At least 7 untitled early Hokusai prints are known for the years *c.* **1782** through **1794** in the vertical *hashira-e*, 'pillar-print' format, depicting figures, animals, Gods of Luck
Signatures: Shunrō, Katsu Shunrō, Katsukawa Shunrō
Publishers: 1 Chichibuya, others unknown
▶ Plate 14; Fig. 5

5 CALENDAR PRINTS

Perhaps a dozen untitled early Hokusai *surimono* (especially *egoyomi*, calendar-prints) are known for the years *c.* **1782** through **1794**, usually in *koban*-size, depicting figures, animals, still lifes
Signatures: Shunrō, Katsu Shunrō, Katsukawa Shunrō, Gummatei, Kusamura Shunrō
(N.B. This period has yet to be studied intensively, and works by Shunrō II are sometimes difficult to differentiate)
▶ Plate 18; Fig. 7

6 *NAKASU HAKKEI*
Eight Views of Nakasu

Fig. 7 (1794)

3 prints known, vertical *koban*, *c.* **1783**
Signature: Mari *ga* (possibly an early pen-name of Hokusai) [F–17]

7 *FŪRYŪ SHIKI NO TSUKI*
The Stylish Moon in the Four Seasons
2 prints known, vertical *chūban*, *c.* **1784**
Signature: (Katsukawa) Shunrō *ga* [F–1, which gives only 1 design]

8 *TŌJIBA HAKKEI*
Eight Views of Health Resorts
1 print known, vertical *chūban*, *c.* **1784**
Seal: Shunrō [F–5]

9 *MIBU KYŌGEN*
The Mibu Farces
11 prints known, vertical *chūban*, *c.* **1785**
Signature: Shunrō *ga*
Publisher: Tsutaya Jūzaburō [F–7, which gives only 7 designs, and misreads subtitles]
▶ Plate 4; Fig. 6

10 *FŪRYŪ EDO HYAKU-HINODE*
Stylish Hundred Dawns in Edo
1 print known, vertical *chūban*, *c.* **1785**
Signature: Shunrō *ga*
Publisher: Jōshūya [F–x]

11 *HANA-KURABE*
Flowers of the Seasons
1 print known, *ōban*, *c.* **1785**
Sealed: Shunrō [F–x]

11a TEA CEREMONY
1 print known, vertical *chūban*, *c.* **1785**
Signature: Shunrō *ga*
Publisher: Tsutaya Jūzaburō [F–x]

12 *FŪRYŪ UJI NO MICHI-NO-KI*
Stylish Record of the Road to Uji
2 prints known, vertical *chūban*, *c.* **1788**
Signature: Shunrō *ga* [F–8, which gives as 'Koban', with subtitle misread]

13 *HAIKAI ODAMAKI*
Haiku Series
2 prints known, vertical *chūban*, *c.* **1788**
Signature: Shunrō *ga*
Publisher: Tsutaya Jūzaburō [F–9, which cites as 'Koban']
Fig. 8

Fig. 8   Fig. 9

14 *HAIKAI SHŪITSU*
Haiku Masterpieces
3 prints known, vertical small-*chūban*, *c.* **1788**
Signature: Shunrō *ga*
Publisher: Eijudō [F–10—which cites as 'Koban', with 2 designs only]
▶ Plate 7

15 *EDO-MI-ZAKA*
Views of Edo Slopes
2 prints known, vertical *chūban*, **c. 1788**
Signature: Shunrō *ga* [F–11—which omits the title and the second design]

16 SUMŌ PRINTS—*AIBAN*
2 prints known, vertical *aiban*, *c.* **1788**
Signature: Katsu Shunrō *ga* [F–x]
▶ Plate 16; Fig. 9

Fig. 10   Fig. 11

17 RYŪKYŪ EMBASSY TO JAPAN
2 prints known, vertical *aiban*, *c.* **1788**
Signature: Shunrō *ga*
Publisher: Harimaya Shinshichi [F–x]

18 [title prefix] *UKI-E* (Perspective-print)
4 prints known, *ōban*, *c.* **1788–89**
Signature: Katsu Shunrō *ga*
Publisher: Eijudō [F–3—for No. 3 (our Fig. 13), *-ganso* should be rendered as part of the prefix-title, and 'Edo' is misread as 'Toto'; there are two versions of this print, of which the earlier, of I/ 1788, is illustrated here]
Figs. 12–14

19 *FŪRYŪ KODOMO-ASOBI GOSEKKU*
Children at Play: Five Stylish Festivals
3 prints known, vertical *ōban*, *c.* **1789**
Signature: Katsukawa Shunrō *ga* (also, sometimes 'Gumbatei' on one design, and sometimes unsigned)
Publisher: Ōmiya [F–2]

20 *TŌTO HŌGAKU*
The Four Directions of Edo
3 prints known, *chūban*, *c.* **1785**
Signature: Shunrō *ga*
Publisher: Eijudō [F–12]

21 **FŪRYŪ OTOKODATE HAKKEI*
Eight Views of Stylish Gallants
6 prints known, vertical *chūban*, *c.* **1789**
Signature: Shunrō *ga*
Publisher: Eijudō [F–13—which gives 5 prints, cites erroneously as 'Koban' and 'Surimono', and misreads the names Aragorō, Denkichi, Yazaemon]
▶ Plate 6; Figs. 10, 11

Fig. 12

Fig. 13 (I/1788)

Fig. 14

22 CHILDREN AT PLAY
5 prints known, vertical *ōban*, *c.* **1789**
Signature: Shunrō *ga*
Publisher: Eijudō [F–14]

23 [title prefix for second edition] *SHIMPAN UKI-E*
(New Perspective-prints)
4 prints known, *ōban*, *c.* **1790** (in second edition only, titles in margin)
Signatures: Shunrō *ga* / Katsu Shunrō *ga*
Publishers: Eijudō and Iwatoya [F–4, which cites only Eijudō edition]
▶ Plates 8, 17

24 *TŌSEI ASOBI*
Modern Games
1 print known, vertical *chūban*, *c.* **1790**
Signature: Shunrō *ga* [F–15]

25 *FŪRYŪ MITATE KYŌGEN*
Stylish Kyōgen Parodies
5 prints known, vertical *chūban*, *c.* **1790**
Signature: Shunrō *ga*
Publisher: Tsutaya Jūzaburō [F–x]
Fig. 15

Fig. 15   Fig. 16

26 *TAKEDA NI-JŪ-SHI-SHŌ E-ZUKUSHI SHIMPAN*
New Twenty-four Generals under Takeda
1 print, vertical *aiban*, *c.* **1792** (*kiwame* seal)
Signature: Shunrō *ga*
Publisher: Tsutaya Jūzaburō [F–6]

27 TOY PRINTS—*HOSOBAN*
Several *omocha-e* ('toy-pictures') actor-prints are known for the period *c.* **1792**, in vertical *hosoban* size, intended as cut-out playthings for children
Signature: Shunrō *ga*; *kiwame* seal
Publisher: Tsutaya Jūzaburō
▶ Plate 2; Fig. 16

28 *NIWAKA KYŌGEN*
Yoshiwara Festivals of the Twelve Months
16 prints known, vertical *chūban*, *c.* **1793** (*kiwame* seal)

Signature: Shunrō *ga*
Publisher: Tsutaya Jūzaburō [F–16, which gives only 12 designs, cites as 'Koban', and misreads several subtitles]

29 MISCELLANEOUS *SURIMONO*: SMALL
Over 100 untitled smaller *surimono* by Hokusai are known for the years *c.* **1795** through *c.* **1812**, depicting genre scenes and still lifes
Signatures: Sōri, Sōri Hokusai, Hokusai Sōri, Hokusai, Kakō, Tokimasa, Kintaisha, Gakyōjin, Kyūkyūshin, Gakyō-rōjin (plus the questioned works, probably by pupils, signed Hyakurin Sōri and Tawaraya Sōri)
▶ Plates 18, 19, 24, 196–200, 201–4, 218; Figs. 17–19, 36

30 MISCELLANEOUS *SURIMONO*: LARGE
Over 100 untitled long-*surimono* by Hokusai depicting genre scenes and still lifes are known for the years *c.* **1795** through *c.* **1812**
Signatures: Sōri, Hokusai Sōri, Hokusai, Kakō, Tokimasa, Kintaisha, Gakyōjin, Kyūkyūshin, Gakyō-rōjin (plus the questioned works, probably by pupils, signed Hyakurin Sōri, Tawaraya Sōri, Shunrō [II])
▶ Plates 25–30; Figs. 20–25

Fig. 17 (1799)

Fig. 18 (*c.* 1800)

Fig. 19 (*c.* 1810)

Fig. 20

Fig. 21

Fig. 22 Original format of 'long-*surimono*', with
announcement text on same large sheet of paper,
planned to be folded at centre for distribution

Fig. 23 (*c.* 1805)

Fig. 24

Fig. 26 Second editions of prints 33–2 and 33–3, with
titles removed. Such smaller colour-prints were often
engraved two-to-a-block, and divided after printing. In
this specimen, unusually, the full sheet is extant, uncut

Fig. 27

Fig. 28

31 THE SEVEN GODS OF LUCK
7 prints (of which 2 by Utamaro), *chūban surimono*,
c. **1797**
Signatures: Sōri *ga* and Hokusai Sōri *ga* [F–21]

32 SHIMPAN UKI-E CHŪSHINGURA
New 'Chūshingura' Perspective-pictures
11 prints, *aiban*, *c.* **1798**
Signature: Kakō *ga*
Publisher: Iseya Rihei [F–27, which cites
erroneously as *ōban*]
▶ Plate 85

**33 *EIGHT VIEWS OF STAR-CROSSED
LOVERS**
6 prints known, vertical small-*chūban*, *c.* **1798**
Signature: Kakō *ga* [F–28—which cites as 'Koban'
and omits the sixth design]
1 **O-Hatsu Tokubei: shūgetsu**
   O-Hatsu and Tokubei: the Autumn Moon
2 **Azuma Yogorō: zansetsu**
   Azuma and Yogorō: the Lingering Snow
   ▶ Plate 65; Fig. 26
3 **Date Yosaku Seki no Koman: sekishō**
   Date Yosaku and Seki no Koman: towards Dusk
   ▶ Plate 65; Fig. 26
4 **O-Some Hisamatsu: shunka**
   O-Some and Hisamatsu: the Spring Flowers
   Fig. 27
5 **O-Ume Kumenosuke: banshō**
   O-Ume and Kumenosuke: the Vesper Bell
   ▶ Plate 63
6 **O-Hana Hanshichi: rakugan**
   O-Hana and Hanshichi: Wild Geese Descending

34 *FŪRYŪ NAKUTE NANA-KUSE
Seven Stylish Foibles
2 prints known, vertical *ōban*, *c.* **1798**
Signature: Kakō *ga*
Publisher: Tsutaya Jūzaburō [F–26]
1 **Woman and Girl with Telescope**
   ▶ Plate 68
2 **Girls at Toilette**
   ▶ Plate 66

**35 TSUCHINOTO-HITSUJI: BIJIN-AWASE-
NO-UCHI**
Series: Beautiful Women of 1799

3 prints known, *koban surimono*, **I/1799**
Signature: Sōri *aratame* Hokusai *ga* [F–x]
▶ Plate 21

36 TŌSEI BIJIN-AWASE
A Comparison of Modern Beauties
9 prints known, *koban surimono*, *c.* **1799**
Signature: Sōri *aratame* Hokusai *ga* [F–22; title
misread and only 8 prints cited]

36a [SARUHASHI]
Ōtanzaku/naga-ōban sizes, *c.* **1799** (?)
(known only in early reproductions)
Signature: Sōri *aratame* Hokusai *ga* [F–x]

37 WINTER SCENES
2 prints known, *koban surimono*, *c.* **1799**
Signature: *saki-no* Sōri Hokusai *ga* [F–23]

38 FŪRYŪ YAMATO NISHIKI
Fashionable Yamato Brocades
1 print known, *koban*, *c.* **1799**
Signature: *saki-no* Sōri Hokusai *ga* [F–24]

39 SHŌFŪDAI SHICHIKEN-NO-UCHI
*Shōfūdai Club: Seven Sages [of the Bamboo
Grove]*
8 (not 7) prints, vertical *surimono*, dated **1800**
Signature: Hokusai *ga* [F–40; title **KEN** misread as
'Kenjin', only 7 designs cited, and date missed]
▶ Plate 23; Fig. 28

40 SHI-NŌ-KŌ-SHŌ
The Four Classes
Set of 4 *koban surimono*, datable to **1800**
[F–x]
▶ Plate 22

41 NOROMA KYŌGEN
Comic Interludes
4 prints known, *koban*, *c.* **1800**
Signature: Gakyōjin Hokusai *ga* [F–x]
▶ Plate 67

42 THE DEAF, THE DUMB, THE BLIND
3 prints, *koban* vertical *surimono*, *c.* **1800**
Signature: *saki-no* Sōri Hokusai *ga* [F–25; for
correction of one subject, see page 34, note 6]
▶ Plate 20

43 THE CHILDHOOD OF FIFTEEN HEROES
15 prints (?), *surimono*, *c.* **1800** [F–46]

44 EDO HAKKEI
Eight Views of Edo
8 prints, vertical *chūban*, *c.* **1801**
Publisher: Iseya Rihei [F–35—where given as
'Koban', only one design cited, and subtitle
misread]

45 TŌTO JŪNIKEI
Twelve Views of the Eastern Capital
17 prints, *koban*, *c.* **1801**
(9 prints by Hokusai, 8 by Shuntei; but

Fig. 29

Fig. 25 (*c.* 1805)

'overlapping' for 5 of the designs)
Signature: Hokusai *ga*
Publisher: Iseya Rihei [F–36—incomplete]

46 EIGHT VIEWS OF LAKE BIWA
8 prints, vertical *chūban*, c. **1801**
Signature: Hokusai *ga*
Publisher: Iseya Rihei [F–37 ?]
Fig. 29

47 ŌMI HAKKEI
Eight Views of Lake Biwa
8 prints, vertical *chūban*, c. **1801**
Signature: Hokusai *ga*
Publisher: Iseya Rihei [F–38, which cites as 'Koban' and omits publisher]

48 SHIMPAN ŌMI HAKKEI
New Eight Views of Lake Biwa
8 prints, vertical *chūban*, c. **1801**
Signature: Hokusai *ga* [F–39, which cites as 'Koban']

49 KANA-DEHON CHŪSHINGURA
The Syllabary 'Chūshingura'
1 print known, *koban*, c. **1801**
Signature: Hokusai *ga*
Publisher: Iseya Rihei [F–41]

50 KANA-DEHON CHŪSHINGURA
The Syllabary 'Chūshingura'
12 prints, vertical *chūban*, c. **1801**
Signature: Hokusai *ga*
Publisher: Iseya Rihei [F–42]
▶ Plate 86; Fig. 30

Fig. 30

Fig. 31 (Compare the similar 'Goyu' in Hiroshige's *Hōeidō Tōkaidō* series)

50a KANA-DEHON CHŪSHINGURA
The Syllabary 'Chūshingura'
12 prints, vertical *chūban*, c. **1801**
Signature: Hokusai *ga*
Publisher: Iseya Rihei [F–x]
(Note: unlike No. 50, includes subtitles)

51 THE FIFTY-THREE STATIONS OF THE TŌKAIDŌ
54 prints, *koban*, c. **1801**
Signature (on most): Hokusai *ga* [F–34]
▶ Plates 69–71; Fig. 31

51a CHŪSHINGURA
2 prints known, *koban surimono*, I/1802
Signature: Gakyōjin Hokusai *ga* [F–x]

52 KANAZAWA HAKKEI
Eight Views of Kanazawa
1 print known, large *koban surimono*, c. **1802**
Signature: Hokusai *utsusu* [F–29, which implies 2 designs but describes only one, and misreads *utsusu* in signature as 'Egaku']
▷ Lane, Richard: 'Hokusai's Exotic Decade', in the journal *Andon*, in press
▶ Plate 80

53 ORANDA GAKYŌ [EKAGAMI]: EDO HAKKEI
Eight Views of Edo: Dutch-style Mirror-pictures
8 prints, *koban*, c. **1802**

Fig. 32

Signature (on wrapper): Hokusai *sensei zu*, with title and publisher, Sōshūya [F–33 omits publisher]
▶ Plate 76; Fig. 32

54 ROKKASEN-NO-UCHI
Six Famous Poets
6 prints, vertical *koban*, c. **1802**
Signature: Hokusai *ga*
Publisher: Iseya Rihei [F–48]

55 MU-TAMAGAWA
The Six Jewelled Rivers
1 print known, *koban*, c. **1802**
Signature: Hokusai *ga* [F–49]

56 THE FOUR DIRECTIONS
2 prints known, *koban surimono*, c. **1802**
Signature: Gakyōjin Hokusai *ga* [F–82]

57 BYŌBU ISSŌ-NO-UCHI
From a Pair of Folding Screens
11 prints known, *koban surimono*, c. **1802**
Signature: Gakyōjin Hokusai *ga* [F–83]

58 NANA-KOMACHI
The Seven Komachi
3 prints known, *koban surimono*, c. **1802**
Signature: Gakyōjin Hokusai *ga* [F–84]

59 NOTED PLACES IN EDO
14 prints known, *ōban*, c. **1802**
Signature/seals: Hokusai/Gakyōjin [F–50; seal 'Ho·ku·sa·i' misread as 'Gakyōshi', and only 8 designs recorded]

60 FŪRYŪ MU-TAMAGAWA
The Stylish Six Jewelled Rivers
6 prints, *koban surimono*, c. **1802**
Signature: Hokusai *ga* [F–51]

61 MU-TAMAGAWA
The Six Jewelled Rivers
2 prints known, *koban surimono*, c. **1802**
Signature: Hokusai *ga* [F–52]

62 TAMAGAWA
Jewelled Rivers
1 print known, *koban surimono*, c. **1802**
Signature: Hokusai *ga* [F–53]

63 ZASHIKI HAKKEI
Eight Views of the Parlour
6 prints known, *koban surimono*, c. **1802**
Signature: Hokusai *ga* [F–54; title misread/mistranslated]

64 TŌKAIDŌ GOJŪSAN-TSUGI
The Fifty-three Stations of the Tōkaidō
56 prints, *koban*, c. **1802**
Signature (on 6 of the designs, for at least one edition): Hokusai *ga*

Fig. 33 Four designs from this set, in the original uncut form, showing how they were originally printed, 4 to a larger sheet of *ōban* paper

Publisher: Iseya Rihei
(Note: the numbering on prints 23 and 33 is transposed; title of final print is variant) [F–55]
Fig. 33

65 *LANDSCAPE PRINTS IN WESTERN STYLE
4 prints known, large-*koban*, c. early **1800s**
Signature: Hokusai *utsusu* [F–x]
▶ Plate 79

66 ODORI-ZUKUSHI
Series of Dances
10 prints known, *koban surimono*, **1803**
Signature: Gakyōjin Hokusai *ga* [F–86; only 4 designs cited, and lacking date]

67 SHOGEI SANJŪROKKU [NO] TSUZUKI
The Thirty-six Accomplishments
3 prints known, small-*chūban surimono*, **1803**
Signature: Gakyōjin Hokusai *ga* [F–90; misdated and title partially misread]

68 SUMIDA RIVER SURIMONO
10 prints known, small-*chūban surimono*, **1803**
(Several of the compositions reappear in Hokusai's picture-book, Fig. 185 below)
Signature: Gakyōjin Hokusai *ga* [F–91—4 designs only, lacking date]

Fig. 34

Fig. 35

Fig. 36

Fig. 38 (Compare the right, 'Kambara' design with our Plate 269)

Fig. 39

69 *LANDSCAPE PRINTS IN WESTERN STYLE
5 prints known, *aiban*, c. **1803** [F–30]
1 **Haneda Benten no zu**
Benten Shrine at Haneda
▶ Plate 77
2 **Kanagawa oki Hommoku no zu**
View of Hommoku off Kanagawa
▶ Plate 88
3 **Takinogawa Iwama no zu**
View of Iwama at Takinogawa
Fig. 34
4 **Nihon-zutsumi yori denchū wo miru no zu**
View of Paddies seen from Nihon Embankment
Fig. 35
5 **Azuma-bashi yori Sumida wo miru no zu**
The Sumida [River] seen from Azuma Bridge
▶ Plate 78

70 SHŪITSU MU-TAMAGAWA
The Splendid Six Jewelled Rivers
6 prints known, vertical *chūban*, c. **1803**
Signature: Hokusai *ga*
Publisher: Iseya Rihei [F–56; 5 prints, cited as 'Koban', and with misreadings of most subtitles]

71 EIGHT VIEWS OF EDO
2 prints known, *koban*, c. **1803**
Signature: Gakyōjin Hokusai *ga* [F–x]

72 GODAIRIKI
The Five Strengths
5 prints, *koban surimono*, c. **1803**
Signatures: Gakyōjin Hokusai *ga*/Hokusai *ga* [F–80]
Fig. 36

73 MITATE CHŪSHINGURA
'Chūshingura' Pastiche
8 prints known, *koban surimono*, c. **1803**
Signature: Gakyōjin Hokusai *ga* [F–85]

74 JŪNI-SHI-NO-UCHI
The Twelve Zodiac Symbols
4 prints known, *surimono*, c. **1803**
Signature: Gakyōjin Hokusai *ga* [F–87]

74a FAN PRINTS
3 prints known, *uchiwa-e*, c. early **1800s**
Signatures: Hokusai *egaku*, Hokusai *ga*, Hokusai *hitsu*

Publisher: Yamaguchiya [F–x]

75 RAT SERIES
4 prints known, *koban surimono*, **1804**
Signature: Gakyōjin Hokusai *ga* [F–x]

76 THE FIFTY-THREE STATIONS OF THE TŌKAIDŌ
59 prints, *koban* or *tanzaku-ban*, dated **1804**. Some scenes are known with verses added.
(The first edition includes 8 prints in the long, horizontal, *tanzaku* format, which were replaced with *koban* scenes by Hokusai's pupil Yanagawa Shigenobu in later editions. This latter version was posthumously reprinted in book form—both in colour and monochrome editions—under the title *Hokusai kyōga: Tōkaidō gojūsan-eki* (Hokusai's Cartoons: the Tōkaidō 53 Stations), with title-page subtitle *Hokusai-ō michi-no-shiori* (Old Hokusai's Guide to the Road), 2 vols., 1862, with the addition of frontispiece-map and miniature illustration by Sadahide.)
Signatures: Gakyōjin Hokusai *ga*/Hokusai *ga* [F–81—which erroneously cites 'made in collaboration with Yanagawa Shigenobu']
▶ Plates 72–73; Fig. 37

76a TŌKAIDŌ GOJŪSAN–TSUGI EZUKUSHI
The Fifty-three Stations of the Tōkaidō: A Pictorial Compendium
60 prints, square *koban*, dated **1810** (also, album-format)
(Title appears on wrapper/cover; extra designs for Akiba and Hōraiji; Nihon-bashi, Shimada and Kyōto are diptychs)
Wrapper signed: Katsushika Hokusai *ga*
Publisher: Tsuruya Kinsuke [F–x]
Fig. 38

76b TŌKAIDŌ SERIES
56 prints, vertical *koban*, c. **1804**
(No series-title; location given in mixed *gyōsho/hiragana*, within cartouche; 2 separate designs for Kyōto) [F–x]
Fig. 39

76c TŌKAIDŌ SERIES
56 prints, *koban*, c. **1804**
(No series-title; 2 designs for Kyōto)
Signature: Gakyōjin Hokusai *ga*
Publisher: Yoshinoya Tokujirō [F–x]

77 CHŪSHINGURA SERIES
2 prints known, vertical *koban*, c. **1804** [F–57]

78 SANSEKI
Three Poetic Evenings
3 prints, *koban*, c. **1804**

Fig. 37

Signature: Hokusai *ga* [F–45; title misread, cited as 'surimono', and only 2 designs noted]

79 HACHIBAN-TSUZUKI
Series of Eight
1 print known, *koban surimono*, c. **1804**
Signature: Hokusai *ga* [F–x]

80 NIJŪSHI-KŌ
Twenty-four Paragons of Filial Piety
9 prints known, *koban surimono*, c. **1804**
Signature: Gakyōjin Hokusai *ga* [F–92; 6 designs cited]

81 JIKKAN-NO-UCHI
The Ten Celestial Stems
2 prints known, *koban surimono*, c. **1804**
Signature: Gakyōjin Hokusai *ga* [F–93]

82 THE SIX JEWELLED RIVERS
6 prints, *koban*, c. **1804**
Signature: Hokusai *ga*
Publisher: Iseya Rihei [F–58]

83 FŪRYŪ EDO [TŌTO] HAKKEI
Eight Fashionable Views of Edo
8 prints, vertical *chūban*, c. **1804**
Signature: Hokusai *ga*
Publisher: Iseya Rihei
(Only one of the series is signed; very similar prints by Sekijō and Utamaro [II?] are known)
[F–59, where cited as 'Koban']

84 SAN BENTEN
The Three Benten Shrines
2 prints known, *koban surimono*, c. **1804**
Signature: Hokusai *ga* [F–x]

85 SANKYOKU
Three Musical Instruments
1 print known, *koban surimono*, c. **1804**
Signature: Gakyōjin Hokusai *ga* [F–x]

86 [title prefix] SHIMPAN UKI-E
New Perspective-prints
13 prints known, *ōban*, c. **1804**
Signatures: *eshi* Hokusai *ga*/Hokusai *ga*
Publishers: Iseya Rihei and Yamaguchiya Tōbei
[F–60—which cites only 11 designs, and misreads Mimeguri as 'Mii']

87 *LANDSCAPE PRINTS IN WESTERN STYLE
5 prints known, *chuban*, c. **1805**
Signature: Hokusai *egaku* [F–31]

1 *Takahashi no Fuji*
Fuji under High-Bridge
Fig. 40

2 *Yotsuya Jūnisō*
Jūnisō Shrine at Yotsuya
► Plate 89

3 *Kudan Ushigafuchi*
Ushigafuchi at Kudan
► Plate 92

4 *Oshiokuri hatō tsūsen no zu*
Cargo Boat passing through Waves
► Plate 81

5 *Gyōtoku shiohama yori Noboto no higata wo nozomu*
Seashore at Noboto from Gyōtoku Beach
Fig. 41

88 THE FOUR SEASONS
4 prints, *surimono*, *c.* **1805**
Signatures: Hokusai *ga*/Gakyōjin Hokusai *ga*
[F–79]

89 *HANA-AWASE*
A Comparison of Flowers
2 prints known, *surimono*, *c.* **1805**
Signature: Gakyōjin Hokusai *ga* [F–88]

Fig. 40

Fig. 41

90 *EZŌSHI-AWASE*
A Set of Picture Books
1 print known, *surimono*, *c.* **1805**
Signature: Gakyojin Hokusai *ga* [F–89]

91 *ŌMI HAKKEI*
Eight Views of Lake Biwa
1 print known, vertical *chūban*, *c.* **1805** [F–61]

92 *TENJIN* SERIES
3 prints known, *koban surimono*, *c.* **1805**
Signature: Gakyōjin Hokusai *ga* [F–x]

93 *ROKUJO SŌSHI*
Six Females Booklet
1 print known, *koban surimono*, *c.* **1805**
Signature: Gakyōjin Hokusai *ga* [F–x]

94 *GOGEN-NO-UCHI*
The Five Elements
1 print known, *surimono*, *c.* **1805**
Signature: Kyūkyūshin Hokusai *ga* [F–94]

94a *KYŌKA GOSHIKI–ZURI*
Verses in Five Colours
1 print known, large-*koban surimono*, *c.* **1805**
Signature: Hokusai *ga* [F–x]

95 THE HUNDRED POETS
100 *KYŌKA* prints, *koban*, vertical *surimono*,
c. **1805**
Signatures: Hokusai *ga*/Sōri *ga* [the pupil?]/
Kyūkyūshin Hokusai *ga* [F–68]

96 *FUJI HAKKEI ZU*
Eight Views of Mt Fuji
1 print known, *ōban*, *c.* **1805**; alternative title: *Fuji-no-mine zu* (View of Mt Fuji); note that this design may well derive from a similar *ōban uki-e* landscape by Hokusai's predecessor Toyoharu: *Tago-no-ura haru-no-Fuji* (Fuji in Spring with Tago Bay)
Signature: Katsushika Hokusai [F–95]
► Plate 93

97 *GOGAKU-NO-UCHI*
From the Five Sacred Mountains [of China]
3 prints known, *koban surimono*, datable to Spring **1806** [F–x]

98 *KANA-DEHON CHŪSHINGURA*
The Syllabary 'Chūshingura'
11 prints, *ōban*, IV **1806** (date-seal: Tiger/IV, censor's seal: *kiwame*)
Unsigned (one state allegedly bears the signature 'Gakyōjin Hokusai', but this probably refers to a set of revised Meiji reproductions featuring added subtitle and altered title-cartouche, with that signature interpolated).
Publisher: Tsuruya Kinsuke (but for second and third editions—lacking earlier date-seal—Izumiya Ichibei) [F–71, which mis-cites 'Tiger 6' seal also]
► Plates 87, 95

99 *MU-TAMAGAWA*
The Six Jewelled Rivers
1 print known, vertical *chūban*, **1806** (date seal: Tiger/XI, censor's seal: *kiwame*)
Signature: Hokusai *ga* [F–70]

100 *TŌKAIDŌ GOJŪSAN-TSUGI*
The Fifty-three Stations of the Tōkaidō
56 prints plus wrapper, vertical *chūban*, *c.* **1806**
Publisher: Iseya Rihei
Unsigned except allegedly on final scene in first issue. (Later published as a set, in album format, under the title *Tōkaidō gojūsan-tsugi: ekiro-no-suzu* [. . . Packhorse Bells])
[F–72—which omits much of the above data]
▷ *Hokusai—53 Stationen der Tōkaidō*. Nuremberg, 1978
► Plate 74; Fig. 42

101 *MITATE NIJŪSHI-KŌ*
'24 Filials' Pastiche
1 print known, vertical *chūban*, *c.* **1806**
Signature: Gakyōjin Hokusai *ga*
Publisher: Moriya Jihei [F–x]

102 *TŌTO MEISHO*
Noted Places of the Eastern Capital
12 prints known, *ōban*, *c.* **1806**
Signature: Hokusai *ga*
Publishers: Eijudō/Yamamotoya [F–73]

103 *SANGOKU YŌKO-DEN*
The Three Kingdoms Magic-Fox Legend
2 tableaux known, *ōban*, vertical *diptych*, III/**1807** (date-seal: Hare/III, censor's seal: *kiwame*)
Signature: Hokusai *ga*
Publisher: Tsuruya Kinsuke [F–74 cites publisher as Kiemon, and 'Hare 2' date, erroneously]
► Plate 198; Fig. 43

104 ACTOR PRINTS—*ŌBAN*
2 prints known, vertical *ōban*, III/**1807** (date-seal: Hare/III, censor's seal: *kiwame*) (Note: month of

Fig. 42

date-seal in Nos. 103–4 is ill-drawn, but definitely 'III')
Signature: Hokusai *ga* [F–75, which cites as 'Hare 1' and misreads actors' names Ronosuke and Sawamura]
► Plate 194

105 *MOMO-SAEZURI* PLATES
7 prints, *ōban*, *c.* **1807**
Signature: Hokusai *ga*
Publisher: Eijudō
(Single-sheet colour-prints reissued from the book *Momo-saezuri* of 1805; see Books, No. 117 [F–x]
► Plate 82

106 *EDO HAKKEI*
Eight Views of Edo
8 prints, *chūban*, *c.* XII/**1807/08** (seal on two of the prints presumably represents Twelfth Month of Bunka IV, which would run into Jan. 1808) [F–x]

107 STILL-LIFE SERIES
Number unknown, *koban surimono*, *c.* **1808**
Signature: Hokusai [F–69]

108 *SURIMONO*-STYLE *ŌBAN* LANDSCAPES
At least a dozen *ōban* landscape prints are known from the mid and late **1800s**, both titled and untitled, generally unsigned but by Hokusai; some are clearly revised versions of long-*surimono*.
► Plates 83, 94; Figs. 44–6

109 *NANA-YŪJO*
Seven Courtesans
7 prints, *koban surimono*, *c.* **1808**
Signature: Katsushika Hokusai *ga* [F–96]

Fig. 43

Fig. 44

Fig. 45

Fig. 46

Fig. 48

Fig. 49

110 SHIMPAN KUMIAGE-DŌRŌ-E: KYŌ KIYOMIZU HANAMI-NO-ZU
Newly Published Assemblage Lantern: Flower-viewing at the Kiyomizu Temple in Kyōto
2 prints, *tate-banko, ōban, c.* **1808**
Signature: Hokusai *ga*
Publisher: Maruya Bun-emon [F–67]

110a FŪRYŪ GENJI UTA-GARUTA
Stylish Genji Poem-cards
Ōban tetraptych, dated VIII/**1809**
Signature: Katsushika Hokusai *ga*
Publisher: Daikokuya (later edition: Izumiya Ichibei) [F–x]

111 SANKEI
Three Views
3 prints, *surimono, c.* **1800s**
Signature: Hokusai *ga* [F–43]

112 UNTITLED SURIMONO SET
6 prints known, *surimono, c.* **1800s**
Signature: Hokusai *ga* [F–44]

113 EIGHT VIEWS OF EDO
2 prints known, *koban, c.* **1800s**
Signature: Gakyōjin Hokusai *ga* [F–x]

113a ASUKA-YAMA
Mt Asuka
1 print known, *koban, c.* **1800s** [F–x]

114 THE SIXTY-NINE STATIONS OF THE KISO-KAIDŌ
4 prints known, *koban, c.* **1800s**
Signature: Hokusai *ga* [F–47]

114a ŌMI HAKKEI
Eight Views of Lake Biwa
8 prints, *koban, c. late* **1800s**
Signature (on 2 designs): Hokusai *ga*
Publisher: Iseya Rihei [F–x]

115 SHISUI SHUNSHO
The Four Sleepers in Spring Dawn
3 prints known, long-*surimono, c.* **1810**
Signature: Katsushika Hokusai *ga* [F–97; title misread 'Shunsei']

116 LARGE SURIMONO SERIES
12 prints known, *ōban surimono,* allegedly *c.* **1810**
Signatures: Hokusai *ga* and Katsushika Hokusai *ga* [F–98; though not so noted in Forrer, the series is probably spurious, the designs being taken from two Hokusai picture-books]

117 PUBLIC BATH-HOUSE
5 prints, *tate-banko, ōban, c.* **1810**
Signature: Hokusai *ga*
Publisher: Maruya Bun-emon [F–66, which misreads as 'Tatehonko']
(Note: see also No. 110; a half-dozen other 'assemblage-prints', on historical, legendary and genre subjects, are known by Hokusai from this period.) [F–x]
Fig. 47

Fig. 47 Reconstructed *tate-banko*

118 THE SIX POETS
6 prints, vertical *ōban, c.* **1810**
Signature: Katsushika Hokusai *ga*
Publisher: Ezakiya Kichibei [F–99]
▶ Plate 197

119 *PILLAR PRINTS
Several prints in the *hashira-e* format are known for the period *c.* **1810**
Signatures: Gakyō-rōjin Hokusai *ga*
▶ Plate 195

120 ŌMI HAKKEI: DŌBAN
Eight Views of Lake Biwa: in Copperplate
8 prints, *koban, c.* **1811**
Signature (on wrapper): Hokusai *ga*
Publisher (also on wrapper): Sōshūya
[Correct F–32, which gives much earlier date and omits publisher]
Fig. 48

121 WAKA SANJIN
The Three Gods of Poetry
3 prints, *koban,* vertical *surimono* triptych, *c.* **1812**
Signature: Hokusai *ga* [F–x]
Fig. 49

122 TOBA-E SHŪKAI
Gathering of Caricatures
12 prints known, vertical *chūban, c.* **1815**
(Title appears only within one design)
Signature: Hokusai *ga*
Publisher: Yamashiroya Tōemon [F–62 gives as Yamaguchi-ya Tōbei, and only 9 designs]

Fig. 50

Fig. 50

▶ Plate 216; Fig. 50

123 TOBA-E CARICATURES
6 prints known, vertical *chūban, c.* **1815**
Signature: Hokusai *ga*
Publisher: Iseya Rihei [F–63]

124 TOBA-E CARICATURES
84 prints known, small *chūban, c.* **1815**
Signature: Hokusai *ga*
Publisher: Iseya Rihei [F–64]
▶ Plate 217

125 *FŪRYŪ ODOKE HYAKKU*
One Hundred Fashionable Comic Verses
30 prints known, *koban*, *c.* **1815**
Signature (intermittent): Hokusai *ga*
Publishers: Iseya Rihei and Yamashiroya Tōemon
[F–65 cites as Yamaguchi-ya Tōbei, and title
misread as 'Hyakunin']

125a FAN PRINTS
1 print known (proof only), *uchiwa-e*, *c.* **1816**
Signature: *zen*-Hokusai Taito *hitsu* [F–x]

126 FISH AND SHELLFISH
15 prints known, *koban*, *c.* **1816** [F–76]
Fig. 51

Fig. 51

127 *WASHO-KURABE*
A Comparison of Texts
1 print known, *surimono chūban*, *c.* **1821**
Signature: Hokusai *ga* (but another specimen is
signed Hokkei) [F–77]

127a *JŪNI-KA-GETSU*
The Twelve Months
Wrapper for a lost series of 12 *aiban* (?) prints, *c.*
late **1810s** (?)
Signature: Katsushika Hokusai-*ō-hitsu* [F–x]
▶ p. 188, Note 1 and text fig.

128 *FŪRYŪ SUMIDA-GAWA HAKKEI*
Eight Fashionable Views of the Sumida River
2 prints known, *koban*, *c.* **1819**
Signature: Hokusai *ga* [F–78, where Mimeguri is
misread 'Mii']

129 *TŌTO GOJŪSAN-EKI*
53 Stations of Edo
Set of 53 *koban* prints, dated **1820** [F–x]

130 *MUKASHI-BANASHI: CHI-JIN-YŪ*
Legends of Wisdom, Benevolence, Courage
1 print known, *chūban surimono*, *c.* **1820**
Signature: Katsushika Iitsu *hitsu* (others of the
series are by Shuntei) [F–100]

**131 *WAKAN BUYŪ-AWASE SAMBAN
NO UCHI***
Chinese and Japanese Heroic Poems
6 prints known, *koban surimono*, *c.* **1820**
Signature: Hokusai Taitō *aratame* Katsushika Iitsu
hitsu [F–101]

132 **GENROKU-KASEN-GAI-AWASE*
Genroku Poetry Shell-Game
36 prints, vertical *chūban surimono*, **1821**
Signatures: Getchi-*rōjin* Iitsu *hitsu*/Getchi-*rōjin*
hitsu
(The traditional dating '*c.* **1828**'—F–126—is dis-
proved by the 'Snake Year' notation on one print; cf.
▷ Forrer, M. and Keyes, R.: 'Mighty Like a
Whale'—Hokusai's Illustrations for the Genroku
Poem Shells', in *A Sheaf of Japanese Papers*, The
Hague, 1979)
▶ Plate 208; Fig. 52

133 *UMA-ZUKUSHI*
Horse Series
33 prints known, *chūban surimono*, **I/1822**

Fig. 52

Fig. 53

Signature: Fusenkyo Iitsu *hitsu* [F–103, which fails
to note that some of the designs include the date]
Fig. 53

134 *SHISEI-NO-UCHI*
The Four Clans of Japan
4 prints, *chūban surimono*, *c.* **1822**
Signature: Fusenkyo Iitsu *hitsu* [F–102]

135 *HITOMANE SURU*
Imitations of People
5 prints known, *koban surimono*, **1824** (Year of the
Monkey)
Signature: Katsushika *no oyaji* Iitsu *hitsu* [F–104]

136 *SHIMPAN DAIDŌ-ZUI*
New Scenes on the Road
Set of 12 prints in wrapper, *koban*, *c.* **1825**
Publisher: Akamatsu Shōtarō (?); one print
includes names of Iseya Rihei and other
publishers; the set is cited in an advertisement of
Eijudō, as 'for *harimaze*' (mounting on boxes,
screens, etc.); text of 'Nihon-bashi' cites 'Peasant
Hokurobei [= Hokusai] of Katsushika County,
sightseeing in Edo . . .'
[F–121 gives as *surimono*, and with incorrect title
(title appears in irregular calligraphy and has
often been misread—see also e.g. *Zaigai hihō* IV,
p. 94, and Nagata, *Nempu*, p. 214)]
▶ Plate 239

137 *GOKASEN*
The Five Poets
5 prints, *chūban surimono*, *c.* mid **1820s**
Signature: Hokusai *aratame* Iitsu *hitsu* [F–105]

**138 *OSANA-ASOBI KEN SAMBAN-TSUZUKI-
NO-UCHI***
Series of Three Youthful Diversions
2 prints known, *chūban surimono*, **1823** (Year of the
Goat)
Signature: Hokusai *aratame* Iitsu *hitsu* [F–106; title
misread/mistranslated, misdated and only 1 print

Fig. 54

cited. *Ken* here refers to the children's finger-game
of *gū-choki-paa*—stone/scissors/paper]
Fig. 54

138a *TŌTO HYAKKEI*
100 Views of Edo
9 prints known, *koban*, intended as stationery
envelopes; *c.* mid **1820s**
Signature: Hokusai *aratame* Iitsu *hitsu*
Publisher: Yamaguchiya [F–x]

**139 *SARUGAKI-REN GOBAN-NO-UCHI
WAKAN E-KYŌDAI***
***Five Japanese-Chinese 'Brother Pictures' of the
Sarugaki Club***
4 prints known, *chūban surimono*, *c.* **1828**
Signature: Getchi-*rōjin* Iitsu *hitsu* [F–125; Sarugaki
misread as 'Baigaku']

139a LARGE FLOWER-AND-BIRD PRINTS
1 print known, 'Falcon and Dawn Sun', *kake-
mono-e*, *c.* **1828** (?)
Sealed: Fusenkyo
Publisher: Wakasaya [F–x]
Fig. 55

Fig. 55

139b FAN PRINTS: *KACHŌ* THEMES
1 print known, *uchiwa-e*, *c.* **1828**
Signature: Getchi-*rōjin* Iitsu *hitsu*
Publisher: Aritaya Seiemon [F–x]

140 *TANZAKU* SERIES
11 prints known, *tanzaku-ban*, *c.* **1830**
Signature: *zen*-Hokusai *ga*/*zen*-Hokusai Iitsu *hitsu*

(see also Nos. 147 and 148, which may be related, though slightly different sizes)
Publisher: Moriya Jihei [F–128—which cites 2 examples only, but see note above]
▶ Plate 240

141 *FUGAKU SANJŪ-ROKKEI
Thirty-six Views of Mt Fuji

Hokusai's most famous series, 46 prints in ōban size, c. 1830–32; many of the prints bear Eijudō and kiwame (censor's) seals on early editions
(In addition to the original 36, there are ten supplementary prints—the so-called ura-Fuji [Fuji from the Other Side]. These are known only with black key-block impressions, whereas early impressions of the first 36 designs feature outline in dark blue. This series is neither numbered nor dated. For convenience of reference, our order follows that of vol. 13 in the Shūeisha* Ukiyo-e taikei series Fugaku sanjū-rokkei [ed. T. Kobayashi, Tōkyō, 1975], in the deluxe edition of which the complete set is illustrated full size and in colour [but not always from the best impressions].)
[Note: the earliest reproduction of this series seems to be that dated 1889 in margins—lacking title-cartouches and with altered colouring, the new title being added: Zen-Hokusai Fuji Shōkei (Fine Views of Fuji by the former Hokusai).]
Signatures: Hokusai aratame Iitsu hitsu/zen-[saki no] Hokusai Iitsu hitsu/Hokusai Iitsu hitsu
[F–107; see also Lane, Richard: 'On the Dating of Hokusai's Fuji', in Andon, No. 23, 1986]
Publisher: Eijudō
▷ Anon.: Fujiyama der ewige Berg Japans. N.p., 1956
▷ Kondō, I. (adapted by Terry, C.): Hokusai's Thirty-six Views of Mount Fuji. Tōkyō, 1959; reprinted Honolulu, 1966, as The Thirty-six Views of Mount Fuji by Hokusai
▷ Narazaki, N. (adapted by Bester, J.): Hokusai— 'The Thirty-six Views of Mt Fuji'. Tōkyō, 1968
▷ Kikuchi, S. (translated by Kenny, D.): Hokusai. Ōsaka, 1970
▷ Lane, Richard: Images from the Floating World: The Japanese Print—Including an Illustrated Dictionary of Ukiyo-e. 1978. (Pp. 161–8, 260–5)
▷ Hokusai—Twelve Views of Mount Fuji. Introduction by L. Smith. London, 1981
1   Kanagawa-oki nami-ura/Under the Wave off Kanagawa
     Three boats at the foot of a great wave in the wild sea, Mt Fuji in distance
     (Note: the sky pigments are rather fugitive: the yellowish cloud-formations tend to disappear, and even the colour of the sky itself may fade somewhat—or turn to beige—on prolonged exposure to light. Note also that in late editions the blocks are partially re-engraved.)
     ▶ Plate 247
2   Gaifū kaisei/South-Wind, Clear-dawn
     Reddish-brown mountain against blue sky with cloud-strata
     (Note: the colloquial appellation for this print, Aka-Fuji, 'Red Fuji', is not necessarily a modern nickname, for this aspect of the mountain—peak red and sky as viewed at dawn from the Lake Kawaguchi region—is known locally as beni-Fuji, 'Rose Fuji'; and indeed, the earliest impressions of this print delineate the mountain in lightish sienna colouring)
     ▶ Plate 245
2a   Variant, late edition in shades of blue, showing the summit in white with cloud-strata visible only at top
     ▶ Plate 246
3   Sanka haku-u/Thunderstorm beneath the Summit
     Clouds in the distance and lightning at the foot of the dark mountain
     (Summit lines recarved in late editions)
     ▶ Plates 248, 249

Fig. 56

Fig. 57

3a   A variant, late state adds row of trees (probably from a hand other than Hokusai's) in the foreground
     ▶ Plate 250
4   Fukagawa Mannen-bashi no shita/Under Mannen Bridge at Fukagawa [Edo]
     Figures on arched bridge, cargo boat and fisherman in foreground
     Fig. 56
5   Tōto sundai/Surugadai in Edo
     Wayfarers and buildings in the foreground
     Fig. 57
6   Aoyama enza-no-matsu/The Cushion-Pine at Aoyama [Edo]
     Picnickers at lower right
     ▶ Plate 257
7   Bushū Senju/Senju in Musashi Province [Edo]
     A peasant with packhorse; two men fishing
     ▶ Plate 258
8   Bushū Tamagawa/The Tama River in Musashi Province [Edo]
     A cargo boat crossing the river; peasant leading packhorse at the near bank
     Fig. 58

Fig. 58

9   Kōshū Inume-tōge/Inume Pass in Kai Province
     Travellers and trees in the centre
     Fig. 59
10   Bishū Fujimigahara/Fujimigahara [Fuji-view Fields] in Owari Province
     In the foreground a cask-maker caulks a large tub
     Fig. 60
11   Tōto Asakusa Honganji/Honganji Temple at Asakusa in Edo

Fig. 59

Fig. 60

Fig. 61

Fig. 62

     Roof-tilers at work; a kite flying
     Fig. 61
12   Buyō Tsukuda-jima/Tsukuda Island in Musashi Province [Edo]
     Cargo and fishing boats in the foreground
     Fig. 62
13   Sōshū Shichiri-ga-hama/Shichiri-ga-hama in Sagami Province
     Enoshima in the middle background
     (Note: clouds omitted in later issues. This print and the previous Tsukuda-jima design are mentioned in the publisher's advertisement of 1831—the only specific evidence of publication date for the series)
     Fig. 63
14   Sōshū Umezawa-zai/Umezawa Hamlet-fields in Sagami Province
     Cranes in the foreground and in the air
     (Block-variations in cloud at centre; the last character of the title is sometimes assumed to be a misprint for shō, 'Manor', but zai is probably correct, being an early term for

Fig. 63

Fig. 66

(Post at left recarved in late editions)
Fig. 70

24 ***Koishikawa yuki no ashita***/*Snowy Morn at Koishikawa*
Teahouse on left, ravens in the sky
Fig. 71

25 ***Shimo-Meguro***/*Lower Meguro*
Rustic scene, two falconers on lower right
Fig. 72

26 ***Onden no suisha***/*Waterwheel at Onden*
Peasants working in the foreground
(As the characters indicate, *Onden* originally meant 'Hidden Paddy'—either worked by exiles, or worked surreptitiously without paying taxes)
Fig. 73

27 ***Sōshū Enoshima***/*Enoshima in Sagami Province*

Fig. 64

Fig. 67

Fig. 70

'rustic village' or 'agricultural area')
Fig. 64

15 ***Kōshū Kajikazawa***/*Kajikazawa in Kai Province*
A fisherman and his little helper on a promontory
(Early impressions are generally in shades of blue; later issues sometimes add brick red, orange, yellow)
▶ Plates 252, 253

16 ***Kōshū Mishima-goe***/*Mishima Pass in Kai Province*
Three travellers try to encircle a huge cryptomeria tree
(The version in blue and green is probably earlier than that in blue and brown)
▶ Plate 254

17 ***Shinshū Suwa-ko***/*Lake Suwa in Shinano Province*
Trees and a small shrine on promontory in the foreground
Fig. 65

Fig. 68

Fig. 71

Fig. 65

18 ***Sunshū Ejiri***/*Ejiri in Suruga Province*
Travellers struggle with the wind under bare trees
Fig. 66

19 ***Tōtōmi sanchū***/*In the Tōtōmi Mountains*
Lumbermen at work in the foreground
(There is also a variant, later state with lumber, foreground and horizon all heavily coloured)
Fig. 67

20 ***Jōshū Ushibori***/*Ushibori in Hitachi Province*
A large, inhabited junk moored in the

Fig. 69

foreground
Fig. 68

21 ***Edo Suruga-chō Mitsui-mise ryakuzu***/*Suruga-chō Street in Edo; the Mitsui Shop, Abridged View*
Roof-tilers, and flying kites
(For an earlier Hokusai version see Plate 76)
Fig. 69

22 ***Ommayagashi yori Ryōgoku-bashi no sekiyō wo miru***/*Viewing Sunset over Ryōgoku Bridge from the Ommaya Embankment*
A crowded ferryboat in the foreground on the Sumida River
(Regarding the title, see Note 2, p. 199)
▶ Plate 251

23 ***Gohyaku-rakanji Sazaidō***/*Turban-shell Tower, Five-Hundred-Rakan Temple*
Pilgrims on the tower balcony

Fig. 72

Fig. 73

Fig. 74

Fig. 78

Fig. 82

Fig. 75

Fig. 79

Fig. 83

A distant view, showing inns on the island
Fig. 74
28 **_Tōkaidō Ejiri Tago-no-ura ryakuzu_**/_Tago Bay near Ejiri on the Tōkaidō, Abridged View_
Two junks in the foreground
Fig. 75
29 **_Tōkaidō Yoshida_**/_Yoshida on the Tōkaidō_
Travellers in the foyer of the 'Fuji-view Teahouse'
Fig. 76
30 **_Kazusa no kairo_**/_At Sea off Kazusa_
Two large junks in the foreground
Fig. 77
31 **_Edo Nihon-bashi_**/_Nihon-bashi [Bridge], Edo_
Crowds crossing the bridge, storehouses along the canal, Edo Castle at rear
Fig. 78

Fig. 80

Fig. 76

Fig. 77

Fig. 81

32 **_Sumida-gawa Sekiya no sato_**/_Sekiya Village on the Sumida River_
Three express riders depart Edo at dawn
Fig. 79
33 **_Noboto-ura_**/_The Bay of Noboto [Shimōsa Province]_
Shellfish-gatherers in the foreground; two _torii_ in the water
Fig. 80
34 **_Sōshū Hakone no kosui_**/_Hakone Lake in Sagami Province_
Placid lake with trees and hills
Fig. 81
35 **_Kōshū Misaka suimen_**/_Reflection in Lake Misaka, Kai Province_
(The reflection is shown off-centre, doubtless for variety of composition)
Fig. 82

36 **_Tōkaidō Hodogaya_**/_Hodogaya on the Tōkaidō_
Travellers seen before a row of pines
▶ Plate 255
37 **_Honjo Tatekawa_**/_Tatekawa in Honjo_
The timber yard at Tatekawa [Canal] in Edo.
(On the improvised gate at lower right appear the publisher's name and address and the note 'New Edition, _36 Fuji_ Completed', probably indicating that this represents the first of the supplementary series of 10 prints)
A similar lumberyard scene will be found in Hokusai's _yomi-hon_ of 1808, _Nanka no yume_.
Fig. 83
38 **_Senju kagai yori chōbō no Fuji_**/_Fuji seen from the Senju Pleasure Quarter_
A _daimyō_'s procession and a teashop
Fig. 84

Fig. 84

Fig. 85

Fig. 86

Fig. 87

Fig. 88

Fig. 89

39 **Tōkaidō Shinagawa Goten-yama no Fuji**/*Fuji from Goten-yama, at Shinagawa on the Tōkaidō*
Sightseers and revellers amid cherry trees
Fig. 85

40 **Sōshū Nakahara**/*Nakahara in Sagami Province*
Peasants and travellers at stream with bridge
Fig. 86

41 **Kōshū Isawa no akatsuki**/*Dawn at Isawa in Kai Province*
A rustic village, travellers departing at dawn
Fig. 87

42 **Minobu-gawa ura Fuji**/*Fuji from Minobu River*
Porters, travellers and packhorses in the foreground
Fig. 88

43 **Sunshū Ōno-shinden**/*The Paddies of Ōno in Suruga Province*
Peasants lead oxen laden with rushes;

women carry the harvest on their backs.
Fig. 89

44 **Sunshū Katakura chaen no Fuji**/*Fuji from the Tea Plantation of Katakura in Suruga Province*
Women picking tea leaves, which workers carry into a storage shed
Fig. 90

45 **Tōkaidō Kanaya no Fuji**/*Fuji from Kanaya on the Tōkaidō*
Travellers and freight being carried over the turbulent Ōi River by porters
▶ Plate 259

46 **Shojin tozan**/*Groups of Mountain Climbers*
Pilgrims at the summit and resting in grotto
Fig. 91

Fig. 90

Fig. 91

Fig. 92

142 *AIZURI* SERIES
9 prints known, vertical small-*chūban*, *c.* **1831** (censor's seal: *kiwame*)
(Landscapes, figures, *kachō-ga*, fish, mainly in *aizuri* colouring)
Signature: *zen*-Hokusai *hitsu*, *zen*-Hokusai Iitsu *hitsu*
Seals: *Iitsu*/*Shichijūni-ō* ('in 72nd year')/*Kakō*/*Fuji-no-yama*/*Nishi-nishi-nishin*/*Jimbutsu-nitai*
Publisher: Moriya Jihei [F–127; cites as 'Koban']
Plate 272

143 *HYAKU-MONOGATARI*
Ghost Tales

Fig. 93   Fig. 94

5 prints known, vertical *chūban*, *c.* **1831**
Signature: *zen*-Hokusai *hitsu*
Publisher: Tsuruya Kiemon
(Regarding the dating, see Note 1, p. 230; of this series there is also an excellent set of early woodblock-printed reproductions, published in 1893) [F–130]
1 **O-Iwa-san**
▶ Plate 277
2 **Warai-Hannya**
Laughing Demon
Fig. 92
3 **Kohada Koheiji**
▶ Plate 282
4 **Sara-yashiki**
The Plate-mansion Ghost
Fig. 93
5 **Shūnen**
Haunted Revenge
Fig. 94

144 HUMOROUS CARICATURES WITH VERSES
9 prints known, vertical *chūban*, *c.* **1832** (*kiwame* seal)
Signatures: *zen*-Hokusai *ga*/*zen*-Hokusai *hitsu*
Publisher: Moriya Jihei [F–129, where 7 designs given, cited as 'Surimono']

145 *SETSU-GEKKA*
Snow/Moon/Blossoms
3 prints, *ōban*, *c.* **1832** (censor's seal: *kiwame*)
Signature: *zen*-Hokusai *hitsu*
Publisher: Eijudō [F–114]
1 **Sumida [yuki]**
Snowscape by the Sumida River
▶ Plate 263
2 **Yodo-gawa [tsuki]**
Moonlight on the Yodo River
Fig. 95
3 **Yoshino [hana]**
Cherry Blossoms at Yoshino
[title is miswritten 'Setsukagetsu']
Fig. 96

146 *LARGE FLOWER-AND-BIRD PRINTS*
5 prints known, vertical *naga-ōban*, *c.* **1832–33** (censor's seal: *kiwame*)
Signature: *zen*-Hokusai Iitsu *hitsu*

Fig. 95

Fig. 96

Fig. 97   Fig. 98

Publisher: Moriya Jihei (and possibly others)
[F–115]
1 **Falcon and Cherry-Blossoms**
2 **Swimming Tortoises**
   ▶ Plate 287
3 **Carp in Cascade**
   Fig. 97
4 **Cranes on Pine Tree**
   Fig. 98
5 **Horses in Pasture**
Note: there is also at least 1 landscape known in
this format:
6 **Crossing the Ice at Lake Suwa in Shinshū**
Data and signature: as above [F–x]
(Distinguish No. 139a above, which resembles
this series but is of larger format)

147 *TANZAKU* SERIES
9 prints known (?), vertical *tanzaku-ban*, *c.* **1832–33**
(censor's seal: *kiwame*)
Signature: *zen*-Hokusai Iitsu *hitsu*
Publisher: Moriya Jihei [F–118]

148 *AI-ZURI TANZAKU* SERIES
3 prints known, vertical *tanzaku-ban*, *c.* **1832–33**
(censor's seal: *kiwame*)
Signature: *zen*-Hokusai Iitsu *hitsu*
Publisher: Moriya Jihei [F–119]

149 *SHŌKEI SETSU-GEKKA*
Fine Views of Snow/Moon/Flowers
9 prints known, *koban*, *c.* **1832–33** (censor's seal:
kiwame)
Signature: *zen*-Hokusai Iitsu *hitsu*
Publisher: Akamatsu Shōtarō [F–120, with minor
errors]
▶ Plate 271

149a *EDO HAKKEI*
Eight Views of Edo
1 print known, 'Evening-snow at Ryōgoku,'
intended as wrapper for confections; *c.* early **1830s**
Signature: *zen*-Hokusai Iitsu *ga* [F–x]

150 *FAN PRINTS

3 prints known, *uchiwa-e*, one datable to **1833**, one
to **1835**
Signature: *zen*-Hokusai Iitsu *hitsu*
Publisher: 'Tsujiya Yasubei'
(On the latter dating, see Note 3 on p. 230)
▶ Plates 278, 288, 289

151 *FAN PRINTS
3 prints known, *uchiwa-e*, *c.* **1833**
Signature: *zen*-Hokusai Iitsu *hitsu* (with variations)
Publisher: 'Yama-Den'
Fig. 99

Fig. 99

152 *SHOKOKU TAKI-MEGURI*
A Tour of Japanese Waterfalls
8 prints known, vertical *ōban*, *c.* **1833–34** (censor's
seal: *kiwame*)
Signature: *zen*-Hokusai Iitsu *hitsu*
Publisher: Eijudō [F–112; there is a set of excellent
woodblock-printed reproductions of the 1890s—
see ▷ Keyes, R. and Morse, P.: 'Hokusai's
Waterfalls and a Set of Copies', in *Oriental Art*,
XVIII-2, 1972]
1 **Shimotsuke Kurokami-yama, Kirifuri-no-taki**
   Fig. 100
2 **Kiso-kaidō, Ono-no-bakufu**
   Fig. 101

Fig. 100   Fig. 101

Fig. 102   Fig. 103

3 **Tōkaidō Sakanoshita, Kiyotaki Kannon**
   Fig. 102
4 **Washū Yoshino, Yoshitsune Umaarai-no-taki**

Fig. 104   Fig. 105

▶ Plate 261
5 **Kisoji no oku, Amida-ga-taki**
   ▶ Plate 260
6 **Tōto, Aoigaoka-no-taki**
   Fig. 103
7 **Sōshū Ōyama, Rōben-no-taki**
   Fig. 104
8 **Mino-no-kuni, Yōrō-no-taki**
   Fig. 105

153 *EDO HAKKEI*
Eight Views of Edo
8 prints, *kōban*, *c.* **1833**
Signature: *zen*-Hokusai *aratame* Iitsu *ga*
Publisher: Akamatsu Shōtarō [F–122, with minor
errors]
Fig. 106

Fig. 106

154 *RYŪKYŪ HAKKEI*
Eight Views of Ryūkyū
8 prints, *ōban*, *c.* **1833**
Signature: *zen*-Hokusai Iitsu *hitsu*
Publisher: Eijudō (later edition from Moriya Jihei)
[F–123]
1 **Jungai sekishō**
   Evening Glow at Jungai
   Fig. 107
2 **Ryūdō shōtō**
   Pines and Waves at Ryūdō
   Fig. 108
3 **Rinkai kosei**

Fig. 107

Fig. 111

Fig. 115

Fig. 108

Fig. 112

Fig. 116

Fig. 109

Fig. 113

Fig. 117

Fig. 110

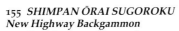

Fig. 114

Fig. 118

Voice of the Lake at Rinkai
▶ Plate 266
4 **Senki yagetsu**
Night Moon at Senki
Fig. 109
5 **Jōgaku reisen**
Sacred Fountain at Jōgaku
Fig. 110
6 **Sanson chikuri**
Bamboo Grove of Sanson
Fig. 111
7 **Chōkō shūsei**
Autumn Weather at Chōkō
Fig. 112
8 **Chūtō shōen**
Banana Groves at Chūtō
Fig. 113

155 SHIMPAN ŌRAI SUGOROKU
New Highway Backgammon
2 sections known, *aiban, c.* **1833**
(Probably complete in 4 sections)
Signature: *zen*-Hokusai Iitsu *zu*
Publishers: Nishimuraya Yohachi, Tsuruya
Kiemon and Jōshūya Jūzō [F–124]

156 *LARGE-FLOWERS SERIES
10 prints, *ōban, c.* **1833–34** (*kiwame* seal)
(Note: there is an excellent woodblock-printed set
of copies, dating from *c.* **1890s**)
Signature: *zen*-Hokusai Iitsu *hitsu*
Publisher: Eijudō [F–110—which includes an
unrelated, eleventh print, 'Narcissus']
  1 **Chrysanthemums and Horsefly**
    Fig. 114

2 **Irises and Grasshopper**
(Note: this print is thought to have been the
inspiration for Van Gogh's famous *Irises* of
1889)
Fig. 115
3 **Lilies**
Fig. 116
4 **Morning-glories and Tree-frog**
▶ Plate 280
5 **Orange Orchid**
Fig. 117
6 **Peonies and Butterfly**
Fig. 118
7 **Cotton-rose and Sparrow**
Fig. 119
8 **Poppies**
▶ Plate 281

Fig. 119

Fig. 120

Fig. 121

9   **Hydrangea and Swallow**
    Fig. 120
10 **Chinese Bellflower and Dragonfly**
    Fig. 121

157 *CHIE-NO-UMI
Oceans of Wisdom
13 prints known (block-sketches for 10 other
designs are also extant), *chūban, c.* **1833–34**
(censor's seal on most designs: *kiwame*)
Signature: *zen*-Hokusai Iitsu *hitsu*
Publisher: Moriya Jihei [F–116—which omits
notice of proofs/sketches; see also ▷ Izzard, S.:
'Hokusai's *Chie no umi*, The Oceans of Wisdom',
in *Impressions*, No. 9, 1984, and text p. 207 ff.]
    1   **Kōshū hiburi**
        Fishing by Torchlight, Kai Province

Fig. 122

Fig. 123

Fig. 124

Fig. 125

    ▶ Plate 268
    2   **Sōshū Tonegawa**
        Tone River, Shimōsa Province
        Fig. 122
    3   **Sōshū Chōshi**
        Chōshi in Shimōsa Province
        ▶ Plate 269
    4   **Sōshū Uraga**
        Uraga in Sagami Province
        Fig. 123
    5   **Gotō kujira-tsuki**
        Whaling off Gotō
        ▶ Plate 267
    6   **Kabari-nagashi**
        Fly-hook Fishing
        Fig. 124
    7   **Shimōsa Noboto**
        Noboto in Shimōsa Province
        Fig. 125
    8   **Miyato-gawa naga-tsuna**
        Line-fishing in the Miyato River
        Fig. 126
    9   **Machi-ami**
        Fishing with Net on Poles
        Fig. 127
    10 **Kinu-gawa hachi-fuse**
        Basket-fishing in the Kinu River
        ▶ Plate 270
    11 **Shinagawa** [known in proof-version only]
    12 **Kazusa Bay** [known in proof-version only]

Fig. 126

Fig. 127

    13 (title uncertain) [known in proof-version
        only]

158 *SHIIKA SHASHIN-KYŌ
A Mirror of Chinese/Japanese Verse
10 prints known, vertical *naga-ōban, c.* **1833–34**
(censor's seal: *kiwame*)
Signature: *zen*-Hokusai Iitsu *hitsu*
Publisher: Moriya Jihei [F–117; *kyō* of title misread
as 'Kagami']
    1   **Haku Rakuten**/*Po Chü-i*
        Fig. 128
    2   **Minamoto no Tōru**
        Fig. 129
    3   **Tokusa-gari**/*Peasant carrying Rushes*
        Fig. 130
    4   **Ri Haku**/*Li Po* (there appear to be two
        versions of this print)
        Fig. 131
    5   **Ariwara no Narihira**
        Figs. 132, 133
    6   **Tōba**/*Su Tung-p'o*
        ▶ Plate 273

Fig. 128

Fig. 129

Fig. 130   Fig. 131   Fig. 136

Fig. 139

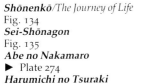

Fig. 133 Preliminary sketch for the figure-detail of print 158(5); from the same miniature album of drawings as Plates 334–338. (The design has been 'cancelled' by impression from an inked coin)

Fig. 132

159 *SHOKOKU MEIKYŌ KIRAN
Rare Views of Famous Japanese Bridges
11 prints known, ōban, c. 1834 (kiwame seal)
Signature: zen-Hokusai Iitsu hitsu
Publisher: Eijudō
(There are variations in cartouche colour; also, there is a late reissue of several scenes, with design trimmed and margins added.) [F–111]

1   **Yamashiro Arashiyama Togetsu-kyō**
    'Crossing-Moon Bridge' at Arashiyama, Yamashiro Province
    Fig. 137
2   **Kōzuke Sano funabashi no kozu**
    Pontoon Bridge at Sano, Kōzuke: Former View
    ▶ Plate 264
3   **Ashikaga Gyōdōzan Kumo-no-kakehashi**
    'Cloud-Hanging Bridge' at Mt Gyōdō, Ashikaga
    Fig. 138
4   **Hi-Etsu no sakai tsuribashi**
    Suspension-Bridge between Hida and Etchū
    (Second state: mountain below bridge revised)
    ▶ Plate 265
5   **Suō-no-kuni Kintai-bashi**
    Kintai Bridge, Suō Province
    Fig. 139

Fig. 140

Fig. 141

7   **Shōnenkō**/The Journey of Life
    Fig. 134
8   **Sei-Shōnagon**
    Fig. 135
9   **Abe no Nakamaro**
    ▶ Plate 274
10 **Harumichi no Tsuraki**
    Fig. 136

Fig. 137

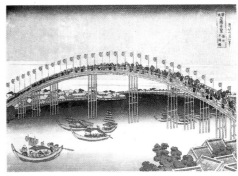

Fig. 142

6   **Tōkaidō Okazaki Yahagi-no-hashi**
    Yahagi Bridge at Okazaki on the Tōkaidō
    Fig. 140
7   **Kameido Tenjin taiko-bashi**
    Drum-Bridge at the Kameido Tenjin Shrine
    Fig. 141
8   **Sesshū Temma-bashi**
    Temma Bridge, Setsu Province
    Fig. 142
9   **Echizen Fukui-no-hashi**
    Fukui Bridge, Echizen Province
    Fig. 143
10 **Mikawa no Yatsu-hashi no kozu**
    'Eight-Parts Bridge' in Mikawa, Former View
    Fig. 144
11 **Sesshū Aji-gawa-guchi Tempōzan**
    Mouth of the Aji River, Tempōzan, Setsu Province
    Fig. 145

Fig. 134   Fig. 135   Fig. 138

Fig. 143

Fig. 144

Fig. 145

Fig. 146

Fig. 147

Fig. 149

Fig. 151

Fig. 153

Fig. 148

Fig. 150

Fig. 152

Fig. 154

160 *HEROES IN COMBAT

5 prints known, *ōban*, *c.* **1834** (censor's seal:
kiwame)
Signature: *zen*-Hokusai Iitsu *hitsu*
Publisher: Yamamotoya Heikichi [F–108 cites as
'Yamakiu', with earlier date, and misreads several
of the warriors' names]
▶ Plate 290; Fig. 146

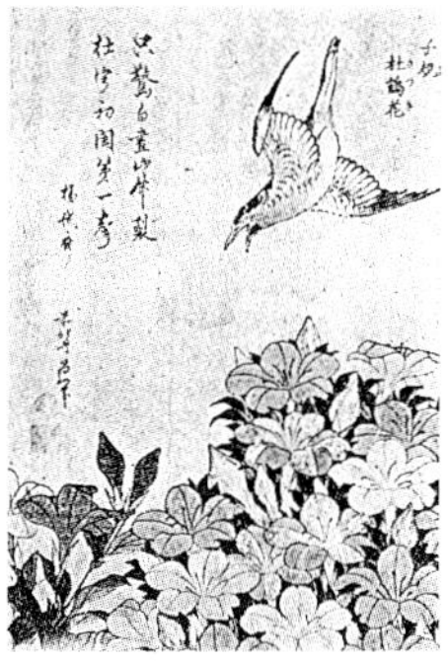

161 *SMALL-FLOWERS SERIES

10 prints, vertical *chūban*, *c.* **1834** (*kiwame* seal)
Signature: *zen*-Hokusai Iitsu *hitsu*
Publisher: Eijudō (later issues bear variant
publisher's seal, or none at all) [F–113]
1   *Crossbill and Thistle*
    Fig. 147
2   *Bullfinch and Weeping-Cherry*
    ▶ Plate 283
3   *Cuckoo and Azaleas*
    Fig. 148
4   *Java Sparrow on Magnolia*
    Fig. 149
5   *Canary and Small Peony*
    Fig. 150
6   *Wagtail and Wisteria*
    ▶ Plate 286
7   *Nightingale on Roses*
    Fig. 151

8   *Grosbeak on Mirabilis*
    Fig. 152
9   *Swallow and Shrike with Strawberry and
    Begonia*
    Fig. 153
10 *Kingfisher with Pinks and Iris*
    Fig. 154

162 *SHŌKEI KIRAN

Rare Views of Famous Landscapes
8 prints known, large-*chūban*, *uchiwa-e*, *c.* **1834–35**
Signature: *zen*-Hokusai Manji (*hitsu*) [F–131]
▶ Plates 275–276; Fig. 155

163 FLOWER-AND-BIRD SERIES—ŌBAN

At least 14 prints known, *ōban*, in Hokusai's style
of the early–mid **1830s**
Signature: *zen*-Hokusai Iitsu *hitsu*
(A disputed work, often given to Taito II [see F–
109], but the impressions commonly seen would
appear to be Meiji imitations, done after Hokusai
designs)

Fig. 155

Fig. 156

164 FAN PRINTS—*KACHŌ* THEMES

1 print known, *uchiwa-e*, *c.* mid-**1830s**
Signature: Gakyō-*rōjin* Manji [F–x]
Fig. 156

165 FAN PRINTS—LANDSCAPE THEMES

c. mid-**1830s** [F–x]

166 *HYAKUNIN ISSHU UBA-GA-ETOKI

*The Hundred Poems [by the Hundred Poets]:
Explained by the Nurse*
28 prints known, each bearing the poet's name
and his verse, *ōban*, *c.* **1835–36** (*kiwame* seal)
(Notice of this series appears in a Nishimuraya
Eijudō advertisement of 1835, and it is likely that
most of the designs were made about this time,
though publication delayed or cancelled.)
Signature: *zen*-Hokusai Manji
Publishers: Nishimuraya Eijudō and Iseya Eijudō
(Cartouche colours vary in later issues. Note:
Hokusai's original drawings for at least 62 other
designs are also extant, though not known to have
been published; four additional designs were
reproduced by woodblock in 1921, but the original

Fig. 157

Fig. 158

Fig. 159

Fig. 160

sketches were subsequently lost; for some scenes, the first issue is characterized by presence of publisher's red seals.) [F–132—which omits much of the above data, and cites second publisher as 'Eikōdō'; also see ▷ Bruijn, R. de: '"The One Hundred Poems Explained by the Nurse"', in *The Fascinating World of the Japanese Artist*, The Hague, 1971, and ▷ Lewis, R. E. (ed.), *Hokusai's 'Hundred Poems explained by the Nurse'*, Calif., 1982]

1   *Tenchi-tennō*
2   *Jitō-tennō*
3   *Kakinomoto no Hitomaro*
     Fig. 157
4   *Yamabe no Akahito*
5   *Sarumaru-daiyū*
6   *Chūnagon Yakamochi*
     Fig. 158
7   *Abe no Nakamaro*
     Fig. 159

8   *Ono no Komachi*
9   *Sangi Takamura*
      ▶ Plate 284
10   *Sōjō Henjō*
11   *Ariwara no Narihira ason*
      Fig. 160
12   *Fujiwara no Toshiyuki ason*
13   *Ise*
14   *Prince Motoyoshi*
      ▶ Plate 285
15   *Kan-ke*
16   *Teishin-kō*
17   *Minamoto no Muneyuki ason*
      Fig. 161
18   *Harumichi no Tsuraki*
      Fig. 162
19   *Kiyowara no Fukayabu*
      ▶ Plate 291
20   *Funya no Asayasu*

Fig. 161

Fig. 162   (Compare the *Fuji* scene of Fig. 67)

Fig. 163

Fig. 164

Fig. 165

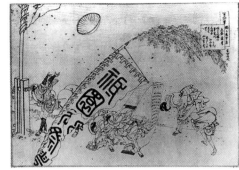

Fig. 166

21   *Sangi Hitoshi*
22   *Ōnakatomi no Toshinobu ason*
23   *Fujiwara no Yoshitaka*
      Fig. 163
24   *Fujiwara no Michinobu ason*
      ▶ Plate 279
25   *Sanjō-in*
26   *Dainagon Tsunenobu*
      Fig. 164

Fig. 167

Fig. 168

Fig. 169

27 **Gonchūnagon Sadaie [Teika]**
    Fig. 165
28 **Mibu no Tadamine**
    [known only in proof-version]

Fig. 170 Detail of large *surimono*

29 **Funya no Yasuhide**
    (example of Hokusai's original block-sketch,
    never published)
    Fig. 166

167 MISCELLANEOUS *SURIMONO*
A large number of untitled *surimono*, mainly in
chūban-size, are known for the years *c.* **1811** to
1844
Signatures: Gakyō-*rōjin*, Katsushíka, Taito,
Raishin, Fusenkyo Iitsu, *zen*-Hokusai Iitsu,
Getchi-*rōjin*, Manji (with variations)
► Plates 201–204, 207–209, 218, 241, 332, 333;
Figs. 167–70; also Figs. 52–54

168 LARGE TOPOGRAPHICAL PRINTS
Several topographical/panoramic prints in double-
ōban size are known for the period *c.* **1820–40**,
including pictorial maps of the Chiba Peninsula,
the Tōkaidō, the Kiso Highway, the Shiogama-
Matsushima region, the Chinese sub-continent, a
landscape-surveying scene, and the
comprehensive 'Hundred Bridges' landscape
shown in Plate 262
Signatures: Katsushika *zen*-Hokusai Taito,
Hokusai *aratame* Iitsu, *zen*-Hokusai Iitsu, Gakyō-
rōjin Manji (and variations)

III

Hokusai's Illustrated Books and Albums

This bibliography includes several innovations. It
is the first in the West to cite month of publication
as well as year—and to be adjusted to the
Gregorian calendar. Further, full translations are
included of all titles (titles within titles appear in
quotes), and bibliographical details are given of
prior studies in the Occident—scarce though they
are. Attention has also been paid to reissues and
revisions of Hokusai's published works, generally
neglected by previous students. Unless there are
significant variations, retitled reprints have
generally been consolidated under the first entry
(considerably reducing the total number of main
entries, but giving a more valid picture of the
artist's actual output). In some cases, Hokusai
books are best known abroad under the titles of
later editions; for these, the reader should consult
the Index. Where not cited, works are unsigned
(or signature unrecorded).
    Data on titles and even signatures is not
intended to be definitive: differing forms may
appear not only on a book's wrapper, cover, title-
page, preface, table of contents and colophon, but
may also be changed for subsequent editions. For
the general purposes of this book, I have often
simply selected the most frequently used of these
multiple possibilities.

BOOK SIZES: may be approximately summarized
as:
chūbon: 18 × 12 cm/7¼ × 4¾ in. (*kibyōshi/sharé-
hon*, some picture-books)
hanshi-bon: 23 × 16 cm/9 × 6¼ in. (*yomi-hon*,
artists' manuals, some verse-collections and
picture-books)
ōbon: 27 × 19 cm/10½ × 7½ in. (many verse-
collections and most albums and picture-books)

BOOK CATEGORIES:
kibyōshi: light novelettes in picture-book format
sharé-hon: Yoshiwara novelettes, with minimal

illustration
hanashi-bon: *conte* booklets
gōkan-bon: lengthy *kibyōshi*
yomi-hon: lengthy 'Gothic' novels
kokkei-bon: comic novels/novelettes
ehon: picture-books
e-dehon: instructive picture-books for aspiring
artists
orihon: album (see text, pp. 35, 44)
yoko-bon: narrow horizontal format

Note: Only differences/corrections of special
significance have been cited vs. the listing in J.
Hillier's useful *The Art of Hokusai in Book Illustration*
(which includes Japanese characters, and limited
reference to other published sources). In all cases
the present data takes precedence over that
included in my earlier *Images from the Floating
World.*
    Subtitles—which appear at head of title in
Japanese books—have usually been omitted
when printed small in the original—i.e., not part
of the primary title. Translations of fanciful titles
are only approximate; with some complex titles,
simplified form—and translation—is adopted in
the main text, but full form in this detailed listing
(with both forms indexed). Unless otherwise
stated, all works are in one volume. Where month
of publication is known, it is given in Roman
numerals. (The Twelfth Month of the lunar
calendar usually falls in January of the Gregorian,
here indicated by the subterfuge 'XII/1798/99'.
'c. I/1780' implies that the *month* is approximate,
not the year.) Items in brackets are derived from
secondary sources. (Hokusai's erotica will be
found in a separate listing, under Part IV.)
    Finally, a practical note for the reader who seeks
a supposed Hokusai title but does not find it here
(or in the Index): 1. Add or deduct possible title-
prefix such as *Ehon*, *Kyōka* or *Shimpen*. 2. Consider

the possibility that the work may be by a pupil
bequeathed the Master's *nom d'artiste* (on which,
see pp. 311–15). 3. If neither of these leads proves
fruitful, report your find to the nearest museum.

1 **GAKUJO-KŌSHI**
   Singing-girls behind the Bars
   Sharé-hon by Sanchō, **1775**
   (Text said to have been carved by Hokusai at
   age 15 during his period of apprenticeship to
   a woodblock engraver, hence his first
   published work)
   Fig. 171

2 **IKI-CHONCHON KURUWA NO CHABAN**
   A Gallant's Farce in the Pleasure Quarter
   Kibyōshi text by Mari (possible pseudonym of
   Hokusai), 2 vols., I/**1780**
   Signature: Katsukawa Shunrō [=Hokusai]

3 **MEGURO NO HIYOKU-ZUKA**
   The Love Mound of Meguro
   Kibyōshi, 2 vols., I/**1780** (author not recorded,
   possibly Hokusai)

Fig. 171

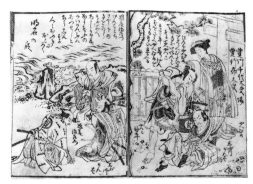

Fig. 172

Signature: Katsukawa Shunrō
▶ Plate 9; Fig. 172

4 *[ISSHŌ TOKUBEI SAN-NO-DEN*
Three Tales of Tokubei]
Kibyōshi by Tsūshō, 3 vols., **1780**
[Hokusai attribution questioned]

5 *NICHIREN ICHIDAI-KI*
Life of St Nichiren
Kibyōshi by Mari-ko (= Hokusai?), 3 vols.,
c. **1780**
Signature: Katsukawa Shunrō

6 *ARIGATA TSŪ-NO-ICHIJI*
The Happy Word 'Gallant'
Kibyōshi by Korewasai (pseudonym of
Hokusai[?]), 2 vols., I/**1781**

7 *KŌDAI NO MUDAGOTO*
Idle Talk on Gallantry
Sharé-hon by Takōjin, **1781**
Signature: Katsukawa Shunrō

8 *[MAME-BATAKE*
The Bean-field]
Hanashi-bon, **1781**
Signature: Katsukawa Shunrō
(Distinguish p. 310, No. 3)

9 *KYARA-DAIKON*
The Fragrant Gallant
Sharé-hon by Rihaku-sanjin; c. **1782**
Signature: Shunrō

10 *KAMAKURA TSŪSHINDEN*
The 'Gallant' Samurai of Kamakura
Kibyōshi by Gyobutsu, 2 vols., I/**1782**
Signature: Shunrō

11 *SHI-TENNŌ TAITSŪ-JITATE*
The 'Four Kings' as Gallants
Kibyōshi by Korewasai (Hokusai[?]), 2 vols.,
I/**1782**
Signature: Shunrō

12 *FUKAGAWA HAIKEN*
Views of Fukagawa
Sharé-hon by Kikyō, **1782**
Signature: Shunrō
▶ Plate 11

13 *KAN-YŌKYŪ TSŪ-NO-YAKUSOKU*
The 'Gallant's' Promise in the Dragon-King's
Palace
Kibyōshi, 2 vols., c. I/**1783**
Signature: Shunrō

14 *UN-WA-HIRAKU ŌGI NO HANA-KA*
Luck of The Perfumed Fan
Kibyōshi, 2 vols., Spring/**1784**
Signature: Shunrō

15 *KYŌKUN ZŌ-NAGAMOCHI*
The Chest Replete with Teachings
Hanashi-bon, 5 vols., I/**1784**
Signature: Katsukawa Shunrō
(the text is a reprint of a 1752 work)

16 *NOZOKI-KARAKURI YOSHITSUNE*
YAMA-IRI
Peeping on Yoshitsune's Escape
Kibyōshi by Ikuji-mo-nai, 3 vols., I/**1784**
Signature: Katsu Shunrō

17 *OYA-YUZURI HANA-NO-KŌMYŌ*
Pride of High Parentage

Kibyōshi by Jakusei, 3 vols., **1785** (Retitled
reprint of 1801: *Gekai-sawagi tawake-tengū*
[Pandemonium and the Fall of Pride]
Signature: Shunrō *aratame* [changed to]
Gumbatei

18 *ONNEN UJI NO HOTARUBI*
Revenge: Fireflies on the River Uji
Kibyōshi, 2 vols., **1785**
Signature: Katsu Shunrō

19 *NIICHI-TENSAKU NISHIN-GA-ISSHIN*
Two-and-One Arithmetic Reckoning
Kibyōshi by Tsūshō, 3 vols., **1786**
Signature: Gumbatei [Hokusai]
(Later reissued under the title *Ningen banji
niichi tensaku-no-go* [Life is But an Arithmetic-
calculation], 1788 and 1800; for an interesting
predecessor, see the *aohon* by Kiyomitsu of
1765, *Niichi tensaku-no-go*)

20 *ZEN ZEN-TAIHEIKI*
The Earlier 'Pre-Taiheiki'
Kibyōshi by Unubore-sanjin [Hokusai(?)],
5 vols., I/**1786**
Signature: Shunrō
▶ Plate 10

21 *JABARA-MON HARA-NO-NAKACHŌ*
A Snake-skin Crest in Main Street
Kibyōshi by Hakusekkō, 2 vols., I/**1786**
Signature: Shunrō *aratame* Gumbatei

22 *[DAIBUTSU HIDARI-YORI*
The Left-handed Great Buddha]
Kibyōshi, 3 vols., **1786**
Signature: Hakusanjin Kakō [Hokusai (?)]
(Later reprinted as *Azuma-daibutsu momiji no
meisho* [The Eastern Great Buddha: Famous
for Autumn Maple Leaves], 1793)

23 *WAGA-IE RAKU NO KAMAKURA-YAMA*
Our Happy Home at Mt Kamakura
Kibyōshi, 2 vols., I/**1787**
Signature: Gumbatei [Hokusai]
Fig. 173

Fig. 173

24 *ŌICHŌ KONGEN-SOGA*
The Soga Brothers' Great Ginkgo-tree
Kabuki picture-book for a performance of
I/**1787** at the Nakamura-za, Edo; 2 vols.
Signature: Shunrō

25 *[JINKŌKI NISHIKI-MUTSUKI*
Arithmetical Descriptions of Two Wars]
1788. Signature: Gumbatei (?)

26 *FUKU-KITARU WARAI NO KADOMATSU*
The Pine at the Gate Inviting Happiness
Kibyōshi by Tsūshō, 2 vols., c. I/**1789**
Signature: Katsu Shunrō

27 *KUSAKI MO NABIKU HIRIKURA-NO-*
SAKAE
Wind-breaking of Good Fortune
Kibyōshi by Kentō, 2 vols., **1789**
Signature: Shunrō

28 *[YOROZUYA TOKUZAEMON*
(A Rich Merchant of Kamakura)]
Kibyōshi, 2 vols., c. **1789**
Signature: Katsu Shunrō (?)

29 *ROKKASEN KYOJITSU NO TENSAKU*

The 'Six Poets' Corrected
Kibyōshi by Nanri, 2 vols., **1789**
Signature: Shunrō

30 *HAYARI-UTA TORIKOMI-SHŌBU*
Imbroglio to a Popular Tune
Kibyōshi by Zōsui, 2 vols., **1789**
Signature: Shunrō

31 *HEIJI TAIHEIKI*
The 'Heiji' Epic
Kibyōshi by Tsūshō, **1789**
Signature: Shunrō

32 *HANA NO O-EDO MASAKADO-*
MATSURI
Flowery Edo: the Masakado Festival
Kabuki picture-book for a performance of XI/
1789 at the Ichimura-za, Edo

33 *[KOMAGUMI DŌKANSHŌ*
Guide to Placing the Pieces]
Chess handbook, **1790**

34 *[MITATE CHŪSHINGURA*
The 'Chūshingura' in Modern Dress]
1790

35 *TATSU-NO-MIYAKO SENTAKU-*
BANASHI: IMO-TAKO NO YURAI
Laundry at the Dragon's Palace: The Origins
of 'Fish and Chips'
[potatoes and octopus in this case]
Kibyōshi, 2 vols., I/**1791**
Signature: Shunrō

36 *[MIBU KOWAIRO NADAI-NO-FURISODE*
Mimicking a Mibu Actor in His Regalia]
Kibyōshi by Shinkō, 2 vols., **1791**
Signature: Shunrō (?)

37 *[TENJIN SHICHIDAI-KI*
The Seven Generations of Tenjin]
(Alternative title: *Masumi no kagami* [Mirror of
Success])
Kibyōshi, 3 + 2 vols., **1792**
Ascribed to Shunrō

38 *NUE YORIMASA NAUTA-NO-SHIBA*
Yorimasa and the Monster: Poetry-lawns
Kibyōshi by Somabito, 2 vols., I/**1792**
Signature: Katsukawa Shunrō
(an earlier edition of 1788 is also alleged)

39 *JITSUGO-KYŌ OSANA-KŌSHAKU*
A Lecture for Children on the 'Jitsugo-kyō'
Kibyōshi by Kyōden (in collaboration with
Bakin), 2 vols., **1792**
Signature: Katsu Shunrō

40 *ONNA-SŌJI KOCHŌ-NO-YUME*
Woman-philosopher: Butterfly Dream
Kibyōshi by Kuroki/Bakin, 2 vols., **1792**
Signature: Shunrō

41 *HANA-NO-HARU SHIRAMI NO*
MICHIYUKI
Flower Spring: Bedbugs' Love-journey
Kibyōshi by Bakin, 2 vols., **1792**
Signature: Katsu Shunrō

42 *MOMOTARŌ HOTTAN-BANASHI*
The Origins of Momotarō
Kibyōshi by Kyōden, 3 vols., **1793**
Signature: Shunrō

43 *[SHIOYAKI BUNTA MIYAKO*
MONOGATARI
Bunta the Salt-Gatherer: in the Capital]
Kibyōshi, 3 vols., c. **1792**
Signature: Katsukawa Shunrō (?)

44 *HIMPUKU RYŌ-DŌCHŪ-NO-KI*
The Two Roads of Poverty and Riches
Kibyōshi by Kyōden, 3 vols., I/**1793**
(second edition, 1795)
Signature: Shunrō

45 *CHIE-SHIDAI HAKONE-ZUME*
Keeping One's Wits at Hakone
Kibyōshi by Kusaki, 3 vols., **1793**
Signature: Shunrō

46 *[KABUKI PICTURE-BOOK, TITLE LOST]*
From a performance of Autumn **1793** at the
Kiri-za, Edo

47 [KAKEAI KYŌKA-MONDŌ
   Kyōka Duet]
   Kyōka anthology, c. early **1790s**
   Signature: Katsukawa Shunrō

48 FUKUJUKAI MURYŌ NO SHINADAMA
   Jewel of the Sea of Everlasting Life
   Kibyōshi by Bakin, 3 vols., **1794**
   Signature: Shunrō

49 KOBITO-JIMA NANASATO-FŪKI
   Happy Island of Midgets
   Kibyōshi, 2 vols., I/**1794**
   Signature: Shunrō

50 NOZOITE-MIRU TATOE-NO-FUSHIANA
   A Peek through the Proverbial Keyhole
   Kibyōshi by Tsubohira, 2 vols., I/**1794**
   Signature: Shunrō

51 TEMAEZUKE AKŌ-NO-SHIOKARA
   Spicy Tales of the 'Chūshingura'
   Kibyōshi by Tsubohira, 2 vols., Spring **1794**
   Signature: Shunrō (?)

52 [TSURANE-AWASE ONNA-
   SHINASADAME]
   Conglomerate Types of Women
   Kyōka anthology, IV/**1794**
   Signature: Kusamura Shunrō [possibly
   Shunrō II]

53 SAIFU-NO-HIMO SHIWAMIUSE-GUSURI
   The Purse-string: Prescription for Losing
   Wrinkles
   Kibyōshi by Tsubohira, 3 vols., Spring **1795**
   Signature: Shunrō

54 KYŌKA SAITAN EDO MURASAKI
   The Purple of Edo: New Year Verses
   Kyōka anthology, I/**1795**
   Signature: Sōri (seal: Kan) [= Hokusai]
   (With Toyokuni, Eishi, Utamaro, Kyōden,
   Keisai, Kikōtei)

55 KYŌKA ANTHOLOGY
   c. **1795**
   Signature: Sōri (but rather in Toyokuni style)

56 SHIKINAMI-GUSA
   Grasses of the Four Seasons
   Kyōka anthology, c. I/**1796**
   Signature: Hyakurin Sōri [there is doubt that
   this name is identical with Hokusai]

57 YOMO NO HARU
   Spring All Over
   Kyōka anthology, **1796**
   (With Kyōden, Gentai, Sō-Shizan et al.; a
   different work from No. 61)

58 KYŌKA ANTHOLOGY
   1796
   Signatures: Hokusai Sōri/Sōri

59 ASAHINA OHIGE-NO-CHIRI
   Dusting the Whiskers of Asahina
   Kibyōshi by Jihinari, 2 vols., **1796**

60 MOMO-SAEZURI
   The Twittering of Birds
   Kyōka album, **1796**
   Illustrated by Hokusai, Shumman et al.
   (distinguish No. 117)

61 *YOMO NO HARU
   Spring All Over
   Kyōka anthology (album), **1796**
   Signature: Hokusai Sōri
   (With Eishi and Masayoshi; distinguish No.
   57)
   ▷ Forrer, M.: 'Kyōka Albums of the Kansei
   Period', in Essays on Japanese Art, London,
   1982
   ▶ Plate **32**

62 KYŌKA EMA-AWASE ONNA KANA-
   DEHON
   Female 'Chūshingura' in Ema-panels
   Kyōka anthology, c. **1796** (second edition 1799)
   Signature (on verse): Hyakurin Sōri [cf. No.
   56]

63 *SANDARA-KASUMI
   Mists of Sandara

Kyōka anthology (album), **1797**
Signature: Hokusai Sōri
(With Shigemasa and Ittei;
a different work from No. 68)
▶ Plate **34**

64 *YANAGI-NO-ITO
   The Willow-branch
   Kyōka anthology (album), **1797**
   One print signed Hokusai Sōri
   (With Eishi, Shigemasa, Tōrin, Rinshō)
   ▶ Plate **31**

65 SHUNKYŌ-JŌ
   Album of Springtime Diversions
   Kyōka anthology, 2 vols.
   One print signed Sōri in first vol., dated **1797**;
   one signed Hokusai Sōri in second vol., dated
   1798

66 MIYAMA UGUISU
   Nightingale in the Mountains
   Kyōka anthology (album), I/**1798**
   Signature: Hokusai Sōri
   (With Shigemasa)

67 BAKEMONO YAMATO-HONZŌ
   Botanical History of Japanese Ghosts
   Kibyōshi by Kyōden, 3 vols., I/**1798**
   Signature: Kakō [Hokusai]

68 *SANDARA-KASUMI
   Mists of Sandara
   Kyōka anthology (album), I/**1798**
   Signature: Hokusai Sōri
   (With Shigemasa and Settan; a different work
   from No. 63)
   ▶ Plate **35**

69 *OTOKO-DŌKA
   Men's Dance of Spring
   Kyōka anthology (album), I/**1798**
   Signature: Hokusai Sōri
   (With Shigemasa, Utamaro, Tōrin, Ekiji,
   Eishi)
   ▶ Plate **36**

70 KYŌKA HATSU-WAKANA
   First Young Herbs
   Kyōka anthology (album), I/**1798**
   Signature: Sōri aratame [changed to] Hokusai
   (with other artists)
   ▶ Plate **33**

71 SASHIIRE HANA-NO-FUTAMI
   Views of Flower-arrangement
   1798, alternative title: Rakumon binka-fu
   (Flower-arrangement of the Raku School)
   Signatures: Hokusai/Sōri; seals: Kanchi/
   Hyakurin (in collaboration with Kansai Sōrin)

72 [HAIKAI SHIJIKU-ZŌSHI
   Verses of the Four Seasons]
   Haiku anthology, **1798**
   One print signed: Sōri aratame Hokusai
   Tokimasa

73 [HANA-NO-ANI
   The Eldest of the Flowers]
   Kyōka anthology, **1798**
   Two prints, one signed zen-Sōri Hokusai, the
   other Hokusai Tokimasa

74 *HARU-NO-MIYABI
   Elegance of Spring
   Kyōka anthology (album), c. **1798**
   Signature: Hokusai Sōri
   ▶ Plate **40**

75 TARŌ-ZUKI
   The First Moon
   Kyōka anthology (album), c. **1803**
   One plate, signed Sōri (most probably the
   work of Hokusai's pupil, Sōri III)
   ▶ Plate **37**

76 SHUNKYŌ-JŌ
   Album of Springtime Diversions
   Kyōka anthology (album), c. **1798**
   Signature: Hokusai Sōri
   (With Shiransai, Shigemasa et al.)

77 *AZUMA ASOBI
   Dances of the East
   Kyōka anthology, Spring/**1799**
   (Due to the diverse contents, and
   contributors from distant provinces,
   production of the volume probably spanned
   the years 1797–98, when Hokusai was yet in
   his 'Sōri Period')
   Signature: Hokusai
   (Later, alternative editions printed in colour,
   1800/1802; see No. 85)
   ▶ Plate **44**; Fig. 174

78 KYŌKA ANTHOLOGY
   1799
   One plate signed Sōri

79 KOZUE NO YUKI
   Snow on the Branches
   Kyōka anthology, c. XII/**1799/1800**
   Signature: Fusenkyo Hokusai
   (with other artists)

80 SHUNKYŌ-JŌ
   Album of Springtime Diversions
   Kyōka anthology, c. late **1790s**
   Signature: Sōri
   (With Utamaro and Toyohiro)

81 [SHUNKYŌ-JŌ
   Album of Springtime Diversions]
   Kyōka anthology, c. late **1790s**
   Illustrated by Sōri and Kyōden

82 [SANGOKU-SHI
   Chronicle of Extremes]
   Hanashi-bon by Chiyo-okagusa, late **1790s**
   Signature: Hokusai (?)

83 *TŌTO MEISHO ICHIRAN
   Famous Views of the Eastern Capital
   Picture-book, 2 vols., I/**1800**
   Signature: Hokusai Tokimasa
   Alternative title of later editions: Tōto shōkei
   ichiran; reprinted 1815—signature on
   wrapper: Gakyōjin Hokusai
   ▶ Plates **46, 47, 50**

84 KAMADO-SHŌGUN KANRYAKU-NO-
   MAKI
   Tactical Treatise of General Oven
   Kibyōshi, 3 vols., c. I/**1800**
   Text and illustrations signed: Tokitarō Kakō
   ▶ Plates **90, 91**; Fig. 175

Fig. 174

Fig. 175

Fig. 176 Title-slip to Vol. I

85 *EHON AZUMA-ASOBI
Dances of the East Illustrated
Picture-book, 3 vols., Spring/**1800**
(Reissue of the 1799 book [No. 77] with some
plates and most poems omitted and colours
added; also reprinted in 1802, in the 1830s,
and again in the 1880s)
Signature: Hokusai
(Note: Hillier, p. 43, also cites an edition of
1801, presumably an error; the first, 1800
issue is rare—one example in the Art Institute
of Chicago and another recorded by Hillier in
the London Sotheby sale of 25 Oct. 1978)
▶ Plates **44, 45**

86 [ANATA YOMO-NO-HARU
Poems on Spring]
Kyōka anthology, *c.* **1800**
Signature: Hokusai
(With Tsunezune and Eishi)

87 KYŌKA SANJŪ-ROKKASEN
Thirty-six Poets of Kyōka
Kyōka anthology, *c.* **1800**
Signature: Hokusai Tokimasa
(Distinguish Nos. 123 and 215)

88 [TŌTO MEISHO ZUKA-SHŪ
Views of Edo with Poems]
c. **1800**

89 CHIGO-MONJU OSANA-KYŌKUN
Juvenile Instructions of the Boy-Monju
Kibyōshi, 3 vols., I/**1801**
Text and illustrations signed: Tokitarō Kakō
Fig. 176

90 HARU NO ZARE-UTA
Playful Verses of Spring
Kyōka anthology, *c.* **1801**
Signature: Gakyōjin Hokusai
(With Busentei Eiri; cover-design by Hokkei)

91 NISHIKI-ZURI ONNA-SANJŪ-
ROKKASEN
Brocade Prints of the Thirty-six Poetesses
Picture-album, Spring, **1801**
Frontispiece signed: Gakyōjin Hokusai
(The plates of the poetesses, by Eishi)
▶ Plate **38**

92 BON-ODORI
Summer Dances
Kyōka anthology of the Shishōan Club, *c.* **1801**
Signatures: Hokusai/Gakyōjin Hokusai

93 ADA-DEHON
Models of Rakish Vendetta
Sharé-hon by Atsumaru, *c.* **1801**
Signature: Gakyōjin Hokusai
(For sequel see following item)

94 TSŪSHIN-MUDA
The Rakish Rōnin's Revenge
Sharé-hon by Atsumaru, *c.* **1802**
Signature: Gakyōjin Hokusai
(Alternative title: *Tsūshin-gura*; sequel to the
preceding item)
[N.B. Hillier Nos. 95 and 102 are duplicative]

95 *FŪRYŪ GOJŪNIN ISSHU: ISUZU-GAWA
KYŌKA-GURUMA
Fifty Fashionable Poets, One Poem Each:

Fig. 177 Details

Humorous Odes of The Isuzu River
I/**1802**
Signature: Hokusai Tokimasa
▶ Plate **49**; Fig. 177

96 *ITAKO ZEKKU-SHŪ
Songs of Itako
Kyōshi anthology, 2 vols., *c.* I/**1802**; also one-
vol. edition with supplementary text by
Bakin, and one-vol. retitled edition, *Ehon
Itako-no-hayashi* (The Itako Chorus: a Picture-
book), both *c.* 1800s
Unsigned but known from contemporary
records to be illustrated by Hokusai
▶ Plates **48, 55**; Fig. 178

97 EHON CHŪSHINGURA
Picture-book 'Chūshingura'
2 vols., I/**1802**
(Inner-title: *Chūshingura yakuwari kyōka*
[Humorous Poems on the *Chūshingura*
Roles]). Text by Jihinari
Signature: Hokusai Tokimasa
(There is also a monochrome edition)
▶ Plate **57**; Fig. 179

Fig. 178

Fig. 179

98 *MIYAKO-DORI
Birds of the Capital
Kyōka anthology (album), *c.* **1802**
Signature: Gakyōjin Hokusai
▶ Plate **42**

99 [FUDE-HAJIME
First Writings]
Hanashi-bon, **1802**

100 AMA-NO-SUTEGUSA
The Fisherman's Reeds
Yomi-hon by Hirozumi, 6 vols., I/**1803**
Signed: Gakyōjin Hokusai

101 BUCHŌHŌ SOKUSEKI-RYŌRI
An Improper/Impromptu Feast
Kibyōshi, 3 vols., I/**1803**
Text and illustrations signed: Tokitarō Kakō
(The original manuscript-version of this book
is in the Tenri Library, Nara)

102 KUGAI JŪNEN: AA SHINKIRŌ
The Bitter World: Ah, The Mirage
Kibyōshi by Onitake, 3 vols., I/**1803**
Signature: Katsushika Hokusai

103 HARU-NO-FUJI
Fuji in Spring
Kyōka anthology (album), I/**1803**
Signature: Gakyōjin Hokusai
▶ Plates **39, 43**

104 EHON OGURA HYAKKU
Verses after the 'Hundred Poems'
Kyōku anthology by Hakuen (the actor
Danjūrō V), I/**1803**
Signature: Hokusai Tokimasa
▶ Plate **53**

105 SANGOKU MUKASHI-BANASHI:
WAKARAN-MONOGATARI
*Incomprehensible Tale of Three Countries—
East and West*
Kibyōshi by Onitake, 3 vols., Spring, **1803**
Signature: Kakō

106 MUNAZANYŌ USO-NO-TANAOROSHI
Facetious Calculations
Kibyōshi, 3 vols., **1803**
(Subtitle and turnover-title: *Jinkō-ki*)
Text and illustrations signed: Tokitarō Kakō
Fig. 180

107 HASHIKA OTOSHI-BANASHI
Jokes on Measles
Hanashi-bon, **1803**
Signature: Senzankō (?)

Fig. 180

108 [HINAUTA] TSUKI-KUWASHI
Rustic Moon-lit Verses
Kyōka anthology, **1803**
Signature: Gakyōjin Hokusai

109 [FUJIMI NO TSURA
On Viewing Mt Fuji]
Kyōka anthology, **1803**
Signature: Gakyōjin Hokusai

110 *[EHON KYŌKA] YAMA-MATA-YAMA
*Mountain upon Mountain: [with Verses,
Illustrated]*
Picture-book with *kyōka*, 3 vols., I/**1804**
Signature (on wrapper): Hokusai-*shujin*
(Regarding the title, see Note 3 on p. 54—to
which I may add that the curious Forrer
[/Keyes?] interpretation is further amplified
in his Hillier review in *Impressions* No. 6, 1981,
p. 7, but then ambiguously modified in the
Eirakuya monograph, pp. 226–7)
▶ Plates **52, 56, 59**; Fig. 181

111 MUSUME KATAKIUCHI IMOSE-NO-
TOMOZUNA
The Faithful Daughter's Revenge
Kibyōshi by Korori, 2 vols., I/**1804**
(Alternative title: *Ryōmen-shusse sugata-kagami*
[A Mirror of Double-success])
Signature: Tokitarō Kakō
Fig. 182

112 SHŌSETSU HIYOKU-MON
A Novel of Two Lovers
Yomi-hon by Bakin, 2 vols., I/**1804**
Signature: Hokusai Tokimasa
(Reissued in 1807 in *gōkan-bon* format, 2 vols.,
under the title *Yūkun-no-misao renri no*

Fig. 181

Fig. 183

Fig. 186

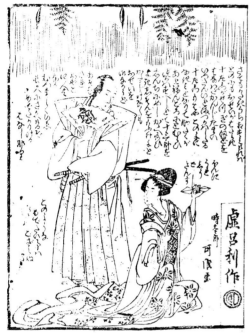

Fig. 182

Fig. 184

Fig. 185

mochibana [The Flower of a Courtesan's
Fidelity]; signature: Gakyōjin Hokusai)
113 **[MISOKA-TSUZURA**
A Month-end Collection]
Collection of poetry and designs, **1804**
Four are signed: Gakyōjin Hokusai
114 **TOSHI-OTOKO WARAI-GUSA**
New Year's Jokes
Hanashi-bon by Ki-no-Osamaru, **1804**
Signature: Tokitarō Kakō
115 **OTOGI YAMAZAKI KASSEN**
Tale of the Battle of Yamazaki
Kibyōshi, **1804**
Signature: Gakyōjin Hokusai
116 **HANASHI-GAME**
Turtle Tales
Hanashi-bon by Fukusuke, **1804**
Signature: Tokitarō Kakō
117 **MOMO-SAEZURI**
The Twittering of Birds
Kyōka anthology, Spring, **1805**
Signature: Gakyōjin Hokusai
(See Hokusai **Prints** No. 105 for reissue in
single-sheet format, with colour-printing)
(Distinguish No. 60)
▶ Plate **54**; Fig. 183
118 **EHON AZUMA FUTABA-NISHIKI**
Young Brocade of Edo Illustrated
Yomi-hon by Shigeru, 5 vols., I/**1805**
Signature: Gakyō-rōjin Hokusai
▷ Lane, Richard: 'Hokusai's Gothic
Connection: the Yomi-hon,' in Andon, No. 24,

1987, reprinted in Studies in Edo Literature
▶ Plate **96**; Fig. 184
119 ***EHON SUMIDA-GAWA RYŌGAN**
ICHIRAN
Views of Both Banks of the Sumida River
Picture-book, 3 vols., c. **1804–05** (an earlier
date of 1803 has been proposed, but based
mainly on the evidence of a related surimono
series of that year—see Prints No. 68 above)
Hokusai's name is mentioned in the preface
▶ Plates **60, 61**; Fig. 185
120 **KYŌKA ANTHOLOGY**
c. **1805**
One plate signed Gakyōjin Hokusai
121 **KYŌKA SAN-AI-SHŪ**
Verses: Three Loves
Kyōka anthology, c. **1805**
Signature: Hokusai
▶ Plate **51**
122 **[ŌTSUDOI**
The Great Gathering]
Kyōka anthology, c. **1805**
Illustrations by Hokusai and Rankei
123 ***KYŌKA SANJŪ-ROKKASEN**
Thirty-six Poets of Kyōka
Kyōka anthology, c. **1804–05**
(Distinguish Nos. 87 and 215)
▶ Plate **58**; Fig. 186
124 **HITORI-HOKKU**
Lone Haiku Verses
Haiku anthology, 2 vols., c. **1805**
Signature: Gakyō-rōjin Hokusai

(With Hōchū, Hōitsu, Kōkan, Sūkoku et al.)
▶ Plate **177**
125 **SHIMPEN SUIKO-GADEN**
The New Illustrated 'Suihuchuan'
Yomi-hon by Bakin and Ranzan, 56 vols.:
IX/**1805**, I/**1807**, I/**1829**, Autumn/**1833**, **1835**,
1838
Signatures: Katsushika Hokusai/Hokusai
Taito-rōjin/zen-Hokusai Iitsu-rōjin
126 **[TŌKAIDŌ GOJŪSAN-TSUGI EZUKUSHI**
Fifty-three Stations of the Tōkaidō]
Album-format of Prints, No. 76a
127 **[SHIMPAN ŌMI HAKKEI**
New Eight Views of Lake Biwa]
c. **1806–08**
Signature: Hokusai
[possibly related to, or confused with,
Hokusai's print-series No. 91]
128 **EHON TAMA-NO-OCHIBO**
Jewelled Gleanings Illustrated
Yomi-hon by Shigeru, 10 vols., I/**1806** and
I/**1808**
Signature: Katsushika Hokusai
(Later reissued as Ehon Nitta kōshinroku [The
Loyal Retainers of Nitta Illustrated], I/**1841**;
by one account it was quarrelling over this
work that led to the initial break-up of the
Bakin–Hokusai collaboration)
129 **[UWAKI SŌSHI**
Book of Philandering]
Kibyōshi by Ran-i, 3 vols., **1806**
Signature: Hokusai
130 **JIMOKU-SHŪ**
Ears and Eyes Collection
Kyōka anthology, **1806**
Frontispiece signature: Hokusai
131 **JIRAIYA SETSUWA**
Legends of Jiraiya
Yomi-hon by Onitake, 11 vols., **1806**
Signature: Hokusai
132 **KARUKAYA KŌDEN TAMA-KUSHIGE**
Tale of Karukaya: The Jewelled Comb
Yomi-hon by Bakin, 5 vols., I/**1807**
Signature: Katsushika Hokusai
(Reissued in gōkan-bon format, 3 vols., 1809,
retitled Ishidōmaru Karukaya monogatari [Tale
of Ishidōmaru and Karukaya], with new
cover-print by Shuntei)
133 **KATAKI-UCHI URAMI KUZU-NO-HA**
The Vengeance of the Fox
Yomi-hon by Bakin, 5 vols., I/**1807**
Signature: Katsushika Hokusai
Fig. 187
134 **CHINSETSU YUMIHARI-ZUKI**
Strange Tales of the Crescent Moon
Yomi-hon by Bakin, 29 vols.: I/**1807**, I/**1808**,
XII/**1808**/09, VIII/**1810**, III/**1811**
(Note: this novel proved so successful that it
was adapted to a jōruri play in Ōsaka, in
1808—as also were Nos. 141, 147 and 151)
Signature: Katsushika Hokusai
▶ Plate **101**; Figs. 188, 189
135 **SONO-NO-YUKI**

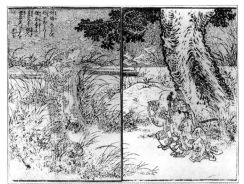

Fig. 187

Fig. 188

Fig. 189 (Compare Plate 124; this illustration is also copied in a book of Taito II, *Eiyū-zue* [Illustrations of Heroes], *c.* 1820s)

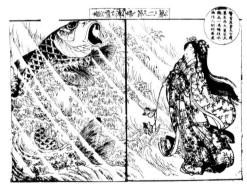

Fig. 190

Snow in the Garden
Yomi-hon by Bakin, 5 parts in 6 vols., I/**1807**
Signature: Katsushika Hokusai
► Plate **100**; Fig. 190

136 *SUMIDA-GAWA BAIRYŪ SHINSHO*
Plum-and-Willow on the Sumida River
Yomi-hon by Bakin, 6 vols., I/**1807**
Signature: Katsushika Hokusai
► Plate **97**; Fig. 191

137 *SHIN KASANE-GEDATSU*
MONOGATARI

Fig. 191

New Tale of the Salvation of Kasane
Yomi-hon by Bakin, 5 vols., I/**1807**
Signature: Katsushika Hokusai

138 *YURIWAKA NOZUE-NO-TAKA*
The Wild Falcon of Yuriwaka
Yomi-hon by Sōba, 5 vols., I/**1808**
Signature: Katsushika Hokusai

139 *ONNA-MOJI NUE MONOGATARI*
Simplified Story of the Monster Nue
Yomi-hon by Nagane, 5 vols., I/**1808**
Signature: Katsushika Hokusai

140 *KATAKI-UCHI MIGAWARI-MYŌGO*
Vengeance by Substitute Invocation
Gōkan-bon by Bakin, 2 vols., I/**1808**
Signature: Katsushika Hokusai

141 *SAN-SHICHI ZENDEN NANKA NO*
YUME
Complete Story of Sankatsu and Hanshichi:
A Dream of Nanka
Yomi-hon by Bakin, 6 vols., I/**1808** (but
actually put on sale in late III/**1808**)
Signature: Katsushika Hokusai
(See caption to Plate 193)
(Sequel: No. 169)

142 *KYŌKUN ONORE-GA-TSUE*
Didactic Tales: My Staff
Gōkan-bon by Ikku, 5 vols., **1808**
Signature: Ĝakyōjin Hokusai

143 *SHIMOYO-NO-HOSHI*
Stars on a Frosty Night
Yomi-hon by Tanehiko, 5 vols., **1808**
Signature: Katsushika Hokusai
► Plate **98**

144 *KITABATAKE ONNA-KYŌKUN*
Instructions in Women's Bravery
Gōkan-bon by Ikku, 5 vols., **1808**
Signature: Gakyōjin Hokusai
(Later reissued as *Yūryaku onna-kyōkun*
[Instructions in Women's Tactics], *c.* 1810)

145 *KASA-ZUKUSHI*
Medley of Caps
Theatre booklet by Bakin, *c.* IX/**1808**
Cover signed: Katsushika Hokusai
► Plate **193**

146 *KATAKI-UCHI MUKUI NO JA-YANAGI*
The Vengeance of the Snake-Willow
Gōkan-bon by Sanwa, 6 vols., **1808**
Signature: Hokusai

147 *RAIGŌ-AJARI KAISŌ-DEN*
The Ghostly Rat and the Priest Raigō
Yomi-hon by Bakin, 8 vols., I–XI/**1808**
Signature: Katsushika Hokusai

148 *AWA-NO-NARUTO*
The Maelstrom of Awa
Yomi-hon by Tanehiko, 5 vols., I/**1808**
Signature: Katsushika Hokusai

149 *ANOKUTARA KEN MONOGATARI*
A Tale of Peerless Wisdom
Yomi-hon by Shinrotei, 5 vols., *c.* I/**1808**
Signature: Katsushika Hokusai

150 *KANA-DEHON GONICHI-NO-BUNSHŌ*
The 'Chūshingura': A Sequel

Yomi-hon by Emba, 5 vols., I/**1809**
Signature: Katsushika Hokusai
► Plate **102**

151 *HIDA-NO-TAKUMI MONOGATARI*
Story of the Craftsman from Hida
Yomi-hon by Rokujuen, 6 vols., I/**1809**
Signature: Katsushika Hokusai
▷ *Hida No Takumi No Monogatari.*
Translated by F. V. Dickins. Glasgow, 1912
(reprinted Tōkyō, 1965)
► Plate **99**

152 *CHŪKŌ ITAKO-BUSHI*
Loyal Songs of Itako
Yomi-hon by Emba, 5 vols., I/**1809**
Signature: Katsushika Hokusai

153 *YUME-NO-UKIHASHI*
The Bridge of Love-Dreams
Yomi-hon by Tōei, 3 vols., Spring, **1809**;
second part, 5 vols., **1814**
Signature: Katsushika Hokusai
► Plate **103**

154 *SANSHŌ-DAYŪ EIKO-MONOGATARI*
The Rise and Fall of Sanshō-dayū
Yomi-hon by Kokuga, 5 vols., I/**1809**
Signature: Katsushika Hokusai

155 *AGEMAKI MONOGATARI KŌHEN*
The Story of Agemaki: A Sequel
Yomi-hon by Tanehiko, 2 vols., I/**1809**
Signature: Katsushika Hokusai
(Retitled reissue: *Edo-murasaki sannin-dōhi*
[Purple of Edo: Three Comrades], 1843)
(First part illus. by Tōsen previous year)

156 *KI-NO-HANA-ZŌSHI*
Tale of Umegawa and Chūbei
Yomi-hon by Shigeru, **1809**
Signature: Katsushika Hokusai

157 *SHIRAITO-SŌSHI*
Story of Shiraito
Yomi-hon by Nagane, 5 vols., I/**1810**
Signature: Katsushika Hokusai Tokimasa

158 *ONNYO IMOSE-YAMA*
The Mountains of Husband and Wife
Yomi-hon by Shinrotei, 6 vols., I/**1810**
Signature: . . . Katsushika Hokusai

159 *ONO-GA-BAKAMURA MUDAJI-*
EZUKUSHI
Foolish Ono's Nonsense Picture-Dictionary
Picture-book, text by Sensō, **1810**/*c.* **1810**
Signature: Katsushika Hokusai
(Retitled editions with revisions, some with
colour-blocks added: *Ryakuga hayamanabi*—
preface, Autumn 1814; *Gadō hitori-geiko:*
Ryakuga haya-oshie, Series III; and *Hokusai*
manga haya-oshie: Series II; *c.* 1840s [Hillier
No. 181 presumably represents retitled
editions of his No. 166])
► Plates **130–131**

160 *[CHAMISE SUMINOE-ZŌSHI]*
The Teashop Suminoe Booklet]
Theatre book, 9 vols., **1810**
Frontispiece signed: Katsushika Hokusai

161 *FUJI-MI JŪSANKEI: KYŌKA TŌMEGANE*
Thirteen Views of Fuji: The Verse
Telescope
Kyōka anthology, *c.* **1810**
Signed: Gakyōjin Hokusai
(With 12 other artists)

162 *SETA-NO-HASHI RYŪNYO-NO-HONJI*
The Dragon-lady of Seta Bridge
Jōruri yomi-hon by Tanehiko, 3 vols., I/**1811**
Signature: Katsushika Hokusai
(Also reissued in 1813 and 1823)
Fig. 192

163 *TSUYU-NO-FUCHI*
Vale of Dewdrops
Kyōka anthology (commemorating the death
of Kikunojō III), XII/**1811**/12
Signature: Hokusai
(With Hokuba, Shūri, Gosei, Kiyonaga,

Fig. 192

Fig. 193

Fig. 194

Shuntei, Toyokuni, Hokuju, Shinsai, Shun-ei, Chiyogiku)

**164　*ZOKU HIZAKURIGE*
'Hizakurige' Sequel**
Kokkei-bon by Ikku, 2 vols., **1811**
Signature to Frontispiece: Hokusai

**165　*SHIMPEN TSUKI-NO-KUMASAKA*
The New 'Brigand Kumasaka'**
Gōkan-bon, 3 vols., c. I/**1811**
Signature (text and illustrations): Tokitarō
[=Hokusai] (covers illustrated by Kunimaru)

**166　*KOKKEI FUTSUKA-YOI*/
JŌDAN FUTSUKA-YOI
A Comic Hangover**
Kokkei-bon by Ikku, 2 vols., **1811**
Illustrated by Hokusai and Hokusū
(Reprinted in 1825 with the artists' names removed, and under the alternative title cited above; also, new edition of 1882)

**167　*HORIKAWA TARŌ HYAKUSHU DAI-KYŌKA-SHŪ*
First Hundred Verses at Horikawa**
Kyōka anthology, 2 vols., c. **1811**
Signature: Katsushika Hokusai
(With Shigemasa, Shumman, Kanrin, Kikkei, Kiyozumi, Shūri)
▶ Plate **178**

**168　*KANTŌ HYAKUDAI KYŌKA-SHŪ*
One Hundred Mad Verses of East Japan**
Kyōka anthology, 2 vols., c. **1811**

**169　*YUME-AWASE NANKA KŌKI*
New Dreams of Nanka**
Yomi-hon by Bakin, 8 vols., I/**1812**
(A sequel to *San-Shichi zenden*, No. 141)
Signature: Katsushika Hokusai Tokimasa

**170　*MATSUŌ MONOGATARI*
The Story of Matsuō**
Yomi-hon by Shigeru, 6 vols., I/**1812**
Signature: Hokusai

**171　*RYAKUGA HAYA-OSHIE I*
Quick Guide to Drawing, Series I**
c. I/**1812** (Series II: see No. 180; Series III: see No. 186, and also No. 159)
Signatures: Hokusai-*rōjin*/Kyōrian Bainen
(in advertisements: Taito)
▷ Tōgasaki, F.: 'Certain aspects of the basic compositional elements in Hokusai's work . . .,' in *Ukiyo-e Art*, Nos. 51–52 (1976)
▶ Plates **132–133**; Fig. **193**

**172　*KYŌKA ICHIE ŌZUMŌ*
Sumō Chances**
Kyōka anthology, **1812**
Signature: Hokusai

**173　*AOTO FUJITSUNA MORYŌ-AN*
The Ambiguities of Aoto Fujitsuna**
Yomi-hon by Bakin, in 2 series of 5 vols. each, XII/**1812**/**13**
(Adapted to the Kabuki stage in Edo, 1814)
Signature: Katsushika Hokusai Raishin

**174　*OGURI GAIDEN*
The Legend of Lord Oguri**
Yomi-hon by Shigeru, 15 vols.: I/**1813**, I/**1814**, I/**1815**
Signature: Katsushika Hokusai

Fig. 195

**175　*[NICHIREN-SHŌNIN ICHIDAI-ZUE*
A Pictorial Life of St Nichiren]**
Yomi-hon, 6 vols., **1813**

**176　*HOKUETSU KIDAN*
Strange Tales of Northern Echigo**
Yomi-hon collection by Shigeyo, 6 vols., IX/**1813**
Signature: Katsushika Hokusai (some illustrations by author)
▶ Plate **179**; Fig. **195**

**177　*KATSUSHIKA-ZUSHI TEGURI-BUNE*
The Fishing Boat of Katsushika**
Kyōka anthology and gazetteer, **1813**
Signed: Hokusai
(With Tōrin, Bunchō, Nanrei et al.)
Fig. **196**

**178　**HOKUSAI MANGA I*
Random Sketches by Hokusai, Series I**
c. I/**1814**

Fig. 196

Signature: Katsushika Hokusai (Note: this is the signature for the Nagoya editions of the first 10 *Manga* series; for the Edo editions the more 'current' *nom d'artiste* appears: Hokusai *aratame* Katsushika Taito)
(Preface dated 'Autumn, 1812'; thought to have been issued first in early Spring, 1814; at head of title [for all of the series]: *Denshin kaishu* ['A Primer for Transmitting the True Spirit'—i.e. for aspiring artists; on this term see my translation from Series I of the *Manga*, cited below])

(First issue omits Series-number from title-slip; blocks recarved for edition of 1829; reduced-size reprint titled *Hokusai gafu*.
(For the subsequent Series of the *Manga*, see Nos. 183, 184, 190, 191, 193, 194, 197, 200, 201, 236, 238, 265, 269, 274)
▷ Dickins, F. V.: *The Mangwa of Hokusai*. London, 1905
▷● Michener, James A.: *The Hokusai Sketchbooks: Selections from the Manga*. (With translations by Richard Lane.) Tōkyō, 1958
▷ Various: *Hokusai manga*. 2 vols., Tōkyō, 1976 (in Japanese)
▷ Forrer, M.: *Eirakuya Tōshirō, Publisher at Nagoya*. Amsterdam, 1985 (p. 195 ff.)
▷ Nagata, S. (ed., with Asakura, H.): *Hokusai manga*. 3 vols., Tōkyō, 1986 (in Japanese)
▶ Plates **136–139, 147, 148, 153**; Fig. **194**

**179　**HOKUSAI SHASHIN GAFU*
Hokusai's Album from Life**
Album, preface dated III/**1814** (first dated colophon, 1819)
(There is also a much expanded—though hardly authoritative—re-engraved edition of 1890)
▶ Plates **180, 187**

**180　*RYAKUGA HAYA-OSHIE II*
Quick Guide to Drawing, Series II**
c. **1814**
(Series II of No. 171 above; alternative title, *Ryakuga haya-manabi* [Quick Learning of Drawing].) (Partly reissued in 1857 with colours added; and again, c. 1890s, combining Nos. 171 and 192)
Signature: Tengudō Nettetsu
▶ Plates **134–135**, Fig. **197**

Fig. 197

Fig. 198

**181　**EHON JŌRURI ZEKKU*
Mixed Verses on Jōruri**
I/**1815**
Signature: Katsushika Hokusai
(Note: There is an alternative edition with colouring added—but fewer illustrations—entitled *Ehon Chōseiden* [Picture-book of

Longevity Hall (an elliptical reference to the
jōruri genre)], 2 vols., *c.* 1814/15; it has yet to
be determined which edition is the earlier.
There are also editions on large-size paper
(*ōbon*), in 1 or 2 vols.; and an 1891 reprint of
the plates only, entitled *Jōruri zue*)
▶ Plates **210, 211**

182 *BEI-BEI KYŌDAN*
  A Rustic Tale of Two Heirs
  Yomi-hon by Bakin, 6 vols., I/**1815**
  Signature: *zen*-Hokusai Taito
  (The blocks were lost in the Edo Fire of 1829,
  and recarved for the reprint of 1858)
  Fig. 198

183 *HOKUSAI MANGA II*
  Random Sketches by Hokusai, Series II
  Spring, **1815**
  Signature: Katsushika Hokusai (see No. 178)
  ▶ Plates **149, 156, 182**

184 *HOKUSAI MANGA III*
  Random Sketches by Hokusai, Series III
  Spring, **1815**
  Signature: Katsushika Hokusai (see No. 178)
  ▶ Plates **138, 140, 159**; Fig. 199

Fig. 199

185 *MONGAKU-JŌNIN HOSSHIN-NO-KI:*
  HASHI-KUYŌ
  The Enlightenment of St Mongaku:
  Mass for the Bridge
  Yomi-hon by Shigeru, 5 vols., **1815**
  Signature: Katsushika *zen*-Hokusai-*ō*
  (With Raishū)

186 *ODORI HITORI-GEIKO*
  Teach Yourself the Dance
  Preface dated Summer, **1815**
  Signature: Katsushika Hokusai-*oyaji hitsu*
  (Nominally, constitutes Series III of No. 171
  above; reprinted Summer, 1835)
  ▶ Plate **161**; Fig. 200

187 *[KAGEKIYO GAIDEN*
  The Story of Kagekiyo]
  Yomi-hon by Shigeru, 5 vols., *c.* **1815**

188 *NIHON SAIJIKI KYŌKA-SHŪ*
  Kyōka of Japanese Festivals
  c. mid-**1810s**
  Signature: Taito

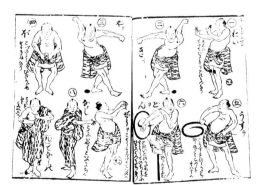

Fig. 200

Fig. 201

Fig. 202

189 *SANTEI GAFU*
  Painting in Three Aspects
  c. Spring, **1816** (a wrapper is extant, dated
  1815, which is also date of preface)
  Signature: Hokusai *aratame* Katsushika Taito
  (Turnover employs different character for *fu*;
  the more customary reading of the title is
  Santai: the form -*tai* appears, e.g., in an
  advertisement in No. 210 below)
  ▶ Plates **162–165**; Fig. 201

190 *HOKUSAI MANGA IV*
  Random Sketches by Hokusai, Series IV
  Summer, **1816**
  Signature: Katsushika Hokusai (see No. 178)
  ▶ Plates **150–151, 154**

191 *HOKUSAI MANGA V*
  Random Sketches by Hokusai, Series V
  Summer, **1816**
  Signature: Katsushika Hokusai (see No. 178)
  ▶ Plate **157**; Fig. 202

192 *EHON HAYABIKI*
  The Quick Pictorial-Dictionary
  Series I, **1817**; Series II, **1819**
  Signatures: Katsushika Hokusai Taito-*rōjin*/
  zen-Hokusai Taito
  (Sequels to *Ryakuga haya-oshie*, No. 171)
  ▶ Plates **166–167**

193 *HOKUSAI MANGA VI*
  Random Sketches by Hokusai, Series VI
  1817
  Signature: Katsushika Hokusai (see No. 178)
  ▶ Plate **141**

194 *HOKUSAI MANGA VII*
  Random Sketches by Hokusai, Series VII
  1817
  Signature: Katsushika Hokusai (see No. 178)
  ▶ Plates **152, 155, 158**; Fig. 203

195 *HOKUSAI GAKYŌ*
  Mirror of Designs by Hokusai
  1 vol., preface dated Spring **1818** (new
  edition, 1834); alternative title: *Denshin gakyō*
  (Mirror of Designs to Transmit the [Artist's]
  True Intent)

Fig. 203

(At head of title: same subtitle as the *Manga*,
No. 178 ff. Many of the designs are patterned
on the work of the genre-painting pioneer
Hanabusa Itchō [1652–1724], as conveyed in
the copy-book of 1758/73, *Eihitsu hyakuga* [A
Hundred Sketches by Hanabusa]; indeed,
one edition features separate title-page citing
the volume as a 'Sequel' to the latter)
Colour edition, retitled *Shūga ichiran*
(Excellent Pictures at a Glance), *c.* Spring 1819
(omits 4½ spreads of illustrations
from the *Hokusai gakyō*; one early impression
includes touches of 'gold'-dust and mica; an
earlier, *kyōka-bon* version is also alleged;
abridged edition, *Hokusai gakan*, published in
1858; see also No. 272)
Signature: Katsushika Hokusai
▷ Ouwehand, C.: 'An Annotated
Description of Hokusai's *Shūga Ichiran*', in
*Mededelingen van het Rijksmuseum voor
Volkenkunde*, No. 15, Leiden, 1962
▶ Plates **188–189**; Fig. 204

Fig. 204

Fig. 205

196 *HYŌSUI KIGA*
  Strange Pictures by Chance Encounter
  Haiku anthology, 2 vols., II/**1818**;
  landscapes by Ryūkōsai, figures by Hokusai
  (see text, p. 148)
  Signature (on wrapper): Hokusai Taito
  (Later reissued as *Hakoya-no-yama* [Mountain

Fig. 206   Fig. 207

Fig. 208

of the Immortals], 1 vol., I/1821, and *Ehon ryōhitsu* [Picture Book from Two Brushes], 1 vol., *c.* 1820s
▷ Hillier, J. and Suzuki, J.: 'The Hokusai/ Ryūkōsai *Hyōsui Kiga* and *Ehon Ryōhitsu*', in *Ukiyo-e Art*, No. 13 (1966)
Fig. 205

197 **HOKUSAI MANGA VIII**
Random Sketches by Hokusai, Series VIII
I/**1819** (the date on blocks is 1818 but actual publication was Spring of 1819)
Signature: Katsushika Hokusai (see No. 178)
▶ Plate **142**; Fig. 206

198 **KOMAWAKA ZENDEN: SAKARŌ NO MATSU**
Story of Komawaka: The Tower-Pine
Yomi-hon by Kiraku, 6 vols., I/**1819**
Signature: Katsushika *zen*-Hokusai Taito (With Hokuun)

199 ***HOKUSAI GASHIKI**
The Hokusai Painting Style
IV/**1819**
Signature: Katsushika Taito
▶ Plates **181, 184–186**; Fig. 208

200 **HOKUSAI MANGA IX**
Random Sketches by Hokusai, Series IX
Spring, **1819**
Signature: Katsushika Hokusai (see No. 178)
▶ Plates **143–145, 160**; Fig. 207

201 **HOKUSAI MANGA X**
Random Sketches by Hokusai, Series X

Fig. 209

Spring, **1819**
Signature: Katsushika Hokusai (see No. 178)
▶ Plate **146**; Fig. 209

202 **[HOKUSAI GAFU   A Hokusai Album]**
1820
(Supplement to the preceding *Hokusai gashiki*, No. 199)

203 ***RYŌBI SHAHITSU**
Elegant Brushstrokes
Picture-book, *c.* V/**1820** [*saihitsu* is the more usual reading, but in the sense of 'flowing brushstrokes', *shahitsu* seems preferable]
(Retitled reissue—by which the work is more commonly known: *Hokusai soga* [Designs by Hokusai], *c.* early 1820s; see also No. 263 below)
Signature: Katsushika Taito
[*Note to Plate 192*: perhaps the first rule of ukiyo-e research is not to be lulled into assuming a relationship between prints of the same title, subject, or even composition. In the present instance, however, it was only upon contemplating the similar titles of the originals that the thought flashed into my mind: could not this Hokusai design have been the ultimate inspiration for Hiroshige's ultimate masterpiece, *Snowy Night at Kambara* (1833—Fig. 213)? Indeed, the basic elements are all the same, and this is a source that the younger artist surely studied in his youth. This new hypothesis must, certainly, be belatedly added to the Addenda of my monograph (the first, I might add, on a single ukiyo-e print), *Hiroshige: 'Kambara'—the Anatomy of a Japanese Print* (1984).]

Fig. 210

Fig. 211

▶ Plates **190–192**; Figs. 210–212
204 **WAGO INSHITSU-BUN ESHŌ**
Divine Providence Illustrated
I/**1820** (On the basis of style, probably the work of Taito II—who had received this art-name several months before)
Signature: Katsushika Taito

Fig. 212

Fig. 213

205 **KUSA-NO-HARA**
Grassy Plains
Kyōka anthology, *c.* **1821**
Illustrated by Hokusai, Hokkei, Hōitsu et al.

206 **TŌKAI TANGO**
Searching the East Highway
Sharé-hon by Miyoshino, **1821**
Signature: *zen*-Hokusai Iitsu
(Frontispiece by Hokusai, illustrations by Hokushū; freer translation of title: *Last Tango in Edo*)

206a **TŌ-NO-SHIRANAMI**
(Life of the Swashbuckler Ippondaemon)
Yomi-hon by Ikku, 3 vols., **1822**
Unsigned (but publisher's advertisement cites as 'By Katsushika Hokusai')

207 **EDO RYŪKŌ RYŌRI-TSŪ**
Fashionable Edo Cookery
A guide to cookery of the Yao-Zen Restaurant in Edo, 4 Series, **1822–35**
Various illustrators (including Hōitsu and Tani Bunchō), Hokusai's contributions appearing in Series II (II/1822, signed Hokusai *aratame* Iitsu) and Series IV (II/1835, signed *zen*-Hokusai Iitsu, in 75th year)
(Reprinted in 1903 as *Ryōri haya-shinan—* Quick Guide to Cookery)
▶ Plate **229**; Fig. 217

208 **SHUNJU-AN YOMIHATSU-MUSHIRO**
Shunju's New Year Poems
c. **1822**
Signature: Getchi-*rōjin* Iitsu

209 **[KYŌKA MUMA-ZUKUSHI**
Comic Poems on Horses]
c. **1822**
One design signed: Getchi-*rōjin* Iitsu
(Possibly confused with the *surimono* series cited under **Prints**, No. 133)

210 **IMAYŌ SEKKIN [KUSHI-KISERU] HINAGATA**
Models of Modern Combs and Pipes
3 vols., *yoko-bon*, **1822–V/1823**
Signature: *zen*-Hokusai *aratame* Katsushika Iitsu
(See also No. 256 for various reissues)
▶ Plates **168–171**; Fig. 214

Fig. 214

211 IPPITSU GAFU
Drawings at One Stroke
Spring, **1823** (but prepared *c*. 1817)
Signature: *zen*-Hokusai Taito *sensei/*
(wrapper) Hokusai Taito *sensei*
(At head of title: same subtitle as No. 178.
According to the preface and wrappers,
Hokusai's inspiration was a series of [MS]
sketches in similar abbreviated manner done
by the early Nagoya Nanga master Fuku-
zensai [Niwa Kagen—1742–1786]; no such
work has been traced; see also No. 252.)
(Note: the notion that the signature 'Taito'—
appearing on three plates of this volume—
indicates collaboration with the pupil Taito
II seems to me quite erroneous [see M.
Forrer in *Hokusai and His School* (Haarlem),
p. 76, and J. Hillier in *The Art of Hokusai in Book
Illustration*, p. 191; with a further ambiguous
and confusing note in the Forrer *Eirakuya
Tōshirō*, p. 227]. My first reason is that the
expression '*Mâitre* Taito' appears on the
wrapper to the book [Hillier, Pl. 174], here,
clearly indicating *only* Hokusai: being part of
the subtitle 'Inheriting the Concept [of
Fukuzensai]'. My other reasons are that the
plates in question appear at the *head* of the
volume, are entirely in Hokusai's style, and
there is no other evidence to assume any
Taito II relation to the book; and—as cited in
Note 7 on p. 141—Hokusai was inextricably
associated with the name Taito in Nagoya,
due to his famous 'Great Daruma Exhibition'
there.)
▶ Plates **173–176, 183**; Figs. **215, 216**

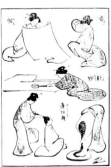
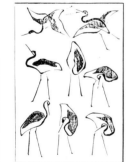

Fig. 215   Fig. 216

212 KYŌKUN KANA-SHIKIMOKU
Ethical Laws in Popular Language
I/**1824**
Signature: *zen*-Hokusai Iitsu
213 KYŌKA KACHŌ-FŪGETSU-SHŪ
Poems on Birds/Flowers/Wind/Moon
Kyōka anthology, **1824**
Signature: Katsushika Iitsu
(With Hokusen)
214 SHINGATA KOMON-CHŌ
New Models for Kimono-patterns

Fig. 217

c. III/**1824**
Signature: *zen*-Hokusai Iitsu
(Reissued in 1884 as *Hokusai moyō gafu*
[Hokusai's Pattern-album], reprinted 1891)
▷ Amstutz, W. (ed.): *Japanese Emblems and
Designs*, Zürich, 1970
▶ Plate **173**
215 [KYŌKA SANJŪ-ROKKASEN
Comic Verses on the Thirty-six Poets]
c. **1824**
Signature: *zen*-Hokusai
216 KYŌKA KUNI-ZUKUSHI
Verses on the Provinces
c. **1810** (later edition of 1825, with *kyōka*
replaced by *senryū* verses) (Date-order
wrong, as very recently revised)
Signature: Hokusai
(With 15 pupils)
217 RENGE-DAI
The Lotus-pedestal
Kyōka anthology, VI/**1826**
Signature: Iitsu
(With Hokuba, Hokkei, Kunisada, Hōitsu et
al.)
▶ Plate **228**
218 SUKI-GAESHI
A Random Miscellany
Miscellany by Tanehiko, 2 vols., XI/**1826**
Illustrations copied by Hokusai from earlier
works
Signature: Katsushika Iitsu
219 [AKI NO HANA-TORI SHŪ
Autumn Flower Gathering]
1826
Illustrated by Hokusai, Hokkei, Gyokkei
220 KYŌKA SEIRYŪ HYAKKACHŌ
One Hundred Kachō Verses
c. **1826**
Signature: Hokusai (with Hokkei)
221 HAIKAI SANJŪROKKASEN
Thirty-six Poets of Haiku
Verse anthology, **1827**
Signature: Katsushika Iitsu
222 ASHI-NO-HITOMOTO
A Single Reed
Haiku commentary on Bashō, Summer /**1827**
Signature: Hokusai *aratame* Iitsu

Fig. 218   Fig. 219

223 KACHŌ-GASAN UTA-AWASE
Illustrated Verses on Flowers-and-Birds
Kyōka anthology, **1828**
Signature: Getchi-*rōjin* Iitsu
▶ Plate **227**
224 BONGA HITORI-GEIKO
Teach Yourself Sand-painting
1828
Frontispiece signed: Iitsu (with Kōitsu)
▶ Plate **230**
225 SHOKKŌ HINAGATA KINTAI GASŌ
Models for Master Craftsmen
1828
Signature: Hokusai
226 EHON TEIKIN ŌRAI
Illustrated Home Precepts
Series I: Autumn/1828; Series II: *c*. 1830s(?);
Series III: 1848
Signature: *zen*-Hokusai Iitsu (and in Preface
to Series I: Getchi-*rōjin*)
(Later combined in one volume, *c*. 1850)
▶ Plates **231–232**; Fig. **218**
227 SUIKODEN YŪSHI-NO-EZUKUSHI
Heroes of the 'Suihuchuan' Portrayed
I/**1829**
Signature: Katsushika *zen*-Hokusai Iitsu-
rōjin
(Although the *kana* reading remains the
same, the title page appears in two forms:
with the *kanji* written *Hyaku-hachi seitan shōzō*
(Portraits of the 108 Stars) and in a later
edition, *Ehon Suikoden*; cover-title: *Chūgi
Suikoden ehon*—which also appears on the
title-page in a later edition)
(Reprint edition: *Ehon Suikoden*, *c*. 1840s)
▶ Plates **234–236**; Fig. **219**
228 [KYŌKA SHOGA-JŌ
Pictorial Album of Verses]
Kyōka anthology, *c*. later **1820s**
Signature: Hokusai *aratame* Iitsu
229 EHON ONNA IMAGAWA
Women's Precepts Illustrated
(Stylistically this work would seem to date
from the late **1820s**: there is also mention of
it in a Hokusai letter to the publisher
Eirakuya of that period; the only dated
edition is from 1844; some editions have
colours added, and the title *Hokusai Onna
Imagawa* on title-page)
Signature: (on wrapper): Katsushika
Iitsu-*rōjin*
▶ Plate **237**
230 RESSEN GAZŌ-SHŪ
Portraits of the Immortals
3 vols., **1829**
Signature: Hokusai *aratame* Iitsu
(With Hokuga)
▶ Plate **233**
231 HOKUSAI DŌCHŪ GAFU
Hokusai's Pictures on the Road
Picture-book, **1835** (with several reissues)
(Revised version of a work by Hokusai's
pupil Hokkei, *c*. 1830, only the frontispiece
and first illustration being by Hokusai; also
found in 2-vol. editions, n.d. and 1881)
▷ Forrer, M.: *Eirakuya Tōshirō* . . . Chapter I
and infra
232 ONNA ICHIDAI EIGA-SHŪ
Lives of Flourishing Women
Kyōka anthology, III/**1831**
Signature: *zen*-Hokusai Iitsu, in 72nd year
▶ Plate **238**
233 HANA-FUBUKI EN-NO-SHIGARAMI
Snow-blown Chains of Fate
Gōkan-bon by Isobe; 6 fascicles in 4 vols.,
Spring/**1832**
Signature: *zen*-Hokusai Iitsu

Fig. 220

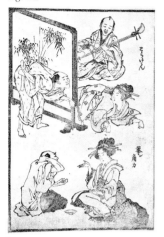

Fig. 221

(Cover-design by Hokusai and Kuniyoshi, illustrations by Kuniyoshi)

234 TŌSHISEN EHON
'Chinese Verses' Illustrated
By Takai Ranzan. Series VI: *gogon-ritsu*
(signed *zen*-Hokusai Iitsu), 5 vols., I/**1833**;
Series VII: *shichigon-ritsu* (signed Gakyō-*rojin*
Manji-*ō*), 5 vols., IX/**1836** (title-page: *Ehon
Tōshisen*)
(The earlier series were illustrated by Seppō,
Fuyō, Enjō, Shigemasa and Suikei; see also
No. 273)
▶ Plate **312**; Fig. 220

235 SHUSSE YAKKO-KOMAN-NO-DEN
The Story of Koman's Success
Gōkan-bon by Tanehiko; 4 fascicles in 2 vols.,
I/**1833**
(Covers signed: *zen*-Hokusai Iitsu;
illustrations by Kuninao; covers only,
reissued for a novel of 1842, *Oshidori
monogatari*, with Kunisada's name
interpolated)

236 HOKUSAI MANGA XI
Random Sketches by Hokusai, Series XI
c. **1833**; unsigned
▶ Plates **307–308**; Fig. 221

237 EHON CHŪKYŌ
'The Canon of Loyalty' Illustrated
I/**1834**
Signature: Katsushika *zen*-Hokusai Iitsu-
rōjin
▶ Plate **313**

238 HOKUSAI MANGA XII
Random Sketches by Hokusai, Series XII
I/**1834** (date of preface); unsigned; first
edition—and all Edo issues—omits tints
▶ Plate **309**

239 *FUGAKU HYAKKEI*
The Hundred Views of Fuji
Vol. 1, III/**1834**; vol. 2, III/**1835**; vol. 3,
engraved *c.* **1835** but not published until at

Fig. 222

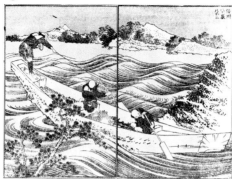

Fig. 223

Fig. 224

Fig. 225

Fig. 226

least a decade later
(Note: as cited above—p. 188, Note 3—the
reading *Fuji* is also possible for the title;
however, in Series III–15a appears a parasol
bearing the inscription in *kana*—a concealed
publisher's blurb—*Fugaku*: which would
support the view that *either* reading was
correct at the time)
(On the engraving of this work, see
Hokusai's letter quoted in the text, p. 120;
future students of this and other ukiyo-e
masters may do well to scrutinize the
influence of the woodblock-carvers—not to
mention the printers—on the effectiveness
of the final printed works)
Signatures: *zen*-Hokusai Iitsu *aratame*/
Gakyō-*rōjin* Manji (in 75th/76th years)
▷ Dickins, F. V.: *Fugaku Hiyaku-kei* or *A
Hundred Views of Fuji (Fusiyama): By Hokusai*
London, 1880 (commentary only)
▷ *One Hundred Views of Fuji.* Introduction
by Jack Hillier; descriptions of the plates by
F. V. Dickins. New York, 1958. (With com-
plete reproduction of plates, but all, mirror-
reversed, 'for reading from left to right')
▷● Suzuki, J.: *Hokusai: Fugaku hyakkei.* 4
vols., Tōkyō, 1972 (reprinted in 1 vol., 1986;
in Japanese)
▷ Winzinger, F. (ed.): *Die Hundert Ansichten
des Berges Fuji*, Dortmund, 1981
▷ Smith, Henry II (ed.): *Hokusai: One
Hundred Views of Mt. Fuji*, New York, 1988
▷ Lane, Richard: 'Hokusai towards the
Summit: *The Hundred Views of Fuji.*' In *Arts of
Asia*, Jan.–Feb. 1989
▶ Plates **292–306, 359**; Figs. 222–226

240 HOKUSAI MANGA HAYA-SHINAN
Hokusai's Book of Quick Sketching
c. **1834–35**
Signature: *zen*-Iitsu-*rōjin*

241 EHON KŌKYŌ
'The Canon of Filial Piety' Illustrated
The Chinese *Hsiao ching*; 2 vols, Spring/**1834**
(Wrapper and inner-title: *Ehon kobun*
[Ancient] *Kōkyō*; reissued in 1850 and 1864)
Signature: Katsushika *zen*-Hokusai Iitsu-*ō*
▶ Plate **315**

242 EHON SENJI-MON
'The Thousand-Letters' Illustrated
The Chinese classic *Ch'ien-tze wen*; **1835–36**
Signature: Katsushika *zen*-Hokusai Iitsu
(Frontispiece by Shōdō)
▶ Plate **314**

243 WAKAN EHON SAKIGAKE
Warriors Illustrated: China and Japan
I/**1836**
Signature: *zen*-Hokusai Iitsu *aratame* Gakyō-
rōjin Manji, in 76th year (and variations)
(Second edition of 1887; for sequel see
following item)
▷ Fagioli, M.: *Hokusai, Wakan Ehon
Sakigake.* Florence, 1978
▶ Plates **319–320**; Fig. 227

Fig. 227

244 **EHON MUSASHI-ABUMI**
'The Stirrups of Musashi' Illustrated
VIII/**1836**
Signature: *zen*-Hokusai Gakyō-*rōjin* Manji,
in 77th year
(Second edition of 1887; a sequel to No. 243)
▶ Plate **321**

245 **EHON WAKAN-NO-HOMARE**
Heroes of China and Japan Illustrated
c. **1836/50** (Note: colophon cites 'in 76th year
[i.e. 1835], while on travels in Izu-Sagami';
earliest dated edition: 1850 [Nagata, *Nempu*
p. 110, cites as 'Kaei I', 1848, presumably a
misprint]; I have seen undated editions
which seemed—on the basis of printing,
binding and paper—to predate that of 1850,
and have hence tentatively listed under the
ambiguous date '*c.* 1836/50')
Signature: *zen*-Hokusai *aratame* Gakyō-*rōjin*
Manji, in 76th year
▶ Plates **322–323**

246 **SHOSHOKU-EHON SHIN-HINAGATA**
New Designs for Craftsmen Illustrated
I/**1836**
Signature: *zen*-Hokusai Iitsu *aratame*/Gakyō-*rōjin* Manji (and variations)
(Reprinted, *c.* 1840s as *Katsushika shin-hinagata*, and in 1877 as *Hokusai shin-hinagata*)
▶ Plates **317–318**

247 **UTEI EMBA GASHŌ**
Honouring Utei Emba
Kyōka anthology, *c.* **1830s**
Signature: Hokusai Iitsu

248 **NIKKŌSAN-SHI   A Guide to Nikkō**
5 vols., I/**1837**
One four-page plate in vol. 4, signed:
Gakyō-*rōjin* Manji, in 77th year [due to
block-damage, also readable as '72nd']
(With Kazan, Tani Bunchō, Chinzan,
Hokuga, Shigenobu II)
▶ Plate **324**

249 **WAKAN INSHITSU-DEN**
Divine Providence in China and Japan
II/**1840**
Signature: *zen* Hokusai *aratame* Gakyō-*rōjin*
Manji
▶ Plate **325**

250 **SHAKA GOICHIDAIKI-ZUE**
Life of Sakyamuni Illustrated
Yomi-hon, 6 vols., IV/**1841**
(Engraving details are mentioned in a
Hokusai letter dating from several years
prior to publication)
Signature: *zen*-Hokusai Manji-*rōjin*
(Reissued in 1845, and in 1884 with
copperplate re-engraving)
▶ Plate **327**; Fig. **228**

Fig. 228

251 **NAGASHIRA MUSHA-BURUI**
Warriors Classified
Autumn/**1841**
Signature: Hokusai *aratame* Katsushika Iitsu
(Abridged edition: *Musha-zukushi e-dehon*

[The Compleat Warriors: Artist's-guide],
c. 1840s; see also No. 257)
▶ Plates **326, 336**

252 **IPPITSU EHON**
Picture Book: with One Brushstroke
III/**1842**
(Reduced-size version of the *Ippitsu gafu* of
1823, No. 211 above; cited as 'by *maître*
Hokusai')

253 **HANA-NO-JŪMON**
Flowers of Sixpence
A geographical work, *c.* **1842** (with Hokkei)
Signature: Gakyō-*rōjin* Manji, in 82nd year

254 ***MANJI-Ō SŌHITSU GAFU**
Old Manji's Cursive Album
Picture-book, I/**1843** [1832]
Signature: *zen*-Hokusai Manji-*ō*
(Also coloured edition under the title
Hokusai manga/sōhitsu-no-bu [Hokusai's
Sketches in Cursive Style], same date; and
reissued with other works in 1877 as *Hokusai
gaen* [A Garden of Hokusai Sketches])
(In Hokusai's style of *c.* 1832—which is date
of the preface and for which date, indeed, an
edition is alleged)
▶ Plates **328–330**

255 **EHON KAN-SO GUNDAN**
The Wars of Han and Ch'u Illustrated
Yomi-hon adapted from a Chinese novel,
translated by Shunsui after an earlier version
by Bakin; 20 vols.: X/**1843**, I/**1845**
Signature: Katsushika Manji-*rōjin*
Hachiemon
▶ Plate **331**

256 **HOKUSAI MANGA**
Random Sketches by Hokusai
1845
Signature: Katsushika Hokusai
(A separate work from the famous 15-
volume series—No. 178 ff. above—being a
reissue of No. 210; also retitled *Iitsu manga*
[1841], and again reissued, *c.* 1850s, as
Banshoku zushiki [The Crafts Illustrated],
with reprint in 1880; also known under the
titles *Kachō-sansui zushiki* [Flowers/Birds/
Landscape Illustrated], and as part of the
two series *Saiga zushiki* [Miniatures
Illustrated] and *Hokusai zushiki* [Hokusai
Illustrated], 1860s–1870s)

257 **EHON MUSHA-ZOROI**
Picture-book: The Compleat Warriors
c. mid-**1840s**
(An abridged version of No. 251, with
colours added)

258 **GENJI ITTŌ-SHI**
The History of the Minamoto Unification
Yomi-hon by Yasusada, 5 vols., **1846**
(reissued 1850)
Signature: Hokusai Iitsu-*rōjin* Hachiemon

259 **RETSUJO HYAKUNIN ISSHU**
One Hundred Poems by Famous Women
1847
Signature: Katsushika Manji-*rōjin*
(with Kunisada)

260 **EHON SAISHIKU-TSŪ**
On the Use of Colouring
Series I and II, I/**1848**
Signature: Gakyō-*rojin* Manji
▶ Plates **352–354**; Fig. **229**

261 **SHŪGA HYAKUNIN-ISSHU**
One Hundred Poems of Elegance
I/**1848**
Signature: Old Manji, in 88th year
(In collaboration with Kuniyoshi, Shigenobu
II, Eisen, Kunisada)

262 **SOKUSEKI HŌCHŌ**
The Ready Cleaver
A miniature cookbook with coloured
frontispiece by Hokusai, *c.* **1848**

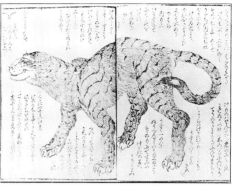

Fig. 229

Signature: Manji Iitsu, in 89th year

263 **[HOKUSAI GAFU**
A Hokusai Album]
3 vols., **1849**; a combined edition of the
Gashiki [No. 199], *Gafu* [No. 202], and *Soga*
[No. 203], in reduced size

264 **ZOKU EIYŪ HYAKUNIN ISSHU**
One Hundred Poems of Heroes: A Sequel
I/**1849**
Signature: *zen*-Hokusai Manji-*rōjin*
(With Kuniyoshi, Shigenobu II, Kunisada,
Sadahide)

POSTHUMOUSLY PUBLISHED WORKS

265 **HOKUSAI MANGA XIII**
Random Sketches by Hokusai, Series XIII
c. Autumn/**1849**; unsigned (first edition
omits tints)
▶ Plate **310**

266 **GIRETSU HYAKUNIN ISSHU**
One Hundred Poems of Celebrities
1850
Signature: *zen*-Hokusai Manji-*rōjin*
(With Kuniyoshi, Yoshitora, Kunisada,
Sadahide)

267 **SŌZAN CHOMON-KISHŪ**
Strange Tales by Sōzan
3 vols., **1850**
Two designs signed: Manji, in 88th year

268 **KIJIN HYAKUNIN-ISSHU**
The 'Hundred Poems' by Eccentrics
Verse anthology, **1852**
(In collaboration with Utagawa artists;
several original Hokusai sketches for this
book are extant)
▶ Plates **337–338**

269 **HOKUSAI MANGA XIV**
Random Sketches by Hokusai, Series XIV
c. early **1850s**
(Though undated, the first impression
features advertisements, paper and
colouring very similar to Series XIII)
▶ Plate **311**

269a **HOKUSAI ZUKŌ I**
Hokusai Designs, Series I
c. 1850s (possibly after Hokusai sketches, but
ill-copied)

270 **KANNON-KYŌ WAKUN-ZUE**
The Sutra of Kannon Illustrated
Yomi-hon-style Buddhist text by Tsunetoshi,
2 vols., **1862** (Preface 1849; reissued in 1891;
turnover-title: *Kannon-kyō ryakuzukai*)
Signature: Katsushika Hokusai

271 **HOKUSAI KYŌGA: TŌKAIDŌ
GOJŪSAN-EKI/HOKUSAI-Ō
MICHI-NO-SHIORI**
1862; see **Prints**, No. 76 (p. 284)

272 **HOKUSAI MANGA XV**
Random Sketches by Hokusai, Series XV
September **1878**
(Hokusai's sketches [including many plates

reprinted from No. 195] supplemented by the work of the Meiji Nagoya artists Oda Kyōsai and Numata Gessai II)
▶ Plate **316**

273   EHON TŌSHISEN
'Chinese Verses' Illustrated

2 vols., January **1880**
Signature: *kojin* [deceased] Katsushika Iitsu
(A supplement—comprising *gogon-zekku* verses—to No. 234)

274   HOKUSAI RINGA I
Copies from Hokusai, Series I

c. **1880s**; second edition, 1911
(Based on *Hokusai gaen* and *Hokusai zukō*)

275   HOKUSAI KOPPŌ FUJIN-ATSUME
Women in Hokusai's Brushwork
1897 (From drawings made *c.* 1822)

IV

Hokusai's Erotica: Prints, Albums, Books

(The order follows that of my monograph 'Hokusai's Erotica', in *Hokusai and Hiroshige*, 1977, where many of the works are illustrated)

1   EHON KURAGARI-ZŌSHI
Erotica: Groping in the Dark
Preface datable to **1782**
Signature: Katsu Shunrō
▶ Plate **12**; Fig. 230

2   [TITLE LOST]
Small *yokobon*, *c.* **1789**
Signature: Gankō
▶ Plate **15**; Fig. 231

Fig. 230

Fig. 231 Detail

3   MAME-BATAKE
The Bean Field
c. **1792**
Signature: Shunrō, Shishoku Gankō
(Distinguish **Books**, No. 8, p. 299)

4   [EHON HARU-NO-IRO
The Colours of Spring]
c. **1790s**
Signature: Katsukawa Shunrō

5   [EHON MATSU-NO-UCHI
The New Year's Season]
3 vols., *c.* **1794**
Signature: Shishoku Gankō

6   [EHON IRO-NO-WAKABA
Young Leaves of Eros]
c. mid-**1790s**
Signature: Shishoku Gankō

7   MINIATURE SHUNGA PRINT-SERIES
Well over 200 unsigned, *koban*-size shunga *surimono* printed in colour are known, done in

Fig. 232 Miniature shunga, 1811

Fig. 233 Miniature shunga, 1811

the distinctive style of Hokusai's middle period (but among them, related works in Hokusai style by pupils). Many of these are *e-goyomi* (calendar-prints), datable to the years 1805, 1811–14. The formats are both vertical and horizontal. Many must first have been issued in sets, enclosed in wrappers. (Some such prints originally included a *shikake-e* [hinged] device—which is often lost)
▶ Plates **201–204**; Figs. 232, 233

8   EHON FUTAMI-GATA
Conjugal Eddies
3 vols., *c.* **1805**
(Attributed to Hokusai by some students, though very much in imitation of the late Utamaro style)

9   *EHON TSUHI NO HINAGATA
Illustrated Models of Loving Couples
Shunga album with 12 *ōban*-size colour prints, early **1810s**
Signature: Shishoku Gankō
(At least two versions are known, printed from different blocks; there is also a late edition trimmed to *aiban* size, and a Meiji reproduction of 5 plates—see 13E(2) below)
▶ Plates **214–215**; Fig. 235

Fig. 234

10   *EHON AZUMA NISHIKI
'Brocade of the East' Illustrated
Shunga album with 12 *ōban*-size colour prints, early **1810s**

Fig. 235

Fig. 236

Fig. 237

Unsigned
(Plates from this series are sometimes found combined with incomplete sets of Hokusai's better-known *Ehon tsuhi no hinagata* [No. 9] and were hitherto thought to be alternative plates of the latter work; however, our recent discovery of a complete, integral set proves that this is an independent series)
▶ Plates **219–220**; Fig. 234

11   *KINOE-NO-KOMATSU
Pining for Love
3 vols., preface datable to **1814**
Signature: Shiun-an Gankō
▶ Plates **205**, **222**; Fig. 236

12   TSUMA-GASANE
Overlapping Skirts
3 vols., *c.* **1820**

Fig. 238

Fig. 239

Fig. 240

▶ Plate **223**; Fig. 237

13 *FUKUJUSŌ*
The Adonis Plant
'NAMI-CHIDORI'
Plovers above the Waves
EHON SASEMO-GA-TSUYU
Dew on Love's Grasses
Shunga album with 12 ōban-size colour prints,
c. **1820**
Several variant editions of this famous work
are known:
A. *Fukujusō* employs full colour printing; the
text is printed above the figures and this may
represent the earliest version of the album;
but there are also late impressions of this
state.

Fig. 241

Fig. 242

▶ Plate **221**; Fig. 238
B. 'Nami-chidori' is the popular title of the set
in general, derived from the pattern
appearing on the covers of this edition. This
state, which is largely from different blocks,
features a white mica ground and extensive
hand-colouring but omits the text above the
figures, as well as background elements and
many printed details. [In one variation the
eleventh plate features a *shikake-e* device.]
▶ Plate **224**; Fig. 239
C. *Ehon sasemo-ga-tsuyu* is basically similar to
'Nami-chidori' but features a pink mica ground
Fig. 240
(Note: As I have recorded elsewhere, this
Hokusai tableau—which represents, to some
degree, a subject traditional in shunga—
bears striking affinities to a plate by Sugimura
Jihei in the Genroku Era, well over a century
earlier. See *Ukiyo-e*, No. 76, 1979, 'Sugimura
and "Love's Naked Forms"'.)
D. A later (Kamigata?) version employs
colouring by stencil
E. There are also Meiji (1890s) facsimile
editions: (1) 6 plates from 'Nami-chidori',
combined with 6 other ōban-size plates by Eiri
et al.; (2) a reproduction combining 7 plates
from *Fukujusō* with 5 plates from *Tsuhi no
hinagata*, plus new frontispiece in Hokusai
manner showing the Sex Gods of Mt Tsukuba
14 *'NAMI-CHIDORI'*. See 13B above

15 *EHON SASEMO-GA-TSUYU.* See 13C
above
16 *TAMA-KAZURA*
The Jewelled Merkin
3 vols., c. **1820**
▶ Plate 213
17 *MAMPUKU WAGŌ-JIN*
The Gods of Intercourse
3 vols., postface datable to 1821
(There is also a reworked, Meiji [1890s]
reproduction of this set—combining two
scenes on one ōban-size plate—under the title
Kuni-no-sakae [The Nation Flourishes]; the
cover bears the notation 'By Katsushika
Hokusai')
▶ Plates **206**, **212**; Fig. 241
18 *EN-MUSUBI IZUMO NO SUGI*
The Lusty God of Nuptials
Shunga album with 12 *chūban*-size colour
plates, preface datable to **1822**
(Meiji [1890s] reproduction under the title
Tsuyu-no-hinuma [Before the Dewdrops Dry])
▶ Plates **225–226**; Fig. 242

(Note: A number of rather similar shunga
books and albums in Hokusai style were
produced during the 1820s by his followers
Eisen, Shigenobu, Hokuba et al., which must
be the subject of a special study. Note also
that there is a tendency for writers unfamiliar
with shunga—or with Hokusai's distinctive
figure style—to rely on the prolific studies of
Y. Hayashi: an excellent editor of Edo texts
but no authority on ukiyo-e as art—whose
hypotheses are all too often based merely
upon certain coincidental resemblances of
subject, language, calligraphy, names etc.
See, for example, R. Keyes (after J. Hillier?),
in the monumentally disorganized Paris
catalogue *Hokusai et son temps*, 1980, pp. 379–
83.)

▷ Hayashi, Y.: *Ehon kenkyū: Eisen to O-Ei*,
Tōkyō, 1968 (in Japanese)
▷ Lane, Richard: 'The Shunga in Japanese
Art', in *Erotic Art of the East*, New York, 1968
▷ Hayashi, Y.: *Ehon kenkyū: Hokusai*, Tōkyō,
1968 (in Japanese)
▷ Lane, Richard, Beurdeley, M. et al.: *Le
Chant de L'Oreiller*, Geneva, 1973 (English
version, *The Song of the Pillow*, N.Y., in press)
▷ Evans, T. and M.: *Shunga, the Art of Love in
Japan*, London, 1975
▷ Lane, Richard: 'Hokusai's Erotica', in
Ukiyo-e: a Journal of Floating-World Art, Special
Issue, 1977 (reprinted, with unexpurgated
supplement, in my *Hokusai and Hiroshige*, 2
vols., 1977)
▷ Lane, Richard: 'Hokusai's Erotica
Revisited', in *Ukiyo-e* No. 76 (1979)
▷ *The Gifted Venus*, by Katsushika Hokusai,
n.p. [Los Angeles], 1980

V

Hokusai's Pupils and Followers: A Checklist

Note: A detailed study of Hokusai's pupils and
followers has yet to be made, but a useful listing
by S. Nagata will be found in the Japanese journal
Ukiyo-e Art, No. 68, 1980—with notable
predecessors in M. Narazaki's *Hokusai ron* (1944),

as well as G. Yasuda's *Gakyō Hokusai* (1971) and
subsequent articles in the journal *Ukiyo-e*; useful
material will be found also in R. Keyes and K.
Mizushima, *The Theatrical World of Osaka Prints*
(Philadelphia, 1973); and some preliminary notes,

with figs., appear in my own 'Illustrated
Dictionary of Ukiyo-e' (1978). (Curiously enough,
fully nine of the artists of the present checklist
were 'discovered' by the present writer during
desultory research over the past three decades:

surely some indication of the yet pioneer nature of ukiyo-e studies.) Data follows the general format adopted for my 'Illustrated Dictionary of Ukiyo-e': principal *nom d'artiste*/(dates)/brief biographical note/*art-surname/(family surname)/art names [alternative readings]/familiar names. (It has not been possible to include characters for the names here: for most, cf. Nagata.)

Baen   (fl. 1810s)
Hokusai pupil, noted for his *yomi-hon* work.
* Batatsu, Ippōsai

Bokusen   (1775–1824)
Nagoya samurai and ukiyo-e painter, print and *dōban* artist; when Hokusai came to Nagoya in 1812, Bokusen helped in the preparation of the first volume of the *Manga*; originally a pupil of Utamaro. (See p. 113 and infra.)
* Maki, Utamasa, Shin-ei [Nobumitsu], Gessai I, Gabimaru, Hokutei, Hyakusai, Tokōrō

Bokuzan   (fl. c. 1810s)
Kansai pupil of Hokusai.
* Hokudō, Hokutei

Chitora   (1836–1902)
Nagoya samurai, son of Yoshimasa, pupil of Gessai II.
* Kawasaki, Genroku, Tomotarō

Eisen   (1790–1848)
Pupil first of the Kanō artist Hakkeisai, then of the ukiyo-e master Eizan. Strongly influenced by Hokusai, especially in his shunga and his landscapes.
* Ikeda, Keisai, Yoshinobu, Konsei, Hokugō, Hokutei, Ippitsuan, Kakō, Kakushunrō, Mumei-ō, Zenjirō, Teisuke

Empo   (fl. c. 1800s)
Osaka pupil of Baen.

Gakutei   (c. 1786–1869)
Ukiyo-e print artist, studied under Tsutsumi Shūei and Hokkei; much influenced by Hokusai. Of samurai stock and a writer as well, Gakutei often employed the *nom de plume* Gogaku and left a number of skilled *surimono* and book illustrations, among which his impressionistic landscape scenes are notable. Though a native of Edo, Gakutei lived in Ōsaka during the early 1830s, and one of several souvenirs of that sojourn is his best-known work, the series of landscapes *Tempō-zan shōkei ichiran* [Fine Views of Tempō-zan (Ōsaka)]; published in 1834.
* Yashima (Sugawara), Gogaku, Harunobu, Teikō [Sadaoka], Hōkyō, Gakuzan, Ichirō, Kaguradō, Kōen, Nanzan, Ryōsa, Shingakudō, Shinkadō, Yōsai, Yōsei, Horikawa Tarō, Maruya Onokichi

Gessai II   (1787–1864)
Nagoya samurai, pupil of Bokusen and Hokusai; later turned to Nanga painting.
* Numata, Masatami, Utamasa II, Shii, Ryōun, Hanzaemon

Goryū   (c. 1820s)
Pupil of Gosei.

Gosei   (fl. c. 1800s–30s)
Noted ukiyo-e painter in the Hokusai manner.
* Sunayama, Hōtei [see note under *Hokuga* (1)]

Gyokusen   (1791–1864)
Pupil of Bokusen (also of Ikkei and Chikutō). Leading genre painter in Nagoya.
* Mori, Takamasa (Kōga), Kaō, Kikutei, Sankōdō

Hakuei   (fl. c. 1820s)
Pupil of Hokusai.
* Katsushika

Heishi   (fl. 1810s)
Pupil of Hokusai.

Hokkei   (1780–1850)
Ukiyo-e painter, print artist and illustrator; originally a fishmonger [hence the name Totoya], he studied painting under the Kanō master Yōsen-in, later becoming a pupil of Hokusai. Hokkei excelled in elaborately executed *surimono* and in landscape panoramas that convey well the technique of Hokusai but add a vaguely formal yet other-worldly atmosphere seldom found in that earthy master.
* Totoya [Uoya], (Iwakubo), Kien, Aoigaoka [Kikō], Kyōsai, Tatsuyuki, Shogorō, Kin-emon

▷ Hillier, J.: *The Japanese Print. A New Approach* (Ch. XV). London, 1960

Hokkei   (fl. c. 1810)
Pupil of Hokusai.

Hokkei   (fl. 1810s–20s)
Ōsaka pupil of Hokushū and Hokusai.
* Shun-yōsai, Kintarō

Hokkei   (fl. 1830s)
Ōsaka pupil of Hokushū.
* Ran-yōsai

Hokki   (fl. early 19th century)
Ukiyo-e print artist, pupil of Hokusai.
* Katsushika (Edogawa), Sumpō

Hokkō   (fl. c. 1820s)
Ōsaka pupil of Hokusai.
* Gakyōjin

Hokkō   (fl. c. 1810s–20s)
Ōsaka pupil of Hokusai.

Hokkō   (fl. c. 1820s)
Pupil of Hokusai.
* Katsushika

Hokkon   (fl. c. 1820)
Pupil of Hokusai.
* Katsushika, Joren

Hokkyō   (fl. c. 1810s)
Pupil of Hokusai.
* Katsushika

Hokuba   (1771–1844)
Ukiyo-e painter, print artist and illustrator; retired samurai and an outstanding pupil of Hokusai; designed many *surimono* and illustrated a number of *kyōka* books; also known for figure paintings.
* Arisaka (Hoshino), Teisai, Shūen, Shunshunsai, Shunshuntei, Gohachirō

Hokuba II   (fl. c. 1840s–50s)
Son and pupil of Hokuba.
* Arisaka, Gembei

Hokuchō   (fl. c. 1820s–30s)
Ōsaka pupil of Hokushū.
* Inoue, Shungyōsai

Hokuei   (fl. early 19th century)
Ukiyo-e print artist, pupil of Hokusai.
* Tōkaen

Hokuei   (fl. c. 1830)
Pupil of Hokushū.
* Shunkō, Shunkōsai

Hokuei   (fl. c. 1820)
Pupil of Hokusai.
* Katsushika

Hokuen   (fl. c. 1800s–10s)
Pupil of Hokusai.
* Katsushika

Hokuen   (fl. c. 1810s)
Possibly pupil of Hokusai.

Hokuga   (fl. early-mid 19th century)
Ukiyo-e print artist, illustrator, pupil of Hokusai (later, expelled) [sometimes cited as identical with Gosei (q.v.), a hypothesis I would consider untenable on stylistic grounds].

* Mita, Toraya, Hōtei, Tōitsu, Kosaburō, Manjirō

Hokuga   (fl. c. 1800s–30s)
Painter, print artist, pupil of Hokusai.
* Katsushika (Yamadera), Karyōsai, Ginsetsu II, Nobuyuki, Myōnosuke

Hokugai   (fl. c. 1810)
Possibly pupil of Hokusai.

Hokugai   (fl. 1820s)
Son and pupil of Taito II.

Hokugan   (fl. 1810s–30s)
Ōsaka pupil of Kuniyoshi, later Hokushū.
* Shunkisai, Toshikuni, Shun-yōdō

Hokugyū   (fl. c. 1820s)
Pupil of Hokusai.
* Katsushika, Taiga

Hokui   (fl. 1830s–80s)
Ukiyo-e print artist, pupil of Hokusai.
* Katsushika (Fukao), Hakusanjin

Hokuitsu   (fl. c. 1804–30)
Skilled ukiyo-e painter and print artist, pupil of Hokusai.
* Katsushika, Kōgyōsai, Shikōsai

Hokuju   (1763-mid 1820s)
Ukiyo-e painter and print artist, one of the foremost pupils of Hokusai. Of all Hokusai's pupils Hokuju made the largest contribution as an original landscapist; his cubist landforms, highly stylized clouds and near-photographic figures and dwellings provide a curiously modern concept of the world. This is not entirely coincidence, for Hokuju was influenced by what little he knew of European art: yet the result must be considered one of the most notable of the Japanese variations upon what were then only dimly apprehended concepts of Western forms.
* Shōtei, Shōsai, Kazumasa

Hokuju II   (fl. c. 1850s)
Pupil of Hokuju.
* Shōtei

Hokuju   (fl. 1840s–50s)
Pupil of Hokusai.
* Katsushika

Hokumei   (fl. c. 1810)
Pupil of Hokusai.
* Ikuta

Hokumei   (fl. c. 1810s–20s)
Ukiyo-e painter and illustrator (probably female), pupil of Hokusai (see p. 108; there may well be two different artists of this name).
* Katsushika (Inoue), Gakyōjin, Kyūkyūshin [Masa-jo]

Hokumei   (fl. c. 1810s–20s)
Pupil of Hokusai.
* Katsushika

Hokumoku   (fl. c. 1800s)
Pupil of Hokusai.
* Katsushika

Hokumyō   (fl. c. 1820s–30s)
Ōsaka pupil of Hokusai.
* Shumpusai, Sekkōtei

Hokuō   (fl. c. 1818)
Nagoya pupil of Hokusai.
* Juju, Katsushika

Hokurai   (fl. c. 1820)
Pupil of Hokusai.
* Katsushika (Inoue)

Hokurei   (fl. c. 1840s)
Pupil of Hokusai.
* Irie, Kōchō, Zenkichi

Hokuri   (1772–1815)
Samurai (later, *rōnin*), pupil of Hokusai.

* Sakai, Isaka, Shinzaemon, Masaaki

Hokuri   (–1826)
Samurai pupil of Hokusai.
* Ōyama, Shōsuke

Hokuryō   (fl. *c.* 1820s)
Pupil of Hokusai.

Hokuryū   (fl. *c.* 1820s)
Pupil of Hokusai.
* Katsushika

Hokusai II   (fl. *c.* 1810s–1826)
Pupil of Hokusai, Yoshiwara tea-house proprietor (see p. 112)
* Suzuki Tokimasa, Kisaburō

Hokusai III   (fl. 1840s–50s)
Pupil of Hokusai.
* Hashimoto Tokimasa

Note: There are certain other appearances of the name 'Hokusai' on paintings neither by the Master nor apparent forgeries; they may well represent the efforts of anonymous amateurs.

Hokusei   (fl. *c.* 1810)
Pupil of Hokusai.
* Katsushika, Raiei

Hokusei   (fl. *c.* 1810s)
Pupil of Hokusai.

Hokusei   (fl. *c.* 1820s)
Ōsaka pupil of Hokushū.
* Shungyōsai

Hokusen   (fl. *c.* 1810)
Pupil of Hokusai.

Hokusen   (fl. *c.* 1810s–30s)
Pupil of Hokusai.
* Gakei-rōjin, Manji-sai, Masazumi

Hokusen   (1814–after 1893)
Follower of Hokusai.

Hokushi   (fl. 1800s)
Early pupil of Hokusai.
* Reisai

Hokushi   (fl. 1800s–20s)
Pupil of Hokusai.
*Tōtei

Hokushi   (fl. early-mid 19th century)
Pupil of Hokusai.
* Tōtei

Hokushin   (fl. *c.* 1820s)
Pupil of Hokusai.

Hokushō   (fl. 1820–30s)
Ōsaka pupil of Hokushū.
* Shunchōsai

Hokushō   (fl. *c.* 1810s–20s)
Ōsaka pupil of Hokushū.
* Shunchōsai

Hokushū   (fl. *c.* 1800s–30s)
Ōsaka ukiyo-e print artist, pupil of Hokusai; also studied under Shōkōsai Hambei.
* Shunkō, Shunkōsai, Sekkatei

Hokushū   (fl. 1800s–20s)
Pupil of Hokusai.
* Katsushika (Kanazawa)

Hokushū   (fl. 1810s–30s)
Pupil of Hokusai.
* Katsushika (Kijima)

Hokushun   (fl. *c.* 1810)
Pupil of Hokusai.

Hokusō   (fl. *c.* 1830s–40s)
Pupil of Hokusai

Hokusū   (fl. *c.* 1810s–20s)
Pupil of Hokusai.

* Katsushika (Shima), Ransai, Ryūkyo

Hokusui   (fl. *c.* 1820s)
Pupil of Hokusai.
* Katsushika

Hokusui   (fl. *c.* 1840s)
Possibly pupil of Hokusai.

Hokutai   (fl. 1800s–30s)
Ukiyo-e print artist and illustrator; an early pupil of Hokusai.
* Katsushika, Eisai, Raito, Shinshinshi

Hokutei   (–1893)
Samurai pupil of Hokusai.
* Katsushika (Itō), Ichoku

Hokutō   (fl. *c.* 1810s)
Pupil of Hokusai.
* Chizan

Hokuu   (fl. *c.* 1820s)
Pupil of Hokusai.

Hokuun   (fl. early-mid 19th century)
Nagoya ukiyo-e painter and print artist, pupil of Hokusai (formerly a carpenter by trade).
* Katsushika (Ōkubo), Tōnansei, Taiga, Gorō, Bungorō, Kyūgorō

Hokuyō   (fl. *c.* 1800s)
Pupil of Hokusai.
* Eisai

Hokuyō   (fl. *c.* 1820s)
Ukiyo-e print artist, Ōsaka School, pupil of Hokusai.
* Katsushika, Tanseidō, Senkakutei, Senkakudō

Hokuyō   (1822–68)
Pupil of Hokusai, samurai and scholar.
* Homma, Mitsuyoshi, Yūtoku

Hokuyū   (fl. *c.* 1820s)
Pupil of Hokusai.

Hokuyū   (fl. *c.* 1820s)
Pupil of Hokusai.
* Reisai

Ichiro   (fl. *c.* 1830s–50s)
Possibly a pupil of Katsushika Hokuga.
* Hokuyūsai

Idō   (fl. *c.* 1820)
Possibly pupil of Hokusai.
* Masadayū

Iitsu II   (fl. *c.* 1850s–early 1870s)
Nagoya ukiyo-e print artist, pupil of Hokusai.
* Katsushika (Kondō), Getchi-*rōjin*, Meimeikyo, Kozen

Iitsu II   (d. 1893)
Late Hokusai pupil, noted for his sketch of the Master's lodgings (see Plate 349).
* Tsuyuki (Kubota), Kōshō, Tsunejirō

Isai   (fl. *c.* 1830s–50s)
Hokusai pupil (?)

Isai   (1821–80)
Ukiyo-e painter and print artist; studied under Hokusai (who lived in his house for some time).
* Katsushika (Shimizu), Sōji, Suiōrō

Issen   (fl. *c.* 1830s)
Possibly late Hokusai pupil.

Isshō   (fl. *c.* 1840s)
Late Hokusai pupil.
* Manjisai

Issoku   (1824–76)
Hokusai pupil, later noted as metal-craftsman (see Note 6, p. 141).
* Fukawa, Hokurei, Hokushin

Itsuba   (fl. *c.* 1830s)
Pupil of Hokuba.

* Katsushika, Eishin, Ryūsai

Itsuba   (fl. *c.* 1810s)
Possibly pupil of Hokuba.

Iwajirō   (1838–*c.* 1870s)
Pupil of Isai (2), from Obusé.

Jisen   (fl. *c.* 1810s)
Pupil of Hokusen.

Joren   (fl. *c.* 1810s–20s)
Pupil of Hokusai.
* Hokutei

Kakusen   (fl. *c.* 1820s–30s)
Possibly Hokusai pupil.
* Isseisai

Kanga [Sōga]   (fl. *c.* 1840s)
Pupil of Hokuga

Kansai   (fl. *c.* 1860s–70s)
Pupil of Mita Hokuga.
* Ichikawa, Kijirō

Kanto   (fl. *c.* 1800s)
Early pupil of Hokusai.
* Katsushika, Hisanobu, Hyakusai

Kashū   (d. 1901)
Pupil and grandson of Gessai in Nagoya.
* Numata, Masayuki, Bokusai

Kassai   (1792–1868)
Obusé literatus, probably pupil of Hokusai.
* Hiramatsu, Kunai

Katsushika   (*c.* 1820s)
Identity uncertain.

Keiga   (1786–after 1860)
Nagasaki documentary painter, influenced by Hokusai (of whose works he made numerous copies for his patron, Dr von Siebold).
* Kawahara, Toyosuke, Taneyoshi
▷ Lane, Richard: 'Hokusai's Dutch Connection Revisited'. In *Andon*, in press; reprinted in *Studies in Edo Art*.

Keigetsu   (fl. *c.* 1820s)
Pupil of Hokkei.
* Aoigaoka [Kikō]

Keiri   (fl. *c.* 1820s–30s)
Pupil of Hokkei.
* Kyōitsu

Keirin   (fl. *c.* 1820s)
Pupil of Hokkei.
* Tsuruya

Keisai   (1839–*c.* 1880s)
Nagoya pupil of Gessai II.
* Hirose, Takanari

Keisei   (fl. 1820s–30s)
Pupil of Hokkei.
* Aoigaoka [Kikō], Bensendō

Keisetsu   (fl. *c.* 1820s)
Pupil of Hokkei.
* Kishimoto

Keishō   (fl. *c.* 1820s)
Pupil of Hokkei.
* Okada [Kikō]

Keiyu   (fl. *c.* 1820s)
Pupil of Hokkei.

Kidō   (fl. *c.* 1830s)
Pupil of Hokusai (also of Chinzan).

Kitamaro   (fl. *c.* 1830s)
Possibly pupil of Hokusai.

Kiyozumi   (1786–1834)
Kyōka poet (son of Meshimori) and occasional artist in the Hokusai style.
* Nakamura Jingairō, Gyokua, Kiyosaburō

Kōchō (fl. *c.* 1810s)
Pupil of Hokusai.

Koen (fl. *c.* 1810s)
Pupil of Baen.
* Ichiryūsai

Kōitsu (fl. *c.* 1820s)
Possibly pupil of Hokusai.
* Sonsai

Koryū (fl. *c.* 1810)
Pupil of Hokusai.
* Suigetsu

Kōshun [Mitsutoshi] (fl. *c.* 1830s)
Hokusai pupil or follower. (A signed copy of a lost 'Hokusai Iitsu' landscape painting of the 1830s is known by this artist.)

Kōzan (1806–1883)
Noted Obusé literatus, pupil and patron of Hokusai in his late years (see p. 266).
*Takai, Sankurō

Masahisa (fl. 1880s)
Follower of Hokusai.

Nakamura (fl. *c.* 1840s)
Obusé artist, possibly pupil of Hokusai.

Naohisa (fl. 1880s)
Hokusai follower.
* Katsushika

Nobusada (fl. 1820s)
Ōsaka pupil of Shigenobu.
* Yukinobu

O-Ei (fl. 1810s–40s)
Ukiyo-e painter and illustrator; daughter of Hokusai (see Plate 128 and text infra).
* Katsushika (Nakajima), Ōi (from *c.* 1820), Miuraya, Ei, Ei-jo

Ōi ▶ **O-Ei**

Ōtai (fl. 1820s)
Hokusai school.

O-Tatsu (fl. *c.* 1810s)
Ukiyo-e painter, daughter of Hokusai (see Plate 107 and text infra)
* Katsushika (Nakajima), Tatsu-jo [O-Tetsu]

Raisen (fl. *c.* 1810)
Pupil of Hokusai.
* Katsushika

Raishū (fl. *c.* 1800s–20s)
Pupil of Hokusai.
* Katsushika, Hikojirō

Raishū (fl. *c.* 1800s–50s)
Pupil of Hokusai, best known for his copperplate engravings.
* Yasuda, Bunkaken, 'Willem van Leiden'

Raizan (fl. *c.* 1810s)
Pupil of Hokusai.
* Hyakuju

Renshi (fl. *c.* 1830)
Pupil of Hokusai.

Sadamasa (1802–*c.* 1830s)
Pupil of Baen in Ōsaka.
* Ichirōsai

Saiboku (fl. *c.* 1820)
Possibly pupil of Hokusai.
* Saisentei

Senshi (fl. *c.* 1810s–30s)
Pupil of Shinsai.

Setsuba (fl. *c.* 1810)
Pupil of Hokuba.

Shigeharu (1803–53)
Pupil of Shigenobu in Ōsaka.
* Yamaguchi, Ryūsai, Kunishige

Shigehiko (fl. *c.* 1830s)
Pupil of Shigenobu in Ōsaka.
* Ichiryūsai

Shigemasa (fl. *c.* 1830s–50s)
Pupil and son-in-law of Shigenobu.
* Yanagawa (Suzuki), Sagenji

Shigemitsu (fl. *c.* 1850s)
Pupil of Shigenobu.
* Enrōsai

Shigenobu (1787–1832)
Ukiyo-e print artist and illustrator who worked in Edo and, for a short time, 1822–23, in Ōsaka, where his artistic influence was great. Became successively pupil, son-in-law and adopted son of Hokusai.
* Yanagawa [Ryūsen] (Suzuki), Kinsai, Raito, Reisai, Ushōsai, Jūbei

Shigenobu II (fl. *c.* 1820s–40s)
Pupil of Shigenobu.
* Yanagawa (Tanishiro), Shigi, Sesshōsai, Shōei, Risanta

Shinchō (fl. *c.* 1810)
Pupil of Shinsai.

Shingyō (fl. *c.* 1810)
Pupil of Shinsai.

Shin-itsu (fl. *c.* 1810)
Pupil of Shinsai.

Shinsai (fl. *c.* 1780s–1820)
Ukiyo-e painter, print artist and illustrator; studied first under Sōri I, then under Hokusai; noted for his *surimono* and for his landscape prints in semi-European style.
* Mannō, Ryūryūkyo, Ryūkaen, Masayuki, Hanji, Hanjirō

Shinsaku (fl. *c.* 1810s)
Probably pupil of Hokusai.

Shirei (fl. *c.* 1810s)
Ōsaka pupil of Baen.

Shunchō (fl. 1810s–20s)
Ōsaka pupil of Hokushū.

Shunrei (fl. 1800s–10s)
Pupil of Hokusai.
* Katsushika (Azuma)

Shunrō II ▶ **Toyomaru**

Shunshi (fl. 1820s)
Ōsaka pupil of Hokushū.
* Gatōken

Shunshi (d. 1860)
Ōsaka pupil of Hokushū.
* Seiyōsai

Shunsho (fl. 1820s)
Ōsaka pupil of Hokushū.
* Shun-yō

Shunzan (fl. *c.* 1830)
Ōsaka pupil of Hokushū.
* Hokushinsai

Shūri (fl. 1800s–20s)
Pupil of Hokuba.
* Yoshimi, Teisai, Teitei

Sōbu (fl. *c.* 1800)
Probably pupil of Hokusai.
* Gentei

Sōhyaku (fl. *c.* 1800s)
Pupil of Hokusai.
* Jutei

Sōji ▶ **Sōri III**

Sōju (fl. *c.* late 1790s)
Probably early pupil of Hokusai.

Sōri III (fl. 1790s–*c.* 1818)

Early pupil of Hokusai, receiving the Master's *nom d'artiste* Sōri late in 1798. A skilled artist, his works are often confused with Hokusai's. (See p. 23, Plate 75, and infra.)
* Hishikawa, Tawaraya, Hyakurin, Rinsai, Sōji, Tan-unsai, Kanchi
▷ Lane, Richard: 'In the Shadow of Hokusai: a Note on Sōri III', in *Andon*, in press; reprinted in *Studies in Edo Art*.

Taigadō (fl. 1810s)
Pupil of Hokusai.

Taigaku (fl. *c.* 1820s–30s)
Ukiyo-e print artist, pupil of Taito II.
* Endō, Keisai, Unkaku, Hokusen, Manji

Taiho (fl. *c.* 1810)
Pupil of Hokusai.
* Takeshiba

Taiitsu (fl. *c.* 1820s)
Pupil of Hokusai.

Taishin (fl. *c.* 1820s)
Pupil of Hokusai.
* Katsushika (Ishii), Shikan

Taiso (fl. late 1810s)
Nagoya pupil of Hokusai.

Taito (fl. 1810s)
Pupil of Hokusai.

Taito II (fl. *c.* 1810s–53)
Ukiyo-e painter, print artist and illustrator; samurai pupil of Hokusai, who in 1819 gave him his pen-name Taito; he spent his final decade (from 1843) in Ōsaka.
* Katsushika (Fujiwara, Kondō), Beikasai, Beika-dōjin, Beika-sanjin, Dōteisha, Genryūsai, Hokusen, Shōzan, Toenrō, Ryūsai, Masazumi, Fumio, Ban-emon, Kisaburō
[Note: Though not 'Taito III', there was also an unrelated, *non*-ukiyo-e Edo painter of this name, fl. *c.* 1830s. He was a minor samurai of the Okayama *daimyō*, dwelling in Kōji-machi, of the surname Kondō.]
▷ Hillier, J.: *Hokusai Drawings*, Ch. 6

Taizai (fl. 1810s)
Pupil of Hokusai.

Takusū (fl. *c.* 1810)
Pupil of Hokusū.

Tatsu-jo ▶ **O-Tatsu**

Ten-en-dōjin (fl. *c.* 1810)
Probably pupil of Hokusai.
* Shiba, Shō

Tobun (fl. 1810s)
Pupil of Hokusai.

Toen (fl. 1810s)
Pupil of Hokusai.
* Katsushika

Tōkō (fl. *c.* 1830s)
Possibly Hokusai pupil.

Torai (fl. *c.* 1810)
Pupil of Hokusai.
* Untaishi

Toseki (fl. 1810s)
Pupil of Hokusai.

Toshi (fl. *c.* 1820)
Probably pupil of Hokusai.
* Kyūkyūshin

Toyomaru (fl. *c.* 1789–*c.* 1802; d. 1817)
Pupil first of Toyoharu, then of Hokusai, receiving the latter's art-name 'Shunrō [II]' *c.* 1794, but after a time reverted to the name Toyomaru (see text, p. 23). (Note: A recent attempt to theorize that Toyomaru and Shun-ei are identical seems unfounded.)

* Kusamura, Shunrō [II], Jutei

Toyomaru II   (fl. *c.* late 1790s–1800s)
Pupil of Toyomaru.
* Kusamura

Tōzan   (fl. *c.* 1830s)
Possibly Hokusai pupil.
* Katsushika

Unga   (d. 1885)

Late pupil of Hokusai.
* Tomita, Yūjirō

Utamasa III   (fl. *c.* 1820s)
Nagoya samurai, pupil of Gessai II.
* Haniwara, Gessai III, Kunai

Yoshimasa   (1807–81)
Nagoya samurai and pupil of Gessai [II] (father of
the famed Chitora).
* Kawasaki

Yūba   (fl. *c.* 1820s)
Pupil of Hokuba.
* Sōsai

Yukimasa   (fl. *c.* 1830s)
Nagoya pupil of Gessai [II].
* Imai, Hanjirō

Yūsoku   (fl. *c.* 1840s)
Follower of Hokusai.
* Fujiwara

VI

A Hokusai Bibliography

Principal works bear the symbol •. This listing is
relatively comprehensive for Western books—
though there are few solid studies—but highly
selective for those in Japanese (denoted here with
asterisk). Note: Specialized studies are cited not
here, but under specific *Appendix* entries:
Prints, Nos. 52, 100, 132, 141, 152, 157, 166
Books, Nos. 60, 118, 151, 171, 178, 195, 196, 211,
214, 239, 243
Erotica, pp. 310–311

Siebold, P. F. Von: *Nippon Archiv zur Beschreibung
von Japan.* Leiden, 1831
Huish, M. B. (ed.): *Catalogue of a Collection of
Drawings and Engravings by Hokusai at the Fine Arts
Society.* London, 1890
Fenollosa, Ernest F.: *Hokusai and His School:
Catalogue of Special Exhibition No. 1*, Museum of
Fine Arts, Boston, Mass., 1893
• Iijima, K.: *Katsushika Hokusai den.* Tōkyō, 1893.
(Reprinted Tōkyō, 2 vols., 1978, ed. S. Segi.)*
• Goncourt, Edmond de: *Hokusaï.* Paris, 1896
Revon, H.: *Etude sur Hok'sai.* Paris, 1896
Holmes, C. J.: *Hokusai.* London, 1899 and New
York, 1901
Various: *Werke Hokusais* (catalogue). Vienna, 1901
• Fenollosa, Ernest F.: *Catalogue of the Exhibition of
Paintings of Hokusai Held at the Japan Fine Art
Association, Uyeno Park.* Tōkyō, 1901. (Reprinted
Geneva, 1973.)
Perzynski, F.: *Hokusai.* Leipzig, 1904
Asaoka, O.: *Koga bikō.* 4 vols., Tōkyō, 1904
Tomkinson, M.: *Hokusai, Master of the Ukiyo-e
School of Painting.* France Hall, 1904
Strange, Edward F.: *Hokusai: The Old Man Mad
with Painting.* London, 1906
Vignier, C. and Inada, H.: *Estampes Japonaises
exposées au Musée des Arts Décoratifs.* 6 vols., Paris,
1909–14
Focillon, Henri: *Hokusai.* Paris, 1914
Binyon, L. (ed.): *Catalogue of the Japanese and
Chinese Woodcuts in the British Museum*, London,
1916
Oda, Kazuma: *Hokusai.* Tōkyō, 1926 (rev. ed.
1957)*.
Salaman, Malcolm C.: *Hokusai.* London, 1930
Toda, K.: *Descriptive Catalogue of Japanese and
Chinese Illustrated Books in the Ryerson Library of the
Art Institute, Chicago.* Chicago, 1931
Noguchi, Yone: *Hokusai.* Tōkyō, 1932.
Mizutani, Y.: *Kohan shōsetsu sōgashi.* Tōkyō, 1936*
Eisen et al.: *Ukiyo-e ruikō* (ed. K. Nakata). Tōkyō,
1941*; also, ed. Yura, T., Tōkyō, 1981
• Narazaki, M.: *Hokusai-ron.* Tōkyō, 1944*
Gray, B. (ed.): *The Work of Hokusai.* London, 1948
Bruijn, R. de (ed.): *Hokusai, 1760–1849* (catalogue).
Amsterdam, 1949
Hemple, R. (ed.): *Hokusai.* Amsterdam, 1949
Gruyter, W. J. de (ed.): *Rembrandt/Hokusai/Van
Gogh.* Amsterdam, 1951

Ledoux, L. V. (ed.): *Japanese Prints in the Ledoux
Collection.* Vol. V, 1951
Gruyter, W. J. de (ed.): *Hokusai: Drawings and
Water-Colours* (catalogue). London, 1954
Winzinger, Franz: *Hokusai.* Munich, 1954
• Hillier, J.: *Hokusai: Paintings, Drawings and
Woodcuts.* London, 1955. (Reprinted 1957, 1978,
1985.) (German edition, *Hokusai: Gemälde,
Zeichnungen, Farbholzschnitte.* Cologne, 1956.)
Hloucha, Joe: *Hokusai.* Prague, n.d. (Originally
published in German; Prague, 1955.)
Kondō, Ichitarō: *Katsushika Hokusai* (English
adaptation: Elise Grilli). Tōkyō, 1955
Boller, Willi: *Hokusai.* Stuttgart, 1955
Kikuchi, S.: *Hokusai.* Tōkyō, 1957*
Winzinger, F.: *Hokusai.* Munich, 1958
Hillier, J. (ed.): *Hokusai, dessins, aquarelles,
estampes, livres* (catalogue). Paris, 1958
Swann, P., after Kikuchi, S.: *Hokusai.* London,
1959
• Narazaki, M.: *Ukiyo-e: Hokusai/Hiroshige.* In
Nihon hanga bijitsu zenshū, vol. V. Tōkyō, 1960*
[Stern, H. P. (ed.)]: *Hokusai: Paintings and
Drawings in the Freer Gallery of Art.* Washington,
1960
Yamada, C. (ed.): *Special Exhibition of Hokusai . . .*
Haifa, 1960
Lane, Richard: *Masters of the Japanese Print: Their
World and Their Work.* New York and London,
1962. (Also editions in French, German, Italian,
Spanish, Dutch, 1962.)
Connor, R.: *Hokusai.* Hanover, 1962
Fontein, J. (ed.): *Het Landschap bij Hokusai*
(catalogue). Amsterdam, 1962
Ukiyo-e: A Journal of Floating-World Art. Tōkyō,
1962–85. (Includes numerous articles on Hokusai,
No. 50 [1972] being devoted to the artist; in
Japanese, other than articles by the author, which
appear in both languages.)
Ukiyo-e Art [Journal]. Tōkyō, 1962 to date.
(Includes occasional articles on Hokusai; mainly in
Japanese with English summaries.)
*Illustrated Catalogues of Tōkyō National Museum:
Ukiyo-e Prints (3).* Tōkyō, 1963
Suzuki, Jūzō: *Katsushika Hokusai.* Tōkyō, 1963*
Kokusho sōmokuroku. 9 vols., Tōkyō, 1963–76*
Bowie, Theodore: *The Drawings of Hokusai.*
Bloomington, Ind., 1964. [For corrections see my
'Ukiyo-e Paintings Abroad', in *Monumenta
Nipponica*, 1968, reprinted in *Studies in Edo Art*]
• Narazaki, Muneshige: *Hokusai to Hiroshiga.* 8
vols., Tōkyō, 1964–65*. (English version,
Masterworks of Ukiyo-e, 8 vols. Tōkyō, 1967–69.)
Hillier, J.: *Japanese Drawings from the 17th Century to
the End of the 19th Century.* London, 1966. [For
corrections see my 'Ukiyo-e Paintings Abroad', in
Monumenta Nipponica, 1968, reprinted in *Studies in
Edo Art*]
Hillier, J.: *Hokusai Drawings.* London, 1966
• Ozaki, S.: *Hokusai.* Tōkyō, 1967*

Longstreet, S. (ed.): *The Drawings of Hokusai.*
Calif., 1969
• Yasuda, G.: *Gakyō Hokusai.* Tōkyō, 1971*
• Suzuki, J. et al. (ed.): *Hokusai yomihon sashie
shūsei.* 5 vols., Tōkyō, 1971–73*
• Narazaki, Muneshige: *Zaigai hihō/Ōbei shuzō
ukiyo-e shūsei*, vol 4: *Katsushika Hokusai.* Tōkyō,
1972*
Hokusai kenkyū [Journal]. Tōkyō, 1972–80.
(Specialized studies, mainly bibliographical.)*
Yoshida, T.: *Ukiyo-e jiten.* 3 vols., Tōkyō, 1972–74*
Stern, H. P.: *Ukiyo-e Painting.* Washington, 1973
Lane, Richard: 'Hokusai', in *Encyclopaedia
Britannica*, Fifteenth Edition. Chicago, 1974
• Oka, Izaburō (ed.): *Hokusai.* In *Ukiyo-e taikei*,
vol. 8, Tōkyō, 1974*
• Forrer, Matthi: *Hokusai—A Guide to the Serial
Graphics.* Philadelphia and London, 1974
Oka, Izaburō (ed.): *Hokusai.* Tōkyō, 1975*
• Kaneko, F. et al. (ed.): *Nikuhitsu: Katsushika
Hokusai.* Tōkyō, 1975*
Voronova, B. G.: *Katsushika Hokusai* (in Russian).
Moscow, 1975
Various: *Taiyō ukiyo-e series: Hokusai.* Tōkyō, 1975*
Schneeberger, P. F.: *Hokusai et le japonisme avant
1900.* Geneva, 1976
• Lane, Richard: *Hokusai and Hiroshige* (in
English and Japanese). Tōkyō, 1976
Hillier, J.: *Japanese Prints and Drawings from the
Vever Collection.* 3 vols., London, 1976
• Lane, Richard: *Hokusai and Hiroshige.* Tōkyō,
Baltimore and Cologne, 1977; reissue of the 1976
work with addition of the pamphlet 'Hokusai's
Erotica' and original book specimens.
Various: *Hiroshige Hokusai shokoku meisho-eshū.* 3
vols., Tōkyō, 1977*
Various: *Ukiyo-e shūka.* 18 vols., Tōkyō, 1978–83
• Lane, Richard: *Images from the Floating World:
The Japanese Print—Including an Illustrated
Dictionary of Ukiyo-e.* London and New York, 1978.
(Includes lengthy sections on Hokusai, pp. 159–
171, 255–276.) (Translations: *Ukiyo-e Holzschnitte*,
Zürich, 1978; *L'Éstampe Japonaise*, Fribourg, 1979.)
• Suzuki, J.: *Ehon to ukiyo-e.* Tōkyō, 1979*
• Hillier, J.: *The Art of Hokusai in Book Illustration.*
London and Berkeley, 1980
• Various: *Le Fou de Peinture: Hokusai et son temps.*
Paris, 1980
Various: *Genshoku ukiyo-e daihyakka jiten*, vol. VIII.
Tōkyō, 1981*
Andon [Journal]. Leiden, 1981 to date. (Includes
occasional articles on Hokusai, No. 8 [1982] being
devoted to the artist.)
• Various: *Hokusai and his school: Paintings,
Drawings and Illustrated Books.* Haarlem, 1982
• Various: *Hokusai and his school.* Catalogue of the
Collection of Japanese Prints, Part III,
Rijksmuseum, Amsterdam, 1982
• Tsuji, N.: *Hokusai.* Tōkyō, 1982*
• Various: *Nikuhitsu ukiyo-e*, Vol. VII, *Hokusai.*

Tōkyō, 1982*

Gakyōjin Katsushika Hokusai ten. Ōsaka, 1983*

Keyes, Roger: 'Hokusai', in *Encyclopedia of Japan.* Tōkyō, 1983

● Various: *Ukiyo-e hakka*, Vol. V, *Hokusai.* Tōkyō, 1984*

Katsushika Hokusai to sono sekai ten. Sapporo, 1984*

Katsushika Hokusai. Tōkyō, 1984*

Suzuki, J. (ed.): *Kinsei Nihon fūzoku-ehon shūsei.* Kyōto, 1984*

Lane, Richard: *Hiroshige: 'Kambara'—the Anatomy of a Japanese Print.* Tōkyō, 1984

● Forrer, M.: *Eirakuya Tōshirō, Publisher at Nagoya.* Amsterdam, 1985

● Nagata, S.: *Katsushika Hokusai nempu.* Tōkyō, 1985*

● *Katsushika Hokusai ten.* Tōkyō, 1985*

Keyes, Roger: *The Art of Surimono.* 2 vols., London, 1985

● Nagata, S. (ed., with Asakura, H.): *Hokusai no e-dehon.* 5 vols., Tōkyō, 1986*

Boston de mitsukatta Hokusai ten. Tōkyō, 1987*

● *Tokubetsuten: Hokusai.* Nara, 1987*

● Nagata, S. (ed., with Asakura, H.): *Hokusai no ehon-sashie.* 3 vols., Tōkyō, 1987*

Various: *Hizō ukiyo-e taikan/Ukiyo-e Masterpieces in European Collections.* 13 vols. planned, Tōkyō, 1987–*

Hillier, J.: *The Art of the Japanese Book.* 2 vols., London, 1987

Hokusai ten: Peter Morse Collection. Tōkyō, 1988*

Lane, Richard: 'Hokusai's World'. Series of 38 weekly articles, *The Japan Times*, Tōkyō, 11 August 1988ff.

Lane, Richard: 'Labyrinth or Hornet's Nest? A Note on Hokusai's Paintings'. In *Andon*, in press, reprinted in *Studies in Edo Art*, in press

Lane, Richard: 'Hokusai's Dutch Connection Revisited'. In *Andon*, in press; reprinted in *Studies in Edo Art*, in press

Lane, Richard: 'In the Shadow of Hokusai: a Note on Sōri III', in *Andon*, in press; reprinted in *Studies in Edo Art*, in press

Nagata, S. (ed.): *Hokusai no kyōka ehon.* Tōkyō, 1988

Lane, Richard: *Hiroshige—'The Provinces of Japan'.* New York, in press

Lane, Richard: *Studies in Edo Literature.* Tōkyō, in press

Lane, Richard: *Studies in Edo Art.* Tōkyō, in press

Postface

To those readers of some acquaintance with ukiyo-e it might appear that I have waited an inordinately long time to get round to a Hokusai book; this represents, however, not a lack of interest but the vagaries of publishing in such a limited field as Japanese art. In a sense I should have begun it immediately after my first, *Kaigetsudō* monograph—published while I was living in the midst of 'downtown' Asakusa in 1959: doubtless I would, forthwith, have moved a mile across the Sumida River and down to the borderline of Honjo and Fukagawa, where Hokusai was born and lived out much of his life. (Yet, enthused as ever by the colourful, frenetic life of old/new Japan about me I might, indeed, never have completed such a complex book!) This method—which I had earlier employed in my studies of Edo life and literature—worked well enough in the Tōkyō of the 1950s, while the roots of the Japanese populace were still firmly embedded in their glorious native culture. Today, however, they have changed more than I, and it is not without justification that some friends refer to me as 'the last surviving relic of the Edo Period'; others have chided me equally for an exaggerated view of ukiyo-e as the centre of the Universe and a comprehensive *raison d'être*: all, criticisms which I acknowledge with frank pleasure. Thus for better or worse the present volume has been written more in reflection than in the midst of activity— and somewhat removed in space from Hokusai's Edo: most, in the mountains east of the ancient capital Kyōto (to which I escaped, many years ago, for a little peace and quiet); but a good part, in my 'hermitage' amidst the foothills of Eastern Bali (an entranced island where, in middle-age, I rediscovered much of the colour and single-minded vigour of Old Edo, albeit in a different— though surprisingly related—race and civilization, and under the shadow of another sacred mountain than Fuji). The resultant text is probably more philosophical in content than anything I would have written some decades earlier—yet not, I trust, at the expense of that detailed, critical perfectionism that was the ideal of my youth.

Quite by coincidence this book has been written during a 'Hokusai Boom' and a time of exciting scholarly activity both in Japan and in the West. A series of impressive Hokusai exhibitions has resulted in numerous new discoveries— particularly in the field of painting—that have greatly enriched our knowledge of this prolific, prodigious genius; and at the same time, more stringent standards of expertise have resulted in expunging numbers of dubious paintings from the generally accepted canon (which is still far

from consolidation, however). With such a plethora of fresh material it is only natural that my own tentative studies will be revised and corrected by future generations; but a beginning had to be made, and the reader will thus find here an ample sampling of these newly discovered works: most of which have never been published in the West—some, not even in Japan.

I shall not tax the reader's sympathies with an account of the trials experienced in a global pursuit of the many rare objects illustrated in this book. It may be of general interest to note, however, that one cannot merely rely on museums, however renowned, to select their 'best examples': such institutions are customarily understaffed, and where there is no specialized curator have even been known to photograph reproductions by mistake. Collections in Japan are notoriously difficult (and several major collectors customarily refuse all cooperation). Simply locating rare but vital items can prove a full-scale project in itself: I cannot really claim to have obtained ideal examples for more than three-quarters of the Plates; and even for the famed *Fuji* prints—extant in dozens of specimens—there are surprisingly few examples of absolutely first impressions in pristine condition. Coming to the rarer prints (not to mention paintings), the situation is even more acute: one must often really be grateful that there is one example extant, whatever the state. And one's choice must also be influenced by one's purposes: with Plate 5, for example, I could locate only two colour-printed specimens (Berlin and Tōkyō), both trimmed, and chose the former—whereas for a more technically-oriented monograph I might have used the complete, but colourless, original printer's-proof in the same museum. Indeed, had Fate permitted yet another year to work on this book, rather than spending it on the more esoteric details of Hokusai biography/bibliography, I should rather have devoted the time to a worldwide search for superior specimens—and photographed them myself, to achieve some kind of consistency in colour rendition.

In a book prepared without benefit of assistant or computer—and partly on travels—there may well yet remain inconsistencies of detail between the main text and the Appendices: occasioned by the fact that many Hokusai dates represent 'educated guesses', and that Japanese titles are often susceptible to a half-dozen equally correct translations—none of which are yet standardized. I am, perhaps, even more than any of my critics will be, keenly aware of the futility of attempting a truly comprehensive Hokusai monograph at this yet primitive stage of our knowledge; and this is

particularly the case for the lone student, working part-time and without institutional support. It is my firm belief, however, that such tasks should not be relegated to 'project-teams': each scholar a specialist in one narrow field but seldom able to grasp the totality of his subject. The present book thus—though indebted to the piecemeal studies of predecessors—at least represents the intense focus of a single mind, however limited.

Even such a specialized subject as this monograph must inevitably entail a close consideration of all the larger themes and forces of Japan in the later Edo Period: social and literary movements as well as artistic, economic and political influences on the life of the artist, on his publishers and on his audience. I do not pretend to have treated this background as comprehensively as I might have wished. On the other hand, the voluminous Appendices will necessarily seem of limited interest to the casual reader. Yet I hope he may, even skimming through them, perceive something of the profuse and dynamic maelstrom, the often haphazard order in which the artist had to produce his major works. And, with closer scrutiny of this microcosm/macrocosm, it may even be possible to approach realization of that ultimate enlightenment: *What was it like to be Hokusai?*

Having far exceeded my allotted space in the text I can only summarize here certain comments on the scope and methodology of this volume.

Despite Hokusai's fame this would appear to be the first comprehensive and detailed, fully-illustrated monograph on the artist.* In the West, the pioneer work was E. de Goncourt's *Hokusaï* of 1896, a brilliantly written creative essay on the artist, still stimulating reading (if one knows French); it is not illustrated, however, and— though based on research by the pioneer ukiyo-e dealer T. Hayashi—is essentially a literary work, featuring more imagination than fact. In more recent times the standard book in the West has been J. Hillier's *Hokusai: Paintings, Drawings and Woodcuts* of 1955, another excellent introduction to the artist from a strictly Western point of view, but outdated and of limited scope (quite omitting, for example, not only Hokusai's erotica but even his landscapes in Occidental style). In Japan, K. Iijima's *Katsushika Hokusai den* ('Biography') of 1893 was a pioneer compilation of biographical anecdotes, but the first true monograph came late—Professor Narazaki's *Hokusai-ron* ('On Hokusai') of 1944; here one finds a conscientious

* M. Forrer's long-awaited *Hokusai* has just appeared, but is basically an extended commentary on the classic Goncourt monograph of 1896.

compilation of basic material, but often undigested and (being a wartime publication) poorly illustrated. Subsequent Japanese publications, though numerous, have tended either to be specialized studies of narrow facets of the artist's *oeuvre* or 'coffee-table' tomes, lacking solid text matter. (In contrast there are two excellent, comprehensive monographs on *Hiroshige*—by Uchida and Suzuki—an equally prolific but far less complex artist.)**

It has always been my dictum that 'The more Japanese one knows, the less one shows it,' and I have avoided native terms wherever there is a perfectly good English word—even going to the extreme of referring back to the literally dozens of major Hokusai book and print titles by their translations after first appearance (my Index, however, comprehends both forms). Translations, both of titles and text material, are my own and emphasize clarity rather than literalness; future writers may find them of use—and perhaps even improve on them—but I hope with suitable acknowledgement.

Regarding the Plates, after some comparative study I have concluded that, when dealing with those of Hokusai's books in monochrome (and near-monochrome) to begin with, an essentially *graphic* method of reproduction is more effective than the usual, murky halftones. This experiment may offend purists, but the aim is to achieve as close an approximation to the originals as is possible without recourse to actual woodblock-printing.

My interest in Japan, whether in literature, art or actual life, has always been directed to the down-to-earth and plebeian, and I hope that this long experience has enabled me to grasp something of the essence of this complex master's character and circumstances; by the same token, several decades of earnest book-collecting and daily viewing/reading of the original texts, prints and paintings has served to bring me about as close to the original artist as one can get today.

My subject here has been the artist himself and I have purposely eschewed any detailed comment on Hokusai's influence on modern art in the West: such is relative only in that it justifies the Master's own conviction of the future validity of his lifelong effort. Indeed, to appreciate solely the 'modern' elements in Hokusai is not only to miss the greater part of his worth, but may also tend to limit one's perception to a mere confirmation of prejudices already acquired. The fact that even the minor beneficiaries of *Japonisme* fetch greater prices on the market today than the best of Hokusai reflects matters of temporal taste, fashion, format, geography—not the intrinsic

** Though it appeared after my own basic research was completed, S. Nagata's *Katsushika Hokusai nempu* of late 1985 is a useful compendium of chronological data on the artist.

importance of the artist himself. This book is not without its own ulterior motives, however, principal among which is to go beyond the stereotyped image of the 'Artist of Fuji' and show the Master in sufficiently comprehensive detail that something of his true position in world art will become apparent; symbols are important, but they can never represent more than a shadow of the truly creative genius, of the total quality of his achievement. For the assiduous reader this volume may, I hope, represent but the first stage in a quest for the real Hokusai—an artist whose achievement extends far beyond the limits of that strange archipelago called Japan. To me, at least, Hokusai is the example pre-eminent of the *artist*: he quite literally existed for his art and—rather like the Hindu god Indra—formed it out of his own nature. He created a style that, despite hundreds of pupils, belonged to him alone; he did not just talk art, he lived it.

Kyōto and Bali
1983–88   R. L.

Acknowledgements

Naturally enough, the details of this monograph quite supersede the more superficial account of Hokusai and his works that appeared a decade ago in my *Images from the Floating World*; it has been possible here not only to reassess the artist's total life but also his complex, and often bibliographically obscure *oeuvre*; yet this is still but a general book, and as much data and illustration had to be omitted as was actually included.

Acknowledgement for editorial suggestions is due to the producers of this book in London, Messrs John Calmann & King Ltd, and especially to Elisabeth Ingles and Diana Davies. In Japan, fellow Hokusai-students Yoshikazu Hayashi and Seiji Nagata have kindly provided practical assistance; and special thanks are due to my friend of thirty-five years, Jack Hillier—who has, alas, declined the honour of doing a final and definitive Hokusai biography of his own, but offered much helpful advice in the preparation of this one, including the generous opening of his photographic archives. (In striking contrast, the Center for the Study of Japanese Woodblock Prints [Roger S. Keyes, Director]—though massively subsidized by the United States National Endowment for the Humanities and the Burke, Kress, and Japan Foundations—refused all cooperation with my own, quite unsponsored project: on the grounds that it might conflict with its own long-term programme on 'Hokusai's Prints'. Nevertheless, I have opened my own files to this Center, feeling the goal to be more important than such temporal considerations.)

The plates and figures of this volume are the result of some decades of desultory research (and

some collecting) on the artist, and the following list is but an inadequate summary of my debt to the collectors and institutions involved. (In some cases where the present owners could not be traced, I have also had the kind cooperation of Messrs Christie's, New York, and Messrs Sotheby's, London, in obtaining photographs.)

Nakau Collection, Kōbe: 13, 89, 197, Fig. 35
Tōkyō National Museum: 3, 7, 16, 64, 67, 79, 81, 287–9, Figs. 4, 5, 20, 29, 45, 92–4, 97, 99, 161
Japan Ukiyo-e Museum, Nagano: 4, 8, 115, Figs. 6, 16, 55, 98
Museum für Ostasiatische Kunst, Berlin: 5, 240
Art Institute of Chicago: 6, 26, 39, 42, 43, 83
Ōta Memorial Museum, Tōkyō: 14, 106, 195, 278, 357
Museum of Fine Arts, Boston: 17, 63, 80, 92, 128, 129, 227, 276
Hillier Collection, Surrey: 18, 24
Indiana University Art Museum: 19, 27, 75
Walter Collection, Tōkyō: 21
Fogg Art Museum, Cambridge: 20, 25, 75
Cleveland Museum of Art: 28
Honolulu Academy of Arts: 30, 72, 73, 257, 274, 275, Figs. 1, 2, 14, 131
Chester Beatty Library, Dublin: 32, 41, 180, 187
British Museum: 31, 33, 34, 36–8, 56–59, 85, 124, 176, 178, 181, 186, 188–93, 230, 242, 328–30
Morse Collection, Honolulu: 40, 58, 228, Fig. 26
Metropolitan Museum of Art, New York: 66, 199
Uragami Collection, Tōkyō: 68, 249, 251, 253, 255, 279
Kōbe Municipal Museum: 76, Figs. 32, 48
Caplan Collection, Tōkyō: 77, 88, 93, 94, 196, 254, 264, 265, 282, 284, Figs. 21, 52
Musée Cinquantenaire, Brussels: 86, 208, 216, Fig. 50
Los Angeles County Museum: 107
Hokusai-kan, Nagano: 109, 243, 350, 351, 358
Civic Museum of Oriental Art, Genoa: 114
Chaïkin Collection, Venthône, Switzerland: 116
Ujiie Collection, Kanagawa: 119, 126, 345, 347
MOA Museum, Shizuoka: 113
Hie Shrine, Chiba: 127
Ōsaka Prefectural Museum: 123
Rijksmuseum voor Volkenkunde, Leiden: 161, 198, 292, 346
Freer Gallery of Art, Washington: 244, Fig. 164
Shinjō Collection, Ōsaka: 245, 248
Musée Guimet, Paris: 239, 247, 273, 277, 283, 348
Minneapolis Institute of Arts: 280, Figs. 114–20
National Diet Library, Tōkyō: 349
Myōkōji temple, Ibaraki: 356
Worcester Art Museum, Worcester, Mass.: Fig. 27
Nikaidō Ukiyo-e Library, Kamakura: Fig. 156

Other items are from anonymous collectors (principally in Japan), or from the author's collection (mainly books)

Index